To Joe from Bets.

Cunsimas,

The Gravediggers of France

The Literature of France

The Gravediggers of France

GAMELIN, DALADIER, REYNAUD, PÉTAIN, and LAVAL

MILITARY DEFEAT · ARMISTICE
COUNTERREVOLUTION

By

Pertinax [pseud.]

Géraud, André.

Doubleday, Doran & Company, Inc.
GARDEN CITY, NEW YORK
1944

THIS BOOK IS
STANDARD LENGTH,
COMPLETE AND UNABRIDGED,
MANUFACTURED UNDER WARTIME CONDITIONS
IN CONFORMITY WITH ALL GOVERNMENT
REGULATIONS CONTROLLING THE USE
OF PAPER AND OTHER MATERIALS

Preface

I FEEL I OWE THE READER of this book a few words of explanation. More than three and a half years ago I set to work with a strictly limited purpose in mind: to reconstruct from my notebooks the defeat of the French Army, the conclusion of the "separate armistice," the Bordeaux counter-revolution. But once I began the task I saw that a mere recital of everything it had been my fortune to see, hear, feel, and grasp was not in scale with such vast and complex events. I knew enough to create all sorts of problems for myself, but I did not know enough to solve them. So I continued my search. The personal testimony, to which I first wished to limit my narrative, has been checked against the testimony of others and rounded out. Little by little I found myself engaged in writing a historical essay, and I wish that word to be taken in its original sense.

This was, indeed, a very bold attempt, and some will surely reproach me for it. History, they will claim, can deal only with matter which has had a chance to cool off. History shies away from lava which is still in its liquid state. Yet between the tranquil story told by a historian after the evidence of two or three generations has been allowed to settle, after the dregs have been separated from the liquor, and the sketchy reviews published in newspapers or magazines—spotty, riled, partisan—there is room for provisional synthesis. This book is such a provisional synthesis, and it may anticipate on the balanced judgment which shall rest upon the full record. Shall I be thought presumptuous because of my belief that a journalist was perhaps specially fitted for the task, a journalist trained to work upon events which have not yet come to a head or run their full course?

The investigation I have undertaken is needed at this critical moment in French history. Our country lost its independence in June 1940; but, thanks to the growing power of the United Nations, our hope of liberation

v

nears fulfillment. When this volume reaches the public, Allied troops will have been fighting Nazis on French soil for several weeks. For their own future guidance it is vital that French, British, and Americans be enlightened about the causes of our misfortune. To postpone defining them on the ground that only incomplete data are available would amount to groping in the dark by choice rather than moving forward with the torch we do have—however feeble it may be. The full illumination will be tomorrow's. Meanwhile let us not scorn that flickering light. After all, what is essential is perhaps less to detail facts than to find the links between them, to determine their relationship. I believe I have approximated this. French affairs call for decisions which can hardly be more than a gamble if arrived at in ignorance of our country's vicissitudes all through the recent years.

I found it impossible to follow a strictly chronological sequence. I should never have managed to get out of the forest's recesses had I tried to record them tree by tree, bush by bush. So I have held firm to the four protagonists whose trail is the most clearly blazed through the thicket: Gamelin, Daladier, Reynaud, and Pétain. The other characters are related to these four; even Laval would never have emerged had it not been for the marshal's collusion and senility. By this device our mishaps have been grasped at focal points.

The men I have named wielded supreme authority: they are foremost among those who dug the grave of France. They do not all stand on the same level of guilt, and our censure will have to discriminate. Daladier and even Reynaud do not deserve to be arraigned by the side of Pétain, Laval, and their henchmen. From genus to species wide differences may exist, and great heed must be paid to them.

I do not scruple to give this book a generic title, *The Gravediggers of France,* for those words tell everything. Some may object that the choice of so violent an appellation betrays bias, that such crass simplifications are repugnant to history. I answer that strong convictions, with only the partisanship of truth stamped upon them, are useful. France very nearly died because of those who tried not to have convictions. I have never been in any man's service. Temperamentally repelled by abstract political theorizing, I wrote all through thirty years for a Rightist paper. Yet I was born outside Paris, the years of my youth were spent in England, and French conservative circles have always struck me as being singularly narrow. Thus I can lay claim to some degree of open-mindedness. To every French statesman whose foreign policy it was my duty to explain and interpret I have allowed a clean slate at the start, and all the more easily since no personal commitments were there to hold me back. I have judged French ministers by their deeds and by their deeds only. I have meted out to Messrs. Poincaré and Millerand the same treatment as to Messrs. Briand and Blum. Seldom, if ever, have ministerial achievements met with my approval from beginning to end, but I have never shifted my ground for reasons of self-interest, grudge, intrigue, or vanity. My criticism has always been based on reasoning and riveted to a patient observation of the facts, the sovereignty of which I have ever recognized. Judgment once reached about any man, I have never set it aside without good reason. Given our present plight, no one will any longer marvel at my always having used sharp language. To inform French people, as well as our Allies, fearlessly and freely is, today, the more imperative a duty since, of all the fifth columns, the fifth column of lies and concealments was the first to overrun our highways and byways.

In the pages that follow, the reader will find a quantity of diplomatic or political information quoted without reference to sources and sometimes in contradiction to what is commonly accepted. He may rest assured that this was supplied by irreproachable authorities. I have drawn upon my notebooks, upon the diary which I kept more faithfully after 1934 than before that year. For instance, I found recorded therein numerous talks with General Weygand, whom I saw regularly for a dozen years, up to the time when his fascist demon made him lose his head. He may accuse me of publishing statements uttered in confidence, sub rosa, and he may burst forth with denials. But he has long since foregone the privileges of confidence. I am quit of all obligation.

The military section of this book is indispensable, though relatively brief. On this, unfortunately, I have not had the same enlightened assistance which has helped me elsewhere. Despite all my care, inaccuracies have probably crept in, and these I shall hasten to correct whenever they are pointed out. Weak spots will be detected in my work, and I entertain no illusions about them. But, at any rate, some sort of observatory has been built. The reader who patiently follows through to the end will find himself upon a platform, and under his eyes the sinister landscape will unfold as it never did before. Whatever his opinion, he will see more deeply into the case of my country and, besides, into the working of international politics. My purpose will have been fulfilled.

On the conclusion of those introductory notes, my gratitude goes to friendly America, whose hospitality was, in the storm, an unforgettable privilege. Six lectures delivered in Northwestern University on Norman Wait Harris Foundation were the first outline, which I have been gradually filling in. A French edition was published last year. This is, in fact, a revised edition, the labor of the many friends who contributed new data, corrections, and advice.

PERTINAX

Washington, D.C
June 1944

Contents

BOOK ONE

The Men Who Ruled the French Republic at War

SECTION I: GAMELIN: MILITARY DEFEAT

I

Gamelin, Promoter of Resistance, Prophet of Victory

DURING THE OMINOUS YEARS when war was impending—from the summer of 1935 to the summer of 1939—we broadly know where the French and British governments stood. We know that both lacked the courage to halt the German-Italian cataclysm when the threat offered by the totalitarian powers was still indirect, could even appear remote to men living amid illusions—also when the superiority in armed force still unquestionably belonged to Britain and France. Conquest of Abyssinia, military reoccupation of the Rhineland, totalitarian intervention in Spain —the French and the British governments saw it all and did nothing.

We know that the London and Paris cabinets did not decide to act until eighteen and eleven months after the frontier posts had been uprooted in Austria and Czechoslovakia. They waited until Poland had actually been invaded. By then the balance of military power had been altered to their serious disadvantage.

But the mind of the French High Command throughout those crucial years, the mind of that final authority whose function it was to evaluate at each successive moment the chances of victory, has so far attracted very little attention. My initial task must be to explain it.

On March 7, 1936, the Reichswehr entered the demilitarized zone of the Rhine. General Gamelin, for fourteen months commander in chief of the French Armies, took an extremely cautious position. It is not true, as has been alleged, that he refused to occupy the Saar. He was willing to go ahead. At the same time he did not hold as adequate the three army classes Premier Sarraut offered to call up. He insisted that he must have whatever was needed to deal with any contingency; that the government should be prepared to proceed with a general mobilization; that we must be ready to follow up our acts to the extreme limits of their possible consequences; finally, that the government should unequivocally state its resolve, if the Germans left it no other choice, to enforce international law by war. The Army he had taken in charge, toward the end of January 1935, was a compact and rigid machine; to set any of its parts in motion independently of the others seemed to him difficult if not dangerous. There must be no halfway measures, he said. The lack of military elasticity, for which we were to pay so heavily in 1940, was apparent for the first time.

Such was the first position taken by the High Command.

It was once again called upon to state its views in 1938 and in 1939, at the time Czechoslovakia and Poland were faced with the threat of annihilation. General Gamelin repeatedly asserted that victory was certain. And he gave his opinion without waiting to be asked.[1]

In the early days of September 1938 the Nuremberg Congress met in tumult. Probably Premier Daladier was anxious not to have his hands tied and was afraid of being involved further than he thought prudent. He, therefore, did not summon the Supreme War Council, on which generals commanding armies sat as members. Gamelin thereupon went to see him, taking along General Georges and General Billotte, and

---

[1] I need not go into the whole sequence of secondary facts. In October 1937, when Chautemps was Premier, France's commitments with regard to Czechoslovakia were extended to cover the case of internal disorders provoked by Berlin. When consulted, Gamelin approved.

In April 1938, before Daladier's and Bonnet's visit to London, Gamelin explained in a memorandum the methods by which Czechoslovakia could be defended: "Her fate will depend," he said, "on the outcome of the whole war," etc.

And in my diary for October 25, 1937, I find these words of Léon Blum: "As long as I was in power, General Gamelin was always present at private meetings between certain cabinet ministers which I arranged for the purpose of discussing questions of foreign policy involving military commitments—questions that could not be aired in general meetings of the Cabinet."

gave him formal assurances that the democratic nations would dictate the peace. Such was the actual expression he used. Shortly afterward[2] he confirmed what he had said in a letter giving reasons for his confidence.

On September 25 (after the second Chamberlain-Hitler meeting at Godesberg) Gamelin was called to London, and on the twenty-sixth, before Chamberlain, Daladier, and Sir Thomas Inskip—and with the French Ambassador, Corbin, acting as interpreter—he repeated his analysis of the whole military problem with an optimism calculated to hearten the two Prime Ministers.[3]

In casual conversation, however, M. Bonnet laid special stress on a report submitted by General Vuillemin, head of the French Air Force, emphasizing the great weakness of French aviation. It is the whole and not the part that counts, explained the generalissimo. A few days later he took strong exception to a memorandum drawn up at Downing Street or at Whitehall and transmitted to him through the British military attaché in Paris, in which it was apparent that M. Bonnet's arguments had borne more weight than had his own views, at least insofar as certain ministers were concerned. He wrote to Mr. Hore-Belisha, Secretary of State for War, confirming the exposé he had made on the twenty-sixth and reminding him that this remained on record with the Imperial General Staff. Later again, when the Prime Minister visited Paris, Gamelin seized the opportunity to clear any remaining misconception—deliberate or accidental—concerning his statements in London. The step which Gamelin took at that belated hour had no practical importance, for the Munich Pact was already several months old. The general wanted to have a clear conscience: with an eye on posterity, he was taking precautions. He did not wish to be held responsible for the dismemberment of Czechoslovakia.[4]

But the generalissimo went further. Before the Munich Conference he stated to M. Daladier, specifically and in writing, the limits which, according to him, eventual territorial concessions to Germany ought not to transgress. He was determined that, for the future, Czechoslovakia must remain capable of giving effective assistance to France and Great Britain.

[2]Speaking privately at the time, General Georges expressed a widely different opinion. Why, then, did he underwrite Gamelin's views by his presence—and his silence?

[3]There had been a first conversation on diplomatic matters in the Prime Minister's office. This meeting had been suspended by Mr. Chamberlain, and when it was resumed George Bonnet was left with Sir Robert Vansittart and M. Léger in an anteroom while Lord Halifax returned to the Foreign Office.

[4]General Gamelin himself told a friend of mine the whole story.

He deprecated all compromise on essentials, and his memorandum listed them: the main Czechoslovak fortifications, the railroad trunk lines as well as strategically important branch lines and defense industries. Above all, the Germans must not be allowed to cut off the Moravian corridor.

On September 29, in Munich, M. Daladier made his own, to a certain extent, the conditions set forth by the commander in chief, especially in the matter of the Moravian corridor, and persuaded himself that he had been successful in imposing them. It was a relative and precarious achievement. Not for a moment did it prevail against the arbitrary demands of Generals Keitel and Von Brauchitsch at the conference of ambassadors in Berlin, which was charged with translating into physical boundaries the decision of the four participating powers. M. François-Poncet, whose steps M. Georges Bonnet directed by telephone, allowed Hitler's representatives to make a clear sweep of all the limitations which, a few days earlier, had been laid on Nazi claims.[5]

On the evening of March 14, 1939, I met General Gamelin at a dinner given by a foreign ambassador accredited to France. Already German troops were marching on Czechoslovakia, this time to take possession of the whole country, and President Hacha, submitting to a peremptory order, was on his way to Berlin. At intervals telephone messages came for the Czechoslovak Minister, who was one of the guests. The general was not surprised at the news. Like everyone else, he knew that Czechoslovak independence had been doomed for months. It was all too obvious that the German thrust into eastern Europe could no longer be checked by peaceful methods or by any amount of diplomacy. I asked General Gamelin if we would be meeting the test of arms under circumstances less favorable to us than had prevailed before the Munich Agreement. "There can be no doubt about it," he replied. "The balance sheet of Munich is against us."

In *L'Europe Nouvelle,* which I edited at the time, an officer who was soon to be called to an important post on the General Staff had recently discussed this question, basing his articles on information from the Intelligence Service. General Gamelin told me that his own opinion was reflected on those pages.[6] This military expert had written that the hundred German divisions of 1938—of which fifty were insufficiently trained

[5]Georges Bonnet called up M. François-Poncet, the French Ambassador to Berlin, from the Chamber of Deputies. He did not want his own officials to know.

[6]*L'Europe Nouvelle,* "Balance Sheet of Munich," by Polémarque, February 25, March 4, 1939.

and lacked capable officers—had meanwhile increased by 40 per cent in quantity and, as a result of intensive training in the field during the autumn and winter, had gained also in quality. To the three armored divisions of 1938 two more had been added, and this total was, at least, to be doubled within a few weeks.

Not only were the five Czechoslovak armored divisions to be incorporated into the Wehrmacht—with German personnel, of course—but their equipment would provide useful models. German tanks in Spain had still showed some of the faulty construction of the original 1917 type.[7] Marshal Goering's air force now numbered six thousand planes instead of thirty-five hundred or four thousand. The Siegfried lines, which in the summer of 1938 were no more than fieldworks, had been strengthened with great quantities of concrete and steel. For all practical purposes, they had now become permanent fortifications. Day by day Germany was increasing her lead. While our technicians were fumbling over the choice of basic types and laboriously working over details of design, German war industry already worked to capacity with mass production in full swing.

Finally, thirty-five Czech divisions, the Czech fortifications, quantities of matériel, and well-equipped factories had been surrendered to the Reich. Germany was perfectly free, therefore, to concentrate in the west the fifty divisions she would have had to use in the east had it proved necessary to subdue Masaryk's nation by force. It was, of course, still possible to hope that Poland—linked to Germany since the declaration of January 26, 1934—might now return to her alliance with France and fill the gap. But General Gamelin did not rely on the team Poland-Russia as he did on the team Czechoslovakia-Russia.[8]

While he recognized that our military power had seriously decreased since September 30, 1938 (with the exception of the Air Force, where

---

[7]At the time of Munich the German Army was inferior to the French and Czech armies taken together with regard to the quantity and quality of its tanks.

[8]Concerning the results of Munich and the increase in the relative military strength of Germany, Chancellor Hitler agreed with General Gamelin, according to Mr. Burckhardt, High Commissioner for the League of Nations in Danzig, who was received at Berchtesgaden on August 11, 1939. "A year ago my generals did not want to go to war," was the gist of Hitler's statement to him. "This year they are eager for war." And according to a statement made by Burckhardt to Edouard Herriot, Hitler is reported to have said also: "When, after Munich, we were in a position to examine Czechoslovak military strength from within, what we saw of it greatly disturbed us: we had run a serious danger. The plans prepared by the Czechoslovak generals were formidable, although they were more the work of students in war games than of seasoned leaders. So I understood why my own generals had urged restraint."

the Franco-British inferiority stood now roughly at three to ten instead of one to ten), the commander in chief of the French Army still kept faith in Allied victory. I saw him again in July: his opinion was unchanged. He considered war inevitable and he set September 20 as the dead line. He thought this the most likely date since he felt Italy would prefer not to fight at the side of her ally until safely protected against a French offensive by snow in the Alps.

On August 23 came the Molotov-Ribbentrop "Non-Aggression" Pact. We had lost Russia. The Anglo-Franco-Russian military discussions in Moscow had failed just as the political talks had failed before them. Here was an appalling check to French and British diplomacy. We felt, all of us, that our whole plan was shattered. We saw that the German General Staff had, at last, rid itself of its most harassing worry, born of the experience of 1914–18. No matter what it might cost, Germany meant to avoid a war on two fronts; she meant to wipe out Poland, mass the Army in the west, and then strike France a crushing blow. And we also recalled what General von Fritsch, at that time in command of the Reichswehr, had told the Belgian military attaché in 1936: "We shall never forgive Hitler for giving France a chance to win over Russia." Hitler's error of 1934 was now corrected.

I learned only at secondhand the views of the commander in chief during the interval between the defection of Russia and the German offensive against Poland. But I know he spoke encouragingly at the meeting of ministers concerned with national defense and chiefs of staff —called by Daladier on the evening of August 23—to appraise the military implications of the Soviet *volte-face* and to reach a decision on war and peace.[9] It seems that Gamelin calmly accepted the disappearance of any prospect of keeping the Reich busy in the east, of having it caught up in a war of movement, the only kind of warfare which can be fought on the Central European plain, between the Baltic and the Carpathians, where fortified lines cannot be set up and where tactics of attrition[10] are out of order. As he saw it, there was indeed a substitute—the Polish

[9]At Riom, during the preliminary investigation, Gamelin sought to cast doubt upon the accuracy of the minutes of this meeting, which had been recorded by General Decamp of Daladier's military secretariat. Gamelin insisted that he was only answerable for mobilizing and assembling the Army.

In his testimony before the Riom magistrates (July 7, 1941) Georges Bonnet stated that, not being aware of the lack of preparedness in our defense, he went away from the meeting of August 23 with the impression that considerations of our military possibilities need no longer fetter our foreign policy.

[10]At any rate, in the summer of 1939, the French High Command thought so.

Army. Without Soviet support, it would be able to carry on until spring. However modest were Gamelin's expectations in that respect, he took too much for granted, as subsequent events were to prove. But even at his own valuation of Poland's staying power, the loss suffered from Russia's newfangled neutrality was enormous. Yet he readily resigned himself to the sudden reversal of his General Staff's calculations.

Like Weygand, and as early as 1933 and 1934, Gamelin had advised Paul-Boncour and Barthou, who held the portfolio of foreign affairs in succession, to enlist Russian co-operation. This co-operation, they said, would close an important source of raw materials to the Reichswehr, free our allies or associates in eastern Europe from the Soviet menace, and enable us to send them supplies—which we could never forward across the Italian barrier. Above all, it would rally Turkey to our cause. In February 1934 Gamelin urged me to explain to the reading public the necessity for a new policy toward Moscow. On July 1, 1935, at a time when Laval was busy delaying the ratification of the Franco-Soviet treaty he had signed two months before, by arousing the press against the Soviets and accusing them of subversive propaganda and treachery, I called on the generalissimo and asked him whether, during the last fifteen months, he had changed his mind about our future relations with Russia. "By no means," he replied. "To your knowledge," I asked, "are the Communists at work again in the Army, and, if so, is their propaganda inspired by the Third International?" "No," Gamelin said, "and if this kind of game had been resumed we should be quick to detect it because it is a very old one and we had to suppress it in the past." "Then M. Laval is only playing politics?" The general said: "It is permissible to think so." Gamelin's remarks are interesting because they show how large Russia loomed in his strategical plan.[11] He was not prepared to part with her in deference to Laval's wishes.

I have no precise notes on what he said about Russia between 1936 and

---

[11]General Gamelin added that he had brought the Russian problem for discussion before the Supreme War Council; that his views had been approved unanimously and that no one differed with him. However, I find in my diary that, by August 19, Gamelin had changed his tune. He then believed that communist propaganda was being carried out among the non-commissioned officers. In spite of this, he would let General Loiseau go to Russia, he said, but to show his mistrust he was breaking off staff conversations. These conversations were renewed later. They were going on during the autumn of 1936. On November 22, 1935, a staff officer close to headquarters said to me: "Ever since 1932 or 1933 there has been no more Soviet propaganda in the French Army. Whatever you hear of the sort is talk." At heart Gamelin held the same opinion; what he said on August 19 was nothing more than pandering to ministerial power. Later on he kept reassuring Daladier about communism: "The NCOs are inoculated against the virus." (See page 72, note 16.)

1938. During that period most French conservatives were bitterly assailing those who followed the line of the General Staff and who dared suggest that it would be useful to have Moscow on our side. He was no man to face a storm. He used to go to the Quai d'Orsay every month to see which way the wind was blowing. There he would listen passively to what they told him, giving no sign of what he felt. To friends, however, he talked with greater freedom.

The French General Staff was always extremely cautious when estimating the positive help Russia could furnish.[12] Nevertheless, the missions to Moscow (one headed by General Loiseau, in 1935, the other by General Schweisguth, in 1936, both assistant chiefs of General Staff) had brought back favorable reports on the quality of Russian equipment.[13] On the day the Russo-German agreement of August 23 was announced I was traveling with an important official of the War Ministry. He was overwhelmed by the news and could not believe it. This is enough to emphasize Gamelin's amazing complacency at a moment when the whole strategic structure was crumbling to pieces.

Our position had been impaired and imperiled by the Russian "default," but on September 3 we had an opportunity to re-establish it. Italy declared her neutrality—a novel and peculiar neutrality within the framework of the "Steel Pact," the war alliance which the Führer and the Duce had signed on May 22. Mussolini now claimed the right to stand at Germany's side, giving Germany all aid short of actual war, and yet insisted on being given the privileges of a neutral state and even of a great neutral state. That is what was meant by the policy of "non-belligerency" as set in motion by the telegrams exchanged between the two despots. Were we to bow quietly to this curious arrangement, or should we insist on Italy redefining her neutrality in a correct and traditional manner, if not in a manner which would favor our cause?

I had a conversation in October 1939 with the most qualified French observer of Italian affairs. In spite of the clause in the Steel Pact which relieved Italy for three years of any obligation to join Germany on the

---

[12]Weygand said of the Red Army: "It's an internal constabulary which will never be able to leave Soviet territory." And Gamelin said: "It's the old Russian Army plus equipment. But what can be expected of it after its generals and high-ranking officers have been put to death by the thousands?" How ironical these words sound today.

[13]After the maneuvers were over, the Russians said to General Loiseau and to General Maindras, former military attaché at Moscow, who was in his party: "Go wherever you will throughout the country; visit whatever factories you come across." Both men were astounded by what they saw. "The Soviets," one of their intimate friends told me, "have produced an army in the best physical trim, full of buoyancy and combativeness."

battlefield, and in spite of the fact that Ciano had used this clause to the full at Salzburg—and had been thoroughly insulted by Hitler for doing so—Mussolini, on September 3, wanted to enter the war at once. Badoglio and the other army leaders restrained him: "Impossible to fight without artillery, etc." My informant—I repeat that he was exceptionally well placed to know the truth—added: "The Italian High Command would not have stopped even at a military *coup d'état* had the dictator paid no attention to its warnings. Italy lacked many of the most elementary supplies. She had built hardly an aircraft since September 1938; she was in no position to choose freely between war and peace. We had only to 'put her on the spot' while Germany was beating Poland down. Her people was in a panic: she would have yielded to 'some plain speaking.' It would have meant a more effective blockade of Germany; direct access for us to the eastern Mediterranean and to the Balkans would have been implied. We could have established an Eastern Front, that Eastern Front which General Weygand and his three divisions were destined, month after month, to pursue as one pursues a mirage, with the British unceasingly objecting that nothing could be done 'as long as Italy remains hostile.' ('As long as Italy remains hostile'—what a terrible misreading of Mussolini's policy is in those words!) By the reversal of Russian policy, the chain which we had tried to forge around Germany was shattered, and now, by Italian 'non-belligerency,' another chain was being forged which threatened to lock us up in western Europe. By intimidating Italy we could have reversed the process, regained a means to besiege the enemy."

General Gamelin did not see how precious an opportunity lay open to us in the Italian Peninsula. Like the Daladiers, the Bonnets, and the great majority of French politicians, he simply ignored it. In April 1935, after the Mussolini-Laval agreement, he had discussed with Badoglio the articles of the military protocol with which Mussolini tried to inveigle us in order to make sure that we would not move when he undertook his Abyssinian adventure. Gamelin knew that Italian support against Germany must remain illusory as long as the old quarrel between Italy and Yugoslavia persisted—a quarrel which Mussolini settled overnight the instant Prince Paul turned his back on France, but which he had till then continuously described as an insuperable difficulty as long as Yugoslavia remained bound to us in friendship.[14] In common with

---

[14]"The two General Staffs worked on the basic assumption of Italian-Yugoslav-Little Entente military co-operation." (Conversation with Gamelin, July 1, 1935.) Gamelin was so foolish as to suppress the Italian section of military intelligence as early as the summer of

many others, however, Gamelin stubbornly persisted in finding an anti-German interpretation for Mussolini's political actions. Up to a few months before the war Gamelin still corresponded with Badoglio, who would in all probability have cast his lot with us had the decision depended upon him. Nonetheless, months earlier, Gamelin had exclaimed, "The Paris-Rome settlement was merely a beautiful dream."

After the shocking surprise of the Russo-German Pact, Gamelin does not seem even to have considered the possibility of re-establishing our strategic position via Italy. Toward the end of August, at a session of the Permanent Committee for National Defense, a discussion took place as to what we could do if Italy went to war. General Vuillemin felt that he would be able to send what bombers we then had, which were stationed in Tunisia, over any part of the whole Peninsula. All Gamelin said was that he would "go out on the balcony," meaning that his troops would seize the commanding heights in the Alps and later on, in the spring of 1940, move down toward the Po. Darlan, chief of the naval forces, who liked to brag of his dashing and hard-hitting leadership, said nothing at all. It is only too clear: the true problem, Italy's non-belligerency, was left aside. I am told that General Weygand had a clear idea of the action required by French interests. But he had not yet even been called back to active service, and the information comes to me secondhand. General Georges, speaking to an American writer on military affairs, is said to have told him that he was in favor of sending an ultimatum to Italy. But no one asked his advice.[15]

1935, thus sacrificing further knowledge of the Italian Army. We had already overestimated its strength through the reports of General Parisot, our military attaché at Rome, who was dazzled by the honors showered upon its military chiefs.

[15]According to the minutes of the meeting of August 23, mentioned above, Gamelin and Darlan there asserted that "it was important to secure Italy's absolute neutrality." Yet they were content with Georges Bonnet's vague reply: "We can try something along that line."

2

The Credo of the Maginot Line: Doctrinal Unity in the High Command. Charles de Gaulle, The Rebel

How CAN ONE EXPLAIN the immovable calm of the generalissimo, the confidence with which he looked forward to a future of flame, steel, and blood? The answer is that General Gamelin had settled down into the certainties of what may be called the *Credo* of the Maginot Line. Here are the central articles of this faith:

1. Men defending fieldworks can hold out against an offensive, even if they are outnumbered three to one, or if the attack is carried out with bombers and tanks in massive quantities. This is even more true of the defense of concrete and steel fortifications. In order to do this successfully, they need only know how to handle their automatic rifles, machine guns, mortars, grenades, trench cannon, anti-tank and anti-aircraft cannon, avail themselves of the various types of artillery, and, in counterattacks, combine planes and tanks with all other arms.

The French Command was well aware that tanks would be launched against our lines in a density of one hundred units to the kilometer: the military writer in *L'Europe Nouvelle,* whom I have already mentioned, clearly said so in one of his articles.[1] But this avalanche of steel did not worry the High Command. Besides, they ignored that there was such a thing as air artillery which was to work in conjunction with fortresses on wheels. To a friend of mine General Georges bluntly declared that the German Panzer tactic was a terrible blunder. "Their tanks will be destroyed in the open country behind our lines if they can penetrate that far, which is doubtful." The French Staff had convinced itself that the new weapons were more effective when integrated into massive bodies of troops, in accordance with old-fashioned tactics, than when used independently for offensive action, in drives deep into the adversary's terri-

---

[1]February 2, 1939. And Marshal Pétain, in the *Revue des Deux Mondes,* as early as March 15, 1935, spoke of onslaught by planes and tanks.

tory, where they would be overwhelmed from all sides and the halter of an organized field of battle would strangle them. Above all, French tanks were intended to fight in support of infantry.

2. The ground gained by an enemy attack will always be limited, since it will be easier for the defense to organize resistance than for the attack to assemble the fresh troops required to widen the breach it has made. In the days that followed World War I, Marshal Pétain was wont to explain the relative impregnability of the defensive by the fact that heavy artillery never could keep up with an infantry attack and therefore could not effectively shell the new enemy position until after the determining moment had passed. "But if ever it becomes possible for artillery to follow quickly enough, then, without exaggeration, we may expect to see once again the quick-paced victories of the past with all their classical finality."[2] So much might happen someday. However, for the time being, the problem of the break-through still awaited a solution. The plane and the tank would not succeed in doing what, in the last war, the combination of artillery and infantry had failed to accomplish and was still incapable of accomplishing. In the spring of 1939 it did not appear that the opinion of the old soldier had changed, judging by the preface he wrote for the book *Is Invasion Still Possible?* by General Chauvineau, of the Engineers.[3]

General Gamelin and those close to him also refused to believe that any new means had been found whereby the offensive could once again come into its own. In 1938 I had asked General Armengaud of the Army of the Air to write an article, "Aviation—Artillery of the Battlefield."[4] He was willing to concede that planes, to a limited extent, could function as cannon, but a year later, in the *Revue des Deux Mondes,* he retracted what he had written.[5] "Barring complete surprise, which we must eliminate as a possibility on either side, barring also a collapse in morale, which nothing leads us to expect, we will again pass through the slow and discouraging vicissitudes of 1914–1917."[6]

[2]Quoted by General Armengaud, of the Air Force, in *L'Europe Nouvelle,* May 28, 1938.
[3]See Appendix 1.
[4]*L'Europe Nouvelle,* May 28, 1938.
[5]*Revue des Deux Mondes,* April 1, 1939: "Towards Stabilization in the Air Force." However, after witnessing the war in Poland, General Armengaud sent a thoroughly documented warning to the General Staff. His extremely precise account of plane and tank attacks in Poland was the source from which a note was drafted by the 3rd Section of the General Staff (Bureau of Operations), dated September 14, 1939. This text is published by Paul Allard in *Corap and the Loss of the Meuse Line,* a plea in favor of General Corap (1941).
[6]See also on this subject various numbers of the *Revue des Deux Mondes* in the autumn of 1939. In his reports Colonel Didelet, French military attaché in Berlin, did not correctly

3. Besides, the Maginot Line has replaced the fieldworks of twenty-five years ago. These works were continuous; the Maginot Line is not only continuous, it has a strength far above anything we have ever seen. True enough, it lacks depth and elasticity. The lack of these is the price we paid for building strength into continuity and permanence. All in all, nevertheless, this combination probably excludes the possibility even of a minor break-through.[7] In 1914 we had to win the Battle of the Marne to check the war of movement where the superior man power and matériel of the Germans might have overwhelmed our forces. That first blitzkrieg of our enemies played into our hands and we secured a stabilized front, in other words, the respite of several years our inadequate preparation made imperatively necessary. But today, thanks to the Maginot Line, we start out with an achieved stabilization of capital importance to us. It will be ours to determine at will the time for the offensive to break Germany; meanwhile we will have opportunity and time to train our army for modern war—an army in which the proportion of reserves to regulars is much higher than in the last war.[8] The Maginot Line presents the Germans with this dilemma: either they attack at once and pay a fearful toll in lives—presenting us also with the

appraise the actual strength of the German armored divisions. Regarding aviation, however, the French Staff had a clearer picture of the real state of affairs after General Vuillemin's trip to Berlin (July 1938). General de Geffrier, moreover, air attaché from July 1937, insists that he had described in detail the increase in strength of German aviation. A great deal could be said about the carelessness with which our military attachés in Berlin were chosen during the twelve years preceding the conflict. Neither Didelet's predecessor nor his predecessor's aide spoke German. Had Weygand, who appointed them, forgotten that our operations in August 1914 were faultily planned because of the reports made by Colonel Serret, military attaché in Berlin before World War I? Serret had maintained that the German Command did not intend to use its reserve divisions in the initial phase of the campaign.

[7]In contrast, the Germans, when they built the Siegfried Line in 1938–39, made sacrifices to depth. Their individual works were weaker than ours but were built checkerboard fashion, extending four, five, twenty, thirty kilometers to the rear. This scheme had had its advocates among the French in 1925 and 1927 at the meetings of the Superior War Council. But in 1939 it was thought by our General Staff that the two systems would, in the long run, become very much alike. In fact, while the Germans were strengthening their works we were completing, or we intended to complete, ours in depth by field fortifications. There remained a capital difference. In German strategy, forts served merely as springboards for the offensive.

[8]There were 30,482 regular army officers against 98,000 reserve officers, more or less well trained. In 1935 Weygand told me that out of these reserve officers only 50,000 had attended the voluntary lecture courses and maneuvers organized for them at the training centers. Attendance at these courses was not to become compulsory for first-line reserves until March 14, 1939. Weygand added that, out of 350,000 non-commissioned reserve officers, 30,000 at the most had gone to the same trouble. Out of the 115 divisions which made up the French Army at the time of mobilization, only sixty-five existed in peacetime, and the nineteen divisions described as being in Series B were of second-rate quality. Moreover, thirteen "fortress" divisions were not suited for rapid evolutions in the field.

opportunity for effective counterattack—or they temporize, and thus permit us to sap the fighting strength of the Wehrmacht by undermining the nation's economic structure through the blockade. We do not exclude the possibility of our turning suddenly to a war of movement should we obtain free access through Belgium to a weakly held German sector or should it become possible to make a surprise attack on a Wehrmacht caught badly off guard. In the *Instruction Manual of 1921,* "On the Tactical Handling of Large Units," some considerable stress had been laid on the need of finding free and open terrain in which to maneuver.[9] How odd to see surging up in the midst of the whole defensive pattern that legacy of the offensive theory which, in 1914, had so powerfully swayed the High Command. Was that strange survival more than a compliment reverently paid to the Napoleonic doctrine? Yes. Events would show how the old generals could be swept off their feet.

The Maginot Line ends at Montmédy; from the Meuse to the Pas-de-Calais the terrain is open or slightly protected. How were we to ward against the dangers which arose from this solution of continuity, supposing that we did not get the hoped-for chance to attack along the Belgian-German frontier? Various answers were given. They amounted to this: fieldworks will be constructed. The natural obstacle which consists of the Ardennes Forest and the Meuse River rules out a breakthrough in that area. And the French-British-Belgian armies will be able to get to the relatively narrow stretch of territory between Givet and Antwerp quickly enough to prevent an enemy outflanking action. In the defensive credo here was the point which remained ill defined and vague.[10] But this must be emphasized. Under the military philosophy

[9]Unless I am mistaken, this *Instruction Manual of 1921* was never revised after the completion of the Maginot and Siegfried lines. Yet the whole problem was altered by their existence. But in the neighborhood of the Belgian frontier the Siegfried Line was not built until the spring of 1940.

[10]The French High Command was forever hesitating and changing its mind on this major point. As early as 1932, apparently, it thought that to extend the fortifications to the sea was to encourage the Belgian inclination toward neutrality and, at the very least, to discourage Belgian military preparedness. It is a fact that the Brussels Government, contrary to what was widely believed, wanted France to complete her shield of fortifications. Besides this preoccupation with the effect upon our neighbor, it was felt that reinforced concrete should not be the first and last word of our national defense. The High Command was chary of putting all its eggs in one basket. It was not resolute enough to thoroughly carry out its timid strategical conception. In short, three kinds of works were either built or planned:

1. First of all, from 1930–31 on, the mighty bulwarks which stopped at Longuyon, near Montmédy. They were designated as "old fronts."

2. In 1935, and later, similar but weaker works (called "new fronts") at Rohrbach (Saar), where a gap had been left open, and at Montmédy, Maubeuge, Valenciennes.

3. Following a tour of the region between Montmédy and the sea by M. Daladier and

which goes by the name of Maginot an appendix was set apart for strategy in open space. The "Maginot" credo was not a closed one—and that was the worst of it. In May–June 1940 the fortifications were not actually stormed by the enemy. They were turned.

There is no need to enter into greater detail. We may remark, however, that for anyone holding such views on the nature of the war to come, the numerical disparity between the French and German effectives was only a matter of secondary importance.[11] So much so that General Gamelin did not deem it necessary to conform to the precedent set in 1914 and to call up the 1940 class in advance of the due time.

Despite constant complaints about British procrastination, General Gamelin and Premier Daladier, when they attended the Supreme War Council, never went so far as to insist that British troops be sent to the Continent in greater numbers and with greater speed. The French Ambassador in London repeatedly called the attention of both men to this question and urged them not to neglect it. He argued that the military aspect was not the only issue involved, that France, to maintain her civilization and economic strength, had a moral duty to see to it that the burden of supplying man power for the front line should be less unequally distributed between the two allies. But all he could get from them was some such answer as this: "The English are doing what they

---

General Gamelin (autumn 1936), a "semipermanent framework within which to fashion, in case of need, the organization of a defensive field of battle, by means of field fortifications."

The last phrase is revealing. A German invasion would be forced to go round the Maginot Line to the west, and there, if for one reason or another we did not move into Belgium, we would counterattack on a terrain made ready beforehand. Thus the High Command hoped that somehow the war of movement would come back into its own west of the Longuyon-Montmédy breakwater. Yet, to give no encouragement to Belgian military laxity—doubtless this was the motive—the ground was but feebly shaped for defense. The Command was convinced that, most probably, the Belgians would let us get in before they were themselves attacked and that we had better not waste our concrete along the French frontier. When Belgium withdrew from her alliance with us the High Command did not do more than fortify Montmédy.

[11] In May 1940 the French Army numbered 115 divisions, not counting various scattered forces, a total strength equivalent to some ten divisions. Twenty-four of these were stationed in the Alps, in the Levant, and in North Africa. So there remained ninety-one for the north-east front. Counting the British divisions on French soil and the Polish division, there were altogether 102 divisions, of which thirty were of inferior quality. To this total must be added twenty-two Belgian divisions, and, indeed, one of the purposes of the Belgian campaign was to bring them in. All in all, then, 124 divisions. On March 23, 1940, General Gamelin, speaking to one of my friends, estimated that Germany would have 175 divisions by July and 200 by the end of 1940. To meet this increasing weight he could rely only upon fifteen additional British divisions (by November 1940). The German Command had 140 divisions available for the Battle of Belgium in early May. Germany had only 23,000 to 25,000 regular officers, but its reserve officers were magnificently trained.

can; we must not push them too hard." It is worth noting that Gamelin never spoke at Interallied Meetings unless asked to do so. His extreme reserve and his caution seemed to say: "It's up to you to let me know if you want my opinion." Instinctively he behaved like a subordinate whenever he had dealings with the political power.

It seems clear to us now that there were ways to compensate for the slow British mobilization. During the first year, with four or five million men in service,[12] France could easily have formed a greater number of divisions. Her recruiting could not have kept them up to strength over a protracted period. But why was it not foreseen that the number of these excess units would be decreased gradually as the British Expeditionary Forces grew in size? In the eight months between September 3, 1939, and May 10, 1940, the German Command formed more than fifty new divisions. We did not even get under way with the ten divisions planned when war was declared.

But even the men with the colors were not put to the best use. In the pangs of the collapse the government at Bordeaux ordered a line to be organized along the Dordogne for defense; it was found that 30,000 effectives were scattered in regimental depots throughout that region.

Inferiority in numbers, although by no means a negligible one, was probably not the determining factor in the fall of France. On November 17, 1934, I put down in my diary these words of General Weygand's: "The practical effects of a numerical inequality between armies diminish when the belligerent who is weaker in man power still succeeds in gathering together several million men. Then, too, fortifications make up for deficiency in numbers." But Weygand also said: "Abundance of matériel means an economy in human lives, not in man power." Conversely, on the basis of that aphorism, comparative lack of matériel ought to have increased the requirements of the French Command in fighting troops. Let us bear in mind that the French Command never believed it would be short of effectives. Being thoroughly skeptical of the blitzkrieg, it could not realize that the scales had been turned and that in the new mode of warfare much more men and matériel were needed for resistance than for attack.[13]

This pattern of theories concerning the superiority of the defensive was by no means the property of General Gamelin, the intellectual heir

---

[12]On March 1, 1940, 4,895,000, of which 2,775,000 were with the armies in the field. On May 1, 1917, after suffering heavy losses, we had 3,280,000 men on the various fronts.

[13]See Appendix 4, testimony of General Keller at Riom.

to Joffre. General Weygand, the intellectual heir to Foch, was full of the same notions. And we have seen, too, that they hemmed in Marshal Pétain. Weygand, for instance, often said to me, in 1930–35, that he thought most people exaggerated the part aviation was to fulfill. "You can't hold the ground with planes," he said. He must know now that this was not the point. It was not a matter of deciding whether aviation could or could not hold the ground, but of whether, when acting in liaison with tanks, it could make a breach for the infantry and artillery which would hold the ground.[14] The fact is that the three great leaders of the Army and their vast following kept repeating that when war broke out the enemy's planes would be employed in ambitious raids intended to terrorize the civilian population, paralyze French mobilization, disorganize the country's economic life (following the Italian General Douhet's doctrine), that they would not achieve their purpose, that the losses in planes would exceed the supply of new matériel, and that the threat from the sky would swiftly disappear. "Civilians will suffer," Gamelin used to sum it up, "and that will be extremely deplorable, but the military instrument proper will not suffer much harm—and we need not bother too much about the rest."

Weygand had quarreled persistently with Gamelin and Pétain in the past. It was something to listen to him excoriating Gamelin who, as chief of the General Staff, considered that he should take his orders from the Minister of War rather than from the commander in chief, and consequently gave no support to Weygand's suggestions. Weygand loved to call him a liar. He also loved to dwell upon Pétain's inertia when the latter served as Minister of War and generalissimo. But of what importance are these bickerings? The fact remains that the commander in chief in 1940 and his predecessors were agreed on their broad conception of the war to come. And generals like Georges and Billotte and Prételat and Besson and Bineau and Doumenc and *tutti quanti* thought

[14]In the course of that same talk with Weygand on November 17, 1934, this is the substance of what he said to me: "I worked to get the two-year period of military service reestablished: it will be for my successor to forge the spearhead, taking circumstances into account, and once we are free of the difficulties arising from insufficient man power in the generation born during the last war." By this he meant making the French Army capable of taking the offensive. Perhaps de Gaulle's theories worried him more than he was willing to admit. In the *Revue des Deux Mondes,* October 15, 1936, Weygand denounced the excesses of the defensive spirit. But he hardly went beyond the commonplaces and criticized the existing system only in matters of detail. Once again he refuted the theory of de Gaulle's "separate army." At the sitting of the War Committee held on April 3, 1940 (see page 44), Weygand expressed the view that, in the present war, air forces would not fulfill a great part.

no differently.[15] For them one fact took precedence over everything else: the combined resources of the French and British empires (which were *not* fully mobilized) surpassed the resources of Germany (which had been strained to the utmost even before war began), and there would be time enough behind the shield of the Maginot Line to collect these resources and throw them into the battle. Before their eyes a vision of victory, to materialize after two or three years, took shape automatically.

Around 1935 they went through a pessimistic phase: the trouble was that in a French Army functioning on the basis of one-year military service, with contingents of recruits called up each April and October, the units were no more than perpetual skeleton outfits. It was impossible to cover those bones with living flesh. Feeling that it was hopeless to give men serious training when the arrival of new recruits and the release of those who had served their twelve months created utter confusion twice a year, they were prone to credit the Reichswehr with a power it had certainly not yet acquired. It was a natural reaction to the handicaps they had to face inside the French military system. But in the spring of 1935 the length of military service was increased to two years. The outlook of the upper spheres in the military hierarchy was promptly reversed. The generals felt that they had got the engine running again. This gave a new life to their optimism,[16] and they gradually

---

[15]Billotte, commanding Army Group No. 1, sent to Belgium on May 10; Prételat, commanding Army Group No. 2 (fortified region); Besson, commanding Army Group No. 3 (Haute-Alsace), transferred to the Somme, the Aisne, the Ailette at the end of May; Bineau, chief of staff of the armies in the field (major general), succeeded in December by Doumenc. However, Doumenc and Billotte are perhaps to be placed, as regards military doctrine, in a category of their own. Billotte, according to Daladier's testimony at the Riom trial, foresaw as early as the end of 1939 that the Germans would start their Polish blitzkrieg west of the Meuse. And he urged that armored or mechanized divisions should be assembled at once by means of detaching what was necessary from the forty battalions of tanks scattered everywhere in support of infantry. Concerning certain of Gamelin's unfulfilled intentions see page 26, note 8.

[16]I find these sentences of Weygand's in my diary: "The two years' service is re-established. You can liken the French Army to a drowning man whose foot touches the bed of the river and who kicks his way up to the surface." At Lille, on July 4, 1939, Weygand, who had come to preside over the horse show, did not hesitate to insert in his speech these phrases: "You ask me what I feel about the French Army. I shall answer candidly, my sole purpose being to tell the truth, which I don't find difficult to face. I believe the French Army to be more efficient today than at any other moment in the past. It is provided with a matériel of first quality, first-rate fortifications; it has an excellent morale and a remarkable High Command. In our land nobody wishes for war, but I affirm that we shall again win the battle if compelled to do it." In the same spirit he had written in the *Revue des Deux Mondes,* as early as October 1936: "The French Army is as good as it can be, given the laws which govern it."

discovered all manners of deficiencies in the German military system. Curiously enough, the German and Italian military attachés in Paris actually seem to have endorsed the congratulatory testimonials which the generals were bestowing on themselves.[17]

As early as 1934 a young officer named Major de Gaulle told them to their faces that they were wrong. In his book *Toward a Professional Army* he described with astonishing foresight the disaster that awaited the French. The pages in which he showed how easily the line of the Meuse could fall and pictured and projected into the future the ambiguous path followed by Leopold III are there for all to read. He had only one trait in common with the great military leaders of whom I have been speaking: he also believed that the value of effectives lies in quality rather than in quantity. But in his case this statement was related to a broad plan very different from theirs: he wanted some hundred thousand professional soldiers to be thoroughly trained so that they could fight in tanks and planes with the purpose of breaking through the front and destroying the enemy rear. These men would renew the cavalry exploits of yore. I shall always remember de Gaulle's arrival at my house ten years ago. There he met one of the most prominent officers on Weygand's staff, an extremely intelligent and courageous soldier who was to give a fine account of himself in the battles of May and June 1940. Colonel de Lattre de Tassigny assailed de Gaulle's revolutionary thesis; de Gaulle, with an abundance of argument and considerable violence, held his ground. At the time my wife and I felt that the controversy was exceedingly unpleasant to listen to. We could hardly be expected to realize that in that clash of opinion the fate of France was at stake. Around 1935 de Gaulle wrote the chapter on military affairs for a book in which Paul Reynaud proposed a general program for revitalizing the state. Weygand sent this note to Reynaud: "What you have written has deeply interested me, but I do not agree."[18]

[17]But not the American military attaché, Colonel Fuller.

[18]De Gaulle seems like a voice crying in the wilderness if one considers only the French High Command. But, as early as 1934 and 1935, it was not at all uncommon for young staff officers to inveigh against the "army of concrete." For instance, in 1936 I made a note of the remarks of a young captain who was preparing General Weygand's son for the War School. "Concrete and still more concrete. Static security: but it can never be complete. The High Command is bothered day after day by Chambers of Commerce in the north writing to call attention to a hole in the defensive fence. The High Command cannot make up its mind about the new forms of war, about the mechanized force. It fears the unknown. The High Command prefers to stick to the rules of 1914–18. But 'concrete' will provide for no more than an army comparable to that of 1870. With us, for all immediate purposes, the offensive

3

The "Phony War," September 1939–May 1940. Gamelin Does Nothing To Spur Armament Production. He Allows His Armies To Become Soft

EUROPE WENT TO WAR. In eighteen days tanks and planes broke Poland. From the very start the Polish Staff lost control of its military machine. The fate of a guinea pig in a laboratory experiment tells the tale of the Polish Army: once the hinterbrain has been cut all power of co-ordination is lost. Then Gamelin's great mistakes began. He deliberately rejected the Polish lesson, just as he had paid no attention to the lesson of Spain.[1] It was simple enough, he thought: the planes and the tanks had smashed everything in Poland because they had met with neither fortifications, nor anti-tank and anti-aircraft cannon, nor trained artillery, nor competent officers, nor adequate staffwork. I was told that neither he nor the director of operations could find any time to spend on the Polish files at French General Headquarters.[2]

Thus they threw away the last opportunity to revise existing tactics, to devise the means of stopping the blitzkrieg, to use tanks and planes after the German pattern, to mechanize the Army in the right manner, and to "motorize" it, to introduce the notion of "movement" into our

is no longer anything but a tactical notion. The strategical offensive is to come into play only after the strategical defensive."

It was said that among the generals at the top of the French Army, next to Georges and Gamelin, some had been won over to the new ideas. Doumenc, to quote one name. Yet how explain their passive behavior in the Superior War Council?

[1] General Duval discussed the Spanish War in two books published in 1938 and 1939. He brought back from the Peninsula nothing which did not confirm the notions of the French General Staff on airplanes and tanks. Masses of planes attacking by dive-bombing? Impossible! Tanks used in advance of infantry? They would be doomed! Weygand, in a preface written for the first book (*Lessons of the Spanish War in 1938*), approved of these conclusions.

[2] Today General Georges washes his hands of the whole business by producing the memorandum of September 14 (see page 12, note 5), which issued from the Bureau of Operations. Gamelin is supposed to have given no heed to this. But was this memorandum anything more than a routine recording of the Armengaud report by the proper military officials?

doctrine of warfare. In May, French soldiers had to enter the fight after marching thirty, forty, or fifty kilometers with a full load on the back. Paul Reynaud, Minister for National Defense, received a pathetic letter from a colonel, stating that he was about to kill himself in the hope that his sacrifice would awaken those whom all argument had failed to convince.[3]

It was too late. The General Staff was haunted by fear of traffic jams on the roads. Whether true or false, a story went the rounds about the Germans having had trouble with their armored divisions when they marched on Vienna in March 1938. So long as the war lasted it was only in exceptional cases that French infantry was provided with motor transportation. Most of our field artillery and some of our heavy artillery were drawn by horses. The engineers and the supply services labored under the same handicap. And what adventures we had with requisitioned trucks! Besides, there was a lack of remounts. "Large-scale movements were simply not within the power of the French Army," said General Carence to the Riom judges. If the French General Staff was so deeply concerned about possible military stoppages on the roads, it might conceivably have foreseen what assistance the uncontrolled exodus of refugees would give the enemy. But that side of the question caught it unawares.

Meanwhile, on the western front, the eight months' lull began—to all intents and purposes a *de facto* armistice conceded us by the Germans. Superficially it seemed to support the official French thesis—the impregnability of the defensive. Yet this unexpected reprieve did not mean that the Germans were still in doubt as to the methods for breaking through defensive positions. It meant simply that their matériel, especially their tank matériel, was not sufficiently perfected or had not come out of their factories in adequate quantity, that they still had to staff the command of their armies with capable officers and to increase the number of their effectives. Perhaps the delay also meant that Hitler was reluctant to stake his all while he could still hope, as he had always obstinately hoped, that France would collapse internally and submit.

Gamelin joyfully pocketed this unearned profit. He had feared that heavy bombing might hamper the mobilization and grouping of his armies; no such interference occurred. In September 1939, not having dared request or having failed to obtain from the government a decision to go into Belgium, he had been afraid, on the declaration of war, lest he would not have time to build the network of field fortifications which

[3]Reynaud ordered an investigation, and the officer's suicide was ascertained.

was to extend the Maginot Line to the sea. Now he was given time to fill the gap. His stock piles of matériel and munitions were so inconsiderable that the problem of how to hold out, even in moderately severe engagements, until the factories should come into full production, must have been agonizing for him. Incredible luck—he now had time to build up his supplies. Prior to April 9, 1940, the French artillery fired only 304,000 shells as against a monthly average of 5,500,000 in 1918.

Amazingly enough, the generalissimo did not appreciate the solemn, decisive importance of this gift that had been bestowed upon him, of this fleeting hour. He was responsible for the nation's fate: he should have asserted his leadership, forced action, if necessary, from ministers and Parliament, compelled everyone to conform to his will, imposed upon established institutions the technical dictatorship needed for victory. He did nothing of the kind. He continued to handle the wheel with soft fingers.

In 1936 he had shunned the task of supervising the rearmament of the French Army, as defined in the program which the "Popular Front" Ministry had agreed upon on September 6. He had seen in that rearmament an undertaking outside the scope of his direct control; perhaps he feared to clash with the powerful officials and vested interests which, sooner or later, might make it their special concern. His General Staff, of course, had submitted plan after plan for carrying out the 1936 program: indeed, it had submitted altogether too many of them. It had proved unable to stick to an unwavering production schedule extending over several years. Everything had been kept in flux because of its shaky tactical and strategical constructions. Gamelin had punctiliously presided at meetings of the consultative committee on armaments and had always had a representative on the production board, the "vigilance" board, etc. But directly his orders had been transmitted to the Bureau of War Fabrications (in the Ministry of National Defense), he had felt that he was no longer responsible. He had not eagerly watched deliveries nor made a point of protesting to the Minister if time was being wasted.

Having once forwarded his demands and "plans" to the Bureau of War Fabrications, he had taken no personal interest in what became of them. He had assumed the attitude of a customer toward a monopolist merchant—the Ministry of National Defense—rather than behave as a chief toward subordinates. When mobilization came a dreadful lag faced him: the D 1 plan (1936) would be completed one year late. The E plan, which was to succeed it and had been adopted in January 1938, was in its preparatory stages, and the E 1 plan, intended to be the corrective of the latter, had not yet been given serious attention. Let us not forget that all those "plans" were merely the small change for the full coin, the program of 1936.

In the second week of the war, on September 14, 1939, an Armament Ministry was set up under a staunch patriot—Dautry. At one single stroke Jacomet, Chief of the Secretariat in the Ministry of National Defense and War, and the officials of the Bureau of War Fabrications were pushed to the background. Up to that day Gamelin had laid blame on them for everything that went wrong. Was he going to make a new departure, to assert his authority over Dautry, to look upon him as his lieutenant? Would he adhere to the letter and the spirit of the two decrees of January 18, 1935, which gave him powers over rearmament and industrial mobilization, powers which Weygand had never had?[4] Was it not of vital importance that a new program be worked out, molded upon realities now become tangible, and that not an hour be lost?

Gamelin changed not a whit. He knew what had to be done, but neither to civilians, who were his superiors, nor to soldiers, who were his subordinates, has he ever said, "This is my will." He let everything languish and dissolve into technical research and argument. The military bureaucracy, the civilian bureaucracy—he let both slumber on peacefully. Indeed, the High Command itself had become bureaucratic. On the General Staff a colonel of middling reputation was head of the armament services, which worked with Dautry without any sense of urgency.

In September 1939 the French Army had at its disposal the arms and munitions necessary to wage war in 1914-18 fashion. It had them and knew how to handle them. As for the arms which we generally describe as "modern"—tanks, planes, anti-aircraft artillery, anti-tank artillery, mines, communications—it was grossly short of them, and, more important still, its leaders had not yet learned how to use them. But let us leave aside the question of their use. Let us concern ourselves only with matériel itself.

According to the inventory taken at the beginning of operations, this matériel could scarcely meet the requirements of the first six or seven months were the struggle to reach some degree of intensity. From every point of view, then, it was essential that the full flow of new supplies should come forth by the end of March 1940. Gradually it became apparent that, at best, we should not be ready before the following autumn, or even the end of the winter of 1940-41. It is a long, sad tale which, in

[4]See page 325, note 10.

many respects, still baffles investigators. At the Riom trial certain figures were given by the military witnesses called before the court and by the state attorney in his general statement of the case. On the face of it, the latter was tricky with the truth, perhaps because he feared that the truth might break through any bounds he sought to set and might escape his control. I have been able to check in part the information contained in the dubious document produced under his name, thanks to sources connected with the Ministry of Armaments.

The infantry lacked rifles. Only 100,000 or 200,000 of the 1936 model were available. Our soldiers, therefore, went out to fight with the perennial Lebel rifle of 1886 and even with Gras rifles of an earlier day. But has the common soldier's rifle much importance in the battles of our time? The production plan formulated in 1936 would seem to indicate that it has not. As for other arms, the infantry had its full complement of automatic rifles of the 1924–29 type and of machine guns of the 1914–18 type; in both cases, however, the auxiliary parts required for anti-aircraft fire were absent. Up-to-date tommy guns and automatic pistols had not yet left the factories. The infantry possessed all the trench mortars asked for by the General Staff, but it had only superannuated types of hand grenades and grenade throwers. There were not enough caterpillar trucks: almost a quarter of those ordered were never delivered.

But there is a very serious point. Excellent 25-mm. anti-tank and anti-aircraft cannon had kept a host of experts busy since 1934. About two thirds of the anti-tank 25s requested for the infantry were at the disposal of the Command. The second reserve divisions, therefore, were left out of the distribution. They had to fall back on the 37-mm. infantry gun, which was out of date and could achieve an initial velocity of only five hundred meters, less than half that needed to pierce armor. A special shell was improvised in a hasty attempt to correct that defect.[5]

Where the artillery was concerned things looked better. There was plenty of matériel: almost six thousand 75s, including the new model with a range of eleven kilometers, almost four thousand heavy old model 155s, both short and long. The factories concentrated on the four types of the new 105s—one of which was built to take the place of the 75. In all, there were one thousand and five hundred of those new weapons in service on May 10, 1940. The supply of shells was uncertain, except for the 75s, for which there was a sufficiency as early as March–April 1940.

[5] As to grenade throwers, caterpillar trucks, the anti-tank 25s, etc., Daladier questioned the figures given in the statement. Those on which he insisted were higher. (Cf. Appendix 4.)

The 105, the 155, the 25 anti-aircraft were all short of ammunition. A great debate went on endlessly between various army services as to what kind of fuse should be employed for the first two of these guns.[6]

Generally speaking, the High Command had not yet decided, even by April, whether it should set the figure of its monthly needs at three, four, or five million shells, and, as far as specifications were concerned, it was still undetermined as between the steel shell and the steel-jacketed cast-iron shell: the latter could be manufactured more cheaply and in larger quantities; the former was more efficient.

We had two weapons which, apparently, were unequaled in other countries: the 47 anti-tank gun and, above all, the 90 anti-tank and anti-aircraft gun, which could pierce a 90-mm. armor plate at a range of one thousand and eight hundred meters. It is a difficult and tedious job to manufacture this gun. A sleeve of steel has to be forced into its barrel. The metal of this barrel for weeks on end subjected to terrific pressure, becomes more and more close-grained, thereby making possible a greater and greater explosive charge with corresponding initial velocities. Unhappily, there was little or no supply of shells for these 47 or 90 guns. The first thousand of 90s shells was not delivered until April 1940. By the end of May only five thousand in all had come off the production lines. And so, when the storm broke over us, we had to fall back on the anti-tank 25 and the 75, the 75 adapted to an improvised use with an improvised shell, not to mention the old 37.

With regard to armored equipment, we were perhaps better off than most people think. We began the war with 2,484 tanks, and we had 3,186 of them on May 10 (plus some three hundred in North Africa) as against four thousand and two hundred German tanks at the earlier date and seven or eight thousand at the later.[7]

It is unanimously agreed that this matériel was outstanding, superior both in firing power and in armor to that of the enemy. There were 636 heavy tanks of twenty-seven to thirty tons, 2,710 light cavalry or infantry tanks. The S.O.M.U.A. 20-ton tank was the triumph of our engineers. One of these vehicles held up under a direct bomb hit: all of its crew

[6] The special type of heavy artillery required for destroying heavy fortifications was not at hand. Nothing had been ordered—neither guns nor shells specially designed to make old matériel equipment serve this purpose. Therefore the French Army was hardly in position to attack the Siegfried Line. Planning and research were still in full progress.

[7] At Riom, Gamelin insisted that certain of our armored cars of the latest model could be included with the tanks in any comparative figures. On May 10 the High Command had more than six hundred of these vehicles.

was killed, but it was able to move on with another crew. Four thousand of those magnificent weapons were to flow out of our plants by September–October 1940.

Where, then, were the weak spots? The heavy tanks were equipped with insufficiently large fuel containers and, consequently, had not a wide radius of action. Their speed was limited. Many of the light tanks were armed only with old 37s (rather than new guns of the same caliber, produced as early as 1938); the projectiles of these out-of-date weapons, we know already, were ineffective against enemy armor. Our radio transmitters were no good. They had a range of only fifteen kilometers. Indeed, some tanks had no sending apparatus whatever. We had only seventy self-propelled cannon approximating the type favored by the Germans. The order had been given too late. Few fuel trucks were to be seen. Normally each unit needs three of these—one close by, the other on its way to or from the base, and the third refueling. We had to depend on makeshifts. During the night of May 15–16, south of Dinant, between Flavion and Ermeton, the 1st Armored Division, having run out of gas, had to take position on two parallel lines and, paralyzed, await the enemy.

All of these mistakes sprang from an unsound tactical doctrine. French tanks, looked upon as defensive weapons, burned up their fuel supply in three or four hours. German tanks, intended for the offensive, were more generously provisioned. "Our best tank, (the B 1 bis, thirty tons), in addition to a 47 and two machine guns, carried a 75 able to shoot only along the tank's main axis; the heavy German tanks were mounted with a 75 or a 105 shooting from a turret in any direction."[8]

[8]Jean Labusquière, *Vérité sur les Combattants,* 1942. But, worst of all, was the carelessness or the perpetual hesitation of the General Staff over the use of this matériel. Only in December 1938, "after superficial and very limited experiments," writes the state attorney in his introductory statement at Riom, "did the Superior War Council provide for the creation of two armored divisions, and these were not to be ready until 'October 1940.'" The Nancy tank training unit was to be split in two by September 1939. Out of the nuclei which were thus released, the two divisions gradually expanded. They were formally set up on January 16, 1940, but not at full strength. The 3rd Armored Division was constituted on March 15, 1940: by May 10 it was not entirely ready for action. On that date the fourth began to be roughly put in shape. Its tanks were hurled into combat the moment they came out of the factory doors. On the other hand, two light mechanized divisions were already in existence, and a third was added to them on January 1, 1940.

Our armored division normally included sixty heavy and ninety light tanks; our light mechanized division, 160 light tanks. A Panzer division included about four hundred tanks, of which 185 were heavy. It was much more generously supplied with anti-aircraft guns than the French opposite number. The proportion of light tanks in our units exceeded the German. In Riom, Daladier set the number and size of German tanks at much lower figures. More than half of our tanks (that is, some two thousand) were scattered about in forty

The new style of warfare called for new devices in the equipment of the engineers, in mines and communications. With us, all remained obsolete. For instance, the engineers had no appliances for crossing the rivers with heavy tanks. We still resorted to the old collapsible raft while experts were poking around to find the right pneumatic raft. On the Meuse the Germans brought forward precisely what we had failed to find. With regard to mines, also, the Germans were our masters. We did have the light mines of the model singled out by the General Staff. But as far as other types were concerned, those which were to prove most deadly to infantry troops, "our investigations had not been concluded until shortly before May 1940." (Riom statement.)

Our communications had been neglected. Not only was radio matériel not up to schedule, not only were the infantry and cavalry tanks not equipped with it except after "considerable delay," not only were units without their full allotted share of it, but a third of the necessary light wires and telephone apparatus for current use had never come to hand. Once again the technical services had been unable to terminate their wrangling in time. And now we have to tackle the most obscure matter of all—aviation.

Here we find all the military witnesses at one. In the quantity and quality of our machines, in spare parts, in accessories, and even in the training of pilots, our failure was dismal. "The training courses had to be extemporized, almost from the whole cloth, in September 1939" (General Mouchard). Two groups of parachute troops had been formed in September 1937. The High Command, always puzzled by novelties, gave this "air infantry" no status until January 1939. In Germany at this date a whole division of such troops had already been trained. Thereafter, to the best of my knowledge, nobody ever heard anything more about French parachutists.

But let us try to take stock of pursuit, reconnaissance, observation, and bombing planes. On paper the total comprised 1,241 aircrafts on September 3, 1939, excluding the 131 Bloch planes which were antiquated.

---

battalions attached to various army corps, armies, etc., in conformity with the past and the present ideas of our military leaders. According to Colonel Perré, of the 2nd Armored Division, General Gamelin, in instructions dated December 17, 1937, and June 28, 1938, had foreseen the possibility of a massive use of tanks along the extended fronts: "Whereas the tank, with little support from other arms, can achieve very great results against the enemy while he is on the march or is disorganized by combat . . . the tank should not depart from co-operation with other arms when it is up against an enemy on guard and in possession of all its resources." This notion, halfway between the German and that of the old French school, remained a dead letter. It probably merely reflected one of Gamelin's passing thoughts. (Cf. Appendix 4, pages 595–96.)

But General Vuillemin, commander in chief of our Air Forces, asserts that he could only rely, then, on 494 "modern" planes. And he will not allow the adjective "modern" to be applied to the 390 bombers appearing on the list. On May 10, 1940, this same general asserts that the number had increased from 494 to 1,310: 790 pursuits (fighters), 140 bombers, 170 reconnaissance and 210 observation planes.[9] Counting reserves and outmoded aircraft, we were to have at the time of the armistice some forty-two hundred planes, if not more. It goes without saying that

[9]Here we come upon a mystery. After the informal meeting of August 23, 1939 (at which it was, in fact, decided to back up Poland), the Air Minister, Guy la Chambre, begged Vuillemin to confirm in writing the encouraging account he, La Chambre, had given verbally. And Vuillemin did this on the twenty-sixth, in words surprisingly at variance with the figures given above. "Our pursuit planes," he said, "could by day assure protection to planes on local missions along the lines and cover us against enemy attacks." By night, in view of the reduced power of our searchlights, we could not look to any particularly efficient work by specialized aircrafts. As for reconnoitering, things had improved and there would be "quick progress in the near future." In the matter of observation, we should have to wait, probably a fairly long time. "Our bombing potentialities have not changed since September 1938." We should be limited to "night actions at short distances or daylight actions close to our lines, under favorable weather conditions and against objectives familiar to us and weakly defended." With all that, Vuillemin took for granted "considerable British support." He ended on that conclusion: "The air power of the principal allied or friendly nations is still widely exceeded by that of Germany and Italy. All the same, the mighty efforts of the last year have enabled us to improve somewhat the flagrant disproportion of September 1938 in relative strength. Great Britain and France are on the way to an even sharper recovery if one takes into account the matériel of high quality about to be put in line. Within six months, provided our means of production are not weakened by the enemy's offensive air action and the Soviets do not join the war, Franco-British air power should succeed in counterbalancing fairly satisfactorily the German and Italian air armada. . . ." Be it recalled that, on May 10, Germany had five thousand planes available, with plenty in reserve. Was not all this talk merely window dressing conceded to La Chambre? This would hardly fit Vuillemin's character. The riddle was not solved in the Riom trial. The figures which Vuillemin quoted in his letter to bolster his statements are in no way comparable to those I give above, for in it he lumps together the English and the French forces. The Allies, he said, had thirty-eight hundred first-line and nineteen hundred second-line machines. The Axis, sixty-five hundred and six thousand respectively. In the last paragraph of his letter Vuillemin insisted that our anti-aircraft defenses should be strengthened.

On September 3, 1939, these were at their lowest ebb, the Air General Staff having always believed that the pursuit offered the only real protection. To stop planes flying at low altitudes we had only three hundred and sixty-nine guns of small caliber on September 3 (i.e., one fifteenth of the January 1938 program), and most of these were purchased abroad. By May 10, nine hundred and fifty 25s had been added. Against planes at middling altitudes (fifteen hundred to five thousand meters) we had, on September 3, one hundred and twenty-four modern 105s, and in May, at most, nine hundred and eighty-eight 75s (old model) and eight hundred and forty-two 75s (new model). Finally, against high-altitude flights, in September, we had nothing and borrowed some 90s from the more foresighted Navy, which had set the Creusot to work upon them as far back as 1930. Our British allies also lent us some 94s. At last seventeen of the 90s included in our plans were delivered in May.

the French, no more than the British, thought it worth their while to manufacture anything like the German Stuka, the tool which worked such wonders breaking our front.

Such details lift the veil on the whole picture. Gamelin and the other army heads were positive that the crisis would come in the spring: however, they made little attempt to accelerate from outside the tempo on which the Armament Ministry expedited its business. They failed to take obvious and simple preparatory steps even in items easiest to procure. For instance, the maps of Norway distributed to the troops when they embarked for that country in April were, from a military point of view, practically worthless. An even more surprising fact: we apparently forgot to print good maps of Belgium. And in the Alps the artillery had no distance tables.

The Supply Services Corps was violently and not undeservedly criticized. It was not merely that boots and blankets were missing when winter came.[10] An entirely trustworthy officer has to say that his regiment—a crack regiment—did not receive until January the ammunition needed to try out its machine guns. Mobilization itself, however, unrolled with clockwork accuracy.

The most serious charge of all must now be leveled at Gamelin and the entire High Command. It regards preparedness. There was no intensified training of the soldiers on duty in the Army Zone. These men were destined soon to face those fanatical young Hitlerites who with linked arms advanced to die at the crossing of the Scheldt shouting "Heil Hitler," knowing that the first ranks would be mowed down but that the others would get through. It was all-important that the men who were to face that kind of enemy should be vigorous fighters, fully seasoned for battle. We should have filled those eight free months granted us by the adversary with unceasing maneuvers, not only with the mimic warfare of peacetime, but with a continuous series of minor front-line operations against the Nazis. It was vital that every soldier should pass through the school of actual combat, all the more so since none were at home with the new weapons which trickled to the front.

It is a commonplace of military tactics that a defense which does not occasionally throw out offensive spearheads and lacks dynamism is done

[10]Daladier had cut down the appropriations allocated to the supply services in the rearmament program: four billion two hundred million had been granted as against seven billion requested. Besides, these services did not see to it that what they had stored should reach the troops. In Troyes huge stocks of blankets, boots, etc., were overlooked and left unused. Meanwhile, in answer to a call for help from General Giraud, Mr. William Bullitt had given that army commander twenty thousand dollars to purchase blankets.

for. In war everything that does not move is doomed to destruction. But what actually happened? There were whole sections of the front, notably along the Rhine, on which the two armies, by tacit agreement, spared each other any annoyance. There was implicit understanding that certain roads must not be shelled at, and artillerymen and machine gunners were not to break this truce, which was certainly not a truce of God. There is the story of the group of German soldiers who had the hardihood actually to come to buy minor necessities from a roadside shop frequented by French troops. They were captured, of course. They had gone a little too far. We were not quite so casual as that. But the incident testifies to the atmosphere of the front. Strange, certainly, was the sight at the Kehl bridge. Halfway across it a barricade separated the two armies: on each side of this barricade anglers cast their lines. But was our passive attitude matched by the Germans? In the advanced lines, perhaps. In the rear, we do not know. Anyhow, for many months or years they had been molded very differently.

Propaganda and psychological warfare were in their element. Repeatedly, and in many different places, the Germans tried various experiments in fraternization—after the Bolshevik manner of 1917 and 1918. Near Forbach they engineered an apparition of the Blessed Virgin. They took a statue from a near-by church, and the statue slowly rose in a glow of light above the trees. The Breton soldiers, for whose benefit this performance was staged, knelt and wept. Soon, of course, French machine gunners put an end to the show. And it must be admitted that there were odd happenings among the Germans, incidents which disclosed a very strange state of mind. An army doctor heard that the Gestapo was looking for him in connection with "a crime against the race." He consulted a company commander. "You had better desert; there's nothing else you can do," said the officer. "But where in the world can I find shelter? It will be all the worse for me if they catch me." "Don't worry," said the officer. And he led the army doctor carefully through the German mine fields to one of our small outposts. Taken to an army headquarters, the deserter managed to create a sympathetic interest in his case. He got himself into our radio propaganda, volunteered advice. Higher military authorities insisted that he be sent on to them; his fortuitous hosts were reluctant to let him go.[11]

The newspapers of the period talked a good deal about night raids undertaken to feel out the enemy and accustom the men to fighting.

[11] It would be a mistake to think of German morale as being like a block of granite during the early months of the war. The block had cracks which we should have tried to enlarge.

These raids, however, were exclusively the task of special groups, made up from each regiment by calls for volunteers. Side by side were priests, schoolteachers, toughs, daredevils of every kind and from every class— all of them born fighters to whom continued inaction was intolerable. But the general mass of soldiers came to believe that perilous expeditions were none of their business: all they had to do was to wait patiently in the safety of their forts until the German power crumbled by itself.[12] "A colonel who does not put his men to work and leaves them idle is a criminal," one old general exclaimed in my presence.

It was in January that I noted this in my diary, without suspecting how vast and how real was the evil to which it referred. In their billets and encampments the men were bored.[13] Every evening Ferdonnet, the French traitor who spoke on the Stuttgart radio, had attentive listeners. Discipline grew lax: respect for the property of the evacuated inhabitants of the frontier regions was less even than might be expected. An officer has written: "I saw soldiers coming back from the front indescribably fitted out: several wore furs obviously stolen from the quarters they had occupied during their last rest period. None of their officers had done anything about it." There was another very bad sign, which was not taken as seriously as it should have been: the Germans took an average of four prisoners to our one. Also there were suicides. And what can be said of officers who read *Gringoire, Je Suis Partout,* and other such papers, which, as they were never tired of damning the Soviets and Léon Blum, were apt to look on Hitler and Mussolini as pillars of traditional society? Suppose our revolutionary soldiers of 1794 had been led under fire by the Royalist émigrés who actually fled to Coblenz. Neither Fleurus nor Jemmapes would be inscribed on our battle flags.

Although the High Command's failure regarding armament cannot be excused, at least it can be accounted for. After all, a separate ministry was committed to do the work. Gamelin had long since made up his mind to be nothing more than an interested spectator where this min-

[12]Almost all divisions of the French Army served in turn on the Lorraine front—the most active sector. But the short stay of each individual soldier at his front-line post—less than a week on the average—was not, in the circumstances, a real baptism of fire.

[13]Orders were that they should be kept entertained. In the little town to the south of Saverne, where he had set up his army headquarters, General Bourret spent two million francs building moving-picture theaters, recreation halls, etc. For all that, the living quarters were very inadequate. One of my friends visited Gamelin at Vincennes, where he noted on December 2: "All are worried about the enforced idleness of the troops, the psychological effect of that endless waiting. The morale of the reserve officers is second rate; they are not taking care of their men. They are bored."

istry was concerned. But how can it be explained that simple army routine and a sort of habitual pace and acquired momentum didn't at least keep the troops awake and thoroughly busy? Obviously the commander in chief failed in his duty. But there still remains the fact that so many generals commanding armies, army corps, divisions, and brigades, not to speak of the colonels under them, never shook off the all-pervading slackness, if only in the normal fulfillment of their daily tasks.[14]

Gamelin and Georges did not even faintly sense how imperative it was for them, under the impending menace of the enemy, to re-endow the nation in arms with a sense of its moral unity. Through the long autumn, through the winter and spring not a single order of the day was issued by them to infuse some thought or feeling into their troops. One of my friends who called at General Georges's house during the summer of 1939 heard Madame Georges exclaim: "It's pretty hard, after all, to have to fight for Poland." "Don't say such foolish things," the general answered. "It is France we're fighting for." Why were words like that not spoken again and again, in whatever form was fitting, loud and clear over the whole country?

When disaster came, when the military structure went down, great masses of Frenchmen asked themselves these questions to which there were no answers, and they concluded—as was inevitable—that they had been betrayed. The truth is that proven acts of specific treachery were very few. I was told the story of an aviation officer who rode a motorcycle from airfield to airfield, informed the Germans as to what he had observed of interest to them in his rounds, and promptly was shot. There was the dealer in medicinal herbs at Epinal who had installed three short-wave sending sets—one in town, two in the country—and who, availing himself of the lessons he had been taught at the Karlsruhe

---

[14]Gamelin and Georges tell us that all proper orders and instructions were issued repeatedly. The building of field fortifications in the "defense sectors" all along the front, and notably in the sector running from Longuyon to the sea, coupled with the movements of divisions taking their turn in the advanced lines, might cause superficial observers to believe that all men and things were kept moving. But none of this could be called preparation for fighting, and the army leaders ought to have known better. In January 1918 the commander in chief of the French Army was Pétain. As usual, he took the most pessimistic view of the future, but in this instance his pessimism led him to be concerned lest the troops become dull and listless. In an order dated December 30, 1917, he prescribed that troops should be given training for a war of movement on open ground, and by doing so he brought upon himself the wrath of Clemenceau's military cabinet, where anything that was not trenches and barbed wire was considered mere waste. The loss of the Chemin des Dames (May 1918) was attributed to the fact that General Duchêne had not followed the commander in chief's instructions. In 1940 the Pétain school of thought had forgotten the only lesson taught by the Pétain of 1918 that was applicable to the new mode of warfare.

school for spies, made his reports to the enemy. And he did that dirty job for a yearly salary of fifty thousand francs.

But the most exciting stories circulating about Paris were fanciful. I do not believe that treachery, in the strict meaning of the word, played an important part in our defeat. But petty treachery, which is bred of neglect and apathy, of leaders great and small who are forgetful of their trust, or rather believe that they can discharge it by the fulfillment of routine duties, that kind of treachery was often to be met. Something more serious than a shortage of indispensable arms afflicted the French Army. Something was amiss. At a juncture most critical for the fate of France the army was no longer the source of inspiration and strength it had always been to the nation. This time it did not rejuvenate patriotism. "If only the civilians hold firm." That is what Forain quoted Verdun's defenders as saying in the last war. The phrase would have been meaningless in 1939 and 1940. The Army was the epitome of a nation cut to its depth by political and social quarrels. Of course there had been reconciliation as the war drew nearer and nearer. But the passionate element in individuals often seemed to be kept in reserve for tasks other than fighting the enemy.

4

Gamelin, an Aged Leader Turned Academic. A Badly Organized High Command. The Clique Spirit—Darlan—Vuillemin

AT THE TOP of the military pyramid stood General Gamelin, a highly intelligent man, perhaps more so than his rival generals, past or present. He was sixty-eight years old but, seemingly, had lost no vigor of mind and body. His statements before the National Defense Committee were lucid and precise—models of their kind. Léon Blum, so completely an intellectual and with so highly a critical mind, openly admired them. Gamelin got the better of the men with whom he had to confer, notably at the Franco-British Supreme Council. Usually the last word was his.

Where was the flaw in the metal? "Gamelin is not a fighting man."

Lord Gort kept telling the British ministers. Yet he certainly earned the right to be called a fighting man when he kept a division in action after it had been almost completely surrounded, in 1918. Nor had he lacked imagination when, as an operations officer for Marshal Joffre, he was the first to grasp the opportunity for the counteroffensive which developed into the Battle of the Marne and to make the right suggestion as to the timing. The truth is that, as years passed by, he became "academic." He burdened himself with what he thought were the "lessons" of the war. All his learning sank into a set of fixed certainties which he was loath to check against changing reality. His prejudices told him that safety lay in avoiding whatever might disturb the general balance of his system. He was as quick as ever at arguing a point, but he failed to notice that the experimental data upon which his arguments rested had gradually become obsolete.

As to military doctrine, he felt that he had foreseen everything, calculated everything, fitted all the pieces together, and that there was nothing left for him to do. "On the seventh day he rested." The military creator looked at his work and found it good. Aristotle had fallen into a degenerate scholasticism. Of course he was willing to incorporate new technical processes in his system, if necessary. Sometimes he could be heard cleverly expatiating upon them. He made British generals believe that he was not entirely unreceptive to Germany's innovations in warfare. He was probably trying to dispel the suspicion that he wore blinkers and to parade his intellectual brilliancy. But the system itself, with the final adjustments it had undergone, was his, and he would not countenance any change. At any rate, he hoped that in the clash with the Nazi war machine all respite would not be denied to him to correct his technique if necessary. This time the Knight of Crécy condescended to use bombards, but he refused to alter in any way his scheme of fighting.

He did not inspire, he did not animate. Fundamentally he was a quietist, a self-satisfied thinker, and any great public service which is not incessantly prodded by the man who leads it tends to slumber. No one who ever talked with Gamelin would say that he was lethargic or deprived of intellectual curiosity. Yet he allowed routine, that sleepiness of the mind, to invade the military community. In June 1940 General Weygand told the story of a divisional commander who, upon receipt of special instructions as to the various ways of putting tanks out of action, inquired from G.H.Q. by telephone which paragraph in the printed army regulations covered throwing bottles of burning gasoline —one of the special means Weygand had suggested. In Gamelin thought and action were not linked together. His mind moved rather freely; his acts seldom ventured outside time-honored patterns.

There was no human and personal relationship between the generalissimo and the Army. Gamelin remained a cold light, an abstraction. How different from Foch! Lord Oxford told me how he had been struck, at the very first Franco-British conference in Boulogne, by the thoughtful and fervent mold of Foch's face. Foch seemed almost physically incapable of despair and of resignation. The paradoxical feature was that Gamelin (if his own words are to be taken literally) regarded war, not unlike Foch, as a huge gamble where the most elaborate calculations could be set at nought by a stroke of fortune, where the dice might suddenly favor those against whom they had been cast, however disastrously. Thus, to all appearances, he stood poles apart from the Pétain-Weygand type of military leadership, from those General Staff officers seated before their chart of military possibilities as if at a game of chess, quite capable, at a given moment, of saying, "I yield," and sweeping the chessmen. Gamelin was wont to emphasize that, in battle, the human element settled the issue rather than any amount of material force. But, coming from one who "took it easy," who was always on the lookout for his own ease, comfort, and advantage, was it possible to treat very seriously such professions of faith in collective and individual energy? Indeed, with some outward characteristics of a man of will, of a man of foresight, Gamelin was a fraud. Few were not caught.

With the passing of time General Gamelin had changed from a soldier into a high functionary of the type who feels his responsibility safely sheltered once he has written a letter to the Premier withholding complete agreement or making agreement conditional. Gamelin was not impelled by a burning passion for getting results. Having fallen to the moral level of an officeholder, he created round him, in his image, a hierarchy of officeholders. In the memorandum submitted to the Riom Court, explaining why he had not made use of his powers over rearmament and industrial mobilization, he argued, twisting the language of the decrees, that only a work of "co-ordination" was expected of him. He hit upon precisely the right word. His method savored of the coordinator's.

The Third Republic had inherited from December 2, 1851 (seizure of power by the ruler who was to style himself Napoleon III), and from the Boulanger episode, a fear of "men on horseback." The Republic, however, thought the Dreyfus case had rooted out this breed of generals. Doubtless it had succeeded, but at the expense of character and temperament in military leaders. Stendhal, in one of his novels, pictures a veteran officer back from the emperor's wars, with wounds received on a dozen glorious battlefields, who is in charge of a regional military subdivision under the July Monarchy, and who trembles before the local subprefect. Turn that general's career the other way round: suppose that he had gone to war only after laboring for years in administrative harness; probably he would never have been a hero.

Gamelin formed the habit of solving by compromise his difficulties with the political power. Instinctively he sought the middle course. In certain stages of his career he was even servile. A diplomat who closely followed his work in Beirut said that he never came to any decision concerning personnel (promotions, new assignments, etc.) until he had consulted the local Free Masons.[1] He did not get along as smoothly with Daladier as people have tried to make out. Between January and March 1940, as he himself has said, he offered to resign on no fewer than eight different occasions. Gamelin protested against a series of demobilization measures which were carried out under parliamentary pressure: among others, the release, between October and May, of several hundred thousand men.

Daladier was irritated by his critical and negative turn of mind. "The Premier does not understand me," said Gamelin, "and I do not understand the Premier." Like a lawyer, he presented brief after brief in an untiring effort to convince the Prime Minister or to overcome some political obstacle standing in the way of some military necessity. He never lost his temper: patiently, point by point, he kept spinning out his neatly prepared argument. Occasionally Daladier would have enough of it and break away, avoid seeing Gamelin for a week or two. When this occurred Gamelin would appeal to high officials, to men close to the chief. "I need help," he would say. "Really, I'm discouraged. For a whole month now I haven't been able to make him listen to reason. Won't you come out to Vincennes for lunch? I would like to tell you what it's all about. Won't you ask him to send for me?" When Gamelin talked that way it was with a deep and real sadness.

The day that Paul Reynaud became Premier, Gamelin hastened to

---

[1]It is not true—as some partisan commentators have stated—that Gamelin reached the post of commander in chief through the influence of the Popular Front. André Tardieu had known him in 1914 at Joffre's headquarters. When, in 1929, at the request of Pétain, then commander in chief, he appointed Weygand as chief of General Staff, with the understanding that the latter would succeed Pétain, Tardieu stipulated that Gamelin should be next in line. And it was during the premiership of Flandin, with Laval as Minister of Foreign Affairs and General Maurin as Minister of War, that Gamelin, in January 1935, was named generalissimo.

invite those who he thought would be influential under the new regime. The recipients of so sudden an invitation were highly amused. It was generally thought that he was not entirely straightforward. For one thing, he rarely looked directly at you when he spoke. He was extremely courteous, but it was disturbing, certainly, to turn to say good-by, as he accompanied you to the door, only to find him already politely bowing, with his glance fixed on his shoes. Yet it is only fair to say that in my conversations with him he spoke clearly and without evasions of any sort.[2]

At Vincennes, where the keep had been fitted out for his headquarters, he lived surrounded by flattery and adulation. In place of a regularly constituted military staff there was a personal secretariat composed of some fifteen officers all known for their devotion to his interests. Not one of them ever spent any time at the front. This little group plumed itself on its high level of culture; books on the history of art were specially in vogue. One officer passed two weeks there, after having served in a combatant unit, and never once was questioned about his experiences with the troops.

In September 1939 the General Staff—in the proper sense of the term, the General Headquarters—was located at La Ferté-sous-Jouarre, and General Georges, deputy commander in chief and himself in command of the northeastern theater of operations,[3] extending from the North Sea to Switzerland, was in the center of the show. All the scholarly celebrities of the Army were collected there, all the number-one men of examinations and competitions: a thousand officers at least. Too many "professors" were among them. Someday the controversies among these intellectuals secluded in a military convent will make interesting reading, but most likely we shall have to wait a long time before the story is written.[4]

General Georges came from Foch's staff, and Weygand, had he possessed authority to do so, would have elected him as his successor in

[2]Léon Blum devised this formula: "Gamelin is intelligent and limited."

[3]According to a warrant countersigned by the President of the Republic—that is, the equivalent of a decree.

[4]At La Ferté-sous-Jouarre, the head of the Operations Bureau was Colonel Préaud, a friend of Gamelin's, an officer of less marked personality than Colonel Gaucher and Major Baril of the Intelligence. Préaud differed with these officers on many subjects, notably on the lessons to be drawn from the war in Poland. In May 1939 Colonel Revers had been named to replace him, but never took up his functions and later was appointed chief of General Georges's secretariat. Disgusted with this job, he applied, in December, for an active command. He was to reappear, much later, as aide to Darlan.

January 1935. He was reputed to be a strong leader, and the Army trusted him more than Gamelin. But he had been very seriously wounded on October 9, 1934, in Marseilles, by the side of King Alexander and M. Barthou, and he had never completely recovered. He had formed a close friendship with Colonel Fabry, a politician of the Right, Minister of War under Laval in 1935, a henchman of Léon Bailby and then of Bunau-Varilla, owners respectively of *L'Intransigeant* and of *Le Matin,* whose baseness was notorious. General Georges certainly had little of Gamelin's intellectual capacity. Would his share in the combination be to supply driving power? I admit that I cannot answer the question. I remember traveling with him in a train many years ago: that trip left me with the impression that he was vigorous and slightly vulgar. In any case, he was treated rather badly by the generalissimo, who regretted having delegated to him such extensive authority. Whatever his personality may have been, the part he played in the campaign cannot be easily disentangled.

The framework of the High Command was designed and its personnel selected at a time when General Gamelin was convinced that he would have under his charge armies fighting on several fronts (an Italian, a North African, an eastern European front, in addition to the north and northeastern fronts in France); at a time also when he was entitled to believe that his capacity as chief of staff for national defense—a title conferred upon him by a decree dated January 21, 1938—would give him supreme authority over forces on land and sea and in the air. If the abovesaid decree had been fully enforced, Gamelin would have ceased to be chief of the General Staff—that is, commander in chief of the land forces in wartime—and Georges would have succeeded him in that respect. In brief, the functions with which General Keitel was vested in Germany would, in the French Republic, have devolved upon Gamelin and those of General von Brauchitsch upon Georges.

Indeed, such was the arrangement which Daladier planned to carry out. But he ran headlong into the bitter refusal of Darlan, who cherished the ambition of becoming the French Keitel. The Prime Minister wobbled during two long months and then gave it up: "They are a damn nuisance—to hell with them!" All things remained as they were, although Gamelin could boast of another high-sounding title. When the bill for the wartime organization of the country came for discussion before the Chamber of Deputies on March 22, 1938, Daladier attempted to conceal his inconsistency and produced those wonderful words: "Is it to be wished for that the chief of staff for national defense should in peacetime, without any further delay, become the generalissimo?" His answer, of course, was an emphatic no. "Care must be taken not to paralyze the creative spirit."[5]

Because of Russia's reversal of policy and Italy's "non-belligerency," and because of vanity and personal interest standing in the way, coupled with Daladier's helplessness, Gamelin's field of authority shrank until it was no larger, or practically no larger, than the province he had originally allotted to General Georges. As a result the two men were acting in the same zone and as rivals. Gamelin never allowed Georges to forget for a single instant that, even in the north and northeast, his was the last word.[6] The paradox was that the General Staff, an instrument of the High Command, should have grouped round one who was only second in command.

In order to recoup himself and recover the means of asserting superior authority, Gamelin persuaded Daladier to effect the reorganization of January 11, 1940, in direct contradiction to the decree of January 1938. Georges was no longer "deputy commander in chief." He was no

---

[5]Here is the story in detail. The object in view was unified command of all the armed forces—on land, on sea, in the air.

A first decree of January 21, 1938, reorganized the Ministry of National Defense (formerly Ministry of War) in order to widen its scope and to extend its control over the air forces and the Navy. By a second decree (bearing the same date) Gamelin was appointed chief of staff for national defense. It was his task to "co-ordinate" all strategical plans. Whenever he thought it wise, he summoned the chiefs of General Staff for Navy and Air, Darlan and Vuillemin. The general secretariat of the Superior Council for National Defense was his research staff. The Act of July 11, 1938 (organization of the nation in wartime), confirmed that state of affairs. But its Article 5 (Title 1) was so phrased as to differ somewhat from the January decree. "The Prime Minister or, subject to his high authority, the Minister of National Defense, charged with co-ordinating all operations by the land Army, the Navy, the Air Force, shall be assisted in this task by a Chief of Staff for National Defense, chosen from among the Chiefs of Staff of the Army, the Navy, the Air Force." Thus, through the years to come, Darlan might hope to get the promotion he still coveted. But this verbal concession in no wise changed the admiral's attitude—he was determined to remain independent. Once war was declared, a new adjustment came about. The secret decree of September 7, 1939, made Gamelin the executive of the "War Committee." Darlan and Gamelin belonged also to that body and sat beside the Prime Minister together with the Ministers for National Defense and War, for the Navy, Air, etc. But they were given only a consultative voice, whereas Gamelin had a regular vote, which testified to his higher status. What happened was that each pulled his own oar. Under Daladier's leadership the "War Committee" scarcely ever met.

[6]Colonel Petitbon, chief of Gamelin's military secretariat, said one day to General Howard Wise, head of the British Mission at Vincennes: "Everything, absolutely everything, must go through me." He was reputed to have put spokes in the wheels merely to vindicate the authority of his chief. He had been at Gamelin's side for more than twenty years, save for eighteen months when he commanded the 142nd Infantry at Rheims.

longer "commander of the northeastern theater of operations," but, more modestly, "commander in chief on the northeastern front."[7]

Moreover, Gamelin permanently retired General Georges's chief of staff (major general), General Bineau, who had passed the age limit two years before and had been called back to active service with other veterans, in September 1939, on a temporary and emergency basis. Then he decided that Bineau's successor, General Doumenc, was not to be stationed at La Ferté-sous-Jouarre, but at a point halfway between that place and Vincennes, taking with him some elements of the Third Bureau of the General Staff (operations outside the northeast front) and the entire Fifth Section (espionage and counterespionage). The commander in chief argued that he was only taking back what belonged to him. In truth, he deliberately created a confused state of affairs in which he was free to interfere at will with the necessary autonomy of his principal lieutenant.

To sum up: the commander in chief and a military secretariat were at Vincennes; G.H.Q. number 1 was at La Ferté-sous-Jouarre; G.H.Q. number 2 was at Montry, near Meaux—not to mention General Colson's staff, which, from Paris, supervised the forces in the interior of the country. Everything was at loose ends. Authority was thoroughly dispersed.[8]

Already in the past General Georges had been forced to realize that the gravest decisions were reached without his being consulted, and he had keenly resented it. But henceforward he was denied the right to choose the generals who were to be under his command, and he felt aggrieved about it. Stripped of that power, he said, his authority was hardly more than an empty shell.[9] The fact is that the Army's two highest-ranking officers did not like each other: the men around them, as is always the case, saw to it that each of them heard anything particularly disagreeable said by the other. I find in my diary one of my friends' conversation with Gamelin on March 24. "For the whole of two hours he

---

[7]In contrast, Weygand continued as "commander in chief of the theater of operations of the Eastern Mediterranean" and Noguès as "commander in chief of the theater of operations in North Africa." Gamelin's actual authority on the northeastern front varied, from day to day, in accordance with his whim and readiness to assume responsibility.

[8]Here is an example of how things were managed. Certain general officers of the British Imperial Staff came to a meeting on Intelligence. This meeting was presided over by General Koeltz, deputy chief of staff of the Army (assistant major general), stationed at the Villa Marguerite in Vincennes. There were present: Colonel Gaucher, chief of intelligence from headquarters in Meaux, Major Baril, head of the 2nd Bureau from headquarters in La Ferté-sous-Jouarre.

[9]Both Weygand and Noguès selected their subordinates.

complained that Georges was never willing to act. He's always putting on the brakes . . . he objected to carrying out an important local action which might have been fruitful. It was his fault that we did not go into Belgium on January 16. From the start it has always been the same story: he opposed our taking a strong stand with Italy." General Georges's friends tarred Gamelin with the same brush. Georges himself told General Sikorski, the Polish Premier, that on September 25 he had wanted to launch an offensive toward Trier. And he told Charles Reibel, on June 14, that if the decision had rested with him, he would have set a limit for the offensive in Belgium. We will not attempt to navigate that contradictory flood of statements and denials. That would be futile. It is obvious that the personal relations of the two generals did not make for teamwork.

A similar friction existed between Gamelin and Darlan, commander in chief of the Sea Forces, or, as he called himself, "Admiral of the Fleet," thereby appropriating to himself a British appellation, the meaning of which he magnified. A curious fellow, that Darlan. Son of a politician from the south of France—his father was Minister of Justice from 1896 to 1898—he clambered up the ladder with the help of two of the great consular figures of the Republic, Fallières and Georges Leygues, both of them elected representatives from his native department, Lot-et-Garonne.

Unable to become chief of staff for national defense, that post being held by Gamelin, Darlan intrigued hard to rob it of all its substance.[10] He affected the plain, gruff language of a sea dog, and this served happily to conceal his basic vulgarity. At the private military meetings in Daladier's office, at sittings of the War Committee, day after day he rubbed elbows with the generalissimo. He did not like to be called on to speak or to be asked to develop his ideas at any length, for he lost his way very quickly in verbal exposition. He would sit there scribbling on his blotter while the others discoursed, now and then contributing to the debate a short sentence or two, an exclamation, fragments of a dialogue with himself. Gamelin exasperated him, and the admiral never missed a chance to do the general a bad turn.

As for his Navy, his attitude was that there was no task, however hard, it could not perform and that he had no need whatever for British assistance. Driven into a corner after having recommended independent action, at Petsamo, for instance, and in the Black Sea, he met the difficulty by means of that simple subterfuge which consists of making the im-

---

[10]He had a reasonable excuse, which was his subordination to the British Admiralty, to which, let it be said, he bowed with small grace.

possible a preliminary condition: "If these diplomats of yours don't know their own business, if they can't provide me with the two ports I need, then don't ask me for anything." He used the same trick for Norway and for Turkey. He flattered the British and got all sorts of honors from them. At heart he hated them: "I wouldn't go shouting it from the housetops, but if I hadn't lent them six destroyers . . . etc. . . ." As for his general view of the war, this indication will suffice: "I won't believe in German aviation until I see it at work. If it possessed the efficiency you mention, do you suppose it would not be already at work?" Still, he had certain real qualities, a taste for detail, organizing ability. He had a far better hold on his personnel than had his predecessor, Durand-Viel, whose high-mindedness and intellectuality were above the heads of most men.

Gamelin's other associate on the War Committee was Vuillemin, chief of the Air Force, a very brave pilot in World War I, liked by his soldiers, but whose own "ceiling" was regrettably lower than that to which his planes could ascend in the skies. Gamelin, who kept insisting that someone else be put in Vuillemin's post, succeeded in having General Têtu assigned to help the latter as chief of staff. This officer was considered remarkably competent, and thereafter Gamelin had no more trouble with the Air Command.

High French army circles remind one too often and too vividly of some club, or caste, insufficiently open to the outer world. It can hardly be gainsaid that the officers trained by Joffre and Foch, and, to a lesser extent, those trained by Pétain, enjoyed, between 1920 and 1940, the privileges of a sort of apostolic succession. In practice, the ruling set in the Army was largely recruited by "co-optation" under a self-perpetuating system, with all dissenters being deliberately hindered in their careers and persecuted. Once Paul Reynaud set himself to find out why de Gaulle had not been promoted to brigadier general and why promises given on that account had not been kept. It turned out that someone had slipped an unsigned note into the de Gaulle file, advising strongly against further promotion.[11]

Enforcement of age limit normally acts as a guaranty against the formation of cliques and monopolies. In France, ever since 1919, the age limit was rendered inoperative, through repeated exceptions to the rule, regarding men at the top. This was so true that when Darlan's predeces-

---

[11]On the ground that, since he had been taken prisoner during the war of 1914–18, he lacked essential experience. Yet he had been mentioned seven times in dispatches and had been wounded at Douaumont.

sor, Admiral Durand-Viel, refused such favors, his action was considered worthy of mention and praise. Marshal Pétain relinquished command of the French Army in 1931, when he was seventy-five; General Weygand in 1935, when he was over sixty-eight. The human figures and faces which took their turn at 4 bis Boulevard des Invalides, peacetime seat of the High Command, were varied indeed; but a dramatist would have discovered in them all a single character—a General Methuselah. Compare this permanence of senility to Hitler's sudden gesture of February 1938, when he put two sturdy men of fifty at the head of the Wehrmacht and the Reichswehr. From 1919 on, remarkable soldiers have led the Reichswehr: Von Seeckt, Von Hammerstein, Von Fritsch. No one of them stayed there unduly long. And once gone—even if only because of some political accident—not one of them ever returned.

Whereas Joffre, in August and September 1914, retired more than a hundred generals, Gamelin hardly ever dismissed anyone during the period of the *de facto* armistice.[12] Yet even on that quiet and inactive front errors had been made, and since achievement in actual combat often differs from the rating accorded by peacetime standards, a generalissimo aware of his duty should have been on the alert to get rid of those who proved incapable or weak. Generals of long experience have told me that when the Forest of Warndt near Forbach was evacuated in October, because of an order either badly drawn up or wrongly interpreted, the general commanding the army involved, and not merely his chief of staff, should have been relieved of his function.

5

Gamelin: Norwegian Expedition and Assistance to Belgium. From Hesitation to Foolhardiness

Now WE MUST FOLLOW GAMELIN into action and into tragedy. After Russia made her pact with Germany, on August 23, 1939, and after Italy

[12]An exception: General Montagne, who explained to the Duke of Windsor how he would go about breaking through the Maginot Line. Although perhaps unfortunate in his choice of a confidant, he had not thereby demonstrated that he was lacking in technical capacity. It was not always because they were deficient in the art of warfare that officers got into trouble.

proclaimed her non-belligerency, the commander in chief never wanted to carry the war—that is to say, the war on land—outside of western Europe. For he was convinced that, sooner or later, the Wehrmacht would be hurled against the Low Countries and France. He thought the attack imminent on October 15 or November 12 (when there was a heavy concentration of German troops in the direction of Belgium and Holland) and on January 15—although at this juncture he did not share entirely the alarm felt by the Brussels General Staff.

At the War Committee of April 3, General Weygand, commanding what was called the Army of the Eastern Mediterranean, held forth in a long monologue. He wanted to create a front in the Balkans. He based his plan on the assumption that the four countries in this peninsula favorable to the Allies had some hundred divisions between them, that these could unite under French Command, and that the three divisions of Syria, plus a fourth brought from Toulon or Tunis, would leaven this mass. A futile dream. Three times before, England had refused even to consider it, so long as Italy persisted in her equivocal non-belligerency, and the Quai d'Orsay, which had favored the enterprise in the autumn, now declared it impracticable. To cap it all, Weygand had to concede that he could not have his forces ready for action at Salonika until four months after he had begun his preparations to go there, whereas no more than two or three weeks would elapse before motorized German forces reached Bucharest. While Weygand read his memorandum Daladier mumbled and shrugged. Gamelin sat in silence, impatiently raised his eyebrows. The whole thing seemed to him absurd and exceedingly dangerous. To his friends he explained privately that, of course, it would be highly desirable for Germany to be forced to fight in the east as well as in the west. But the hour for the western offensive was near. By July the Reich would have 175 divisions in line, 200 toward the end of the year; we had only ninety-one in the north and northeast, plus nine British divisions which would not be reinforced by more than fifteen or eighteen others, at the most, and then only toward the beginning of winter. From such limited strength nothing could be subtracted. Gamelin was right.[1]

[1]As to the eastern front, Gamelin had definite views of his own. His forecast was that the key of victory was to be wrested in North Africa and in the Near East once Germany had been undermined by the blockade. A large-scale offensive would be unleashed from Tunisia, sweep across Italian Libya, carry with it Turkey and the Balkan States as it gained momentum. Finally, on the Danube, it would strike at the heart of the Nazi Empire. Such was the plan which the building of the Mareth Line connoted. But Gamelin did not believe that it could be brought to maturity except after two or three years.

However hostile Gamelin was to dispersed effort and "expeditions" as means to compel the Reich to fight on two fronts, it was impossible for him to take a wholly negative position with regard to projects for intervention in Scandinavia, and even in the Caucasus, since these projects meant tightening the Franco-British blockade—the "keystone" of the defensive credo. From November to February, under neutral pressure, and especially pressure brought to bear by Italy and the United States, the initial French decrees and British orders in council had been rather loosely applied. On November 26 Paris and London decided to strike at German exports as well as imports, but in vain; the rule was not too strictly interpreted, and all manner of exceptions were granted; and far too many goods continued to evade control by being forwarded through indirect channels. American statistics show this clearly. In the last war a greater number of nations co-operated in the blockade: nonetheless, it never was made entirely effective until 1918. Why not resort to more drastic methods than piecemeal restrictions which are bound to operate slowly? Moreover, concerning iron and oil, no other course was open to us but to strike directly at the source in the producing countries, since we could not be sure of intercepting them on their way to Germany by sea, not to speak of transport across Russia, which was out of reach. Iron and oil were weak points in the German war economy. If Germany could be cut off from Scandinavia, seven or eight months of intensive warfare would exhaust her iron-ore reserves. Likewise, her oil supply would fail were purchases to cease in Rumania and in the Caucasus.

Of necessity, the blockade had an important place in General Gamelin's strategic creed (see the articles of this creed as I have formulated them in previous pages). The inner logic of his own doctrine compelled him to lend a receptive ear when Daladier weighed and was inclined to favor armed intervention in Finland, as well as naval and air action in the direction of the Caucasus.

At bottom he was torn—as was Daladier—between two conflicting desires: not to scatter his forces, not to make any hazardous excursions into distant corners of the landscape that would set an avalanche in motion; at the same time, to employ forceful measures to break the primary supply lines of the German war machine. And here a very serious flaw appears in the theory of the defensive war.

Following his natural inclination, he took a middle and wavering line. The English could not see their way clear to conducting air raids on the oil fields of the Caucasus. London's air defense was their main con cern, and this required all their bombers—they dared not spare a single plane. In spite of Darlan's bombast, we had to bow to their decision.[2] On the other hand, our Allies were anxious to destroy the stores of synthetic gasoline in the interior of Germany. But this the French Premier, supported by the generalissimo, vetoed in turn—notably at the Supreme Council on February 5—a veto which was not withdrawn until two and a half months later by Paul Reynaud, and then on the condition that the Germans had first invaded Belgium.[3] Thus the two heads of the nation, the political and the military, resigned themselves to taking no action on the essential problem of gasoline—in one case because they had to comply with the British, and, in another, because they did not want to provoke an enemy offensive before the French defensive apparatus was ready.

As to iron ore, they were bolder. As early as January 1940, Marshal Mannerheim asked for men in addition to the arms he had already secured, and they soon began to form an expeditionary force. To go to Finland meant taking Narvik on the way, that principal North Sea outlet for iron ore, and possibly something more. Still Gamelin followed Daladier reluctantly in the matter: quite properly, he was worried that the Finnish adventure might expand inordinately under the spur of conservative public opinion, then, as always, apt to take fire against the Soviets.

The Helsinki Government having rid us of the issue by signing peace with Moscow on March 12, 1940, Gamelin permitted the Navy, in search of tonnage for our supply line to Morocco, to take back the transports detailed to the expeditionary force. Moreover, the fifty-eight thousand French and British soldiers assembled for the expedition could not remain waiting indefinitely in port; they were diverted to other tasks. The English contingent was sent to France at the request of the generalissimo, who took this opportunity to assign the French alpine regiments back to the Jura.[4]

This left Gamelin at a loss when Reynaud, at the Supreme Council in

[2]However, in March–April, British and even Turks began to move in the direction of the French plan, which provided not only for air raids on oil wells in the Caucasus but also for naval action in the Black Sea. The French Ambassador in Ankara, M. René Massigli, was at the hub of the diplomatic wheel.

[3]Mr. Chamberlain finally won his point at the meeting of the Supreme Council on April 27. If British aviators spent the winter of 1939–40 dropping bundles of printed matter on German cities, they did so as a result of the French veto.

[4]Later this was one of Reynaud's grievances against Gamelin—a grievance not free from prejudice.

London on March 28, bringing up the Scandinavian project from another angle, won Chamberlain over to this plan for action in Norwegian territorial waters as preliminary to an attack on Narvik. He had to reassemble the scattered Norwegian Expeditionary Force and, for doing this, he had to indulge in a good deal of improvisation, which greatly influenced subsequent developments as the experts of the day understood them. Besides, he did not seem to set about the task with great haste. Notwithstanding, Reynaud benefited by his support in the difficult Downing Street discussion on March 28. Gamelin never overlooked that the German battering-ram was threateningly poised on the north and northeast frontiers of France, but it did not entirely prevent him from being alive to the need of risking something in the struggle for iron. At the meeting of the War Cabinet in Paris, after the London conference, he upheld Reynaud against Daladier, who had the backing of General Georges. With Reynaud, and again in opposition to Daladier, he favored granting the British demands for the placing of mines in the Rhine, etc.[5] On the whole, Gamelin followed no constant line; he groped in the dark. All was tentative. Neither Daladier nor his successor ever forgave Gamelin his timid and costly empiricism.

Allied mine fields were laid in Norwegian waters (April 8); Denmark and Norway were invaded (April 9); Narvik fiord was taken by the British (April 13). The fighting started north and south of Trondheim. Things went awry. Mr. Chamberlain and, it seems, Mr. Winston Churchill had not authorized the British fleet to force an entrance into Trondheim fiord defended by land batteries in German hands. The French and British were at an obvious disadvantage; first, because their planes, outnumbered as they were, had to use frozen lakes for airfields when the ice was dangerously thin and already breaking in parts; second, because they had been unable to find suitable places to land their heavy matériel outside Trondheim, which was shut against them. The Germans, on the other hand, were having no trouble in unloading their tanks at Oslo, and General Milch had several regular airports at his disposal.

---

[5] When the British Government yielded to Reynaud's plea for action in Norwegian waters (March 28), it seized the opportunity to revive its proposal to use river mines. The British had urged this plan as early as January, and, with Daladier's consent, all sorts of tests and experiments had been carried out in the sector held by General Bourret's army. But at the meeting of the War Committee convened immediately before Daladier's resignation, the President of the Republic had objected to the project, fearing it would provoke retaliatory bombing of cities in eastern France—easy targets for German aviation—and the Premier had agreed with him.

On April 27 the Supreme Council in London decided to evacuate the Trondheim area. Central Norway was lost. Only under the most favorable circumstances could we continue to hold in the north. Reynaud urged persistence but backed down—he had to, whether he would or not. Later he complained that Gamelin did not possess any moral authority over the British, that he might even have deliberately played a double game. All things went differently when Foch was there to talk to the British, Reynaud's friends kept saying. What was true, of course, was that the generalissimo could not look favorably upon any further increase in our commitments in Norway, upon the increasing numbers of men, arms, and munitions they threatened to absorb. Fourteen thousand French soldiers already had gone there or were on the way. That was enough. The whole expedition had been ruined by Ironside's incompetence, he sighed, and we had to call a halt. Now he agreed with Daladier.

In the Norwegian venture two specific charges were brought against Gamelin in addition to general criticism for his evasive and shifting attitude. Darlan went about exposing what he called Gamelin's carelessness in London on March 28. A memorandum embodying plans for the operations then under discussion had been stolen by an Italian servant from his hotel room. Thus it was possible that the Germans had known in detail the Franco-British arrangements, and that their onslaught upon Scandinavia as early as April 9, twenty-four hours after mine fields were laid, had not been simple coincidence. Furthermore, Darlan, again on March 28, foreseeing an immediate German reaction, had asked Gamelin: "Will you be ready to strike back?" Gamelin had said that he would. But, as we have already noted, the effectives gathered for use in Finland had been spread about and all preparations had had to be made anew.

Now indications pointed to an impending German offensive on Belgium. Undoubtedly the setback we suffered in Norway and the rising tide of war fabrications put an end to the hesitation of which Hitler had given signs in November and January with regard to the Low Countries. On May 10, German troops entered Holland, Belgium, and Luxembourg. Immediately Gamelin rushed aid to the twenty-two divisions of the Belgian Army: twenty French divisions selected from among the best, including three light mechanized divisions and two motorized divisions. In addition he sent five cavalry divisions and nine British divisions.[6] For Gamelin the crucial hour had struck.

[6]Here is the line-up: 7th Army (Giraud): four infantry divisions, one light mechanized division, two motorized divisions; British Expeditionary Forces: nine divisions. First Army

Again and again he had declared to all French Premiers since 1937—the year in which the Belgians had adopted their new policy of "independence and neutrality"—that, having no staff agreements with Brussels and being unwilling to run excessive risks, he would be compelled, when the time came, to hold to a minimum any assistance he might send to Belgium. The formal warning which he forwarded to the Belgian General Staff on January 16, through Daladier and the Belgian Ambassador, expressed a similar determination.

The day before, when Brussels sounded the alarm, French divisions had taken up advance positions and were ready to march. The gist of Gamelin's statement was this: "We cannot possibly continue every two months to undertake the immense and dangerous business of shifting troops about; this invites air attack. Make up your mind before eight o'clock tonight. Either you call us in before you are attacked and we stake everything on the issue while the German armies are not on the alert along your frontiers, and we believe them firmly convinced that you will never give us the initiative and that even if you did we should be afraid to take it.[7] Or, if you really are determined not to call upon us until after you are actually invaded, our divisions will return tonight to their former positions, and afterward you must not expect that on the day of German invasion they will be able to move far beyond the French frontier." In 1937 M. Léon Blum had written to a Belgian Minister—I think it was M. Spaak—on the same lines: "We do not want another Charleroi." That was clear enough. Unfortunately, in all the actions we

(Blanchard): six divisions, including two light mechanized divisions. Ninth Army (Corap): seven divisions, of which one was of motorized infantry, two divisions and a brigade of cavalry. Moreover, of Huntziger's 2nd Army, five infantry divisions constituted the hinge of the whole advance in Belgium. His cavalry (two divisions and a brigade) pushed through into the Belgian Ardennes. Behind the 1st and 9th armies five infantry divisions and three armored divisions were kept ready for massive action at a selected point. This figure of five infantry divisions seems conjectural. Behind the 2nd Army there were in reserve two infantry divisions, of which one was motorized, both being at the disposal of General Headquarters. In the Riom statement it is asserted that Gamelin never had more than three divisions available for his general reserves—an assertion also subject to scrutiny.

[7] I repeat: Gamelin's doctrine of defense not only included the possibility of a counteroffensive against enemy forces, dislocated after an attack against fortified lines, but didn't rule out a search for the opportunity to fight on open ground a war of movement—on condition that the initiative were ours and the surprise factor in our favor. General Giraud shared Gamelin's views. After receiving the negative answer from Brussels brought to him by the Belgian Ambassador on January 16, Daladier, who was confined to his bed as a result of a riding accident at Rambouillet, bitterly regretted the lost opportunity: "Now the war will drag on indefinitely." Daladier was highly enthusiastic over the working of the military machine on January 15 and 16: "Unquestionably, Gamelin knows his job."

took, there remained some ambiguity which persisted until May 10, when it resolved itself into a rash decision.

The French and British governments never repudiated the declaration of April 24, 1937, by which they pledged themselves to defend the territory of the little nation which parted with their alliance. There was no repudiation either before or after January 16. In fact, previous to January 16, they had even worked on a plan for carrying out their obligation. In November 1939, following on the alarm of the twelfth, staff officers of Gamelin and King Leopold, as well as British military representatives, met and discussed plans for eventual Franco-British intervention in Belgium, one providing for an advance to the line of the Scheldt and the other to the line of the Dyle, the "second position" of the Belgian Army which ran through Givet-Namur-Louvain-Antwerp.[8] It has been said that the British Cabinet brought pressure to bear on the French High Command at that time in their anxiety to keep the Germans away from the Belgian coast. Probably this is not true. The British Imperial Staff only agreed to the French scheme after a discussion that lasted several days.[9] Through the early months of 1940 the question was left where it was. Neither Chamberlain nor Daladier, in their communications with Brussels, altered their policy. They even asserted it more definitely at the Supreme Council on April 8.

When all is taken in account, Gamelin's "ultimatum" of January 16 had only a restricted bearing. It meant simply that he reserved the right to adjust his actions to the circumstances. But the fact of capital importance is that Gamelin, who never felt it his duty to demand that Chamberlain and Daladier should cancel the 1937 declaration, and who,

[8] If we had taken our position along the Scheldt instead of along the Dyle, it is possible that the consequences of the battle of the Ardennes and of Sedan might have been limited. The Belgians favored the selection of the Dyle line. The preparations made by the French General Staff seem to have shifted from the Scheldt to the Dyle around March 1940. Anyhow, divisional staffs in the 9th Army of General Corap were given formal notice of the new arrangements by the middle of April.

[9] In November 1939, following on the alarm, the Belgian General Staff somewhat departed from its attitude of reserve. It approached the British Imperial Staff and, on the latter's advice, turned to Gamelin. The Anglo-French-Belgian military conference lasted several days. Lord Gort makes no mention in his dispatches of these November military discussions with the Belgian General Staff. Doubtless he was not authorized to discuss them publicly. In these talks the Belgians were more than reticent in furnishing technical information to their guarantors. According to Lord Gort, the emplacement and the characteristics of the anti-tank ditch on the Perwez-Namur-Louvain line were not made known to the French Command or to himself. A reconnaissance action had to be undertaken, on May 11, to find it out. As late as May 8 the British military attaché in Brussels had vainly asked that the exact position of this line be indicated to him. In the name of independence and neutrality, the Belgian Government condemned both French and British to groping blindly in the dark.

The elements of the German plan and the French "Manœuvre Dyle"

in January, had done no more than provide himself with a way out in case of extreme necessity, considered himself bound to do his utmost to fulfill the Franco-British promise. He merely claimed for himself the right to determine how much could be undertaken without incurring prohibitive risks.

At this point heed must perhaps be paid to another set of considerations. Before 1937 Gamelin (and many others) had never made it his business to have the French frontier strongly fortified in the maritime area, because he was afraid of losing the Belgian alliance for good. Gamelin labored under that fear when the alliance did exist and even afterward, when it had been scrapped, as he still hoped to win it back.

Obviously, if there had been an uninterrupted belt of fortifications running to the sea, the Germans would not have found it an advantage to launch their attack against France across Belgium. Consequently, the Belgians would have felt secure, relaxed their military system, and perhaps tried to find final salvation in an arrangement with Berlin. Then the 500,000 Belgian soldiers would disappear once for all from the military balance sheet of the Western Powers. On May 10, having wasted the opportunity of building up fortifications in the West for the sake of resuscitating Belgian military co-operation, Gamelin must have been irresistibly attracted by the high stakes for which he had gambled: the Belgian Army. How galling to be twice despoiled! He ran after his money.

As he came to grip with the Belgian question, which meant life or death for France, the commander in chief was as incapable as he had been in the case of Norway of binding thought and action into one firm purpose.

On the morning of May 10, at six-fifteen, the French 1st Army Group, under General Billotte, and the British were ordered into Belgium; twenty-nine French and British divisions plus cavalry hinging on Sedan.[10] They were instructed to move as rapidly as possible toward the Givet-Namur-Antwerp line, and there to fight and to hold at any cost. No air attack was made on our columns—that attack which the staffs at Vincennes and at La Ferté-sous-Jouarre had for so many months foreseen and apprehended. Instead, enemy aviation bombed the rear, especially

---

[10]Here is the distribution by sectors, from south to north: the 2nd Army, which did not participate in the converging movement but belonged also to the group of armies under Billotte, was in echelon from east of Montmédy to Sedan (included); the 9th Army, from north of Sedan to Namur, along the Meuse; the 1st Army, from Namur to Wavre, southeast to Brussels; the British Army, from Wavre to Louvain, followed the Dyle; the 7th Army covered Antwerp, the mouth of the Scheldt, and extended into Holland.

railroad stations, roads, lines of supply, and airfields. The very ease with which we progressed toward the enemy should have made us suspicious. But there was no anxiety, not even prudence. Daladier told the Riom judges that General Blanchard dispelled his apprehensions. According to original orders, the movement was to take place only by night. In many cases we also went forward by day under empty and serene skies.

6

Gamelin's Performance Not Even Equal to His Planning. The Military Pundit Collapses on the Third Day

WHAT WAS GAMELIN UP TO? What did he have in mind? Here is the criticism commonly directed against him.

He had always thought that the fortified Maginot Line was the equivalent of a victory of the Marne, of a defensive victory automatically won by France on the first day of the war. He had always calculated that the two Western Powers would have time to mobilize their strength behind this massive wall of steel and concrete and that there would be no need for haste. Then why was he now leaving behind what he considered to be the strongest of bulwarks, to embark upon a war of movement and to fight on open ground?

Had he been preparing through the winter months for this campaign in the open? No. We have seen how he tolerated inertia in the manufacture of armaments, lethargy among the troops. On several occasions he said that he would not hesitate to go through Belgium—if Franco-British diplomacy gave him a free rein—in order to catch the Wehrmacht unaware. But on May 10 it was the Wehrmacht which forestalled our soldiers on Dutch and Belgian territory. There could be no question of surprising it: why, then, did the French and British go into Belgium?[1]

Here is the only conceivable answer. The French Army never left the Maginot Line. It remained there in full strength. French divisions with-

[1]General Giraud disapproved in May the operation which he had approved in January. In May, by dint of hard work sustained all through the winter, the Siegfried Line had been continued northward to face the Belgian frontier.

drew only from the indifferent field fortifications hurriedly built, in preceding months, west of Montmédy. No matter how poorly prepared the Belgians might be or how weak their defensive works, we could count on them to hold for five or six days on the Albert Canal, round Liége, in the Ardennes. Their resistance would give us time to organize the Antwerp-Givet-Sedan line, their own second line of defense, which they should in part have already prepared, and to substitute it for the relatively weak string of fortified emplacements and pillboxes coupled with an anti-tank ditch, for the mediocre military barrier running from the Meuse to the sea in a comparatively wide area where the Nazi Command, free to spread out its troops, would quickly find weak spots.

It was, therefore, a question of exchanging one defensive position for another deemed more advantageous. This new arrangement would make it possible for us to counterattack the German Army after it had forced its way past Belgian resistance and had thereby suffered fragmentation and loss. In any case, should we prefer to await a German onslaught, its impact would be less shattering than if the enemy were left free to re-form at its leisure on the Belgian plains. Meanwhile we should be strengthened by some 500,000 of Leopold's soldiers who would fall back on us; we should protect our northern industrial zone as well as all land approaches to the Channel—in other words, England herself. The line from Givet to the delta of the Scheldt (160 kilometers) is shorter by some one hundred kilometers than the French frontier running west of Givet.

On this relatively narrow front it was not possible for heavy German army effectives to deploy as conveniently as further south in proximity to French territory. There, logically, French and British should have sought their Thermopylae from the start. Logically, that is, if they had been able to make their preparations with no other consideration save that of the greatest military gain and with no concern whatever for Belgian susceptibilities. There the Maginot system should have been extended and closed, joining up with the fortified zones of the Belgian frontier, the Albert Canal, and Liége. There French divisions should have established themselves in September 1939, when the Wehrmacht was doing away with Poland, or yet again on November 12, or even on January 16, 1940.

Let us take the argument for granted. But by May 10, with the Germans stealing a march on us, and with the element of surprise on their side, the enterprise was hazardous in the extreme. Our fate hung on that of the Belgian Army. And, balancing all possibilities, it was hard to believe that five days' grace would allow us to dig in so firmly as to be able to master the German Army, even had it been shaken morally and materially by its preliminary encounter with the troops of Leopold III.

At this point a reader who has been anxiously following the vicissitudes of the present war is likely to exclaim: "What is the use of discussing all the schemes and actions of Gamelin? Is it not sufficient to state as an axiom that armies stripped of substantial air power, of anti-air artillery, and at grip with an enemy which rules the sky, are doomed? Dire experience has taught us that land and sea forces keep their military value today insofar as they are backed by aircraft and special guns sufficiently numerous to counteract the enemy above the ground. Gamelin could not hold his own in the air; therefore he was defeated before the battle began. It mattered little that he should make error after error. Suppose he had proved infallible: the outcome would have been no different. Even if he had stuck to the half-fortified battlefield within French territory, he would have been no better off. Anyhow, the French and the British never had a chance in Belgium. What happened after they passed the frontier is of no consequence."

This view is untenable. The so-called axiom about the utter helplessness of armies too greatly lacking in air power is merely an approximation of the truth. Clearly, such armies have a very unequal fight to sustain. But one ought not to deem them so helpless as to deny that in their case leadership, good or bad, can to some degree affect the issue.

A keener French Command would have learned more quickly that tanks should no longer be scattered in independent battalions. It would have unraveled in time the mysteries of defense in depth. It would have made more efficient use, in the struggle, of what aviation it had and stopped the dispersion of planes. The British themselves, appreciating the French Command's adaptability, might have shifted further to the east—instead of folding back—the air "umbrella" they extended from their island. They would not have withdrawn their fighters.

Under existing arrangements each army commander had at his disposal, or was supposed to have, an observation squadron and a group of fighters; each army-corps commander, some observation planes. They very quickly lost them. For any further support—bombing, long-range reconnoitering, counterattacks by fighters, etc.—army commanders were instructed to apply formally to their counterparts in the Air Force, the air army commanders. If a general commanding a division or a brigade needed bombers or fighters, his request had to be transmitted to the general in command of his army, then passed on to the general in command of the corresponding army of the air, then it filtered down to the squadron and group commanders. According to General Héring's testimony at Riom, that cumbrous procedure absorbed no less than five hours.

Conversely, the Luftwaffe was closely dovetailed into the land forces. Just as they infused a new life and a tremendous one into the war of movement of old, by means of the motor, the Germans had not been slow to perceive that a fighting force must not conform to a rigid pattern, that it should consist of variable elements to fit the special tasks for which it is detailed. The French Command was short of matériel, and hours were numbered. Nevertheless, with some insight and strength of will, several happy improvisations were within reach.

Let us bear in mind what was later achieved in Dunkirk—over 300,000 men re-embarking in the midst of the battle and the resistance to the enemy of the British Expeditionary Force, of the 1st French Army which made possible the achievement. Elsewhere comparable achievements would not have been beyond the wit of a more enlightened High Command. At any rate, it was up to the Command to ward off the worst, the crushing worst. On May 10 the Germans were still trying their hands at the blitzkrieg. They must have been in a somewhat experimental mood. When they endeavored to invade England, in September, they ran on a barrier which proved too much for them. Much sooner, on the Continent itself, they might have stumbled, if not upon so decisive an obstacle, at least upon temporary and incomplete ones helpful to our cause.

The faults of omission and commission to be laid at Gamelin's door in the Battle of the Meuse and the Battle of Flanders are, therefore, of great consequence. As we naturally react against the grossly exaggerated estimate Gamelin had of the military instrument in his grasp, we are perhaps too prone to make light of the matériel power vested in the 125-odd divisions arrayed against the Germans, in thirty-five hundred tanks, in the Maginot stronghold. But for huge errors in tactics and strategy coming on top of the old divagations in the doctrine, those tools would not have been annihilated within five weeks.

The campaign in Belgium opened on a fundamental error. Gamelin knew that he would have to deal with a revised version of the Schlieffen Plan, but he failed to understand what this plan had become, under the careful study of the German General Staff, in terms of new circumstances and new weapons.

The Schlieffen Plan, with numerous, ever-changing modes of applications, rests on a geographical fact. France cannot be attacked through Alsace and Lorraine because the Vosges Mountains form a buttress: she is vulnerable along the valleys of the Sambre and the Oise—the breach through which her most successful enemies have always launched their blows. In a wide pivotal movement across Belgium, which Gröner has explained in his discussion of Schlieffen's ideas,[2] the German right will push toward the Channel coast: it will then attack the main French forces and it will be able to strike at their left flank and perhaps at their rear, since the latter will be concentrated between the region of Paris and the eastern frontier. Thus the fate of the French nation—if all goes well on the chessboard—can be settled at one blow, by a battle in which the French will be obliged to turn their backs on Germany in order to face the Germans coming upon them from the west. For the plan to succeed, the French Army must be engaged and anchored as far north as possible. If the French Army is not locked in battle very early, if it is given time to retreat toward the south, the invader will see his lines of communication grow perilously long. In that case he is exposed to the danger of counterattack by an adversary able to use "inner lines," that is to say, railroads and roads grouped on a perimeter narrower than that on which the invader is obliged to move. The Battle of the Marne was a counterattack of that kind. The problem that faced the German Staff in 1940 was simply not to repeat the mistakes of 1914: the wing which had to sweep down the longest arc had then been supplied with insufficient effectives; because Dutch neutrality had not been violated, its drive had been too slow; the marching columns, as they swept down, were prematurely deflected toward the region east of Paris. Moreover, they were too loosely co-ordinated.

The innovations in the Schlieffen Plan by which the German High Command of 1940 hoped to succeed were these: they would stake a much greater proportion of their strength at the outset, leaving to the relatively few troops in the Siegfried Line the task of holding back the 2nd and 3rd French army groups; they would make their main thrust through the enemy's center, instead of seeking to envelop the Franco-British left—relying on circumstances and the inspiration of the moment to decide where and when to execute this last maneuver.[3] Gamelin was

[2] The *Testament of Count Schlieffen.*

[3] "The choice of the exact moment when one must initiate the wing movement and the exact direction one must give it are among the most difficult technical decisions imaginable." (Schlieffen.) In his speech of July 13, 1940, Adolf Hitler asserted, however, that from the outset the break-through at Sedan was contemplated by the German High Command of 1940.

not prepared to meet these two innovations. The Schlieffen Plan had become frozen in his mind, a memory of his younger days, a dead concept. The Germans had tried to apply it in 1914, and with what a result! They would do no better this time, since in the interval between the two wars the defensive strategy had been confirmed in its supremacy. At this point Gamelin stopped short. He did not trouble to know more. He had not followed the growth of German thought, or else misunderstood it. He did not understand that the coming of the tank and the plane revivified Schlieffen's and Gröner's old conception, gave it a power, a suppleness, a variety of possible combinations and means unknown to the preceding generation.

By May 10 it was clear that the German General Staff was operating on a larger scale, with greater violence and decision and with its moves better co-ordinated, than it had twenty-six years before. For instance, by sending troops into Dutch Limburg it now gained more elbowroom for the invasion of Belgium, and as a result it could speed up its timetable. German divisions could move more freely than in 1914: now they were not forced to crowd through the corridor between Liége and Maestricht. Moreover, tanks took the place of cavalry, which in the last war had not been any too effective.

If Gamelin had remembered Schlieffen's and Gröner's writings—on which so many ponderous studies have been produced—he would at least have realized that the German right wing, when it broke into the Low Countries, would be extremely powerful, numbering some one hundred divisions, not including ten or twelve armored divisions. He never would have left more than half the French Army in the Maginot fortified camp, where it was uselessly superior to the forces manning the Siegfried positions. He would either have given up going into Belgium altogether, or he would have added a good deal to the some fifty divisions sent forward, not counting the Belgians.[4]

Gamelin took particular pains to protect himself against the columns hurled on the Albert Canal and on the Liége fortifications. His 1st Army, under General Blanchard—the most strongly constituted—the British

---

[4]To the thirty-one and one half Franco-British divisions composing the Corap, Blanchard, Gort, and Giraud armies may be added Huntziger's seven and one half divisions, which took direct part in the battle, and, although I am not sure of the total figure, the ten divisions—of which three were armored—held in reserve by General Headquarters but very soon involved. The Germans claim not to have outnumbered us in the Belgian campaign. But in making their calculation they credit us with the Dutch Army, with which we were never able to make firm contact, and with the Belgian Army, whose subordination to the High Command was always left in doubt and uncertainty by the king, its commander.

Expeditionary Force, and his 7th Army, General Giraud's which, on May 13, pushed as far as Hertogenbosch to hearten Dutch resistance, were powerful enough to check the northern arm of the Nazi torrent. But the French generalissimo took slight precautions against a German advance through Luxembourg and the Ardennes to the Meuse. The reasons for this neglect were, first, that an advance through this region did not fit his interpretation of the Schlieffen Plan—in which he saw primarily a flanking movement. Second, that he considered this region the most impenetrable of all. So great in his view was the value of natural obstacles that the Sedan-Namur zone, on which the entire French battle order hinged, was the most weakly held and poorly organized.

The 9th Army (General Corap's) was composed of two and one half cavalry divisions and seven infantry divisions, of which one was motorized and four were classed either as second reserves or "fortress" divisions, which implied second-rate effectives and matériel, with an utter lack of mobility. Two hundred thousand men strung out along 105 kilometers—that was spreading the butter very thin. Here too, more than elsewhere, existed a shortage of anti-tank and anti-aircraft guns. Blanchard, Gort, and Giraud, with their three armies, were holding a front only 160 kilometers long, and they were incomparably better equipped.

Corap's 9th Army reached the positions assigned to it, between Flize to the north of Sedan and Namur, tardily, on May 11 and 12. At certain points the Germans reached the Meuse before it did. Along his sector of some one hundred kilometers Corap's main attention was directed toward the north, between Givet and Namur. In that region he placed his three best divisions. (See map, page 63.)

In Corap's area the weak points lay between Givet and Revin, where a single division was stretched out on twenty-four kilometers, and between Revin and Flize, where the Ardennes "fortress division" was stationed. From Flize to Longuyon—that is, from a point north of Sedan to where the Maginot Line ends just east of Montmédy—the 2nd Army, under General Huntziger, held a sector of some fifty kilometers: eight divisions, three of which were made up of reserves, and of these three, two were second reserves. The latter were very feeble, and it was these that were in contact with the most southern, and feeblest, of Corap's divisions. Whether on their own initiative or in compliance with orders, the two generals centered their inferior troops around Sedan.

It is worth reiterating: our defense was based upon our faith in the high value of the Ardennes-Meuse natural barrier.

From Longuyon to the sea, for reasons which could not have been very convincing since they were endlessly challenged even in high quarters, the High Command had decided by 1936 not to do more than organize a "defensive battleground" by means of fieldworks.[5] But the Meuse area did not even get so much from the Committee of Fortifications, presided over by General Prételat, who during the war was in command of Army Group 2 (the Maginot Line). This committee preferred to allocate funds to the strengthening of Montmédy, the western breakwater of the heavy fortifications, to the districts crossed by the Chiers, a tributary of the Meuse, to the fortified town of Maubeuge and to its neighborhood.

Up to October 1938, after Munich, nothing had been done, for we find Prételat contriving on the spot a new program which he completed on December 19. He left to each "military region" the job of building up the blockhouses, various kinds of casemates, rail fields, networks of barbed wire, and anti-tank ditches. This amounted to letting military bureaucrats, helpless in their local offices, apply their own casual ways to the carrying out of the assignment. Oddly enough, before he took up his command of an army, Corap was in charge of the Amiens military region, with the Sedan-Givet sector committed to his care. Moreover, in the Meuse area itself, Prételat and his associates had shown themselves less concerned with taking care of the deep furrow through which the river runs than with the erection of a series of strong points and anti-tank obstacles perpendicular to that valley: a front beginning at Mézières, touching the Belgian frontier at Rocroi, and following it on to Maubeuge.

On September 7, 1939, four days after war was declared, Gamelin was moved to act. He wrote to General Belhague, the great expert in fortifications, the builder of the Maginot Line, and put him at the head of the Fortified Zones Committee with instructions to fill all gaps. Did this learned man plug up the Meuse breach? No. The Southeast-northwest orientation Prételat had imparted to the work was retained until March 1940. This was because the General Staff still conceived that it would eventually limit Franco-British intervention in Belgium to the Scheldt, but it was also because the staff held the view that the river and the forest were able to look after themselves. There is no need to enter into distressing details. No armor plate was provided to protect embrasures in fortified buildings or casemates. There was no position artillery. The field guns of the occupying contingents would, it was said, suffice. When

May 10 came, all the less did these field guns serve the purpose because they had not been delivered to the troops up to the normal complement. The division of second reserves which Corap scattered between Revin and Flize had no 25-mm. anti-tank guns. The old infantry 37 had to do the job. And be it remarked that Belhague, following Prételat's example, had left to the commanders of armies the arrangement of their own front lines. He and his committee catered only to reserve positions. To sum up, around the hinge there was insufficient preparation, strength, and vigilance.

The strangest aspect of Gamelin's strategy in action was the lack of all sense of maneuver. The Germans would have been in serious danger had French divisions in the Maginot Line to the southeast of Sedan threatened them with a flank attack. General Gröner had feared a counteroffensive similar to that made by the armies of Lanrezac, of Langle de Cary, and Ruffey in August 1916, and, without formally excluding it, he had not dared include a break-through at Sedan in his plan. He had recommended that the advance be maintained on an axis drawn toward the southwest. But the German High Command of 1940 knew that Gamelin was determined not to go into the Ardennes to meet the German thrust, knew also the limitless reliance he placed on this natural Maginot Line of rivers, rocks, and trees, created as though to bolster his belief in static defense. It must have known also that the French Government, toward 1937, had informed the Grand Duchess that under no circumstances would French operations encroach upon Luxembourg. Therefore the High Command determined to risk this attack over which Gröner, Hindenburg's former quartermaster general, had hesitated.

A German military writer has noted the perturbation of the German generals in charge of the operation—Von Kleist, Reinhardt, Guderian, etc.—when they learned, on the evening of May 10, that French tanks had left Carignan, Montmédy, and Longuyon to counterattack toward the northeast. For a moment they thought that their advantage in surprise was lost and that their whole operation might fail. Unfortunately, such counterstrokes were not in the repertory of the French General Staff. The report indeed may have seemed plausible, for the garrisons of the Maginot Line were very near. At any age in our military story other than the era of reinforced concrete, except perhaps in 1870, these forces would never have remained idle. But the counterattack amounted only to mediocre reconnaissance-in-strength and attempts at delaying action by the truck-borne cavalry divisions of the 2nd and 9th armies—nine brigades in all.

These exploratory moves were rather loosely co-ordinated. On the evening of May 10, Corap's cavalry had not even crossed the Meuse, whereas Huntziger's men already had met the Germans to the west of Arlon late that afternoon and were retreating on Neufchâteau and Bastogne. The next day the Corap cavalry spread out toward St. Hubert to protect the left flank of their comrades, who had been so much more actively led under Huntziger. They learned that the latter had been defeated near Libramont and were falling back on the Semoy River, and so they themselves withdrew. By then Guderian light tanks were already in Bouillon. The narrow fortified gorges of Neufchâteau had been easily carried. The Belgian division of Ardennes Chasseurs, trained to defend the Ardennes, had melted away.

It is not my intention to relate the campaign from beginning to end. But I must insist on these details, for they dispose of a story which gained currency and distressed the public.[6] Throughout May 10, 11, and 12, four divisions and two brigades of French cavalry engaged the Nazi armored columns; on the twelfth, French aviators even disturbed General Guderian's field headquarters and forced him to move. By two o'clock in the afternoon of the twelfth these French cavalry forces had crossed back to the western side of the Meuse and orders were given to blow up the bridges. The first German Stukas began to strike. German Panzer forces did not succeed in reaching the left bank until the following day. Therefore it is not true that these forces burst unexpectedly upon the Mézières "fortress" division and upon the other effectives in line with it. For three whole days Gamelin, Georges, Billotte, Huntziger, and Corap must have been informed hour by hour of the enemy's progress. Yet everything took place as if they had been taken unawares. The extraordinary apathy shown by the nerve center of the French Army, whether that nerve center be called Gamelin or Georges or Billotte or Huntziger or Corap, is utterly disconcerting.

Here is an example of that apathy which is even more characteristic because it is on a larger scale. Gamelin gave an order to hold fast along the Givet-Namur-Louvain-Antwerp line "with no thought of retreat." *No thought of retreat:* the phrase must be taken literally. He had allowed no place in his plans for the possibility that he might have to withdraw. He had made no allowance for the hypothesis of a retreat similar to that which his master, Joffre, had been obliged to carry out. He had not dared match the German flanking maneuver in Belgium by

[6]A narrative which Reynaud confirmed and even exaggerated in his Senate speech of May 21.

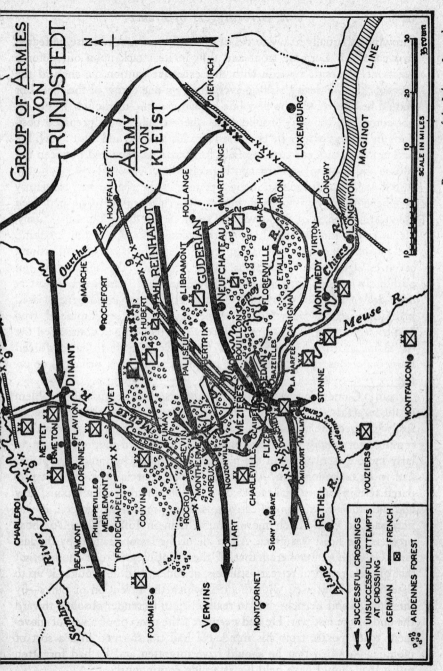

The break-through

By courtesy of the *Infantry Journal*

63

throwing in equally heavy forces of his own, no doubt because he feared
to weaken his Lorraine front and thus invite attack upon our defense
positions. Yet, side by side with this excessive caution, he showed the
most reckless temerity, risking everything on one throw of the dice. For
should he fail to hold the new line he had chosen—or should the enemy
not allow him time to consolidate it—there would be no prepared positions in the rear where he could re-form his defense and start anew. He
had not even ordered that the field fortifications, prepared between the
Meuse and the sea, be permanently manned.

It is true that Joffre's strategical retreat to the Marne and to victory
had been entirely improvised, but at the crucial moment he had been
able to find a mass of maneuver and to piece together Maunoury's army,
etc. Nowhere did Gamelin have anything like this at his disposal. Behind
the 1st, 9th, and 2nd armies, indeed, he had three armored divisions,
seven or eight infantry divisions (these figures for the infantry are not
absolutely certain), two echelons of reserves; but these were almost at
once drawn into the whirlpool of battle. And Corap, who never ceased
protesting against the weakness of the forces under his command, who
had to argue with G.H.Q. for every division that he got, considered the
9th Army as a mere covering force which would have to be reinforced
immediately, as soon as it clearly became the enemy's principal objective!

In 1940 Gamelin's oversight was the more serious because the problem
of the strategical retreat, with planes and tanks as new elements, necessarily had become more complicated than it was in 1914. The procedure
required for setting troops and matériel in backward motion was singularly more difficult than in the past, as harassment by tanks and planes
had to be reckoned with. Anti-tank defense, especially, required a prepared terrain and special tactics, so as to obtain from all weapons, new
and old, their maximum effectiveness. For a retreat to succeed, it was
necessary to yield much more ground than in Joffre's day. To those
problems no heed was given. All in all, of the lessons taught by the last
war, Gamelin remembered that of the "continuous front" and forgot
that of the strategical retreat—still less, of course, had he brought it up to
date. He was obsessed with theories which the invention of tanks—by
the English and French—had in reality begun to render obsolete toward
the end of the last war. He had permitted the concept of a war of movement to evaporate from his mind. He had transformed into a sort of
monomania much that he should have forgotten and he had forgotten
much that should have held his attention continuously.

It has been observed that the principle which Gamelin—and later Weygand—kept reiterating in their orders of the day, "to hold fast with no thought of retreat," brought deadlier results than had the reckless offensive of August 1914. Despite its disastrous outcome, the latter seriously disturbed the smooth operation of the German wheeling movement, and, after all, it had not lacked resiliency. The existence of the Maginot Line perhaps explains this rigidity in combat, this sort of strategical numbness. The question arises as to whether Gamelin had not reached the point where he believed that the introduction into the French military system of fortifications without depth forbade him any large-scale maneuvering in retreat and made it obligatory for him to conquer where he stood or perish. Yet he chose to fight a war of movement on the Belgian plains. What an abyss of contradictions!

I have spoken of Gamelin's intelligence. But of what avail is intelligence when, in action, a man never re-examines his premises and when he is impeded by his ingrained disposition to provide for a thousand different ends at once and by his incapacity to choose one of these and subordinate everything to it? Doubtless we must bear in mind the anxiety caused him by Reynaud's attitude. For two days he had known that Reynaud, who accused him of letting everything drift and of not fighting the war, was determined to relieve him of his command, to have him replaced by Weygand, Giraud, or Huntziger.[7] On May 10, I lunched with an associate of the Premier's. The first thing he said was this: "After all, it's appalling to think that Gamelin has to face the Nazi invasion today without being sure that tomorrow he will still be commander in chief." Can it be possible that Gamelin's rash irruption into Belgium was, psychologically, a flight forward, an evasion toward the Germans? Early in April, Weygand had said to Reynaud when the latter confidentially informed him of his intention to make a change: "Let Gamelin stay where he is. You may be certain that with a dynamic Premier, he will not be the man he was under the static Daladier." The generalissimo must have known each successive phase of the Cabinet's discussions about him. Did he decide to show them what he could do? This may have weighed in the balance.

I do not pretend that this analysis and the foregoing explanations solve the enigma of Gamelin on May 10, the enigma of the foolhardy Franco-British race into Belgium. But here is another almost as troublesome. How, conceivably, could it have taken five days, if not longer, for

[7]The truth was that Reynaud had changed his mind about the offensive in Belgium. See page 190 and note 9.

the generalissmo to realize that his plan had miscarried, that it could lead only to a rout—and that he must give the order to retreat? How were one hundred and forty hours wasted on an enterprise that had become hopeless? How could the General Staff have been so stubborn? The minute Gamelin saw that the Wehrmacht did not even stumble over the Belgian obstacle, but leaped nimbly over it, how could he still persist in so ambitious an undertaking? The list of surprises sprung upon him by the blitzkrieg was a long one. His inertia was a match for it.

The Dutch and Belgians withstood the onslaught neither in Limburg, nor on the Albert Canal, nor in the region of Liége. At the outset of their offensive the Germans captured the bridge on the Meuse at Maestricht and three others, all of them intact. They made use of the bridge on the Albert Canal which carries the road from Maestricht to Liége. On May 11 Fort Eben Emael, near Liége, fell to them. If only our armies could cling to the Meuse between Namur and Sedan, at the "hinge," the whole Franco-British scheme of operations might be persisted in.[8] But during the night of the twelfth, or certainly by the thirteenth, the Meuse began to slip from our grasp. It was not yielded quite so quickly as the Ardennes, but it was merely a matter of degree. Guderian's foot vanguard crossed to the left bank of the river, first at Houx, north of Dinant, during the night of May 12, while German aviation was gathering strength in the air, and then, on the afternoon of the thirteenth, at Monthermé, south of Revin, and at Glaire, where they were closest to Sedan.[9] By May 13, at the latest, it was impossible not to see that the fragile house of cards had been hit in its foundations and was bound to crumble down. There was but one encouraging incident: on the thir-

---

[8]On May 12, Blanchard's mechanized divisions checked the enemy in advance of the Franco-British defensive positions at St. Trond, to the southwest of Hasselt. Not until the thirteenth did the French mechanized cavalry yield the anti-tank ditch—which, according to Gort, the Belgians had laid out rather clumsily along the Perwez-Namur-Louvain line—not until then did they retire to Gembloux, within the main defensive position. The 7th Army held between Bergen-op-Zoom and the canal of Turnhout; British cavalry maintained resistance along the Gette, and the infantry was organizing its position on the Dyle. The "Air Component" of the B.E.F. had slowed down German columns converging toward Tirlemont. If the R.A.F. detachment based near Rheims had come into the fight, a great opportunity—which lasted but a fleeting moment—might have been seized. (Cf. Lord Gort's dispatches.) The Belgians fell back to the Louvain-Antwerp line, on the British left. Thus they had held for three days, but the German Army had come out of the test unharmed. On the night of May 15, writes Lord Gort, the French and British were ahead of schedule in the execution of the Dyle plan.

[9]It should be noticed that, contrary to legend, the Germans captured no bridges. They crossed the river methodically, taking advantage of woods, dykes, and islets, using rubber boats, rafts, pontoons, and trestle bridges. Only two bridges, and those two on the Ardennes Canal and not on the Meuse, fell into enemy hands on May 14: at Omicourt and Malmy.

teenth, at Donchery, south of Glaire, in Huntziger's sector, a German tank division was forced to turn back. But next day it simply detoured through Glaire and all lay open before it.

Where could be found any reason for hope? The French and British positions, extending northward all the way to Holland, were doomed unless Corap's 9th Army could be tightened up. And the German military machine, so complicated in its structure, so direct in its driving power, had been on the job for three days: for three days the effects it had produced on the Allied armies were there to be seen and studied; expectation of success could no longer be entertained. After crossing the Meuse at Monthermé the Germans took our two prepared lines at the rate of one an hour. Both in space and in time this was the origin of the great pocket they were to drive into France.[10]

The German Army operating on the Meuse front was not only that instrument for breaking through which we had expected it to be. It was much more than a mechanism made up of tanks, pursuit planes, hedge-hopping and diving Stukas, heavy bombers, or even flame throwers and screaming sirens. Without worrying about liaison with the main body of its troops, this instrument for breaking through made use of novel and strange auxiliaries once it got to work behind the lines. Immense crowds of refugees, driven methodically along the roads by constant machine-gunning, mired and literally paralyzed the Allied divisions. The spy network was so extensive and so dense that enemy agents were constantly on the spot at the right moment to spread panic, to report back all shifting of headquarters, to disrupt operations by false orders and false information, to prevent the destruction of roads and. bridges, to capture or blow up munition dumps.[11]

Obstacles put in the way of the enemy troops, knowing or unknowing accomplices, swarms of parachutists and motorcyclists, of machine gunners and snipers, tanks, flying artillery, infantry in trucks: such was the assaulting force. "The armored division," writes a German author, "has this distinctive advantage, that it can fight independently of other arms; it has all weapons, and of every type, and its mobility and speed intensify

---

[10]Cf. *Infantry Journal* (April 1941), in which Lt. Paul W. Thompson has analyzed two important studies: "Der Durchbruch über die Maas am 13 May, 1940," by Colonel Soldan (*Militarwissenschaftliche Rundschau*, November 1940), and "Vom Durchbruch zur Einkreisung," by Colonel Deniker (*Schweizerische Monatschrift fur Offiziere aller Waffen*, January 1941). I owe much to those studies.

[11]Lord Gort states in his dispatches that measures had been taken to regulate the exodus of refugees on the roads, but, he adds: "The Belgian authorities, in spite of my request, did nothing to prevent the circulation of private automobiles nor the sale of gasoline."

their efficacy. It has a big volume of fire; it possesses mobility and defense. Its power in attack, however, is greatly lessened if it is not supported by aviation." Aviation is the armored division's heavy artillery. The pundits of the General Staff, with Gamelin at their head, refused year after year to believe in the effectiveness of this boring tool. In March 1935, Paul Reynaud brought up a bill for the creation of twelve armored divisions: they derided him. The tank was invented during the last war by the British and the French, but the French Command, after ten or fifteen years' deliberation, left it to the Germans to draw from this new contrivance all the strategical and tactical implications. Five days was indeed a short time to uproot the prejudice of years. Yet when one thinks what an overwhelming evidence the battlefields of the Ardennes and the Meuse brought forth, the delay of the French Command in revising its opinion seems incredible. One glance should have been enough to see the picture: to look again and again was superfluous.

The complete cutting up of Corap's army represented an extreme case but, to some extent, the same process went on elsewhere. In the sector of Corap it started on the thirteenth and was completed some thirty hours later. At eight-thirty on the evening of the thirteenth an armored unit took the heights of the Marfée, outflanked the 55th and 71st divisions—Huntziger's extreme left wing. These troops retreated in confusion, as they were reservists with only a sprinkling of regular army officers. Their divisional artillery was about one fifth as strong as it should have been and consisted of obsolete 25s and 37s for the most part. On the fourteenth, the 5th Cavalry Division, sorely tried already in the Ardennes fighting, was annihilated. Next day General Huntziger restored some degree of cohesion as he fell back on Stonne to the south. But he was not to fill the breach sixteen kilometers wide open toward Sedan.

Corap's army, which, on the thirteenth, had failed to prevent the enemy from reaching the left bank of the Meuse in the Houx-Dinant area and north of Sedan, was now also outflanked from the south. On the fourteenth, it frittered away.[12] Reinforcements sent Corap (and Huntziger) were quickly cut to pieces. During the night of the fourteenth, General Corap resigned himself to the necessity of abandoning the Meuse. But between Mézières and Fumay his men, attacked from north and south, were held in a vise and they could not escape to reach their second prepared position fifteen kilometers to the rear. They scattered. To the gap of sixteen kilometers which the enemy had opened in the

---

[12]On that date three Panzer divisions were operating on the left bank of the Meuse—two toward Sedan, the other toward Dinant.

2nd Army was now added a breach of some fifty kilometers. Nevertheless, from the time Corap fell back, on the evening of the fourteenth, to the time Gamelin ordered a general retreat, there was an interval of some forty-eight hours.[13] Yet Corap's withdrawal made a general retreat inevitable. When the generalissimo wholly abandoned the operation started on May 10 a German armored column had already reached Montcornet, thirty-five kilometers away from Rethel. Twenty-four hours before the Allies fell back on the Scheldt the enemy was within striking distance of Amiens. In short, the geographical area in which Weygand would have to function was seriously indented. The framework for the forthcoming "battle of France" was badly splintered at the top, whereas the arrangements which had been made for the advance into Belgium had scarcely been modified. Such was the French General Staff in its shining obstinacy. (See map, page 205.)

Should we think of General Corap as a straw caught in a cyclone, or must he be charged with special responsibility within the all-enveloping responsibility of Gamelin, Georges, and Billotte? Reynaud brought the most serious accusations against him in a speech before the Senate on May 21, even insinuating that he would have to pay the supreme penalty. On May 15 Corap was required to exchange commands with Giraud; on the nineteenth, he was relieved of all command. Later he was given a clean bill by General Dufieux, who was appointed by Weygand, on the twenty-first, to investigate the charges against him.[14] The Vichy Govern-

[13]According to Reynaud, the order to retreat was given on the evening of the fifteenth. But Lord Gort states in his dispatches: (1) that he had to request the order from Billotte on the morning of the sixteenth; (2) that the retreat to the Scheldt was to start the night of the sixteenth and that, according to Billotte's instructions, it was to be carried out in three stages in order not to reach that river before the night of the eighteenth. Moreover, Billotte added that there would be two halts along the line of retreat and that in each case a stand might be ordered. Actually, on the seventeenth, General Georges intervened with Billotte because he wanted the British to wait twenty-four hours longer on the line of the Senne (first halt) before continuing to the Dendre (second halt). On Gort's insistence, Billotte's orders were maintained. The movement to the Scheldt was not completed until the nineteenth.

[14]Corap followed the government to Tours and Bordeaux, seeking redress. His meeting with Gamelin, on the nineteenth, is described by Paul Allard (loc. cit.), but it is very probable that we do not find the whole truth in this little book. Gamelin is supposed to have said: "Daladier insisted on your dismissal. But all that's of no importance. We're all sunk. Weygand is going to take over. But what's the use? All is lost." Dufieux probably was the most "reactionary" of all French generals. He was a great friend of Weygand, who, in 1935, was wont to name him after Georges as his own most suitable successor. For several years he had been on the retired list and was the military critic of the *Figaro*. On May 1, 1940, he wrote: "In recent years a new school of thought has been born which asserts that great tank formations will break through the enemy front like an avalanche, crushing the enemy batteries, destroying posts of command, staff headquarters, ammunition dumps, breaking

ment—a military oligarchy naturally hesitant to strike at generals for fear that this game, once begun, might lead far, very far—entrusted Corap with a command in the small army of 100,000 men tolerated under the armistice terms. No one person can be blamed for the catastrophe, it was explained in Vichy. The actual break-through took place in Huntziger's sector, but at the same time he deserves praise because he managed to pull his army together. Then why be so severe about Corap? The temporary failure of the army next to his had made his position untenable.

Sooner or later military trials will be held in an independent France and old verdicts will be revised. Whatever the men of Vichy may say now can carry no weight; the Pétains, the Weygands, the Huntzigers, and their friends are both judges and interested parties. Corap was one of Weygand's satellites and headed Weygand's personal staff from 1931 to 1935. Through the practice of "apostolic succession," he had been promoted beyond his merit. Not Corap but the chiefs who advanced him are accountable for his very inferior leadership. At any rate, it is proper to criticize his lack of foresight and zeal. The failings revealed by even the most cursory study of the Battle of the Meuse reflect on Gamelin, Georges, Billotte, Prételat, Corap, and Huntziger. I shall list those failings but not attempt to apportion individual blame too closely. For the present, justice can speak only in broad terms; later on, justice will particularize.

I have pointed out that Corap, as head of the Second Military Region at Amiens, had formerly been entrusted with the task of fortifying the Meuse country. By a retributory stroke of fortune he was to reappear upon the scene, on May 10, as commander of an army. On arrival, what fortifications did he find between Mézières and Givet, not to mention

---

up reserves before they even can come into action, interrupting communications, annihilating resources of all kinds far back of the lines, thus destroying—and within a very few days —all possibility for the enemy to come back into the fight with the slightest chance of success. But who can imagine any likelihood of things happening in such a manner when adversaries comparable in numbers and in matériel are prepared to oppose the advance of armored units with all the obstacles of terrain, special mine fields, and anti-tank cannons?" Such is the man who passed judgment on Corap. His judgment is worthless. And here again I note the paradox apparent in so many of these military careers. For Dufieux, as chief of Pétain's Operation Bureau, on March 26, 1918, without waiting for orders from Foch— appointed generalissimo that same day—had rushed the Champagne reserves to the aid of the British. It is true that military historians give credit for this to General de Barescut, chief of staff, rather than to Dufieux. Nonetheless, here stands before us an officer whose earlier achievements masked the fact that he had become fossilized. At the Riom trial Corap avenged himself against Daladier by blaming the bad discipline of his troops on the Premier's alleged weakness for the Communists.

Sedan, the perennially neglected? Two lines of defense had been sketchily drawn. Barbed-wire entanglements followed the bank of the river. A few blockhouses had been erected. The bridgehead at Mézières was fairly well provided with blockhouses and anti-tank ditches. To the rear, on the main line of resistance, there were networks of barbed wire, but the real fortifications were still to come. At the most, only a few buildings had been fortified on the road to Mézières and Monthermé. As for the defensive position No. 2, which the Prételat and Belhague commissions had included in their plans, it was to have run from twenty-five kilometers southwest of Sedan to a point northeast of Mézières, but, indeed, had only faintly taken shape along a section of at most fifteen kilometers. In Belgium, from Givet to Namur, what had been done by King Leopold's General Staff did not amount to much.

To be at all satisfied with the little that had been accomplished, it was just as well not to look at details too closely. The blockhouses were not armored. Rail fields did not spread far enough. Anti-tank traps were without blockhouse and, therefore, negligible. In fortified buildings, 37-mm. cannon, substituted for the 25s of which the Army itself was short, were not properly embrasured. The electric wires controlling anti-tank mine fields had not been well insulated: when the time came, they did not work. The four or five men who manned each fortified building, and whose assignment was to hold out until the arrival of the heavy artillery and to smash everything around them, ran away without bothering to destroy the roads. The German tanks had a clear path and advanced without the slightest concern for our slender bodies of troops. Such was the fortification on the Meuse. Corap excused himself by constantly referring to the fact that, month after month, he had harassed G.H.Q. with complaints and demands. He was one of those men whose words carry no weight.

How he actually managed his battle—if he managed anything—it is not possible to judge. He was guilty of neglect in paying far too little attention to the district north of Sedan: but in this he was no more guilty than Huntziger, who placed his two weakest divisions, the 71st and the 55th, around this city and next to the weakest of Corap's. Both men did nothing more than reproduce in their own spheres the error of perspective previously committed by their superiors—that of classing Sedan as a zone of secondary importance, etc. And it must be said also that all of Corap's troops were not in position when the attack came. They were not on the alert. Officers and men were still immersed in the depressing atmosphere of the "truce."

Neither Corap nor Huntziger had their troops in hand. But could even the most energetic leaders have bolstered within a few hours the morale of soldiers suddenly thrown into a battle where, in rapid succession, unheard-of weapons caught them unawares? On this point I cannot pronounce: the evidence is contradictory. In the summer of 1940 the French people convinced itself, through accounts brought back by soldiers, that too many officers had deserted their posts. A hasty, dangerous generalization, unfair to the many who served with honor. We must await history's slow weighing and sifting of the facts. The country's highest leaders, as well as the whole community, were at fault.

On the Meuse front, in some cases, soldiers broke ranks. On the afternoon of the twelfth, south of the bridge at Houx, at the beginning of German infiltration, a battalion of the 39th Infantry turned back instead of counterattacking. On May 13 and 14, Huntziger's two divisions, already mentioned, thinking that they were cut off by tanks, put up no defense. The men had not learned that detachments outflanked by these vehicles are not necessarily lost. They pushed aside the military police which tried to bar their way.[15] Near Dinant, on the fourteenth, a battalion retreated before the German companies that had stolen over to the left bank, and the general temporarily commanding the 22nd Division took no measures to correct this state of affairs until he was directed to do so by Corap and threatened with court-martial. A general order issued by Corap tells the whole story. "Weakness has been shown at certain points. For this the responsibility rests with officers and non-commissioned officers. At a moment when France's destiny is at stake, no such failing can be tolerated. From the highest to the lowest ranks, men in command must set an example and, if necessary, force obedience. Merciless punishment will be visited upon officers who fail to do so."[16]

But when we read this text it is only fair to inscribe alongside the names of four 9th Army generals who fell on the battlefield. They were Buffet, Barbe, d'Argenlieu (Corap's chief of staff), and Augereau. A

[15] In the pamphlet *Corap and the Loss of the Meuse Line* there is the following detail: "By extraordinary luck the 55th Division had anti-tank cannon of 47 mm. together with 3,000 shells to use in them. The guns and ammunition fell into the hands of the Germans, who turned them with great effect against the 3rd Armored Division—thirteen twelve-ton tanks were destroyed."

[16] General Gamelin, like Corap, blamed communist propaganda, and this thesis went the rounds after his fall. "A bad argument," said Georges Mandel. Assuming that the communist infection was especially virulent among the troops defending the Meuse, it was the business of the command to detect it through censorship of the mails and then to check it by whatever reshuffling of effectives might be necessary. But Corap's general order settles the argument. We may note here that, at an earlier date, Gamelin thought he had solved

fifth, D'Arras, was severely wounded, while a sixth, Dauvelure, was taken prisoner.[17] Something else remains to be said. While the whole picture is still wrapped in obscurity, let us keep clear from the belief that in many encounters the French troops did not rise to the call of the fight and prove their mettle, that they did not show any skill in the handling of the new weapons. All they needed to display their true worth was good leadership and not too great unequality in armament. Special mention must be made of the 1st Army between Wavre and Namur, on May 14, and afterward in the areas around the Lys River and Dunkirk. The retreat of the 3rd Army Corps, under General de Fornel de la Laurencie, was a great deed of valor. In the Argonne the 2nd Army was unshakable. In the Alps five or six divisions stopped thirty Italian and prevented them from joining up with the Germans.

Here are a few facts about French soldiers fighting in planes and in tanks. In five weeks the Air Force lost one quarter of its crews. The performance of the mechanized divisions of General Prioux, on May 12, as already said, relieved the Belgians from the enemy pressure. On May 16, "the 4th Armored Division, formed only at the last hour, hastily grouped between Montcornet and Marles, held for two days and threw into considerable confusion the rear of the enemy columns continuing their progress toward the west." We quote from the semiofficial synopsis of operations.[18] It purposely omits the name of the brigadier to whom that achievement must be ascribed: Charles de Gaulle. And the exploits of the 14th Infantry Division, under General de Lattre de Tassigny, near Rethel, between May 15 and May 20, also deserve to be stressed. The division had only five tanks. The Germans lost a minimum of 200 to 250 motorized vehicles, including twenty-five or thirty tanks and armored cars.[19] In this instance the traditional armament, with a slight addition of tanks, held firm against Nazi tactics. Perhaps what happened on the Meuse from the thirteenth to the sixteenth of May bears comparison with the rout of the reserve divisions under General

the problem of communism in the Army by paying special attention to the living conditions of the non-commissioned officers, by providing them with suitable quarters in barracks or near by, etc. Winston Churchill asked him for detailed information on this subject. And Daladier, on the strength of assurances given him by the generalissimo, had stopped worrying about communists in barracks or in the armies; therefore even the most active militants were allowed to rejoin their units.

[17]In contrast, the generals commanding Huntziger's left wing were dismissed.

[18]Published in *Le Temps,* November 1940.

[19]Louis Lévy (*Vérités sur la France*), who visited the 14th Division and reported the testimony of General de Lattre de Tassigny and his officers. They never doubted victory would be theirs.

d'Amade in August 1914. Those badly trained divisions were to re-enter the battlefield, some weeks later, and then did not deflect from the standard set by active troops.

Gamelin realized the full extent of the disaster on May 15, toward eight in the evening. Till then he seems to have comforted himself with the illusion that the gaps could still be "plastered up"—a term and a notion borrowed from the war of 1914–18, which in itself shows how inadequate was his understanding of the operations that were taking place.[20] Suddenly the scales fell from his eyes.

Mr. William Bullitt witnessed the distressing episode. The American Ambassador wholeheartedly served the French cause because the most fundamental interests of the United States, as he saw them, were involved in it. He enjoyed Daladier's unbounded confidence. By 7.45 P.M. he found the latter at the War Ministry, on his return from the Elysées, where the War Committee had been in session. The Minister expressed himself rather optimistically about the prospects of the struggle on the Meuse. Obviously, Gamelin's self-confidence had cheered him up. The telephone bell rang. From General Headquarters at Vincennes the generalissimo asked for him. Daladier listened absent-mindedly. All of a sudden he shouted: "No, what you say is not possible. You are mistaken! It is not possible!"

The fatal piece of news had been broken to him: an armored German column, having made short work of everything in its way, was roaming at will in the district between Rethel and Laon. "You must start an attack immediately!" continued Daladier. "An attack? But there are no reserves at hand to be thrown in!" Lengthy explanations followed, which Mr. Bullitt overheard or guessed. They closed with Gamelin saying: "Between Laon and Paris not a single body of troops can be gathered." Meanwhile Daladier's face shrank and shriveled as he tried hard to regain his composure. The Minister and the generalissimo parted on these phrases: "Then the French Army is doomed?" "Yes, the French Army is doomed." "Not a word to anyone. I shall not even inform the President of the Council." Mr. Bullitt left the Rue St. Dominique at five minutes after nine.

---

[20]It should be noted that on the morning of the fifteenth, Billotte reproached Corap "with having given him, the evening before, an extremely false account of the situation." He thought the report unjustifiably catastrophic. Possibly Billotte's error of judgment stood as a screen between Gamelin and reality throughout the whole fourteenth of May and even until the afternoon of the fifteenth. We have seen (page 69, note 13) that, on the seventeenth, Georges still wanted to slow up the withdrawal to the Scheldt: this stubbornness is incomprehensible when one recalls Gamelin's despair thirty-six hours before.

Does it follow that both men had, at that time, a precise and detailed view of the whole course of the battle? Probably not. Here we must again quote the metaphor applied to the Polish Army when it was at grips with the German tanks and planes—the image of the laboratory guinea pig whose cerebellum has been severed. Most means of communication having disintegrated, no coherent picture of the battle could be pieced together at staff headquarters. There were too many gaps in the complex reports which must steadily converge to make any such picture possible. All too frequently the French Army still depended on field telegraph and telephone. Apparently neither Branly nor Marconi had ever fully worked for it. This old-fashioned equipment helps in some measure to explain the slow awakening of Billotte and Georges, of the General Staff, of Gamelin and Daladier. But how explain that the generals commanding armies and divisions, in closer proximity to the battlefield, were not able to overcome the obduracy of those higher up before the sixteenth? Or is it merely that the latter, having no plan and no preparations made for withdrawal, remained inert simply because they did not know where to turn?

The sudden despair of the generalissimo and of the Minister for National Defense was the despair of men who feel a shock the more intensely because they do not yet know very fully whence it comes. On that evening of the fifteenth Gamelin was only just getting ready to order the armies in the north to retreat![21]

[21]Concerning the incoherence and disorder at the seat of command, Lord Gort's dispatches give appalling testimony.

Here is the gist of it: To begin with, the "Unified Command" was insufficiently organized. The head of the B.E.F. carried out the orders from Gamelin and Georges, and he was in direct communication with them. On May 10, entering Belgium, he was *not* officially under Billotte, commander of the 1st Group of Armies which actually included the British forces. Not until May 12, in the afternoon, at the Château of Casteau near Mons, did Georges ask Gort's chief of staff to agree that Billotte be empowered to co-ordinate the movements of the French and British forces. With the British there were no difficulties. But relations with King Leopold III of Belgium and his military adviser, General van Overstraeten, were an arduous problem. Daladier was forced to come from Paris to get them out of their calculated aloofness. The question seemed to be solved, but the commander of the 1st Army Group made no use of the authority granted him. Gort was left to his own devices. He declares that he received only one order from Billotte, that which provided for retreat to the Scheldt. This order, as we have seen, he had been obliged to solicit himself on the sixteenth. On the seventeenth he had no information as to what the French Command was doing or intended to do in order to close the gap at Sedan. Billotte did not enlighten him until the night of the nineteenth. On May 17, at Georges's request, Gort haphazardly dispatched units which had been guarding his lines of communication to hold the sector Douai-Péronne, without knowing how the French Staff intended to meet the drive of German armored columns toward the Somme. Yet Gort had a representative at G.H.Q. in La Ferté-sous-Jouarre (Brigadier General J. G. des R. Swayne), and liaison officers of all

On May 16, I was called to the telephone at six in the morning. One of my friends repeated what he had just learned from Mme. de Portes, Paul Reynaud's mistress. She had told him at dawn that a German armored column was near Laon. Georges Mandel, the bold Colonial Minister, was greeted with the same rumor when he reached his office around nine o'clock. He telephoned Gamelin. "I found," he later told me, "a man utterly calm and entirely despairing."

Reynaud, on the other hand, had not spoken directly to the generalissimo, whose dismissal Daladier had been refusing him for the last eight days. He felt some embarrassment. Finally he put in the call. Whereupon he heard from Gamelin's own lips that the Germans might reach Paris by nightfall. General Hering, military governor of Paris, insisted that the city should be evacuated by the President of the Republic, the government, and Parliament, since their presence might greatly impede defense measures. Reynaud called a cabinet meeting at eleven o'clock, inviting also the presidents of the Senate and the Chamber of Deputies. The thirty persons thus summoned to deliberate had never suspected the internal weakness of the Army and the Army Command. All of a sudden, without warning, they were told that the capital was wide open to the Germans, that not a single regiment blocked the way. And the commander in chief did not hide that he was at his wits' end. Suggestions flowed in most confusingly. Many of them were of the crackpot variety. Why not, someone proposed, bring up units of the fleet to defend the city? There must be some that drew little enough water to come up the Seine. Orders were given to transfer the seat of government to Tours, and the departure was fixed for four o'clock. M. de Monzie, Minister for Public Works, had few railway cars and fewer trucks at hand. He was to confer with the Prime Minister at three-thirty to take steps. The archives of the Ministry for Foreign Affairs were burned. It was even suggested that they be thrown into the Seine to save time.[22] Meanwhile the German armored units, supplied and pro-

---

kinds were present at all echelons of command. One of Gort's observations, toward the end of his dispatches, partially explains this abnormal state of affairs: "The staff methods of the past proved to be too slow. Headquarters of the various formations were moved about so frequently that conferences followed up by general instructions or isolated messages took the place of formal orders which were the accepted procedure in former campaigns." It will be seen that under Weygand things went no better. Here is a striking instance of the dispersion of plans, decisions, and orders: when the British reached the Scheldt, on the nineteenth, that river was so low that it presented no serious obstacle to the German tanks. The French had tapped the river to flood the region of Valenciennes in order to strengthen their defense. And Lord Gort had not been warned.

[22] For the destruction of the archives see page 238, note 14.

tected from our artillery by a double screen of planes, came no nearer than Marle-le-Château.

General Touchon, at the head of the 6th Army which the High Command was hurriedly forming to breach the gap opened on the fourteenth and the fifteenth, now guaranteed to close the path to Paris. But the Germans made no serious effort in that direction. Their work was accomplished: they had nearly destroyed the 9th Army and pushed back the 2nd. Now, following the general lines of their strategy, they would turn toward the Channel. On the afternoon of the sixteenth, Paris breathed again, and the ministers did not have to pack and run. At half-past three orders for the departure were canceled. Reynaud, in the lobbies of the Chamber, announced that he had just telephoned to 9th Army headquarters and that things were going better.

Gamelin's abrupt collapse is in the center of the drama. On the sixth day of the struggle this military Buddha, with his unequaled serenity, admitted defeat. The system inherited from his predecessors and completed by his own efforts had been bound indissolubly to a rigid structure: now it stood condemned and he found no reprieve. In one lightning flash he had understood at least this: the inventors of the Maginot Line, by sacrificing depth and resiliency to rock-bound strength, had miscalculated.

Could the whole structure hold or fall only in a block? Could it neither be repaired, nor moved, nor reconstructed somewhere else in France—let alone North Africa? In view of the implications of the new weapons, would it have been possible to combine the strategy of the Maginot Line with a strategy borrowed from the Battle of the Marne? In any case, we have seen that neither Gamelin nor his subordinates had threshed out the problem while there was yet time. And now they were called upon to solve it in the midst of a rout.

To Daladier, in the evening of the fifteenth, to Mandel and to Reynaud, on the morning of the sixteenth, Gamelin had spoken with complete frankness. He had in no way concealed what he felt. But he foresaw that Reynaud was about to take action against him, and he turned to a show of impassiveness and confidence. With Daladier's consent, and without having consulted Reynaud, on the evening of the seventeenth he called on his troops, in an order of the day, to "conquer or die"—a striking reminiscence of Joffre's order of the day on the eve of the Battle of the Marne which—who knows?—may have been drafted by Gamelin himself. Certain authors must ever repeat themselves. The wording gave a painful impression of plagiarism. The flourish of words did not ring true. Was Gamelin conforming to what he regarded, in the juncture, as a compulsory rite? Or had he found new courage? Was he acting on sincere conviction? Or was it his own fall rather than defeat that he was seeking to avoid? I cannot pretend to fathom his inner reactions in anguish and sorrow.

That day, at the cabinet meeting, Reynaud did not succeed immediately in obtaining Gamelin's dismissal. The victim was not passive. On the eighteenth, Gamelin went into a long explanation to Pétain, who had just been made vice-president of the Cabinet and chief military adviser to the government. Daladier was present. Both Pétain and Daladier were only too willing to find extenuating circumstances, only too anxious to be convinced. Daladier knew that Weygand, the generalissimo designate, disliked him intensely, and Pétain, although he had chosen Weygand as chief of staff in 1929 and had favored his accession to the High Command in 1931, remembered with bitterness the stinging criticism he had always had to suffer from Foch and his followers.

On May 19, at three in the afternoon, Weygand was placed at the head of France's armies. On the evening before he had engaged in a brief talk with Gamelin and asked him for a complete file of orders. Reynaud and Baudouin have asserted that Gamelin had no such file of orders to show, that he had allowed his subordinates to act as they thought fit throughout the battle, and that he himself had not intervened in any way. Their assertions should not be taken literally. They were afraid that public opinion might be restless during the passage from the old to the new commander in chief, and they considered it only prudent to throw the worst possible light on the man who was going out.

As for Weygand, he confided to his friends that Gamelin had not been able to accurately describe the positions and movements of our various armies, and that the description of the chessboard which he carried away from his meeting with Gamelin was so vague and uncertain that he immediately decided that he must survey the zone of operations in person. This criticism implicitly bore as much on Georges, a personal friend of Weygand's, as it did on Gamelin. On his visit to La Ferté-sous-Jouarre on May 18, Reynaud, in fact, found the generalissimo's chief lieutenant in a state of complete moral breakdown. As Weygand was getting back to his car, after his first call on the Premier, a reserve officer attached to General Headquarters managed to speak to him: "If you want to save anything," he said, "get rid of all the professors at once, dismiss all staff officers above the rank of majors." Weygand shrugged his shoulders.

A report spread rapidly in Paris and throughout France that Gamelin had killed himself. On May 23 a friend of mine found him quietly at home, calm, deliberate, and determined to justify himself. "I want to think only of France," he added. "We are in grave peril, but our cause can still be retrieved." He went on to speak at length and willingly expatiated on communist propaganda in Corap's army. His friends took care to have it known that five hours before his dismissal, that is to say on May 19, at ten in the morning, he had ordered General Billotte to counterattack, but that Weygand's first decision had been to postpone the operation. Here is an indication of the central thesis on which the fallen general will base his pleading whenever the time comes for him to speak.[23] "If they had broken Joffre after Charleroi, if the Premier then in office had denied him the time necessary to extricate the French Army from a campaign which had started badly and to lead it back into battle, the victory of the Marne would not have been won." It is indeed true that the men in power in 1940 were far, very far, from being the equals of the men in 1914, Poincaré and Millerand. And in retrospect the measures planned by Gamelin may perhaps seem preferable to those taken by his successor. But by then he was like a leper, shunned of all men.

7

Gamelin, Prisoner of an Obsolete Military Universe. His Failure To Give France the Requisite Technical Dictatorship

GAMELIN WILL UNDOUBTEDLY PRODUCE, in his own defense, the most ingenious chain of argument and reasoning. We may be sure that he will find a scapegoat for every error with which he is charged. But he will convince no one. No matter from what point of view, he can only be found guilty, completely guilty.

Consider him as the commander during the battle. Examine merely

---

[23]However, in the memoranda and papers he has entrusted to friends who visited him in jail, Gamelin lays the emphasis upon Georges's refusal to carry out his instructions. Gamelin relates this sentence of Weygand uttered during their short talk: "You are Joffre's disciple and I am Foch's. There is nothing I can learn from you."

his reactions to the strategical strokes of the German Command. The only difficulty is to tell at what moment he was most confused. When was it? When he failed to understand the value of the enemy's means for breaking through? When he threw his divisions into Belgium, on May 10, underestimating the numerical strength of the German right wing, neglecting the Sedan-Namur hinge, overestimating the Belgian power of resistance and the natural barrier formed by the Ardennes and the Meuse? Or when he locked his troops in a mad and reckless forward movement, without having prepared beforehand defenses in depth on which to fall back up to the Somme or the Seine? He seemed to ignore the fact that the rigidity of the Maginot Line would make a repetition of Joffre's exploit extremely difficult. Or when he wasted three invaluable days assessing the havoc wrought on the 9th and 2nd armies?

Now let us look at Gamelin from another angle, compare the intentions of the general in his office with what became of them in practical deeds, concentrate on the sequence of his ideas and actions, concerning matters which it was within his power to settle. In other words, let us study the working of Gamelin's mind, his logic. This way of approach leads to the ascertainment of the most damnable facts. What a gap between thought and action!

We shall be generous and grant that Gamelin's conception of the defensive was plausible. Still, it needed being given a fair chance. We don't want to quarrel any more with him about the use he made of his weapons. But he failed to demand in time the weapons he deemed indispensable, did only get them in insufficient numbers, and, moreover, for fighting his great battle, failed to assemble what he had. Such remarks apply to tanks, anti-tank guns, planes, artillery for defense against planes. The Germans of 1943 were outnumbered in tanks and planes. But, well provided with other arms, they gave a convincing demonstration of what Gamelin might have done to check the blitzkrieg with an armament program conceived on a large scale and more punctually fulfilled. Of course a degree of efficient resistance to the blitzkrieg has become possible in 1944, the outcome of deadly experimenting on so many battlefields, to which, in 1940, no army, however well led or supplied, could rise. But, in 1940, Gamelin did not even make the most of his defensive scheme. Moreover, he permitted officers and men to get soft. He trusted in permanent fortifications, yet he put up with a truncated belt of forts.

The line of concrete and steel starting from Alsace ended at Montmédy. It was continued by the construction of fieldworks, especially after the declaration of war. These were casemates armed with two anti-tank 75-mm. guns, four machine guns, one or two 37-mm. cannon; they were garrisoned by a dozen men and they were linked together by specially profiled trenches supposedly capable of stopping tanks. There was a supporting line some distance back. All this differed from one district to another.[1] What casual execution of the program set up by Daladier and Gamelin in the autumn of 1936!

There is no use elaborating again on the irresponsible and haphazard conduct of the General Staff. They staked everything on the belief that the resources of the French and British empires would be mobilized in three years, expected fortifications to provide this respite, left them half completed, and then suddenly rushed into the plains of Flanders, begging for a fight.

In this summary of mistakes the lack of any large strategical reserve, kept clear of the immediate demands of battle, seems perhaps the most shocking item. Toward the end of 1917 the idea had been conceived of placing Foch at the head of a group of divisions specially designated for the function. It was believed that this command, seemingly rather modest, would rapidly confer upon him the supreme control of the war. A mass held in readiness for maneuver is the very soul of any strategy, defensive or offensive. How did this whole notion evaporate from the French mind of 1940? How was it forgotten that a successful defensive must match the dynamism of an offensive? Some authorities maintain that so many troops had to be engaged in the operation on the Dyle that, unavoidably, no surplus was at hand. Then, on that ground only, all advance into Belgium ought to have been ruled out. The very assumption that Gamelin's defensive doctrine was less faulty than is generally supposed makes his execution of it all the more ignominious. Whatever we grant him in the one we must withdraw—and ten times over —from the other.

[1] In the sector assigned to the B.E.F. (Armentières, the Lys, etc.) the latter found, in October 1939, a fairly continuous anti-tank line—a ditch defended by concrete casemates built to contain anti-tank cannon and machine guns. French task troops, under the general commanding the defense sector of Lille, continued to be kept at work on carefully drawn plans. A rather complex scheme: in the forward zone three prepared positions plus another for the army-corps reserves. To the rear still another position. A second anti-tank ditch was planned in the forward zone. Casemates of reinforced concrete were to be constructed in depth throughout the sector to protect the guns forming the backbone of the line of fire. All the plans were ready, and they allowed for the difference between French and British armament. By May 10 the British soldiers had built four hundred concrete casemates; one hundred others awaited completion. A new anti-tank ditch ran for about sixty kilometers. (Lord Gort's dispatches.)

Anyone who persistently investigates the story of the disaster gradually becomes convinced that all these facets do not add up to the true Gamelin. His error was more profound than such details suggest. It was not just because he was mistaken as to the comparative merits of attack and defense or because he misjudged what the Schlieffen-Gröner plan would become in application, it was not because he failed to secure the instruments required by his own defensive concepts or because he did not know how to act consistently with his own doctrine that the generalissimo led France to her doom. These were all secondary causes.

In piercing through to the central cause we are forced to indict the straitened military universe he gradually imprisoned himself in, like a turtle in its shell. It was a world of three dimensions, whereas the German world had four or five. Extreme mobility, the saving of human effort by means of machinery, the stunning surprise effect of new weapons, the political and psychological tricks discovered in the course of civil disturbances in Germany by a regime accustomed to the handling of popular masses, tricks then made part of the traditional armory—all these weapons were as astounding to the French commander and found him as unprepared as if he had been faced with warriors from Mars.

Had the thought ever occurred to him that to spread panic among the enemy is an art?[2] Did he ever suspect the true possibilities of espionage in the new manner and the effectiveness of fifth columns? In these matters we were in a better position to pay the Germans back in their own coin than most people suppose. If the correspondence between the French Staff and its agents in Switzerland is ever made public, for instance, many will be astonished to find what opportunities were offered us which, for reasons of principle, we refused to seize. In the Germany of 1939–40 there were enemies of National Socialism who were willing to take the most desperate risks. This was demonstrated by the bomb which, on November 9, 1939, exploded some ten minutes too late in the Burgerbrau in Munich, where the "hegira" of National Socialism is celebrated each year. That was no work of German *agents provocateurs*. This aspect of the war Gamelin deliberately refused to see. On an ordinary chessboard, under normal rules, he doubtless would have played a losing game. But on a chessboard where pieces he knew nothing about were moving, he was all the more checkmated. He brings to mind those Greek heroes who fought invisible divinities. It was only when wounded or dying that they recognized them.

[2]The French Staff knew about German studies on these subjects and set out to imitate them. But nothing more was done.

It has always been true that to prepare successfully for war a man must have a passionate interest in it and the intuitions of a lover. If the whole thing is simply a job to be done, then it will be done badly, mechanically, and with no spirit of invention. The task certainly did not excite Gamelin emotionally or intellectually, but merely produced sustained, mediocre, and monotonous administrative work which was as far removed as possible from anything forceful or impassioned. I ran into him one afternoon in July 1939, on the steps of a banking house near the Ecole Militaire. He was strolling back to number 4 bis, Boulevard des Invalides, to the building where I had called on Foch so often. Very much the small businessman, taking his little walk before settling down in his leather armchair. The shopkeepers along the way could have set their watches by his daily constitutional.

The Nazi regime has subordinated everything—the nation's institutions, its economy, and even its social customs—to the program of conquest. But in that achievement it has broken with the past less than one might think. It has drawn the full logical consequences from long-existing theories. The writings of Clausewitz, Bernhardi, Ludendorff, each making his own contribution, had formulated the theory of total war. A thorough analysis of the Napoleonic method of warfare, which aims at entirely destroying the enemy's army and not merely at outdoing it in the eighteenth-century fashion, was the starting point. Then, one by one, various closely interrelated notions were introduced into the system: war is nothing more than the continuation of peacetime politics by other means; both in the state and in the people all must be subordinated to this violent and decisive tool; logic requires one to strike at the enemy not only in his own armed forces but in his whole national life, and such a boundless task requires the abolition of all distinctions between the civil and the military power.

The only original contribution of the Führer and his party was that they applied the theory rigorously and without limits, smashing everything that was out of line. No man, alas, was less fitted than Gamelin to bear the brunt of this ethos of blood and fire. Clausewitz said that it is of essential importance that the leader in the war be also a statesman. Gamelin had a civil servant's regard for the limits of his authority. He interfered with what the ministers were doing only by indirection and after the most complete rhetorical precautions. Yet to be a statesman meant that the commander in chief in 1939–40 must provide a France destitute of political leadership with the technical dictatorship she badly needed.

Whenever put to a hard test, he was not a masterful man; and neither Tardieu, who in 1929 insisted on his being made assistant to Weygand, nor Flandin, nor Laval, who made him commander in chief in 1935, can have had any illusions on that score. In choosing Joffre and Foch, their predecessors had been fortunate. Both these men at moments of crisis had known how to speak the language of authority. But Gamelin allowed the civilian government to drift as it pleased. Because of its limitations, the burden of providing the nation with the necessary impetus, of leading it firmly and imperiously, fell upon parliamentary leaders. Daladier and Reynaud after him broke under its weight.

The argument will long continue as to whether the responsibility of the generals in the catastrophe is heavier than that of the ministers, or whether the ministers, by their incapable handling of affairs, did not lose the battle from a distance. It is certainly true that the ministers never were able to unite or strengthen the nation, either before or during the conflict. But the generals, left to their own devices for twenty years, free from any serious supervision or interference, proved capable neither of organizing an adequate national defense nor, when the time came, of directing actual operations.

If only, in those terrible days of May and June, the troops had felt that the High Command was determined to fight it out—what the Red Army must have felt from the outset; if only Frenchmen had found in the communiqués and orders of the day the trace of some intelligible purpose, the "Marseillaise" of 1792, with its inspiring call to battle, would doubtless have amounted to more than just a bas-relief on the Arc de Triomphe. The schism between citizens would not have been healed merely on the surface.

Even more than the politicians, the generals will have to answer for the nation's misfortune. And Gamelin first among them. Either he was deeply convinced that his calculations were right, and he was an incompetent general, or else, knowing the weakness of the military instrument in his hands, he lacked the courage to resign his command so that the nation should be warned, and he was a man of no character.

But this dilemma is not entirely satisfactory. It leaves out an important chapter in Gamelin's record. His desire to remain in power led him gradually to a refusal to face facts, shocking facts. He deceived himself. The capitulation of the French Army was consequent upon innumerable inner capitulations of his own mind and conscience. "Varus, what have you done with our legions?"

SECTION II: DALADIER: POLITICAL AND ADMINISTRATIVE FAILURE

I

A Patriot without Strength of Will

WHEN GEORGES MANDEL, Colonial Minister, decided to fortify Jibuti and to make it impregnable, he found Daladier unwilling to co-operate, haggling over the necessary materials and men. Whereupon he wrote to him substantially as follows: "I have proposed a course of action which you have not deemed advisable to accept. The matter has become your personal responsibility and a time will come when I shall remind you of the fact."

Daladier hated a man to state the cold facts and threaten him with accountability for them. He gave Mandel what he asked for, and, notwithstanding the capitulation of June 1940, the Italians never entered French Somaliland and its capital.

Gamelin was not the man to employ such abrupt and expeditious means. By now the reader is well aware of this fact; he spent his energies in patient and too often futile negotiation. Here I mention Gamelin only by way of introduction to Daladier. In spite of many protests to the contrary, the Premier was grateful to him for never forcing a decision.

Gamelin's twistings and turnings at a time when the fate of a nation depended on the action he took or did not take should quickly have convinced Daladier that it would be better to appoint to the Supreme Command someone endowed with greater determination. It is not at all sure that, intermittently, Daladier didn't faintly perceive the necessity for a change in army leadership. He was heard to complain: "These generals really are too professorial. What will they be like in battle? I don't know . . ." He once said point-blank to General Weygand, then in command at Beirut: "What would you think of a generalissimo who writes this?"[1] And he read aloud a few sentences from a report he had just received in which the tone was legalistic rather than soldierly. Weygand refused to commit himself: "General Gamelin is my superior officer and it's not for me to judge him."

This shows that Daladier had his doubts as to the soundness of the General Staff. He had worked with Weygand and Gamelin in 1932–33 and with Gamelin, uninterruptedly, since 1936. He should have known both men thoroughly. Yet he never bothered to reach some fairly precise judgment as to whether either of them was equal to his responsibilities, whether their strategical conceptions were founded on solid ground. In 1933, the year in which he had to learn his duties as head of the national defense, he freely indulged in polemics with the inspector general—such was the commander in chief's title at the time—on the question of the "hollow years,"[2] refusing Weygand's demand for a two-year training period, trying to get him to accept a makeshift which the latter judged bad[3]—or at least ineffective. He showed a tendency to favor Gamelin, who, as chief of the General Staff, considered himself directly subordinate to the Minister and, therefore, bound in duty to carry out his wishes. Daladier and his close advisers of the period, General Bourret and Colonel Barthe,[4] never really took the trouble to free themselves from current controversy, get down to fundamental questions, and transform their vague impressions into precise opinions.

Later on did the Minister and the men around him give heed to the warnings of independent critics? They did not. The Premier seems to have shared Gamelin's aversion to all innovators, and to Colonel de Gaulle in particular, since he threatened to resign from the Cabinet when the latter, at Paul Reynaud's invitation, was about to become secretary of the "War Committee" in March 1940. Not only did Daladier believe in the inevitably popular credo of the Maginot Line, and never expressed any doubts about it, but he was grateful to Gamelin for letting sleeping dogs lie and found it comfortable to have him at his side.

[1] In December 1939, Weygand came to Paris from Beirut and discussed contemplated operations in the Balkans, the Black Sea, and the Caucasus.

[2] As a result of the extremely low birth rate in the years 1915 to 1919, for four and a half years, young men called to military service at the age of twenty-one numbered 180,000 in 1935, and 120,000 in the years 1936, 37, 38, 39, as against 240,000 in normal years, whence the expression "hollow years." It should be noted that this problem scarcely existed for the Germans, thanks to the very peculiar measures taken to prevent it as early as 1915.

[3] See page 330.

[4] Who held a teaching post, in a low-grade state school, had been a brilliant soldier in 1914–18, won a rank in the Regular Army, and had passed through the War School. Weygand and his followers saw in him only the freemason.

His sluggish temperament could never have put up with Foch's sudden outbursts. One day a friend was urging him to make a clean sweep. He silenced him: "The weakness of democracies is that once a general has been built up in public opinion it becomes impossible to remove him." That was not the case: one could not say that trust in Gamelin was deeply rooted in the French people. For a time the Head of the Government thought of putting Noguès in charge. It was the mere fleeting shadow of a plan.

The Law of July 11, 1938, on the organization of France in wartime, and the secret decree of September 7, 1938, attempted to distinguish between the task that devolved upon the government—the general direction of the war—and that which fell to the commander in chief—the actual conduct of operations. The powers of the civil authority must transcend and include those of the military: yet, in practice, the latter's freedom of decision was safeguarded. The commander in chief was a member of the War Committee, which, with regard to all military matters, wielded every power of government. But he directed military operations under his own responsibility. The War Committee did not have to determine his strategy, and, besides, Daladier hardly ever summoned it.[5]

With all that, defining and limiting the fields of civilian and military authority is well-nigh impossible. They overlap, almost necessarily. It means that the civilian and military heads are most likely to clash if either of them shows strong character and temperament. Moreover, a Premier of the type of Clemenceau or Poincaré would not have tolerated a weakling on supreme command for any length of time.

In the case of Daladier and Gamelin, the Law of July 1938 was of very smooth application, and their quarrels never cut very deep. Unfortunately, this harmony was no ground for satisfaction: it proved only that both men were constantly in the mood for compromise and that neither was capable of fierce resolve. It proved also that Daladier could rely on himself only if he wanted to reform the civilian and military administration, disorganized by twenty years of slackness, carelessness, postponement of overdue decisions—and by a poor selection of personnel. The staff at Vincennes shared the inertia of the Army and the nation. Daladier, alone, now had to provide the nation with the drive and power needed to meet the test of war. From where could he draw that power, that drive? It was asking for something he did not have.

[5]Law of July 11, 1938: General Organization of the Nation in Time of War. Section 3, concerning the Conduct of the War, Article 40. This law was never applied as a whole. Each Premier drew from it what he wanted and forgot the rest.

Daladier's honesty is beyond question. He spent nearly twenty years in that world of politicians where the Oustric and the Stavisky scandals burst forth in quick succession. Gambling on foreign exchange, lucrative friendships with financiers, administrative and even, but in some exceptional cases, judiciary action placed at the service of private interests, tarnished many reputations. In all those years his name has never been associated with anything which savored of money. A baker's son from the little town of Carpentras in Provence, he had the sober, not overimaginative, but still very deep patriotism of the peasant. And a peasant he had remained in his manners. I remembered how upset the French Ambassador in London was when he was host at a luncheon given in 1933 at which Ramsay MacDonald and Sir John Simon were present, eager to meet the new French Premier. The two British cabinet ministers, dignified and solemn, were waiting upstairs in one of the Embassy drawing rooms. Daladier and one of his colleagues—I forget who it was—were late. In the hall downstairs they argued noisily and at length, then they came up to meet the British without even throwing away the butts of their cigarettes.

On the other hand, a witness found these words to describe Daladier's long talk with Mr. Sumner Welles in March 1940: "I kept watching him while he explained to the American Under Secretary of State how any negotiated peace with Hitler would be only a perilous armistice, while he told in minute detail all he had done and was doing to help Finland, while he accused the Swedes and the Norwegians of lacking spirit. He expressed himself slowly and methodically. I had a vision of him in the garb of a plowman walking heavily behind his plow. I had before me a man of the French soil, with his roots deep in it."

He is *"agrégé d'histoire,"* a degree very sparingly granted: out of all the French universities, only fifteen or twenty candidates succeed each summer. This fact implies—or it implied thirty-five years ago—familiarity with the classics and a thorough knowledge of the past. In France and elsewhere we have learned that great culture does not suffice to create a great mind. Yet let us remember this: even in the midst of war Daladier found relaxation at night in reading history. So he took a broad view of the events in which he played a great part; he saw them against the background of the past. He was no autumn leaf swirled by the wind. I have said that he was disinterested as regards material profit. It must be added that he possessed intellectual integrity and was even overscrupulous. He worried ceaselessly as to what he was going to do, what he was doing, and what he had done.

Edouard Herriot, who was a great professor of rhetoric in his day and who taught successively in the Lycée and at the University of Lyons, once told me that he had kept some essays written by Daladier when a student, that they were models of their kind, and that I would be surprised at the promise shown by the young man. Why surprised? In 1914 Daladier had been drafted from his Lycée. Having served four years at the front (a private in an infantry regiment, he came back a captain)[6] and, after the armistice of 1918, having gone in for politics, he affected a sort of rough and rudimentary language. When I called on him from time to time, during his first term as Premier in 1933, I was disturbed by the inferior quality of his statesmanship as reflected in current remarks of his. I can still hear him, the Minister for War, stating as though it were incontestable truth: "The first and the last word in military art is to build a trench and hold it. All the rest . . ." I do not remember the phrase that followed, but surely it ended on the inevitable "that's trash." On another occasion I was asking him about the Anglo-French-Italian-American declaration of December 11, 1932, which granted Germany, in League of Nations jargon, "equal rights in armaments." Germany had slammed the doors on the conference in the preceding month of July. By means of this gift—made without anything more than vague promises being asked in return—the wise men of Paris, London, Washington, and Rome were attempting to pacify her and win her back. "I must confess," acknowledged Daladier, "that the Cabinet ratified this declaration without being aware of what it implied."

Such sentences remained in my mind, and I was prejudiced against the man who uttered them. Herriot, a kind man, tried to change my feelings. Much more convincing testimonials came to me from a civil servant of outstanding merit and from an extremely farsighted financier who both shared to the end in the Premier's counsels. The civil servant vouched for the high quality of Daladier's political intelligence. The banker bore witness that he had an unusual intuition of the most complex monetary questions—and it is well known that most public men run aground on these abstract matters. It was once said in the House of Commons that not more than twenty members, at the most, could possibly follow the treasury experts in some of the ramifications of their thought. Even though I cannot forget that in October 1934, at the congress of the Radical-Socialist party, Daladier, in a fit of demagoguery, flung into the discussion a mad system of "melting money," borrowed from some

[6]The Abbé Desgranges, member of the House of Deputies from Morbihan, served in the same infantry company as Daladier. One day someone asked him: "Is it true that Daladier was a fine officer?" He replied: "Better than that; he was a fine soldier."

Austrian municipal administration, I cannot set myself up against this double testimony to his capacity. But then how is it that so many errors, major and minor, can be charged against him?

The almost unanimous answer is that he has no will power. He reaches a decision only through the most laborious and slow mental processes. He has natural insight—indeed, I have already used the word "intuition." No one has ever denied him a very keen parliamentary sense, at least during his last premiership. Precisely because he is unable to take swift and sharp decisions, he gives free play to what Leibnitz called the "minor perceptions." Unlike the rash and impetuous, he does not choke them off. Not being intellectually alert, he waits until their hidden and unceasing work is accomplished, prepares him for action and moves him forward. Thus he may be clearsighted, but in the manner of those who can never make up their mind. He waits a long time, a very long time, indefinitely, and, while he waits, incessantly reopens the debate within himself.

More often than not he yields to the pressure of persons around him. He is not one of those men all of a piece and impervious to the hurly-burly of the world, immovably fixed in their ideas and feelings. He does not put his mark on men; rather they put their mark on him. His character does not jut out in hard surfaces like that of Clemenceau: it is full of soft spots. His policy is battered by the contradictory forces which hammer at it, and with some cunning he seeks to conceal the dents. I have always been surprised that newspapermen, English and American especially, should have formed the habit of comparing him to a bull. He has the bull's thick neck, perhaps, but certainly not the bull's taste for rushing straight at an obstacle. His taciturn appearance, his sparing speech, his muffled voice and rustic ways explain the metaphor. "This young bull smells of the stable," remarked Caillaux of Daladier when the latter was Premier for the first time in 1933. Thus was scored his political earthiness. But the image should be carried no further. It would be better to remember his thoughtful forehead and his eyes, sad and rather melancholy. True, British cabinet ministers saw him in a different light: when in the thick of a discussion, with no time for introspection and hesitation, he assumed for a few hours all the outward characteristics of resolution and strength. In reality he was weak and irresolute. Events made him a dictator: that was one of life's tricks. He was a dictator in spite of himself.

2

A Dictator in Spite of Himself, and an Inconsistent Man

A STRANGE DICTATOR. He did not secure the exceptional measure of executive authority which spelled practical omnipotence through any patriotic desire, or any ambition to govern the Republic more efficiently, or even because he had a special reverence for the eminent dignity of the state, a feeling which uplifts all statesmen worthy of that name. Nor can we ascribe the rise of the man to a nation in search of a master able to restrain or spur it on—a search which gives a would-be despot his opportunity. "O straight-haired Corsican, how beautiful was France under the high noon of Messidor. . . ." No, there was no poetry and no hero worship. In the case of Daladier the dictator, the part played by any deliberate striving for domination comes down to this: in 1933, when Premier for the first time, he was obliged to recognize that the normal working of French institutions was at a standstill because of the complexity and gravity of the financial problem. He foresaw, perhaps before anyone else, that the French Republic—like the Weimar Republic in July 1930—must allow the chief executive to carry out the most urgent reforms without regular parliamentary discussion and vote; that (within certain necessarily vague limits) it must authorize him to make laws by simple decree, leaving parliamentary ratification to the future.

Daladier was quicker than most in realizing this compelling necessity. However, when he was overthrown in October 1933, and when, after being called back in January 1934 to head the Cabinet, he again withdrew, a few days later, as a result of the tragedy of February 6, he had not even had time to seek the needed enabling bill. It was the tragic state of affairs created by his failure as a leader of government which persuaded Parliament to grant special powers to his successor, Gaston Doumergue. Thereafter (from 1934 to 1938) all French Premiers had these powers at their disposal, except Pierre-Etienne Flandin and Léon Blum, to whom they were refused by one or another of the Houses (May

1935, June 1937, April 1938)[1] and who were compelled to resign. But not until Daladier returned to office on April 10, 1938—to hold it until March 20, 1940—did he himself receive the new "imperium." It was granted him all the more extensively since conditions in France and outside of France, month by month, were growing steadily worse, and since public opinion, wearied by so many contradictory efforts—the Popular Front experiment following that of the National Coalition—was close to despairing of the parliamentary system.

Daladier was given full powers on April 12, 1938, with a time limit set to July 31: full powers again on October 5, and once again on March 19, 1939, for a period lasting, this time, until November. On September 3 the law for the organization of the nation in wartime went into effect: in Article 36 it confirmed and extended the controlling authority granted the Head of the Government. That was still not enough for him. A law dated December 2 added yet more. It is perfectly true, therefore, that Daladier, during the twenty-three months and ten days of his premiership, was in a position to perform the legislative functions of the state in place of Parliament. It is also true that Parliament was forced to ratify, at irregular intervals, measures promulgated and carried out without its participation. But at the origin of this processus no more can be set than Daladier's halting aspirations in the summer of 1933 and Daladier's notorious flinching in February 1934. It is, therefore, impossible to speak of his dogged and clearsighted determination.

To use the word dictatorship and leave it at that is to be superficial. We must lay bare all that existed below the surface. There was, first of all, a country divided within itself; political parties in disagreement on all the questions of foreign or home affairs which required settlement, parties which no longer dared to be outspoken and which survived only to function as electioneering societies. There was a Premier accepted by most people not as a source of energy and action but because he was and had been ever as diverse in his schemes as in his deeds. Politicians of all tendencies, the reformer and the socially conservative, the partisan of resistance to the totalitarian states and the appeaser, each believed or pretended to believe that the "Chief" was his man and that the concessions made to his adversary were only temporary tactics. Those who favored a "strong" policy stood by Daladier for fear that if he were thrown out some "appeaser" would get into the driver's seat—and the appeasers

---

[1] At the moment of his accession to the premiership in June 1936, Léon Blum, supported by a quasi-revolutionary movement, did not consider it necessary to ask for full powers. In fact, he had them.

followed the same reasoning for an opposite purpose. But was the Chief Executive of sufficient stature to be above all these factional interests, to ignore them deliberately and find his only inspiration in the needs of a France at war? The sad fact is that he was only too intensely concerned with day-to-day intrigues, followed them closely, and too often doled out his decisions accordingly. It is at that price that he maintained a pretense of national unity, a veneer which wore off and cracked under the first severe strain.

Such was the real position. Daladier's specious omnipotence sprang from the parliamentary debility which became apparent after the fall of the second Blum Cabinet (April 7, 1938)—that is, after the termination of the Popular Front experiment—and which struck all observers. For instance, the Munich Agreement that so deeply shook the country was discussed by the House of Deputies (October 4) only in the most hasty and futile fashion.[2] Those who rose to speak, with two or three exceptions, used the greatest ingenuity to avoid the real problem, each fearing to lose some portion of his supporters. It was the same story the next day, when the second bill for full powers brought in by Daladier was passed as rapidly and as silently as a letter dropped in a mailbox.

Daladier could not supply the slightest dynamism to make up for Parliament's collapse. In spite of his show of independence, he had for years drawn too heavily upon the small change of politics to nurse his political ascension. Perhaps more than anyone else he must bear the responsibility for the schism that came to exist between Frenchmen. To be sure, he never intended to do things as he did them. Much was accidental, but much was due also to his shilly-shallying and incompetence. I repeat that on the material level his honesty cannot be questioned. But that was not enough. Even under more or less normal conditions, in 1933, he failed to get results from the parliamentary machine because, unlike Clemenceau and Poincaré, he lacked drive. Once that machine was jammed, he was all the more incapable of getting it started again. And, in spite of his claims, he was powerless to govern from above.

To understand what he is and what befell him we must consider the Radical-Socialist party, of which he was the elected "president" and which produced him as a tree produces its fruit.[3] It is not just a political party. The Radical-Socialists represent that class in French society which

---

[2] On the other hand, at a meeting of the House Committee on Foreign Affairs, a few days later, members freely unburdened themselves.

[3] In 1918–19 Daladier was enrolled as a Socialist; he left this party after some six months.

has the greatest stability in its interests, its prejudices, and its feelings. It is made up of peasants who are small landowners, of the lower middle class in the cities, second-rate doctors and lawyers, the personnel of the government services, and most of the retail shopkeepers. By contrast with the conservatives of the Right and Center, who have never succeeded in achieving unity and who are always bickering with each other,[4] the Radical-Socialist structure is built on stable foundations: the administrative agencies of the state, since most government employees belong to the party and the Masonic lodges.[5] All in all, those men have ruled France ever since the Dreyfus affair stripped the "moderates" of the practical monopoly they possessed in government.

During the last twenty years they have lost ground, gradually but seriously, to the Socialists. In the first place, the Socialist party, recruited mainly among the urban and rural proletariat, has also been able to create a steady political machine, because it attracts the lowest ranks of government employees—postmen and teachers in low-grade schools. In the second place, the Socialist ideology cannot but appeal to the underdog. The result was that in May 1936 more Socialist deputies than Radical-Socialist were returned to Parliament. But Radical-Socialist supporters do not melt away. Through all revolutions their mass persists. Toward 1860 these people cheered Napoleon III, just as they cheered, through the last decades, their "presidents"—Herriot, Chautemps, and Daladier.[6] There is in this phenomenon something approaching incompressibility. When individuals belonging to the lower middle class grow richer and rise in the social scale they assume divergent political points of view as

[4]On the Right and in the Center, Louis Marin's Republican Federation and the group of Popular Democrats (Catholic with liberal social views) were the only two properly organized parties possessing stable and uncontested leadership, national headquarters, and regional branches. All the rest was fragmentary and kept forming uncertain and temporary coalitions to defend manifold interests.

[5]Daladier is not a Mason; nor, for that matter, is Herriot. He was wont to remark privately that the most intense patriotism was to be found in the hearts of French priests and friars. Once he pointed to the difference between their conduct and that of the low-grade schoolteachers (*instituteurs*). After a visit from Cardinal Verdier he exclaimed, "Why, the man talks like Archbishop Turpin!" Cardinal Verdier wrote several extraordinarily moving letters to him. The Gestapo knew what it was doing when it attempted to force Cardinal Suhard, the present Archbishop of Paris, to give up his predecessors' papers. The man at the head of the Radical-Socialist Masons, the representative of anti-clerical and even anti-religious laicization, was Camille Chautemps, the most commonplace of the three "presidents" who, in turn, ruled over the party.

[6]The president of the Radical-Socialists was named each year by the delegates of the various local sections. Daladier was elected in 1928 to succeed Herriot, who was serving as a minister of Poincaré's under the banner of national union—a banner which made him temporarily unpopular with his own party.

their new interests become differentiated. But the vast majority almost never change their outlook on public affairs.

France is predominantly a nation of little people whom the Radical-Socialist party typifies pretty well. They were kept away from the broad highways of power by the old monarchy and by the July Monarchy, the latter favoring the upper middle classes and plutocracy in any form. They have had but two regimes after their heart's desire: the Second Empire and, above all, the Republic of 1875—neither Thiers' nor Mac-Mahon's, nor even Gambetta's, nor Ferry's nor Casimir Périer's nor Poincaré's—but the Republic as it took shape at the turn of the century. They made much of the words "radical democracy," but, finding them slightly worn, they enhanced them with the "socialist" label. This needs interpretation.

To a degree that seems atavistic, they mistrusted the central power. This explains why participation in the government meant to them, above all, protection against the state. Protection from the state through participation in the state. They wanted material advantage, various favors from the administration, all that the word patronage implies. Social jealousy, but not hatred, is the mainspring of the Radical-Socialists. To understand their frame of mind, one must have lived among the quarrels of the small French towns and villages, heard interminable stories of the doctor's wife snubbed by the "château" in concert with the rectory, etc. All this closed and bitter life, so often described by French novelists, broadened and softened during the last twenty-five years. The village priest, after the separation of Church and State had deprived him of meager financial support from the public chest and made him dependent on his parishioners' support, took his place among the poor and parted with the country squire. Yet the old rancors persisted in part. Hence a craving for revenge in terms of politics. But the aim was to turn the tables rather than to destroy.

The Radical-Socialist mass was prone to elect men who spoke the language of the doctrinaire republicans of the nineteenth century, who boasted of having no enemies to the Left, and kept on good terms with the Socialists. This association with the Socialists was essential for the simple reason that all the men of the Left would be defeated by the reactionaries if they did not form coalitions. These alone could save the day when a first vote failed to give a candidate an absolute majority and a second vote had to be taken. Thus this same mass incessantly cried for reforms which would bring about social leveling. But on condition that only the wealthy should be affected, the term being interpreted to mean anyone richer than the average. The Radical-Socialists reacted savagely as soon as their pocketbooks were threatened (or rather they were wont to, for recently they had mellowed). Godefroy Cavaignac, one of their leaders, actually won the elections of 1898 on an income-tax platform; but for a long time the rank and file resisted and nullified this tax in country districts.

The life of the party was a painful seesaw between right and left. It always regretted the Golden Age, when "anti-clericalism" and the proposal that the state purchase the railroads were the two main planks in its platform.

Nothing could be more curtailed and narrow than the specifically Radical-Socialist picture of the political universe. The party's annual Congress, held every October before Parliament met, used to be the cartoonist's delight because of the incredible human fossils who attended it, having emerged for a while from the deep caverns of provincial lodges. Here was a closed, a hidebound world, as little fitted as possible to deal with great public questions. Very largely rural, some idea of the part it played in France's political life may be gleaned by comparing it with the American Middle West, a Middle West strongly colored by Tammany. Deeply anchored in certain elemental ideas and feelings that were changeless, it acted like a pendulum. Absorbing the shock of violent pressures from both left and right, it swung to and fro, but always with a tendency to return to center. It gave the nation a sense of balance. And, to vary the metaphor, it was also the crucible in which violent differences were composed through a process of compromise—and compromise is the soul of a regime based on public opinion.

For a long time the Radical-Socialists' ambition did not go beyond this passive, if important, function. They were the strongest party in Parliament, yet they allowed the highest posts—the presidency of the Republic, the Ministry for Foreign Affairs, occasionally even the premiership—to be filled by men who were not of their kind and with whom they could form only temporary alliances. Loubet, Delcassé, Waldeck-Rousseau, Fallières, Rouvier, Poincaré, Jonnart, Millerand, Briand, Viviani—none of these men were Radical-Socialists. As though they had labored under an inferiority complex, the Radical-Socialists felt that their leaders were ill suited to certain positions, especially those connected with foreign affairs, and they feared that if they forced the appointment of one of them, the choice would not be approved by public opinion. Prior to 1914, Emile Combes and Gaston Doumergue, both sprung from well-to-do peasant families, were the only Prime Ministers selected from their midst. But Doumergue turned furiously against them, first as President of the Republic after 1924 and again in 1934 as head of a government of national union. Once showered with public honors, the Radical-Socialist politician easily turned into a conservative die-hard.

Clemenceau, although he was counted as Radical-Socialist, really sprang from a Jacobin model, individualistic, aristocratic, romantic, a type now nearly extinct. He led the party, whip in hand, during his two premierships of 1906 and 1917; split it in two at the 1919 elections, bitterly attacking the fraction which refused to enter his "national unity coalition." And Joseph Caillaux, son of one of MacMahon's ministers, a dandy and an expert in financial matters—if somewhat pedantic—who long bewildered the party as Alcibiades and Catiline would have, influenced it only intermittently.

The Radical-Socialists never really dominated the Republic with leaders of their own vintage until after 1924.[7] Then the era of the three "presidents" we have mentioned opened, and Daladier gradually ran ahead of the other two as the most gifted in the art of government. Easygoing complacency called the tune. Everything went along on a basis of good fellowship. Cabinet followed cabinet—six of them between June 1932 and February 1934—but these crises in government amounted to mere "reconstructions." From ministry to ministry the same men remained in place; they occasionally exchanged portfolios. Thus it happened that Albert Sarraut was a cabinet minister some thirty times, and Queuille, a physician from Corrèze, twenty times. A relative stability was obtained by a sort of high frequency.

The short life of French cabinets has always been criticized; the other side of the picture, in the Republic of 1875, is the way the men who went out so rapidly endlessly came back again. M. de Freycinet, Minister for War in 1871, reappeared as Minister of State during the war of 1914: he was eighty-eight years old. His ministerial longevity, still more surprising than his extreme old age and continued lucidity, was a phenomenon unmatched in Europe. Poincaré, Georges Leygues, Barthou, who were young cabinet ministers in 1893, still held cabinet positions in 1929, 1930, and 1934 respectively. The story of the three dirty shirts is more valid in France than it is elsewhere. A tramp owns three shirts but cannot pay

---

[7]The former *radical* party of Clemenceau, Madier de Montjeau, of Henri Brisson, of Cavaignac, which gradually blended into the Radical-Socialist party, was in reality of a very different nature and tone. Liberal (in the nineteenth-century sense), Jacobin, redolent of the violent ideology of 1793, it originated with the urban middle class, and not with the farm population. It faded little by little under the sobering effect of ministerial responsibilities and under the impact of socialism.

to have them washed. Irresistibly, he thinks that the shirt he wore three days ago is cleaner than the other two.

The great misfortune was that such weak characters as the three "presidents," tied to the narrow outlook of their political following and to their necessary electoral alliance with the Socialists, should have had to handle exceptionally complicated financial, diplomatic, and military problems. It was a great misfortune, furthermore, that the moderate parties—whose leadership was very shortsighted—after making the most serious errors themselves, should then have failed to recognize that the Radical-Socialists stood for truly fundamental elements in France's social fabric. These so-called conservatives thought they could violently assail the Radical-Socialist leaders, vilify them, and destroy their hold on their constituencies. The onslaught drove the latter into the arms of Léon Blum and even of Thorez, the leader of the Communists. The moderates had broken the pendulum.

In 1933, with a policy obstinately centered upon upholding and protecting the gold content of the franc as established by Poincaré seven years earlier, the budget could not be balanced. Daladier made the attempt, as so many were to do after him. He merely united, in opposition to his financial measures, the government employees and the people living on pensions, great and small. In December the Stavisky scandal brought to public attention the fact that it was within the wit of a common criminal not only to avoid going to prison but even to swindle huge sums of money and find accomplices in influential quarters, some of them among the public prosecutors (submitted to the instructions of the Minister of Justice). This was the spark which set widespread discontent afire. The leagues and factions of the Right tried their hand at street demonstrations and clashes with the police. Taken too lightly by Chautemps, they grew more bitter daily. On February 6 neither Daladier, called back to re-establish order, nor his conceited and shady Minister of the Interior, Eugène Frot, nor his incompetent prefect of police, Bonnefoy-Sibour, could find a way to safeguard Parliament except by firing on the mob. Sixteen were killed. The Premier resigned the next day.[8] Thereby it was known that violence could pay, that seditious men threatened the Republic—and were not easily curbed. The Left turned to reprisals. From then on the nation was split in two. The chasm was made deeper both by the failure of Doumergue's national coalition cabinet and by Daladier's personal reaction. Marked out as a machine gunner, insulted

[8]He did not wish to risk further bloodshed. He resigned for reasons which were humane, but hardly consonant with "reason of state."

and abandoned by everyone, he sought, despite Herriot's advice, to save himself by the creation of a Popular Front, not only with the Socialists but with the Communists. "When one is out of office, the way back starts at the extreme Left." He actually said those words.

That the Radical-Socialist party, with an essentially balanced body of opinion behind it, should take shelter in the fold of out-and-out revolutionaries was a very grave matter. In the elections of May 1936, Léon Blum and the Socialists came to the fore. Daladier, vice-president of the Cabinet, Minister for National Defense, approved by his silence the sit-down strikes as well as the ensuing adventurous social legislation while planning to put an end to the whole experiment as soon as the tide subsided.

In April 1938 the ebb began to make itself felt. Daladier started gradually undoing what could never have been accomplished without him. He started bringing the Radical-Socialists back toward the center. He endeavored to repair the pendulum. Laudable as his belated intention was, great havoc had been made and the nation's unity could not easily be attained again. The wealthy could not forget so many red flags waving above so many silent factories, nor the clenched fists raised at their passing automobiles. A vision of revolution on the march had visited them. It dawned upon them that Hitler and Mussolini were allies of their social class rather than enemies of their country. As for the have-nots, they remembered how the government had yielded to the mob on the Place de la Concorde, they saw that preparations were being made for a Fascist seizure of power, and they blamed the ruin of the Popular Front on the capitalists and on capital. The French people underwent an emotional crisis deeper than that caused by the Dreyfus affair. Neither political nor family group were spared.

It would be unfair to make one man alone bear the responsibility for such tragic inner dissension. However, at the critical moments in the history of this period, Daladier, more than anyone else, by what he did accomplish or failed to accomplish, decided the course of events.

No political career, to my knowledge, includes as many contradictions and changes of attitudes as his does, and no statesman was ever less disturbed at adopting utterly inconsistent policies. He did not even seem to know when he was giving himself the lie. I am not merely alluding to the fact that he called the Popular Front to life and, within two years, pulled it down. In other matters there were similarly complete gyrations. His Finance Ministers, Georges Bonnet in 1933 and Paul Marchandeau in 1938, did not evince much common sense in their conduct of affairs.

He dismissed the latter in November—when pressed by him to adopt a desperate solution, the control of foreign exchange—and replaced him with Paul Reynaud,[9] who, for years, had urged a policy dissymmetrically opposed to that pursued by those two ministers. But was Reynaud selected because his views were considered sound or because they were along the line of least resistance? In 1933, on the subject of disarmament, we listened, time after time, to Daladier's boast that he would not consent to any weakening of the French Army, either in armament or in numbers, unless pacts for mutual military assistance against an eventual aggressor were completed at Geneva. Suddenly he dropped this unceasingly advertised claim and expressed willingness to hold as a valid guaranty a system of international supervision over the military establishments of all countries. Such was his persistence![10]

In June 1933 he signed the famous Pact of the Four Great Powers, which—had not Germany abandoned the League of Nations, the Disarmament Conference, etc., in October—would have harnessed the European continent with a directorate of Paris-London-Berlin-Rome and destroyed the system of French alliances as well as the League of Nations itself. This was an abortive undertaking, but, added to the Declaration of December 11, 1932, on equal rights regarding armaments, it served to throw Poland into Germany's arms. M. Georges Bonnet told me how, while on vacation in September 1933, at St. Georges de Didonne, near the mouth of the Gironde, he received a telegram from Daladier requesting his immediate return to Paris. Upon his arrival the Premier informed him of the strange plan Hitler had just confidentially proposed.[11] The heads of the French and German governments were to meet secretly in the Black Forest. They were to meet periodically (with

---

[9]As early as April 1938, when forming his Cabinet, Daladier had offered Reynaud the Finance Ministry. But Reynaud, influenced by Bouthillier, at that time favored dangerous plans for a further devaluation of the franc: 240 francs to the pound sterling. When it became clear that he was failing in his efforts to convince the Premier, Reynaud declined the Treasury and agreed to become Minister of Justice. He had campaigned brilliantly on financial matters for years; this acceptance of the portfolio of justice seemed a comedown. A few weeks later Daladier was heard exclaiming: "What a dangerous man he is! To think that I was sorry when he refused the Treasury!"

[10]Here is another flagrant instance of his instability. In January 1934, when he sought to form that authoritarian cabinet which so soon was to be slapped down, the first man he turned to was Flandin—that is to say, he turned to the moderates. When he got no response from them he immediately shifted his arrangements toward the Left, and this time succeeded.

[11]Fernand de Brinon and Pfeiffer—former secretary-general of the Radical-Socialist party who later left this position to go into business—both "appeasers," were then close to Daladier.

all newspapermen severely banned) until they had achieved a complete Franco-German reconciliation. Once this result had been obtained, Hitler and Daladier would march toward the Rhine, each at the head of a considerable army, and there, at an equal distance from the two banks of the river, on an island or on a bridge, they would dedicate a monument to the settlement of the centuries-old conflict. "But do you think the secret can really be kept?" objected Georges Bonnet. And he added, when telling the tale: "Daladier clung to this weird dream. The Chamber of Deputies, a month later, brought this castle in the air tumbling to the ground, unawares, by its refusal to deprive government employees and pension holders of the slightest fraction of their salaries." The Ministry, of course, did not survive the vote.

Such had been Daladier's excursions into foreign affairs before 1938, when he took up anew the burden of conducting the nation's business. Sir John Simon and Neville Chamberlain had nothing to envy him in the way of "appeasement." Nevertheless, before and after the Munich settlement, Daladier continuously castigated Bonnet, Minister for Foreign Affairs, and described his dubious management of French diplomacy in the most insulting terms. How much wiser he would have been had he held his tongue and disciplined the men, which he did only by fits and starts.[12]

But of all the performances of Daladier, the most inexcusable occurred on September 30, 1938, when he flew back from Munich to Paris.

In the plane, coming home, he was under no illusions as to the importance of the diplomatic setback he had suffered. He saw the future as the future was indeed to be. He expressed aloud the somber thoughts which disturbed his mind. Meanwhile Le Bourget was drawing near. A great crowd had assembled there. The Premier expected to be hissed when he landed. To his astonishment, Georges Bonnet came running toward him, hat in hand, and threw his arms around him. The crowd cheered. The Premier made no move to stop the cheering. He did not cry out: "Do not rejoice! What this means and what you must remember is that you must be more united, stronger, more resolute." Instead

---

[12]Daladier had a deplorable habit of running down and criticizing several of his colleagues in the Cabinet. Never, by his own words, should he have let anyone think that his choice of cabinet ministers was haphazard. Never should he have forgotten that it was his duty to respect them so long as he maintained them in office. But why had he entrusted the Quai d'Orsay to Bonnet? Because he did not want Paul Boncour, whose reputation was too closely linked with the visionary side of Geneva. Furthermore, his majority was so divided that he needed someone accustomed to double-dealing and deceit. At the time the Cabinet was formed Bonnet made no mystery of his opinions but promised not to be swayed by them.

he bowed cynically to the triumph he did not deserve. How revolting it was to see him standing up in the back of his car, with Bonnet beside him, arm uplifted, and thanking the people of Paris for their applause. I was lunching at Larue's with a foreign diplomat, and our conversation had been rather gloomy. The city was bathed in its mellow September light. Suddenly a great stir in the street and a joyous outcry startled us. Surprised, we hurried out. And then, sick at heart, we understood what the gay clamor meant: France's first capitulation was being hailed as though it were a victory.

Soon afterward, at the Radical-Socialist Congress at Marseilles, Daladier concealed France's humiliated position in the world under a most curious political theory. To the principle of European balance of power, from time immemorial the guide of French diplomacy, he now substituted a policy of withdrawal into the French Empire. "Imperial recession" it was dubbed at the time. Heaven knows he did not believe what he said: he knew perfectly well that colonies are won and lost on continental battlefields. Why all this recantation when, a year later, he was to declare war in order to save the very balance of power he had renounced?

3

His Inner Circle. Hostility toward Reynaud and Blum

THERE STOOD DALADIER, possessed of an omnipotence quite out of tune with his temperament, which he could use only by drastic and uninterrupted self-control. He was sustained neither by any impelling force from within nor by any plan of action adopted once for all. Conscious of his weakness, he feared that all could see it. He was a worried man, quick to take offense, jealous of his authority, readily suspicious, secretive: he had neither the true freedom which comes from a self-sufficient intellect nor that which springs from strength of character. Always instinctively mistrustful of people unless he had known them for a long time, he was to a great extent under the influence of those few who were close to him.

But he was sincerely anxious to rise above his own limitations. And when wise counselors showed him what sort of leader he could be, they aroused in him a keen desire to do his best. After he took the Ministry of Foreign Affairs on September 13, 1939, he conferred twice a day with the Under Secretary of State, Champetier de Ribes, with Alexis Léger, secretary-general at the Quai d'Orsay, and Robert Coulondre, former Ambassador to Moscow and Berlin, head of his private secretariat on foreign affairs. At those daily conferences the two career diplomats methodically laid before him the diplomatic correspondence and fully explained to him the ever-shifting international problems.

With one notable exception, which I will discuss later, his handling of them was on the whole enlightened. I shall give two instances. Mussolini, after Poland's defeat, was convinced that neither France nor England would steadfastly keep on with the war, and that far-reaching negotiations soon would be undertaken for a compromise peace. Bonnet's general attitude toward Guariglia, Italian Ambassador in Paris, had encouraged Rome to nurse such a hope. Daladier put an end to it, in a few sharp sentences, the first time he received Guariglia. As a result the Duce carefully avoided playing the part which Berlin assigned to him—as well as to Stalin—in the "peace offensive" launched by the Führer in his speech of October 6. Thanks to Daladier's firmness, the Fascist dictator remained doubtful of German victory—although passionately desiring it—until January 1940.

About the same time Daladier saved the treaty which Great Britain and France were to conclude with Turkey on October 16 from being emptied of all substance. The Kremlin wanted it to be a hollow shell, and Mr. Saracoglou, the Turkish Foreign Minister, was inclined to listen to Russia. Under no circumstances, according to him, must Turkey be drawn into conflict against Germany. If the treaty, in its final shape, retained some force, this was due to Daladier's firm declaration: "I will have nothing to do with a contract made only for the sake of appearances."[1]

Attached to his secretariat as Prime Minister were three officials—Clapier, "Maître des Requêtes à la Cour des Comptes,"[2] a worthy man who, like Daladier, was of peasant origin; Génébrier, a prefect, and Gen-

---

[1] The President of the Turkish Republic, in a personal letter, had begged him to accept the reservation concerning Germany. This would have permitted Turkey to take a position parallel to that of Russia and the agreement would have been directed solely against an eventual Italian aggression. London, disturbed at the very thought of losing Turkey, was willing to yield.

[2] The special court which exerts control of all public expenditure.

eral Decamp, who, one must admit, was very much of an appeaser. They do not seem to have had any weight with him. Unfortunately, one cannot say as much of the circle of friends to whom Daladier turned for relaxation after his day's work. They did not make it easier for him to perform his task.

Mme. Daladier, whose father was Poincaré's physician, had died many years before. The Premier lived with his two sons and a sister in a small and rather gloomy apartment. Mlle. Daladier served her brother's meals, and, on occasion, even those of his infrequent guests, with the simple dignity of Provençal custom. No luxury, no comfort, no attempt at style in the furnishing of the small suite. Seeing that modest home, one understood at once that Daladier could never be preoccupied with money. But meanwhile Daladier was brought in contact with the wider social life of Paris through the Marquise of Crussol. A spirited woman, rather attractive with her arched nose, but grasping and covetous: it was not for nothing that the lady's Breton family had built up a rather handsome fortune putting sardines into cans. She had a strong business sense. Married to the colorless younger son of a noble family, she ruled the household. More and more, as years went on, she interested herself in collecting and dominating ministers, ex-ministers, high officials, and financiers. Unlike Mme. Hélène de Portes, Paul Reynaud's mistress, Mme. de Crussol did not meddle openly in state affairs. She remained very discreetly in the background. For one thing, the malevolent and spiteful stories which pursued her after the riots of February 6 had shown her the advisability of prudence. For another, Daladier knew how to give her a thorough calling down. She was afraid of him and carefully concealed her game. If she exploited his position, it was never with his knowledge or tolerance.

History has a right to discuss her, because she surrounded Daladier with her intimates. Two especially—Daniel Serruys and Emmanuel Arago—took upon themselves to provide the Minister with an interpretative chronicle of Paris society and of its politics. Daladier had no direct, personal knowledge of current gossip: he was isolated by his task and, moreover, quite unfamiliar with the social register.

Serruys, a Greek scholar, had learned political economy during the war of 1914–18 when, as head of the private secretariat, he assisted Albert Métin, Minister of Blockade, and, I believe, his successors. The Ministry of Commerce was for him the next rung of the ladder: he was entrusted there with all commercial negotiations from 1920 to 1930. Then he branched off toward lucrative business and represented a powerful Paris bank on various boards of directors. For a long time I had greatly enjoyed Serruys' verbal fireworks, although they never cast any lasting light in the darkness they were supposed to dispel.[3] He had long believed in the League of Nations to an unreasonable extent. How and why this virtuoso of political luncheons changed into a totalitarian-minded discourser has puzzled me to this day.

As for Emmanuel Arago, he was unpleasant to look at, common, and embittered because the people at the *Petit Parisien*—founded by his grandfather, Jean Dupuy—kept him from having any connection with it. Consequently he was obsessed by the desire to become a personage in other fields, and he danced attendance on cabinet ministers. Utterly devoted to the marquise, and with unlimited time on his hands, he was the perfect chatterbox who boasts that he knows all the intrigues of the capital, adds a few of his own, and gets quite lost in the maze. The specific harm accomplished by these two men was that they encouraged Daladier in his strong dislike for Léon Blum, and in a feeling for Paul Reynaud which very soon became indistinguishable from actual hatred.

Reynaud had never been on friendly terms with Daladier. He owed his nomination as Minister of Justice in April 1938, and as Finance Minister, seven months later, to Countess de Portes. She had had the cleverness, at the right moment, to ingratiate or to reingratiate herself to the Marquise de Crussol—assisted by Arago, fluttering from salon to salon like a loquacious butterfly. Serruys opposed Reynaud's diplomatic and financial ideas but, behind all questions of doctrine, was really aiming at the man himself. It was not merely a case of rivalry between two talents, two orators—one in Parliament, the other in the salons. Serruys had a special grievance. He had persuaded Daladier to make him High Commissioner for National Economy. Then the Finance Minister had deeply offended him by openly treating his department as nothing more than a subdivision of the Finance Ministry and himself as a usurper and idle talker whose projects were mere rhetoric.[4] He did what he could to injure Reynaud in the Premier's opinion; this was mere child's play, with Mme. de Portes peddling all through Paris her friend's cracks about the "Dictator" and predicting that "he would end

---

[3]Daladier said of the memoranda Serruys used to send him: "By the time I have read sixty pages I not only no longer know what he thinks but I do not even know what I think myself." Two days later he appointed him High Commissioner for National Economy.

[4]It should be noted, however, that in October and November 1938, frightened by Marchandeau's plans for the control of exchange, Serruys recommended Reynaud's accession to the Finance Ministry. But he had not yet become High Commissioner for National Economy.

by losing the war," etc. That constant reviling was disastrous in its consequences. Had they been able to work together, the one compensating for the faults of the other, the two leaders would have better served their country than they did each pulling for himself.

As for Léon Blum, he was doubly mistrusted by the little group, first as Reynaud's personal friend—despite the differences in their programs —and then, above all, as a "Marxist." No matter how well deserved may be the criticism made of Léon Blum as Premier, no matter how irritating the remnants of his ideology in a world so generously fertile in ghastly portents, the fact remains that he used his prestige over the working classes to promote the common good and the defense of the nation. His lucid and thoughtful articles in *Le Populaire* rang out every morning to call men to their duty as citizens. Doubtless the call came from an over-subtle intellectual. Yet it was effective in no small degree against those Socialists who favored national surrender, politicians like Paul Faure and Severac, and labor leaders like Belin and Delmas. Socialist collaboration was indispensable to an energetic conduct of the war. But Daladier, as he sought to get even for his supposed wrongs, joined hands with Blum's rivals within the party and undermined the national discipline that Blum was struggling to implant. There was no superabundance of real patriots in Parliament. This unbroken and deliberate quarreling with Reynaud and Blum necessarily led Daladier to fall back on other ministers and parliamentarians whose dependability as regards war policy was highly questionable.

Daladier, Reynaud, and Blum first clashed seriously toward the end of 1939. Before Daladier could get the two Houses of Parliament to vote the law of December 2, giving the government full powers, he had had to overcome in both a persistent reluctance to follow suit.[5] He suspected Reynaud and Blum of having fostered that sudden flare of hostility. On February 4, 1940, he gave a dinner in honor of Chamberlain, Halifax, and Winston Churchill, who were in Paris for a session of the Supreme Council.[6] The Finance Minister was not invited. In his idle manner Daladier had thought for weeks of reconstructing the Cabinet, a project announced in December, which he never succeeded in carrying out: he suddenly planned to relegate to a subordinate position, if not to

---

[5]There was no question as to the principle of full powers, but this law diminished still further the provision made in preceding laws for ultimate parliamentary control. Specifically, it stated that if the Chambers were not in session, Daladier was under no obligation to recall them, within a month, to ratify his law decrees. To secure this freedom was the main objective of the law.

[6]At which the decision was made to send a Franco-British Expeditionary Force to Finland.

eliminate entirely, the man he had come to regard as an openly declared candidate for the premiership and a personal rival.[7] But he triumphed in the secret parliamentary session of the ninth and tenth of February, when the business on the agenda was approved with hardly any dissent. He felt himself secure enough to be generous and indifferent about the traps he believed were being laid for him: "Let him stay if he wants to, but he must stop repeating that my one idea is to be rid of him and he must stop trying to get my job."[8]

On February 15, Reynaud took the offensive. Following Mandel's method, he demanded in a peremptorily worded note that gasoline and coal be rationed, and he made the specific demand that all ministries handling economic affairs—Commerce, Agriculture, and, it goes without saying, Serruys' Commissariat for National Economy—be placed directly under his authority. In this way he aimed at hewing out for himself a special dictatorship, within the one exercised by the Premier. On the nineteenth the two men met to settle the issue: they had not spoken to each other for nearly three weeks.[9] Reynaud sacrificed his close assistant, Palevsky, a man who was no fair-weather friend. Daladier suspected Palevsky of giving financial assistance to *Le Populaire* and deeply resented his enthusiastic outbursts about his chief's intellectual superiority.[10] The climax came in a Cabinet meeting which Serruys was allowed to attend. Reynaud won out on the question of rationing, but he was bluntly denied what he called the "centralized control of national economy." For a while he thought of asking for the Washington Embassy, then he submitted. To Palevsky, taking his leave, he remarked: "The mountebank won't last long."

[7]His idea was then to call back to the Finance Ministry Bonnet or Marchandeau—that is, men who had opposed and criticized the brilliantly executed recovery which started in November 1938.

[8]Daladier had decided to give the Ministry of Information which he had promised to create to Pomaret, Minister of Labor. On hearing that the latter had dined a few days before with Reynaud, he changed his mind.

[9]Reynaud had told the Socialist Deputy Rive (an appeaser), who in the secret session of February 9 had inveighed against the Premier's policy: "You could have gone much further."

[10]Palevsky had drawn upon himself the dislike of Mme. de Portes, and this undoubtedly contributed to his fall.

4

Daladier Conceives the Right War Policy. The Machinery of Government and Administration Breaks Down

REGARDING THE GENERAL CONDUCT OF THE WAR, Daladier's views were sound. He knew well enough what the French Army lacked before it could face the Wehrmacht on not too unequal terms, and very likely he could not help linking so many deficiencies with a painful memory of the past and an uneasy conscience. In the history of the Third Republic he alone shared with M. de Freycinet the privilege of having been at the head of national defense for five years, four of them without a break. If ever defeat laid bare the weak points of the war instrument, he would unavoidably be held responsible. There would be no way to plead extenuating circumstances, no way to shift responsibility on to some predecessor or successor.

He was aware that the military structure could not be put in good shape before the fall of 1940 or perhaps even before the beginning of 1941. Like Gamelin, he lived in constant fear of the Germans breaking the "truce" and forcing a decision before the essential preparations had been completed. Therefore he took great care to confirm Hitler in the belief that he, Daladier, had never ceased at heart to be the man of Munich throughout all vicissitudes, and that, sooner or later, with his nerves shattered by the war, he would seek a compromise. From month to month he never was at a loss to find excuses for avoiding a treaty that would have ruled out any separate negotiations for an armistice and for peace—a treaty modeled on the Anglo-French-Russian agreement of September 4, 1914, which it would have been normal for the cabinets of London and Paris to conclude after the break with Germany.[1]

[1]Chamberlain also was reluctant to forego his freedom of decision when the time should come for peace. However, as early as October 1939, the staffs of both the Quai d'Orsay and the Foreign Office had started to study the question. Alexis Léger, Sir Alexander Cadogan, Sir Ronald Campbell drew up and discussed drafts for the treaty which took into full consideration and satisfied the requirements of French security, as regards the eventual peace

Daladier went further. Certain peace moves made by M. van Kleffens, the Dutch Foreign Minister, were exploited if not inspired by the French Premier in order to mislead Hitler, to anchor him in the hope that the Nazi Empire might attain continental hegemony without having to fight and risk its all. Was the Führer deceived by these maneuvers? I do not think so, but Germans alone are competent to answer the question. At any rate, Hitler, as already indicated, needed the long "truce" to perfect certain war matériel—for instance, his tanks which, in Spain, had been put to the test and found wanting. He needed also to increase their number and build up reserves of arms and ammunition. Moreover, he foresaw that the French morale would not stand up well under the impact of prolonged inactivity, and that, with large-scale operations put off for an indefinite period, the fifth column might operate in the midst of a general French softening. Hitler did not suffer any loss, although he may not have seen through the game of Daladier.

But the fact to place on record is that Daladier, to the knowledge of a very few, methodically and persistently endeavored to deceive the Nazi dictator, that he brought into play great coolness of judgment and power of dissimulation, that he did not allow his stratagem to lead him beyond the limits he had set himself, and that he resisted men like Bonnet, Laval, and De Monzie, who seized the opportunity to push him into most dangerous backstairs conversations. And in this could be seen how solidly rooted was the decision he had reached in the summer of 1939 to take up the German challenge.

But there is a counterpart, a list of his shortcomings. And it is a long list.

His shoulders were not strong enough to bear the burden. Only a man of gigantic power of intellect and capacity for action could have carried the load and Daladier was of meaner stature. The premiership, the Ministries of National Defense, War,[2] and Foreign Affairs: such multi-

---

treaty. On December 19, at a session of the Supreme Council held in England, Chamberlain proposed that the matter be put on the agenda. The Prime Minister was disturbed at the defeatist activities of so many French parliamentarians and thought it would be prudent to lock the door. Daladier declared that he agreed to the principle of the treaty, but that he did not consider the moment favorable to implement it.

[2]In 1932, for the first time, the Minister of War was given the additional and broader title of Minister of National Defense. His new task was to co-ordinate the work of the three ministries of the armed forces: War, Marine, and Air. But the reform did not materialize until June 6, 1936—the date of the decree Daladier drafted for the purpose. Henceforward industrial mobilization fell within the scope of the Minister. More and more, all through the decree of February 20, 1938, the law of July 11, 1938, for organizing the nation in wartime, and the set of regulations embodied in the decree of September 16, 1939, the task

farious duties were far too much for him and would have been for stronger men than he.

On three occasions since 1934 the premiership had been separated from any special administrative department, as is the English custom. Gaston Doumergue, Pierre-Etienne Flandin, and Léon Blum preferred to devote all their efforts to the general management of state affairs and they concentrated on leadership. To that end the Hotel Matignon, which up to 1914 had been the residence of the Austro-Hungarian Ambassador, was put at the disposal of the Premier, his secretariat, and the bureaus immediately dependent on him. But Laval, succeeding Flandin in June 1935, was not satisfied with such a division of responsibility: when he became head of the government he declined to relinquish the Quai d'Orsay. As he rightly saw it, the direct control over certain important departments of government—that of Foreign Affairs at all times and that of National Defense in wartime—gave the Minister specifically in charge such a direct influence upon the most vital problems of the day as to render illusory the supreme authority of the Premier. The handling of Foreign Affairs, for example, included the doling out of "secret funds" in amounts vastly exceeding those allotted to other ministries—and "secret funds" had a great deal to do with forming public opinion.[3] Daladier thought likewise.

Minister for National Defense, for War, and Foreign Affairs, as he was, Daladier, nevertheless, might have deemed it fitting to take up residence at the Hotel Matignon, for all to see that he thought of himself primarily as head of the government. But he was unwilling to leave the Rue St. Dominique, the old mansion with the walls hung in panoplies, where Clemenceau, in alternating anguish and enthusiasm, had awaited the victory of 1918.

I have already described Daladier's incredible inconsistencies. To any-

of co-ordination entrusted to the Minister seemingly partook of the nature of a control. It even carried with it the right to initiate new measures. But in practice the change from the past did not amount to much, since the High Command of the Navy never submitted to Gamelin's authority as chief of staff of National Defense. Thus the authority over the whole range of military affairs with which Daladier had been invested on paper bore some comparison to Hitler's omnipotence if one can imagine Hitler as a war lord without some Keitel by his side. We know that Daladier was powerless even to unravel the true state of affairs at the Air Ministry. Similarly, Jacomet, general secretary to the Ministry of War and National Defense, who, in all administrative and financial matters, led the military bureaucracy as Gamelin did the armies, seldom if ever made his authority effective beyond the limits of the War Ministry itself, industrial mobilization excepted.

[3]According to one of the Minister's secretaries, in charge of the administration of "secret funds" early in 1934, fifteen million francs were distributed to French journalists, not including the Havas Agency, for which a special appropriation was made.

one charging him with lack of steady purpose, his friends replied that he had always put the Army above the parliamentary and electoral ebb and flow; that one should seek Daladier's principle of unity in the vigilant and militant patriotism of the statesman who had to prepare the nation for its supreme duty. Of course he had bargained with the Left against the Right, and then with the Right against the Left, and his actions had often been in complete contradiction with what he had done in the past. But all his apparent vagaries were accounted for by the fixed idea on his mind: to safeguard national defense. Compared to that high purpose what else could seem of any importance to him? Daladier is not the first politician to have discovered that many a dereliction can be excused because of a well-advertised concern for the strength and well-being of the Army. His disdain for the Hotel Matignon proclaimed to all that he was primarily the civilian head of the armed forces: other things had lesser claims on him.

Daladier took over from Bonnet the Ministry of Foreign Affairs on September 13, 1939, after the failure of the appeasement policy and the declaration of war. We have already seen that Under Secretary of State Champetier de Ribes, a true gentleman, a Catholic of liberal leaning, and a team of ambassadors assisted him. Diplomatic affairs took three or four hours of the Premier's time every day. I repeat that they certainly were not worse administered under this system than under ministers with no other functions to perform. But senators, deputies, and newspapermen were endlessly critical of the plurality of offices and of the omnipotence of permanent staffs which resulted from Daladier's triple set of duties—as if the ministerial permanent staffs were some satanic power! On several occasions Daladier said that the arrangement was only temporary, that he would leave the Quai d'Orsay, but that he must be granted time to find a suitable successor.

As a matter of fact, he never seriously approached anyone except Herriot. And Herriot, discerning Mussolini's latent resolve to fight, took fright of public opinion lest it should interpret his nomination as a challenge to Italy and surge violently against him as Italy broke into full belligerency: he, therefore, kept on conditioning his acceptance on Marshal Pétain's recall from Spain, where he was serving as ambassador, and on the latter's promotion to the rank of minister of state. Thus, before the French conservatives, Pétain would have really cautioned Herriot's good behavior. That initiative on the part of Herriot must be called very unfortunate, however intelligible it may have been at the time. It really helped Pétain to start on his dictatorial career. For that reason the whole incident cannot be dismissed in a few words.

The initial offer to Herriot was made on September 6, that is three days after the declaration of war and a full week before Bonnet's transfer to the Ministry of Justice. On the following day Herriot expressed his readiness to fall in with Daladier's proposal if only the marshal could be persuaded to join. But a strange scene ensued. Laval did all that he could to hold back the veteran as Daladier tugged to win him. The Prime Minister got the better of Laval on the ninth and on the eleventh of September. But Laval scored in the evening of the ninth and, for good, on the twelfth. At that date, in a letter of refusal which Laval may have dictated, the marshal even managed to smear Herriot as unworthy of office. This ought to have put an end to the whole business. But Daladier endlessly persisted in the belief that Herriot might still enter the Cabinet, in the foolish and even undignified delusion (twice he had been abused) that Pétain might be deflected from Laval's influence and direction. A sorry business it was. Daladier was stuck up in the Quai d'Orsay. Meanwhile Pétain, under Laval's guidance, allowed all kinds of intriguers—among others, François Pietri, an Italophile Corsican, and Lémery, Martinique's mulatto senator, who were to visit him in Madrid about December—to advertise what they pleased to call his impending premiership. Let it be remembered that Daladier's and Herriot's clumsy attempt at a very fragmentary ministerial reconstruction made of the marshal a virtual candidate for the most exalted political post. From that day onward he was looked upon as the man who would quickly issue from the background if something went amiss. A wider circle of people began to regard him as a political force. Early in October, Laval openly prescribed as the only way to salvation a Pétain cabinet in which all former Premiers including Daladier would participate. He even invited to luncheon a high official with whom he had often disagreed in the past, for the purpose of asking that official to convince Daladier.[4]

[4]Here is the very illuminating chronology of that incident:

September 6: Daladier presses Herriot to become Minister of Foreign Affairs.

September 7: Herriot accepts, subject to Pétain's participation. Toward 7.30 P.M. the police commissioner at Hendaye, on the request of the Ministry of Foreign Affairs, goes to the other side of the frontier and, from Fontarabia, summons Pétain to Paris, on behalf of Daladier. He does not give him any information as to the reason. Daladier did not want Pétain to consult his friends beforehand.

September 9: On his arrival in Paris, Pétain sees Daladier and by 2 P.M. accepts the portfolio of Minister of State. Later on he meets Laval and at 6 P.M. takes back his word.

September 11: Pétain does not stand by his refusal. Once more he agrees to enter the Cabinet.

September 12: Unknown to Bonnet, Daladier leaves Paris alone for Abbeville, where a

The work of supervision, co-ordination, and arbitration, which every Premier has to accomplish as best he can, was complicated, in Daladier's case, by the patchy Cabinet he had brought in: it was a medley of politicians pulling against one other. I have told how he fought with Paul Reynaud. But quarreling went on everywhere. Concerning international policy, Georges Bonnet, Minister of Justice since September 13, Anatole de Monzie, Minister of Public Works, Pomaret, Minister of Labor—not to mention Camille Chautemps, Vice Premier, who, it is true, was notably pliable and adaptable—were in chronic controversy with Paul Reynaud,[5] with Georges Mandel, Minister for Colonies, with Albert Sarraut, Minister of the Interior, Yvon Delbos, Minister of Public Education, Cesar Campinchi, Minister of the Navy. When forming his Cabinet in April 1938, Daladier had wanted it to be a microcosm of Parliament. In practice he did worse. He allowed more often than not each minister to act as a kind of independent satrap. To all outward appearances the Minister for Air, Guy la Chambre, and the Minister for Armament, Raoul Dautry, behaved as though they were modest Under Secretaries of State and the Premier's immediate subordinates.

From the day war was declared, on September 3, 1939, Daladier should have reconstructed his Cabinet from top to bottom. The example of 1914 testified that a Cabinet of "national union" was desirable to lead the country at war. At that time the socialist Jules Guesde and the royalist Denys Cochin sat side by side in the ministerial councils. But so bitter now was the social struggle that in this war, the leader of the Right, Louis Marin, found it impossible to associate with the leader of the Socialist Left, Léon Blum.[6] Furthermore, by their inclination toward totalitarianism and their activities for appeasement, two former Premiers, Pierre Laval and Pierre-Etienne Flandin, had, on their record,

---

meeting has been arranged with N. Chamberlain. On his return to Paris he finds on his desk a letter from Pétain, who has again canceled his acceptance and is already on his way back to Madrid. In the night Herriot rejects Daladier's offer. Subsequently, Daladier came near to selecting Chautemps!

[5] It is true that Paul Reynaud sought personally to be on good terms with Bonnet. Moreover, in October and November, in parallelism with Laval's propaganda, Hélène de Portes had started her nasty intrigue, fated to become fruitful in the spring of 1940, by advocating in all the salons of Paris a Pétain premiership. But, at that time, what this lady said and did was of negligible importance.

[6] In January, and then in March, 1938, after the annexation of Austria, Léon Blum, who saw that war was coming, offered to set up a government of national union. Two rival formulas were available: "From Blum to Marin," "From Marin to Cachin." Cachin, senator for the Seine, was considered the most harmless of the Communist leaders. Neither formula had any success.

excluded themselves from the work of national salvation. They endlessly called for a government of "national union" (how Laval campaigned for it has already been said). On their lips, the expression bade fair to imply that treason must have its share. Therefore Daladier could not resort to the solution which had been so helpful twenty-five years before.

At least his duty was to remove the "defeatists," the protectors of the fifth column, from the ministerial posts allocated to them in April 1938, at a time when he could not break away from mere parliamentary expediency. In November 1917, when Clemenceau selected his ministers, he placed governmental cohesion above everything else. He even went to the length of gathering about him second-rate men, but men whom he could trust. His conversation with Albert Thomas, who had little faith in the old tiger's star and refused a portfolio, has become famous: "Thomas, you're a quitter." Obviously one could not hope for the same brutal firmness from Daladier.

Thanks to Bonnet, Pomaret, de Monzie, Chautemps, or friends of theirs, Laval had a foot in the door. This amounts to saying that the fifth-column underground passages opened straight into the cabinet council room.

The forthcoming "reconstruction" of the Cabinet which Daladier seldom failed to mention in day-to-day talks never was conceived by him except within narrow limits. To hand over to someone else a share of the work with which he could not cope single-handed, to enlist heads for the new ministerial departments—Armaments, Information—badly needed in wartime: such was Daladier's restricted project. And he never could make up his mind to name a Minister of Information which was incomparably easier than to appoint a Foreign Minister. Georges Mandel told me in March: "I have counted thirty parliamentarians whom Daladier feeds with the hope of promotion to the Cabinet. It's reached the point where this has become one of his techniques of government."

Under the terms of the Law of July 11, 1938, (organization of the nation in time of war), the "War Committee" was to assist the Premier in the general conduct of the war.[7] But Daladier only called it into session at irregular intervals. The major decisions were taken in consultation with Gamelin, with Darlan, with Vuillemin, with Champetier de Ribes, Léger, and Coulondre, summoned separately or together.

All questions of persons put aside, the overhauling of the executive power's structure was overdue at a time of crisis when forceful action

'About the War Committee, the Permanent Committee of National Defense, the Superior Council of War, see Appendix 2.

was required. Daladier made no attempt at reform. In the higher strata of national defense, he never put an end to the overlapping of functions. He tolerated Darlan's interference with the reform he had enacted. Yet in this case he was dealing with soldiers who, after all, knew how to take orders from above and were not wont to have their own way in everything. When it came to ministers able and willing to exploit all the parliamentary and journalistic devices of self-protection, it was all the more obvious that they would not find it very difficult to assert their independence.

With the nerve center of ministerial power thus weakened and lax, the administrative machinery, within and without the Army, was bound to disintegrate further and further. France, ever since the Napoleonic era, had been happily possessed of efficient officials. These had been the permanent backbone of the state throughout all constitutional changes. What had happened to them? In the long run no strong and hard-working body of administrators can exist without a strong and determined government. Devotion to the service of the state inevitably deteriorates under successive ministers who have no will of their own. In addition, the constant trespassing by senators and deputies on the field of executive power had weakened discipline from the turn of the century onward. To expatiate upon that very old story would be a waste of time. Every state employee had in Parliament someone he supported and on whom he relied for support. Finally, inflated and debased currency, maladjustment of salaries, and reduced private incomes contributed to lowering the average standard of public servants. From top to bottom the fear of responsibility prevailed, the search for the easiest and safest line. "Anything to keep out of trouble!" A decision made in the upper ranks of the hierarchy filters down through the administrative agencies. Complementary decisions of a technical nature must necessarily be worked out before they can be embodied in the actual practice and life of the country. If each bureau, instead of assuming responsibility, invents difficulties, refers them back to someone higher up, and meanwhile shelves the matter, everything will remain tentative, nothing will ever really be translated into concrete deeds. Governmental action, already far too weak, was further diluted. It dribbled down until it was lost entirely in the appalling bottlenecks of administrative perplexity. The executive no longer executed: it slumbered in interminable deliberations. It goes without saying that the impulses given from above by Daladier and his assistants were far too uncertain and intermittent to disturb this peacetime lethargy.

5

Failure of Rearmament

WE KNOW that the French Army lacked equipment and that this deficit ranks among the major causes of our military disaster. All due allowance being made for its faulty strategy and tactics, the French Army might perhaps have held the German onslaught in check, if better provided with tanks, planes, and the whole range of modern matériel. In 1936 it devolved upon Daladier to supervise France's rearmament. In the performance of that task, determination and method were certainly not his strong points.

Daladier's business was to carry out the rearmament program decided upon on September 6, 1936: fourteen billion francs (to be increased later on to twenty billion) were appropriated that day by the cabinet council. These huge figures implied—and such was their true significance—that the government had resolved to raise France to Germany's military level. In practice, no limit whatever was set to the undertaking. But it was plain that the French industry of 1936 would quickly be submerged by governmental orders. It had neither the tools nor the trained labor to cope with them. The great preliminary problem, consequently, was to rebuild the industrial system, to bring it up to the quantitative and qualitative requirements of the program. The Ministry of War and all other governmental departments and agencies were obviously helpless to solve it. The whole economic body had to be taken in hand and strengthened. It could not be done without a Ministry of Armament specially organized for the purpose. Well, Daladier never agreed to appoint a Minister of Armament until the war had actually begun.

On March 22, 1938, the bill for organizing the nation in wartime came up for discussion in the Chamber of Deputies. It was a hapless instrument indeed, after ten years at least of drafting and redrafting by both Assemblies. The member of the competent parliamentary commission who reported on the bill insisted on the prompt designation of a Minister of Armament. "I agree to do it on the day mobilization of the armed forces is decreed," retorted Daladier, "but not before!" In support of that statement he put forward all sorts of unconvincing reasons. He said that he did not want to saddle the country, in peacetime, with a war economy, or undo what had already been done for producing armaments, or take away from the various ministerial departments the sections in charge of war production and to make them a distinct administrative whole. He steadily refused to throw everything back into the melting pot. "But," remarked someone, "wouldn't it be better to put up with the melting pot now than when we shall be at grips with the enemy?" A pertinent objection, indeed, to Daladier's thesis. The "reporter" of the bill enlarged upon it by observing that Germany did not expand her Army until her whole industry had been mobilized and that the Ministry of Armament, if postponed until the outbreak of the war, would come too late. But Daladier stubbornly clung to his paradox. He could not be prevailed upon to change his mind.

Daladier's obstinacy resulted in a pathetic spectacle. On the one hand, the Ministry of War strove to copy, in all externals, what he thought a regularly constituted Ministry of Armaments ought to be and, on the other, Jacomet, the secretary-general, tried to put himself forward as a great armorer.

The administrative services which cater to the French Army follow honorable but antiquated and straitlaced traditions. They are famed for their integrity—like the naval bureaucracy—and they are a hard-working lot, but in their own way. Their cautious methods were hardly in harmony even with the tempo of the wars before the blitzkrieg. A decision reached in 1936, to build four powder plants, well illustrates how slow they were in action. By 1940 only one of the powder plants was nearly completed. The frame of another had been erected, an empty shell still to be filled. The ground on which the third was to rise had to be fenced in. The site for the fourth had not yet been selected, and local administrative inquiries were still in progress. Yet no simpler undertaking could be dreamed of. What, then, of the infinitely more complicated tasks which were about to crowd upon the old-fashioned War Department?

A twenty-minute talk with Jacomet was enough to make it clear that he was not the man to regenerate and transform an officialdom in which he had ascended, step by step, to the top position of general comptroller. For several years a member of the French Delegation to the Disarmament Conference, he went on periodically visiting Geneva long after all governments concerned had given up the least pretense of doing away with armed forces or reducing them. Why? He sincerely believed that disarmament could be quietly achieved through close control and limitation of all military budgets by international committees. Year after year I scoffed at that fantastic scheme which he had made his own. Toward 1938 a chance conversation proved that he still had this bee in his bonnet. He enjoyed meddling in diplomacy even from the side lines, and the exalted position of supreme European comptroller, which would be his if only his idea could materialize, dazzled him. The man was more shrewd than intelligent, and politics, I am afraid, were part of his daily fare.

In 1936 he had succeeded Guinand (who was sidetracked to the special Court of Public Accountancy), a very different type of man, rather austere and sharp in manner, distasteful to Weygand, Gamelin, and the whole High Command, all of them harassed and restrained in their initiative by his punctilious reading of army laws and bylaws. The authority of Jacomet, developing as it did parallel to Gamelin's, became more and more all-embracing. At the outset he had a deciding voice in administrative and financial affairs only and, on that account, sat permanently on the Council of National Defense, but his province did not extend any further. It expanded tremendously on January 21, 1938: one of the decrees published at that date made him the alter ego of the Minister and detailed him to carry out and control all the armament program. Moreover, the law of July 11, 1938, as it was enforced, put industrial mobilization under his care. We know that Gamelin had been invested with a concurrent authority but that, for motives of his own, he asserted it less and less.

Under the Daladier-Jacomet partnership, committees and parleys proliferated. A consultative committee on armaments did exist already: a production committee (January 1938) and a vigilance committee (October 1938) were juxtaposed to it. Within the framework of the War Ministry a special section dealt with the making of armaments. The orders issued by the General Staff were sent to it for transmission to the industries concerned. With the decree of March 20, 1939, a Council of Production appeared in the background. A futile craze for synods. Through the old buildings between the Boulevard St. Germain and the Rue St. Dominique, you did not feel that a new spirit was blowing, a new spirit born of new enterprises. For instance, the production of tanks continued to depend, in the Ministry of War, as it had done in the past, upon the time-honored sections or "directorates": infantry, cavalry, artillery. Each of them did its best to monopolize the weapons, to have them specially suited to its own needs. Infantrymen wanted them to be the servant of infantry, and cavalrymen wanted them to fill the part assigned to cavalry. The High Command had maintained all the old categories and classifications. Who could have expected that, in its place, the military bureaucracy should break with the past and treat the tank on its own independent merits?

Toward the end of 1938 the Bureau of War Fabrications warned the Premier that, after January 1939, French industry would be saturated with government orders and that no fresh orders could usefully be added to the list unless part of the work already in hand at the time should be suspended. Here came to light a mistake which dated back to the beginning of France's rearmament. Daladier and his friends had not paid enough heed to the fact that many French industrial plants were worn out and obsolete. There had not been sufficient replacement. The extreme exhaustion of French economy since 1932 and the abstentionist attitude of capital accounted largely for that state of affairs. In any case, the projected rearmament was of such magnitude that the construction of additional factories could not be dispensed with. Short of that huge undertaking, a more enlightened fiscal policy might have, in the meantime, imparted greater resiliency to French industry and eased the problem. Tax exemption on replacement of machinery was still calculated at the price level of 1918, which was grossly inferior to actual costs. Was it so difficult to do away with that prohibitive rule? That rule was left in force. It goes without saying that the tougher and more drastic solution, industrial expansion, advanced slowly. What a contrast with the tremendous planning of Goering, at the very outset of the Nazi regime, and the unflinching action that followed!

We come to another major mistake. On January 21, 1939, a report of the President of the Republic, signed and forwarded by Daladier as a matter of administrative routine, laid bare the gaps still detected in the framework of industrial mobilization. In the several ministerial departments concerned, a special staff was supposed to have been enlisted long ago: even at that late hour it was far from being complete. Many commissions had been formed at the Ministry of National Defense to implement the law of July 11, 1938: metallurgical mining, textile commissions, etc. On these the military authorities, the economic ministries concerned, the employers' associations, and the trade-unions had representatives. It devolved upon them to define each industry's, even each factory's, job, to allocate programs, to draw up production plans, to assign the man power available. In the natural course of things a crop of decrees ought to have issued from their labor. But the most necessary information was not produced by the bureaucrats who had it available. Unavoidably, the introductory report made by the textile commission, among others, was extremely vague: from that flimsy basis no headway could be made.

Mr. Chamberlain and the British conservatives were often derided in France for having waited till May 1939 before bringing the conscription law before Parliament and for having too long held to this watchword: conscription will come into effect the first day of the war and not an hour sooner. Wasn't it a case of plucking motes from other eyes? Our blindness was no less appalling. We waited for Poland to be attacked before mobilizing French industry, although German industry had gone into full war production as early as 1937.

The phrase "go into production" has a precise significance in the light of which French policy is subject to a terrible judgment. To "go into production" means to be able to start mass manufacture of different types of matériel after the models for those types have been thoroughly studied and determined. It presupposes, therefore, that each one of the selected types has been broken down into parts after a very lengthy process of designing and trials, the number of these parts being determined by the necessity for ending up with such basic operations as can readily be performed by machinery. It assumes that production lines have been built "which can be fed a rabbit at one end and produce a hat at the other"; that factories have been tooled and workmen trained; that raw materials have been stocked for all industries involved in the chain of production; and that production by one class will not be threatened by any delay or trouble arising in the production of another on which it depends. It presupposes that high-precision gauges, capable of determining errors from one hundredth to one thousandth of a millimeter, have been set up all along the process of manufacture.

With the passage of years the task has become even more complicated. In 1917 the French Government sent complete plans of the 75-mm. gun to America. By so doing it spared our American friends all preliminary worries and research. Yet it took them no less than eighteen months to go into production. The 75, moreover, had changed a great deal more between 1917 and 1940 than it had during the first twenty years of its existence, from 1895 to 1914. To build it today takes ten times more hours than were needed in 1917. New alloys are now employed which have doubled its original range; it can now use twenty types of shell for various purposes, etc.

In the summer of 1939 we were well provided with prototypes: it cannot be repeated too often that these gave us promise of excellent armaments, quite possibly superior to that of the enemy. But we had only comparatively few items in full production, and our planned schedule gave no hope of reaching full production in the whole range of armaments for three to six months, according to the various patterns. "Three months at least to get the simplest factory production started; three weeks at most to mobilize the troops; evidently, therefore, it was of foremost importance that the mobilization of industry should precede that of man power by nine weeks. It was essential to provide matériel before providing personnel."[1]

How dared Daladier delay to the last moment industrial mobilization of a maximum of man power and work hours? What confidence he must have felt in the defense system and in the stocks of old-type armaments which were supposed to bridge the gap! He had already grievously erred by postponing until November 1938 all steps to lengthen the forty-hour week established by the Law of June 21, 1936. And how could he wait until September 6, 1939 (five days after the mobilization of the Army), to ask sixty hours of work from the men employed in defense industries? Even then, on September 6, no one thought of pointing out that the machinery must be kept running day and night on a 168-hour week.

As for other measures accessory to industrial mobilization, the least said the better. It had repeatedly been stated that national defense required decongesting the Paris area, into which 70 per cent of French production was crammed because of the available labor supply. I recall a conversation with Marshal Pétain at a time when he headed a commission studying the protection of cities against bombardment from the air. He had presented a report which proposed, among other steps, that factories be widely scattered and that an underground capital be built. During the following year (1934) Marshal Pétain was for eight months at a stretch Minister of War. However, the bill he had sponsored did not reach the statute book until May 8, 1935, and even then it mostly remained a dead letter.

The whole story comes to this. Daladier did not get new tools to any appreciable extent, and under him the industrial structure remained practically unchanged. But this was a more damnable omission. Far from reinvigorating French economy, he even failed to relieve it of the grievous policy which his friends had devised for it, a policy all the more grievous since, immediately before, his equally unwise political

[1] *L'Europe Nouvelle,* April 1, 1939, "Industrial Mobilization," by Le Polémarque.

opponents had already impaired the strength of the patient. A millstone hung around the neck of French industry. The knot was not loosened by Daladier.

At this point we can forget M. Jacomet: the political actions of his Ministry now concern us exclusively. As a founder of the Popular Front, he, with Léon Blum, was responsible for the social legislation of 1936: the forty-hour week, paid holidays, transference of armament factories to the state. On principle the soundness of those reforms could hardly be challenged. And, as to the mode of application, however harmful to the national interest they may have been, it cannot be denied that, in the spring and summer of 1936, the quasi-revolutionary movement which swept the country gave the government of the day little scope to do better. But with an ever-growing and ever-closer Hitlerian danger, an average working week of thirty-eight hours seven minutes in 1938 as against forty hours two minutes in 1937 cannot be excused.[2]

In 1936–37 all ministers bowed very low to sit-down strikes. Let us recognize that political necessity hardly admitted of another attitude. But later on political necessity was no longer so imperious. Then the new legislation had been put in force and the claims of the working classes had been fulfilled. The time had come for cabinet ministers to swim against the tide. Yet in 1937, and until the autumn of 1938, as industrial disorders burst forth again and again, the men in office did not even try to rule with a sterner hand, chief among them Daladier, who in every one of the four successive cabinets invariably retained the Ministry of National Defense and the vice presidency of the Council. Cessation of work occurred on flimsy pretexts. The Communists went on with the strange agitation which was to culminate in the attempted general strike of November 30, 1938, when they suddenly steered away from the nationwide movement they had started: the Ministry of the day did not budge. Such passivity is unforgivable.

It would be unfair to overlook that in a morally divided France no government could easily adapt its internal policy to new circumstances or shift its majority. Some still insist that not before November 30, 1938, when resounding insults flung at France from the Italian Parliament tragically synchronized with social disturbances at home, could Daladier have found, among the groups of the Left, enough support or tolerance to revise the social laws of 1936 and bring them in harmony with the requirements of French security. They will say also that, all party considerations brushed aside, he could not, through turning back against labor,

[2]See page 370.

let the French conservatives have their way. The French conservatives were so deeply mixed up with appeasers of all description that even making every allowance for their social conceptions, they could not be trusted to serve national interests. But who will dare assert that, in the factories under the control of the War Ministry, Daladier tried very hard to lay down more elastic regulations under the forty-hours act and to impose overtime on workers and employers who all too often were in accord to reject it? Indeed, as late as March 1938, he stood on his circular letters of July 1936 and May 1937. Any Labor Minister with no special regard for national defense might have signed those circular letters. To say the least, industrial recovery would have been advanced by several months had Daladier shown some energy.

He is still more directly involved in the measure whereby ownership of armament plants was handed over to the state. The Law of August 11, 1936, enabled him to take over, wholly or in part, all factories turning out arms and ammunitions and to put under government control those which he did not want to annex. Plainly, the strength of the French Army was in direct relation to the economic well-being of the country and, as such, was affected by the forty-hours law. But how much more immediate was the bearing upon our military power of the "nationalization" law! Today, as we look back with the knowledge and experience won by our British and American friends, we understand that in order to wage total war, to withstand the onslaught of the Nazis, excessive reliance was placed on individual gain as a stimulus. We are aware that to develop production to the limit, within the shortest time, governmental intervention has to be brought into the creation of military power. The classical argument for free enterprise has been disproved in Germany[3] and in Russia: why should it be held more valid in the case of other nations which, on the battlefields, must match the Nazi standard or perish? Thus judgment cannot be passed against the French ministers of 1936 on the ground that they put an end to private ownership in some portions of the armament industry. But in France the weight of the evidence indicates that until war broke out the kind of state management which was introduced brought in its train laxity of discipline and a lesser rather than a greater yield. In short, the new system proved itself inferior to the old, at any rate in peacetime. Either a much more drastic reform had to be forced through or the old system had better remain untouched. The whole business was conducted so clumsily, along some

---

[3]The Nazi Government did not neglect the stimulus of private profit as a contributing factor.

sort of middle way, that it suffered all the disadvantages pertaining to both economic liberalism and public ownership. In 1936–39 compromise was out of order, even regarding internal affairs.

Discipline and eagerness to work were on the wane because, as they were promoted to the status of state employees, the workers conformed to the practice which had come to stay among officials and availed themselves of trade-unionist influence, of electoral and parliamentary pressure to push their claims forward.

In a normal period industrialists and their technical staff would have flocked around a government resolved on meeting the German menace with a fast-developing industrial production. But from 1936 to 1939 the government found among them many bitter men. They trembled at the idea that their possessions might be torn from them; they felt sure that a state of war would touch off a fresh wave of sit-down strikes, bound to culminate, this time, in wholesale expropriation. Their personal risks haunted them and they could not conceive that life was worth living if the existing social hierarchy was to change. Hence the controversies which arose from the ministerial enactments of nationalization and control. I do not profess to apportion the blame. The Schneiders of the Creusot, the Brandts, started proceedings in the Council of State. Daladier complained that those of the Schneider plants taken away by the state (under the Decree of March 11, 1937) were treated by them as a forbidden land, cut off from all relations with surrounding workshops.[4] The least that can be said is that some manufacturers were not too particular in the selection of their means to win the social battle. Clearly, the other battle, the real one, did not, to the same extent, obsess their minds. Year after year, in England, in France, in the United States, cannon makers had been commonly charged by soapbox orators with the intention of stirring up war and thus drumming up trade. In this juncture they were not too keen to cast the guns.

It devolved upon the newly created corps of "armament engineers" to find substitutes for the experienced technicians hitherto in the service of independent armament businesses who preferred to quit rather than

---

[4]The fabrication of such matériel as steel plates for armored tanks, cannons, etc., suffered in proportion. The government found itself compelled to negotiate with the Creusot for the drafting of a protocol after the latter's action in the Council of State had failed. That was by the end of July 1939. The agreement belatedly came into force by November. Léon Blum told the Supreme Court at Riom that the Schneiders had tried to escape "nationalization" by setting in motion the Soviet Embassy. They promised Ambassador Potemkin that Moscow would find its reward in the speedy delivery of long-ordered matériel. The Brandt Company won its case, but the waste of time was probably no less damaging.

lose caste by continuing as public servants in their old laboratories and workshops. The head of the new service, General Salmon, was indisputably an eminent man, but his lieutenants fell far below his own high standard. In that critical period, with the national destiny at stake, a tumultuous transition from the old order of things to the new had, therefore, to be endured. The dislike of the Popular Front ministers for mass production must also be reckoned with. Mass production, they feared, was an additional cause of unemployment. In the arms to be produced too many parts were still made by hand, with hammer and file. Of course within five or six years everything would have settled down. But Hitler did not grant that needed respite, and Daladier let everyone have his own way.

Ten days elapsed between the declaration of war against Germany and the decision of the Prime Minister to appoint a Minister of Armaments. To do so he ruled out the objections of Gamelin, who was prone to believe that the coming in of a new bureaucracy would not bring in any relief but rather the opposite. And he waved aside the pleadings of the Air Minister, Guy la Chambre, who was all too subservient to a set of officials smarting under supervision and wont to deal with contractors at their own pleasure.

Raoul Dautry, who was given the portfolio, was a first-rate engineer, thoroughly accustomed to large-scale planning and operations, a man of exemplary patriotism. In my diary I have a note of a luncheon with him on October 16. He was rather frail, but there was a quality of youth and energy in his eyes, and I was favorably impressed by his agreeable manners. His first act, he said, had been to summon the heads of the Comité des Forges and of the General Federation of Labor and to force them to make a sort of joint declaration by which they forswore class struggle for the present and the future. He had asked: "Do you agree that between victory and death there is no middle way?" and they had been convinced. But he added: "I am determined to keep free of the personal quarrels and ambitions of the politicians, of the rivalries of the generals and the controversies of the experts. If ever I got entangled in them, I should inevitably be led to push one part of the program at the expense of another, and I should be lost." As I listened to him speaking so reasonably and so gently, I could not help picturing the jungle into which he was about to step and bethinking myself that, whether he wanted it or not, he would perforce have to form ideas of his own and fight for them.

Certain people known for their impartiality have said that M. Dautry has a gift for spurring others on but that he is not a good executive.[5] And what was needed above all was a man capable of originating more fruitful methods of work. Laboring eighteen hours a day, Dautry bent under the load and lost sight of the forest for the trees.

There was insufficient delegation of authority: all too often matters which he had settled long before would return to his desk for further consideration. No one was held responsible for anything.[6] Orders were sometimes transmitted in a haphazard fashion. Decisions concerning the armament program, taken at some session of the Supreme Council in London, were mislaid and forgotten by the Minister's secretariat and reached the proper officials only after two months' delay. Here is an astounding detail: it was not until February that the Supreme Council required a general inventory to be made of armaments existing or in course of production, for the French as well as for the British.

The assumption that the war would last three years misled Daladier and Dautry as, on another plane, it misled General Gamelin and the General Staff. Neville Chamberlain fathered this assumption in the House of Commons in September. It could be interpreted in two very different ways. It could mean that the Allies were determined incessantly to make the greatest possible effort to beat Germany down without being discouraged at the prospect of having to fight for three years or even longer. Or it could mean that the blitzkrieg would not pierce the French defensive lines, that the sea blockade would bring Germany to her knees within three years, that the Western democracies had thirty-six months in which to develop their latent resources, and, consequently, that they need not too painfully strain every nerve in the national body and were free to preserve the comforts of their peoples. The Paris and London cabinets behaved as though the second assumption was their reading of the theory.

Dautry had at his command fifty-two arsenals, each of them the center of an "armament area," some thirty powder plants, and some fourteen thousand factories, big, middling, and small, working exclusively or in

[5]This opinion would apply also, I am told, to his chief of secretariat, M. Bichelonne, who is today an ardent collaborationist, and to his assistant, M. Surleau.

[6]See Daladier's futile complaint before the Chamber of Deputies on December 22, 1939, concerning the "delay caused by bureaucratic methods to which a stop must be put, especially in wartime. . . . There is still the customary shirking of responsibility; what I should like is a state of affairs in this war wherein civilian and military leaders might both be entirely free and entirely responsible [cheers], wherein they would not be buried under mountains of red tape, statements, and reports [cheers], and wherein they could freely assert themselves, limited only by their responsibility to the nation." (Chamber of Deputies, December 22, 1939.)

part for national defense. The production of these factories could have been increased 40 per cent in one way or another. But Dautry did not want to stop at makeshifts. He set his goal much higher. He started building new factories. What a topsy-turvy world! Between 1936 and 1938 industrial mobilization could have been tackled in the grand manner and made to include undertakings of this long-term variety. Except in a relatively few cases, we would have none of them while there was plenty of time ahead. Now time was short, and yet, emboldened by the three-year-war doctrine, we adopted methods which would yield results only after the longest of intervals.

This out-of-season megalomania had its repercussions on French buying in the United States. We ordered planes by the hundred instead of by the thousand as we should have done, at least for the sake of stirring up American industry. Notwithstanding our subsidies for the erection of new plants, the leaders of American industry stuck to the belief that the "phony war" would not develop into a real struggle and that they had better refrain from taking risks. "Raw materials and machine tools!" Dautry kept repeating. Unfortunately he was only too readily listened to. Raw materials accounted for 80 per cent of our imports from America: 80,000 tons of coke a month, 20,000 tons of cotton, etc.—tying up to a corresponding extent the available tonnage. Instead we should have been procuring whatever could be used in the conflict with the least possible delay. Had we taken everything available on the American market, a considerable number of divisions might have been motorized.

We were inordinately meticulous. We had ordered eight thousand trucks, which were indispensable auxiliaries for our tanks. But in our specifications we insisted that the existing model be changed: the steering wheel must be on the right instead of on the left, and the electrical equipment must be more powerful. Thereby delivery was postponed till April. And this is not the end. The members of the purchasing commission in New York then refused to let the trucks be carried on foreign ships. They were afraid of drawing too heavily against the gold reserve. So none of the order reached France before the end came.

I have alluded to the gold reserve. Pierre Fournier, governor of the Bank of France, and even Paul Reynaud,[7] the Finance Minister (the latter giving way to Bouthillier, his factotum), insisted that our purchases in America be spread out over a three-year period and that annual purchases be limited to certain amounts arbitrarily determined. As if, in

---

[7] A curious contradiction in Reynaud's thought for anyone remembering his vivid realization of what the blitzkrieg implied.

the order of national interests, any particular interest, even though it be labeled gold reserve, could possibly be ranked ahead of the tools needed to save the nation![8] Here was Gribouille burning to death because he would not part with the furniture in his blazing house. For that matter, Sir John Simon was carrying on in the same fashion in London. To a subordinate who sought to convince him that, after all, the gold reserve was a secondary consideration he retorted: "You will have to walk over my dead body."

The three-year-war policy brought with it even further consequences. Since there was no need to transform France into a Spartan barracks, since the idea was to mobilize the resources of the nation and the empire only by installments, why not adopt the British slogan, "Business as usual"? As regards England, such an attitude, if not wise, at least was formally logical, since her commitments to the French Government in the main provided that she take care of naval and air warfare and, on the continent, help out with only a rather limited effort. But for France, exposed to the German onslaught!

The Armament Ministry, chief consumer of raw materials, had charge of distributing them to private industry:[9] it did not hesitate to allocate tin, copper, iron, etc., to those who boasted that they added to the Treasury's gold reserve by their sales abroad.

In 1914–18 a similarly easygoing regime had been put to the test and had not come out too badly. It was inevitable that in 1940 the same procedure should be tried again. Effective restrictions would immediately have been described as needless meddling. "Business as usual." In cantonments behind the front, officers and soldiers continued to receive their business correspondence and, from afar, to instruct their agents. They continuously pulled wires to get sent home "on public business" whenever regular leave was too slow in coming. They ended by thinking of the war as an embarrassing mistress, but a girl who was not such a bad sort after all and certainly less exacting than she had appeared at first sight. Of moral and material concentration on one fixed idea and on one fixed task—all-out war—there was little.

If he was to succeed, Raoul Dautry had four formidable barriers to overthrow, four hostile forces to bend to his will: the fossilized bureauc-

---

[8] It is to be noted that General Chauvineau, in his book *L'Invasion est-elle encore possible?*, follows the same line of reasoning as Bouthillier. He dared write that whatever a country might gain in military strength, by means of building tanks and planes, it would lose in economic strength. In December 1939, explaining to the House why he had haggled over appropriations for military supplies, Daladier did not argue differently.

[9] By the Law of July 11, 1938.

racy of the republic, the parliamentary and electioneering demagoguery which interfered even with technical armament matters, the apathetic attitude of the industrialists, and the listlessness of the General Staff. His zeal, his undeniable courage bent in the encounter.

Let us ponder over the case of the four powder plants which we have already come across. It evidences how feebly the impulse given at the top ran down the administrative structure. From floor to floor momentum dwindled away, and this time the social legislature of 1936 is not included among the obstacles. Parliamentary appropriations should never be *a priori* considered credits actually spent. With industrialists negotiations dragged on endlessly. And once they were concluded, month after month slipped by pending the official notification of the award. To circumvent restrictive and paralyzing rules, "letters of commitment" were sent to manufacturers. By these letters the state gave them assurance that they would be paid and urged them to set to work without further delay although contracts still were in suspense.

But, in practice, this device did not operate. The Administration disliked using it, and industry disliked accepting it. Side by side with legal formalism there was the formalism of all administrative services. Instructions were sent to manufacturers even before the armies moved into the field to acquaint them with what they would be expected to do. A most praiseworthy foresight, but immediately frustrated. The instructions were in sealed envelopes which the manufacturers were forbidden to open until mobilization had been decreed. So everything still happened as though the producers concerned had been warned only at the last moment, and even after the last moment. Administrative foresight had come into its own only to automatically cancel itself.[10]

The fear of displeasing Parliament and the electorate played havoc with selective mobilization—that is, the problem of skilled workers liable to be called to the colors as all other citizens but urgently needed for war production. This issue should have been solved long beforehand on the basis of a few general principles, and it devolved upon the Premier himself to explain them to the people. Nothing shocks and infuriates a Frenchman more than an unfair distribution of the military burden. If it had been of long-standing public knowledge that such and such a profession, such and such technical training, whether manual or intellectual, involved other kinds of service than bearing arms, in the interests of the whole community, all forms of social rivalry or class jealousy would have

---

[10]It should be added that these letters were drafted in rather vague terms, since, as we have seen, industrial mobilization had been only sketchily worked out.

been banned on the day of the great trial. But, far from acting on a general plan applicable to all, Daladier—who insisted on handling this question fraught with political consequences—set up as a principle that the number of "special exempt" men should be less than the number actually needed, and that the deficit would be made up, later on, by recalling individuals, not categories, from their military posts. Inevitably, the impression given was that the men withdrawn from the armies zone were recipients of special favors.[11]

Such a hand-to-mouth policy necessarily bristled with abuses,[12] and "business as usual" multiplied them. A reaction set in. Senator Mourier headed a parliamentary committee to hunt out the "specially exempt," who, as they saw it, ought not to have been taken away from their regiments. The newspapers regularly published the number of the men sent back to the front after being dislodged from positions in which, according to the investigators, they were less useful than in fighting units. And at times these men, on being sent back to their regiments, underwent a period of punishment following an automatic decision applied to them as they passed through the Railroad Transport Services in the head stations. Cases were described in which honest fellows who never sought the slightest favor were treated as culprits amid the jeers of their comrades. Here is how all this confusion affected the factories. They started losing, in September, enough of their personnel so that they were unable to function at the tempo that had been foreseen. The Renault works, to quote one single instance, missed a considerable part of their labor force. And when this shortage was made good along came M. Mourier or his delegates on an inspection tour, and at once a "purge" left Renault undermanned again. In like manner and for the same reasons the Bourges Arsenal produced 200,000 shells a month instead of its quota of two million—in spite of its up-to-date equipment.

[11]Actually the problem had been dealt with by the Law of July 11, 1938, which revised and modified a Law of March 31, 1928, and a decree of September 17, 1930, but, being a part of industrial mobilization, shared in its fate. It was left aside. The tendency which grew in strength and found its full expression in the 1938 text was that men in the youngest classes of reservists should not be granted—save in cases of absolute necessity—"special exemption." The hope was that they would be replaced in the factories by calling back workmen on the retired lists, by requisitioning labor, and by enlisting volunteers. In December 1939 there were 900,000 "specially exempt" men, in contrast to 1,150,000 at the end of the war in 1918—when the requirements of matériel had been far less complex. And Daladier, after having quoted these figures (speech of December 22 before the House of Deputies), timidly remarked, "I wish there were some thousands more men at work in the factories."

[12]Daladier, on December 22, 1939, told of an auctioneer set to work making shells: "He is not suited to handle that kind of a hammer."

The reaction of the industry owners to the laws of 1936 has already been described.[13] When war broke out they evinced a greater willingness to serve, but their frame of mind could not be changed overnight. And once more the bureaucracy handled them the wrong way. It still discouraged the spirit of enterprise. M. Bouthillier, secretary-general at the Ministry of Finance, a man of authoritarian temperament, suggested, and was successful in having enacted, complicated legal measures to restrict war profits to 4 per cent of gross income on the average.[14] Large-scale industrial establishments had no reason to look askance at this limitation of profits since their normal gain amounted only to a very small percentage on the total amount of business. But industries not engaged in mass production generally counted on a higher return in relation to sales price, and moreover—an important matter—their bookkeeping methods did not conform to the standards of accountancy required by the authorities. Consequently, the very same small factories and workshops which in 1914-18 had vied in their haste to get contracts now shunned government orders.

In the indifferent contribution of French industry to national defense, technicians and engineers have their share of blame as well as employers, although the major blame goes to those who did not call them to order. Here we come across a mania (a very old one indeed) for endlessly modifying standard types, seeking perfection in detail. A dire penalty had to be paid for it: the production of belated, intricate, and disparate matériel. The craftsman did not care. He delighted in small things, which led to treating armaments as though they were delicate jewelry. Meanwhile argument followed argument, experiments and discussions were never concluded. In April 1940, after months of research, our experts still disagreed on the type of tank truck to be made and on what airplane motors should be definitely adopted—not to mention the matter of shells and fuses. A lengthy enumeration could be made. We did not get rid of those aberrations even under the spur of danger.

Considering industrial conditions as a whole, the mind is again forced

---

[13]The aviation manufacturers must be placed in a class of their own. For a long time the main preoccupation of many of them was to prevent the government from ordering motors and planes in the United States.

[14]It is unnecessary to go into the details of this tangled legislation: Article 21 ter, Law of July 11, 1938; Decree of September 1, 1939, and Law of December 1939; interpretative decree of July 29, September 1, September 9, 1939; and laws of January 30, 1940, which superseded all previous legislation. On the profits between 2 per cent and 8 per cent the tax rose progressively from 28 per cent to 100 per cent. This was the general principle. After September 1, 1939, an attempt was made to make all enterprises subject to the same rule whether or not they worked for national defense.

to face a sinister parallel with Germany which relied, from the outset, on an economic potentiality vastly superior to ours. Her factories' equipment had been renovated from top to bottom, in preparation for war between 1924 and 1930, with British and American capital attracted by high interest rates. When General Vuillemin returned from Berlin in July 1938 he astonished everyone by saying that the Germans had built an airplane factory in eight months and that a plane was, by now, delivered every day, etc.[15] And let us never forget that German industry had gone into full production a good three years, if not more, before a weak French industry had begun to move.

Neither the French General Staff nor Dautry nor his assistants were able to quickly bring order into that chaos. And what did Daladier do about it? When forced to take notice of a too glaring scandal, of a damaging "bottleneck," he would descend from his Olympian heights. He would call for the files, cross-question the men involved, attempt to ascertain the truth. There are some achievements to his credit, but they were not enough to reverse the trend.[16] In the winter of 1939 all armament manufacturing was so far behind the timetable that the arrears could not be wiped out before perhaps another year had passed. Listen to Daladier's naïve confession to the Chamber of Deputies on December 22, 1939: "The armament program to which that money has been assigned [he refers to the fourteen billion francs voted in 1936] would have certainly been completed by the summer of 1940 in the normal course of things, if war had not been sprung upon us when we were in the midst of it." But, in the circumstances, ought not the promoters of the program to have regarded war as a normal possibility for 1939–40?

Whether he liked it or not, he was caught in the controversy which raged in the Senate—from December 1938 to March 1940—between Guy la Chambre and André Maroselli, secretary of the Committee on Aviation. The latter, in a series of letters and reports, gave the lie to official figures. He stated that in February and March 1939 forty-four and thirty-five planes respectively were put into service (American planes excluded); that in April 1939 we had 430 airplanes, and in October of the same year (after six weeks of war) only "a few hundred pursuit planes and light bombers, a few dozen reconnaissance planes, and exactly five

---

[15]After a day passed in visiting German factories, General Vuillemin went to the French Embassy, where a ball was given in his honor. His sadness was apparent to everyone.

[16]He brought his full weight to bear on Paul Reynaud in order to increase the orders given to American industry. Over the heads of engineers and inventors, all at loggerheads, he decided for the "anti-aircraft gun of 25" and for the projectile of the new grenade thrower.

modern bombers." He added that, at the same time, 40,000 men were at work on warplane production, while the program for 4,800 planes, drawn up in November 1938, with one half scheduled for delivery by May 1939 and the other half by May 1940, was based on having 100,000 men in full employment. Furthermore, he charged that this program, which had already broken down, was more and more passing into oblivion. "Monthly deliveries of 255 planes so boastfully bandied about —what a fairy tale! One hundred and fifty Amiots a month were supposed to be coming into service by the spring of 1940. We cannot hope to reach that tempo before 1941 . . . 432 Bloch Pursuit 150s, or modifications of that type, were to have been ready in April 1939. There are only one hundred of them with the squadrons. It had been asserted that fifty-five Bloch 175s would be on hand in July 1939. On December 15, 1939, not a single one was in service. One hundred Moranes were turned over from the plants in May 1939. But in June deliveries had fallen to seventy-nine; in July, sixty-five; in November, ninety-three. I pass no judgment. Events, more or less distant, will speak on my behalf." The letter from which I quote was written on January 9, 1940. Daladier had answered the senator's previous admonitions by merely endorsing whatever argument his Air Ministry pleaded in justification. This time he was silent. We know that he threatened, stormed, and, out of sheer lassitude, closed the file. "It is not a question of correcting administrative methods but of correcting rooted habits," he groaned. It was patent that he despaired of doing so. More and more his only hope for salvation centered on American industry.[17]

[17]I feel unable to unravel the record of the newly created Air Ministry. In the prewar period three ministers were in charge: Pierre Cot (January 31, 1933–February 9, 1934); General Denain (February 9, 1934–June 6, 1936); Pierre Cot again (June 6, 1936–January 17, 1938), and Guy la Chambre until March 20, 1938. French air power certainly sank to the lowest level toward the end of 1937. In November of that year C. Chautemps, the Prime Minister, and Yvon Delbos, his Foreign Minister, went to London and there had to put up with a warning from the British Government. Simultaneously the British air attaché in Paris was instructed to acquaint Léon Blum, then Minister of State, with the real conditions of affairs. As to the production of new matériel, the Air Ministry gave a much worse account of itself than the Ministry of War. The air bureaucracy was of recent origin but of doubtful standing. Politicians were at home in its midst.

6

Daladier Does Not Stamp Out Treason, Does Not Take Public Opinion in Hand

DALADIER NEVER TOOK public opinion in hand. To a remark of his in February, that "time was working for the Allies," Georges Mandel replied: "Possibly. But only provided that you find a way to awaken and keep alive the war spirit of the country." The task was an urgent one. Daladier eschewed it.

In the fight against Germany he had five groups of dissidents to reckon with. The Communists, subservient to the Third International, who had stormed against the false appeasement of Munich up until August 23, 1939, and then, once the Russo-German Non-Aggression Pact was signed, had exposed French imperialism with equal vehemence. The Socialists of the Marceau Pivert persuasion, still engrossed in the anti-militaristic doctrines of the old Marxist theoreticians: however obsolete had those doctrines become during the preceding twenty-five years, all the overwhelming evidence of totalitarian aggression had, nonetheless, been required to reclaim from them Léon Blum and the majority of the party. The conservatives of every variety, the well-to-do or those who thought themselves to be so: in this fluctuating universe they took fright at the tidal waves which revolution and war would surely bring forth and they were inclined to see in the Mussolinian and Hitlerian dictatorships instruments of salvation. The financiers, the economists, the wealthy trembling for their wealth, the timid and the cynical, the ideologists of defeat, convinced that France's great days were over, that the wise course for her was to settle into the happy and tranquil lot of a second-rate nation, guaranteed, as a counterpart, its possession of a colonial empire. The German and Italian fifth columns.

The Hitler-Stalin Pact aroused popular indignation. The Premier was carried away by it, and he struck hard at French affiliates of the Third International: by law decree of September 26 the Communist party was dissolved and its deputies were deprived of their parliamentary mandate unless they made public disavowal of any allegiance to the party. Those of the leaders whom it proved possible to arrest were interned. On November 18 another law decree suspended the guarantees of individual liberty, granted prefects the authority to designate a compulsory place of residence to persons considered dangerous and even to assign them definite tasks in the public interest: it was almost exclusively applied to that crowd.[1] But to take such steps Daladier had to stifle his scruples. Some people worried and even dismayed him through questioning the legality of what he had done.

With him such wobbling was an inevitable preliminary for action. Fairly rapidly he freed himself of it. He has been reproached with not having thrust his scalpel deep into the abscess. His censors maintain that he operated only on the outer surface of Communism, dared not probe into its far-reaching ramifications through factories and workshops, that he was shy of pressing for greater severity from the military tribunals. The judges, mobilized from civilian life, showed in their military garb a leniency and a timidity in repression greater than they would have done had they worn their robes of office in their own courts.

I do not know if Daladier deserves criticism on such counts, but I know only too well that conservative or supposedly conservative groups were allowed unbridled license to undermine that minimum of national unity without which the war could not be carried on. Moreover, these groups were, far more than the "Reds," in a position to influence the nation as a whole. Clemenceau, in 1917–18, had haled Caillaux and Malvy before the High Court. Daladier, had he been of the same temperament as his Jacobin predecessor, would have had even greater justification in visiting with harsh retribution the two former ministers, whom the General Staff, in a voluminous report, accused of having been or being in communication with the enemy. His daring went no further than to have criminal proceedings begun against Marcel Déat, Air Minister in 1936, whose name had appeared among the signers of a manifesto calling on soldiers to desert. A member of the Cabinet, Anatole de Monzie, took the guilty man under his wing. By dint of legal quibbling he urged that some discrimination ought to be made between the act of a man who, physically, with pen and ink, signs his name to a manifesto and the act of one who verbally authorizes his name to be appended to it. The public prosecutor did not move.

Berthoin, head of the Sûreté Générale, whom Daladier trusted (he had

---

[1] A subsequent decree, dated November 29, provided for a consultative commission to assist the prefects, whose power thus became less absolute.

been one of Daladier's pupils), did not believe surgical methods to be suited to the circumstances. He prescribed gentler therapeutics. The mutual reconciliation of Frenchmen, won by the Premier's efforts, was still too recent and too delicate an achievement, he pleaded. It was politically wise to spare it too brutal a shock. This Berthoin was a patriot, one of the few officials in the Ministry of the Interior to appraise correctly the full implications of the war.[2] A phrase of Daladier's shows how timid he was when confronted by the worst perversions of national feeling in men of the Right and the Center. Someone said to him one day that he had made a most serious error in tolerating that Mussolini should have his way when, on September 3, 1939, Italy's ambiguous "non-belligerency" was proclaimed. He answered: "You cannot expect me to take on two dictators at once." The thought back of that phrase was that the French conservatives who gave their support against the Nazis were doing Daladier an immense favor and that the least he could do was to avoid taking advantage of their good nature.

As to assuming command of public opinion, Daladier's sloth became particularly obvious in the department of propaganda and censorship. A few weeks before the war Jean Giraudoux was selected to be its chief.[3] I do not want to disparage this subtle and rather precious mind. Among the politicians seeking the position, he, at least, had the merit of being an honest man, and such a quality was no commonplace. Nor had he any taint of the fascism so wildly rampant in the French Academy. But in Goebbels' brutal universe how old-fashioned and obsolete seemed the elegance of this slender column of water rising from a chiseled fountain and ever falling back upon itself! The worst blasts of wind left it serene; never did it sprinkle very far its shining drops of mist. Such was Giraudoux's propaganda, lovely in itself and futile. To make matters worse he attempted to be politically adroit. In a radio talk to Italian children he placed Mussolini at Dante's side! The Duce, if he heard him that day, must have spat out his contempt in a burst of coarse Romagna insult.

But the "High Commissioner" for propaganda and censorship was not master in his own house—the Hotel Continental—whose personnel he did not choose. He soon fell behind in the race with current business and swollen files, and he never caught up.

[2] He had been head of the Sûreté Générale once before, in 1934, when King Alexander and M. Barthou were assassinated. Clearing him of blame in the matter, his friends explained more or less plausibly that he was inexperienced at making police arrangements of the sort and should never have been detailed for that work.

[3] The Law of July 11, 1938, directed that a Ministry of Information should be created in case of war.

A Radical-Socialist politician and a protégé of the Premier's, M. Martineau-Desplas, took to himself the censorship of magazines and newspapers. As he could go at will to the source of authority, he never paid any heed to Giraudoux. A courteous man, at great pains to conciliate everyone, he had but a ludicrous notion of what should be the press of a nation whose very life was at stake. He would have it a sort of insulator made up of heavy layers of felt whose function was to deaden all sounds from without and, if possible, to prevent their being heard. At the same time the press was to proclaim the glory of the Minister who had appointed him. I remember an article in *L'Europe Nouvelle,* comparing the economic methods of Roosevelt, Léon Blum, and Paul Reynaud, which came back from the censorship with all the passages in praise of our Finance Minister deleted. Thus did Daladier's household treat the Premier's principal colleague. What relation was it possible to detect between an entirely theoretical and technical analysis and the secrets of military operations or of diplomatic negotiations which the censorship is supposed to shield?

In the job assigned to Martineau-Desplas one man only had been fortunate enough to win everyone's approval: Major Nusillard, who served under Clemenceau. The story goes that in September Daladier sent word inviting him to return to his old duties. Nusillard said that he would, but on one condition: that he be given full power to select his whole staff. Whereupon he was passed over.

But within the department itself Martineau-Desplas met his match: the military censors under a certain Colonel de Massignac. These censors must have been chosen years before at the remote end of the War Ministry, in some obscure recess where, section after section, the minutiae of mobilization had to be set down. Indeed, in the plans of the General Staff, supervision of the press must have come very far down the agenda. A few reserve officers had been singled out at first—probably taken at their own valuation—and they had brought in their pals. From top to bottom we invariably meet friends co-opted by friends. Seventy per cent of these military censors came from the devotees of *L'Action Française* and *Gringoire.*

Compelled to pass under their scrutiny, as editor of *L'Europe Nouvelle,* I turned first to M. de Marcilly, who had been French Ambassador to Berne and was supposed to assist Martineau-Desplas as diplomatic adviser. With this open-minded gentleman all went smoothly. I soon found him to be an enlightened guide. But the Radical-Socialist politician and the colonel soon got rid of one who was not of their breed.[4] I then attempted to continue the same frank and open relationship with the two majors in charge of periodicals. After the third or fourth attempt I had to realize that their insolence matched their stupidity. I hung up the telephone and did not bother any more about them.[5]

To keep the public informed as to critical spots in international affairs, the most expedient course was to reprint news from the English papers. The censors hated this device, for they hesitated to cut such matter, dearly as they would have liked to. And so they would argue and strike petty bargains over its use, the while they took their vengeance by underhandedly persuading the proper governmental office to hold up for several days the circulation of the freer newspapers from beyond the Channel. Of all forbidden subjects, Italy was forbidden beyond all others. Anything which might lift the veil on the true nature of "non-belligerency," on Mussolini's drift toward armed intervention, was banned. In October the reconstruction of the Italian Cabinet was interpreted against all the dictates of truth. In January, François-Poncet, our Ambassador in Rome, compared the illusions of the French press with the reality which lay before his eyes. In his alarm he sent word that Italian newspaper articles might be reproduced textually without comment.[6] Thus, through painfully piecing together quotations into some sort of mosaic, we did our best to relieve the public of its illusions. Yet at the end of May 1940, and even in the beginning of June, the censorship refused to allow publication of an old article of the Italian dictator's, an article which cried out his hatred of bourgeois society. And long before, of course, the Italian newspapers had ceased to be sold at the kiosks on the boulevards.

The Premier's attention was often called both to the performances of

---

[4]On the proposal of the permanent staff of the Quai d'Orsay, M. de Marcilly had been appointed chief censor (August 29, 1939). Very soon he clashed with Georges Bonnet, who wanted to have his own defeatism translated into the French press. Giraudoux did not support him, and Martineau-Desplas stepped in. M. de Marcilly survived for a while as diplomatic adviser.

[5]One day, in connection with Poland, I had spoken of the "regime of the colonels." The officers at the Hotel Continental at once assumed that the description was aimed at themselves. But a subaltern was there to disabuse them. Twice in succession the military censors prevented my reprinting *L'Europe Nouvelle's* leading article of June 16, 1939, in which I had called attention to the German-Russian negotiations already under way. Why? Because they did not want it to be proved that our weekly, while it stood for a policy of resistance to the totalitarians, showed some prudence and insight.

[6]On January 21 orders to this effect were sent to the censors. On February 18 François-Poncet renewed his advice.

the "colonels" and other reserve officers, to their connection with *L'Action Française,* and, more generally, to newspapers and periodicals of the *Je Suis Partout* type, which, although less openly than in peacetime, still went on with their totalitarian campaign in an easily recognizable form. On several occasions, notably at the end of January, the prefect of police submitted the results of his investigations to Daladier. Each time he did so the Premier was indignant and furious and announced that he would not stand being fooled any longer. And each time his anger ended in a gesture of impotence. He would close the file abruptly with the perennial utterance: "Let them all go to the devil!" Suspension of publication for three days was the easy penalty imposed on *L'Action Française.* It happened in the first week of February. The paper had hurled insults at officials of the Quai d'Orsay guilty of not attuning themselves to the fascist pattern of M. Charles Maurras.

In that remissive manner was the morale of the country mobilized for battle, if such terms can be coupled together. The country's morale suffered not only from Daladier's omissions, but from certain of his positive deeds and words, especially from his speech before the House of Deputies on December 22: "Aware of its responsibility for the conduct of the war, I repeat, the government, above all things, must seek to be sparing of French blood. Let us assume that alluring plans are being submitted to the government. The government must firmly resist them in the present phase of the war, insofar as they call either for systematic and premature offensives of the kind we all remember so well or for haphazard attacks along the whole front, which once caused us losses greater than those of major onslaughts."[7] With such cheap oratory ringing in their ears, why wouldn't soldiers and citizens have given way to the mirage of an easy victory, a victory which would fall into their laps like a ripe fruit? I shall never forget how disturbed I was, a few days afterward, listening to this outburst of heartfelt happiness on the part

---

[7] "The war, in its present form, has proved bewildering. A phrase has spread from civilians to soldiers and back again: 'This is a phony war.' Certainly those who use the phrase do not think that the war is phony, but they thus express their surprise at new forms of war, completely unforeseen, which line up face to face, each in its fortifications, the two most powerful armies in the world. It is in any case an odd war. Should we regret that it is such? Should we complain? In December 1914 we reckoned our dead at 450,000. We had lost the battle of the frontiers, we had won the Battle of the Marne, but ten French departments remained under the invader's heel. Today, however slight the number of killed, it is still too great for our hearts to accept without sorrow. Yet here are the facts: land forces, up to November 30—1,136 killed; naval forces, up to November 30—256 killed; air force, up to November 30—42 killed. I still prefer the situation as of December 1939 to that of 1914." (Loud cheers.)

of a former Premier: "Isn't it wonderful?" We need not be surprised if, in the long run, many people came to believe that Daladier wanted no more than a show of resistance.[8]

A terrible deficit in the country's moral and material preparation: Daladier's account cannot be balanced otherwise by anyone who prods beneath the surface. It was not easy for us in 1939–40 to get at the truth. Trusting the military authorities, almost everybody believed in the strength of the defensive front. The fact that the Germans did not choose to move, the persistence of the strange *de facto* armistice served to confirm the general optimism. In November 1939 a neutral diplomat friend of mine, out of mere curiosity, went to Berlin and spent a fortnight there. He brought back this verdict: the mass of the German people has no doubt as to victory. But those whose ideas take in a broader horizon, university professors, "intellectuals" of all descriptions, can see nothing but defeat ahead. In the diplomatic corps most considered that Germany was lost. And, not last of them, the Dutch Minister, M. de With, Germanophile as he was reputed to be, who had asked as a favor to be sent to the capital of the Reich rather than to Rome. We all knew that Daladier's work at the War Ministry had produced results falling short of the needs of the Army. But we did not think that our preparedness had sunk so low beneath the 1914 level.

The defeat of May and June 1940 laid bare for all to see what Daladier's management of the country had been. Now to pass judgment upon him we take into consideration, above all, his administrative record. He brought a weak France to her hour of trial, and the rest of the story seems irrelevant. However, between January and March 1940, parliamentarians and journalists had only a confused view of his daily routine, hidden away as it was in the silent depths of government bureaus. Therefore, in ever-increasing numbers, they condemned him for political acts openly accomplished, and especially for the Finnish venture on which he had, indeed, staked his premiership. It was the Russo-Finnish treaty of March 12, 1940, which broke him.

He feared that the Wehrmacht would fall upon our armies along the north and eastern frontier before deliveries of war matériel had increased in volume, and, at the same time, he deliberately undertook a foolhardy campaign in the Scandinavian Peninsula whereby substantial bodies of French and British troops would necessarily be diverted from the principal battlefield. On December 19, at the Supreme Council in London,

---

[8]Daladier corrected himself in a speech of January 29. He said that "total war" was at hand.

Gamelin had frowned on taking in the periphery any action which might weaken military power at the center of the struggle. Despite Gamelin's opposition, Daladier pursued his project with a sort of stubborn violence. As his talk went, the aid planned for Finland was never either sufficiently ample or sufficiently prompt. He kept insisting that additional men and equipment should be thrown into the expedition. And his mistake was the mistake of the whole nation. In the end he was driven from his high office, not because of the accumulation of the all too serious errors he had made, but because he had not gone far enough on the unhappy Scandinavian road. It was a case of collective folly. And it indicates to what an extent all those who shared in determining French policy— ministers, parliamentary leaders, and behind them the French masses— were swayed by a confusion of thought. Here was nothing to be compared with the stable and clear-cut lines on which the diplomacy of Delcassé, of Paul Cambon, of Camille Barrère, had, at the turn of the century, paved the way for the victories of Joffre and of Foch.

No more instructive cross section can be taken than that which reveals the French body politic's leanings, in that juncture, just a few months before the end.

7

Daladier Seeks To Make Help to Finland a Means of Reconstructing National Unity. Mussolini's Intrigues

On NOVEMBER 26, 1939, the Red Army suddenly jumped on Finland. From Right to Left the French people, with the "Russian betrayal" of August 23, 1939, still fresh in their minds, were beside themselves. If all did not agree in their outlook on the war, they at least were swept in the same righteous anger.

Many had long considered the German and Italian dictators to be "pillars of the social order," and they had blamed the Bolshevik rather than the Fascist or the National Socialist revolution for the plight of the European continent. Many had dreamed of a coalition aimed against Moscow in which Franco-German antagonism would melt away. All these men now saw their opportunity to steer the war off to the north and alter its goal and purpose. At once a clamor went up for immediate severance of diplomatic relations with Moscow. If we condoned Russian aggression in Finland, wouldn't we lose all right to excoriate German aggression in Poland? Of that very process of reasoning, Italian newspapers had already made great capital against France, but the fact that it served the political interests of Rome in no way gave pause to our conservatives. On the contrary, they delightedly pointed out that the Fascists vied with most Frenchmen in their anxiety to help the Helsinki Government. Blessed be the day when France and Italy come together again at last!

For their part the ideologists of the Left, always inclined to view events *sub specie aeternitatis,* bethought themselves that the League of Nations, although mutilated, discredited, and moribund, was, however, not dead. Here was a chance to infuse it with new life! Their opponents had called them "fellow travelers of communists" for having been bent on co-operating with Moscow against the Reich. They would silence their opponents by proving that they were not going to spare Stalin any more than Hitler the moment Stalin became an aggressor. And it pleased their fancy to believe that Paris and London, if only they showed themselves able to repress the Bolshevik crime, might win precious support among those Scandinavians whose neutrality was, otherwise, likely to degenerate into *de facto* complicity with Germany, for the simple reason that Germany—unlike the Allies—knew how to threaten and terrorize all within reach. And what about the applause of the American nations? Just listen to their ambassadors!

On the Right, political calculation; on the Left, an emotional surge. With that material Daladier was confident he could build national unity. How? His muddled intuition probably led him to imagine that, through hatred of Russia, the conservatives would acquire fighting spirit. This would tap their old reserves of patriotism and, as regenerated men, make them rise for national defense. At last they would look the brutal world in the face.

Daladier scarcely hesitated at all. He followed the tide. He even tried to get ahead of it. He thought that by means of what was mere political maneuvering he could make up for his casualness, his negligence, his inconsistency. He resolved to avail himself of Finland to show his true measure. But he felt he could not disappoint the hopes he had aroused. He knew he would not be forgiven if he failed. "It's a dangerous business," he said; "it must not be allowed to end badly."

In other words, the forces which strove for appeasing Nazis and Fascists were sure to get out of hand and exact their vengeance if Daladier's effort to channel them into the war through Finland came to nought. Then the political struggle within the country would flare up again and deepen national disunion. To understand Daladier's restlessness, the doings of the appeasers, late in 1939, cannot be left out.

Daladier's calls to action had not yet stirred up the French nation as a whole against Hitler's empire. Even after the war had started, far too much peacetime quarreling still engrossed the country. "We shall soon see each other again," remarked M. Brauer, German chargé d'affaires, to the protocol officials who were seeing him off, on September 4, at the Invalides station. M. Brauer knew what he was talking about. Even at the moment of breaking relations he volunteered an implicit prophecy that the French would not fight in earnest and that, given their feelings about the war, the policy of trying to win a "bloodless victory" had a good chance of success.

We know that such a policy was first set in motion in the Russo-German Agreement of September 29, 1939, and that the idea was squarely expressed in the speech made by the Führer at the Kroll Opera House on October 6. To lead the French to believe that England had thrown them into the conflict entirely against their will, that all they had to do in order to be left by Germany in the peaceful enjoyment of their possessions was to lay down their arms—such was the strategy of an aggressor who stood before them, laden with the spoils of Poland. It never made the slightest impression on Daladier. He always found ways of pointing out in his communiqués that he was not impressed.[1]

But it is impossible to assert with the same certainty that most soldiers and citizens remained as immune as Daladier to the "Perfidious Albion" motif, variations of which were played every evening on the Stuttgart radio by Ferdonnet. Nor were soldiers and plain citizens alone hit by this propaganda; parliamentarians, members of the Foreign Affairs committees of the House and of the Senate, were affected also because they were all too willing to be.

M. Mistler headed the former, M. Bérenger the latter; both were men whose interests intermingled business and politics.[2] Mistler, of a para-

[1] As recorded already, Daladier had had the skill to kindle in Hitler the hope—a futile hope—for a compromise peace. But as soon as any rumored project began to take diplomatic shape he hastened to wreck it.

[2] Why were they re-elected year after year with so little trouble? Because, in the beginning, the Radical-Socialist party had singled them out for those posts, and they could not have been ousted without a considerable fuss. "The game would not be worth the candle," I have

doxical turn of mind, flitted lightheartedly from one international problem to another with the facile irresponsibility of a brilliant undergraduate. He was a versatile writer and novelist. He had brought back from the Hungarian university where he had taught a whole trunkload of prejudices against France's allies in Central Europe.

Bérenger was shady, crafty, greedy, and he cold-bloodedly followed a carefully thought out policy of personal plundering. Of all the French Premiers, Paul Painlevé alone had been bold enough to entrust him with a public mission. He appointed him to the Washington Embassy in November 1925. But all his successors, to whatever party they belonged, made it a set rule to keep him away from all executive posts. And that perpetual exclusion shaped for him a very odd career. M. Bérenger for many years filled one of the most important functions in Parliament. By means of the committee over which he presided, he harassed and discomfited a great number of cabinet ministers. Never, in any governmental crisis, however, was his name mentioned as a possible choice for office. He had been oil administrator in the days of Clemenceau: that was quite enough for everyone. Never, not even in the newspapers, did anybody, no matter how irresponsible, suggest that he might possibly become a cabinet minister—and heaven knows what small fry the run of our ministers has been. His was a case almost without precedent. In the 1938 senatorial elections Georges Mandel, Minister for Colonies, deemed it meritorious to have him expelled from his feudal tenure in Guadeloupe, where, some twenty years before—never having set foot on the island—he had connived to procure himself a seat in the Senate. Mandel failed completely. The easygoing mutual backslappers in power lent Bérenger irresistible help; even M. Lebrun went out of his way and gave a pull.

Mistler, Bérenger, and a few other members of the Foreign Affairs committees privately paid more attention to Hitler's speeches than they deserved. The mediatory proposals made by King Leopold of Belgium and by Queen Wilhelmina of Holland, on November 7, a sequel to Hitler's peace initiative, attracted them also, as they were bound to. Yet no definite moves issued from these committees, beyond Gaston Bergery's report in October on the circumstances which had attended the declaration of war on Germany, a report made to the House Foreign Affairs Committee. In it one could find the hand of Georges Bonnet harping on the theme that peace, after all, could have been preserved. Georges Bonnet had been eliminated from the Quai d'Orsay on Septem-

---

often been told by men who judged both of these politicians mercilessly. In the Senate, however, Bérenger's "appeasement" formulas were found congenial.

ber 13. Consigned to the inferior position of Minister of Justice, he was nursing his resentment. Daladier had taken away from him the direction of the French diplomacy, and this undeniably amounted to passing moral condemnation upon him. Hence the propaganda which spread out in his name: war would not have broken out if Bonnet had been entirely free to act. In a press conference Bonnet went so far as to say, "Against me all means were good, and they have all been used."[3]

But, in the fall of 1939 and the winter of 1940, those who believed that, by general agreement, a Europe could be rebuilt in which civilized men might live, and that the campaign need not be carried to the extent of defeating Hitler on the battlefield, placed their main hope in a Mussolini finally won over to friendship with France. They did not doubt that it fell to the lot of the Duce to rid the Continent of Russian Communism and, simultaneously, to hold in the National Socialist Revolution. Few dared speak openly and straightforwardly in favor of the Führer. Fascist Italy supplied all pro-Germans with an alibi, since all pro-Germans had better watch their steps. On the first of January 1939, Lazard Frères, owners of the financial paper *L'Information,* had cut short Fernand de Brinon's articles, the medium so long borrowed by the Germans to advertise that the Reich had only pacific designs on Austria and Czechoslovakia. Crestfallen, Brinon had retired to the country under police supervision.[4] Otto Abetz had left on July first under threat of expulsion. The France-Germany Committee was all but extinct.

At the end of December 1939 the *Yellow Book* published the dispatches of Robert Coulondre, French Ambassador to Berlin since November 1938, the most impressive day-by-day chronicle of the Nazi leaders' aggressive machinations. And even Georges Bonnet, who never allowed a sense of consistency to interfere with his double-dealing, brought his contribution to the indictment of the German dictator. Forgetful of Bergery's report, he was perfectly willing to be seen in the guise of a foreign minister who knew what he was doing when he declared war against Germany. With his tacit approval the summaries of his telephone conversations with Rome (August 31, September 1 and 2, 1939) were even inserted in the *Yellow Book,* from which it appeared that the Duce, at the critical moment, acted as a faithful signatory to the "Steel Pact." Bonnet, of course, had a construction of his own to place on

---

[3]Whereupon he sharpened the impression he had just given by quoting Alexis Léger's name. See page 410.

[4]It is worth noting that during the war Brinon tried to find shelter in Marshal Pétain's approval, which he claimed to have.

those summaries. But in a more guarded moment he probably would have kept them to himself. For the present, he thought victory possible and, in the event of victory, he wanted to be able to claim his share.

It was toward Fascist Italy, looked upon, against all evidence, as desiring to bring into being a well-balanced Europe (so long, of course, in the phraseology of the period, as some slight account were taken of her own noisy demands), that now all those men turned who read in the *de facto* "truce" a sort of permanent German plea for negotiation. How is it possible to think that they were sincere, that they did not realize what it meant to appease the Fascist Government? According to military reports received by the General Staff, Italy, in September 1939, was capable of three or four weeks' resistance at the most. How did it escape them that by giving orders to Italian industry, paying for them half in gold and half in deliveries of raw materials, we simply were providing Italy with an opportunity to build up reserves, enabling her to add to German strength and, when the time came, to draw her dagger from its sheath? How could they forget the insult hurled at the French Ambassador when, on November 30, 1938, in his presence, the Italian House of Deputies interrupted a speech of Ciano's to howl, "Corsica, Nice, Tunisia!"? The hint was clear enough that the Duce sought the salvation of his regime in the cataclysm to be wrought by Hitler and in widespread territorial changes—even if this were to involve the loss of Italian independence—rather than in the conservative Franco-British system, a system which offered him necessarily limited profits.

How often did I ask these questions of my conservative acquaintances only to infuriate them, alas, and get myself called a friend of Moscow! One day, walking down the Rue de Varenne with Charles-Roux, French Ambassador to the Vatican, we met Count de P. "Well, Mr. Ambassador," said this gentleman who prided himself on his diplomatic acumen, "when are you going to bring us back a pact with Italy? We must have it." The Ambassador looked at him: "A pact with Italy? If that is what you want to get, you'll have to take Tunisia along in your pocket before you even enter the Palazzo Venezia or the Chigi. And even if you proffer Tunisia on a silver platter, you can't be sure of making a deal." Count de P. wrinkled his nose. What a perversion of all common sense!

At the end of 1939 and the beginning of 1940 too many Frenchmen stubbornly persisted in refusing to see that the democracies were on one side and the totalitarians on the other. Mussolini was firmly resolved to stand by Hitler. As long as he hesitated to force upon his General Staff and his son-in-law, Count Ciano, the conclusion regarding German military superiority which he himself had formed during the Polish conquest, he would go no further than scheming and plotting for a "negotiated peace."[5] But the minute the French morale seemed to flinch and he ceased to give the French Army the benefit of the doubt he would take full belligerent action. Most heedlessly, then, did the French Italophiles soften the effect produced on the Duce by Daladier's vigorous and intransigeant statements to the Italian Ambassador, Guariglia, concerning France's absolute determination to continue fighting. Wasn't the Duce fully entitled to see a sign of irremediable weakness in the high-sounding praises so many Frenchmen insisted on showering upon him at a time when he lost no opportunity to insult France? The result was plain. All those who, by basely flattering Italy, thought they could stop the war actually strengthened the "Steel Pact" and Germany's material power and audacity. Little by little, Mussolini settled down on this dilemma: Either the French would break down and abandon Poland to its fate, and Franco-British humiliation would be so great that all the conquests the Fascists had planned could be carried out without a blow, or else the French would go into battle without faith or conviction or modern equipment and they would go straight to destruction. From the middle of January on, the Duce based his policy on the second alternative: the letter sent by Muti, secretary-general of the party, to the Fascist hierarchs, a letter drafted by Mussolini himself, bore witness to the Duce's new trend.

From January 1935 Laval was the moving spirit of the campaign for coming to terms with Italy. But he had been exiled into opposition as early as January 1936, and only gradually did he resume his parliamentary activities. He took no part in the regular sittings. He contented himself with drawing one senator or another aside for private indoctrination. "For Laval's buttonholing requirements," one of them said to me, "the whole Luxembourg Palace has not a sufficient supply of quiet corners." He went on advocating the formation of a Pétain Cabinet for national defense, made up of all former Premiers excepting Léon Blum. We shall meet Laval again; he can be left aside for the moment—his greatest hour has not struck. Bérenger and Mistler have already been mentioned in these pages, but in connection with Italy their names perforce come up again. Both of them admired the Duce and rubbed elbows with his emissaries.

For a full seven years, if not longer, Bérenger had seen in reconcilia-

[5]Mussolini thrice thought, to the knowledge of French diplomacy, to involve Washington in his scheme for a "negotiated peace."

tion with Italy—even if we had to pay a heavy price for it—the solution of our foreign problems. Returning from Rome in December 1933, if I remember rightly, he published in the *Petit Parisien* (whose editor, Pierre Dupuy, cast covetous eyes on the post of French Ambassador at the Farnese Palace) one or several articles in praise of our "Latin sister." Incidentally, in one of these articles, he admitted that Mussolini had claims on Constantinople—a passage suppressed by the newspaper's editor. Among the greatest friends of Italian Fascists deserves also to be singled out M. François Piétri, deputy from Corsica, Inspector of Finances, a cultivated man with a quick mind, but frail in body as in character. This tiny vehicle for a deadly policy was propelled by an oversized motor—a boundless ambition, a reckless desire for self-advancement, which gave him no rest. He had been Minister of the Navy several times between 1930 and 1936. Then he had dropped out of the group of those currently favored for ministerial preferment. A former pupil and protégé of Caillaux, he now was in contact with the Extreme Right, thanks to the family of the portly lady whom he had married late in life. At Bordeaux, in June, he poured out his sorrow over Italy's declaration of war to an Italian anti-Fascist whom he had just met: "Italy," he moaned, "why, my blood is half Italian: my grandparents could not speak French." To which the Italian replied: "If I am to judge by your mood, sooner or later we shall sit side by side in the Roman Senate." Piétri answered heedlessly, "I can't thank you enough for your kind words."

But Mussolini's most dangerous agent in France was Anatole de Monzie, senator and—through Daladier's folly—since 1938 Minister of Public Works.

Balzac would have been delighted with this politician. What a novel he could have built around his career! He came from one of the regions in Aquitaine which has best preserved the characteristics of a feudal province. Its absorption into the France of the North, whether under a monarchy or a republic, grated on him. He took the label of the "Independent Socialist" group, a tag which permitted complete freedom to all who bore it, and he enjoyed posing as a man of the sixteenth century. I heard him one day holding forth against Luther: "That German monk could find no better time to preach his Reformation than at the precise moment when the Papacy was becoming the paradise of humanists and neo-pagans. Result: the Counter Reformation, the Jesuits, a fanatical and mean religion, the bigots in power. It was Luther who did all the harm."[6]

[6]Another characteristic detail about de Monzie: This atheist despised the traditionally irreligious teachers in the state's primary schools. For a long time his department, the Lot,

At the turn of the century four young men, whose friendship proved enduring, all four from the same ancestral countryside, swore to conquer Paris, money, fame, and high position: they were Henri and Robert de Jouvenel, from the Bas-Limousin, Maurice Colrat,[7] and Monzie, from Quercy. We are interested only in the first and the last. They had few scruples; personal fancy was the supreme law by which they lived. But in Monzie, an ugly cripple, flowed more biting juices than Jouvenel even knew, he who was a sort of lady's man, like Maupassant's Bel Ami, superficial, flowery, and shopworn. Monzie operated a legal establishment from which, in preference to learned pleas, there came forth a marvelous series of manipulations involving at once his clients, his opponents, cabinet ministers and their subordinates.[8] Once in a while he would manage to hold office (a short spell as Finance Minister in 1926 cannot but be reckoned a fantastic performance), and this would restore his standing in and around the law courts. During the last ten years— heaven knows why—he became obsessed with glorifying Mussolini against all comers and rendered him services which the Duce could properly have expected only from a fifth columnist. And then he would write books, brilliant yet silly. Such, in broad outline, was this amazing fellow. In 1933 Monzie forced Paul-Boncour to appoint Henri de Jouvenel Ambassador to Italy. At once this vainglorious amateur hastened to conclude the unhappy Four Power Pact of June 16, 1933. In after years Monzie had the brass to tell Boncour whenever he met him: "No matter how long you live, you will never be able to pay back the debt you owed me the day I gave you Henri." The Duce had nothing to complain about his retinue in France. In an earlier time Rakowsky, Soviet Ambassador in Paris, had inspired a similar devotion in Monzie. As far as one can judge, this was because Russia at the time still clung to the Pact of Rapallo—that is, to Germany. Monzie began to hate the Soviets the moment he saw them and France converging into the same policy. For Hungary, whose feudal lords he supported as against Czech and Ru-

---

which he bossed as he liked, was the only department in all France not to possess a normal school in which such teachers are trained. Which, for that matter, was no loss.

[7]Minister of Justice under Poincaré in 1922–24. In those far-off days I once heard him remark, "What can you do with a country where each district would gladly yield its neighbor as the price of its own peace?" He did not approve, but he reduced to absurdity the slackness of his countrymen.

[8]In his legal career Laval did the same sort of business (Cf. Henry Torrès, Pierre Laval). As early as 1922 Jean Parmentier, the head official at the Finance Ministry, cried out against Monzie's and Laval's endless interferences in matters relating to false tax statements, of wartime profits on the part of government contractors, and to the amounts allocated for war damages.

manian agrarian reforms, his heart always warmed up. What he did for Budapest could only result in helping Pan-Germanism. He did not bother. "I hate the Little Entente . . ." Monzie said. "Ever since you failed to save Austria when she was invaded and annexed in March 1938, you no longer have any business to interfere with what goes on along the Danube." That is a small sample of Monzie's absurd talk in Paris society and even in cabinet meetings before and during the war.

Though a member of Daladier's Cabinet, he kept right on in his intrigues with the emissaries of Rome, whether these emissaries were official or unofficial. His telephone conversations with the Italian Embassy were tapped. And certain of his phrases, registered at the time, made a scandalous impression.[9]

Monzie dragged Pomaret and Pomaret's consort in his wake. A team with but a single voice. When Daladier appointed Monzie Minister of Public Works, the latter insisted on having his friend appointed Minister of Labor. Outwardly Pomaret seemed a youth without guile, wide awake, fond of sports, and fond of his native Lozère. He had fought well in the war of 1914–18. But, with his reputation for patriotism assured by his war record, he ostentatiously displayed a complete cynicism. Daladier, attracted by his buoyancy, spoke one day of his intention to promote him to more important work. M. Champetier de Ribes, who happened to hear him, interrupted him: "Mr. Prime Minister, you must not think of doing that. Do you know what he said in my presence the other day? That he was for peace at any price, for he preferred getting a kick in the back to a bullet in the head."

To this gang of "ultramontanes"—to use an old term, secularizing its connotation—we must add the name of Baudouin. But, like Laval, he was reserved by destiny for grander accomplishments. We will not deal with him until later on.

In March 1940 the promoters of the Italian cause made the most of Mr. Sumner Welles's visit to the French Government. The Under Secretary of State had spoken with both dictators before reaching Paris. He gave proof of a remarkable discretion and tact. No one could boast of having been allowed by him to peep into his exploratory work. His mission was to gather information for Mr. Roosevelt and Secretary Hull. It was not for him to undertake the education of French and British

---

[9] On June 5 Reynaud was forced to dismiss him on the basis of what was reported concerning those talks. Furthermore, Georges Bonnet's minutes of his own telephone conversations with the French Ambassador in Rome, Berlin, London (August 31–September 2) plainly refer to the contacts of Anatole de Monzie with the Italian Ambassador in Paris, Guariglia. Those references are not to be found in the *Yellow Book.*

statesmen. Nevertheless, Georges Bonnet, and perhaps Chautemps, who had attended the informal dinner given by Daladier on March 4 in honor of the American envoy, hastily credited him with certain opinions regarding Italy which might help their own pet propaganda. Hitler, and above all Ribbentrop, they explained, had aroused in Mr. Welles the deepest repulsion; whereas Mussolini had deeply moved him by conjuring up the horrid and imminent picture of total war. "Is it not possible that you are in some respects at fault? There is still time to make amends." Of course I do not wish to suggest that the American diplomat uttered such words, but only that Bonnet and all his circle told people he did, and that they used their assertions as a means to broaden the scope of their maneuverings.[10]

It is no easy matter to explain why, in February, Daladier, faced with Reynaud's insistent demand for full power in economic matters, and being more intent than at any other time upon reconstructing his Cabinet, did not realize how salutary it would have been to sweep out altogether the whole Bonnet-Monzie-Pomaret clique. There can be only one key to his ambiguous conduct, to his groping, tentative moves which led nowhere. Had he thrown out these three men and their like, he would have had no alternative but to bind himself to, and be absolutely dependent on, Reynaud, Mandel, Campinchi, Herriot, Sarraut—and even Blum. A cabinet united in the determination to "fight the war"— in the phrase borrowed from Clemenceau by the courageous Mandel— could be formed of no others than these. But in such a cabinet Daladier knew that he would no longer be the master. Already, at the time of Munich, Reynaud, Mandel, and Campinchi had attempted to force his hand. They had come very close indeed to resigning as a body. The Premier did not want to have to resist anew that kind of collective pressure at some trying moment. As against unity in the Cabinet—but a unity which would tie him up in a strait jacket—he preferred an ill-assorted collection of ministers, even if "traitors"—the word is his own, and he used it more than once—should continue to sit at the council table.

His choice of men was determined not on the general ground of principle or program, but on the ground of personal expediency. How other-

---

[10] I find in my diary this comment by a man in high office after the secret meeting of the Chamber on February 10, the outcome of which had been highly favorable to Daladier. "If the debate had not gone the way it did, the mere announcement of Mr. Welles's trip, giving rise, as it seemed, to all sorts of opportunities for a negotiated peace, might have been enough to bring about a catastrophe." Thus were laid bare the unstable foundations of French policy.

wise can one explain his calling in Monzie and Pomaret at the very height of the Czechoslovak crisis in August 1938?[11] No wonder, then, that he never upset the microcosm of parliament which he dubbed his "Cabinet." And this brings us back to Finland: Daladier expected his policy of intervention to bring together in the interests of national defense those who were appeasers and those who were determined on a vigorous pursuit of the war. The Finnish expedition was to work the miracle of welding together into a single mass the disunited Cabinet and Parliament, which Daladier's "dictatorship" laboriously dragged along and which the Premier had neither courage nor power to regenerate or exalt.

8

Clash with Laval. Paradoxically, Daladier Is Censured for Stopping Short in the Finnish Adventure Although War with Russia Might Have Ensued

THE PROFESSIONAL DIPLOMATS, who knew their business, dreaded the swelling wave of public opinion. They tried to divert it into a channel of their own so as to save the French policy from being swirled on the rocks. Their constant preoccupation was to spare Russia. They had always considered the German-Russian agreements of September 29, issuing from the Non-Aggression Pact of August 23, with provisions for territorial adjustment, economic co-operation, and joint action for a negotiated peace, as being no more than temporizing tactics on Moscow's part. They knew that in September the Soviet Union had shared with considerable reluctance in a division of spoils which did not equally strengthen the two partners. They hoped that, sooner or later, a change would come in Soviet policy. For, in their view, Stalin, however much he thought to prolong the war by alternately granting assistance to Germany and withdrawing it, would nonetheless be doomed if Hitler won in the end. They noted that the Soviet Union did not punctually deliver

[11]As successors to Frossard (Public Works) and Ramadier (Labor), who resigned in protest against the gradual whittling down (far too gradual, alas!) of the Popular Front's social legislation.

raw materials. If aid to Finland were given too openly, they feared that the German-Russian partnership would be made closer, whereas it still was loose and uncertain. And they did not forget that the Turkish ministers would never have signed the pact of October 16, 1939, with the Western democracies, but for the belief that the latter intended to do all in their power to rally Moscow to their cause.

With these rather elaborate reservations, the diplomats recognized that it was in the interest of both Paris and London to attract the neutral nations, and the greatest of them all, the United States, into a sweeping movement against aggression. Their dislike for Russia must be used to turn them against the Reich. Above all, assisting Finland must be made an excuse to put a stop to the German supply of iron ore. The policy was a subtle one and not easy to carry out. Aid given to the government of Helsinki must be made to resemble that which the Soviets themselves were granting Chiang Kai-shek, without its bringing them into war with Japan. To sum up, aid to Finland must be considered as a means—the means to close Scandinavia to Germany and to draw the three northern states into our orbit—but it must not be considered an end in itself. If that rule were neglected or forgotten, if we should find ourselves in open conflict with Russia, the net result would be to the advantage of the Hitlerian empire. No acquisition of allies and associates could compensate for the major forces we should then have to send to Finland and for the tightening of Russo-German bonds. Finland itself could not but lose in the process. On the day Russia was at war with Great Britain and France the government of Helsinki must reckon with a German Army aligned by the side of the Russians. And it must reckon also with a hardening of Swedish and Norwegian neutrality. Then neither Norway nor Sweden could be expected to allow British and French a free passage across their territories.

This whole trend of thought obviously was far removed from the aspirations of our so-called conservatives. It postulated that the assistance to Finland ought to stop short of the following four well-defined limits: no application would be made to Russia of Article 16 of the Geneva Covenant in its most rigorous clauses; for sending arms and ammunitions to Finland, secrecy would be the watchword after the Italian and German manner during the early months of the Spanish Civil War; no regular troops, but so-called "volunteers," would be transported across the North Sea, and French and British diplomatic establishments in Moscow would remain as they were.

The British Cabinet saw this whole matter in the same light as the

Quai d'Orsay officials. At first it showed an even greater caution. It proved arduous to secure its agreement to send war matériel. It gave way after lengthy debate at two Supreme Council meetings held in December and January. In the end its attitude was best expressed in the following formula, later devised by Lord Halifax: "His Majesty's Government will not permit itself to be distracted from the pursuit of its principal object, which is to defeat Germany, by any fear that such and such a particular action might endanger its relations with Soviet Russia."[1] Those carefully selected words were freely translated by the French diplomats: "We are opposing Russia only to the degree that she places herself in our line of fire against the German target."

In France that statement of Anglo-French policy will not be found in any official or semiofficial text. I collected it piecemeal from officials who tried to strike a sort of balance between Daladier's impulse and the calm and thoroughly thought out views of the Foreign Office. As such, it was far too complex to be practical. It is all very well for ingenious diplomats to draft their finely shaded formulas, to conciliate on paper irreconcilable terms. Brutal reality quickly brushes away the delicate web their intellects have spun. And, in the end, the very men who spin it are forced to make their choice among far coarser fabrics.

The fact was that, in spite of all attempts to restrain him, either in London or in Paris, Daladier yielded unconsciously to partisan pressure. He was leading both France and England straight into a conflict with Russia. The resolution by which the Council and Assembly of the League of Nations expelled the Soviets from Geneva (December 14) was his work. To push it through, he disregarded not only the hesitation of Finland but the opposition of Sweden, Norway, and Denmark,[2] and also the warnings Lord Halifax gave to M. Corbin, French Ambassador in London (December 11) and M. Butler, Parliamentary Under Secretary of State for Foreign Affairs, to Paul-Boncour, France's permanent delegate to the League (December 12). He suffered the Swiss Federal Council to insist in a note forwarded to Joseph Avenol, secretary-general of the League of Nations, that, by reason of Switzerland's perpetual

---

[1]House of Lords, March 19, 1939.

[2]On December 9, while the Council of the League of Nations was holding its first meeting, it became known that Finland was asking certain neutral nations to solicit German mediation of her dispute with Russia. On December 11, the French Minister in Copenhagen reported in a telegram what he had just learned from M. Munch, Danish Foreign Minister. Finland did not consult any of the Scandinavian states before appealing to Geneva, and those states blamed Finland for the step it had taken. On the fourteenth, Denmark and Norway abstained from voting in the Assembly, and Sweden in the Council.

neutrality, the debate must be limited to Soviet aggression and that no discussion of German aggression could be permitted.[3] This was handling the matter in the manner we most desired to avoid, since it tended to make Russia the principal danger and to push Germany into the background.

Geneva's condemnation, after all, was merely moral, and had as much effect on the masters of the Kremlin as water on a duck's back. But, with this condemnation, planes and weapons and munitions were also on the way. And the shipments were to increase steadily in importance. The turning point was at hand. By the end of January the Premier, insofar as the decision rested with him, was ready to comply with Marshal Mannerheim's request for a large Franco-British expeditionary force and not to bother any more about any pretense of merely tolerating the departure of volunteers. Of course, to his mind, the chief advantage of aid to Finland lay in opening the road to Narvik and in an excuse for land and naval operations which would strengthen the blockade.[4] Herr Thyssen, who had just escaped from Germany, maintained that German reserves of iron ore would be made precarious if all outside supplies were cut off. Thus the plan was fairly well cut out. But the essential point was this: fifty-eight thousand French and English troops were allotted to the Finnish campaign, Helsinki was assured that whatever further effectives were deemed necessary would follow in unlimited numbers,[5] and, if need be, the barriers set up by Sweden and Norway would be overthrown by force. No matter what Daladier's intentions might be, we came very near to being entangled in a war with Russia.

The only thing we were waiting for was to be asked officially to intervene: then everything would be put in motion immediately. On March 1, Daladier telephoned to Helsinki, urging that the call to the Western Powers be sent without delay. On March 7, in a note handed to the Finnish Minister in Paris, he entreated those whom he wished to

[3]The Federal Council was submitting to German demands embodied in a note dated December 7. Joseph Avenol, who had the League's Covenant in his care, simply asked the Federal Council to draw up its request in milder terms, which was done.

[4]It is a known fact that M. Magny, French Minister to Helsinki, gave the Finnish Cabinet no other reasons for his government's policy. And for what at the very least was tactlessness he was at once replaced by M. Vaux St. Cyr—who had been appointed to Cuba but who was still in Paris. Subsequently, M. Magny appears to have persuaded the Vichy authorities that his recall from Helsinki, another dirty trick of the Quai d'Orsay, entitled him to a reward, and, under German domination, he served for several months as prefect of the Seine.

[5]Chamberlain, when he addressed the House of Commons to prove that his government had not haggled over numbers, gave a higher figure. It was at the February 4–5 session of the Supreme Council that the fundamental decision was taken.

save in spite of themselves to apply for help. The Finns made use of the Franco-British preparations to secure milder terms from their enemies. They turned their backs on France and England and sent envoys to Moscow to negotiate. Signatures were appended to the treaty on March 12. The French felt that they had been tricked—those who saw in the adventure a good opportunity to put an end to German iron ore imports, those who dreamed of substituting a campaign against Russia for the campaign against Germany, and also those whose ideological inspiration came from Geneva. At once, under this sudden and terrible blow, the Daladier Government tottered. Daladier had secured the united support of the men who wanted to fight the war and the men who wanted appeasement, but it finally turned out that he had done nothing more than supply them all with proof of his incompetence or his bad luck. The opposing factions he had temporarily reconciled were now to join in bringing him to book.

The Daladier who had to face the approaching storm in Parliament was a man whose physical and moral resistance was at a low ebb. The Marquise de Crussol had persuaded him to buy a small house in the forest of Rambouillet, where he often went to spend the week end. On Sunday, January 7, he fell from his horse and broke an ankle. He asked his doctor, Professor Mondor, to employ the most drastic methods of treatment: ultra-red rays and mechanotherapy. For long weeks he was in great pain.

In the secret sitting of February 10 and 11 he rode a wave of success. Having a week earlier overcome Neville Chamberlain's last soul searchings, he knew that, two weeks later, military transports would be lifting anchor to leave for Finland. He was sailing before the wind—at least he felt so. And he spoke to the deputies with an ease, a candor, an absence of reserve to which he had not accustomed them. Agreeably surprised, the Assembly gave him its warm and quasi-unanimous support. Could it be possible, the deputies thought, that he was rid of the defects for which so many had criticized him in recent months—his inclination to be oversuspicious, his irritability at the slightest provocation? As an indirect result of the confidence he inspired, he even managed to save his Air Minister, Guy la Chambre, who had been hammered fairly severely in the initial stages of the debate.

But, a month later, everything was going wrong. Now he despaired of the Finnish undertaking. Finnish plenipotentiaries were at the conference table in Moscow. A storm of criticism burst on him from every section of the Chamber of Deputies. Fernand Laurent, an utter demagogue of the Right, asked leave of the House to question the Premier on "the tragedy of Finland, on the part played by France in this event, and on the conclusions as to the conduct of the war which the government expected to draw from recent military and diplomatic facts." Louis-Oscar Frossard asked leave for a question on "the events in Finland and their consequences"; Léon Blum, on "the events in Finland." Between March 9 and March 17, eight other members had their names put down for addressing the Chamber: Tixier-Vignancourt and Souriaux, who were insane conservatives; Félix Gras, a conservative of the old school, who was soon to die on the battlefield; Ernest Pezet, a Catholic of liberal political views, a sincere and an ingenuous man; Margaine, a Radical-Independent; Gaston Bergery, the Alcibiades of the Left, etc.

On the twelfth, a short discussion broke out: Daladier asked that the debate be postponed a week on the ground that it would be highly improper for the French Chamber of Deputies to go into the matter while the Russo-Finnish conference was still proceeding in Moscow. But in his anxiety to defend himself, or at least to upset his opponents, who, from the right to the left of the House, laid siege to him in a semicircle, he clumsily tossed out a mass of figures and plunged into a detailed exposition of the aid already furnished Mannerheim's troops: 175 planes, 496 cannon of various types, 795,000 shells, 400 mines, 200,000 grenades, 5,000 machine guns, 20 million cartridges, etc. An evident lack of self-control as well as of diplomatic and military prudence. The Premier was exasperated, and no one could get near him. He would unburden himself against Gamelin, against the British, who, by wasting time, had ruined the whole business. On being informed that Winston Churchill would be in Paris for a few hours, he swore up and down that he would not receive him. But all such talk merely betrayed his mood of disappointment and uneasiness and had no lasting meaning. He was exhausted and he was sick.

At the secret sitting of the Senate, on March 14, Laval opened his attack. He rose to speak, almost for the first time in fifty months. During that long period he stepped into the limelight only when, before the Foreign Affairs Committee, he read from documents favorable to the cause of Mussolini and Franco and pleaded in their behalf. The day war was declared he was alone in voting against the financial appropriation asked for by the Cabinet, but said only a few words in explanation. He brooded on his revenge. He followed Daladier's trail of mistakes as a jackal follows a desert caravan. The Finnish setback supplied him with the moment he was awaiting, and he went into action. This time he came boldly out into the open. He developed this theme: at the juncture we have reached we have no alternative but to fight the war, yet, out of sheer weakness, you are well on the way to losing it. Then he took up again his eternal refrain: in order to prevent the conflict or ensure victory if Hitler remained obdurate, he, Laval, had won Italy to our cause: by the Rome agreement of January 7, 1935, and at the Stresa conference of April 1936. But all his achievement had been ruined by the Popular Front, whose spiteful opposition to the dictators was contrary to the nation's interest. And let no one try to use the Spanish War as an argument against Mussolini. The Duce—Laval can prove it—offered to serve as a matchmaker between Franco and the French Republic. Blum's Cabinet did not even condescend to reply to the offer. And with all that, there were people whom the conclusion of the "Steel Pact" had bewildered! Laval would gladly have gone to Rome to re-establish Franco-Italian friendship. He would still be willing to go.

At this point Daladier broke in upon the hostile speech. He disclosed what Count Ciano, on behalf of his father-in-law, had told François-Poncet, Ambassador to the Quirinal, and one of Laval's own henchmen. If the former Premier should report to Rome on a special mission, he would not be welcome.[6]

To appreciate how venomous and how well aimed that arrow was, it must be remembered that during the Abyssinian campaign Mussolini wrote to Laval and reproached him with not having kept his promise of January 1935. According to the Italian dictator, Laval had committed himself, if not actually to further, at least not to hamper in any way, Italian conquests in East Africa. Indeed, Laval succeeded in limiting the sanctions imposed on Italy by Geneva, but he never vetoed them absolutely. He accepted the Home Fleet mobilization in the Mediterranean and did not reject, once for all, the Admiralty's request for eventual use of French naval bases. All he did was to keep discovering reasons why this pledge could not be redeemed. So that the undeniably real assistance which Laval lent to the Duce throughout the crisis remained a secret assistance and only belatedly fulfilled its purpose. The Duce took the position that the help should have been direct, swift, and drastic, and that, since it was not the case, Laval had not carried out the Rome agreement. He had, in fact, given short measure. Laval had merely thrown a spoke into the wheels of Geneva; he had not seized the horse by the bit. In a written reply to this unpleasant communication Laval

[6]François-Poncet, during a stay in Paris, early in April, expatiated endlessly on the subject of this talk with Ciano.

denied the charge and recalled the services he had surreptitiously rendered the Fascist cause—his refusal to approve the embargo on oil insistently demanded by the English.

But Mussolini did not stop there: he sent a second personal message. On the very day he left the Quai d'Orsay (January 30, 1936), Laval, who was anxious not to be seen by his successors in the light of Mussolini's accusations, decided that it would be wise to have the secretary-general draw up a new rebuttal. Thus he borrowed for the occasion the garb of complete Quai d'Orsay orthodoxy. He appropriated to himself the official version of his private conversation at the Farnese Palace with his Fascist guest, not necessarily and even not probably the true one: he had never strayed from the strict letter of existing treaties; he had granted Italy no more than simple freedom of economic action, with the reservation that already existing French interests must not be harmed. And the letter ended on a denial that verbal assurances had ever been given that went further than the official note on Abyssinia handed Mussolini before his departure from Rome, a note which, at the time, the ministry officials had drawn up. After signing the text drafted by the staff of the secretary-general he was heard to exclaim as he took up his hat to go—and it was the last phrase he uttered as he left the Quai d'Orsay—"After all, Mussolini is a bastard and a dirty peddler!" An admission drunk as nectar by those who heard it. Laval had jeopardized the entente with Britain for the sake of the Duce, and such was the outcome! But in March 1940 he was still holding forth as though he had a monopoly on the friendly feelings of the Italian dictator! That dense set of facts lurked behind Daladier's parry of Laval's thrust.

For a moment the disclosure of François-Poncet's testimony brought the scoffers to the side of the government. But as the exchange of letters between the two partners of 1935 and 1936 had been kept secret, the real import of that testimony was not wholly realized. And Laval, counting on the fact that all or nearly all those present were uninformed, proceeded to argue that the snub relayed by the French Ambassador in Rome (if it were to be taken literally, which he questioned) recoiled on the very man who had made it public. Thanks to the minister in office, the quarrel with Italy had reached a point where the most devoted of all "Latin League" promoters were reduced to helplessness.

The episode had no influence on the general course of the discussion in the Senate, which, determined entirely as it was by the news from Finland, ran against the Cabinet. The usual majority began to melt away: sixty members abstained from voting. In five days the Chamber of

Deputies was to meet in secret session: Daladier was getting off to a bad start. Paul Boncour, addressing the senators, had urged the Premier once again to lighten the load of his multiple and arduous duties, to put someone else at the head of the Ministry of Foreign Affairs, and to keep all his strength for a task of co-ordination. Cabinet reconstruction: that might be the means of salvation. A new deal and a new hand to play. But, morose, inert, and dejected, Daladier refused to condescend to palliatives.

It can in all fairness be said that, throughout the sitting of March 19, in the Chamber of Deputies, Daladier made no real effort to save his ministerial existence. He saw himself falling, and he gave way completely. Léon Blum, his most dangerous critic, attacked his intellectual honesty by challenging the accuracy of the figures he had given on March 12. Daladier had to admit that the number of planes sent to Finland was less than he had said. Had he too hastily examined the figures prepared for him? Were the statistics themselves confused and misleading? At all events, no one can suspect him of having willfully deceived Parliament in the juncture. He himself, when the inaccurate details were brought to his attention, sharply rebuked the bureaucrats who had compiled the report.[7] He was hurt and offended by the Socialist leader's gratuitous insinuation. He saw in it the token of an enmity and even a hatred which Léon Blum no longer took the trouble to conceal.[8] Truly the Premier had plenty of documentary evidence at hand that, for

[7]Here arises the question of Daladier's veracity. Did Daladier and, more generally, ministers and officials dealing with national defense, Pierre Cot, Guy la Chambre, etc., tell the truth to Parliament and to parliamentary committees? This only can be safely said: assuredly, facts and figures were deliberately marshaled and even "weighed," so as to impress laymen favorably. Nearly always, inaccurate information of the kind which could have been easily found out was avoided. Besides, the art of the statisticians can be made subservient to any purpose. A simple device consists of lumping together unlikes and passing over the differences in silence. It is worth pointing out that in the Senate committees, which were, perhaps, more alert than the committees of the Chamber, the doubts expressed about the veracity of the Prime Minister mainly concerned the air forces and the anti-aircraft defense. We already know that Daladier had not been able to ascertain for himself the real state of affairs. There seems to be definite evidence that Guy la Chambre went to the length of ordering even still unfinished warplanes to be delivered to units in the war zone so as to improve outward appearances. In December 1939 and in January 1940, General Vuillemin formally protested in writing against such practices. But when all has been said, it is disturbing to read what Edouard Miellet, a close friend of Daladier, president of the Army Commission in the Chamber, had to say in the sitting of March 22, 1938. He declared that "the Army had been provided with all the weapons, all the matériel required for waging a modern war."

[8]Léon Blum, as a matter of fact, actually wished Daladier well and sought to help him. But the latter, urged on by M. Clapier, treated him unfairly, and Blum ended by losing patience and becoming angry.

once, he had been neither indolent nor neglectful. But since his honesty itself had been doubted, what was the use of arguing?

At three in the morning, on March 20, the critical motion was put to the vote. It expressed the confidence of the Assembly in the government and gave it a mandate to "bring France's strength up to a maximum of effectiveness and carry on to final victory a war which was imposed upon us and to defend not only the security of our country but our freedom and the freedom of the world." The motion was passed, but in what a fashion! Members voting: 240. Absolute majority: 121. Votes in favor of the Cabinet: 239. Against: 1. Members not having cast any vote: 300.

Among these three hundred could be numbered more "all-outers" than "appeasers." Irreconcilable men joined in blaming the Premier for spoiling what to all of them—but for different reasons—had seemed to be a great opportunity.

Those who wanted to fight the war condemned him for his personal weakness and lack of dynamic leadership, even more than they censored what they considered the dilatory execution of the plan for intervention in Finland. They opposed Daladier because they hoped for Paul Reynaud. They wanted a stronger hand at the helm. Someone remarked to Léon Blum that Daladier had not deserved to be so harshly brought to book on the Finnish count. Blum answered: "Let's say that he is paying today for the many occasions on which we let him off too easily."

On the other hand, the appeasers hoped that Daladier would be succeeded by someone more inclined toward compromise with the German and Italian dictators. In February, Paul-Boncour, who was himself against any compromise, told me that if anything happened to Daladier, the Laval-Chautemps team, with or without Pétain, would seize power. "The abscess will burst," he added, "and it won't be long then before we have a real war Cabinet." To welcome weak ministers as the prerequisite of stronger ones was a strange road to travel in the midst of a life-and-death struggle. But Paul-Boncour's remark is worth noting. It accounts for the expectations of the "appeasers" on March 20, as to the character of the Cabinet which would succeed Daladier's. They believed that one of them was about to grasp the wheel.

In the automobile which took him through the night to the Elysée, the Premier repeated several times: "Léon Blum does not like me." Always the same tendency to view a political question in terms of personal relationships. He did not say that the Socialist leader, under the circumstances, had been right or wrong, but only that by his attack he had not lived up to the standards prevailing in the republic of political backslappers. And he thought he could see, back of the parliamentary setting, as a potent element, that community of interests between Blum and Reynaud which had long since irritated him. The vote itself, however, and the affront it was for Daladier, had caught everyone unawares. Louis-Oscar Frossard, one of the chief interpellants, had said before the sitting that the Cabinet would incur no serious danger. And, in fact, taken literally, the parliamentary rule did not oblige Daladier to see in the vote more than an expression of the Assembly's bad temper. Technically he had won a majority—the votes not cast did not count—and nothing forced him to resign. But he was at the end of his rope. When he learned that the Finance Minister had been chosen to succeed him he cried out, "Wait and see. In two months a Flandin Cabinet will make a peace." What he meant was that Reynaud's recklessness would bring the war to a disastrous climax.

There was in the vacillating dictator a fundamental pessimism and fatalism. If one can believe a story told among his friends, which goes back to the time of his first premiership in the summer of 1933, a fortuneteller had predicted that his star would suffer an eclipse, that later on he would return to power and would dominate the nation, but that he would be struck down at last, and politically annihilated. Daladier did not like being reminded of this anecdote and in the end said it was invented out of nothing. At times he labored under a feeling of impending and immense misfortune. He would then be silent for long hours, haggard, fascinated by the fate that awaited him. "The people of France will not forgive the Premier who loses the war, even if he is beyond reproach. A fate awaits you which, compared to what they did to me twenty-two years ago, will be like rose water," Caillaux cried out to him one day, Caillaux, the Prince of Appeasers, whom time had stripped of his former rashness. Daladier accepted the sacrifice he foresaw.

In February 1939 he had considered getting himself elected to the presidency of the Republic.[9] He would have asked for nothing better than to have handed over his heavy burden to someone else. But he could not conscientiously make a bid for the vote of the National Assembly without first having made sure of a capable successor. In September 1920, Alexandre Millerand, in order to go to the Elysée, had left the premiership to a clumsy politician, and the vigorous application of the Treaty of Versailles, begun by him, was the sufferer. The conduct of a man who, in the Europe of 1939, followed his example would be judged even more severely. Another point also had to be considered. For three

[9] The election took place on April 5.

years it had been Daladier's duty to organize the defense of the nation. His becoming President of the Republic would in no way have lightened his responsibility. The events which inevitably were to assay and test his military policy would simply have been set in motion by another hand: there could be no other difference. The ring of fate had closed round him. No way lay open for evasion. If nothing else, the consciousness he had of past mistakes riveted him to his post.

The only strength of this spineless man was that he represented fairly well the average Frenchman of his time. There seems to be no other explanation for the long years of his extraordinary good fortune which caused Camille Chautemps to exclaim with envy: "What insolence there is in his luck!" Daladier was the embodiment of the last ten years of the Republic. Cast in the mold of an easygoing regime, he was no man to make it totalitarian in the face of total war. His success as a politician, his failure as a statesman, France's miserable doom—these were three effects of one single cause.

The very reasons which prevented him from being a true leader enabled him to hold the balance between parties and factions. With his fall there began a series of political convulsions which increased in frequency and intensity while the military body of the nation struggled and died.

SECTION III: PAUL REYNAUD: ABORTIVE ATTEMPT AT DYNAMISM

I

Uneasy Beginnings

ON TWO IMPORTANT OCCASIONS personal decisions of M. Albert Lebrun, President of the Republic, weighed heavily on our country's destiny. At dawn, on March 20, he offered Paul Reynaud the premiership. Three months later, on June 21, the culminating point of disaster, although seemingly determined to transfer the seat of government to North Africa in order to carry on the fight at England's side, he let himself be intimidated by the counterrevolution, shelved the heroic and reasonable plan, and collapsed pitifully amid the ruins of constitutional law. He stood aloof while Pétain and Laval set their dictatorial regime going and imposed unlimited surrender.

Never did the Elysée shelter such a weakling. It is a paradox that, in the long line of French Presidents, Lebrun alone, apart from Jules Grévy, obtained a second seven-year term. One would have thought that such a President of the Republic could be found only in a Labiche comedy. When he was first elected and then re-elected the newspapers printed pictures of Mercy-le-Haut, his native village in Lorraine, and pictures of his brother, the farmer, with legs trussed up in leather. If only Lebrun had remained a tiller of the soil! What a pity that he ever passed the difficult examinations for the Ecole Polytechnique, then graduated at the head of his class, and finally became the most commonplace specimen of middle-class mediocrity! How could a competent engineer be so small a man? Two words describe him: perpetual panic.

Every diplomatic and military move seemed to him pregnant with unspeakable risks. He would put his head in his hands, work himself into a frenzy of worry, moan aloud as he read the diplomatic dispatches, telephone right and left to tell people his anxieties, to advise caution, to ask for explanations, to invoke his patriotic vigilance, to beg forgiveness of those he was bothering and exasperating. At the time of the negotiations with the Turks, in September and October 1939, he kept insisting that everything they asked should be granted them—even if it meant reducing the treaty to an empty shell. Naturally fascist sales talk found him helpless on every occasion. Georges Bonnet never failed to look upon him as an ally.

Over and above all this he was a politician—and far from a brave one. For example, as "co-Prince" of Andorra, he declined to endorse certain dubious contracts—fathered by the Minister of Public Works, Anatole de Monzie—for the establishment of a radio station in that republic. He forced the Minister to stop promoting them. But immediately after doing so he was hard put to it to make Monzie forget that apparent courage which deserved only to be called undiluted fear. He always tried to prevent anyone, especially anyone of "good social position," from harboring any lasting ill feeling toward him.

Women could maneuver him up to a point. An English Becky Sharp, who had spun her web around two or three cabinet ministers, kept writing him political letters to which he was only too inclined to pay attention. His speeches, delivered in a stentorian voice, were sentimental and flowery. Incongruously enough, he had the gift of tears. Two counselors, both unique specimens of the breed, followed in his wake. The secretary-general of the presidency of the Republic was a man called Magre, brother of a fairly well known poet. He reveled in good food, songs, and occasional rhymes, as became an ideal citizen in a republic of Toulouse. His ambition, of course, was to end up in some quiet and comfortable retreat, and rumors and alarms of war were to him merely objectionable, spoilsport nuisances to be held off at a proper distance. The head of the military staff, General Braconnier, grew a beard such as had not been seen in Paris for forty years. That adornment impelled Daladier to exclaim: "Lebrun surely must have fished him out of the 1870 army!" A plump and convivial fellow but also an honest man.

That through the interplay of political rivalry, and thanks to the principle "Let the most insignificant among us come up on top," the republic of Poincaré, Clemenceau, or even Fallières—who was not devoid of shrewdness and who spoke frankly—should have had this silly creature to lead it through the most serious hour of its history is enough to make one believe that it stood judged and condemned by Providence. One Premier after another had held Lebrun up to ridicule. One Premier after another—with scarcely an exception—had helped keep him supreme.

M. Lebrun had no fondness for anyone who strayed from the path of his own petty conformity. The changing of the guard, in the early morning of March 20, with Reynaud and Blum coming in, could not have been a ceremony to his taste. One day Léon Blum, then in office as Premier, had expressed to him the now rather commonplace view that a balanced budget was a mirage in a period of economic crisis. He threw up his hands in horror. Had Blum requested him to stand on his head, he would not have felt more deeply outraged. I imagine that Reynaud, in his attempts to warn him against the disastrous effects of the gold standard, in the years 1934-35, must have seemed to him a sophist and a swindler.

Instinctively he tried to make Daladier change his mind when the latter brought him his letter of resignation. To convince the outgoing Premier that the confidence of Parliament could be easily won back again, he put the most narrowly legalistic construction possible on the vote in the Chamber of Deputies. Moreover, he argued that if the Premier had reconstructed his Cabinet or even had taken the slight trouble to appoint a Minister of Information—as he had promised formally to do before Parliament in December—matters would never have come to such a pass. The errors he had committed could still be retrieved. But Daladier would have none of it. And besides, Jeanneney and Herriot, who were qualified under constitutional practice to express the feeling of the two Chambers, sharply maintained that the premiership had to go to the Finance Minister. Lebrun would have been acting entirely out of character if he had openly resisted them. He yielded and at once sent for Reynaud.

Perhaps he thought that to put Reynaud immediately to the test would very likely be giving him the rope to hang himself. Perhaps Daladier agreed with Lebrun that no better tactics than these were available to get rid of a scatterbrained busybody once and for all.

In normal times this method had been used by various presidents of the Republic to do away with men whose rise to power they wished to prevent but whose claim they were obliged to take seriously. They would not call in the man on whom their heart was set until egoistic ambitions and interests, feverishly unleashed directly the premiership became vacant, had first clashed and then subsided, until the two or three candidates they wanted to keep out had sweated blood at the task of forming a cabinet and had admitted their inability to do so. Reynaud's friends have always suspected that such a trap had been set for him.

Four sets of enemies awaited a chance to knife Reynaud before he could succeed in setting up his ministry. First there was the ex-Premier himself, vehement and angry. Then the great moguls of the Radical-Socialist party, the men who ran the party committees. They clung to the belief that the numerically strongest party in the Senate and even in the House—for the Socialists, discredited by the Popular Front and incapable of uniting the country behind them, did not count—had an innate right to monopolize cabinet leadership. Still more to be feared were the avowed or hidden zealots for immediate peace. Finally, the patriots of the Right had to be reckoned with. While wholeheartedly demanding that the war be pursued with the greatest energy, they keenly resented the anticipated entry of Léon Blum's friends into the Cabinet. In the aggregate a formidable coalition was forming.

Reynaud's alarm lasted but a moment. Then he dove headlong into the deep. I well remember something said by his secretary—then my assistant at the *Echo de Paris*—some fifteen years ago: "He will soon be fifty, and he hasn't yet been a cabinet member!" In 1940 he was over sixty, and he had not yet been Premier. The attraction of the honor he had so long coveted was so strong that it blunted his critical sense. Why did it happen that Mme. de Portes, his mistress, was out of town?[1] Ever since the autumn she had been dreaming of a Ministry of National Union in which Daladier, shorn of his primacy, would serve with "Paul" and Laval as equals under Pétain. Had she been in Paris, she would have rebelled at the inclusion of the "Marxists." Perhaps her wrangling would have shipwrecked the nascent ministerial structure. The name of that woman has already been mentioned incidentally, but henceforward her words and deeds will have their share in shaping events. On March 21 she could only telephone, and that was not enough.

Reynaud won a first advantage, incomplete but greater than it was reasonable to expect. Daladier agreed to remain as Minister for National Defense and for War, and did so without waiting to find out what his party thought about it. This was against the rules, and the moguls protested bitterly. "Patriotism would not allow me to act otherwise," he retorted to them. Patriotism? But since he considered his rival's accession to the premiership a public scourge, what then of patriotism? Let us say rather that he did not openly wish to be the rock on which Reynaud would founder. However, he took care not to lift a finger to secure help for the new Premier from his Radical-Socialist brethren. One word from him would have persuaded Chichery, who headed the Radical-Socialist members of Parliament, to accept Reynaud's invitation and enter the Cabinet. He did not utter that word. His conduct was not unlike "non-belligerency," as the Italians understood it. Besides, as Minister for National Defense in time of war, he would hold the Premier at his mercy and he would be the real master of the government: such was his plan.[2]

Reynaud's second success came from the Socialists. Their parliamentary membership accepted his offer to participate by 81 votes against 7, with 5 abstentions. This was a success which he by no means expected. To avoid offending the Right, no cabinet post was offered Léon Blum, the official leader of the Socialist party. Therefore many party members felt anger and humiliation at being given access to the halls of authority by the back door.

[1]She had gone to Arcachon for her son's first communion. I have been shown a letter she wrote to Reynaud, which strayed into a third person's possession. "You have taken advantage of my absence to let in the Socialists," she said. "You will play no more such tricks."

[2]Cf. A. de Monzie, *Ci-devant:* ". . . I had quite a long telephone conversation with Daladier. . . . I wanted to find out whether or not he was willing to enter Reynaud's cabinet line-up. After having demonstrated that this line-up would not work, Daladier admitted to me that he was willing to participate. In any case, he told me, we had better not leave him all alone."

To offset this gain of the Prime Minister designate, Rucart, Minister of Justice, under the Popular Front and an important Free Mason, immediately mobilized the lodges against the cabinet in process of formation. Foreseeing that his tenure of office would hang by a thread and that his fate might be settled on the first encounter with Parliament, Reynaud—at a time when boldness would have meant wisdom—lacked the courage to play for really high stakes. He dared not shut his ears to the clamor of the cliques; he dared not form a homogeneous, united, determined, and competent cabinet, take from the start a stand far above all considerations of political groups and selfish interests, ordinary politicians' combinations and compromises. Far from it: he stuffed his Cabinet with thirty-five senators and deputies. Twenty-five of them were shabby ministerial hacks, the flotsam of those two dozen cabinets which had for the most part mismanaged public affairs since Poincaré's departure in 1929: Chautemps, Laurent Eynac, Henri Roy, Lamoureux, Sarraut, Frossard, Rio, Marcel Héraud, Hippolyte Ducos, and even the Monzie-Pomaret twins.[3] What hope of giving new life to the government, what break with the past could these worn-out, faded, and discredited puppets bear out? This Reynaud Cabinet was worth just about as much as the one Daladier had not been able to make up his mind to reform. It was not an improvement. Now, as before, the Cabinet was conceived as a microcosm of Parliament, with the grandees of the Republic as monopolists.

Reynaud, shaken beforehand by the blows he knew would fall, did precisely what he had blamed others for doing. The plans he had for drastic reform were left in the cloakroom; he plunged straight into the most sordid parliamentary game. Since he was not a good craftsman on the lower plane of politics, and since he had no flair for backstage arrangements, he at once made a double mistake. Whereas six Socialists were included in the new Cabinet—three of them as under secretaries of state—the most influential group of the Right, the Republican Federation, was left in the cold. That Socialists of proven patriotism should be given cabinet rank and responsibility was entirely proper. It meant strengthening their influence with their own party, where numerous pacifists were buzzing about, and with the working class, where so many men in the allegiance of the Third International continued their

---

[3] Cf. A. de Monzie, *Ci-devant:* "Reynaud entreated me to stay on. I pointed out our differences regarding Italy. 'Monzie,' he replied, 'I repeat that I approve of what you do to make Italy persist in her neutrality. My offer is particularly intended to assert good will toward Italy!'"

undermining activities. But, to balance Socialist participation, those leaders of the Right who had given proof of their devotion to national interests ought to have had a chance to join. Reynaud stubbornly refused to place more than one cabinet post at the disposal of M. Louis Marin, deputy from Nancy and president of the Republican Federation. Marin claimed three and would have settled at two. His enmity could easily have been forestalled. The Premier, who detested him, shrugged his shoulders and went his way. Nor did he avoid another false step. He refused to appoint as Finance Minister M. Abel Gardey, a Radical-Socialist of the conservative type and a power in the Senate, simply not to offend M. Bouthillier, secretary-general at the Ministry of Finance, whom this politician did not like.

In its reaction to the Reynaud Cabinet, the country was rent asunder. The thin veneer of national unity with which Daladier had covered partisan discord immediately cracked up. All those who wanted to revive the policy of Munich while there was still time to do so, thanks to the "truce" granted by Hitler, broke out in a paroxysm of disapproval. They saw the Socialists, who had abstained in a body from taking part in the vote which brought Daladier's fall, now reinvading the Cabinet after two years' absence.[4] How could the evidence be resisted? Obviously the two "warmongers" of 1938–39, Reynaud and Blum, had contrived together to oust from office all their opponents and had brought back the executive authority to the control of the Left—that is, the Popular Front. In Paris drawing rooms, at officers' messes in the field, everywhere, the same charge was made.

Paul Reynaud faced the Chamber of Deputies on March 22. I shall always remember that evening. We sat for hours, awaiting the outcome. As the debate went on a friend telephoned me, an extreme conservative but one who had never been blind to the German peril. He found it hard to keep calm. "The House is split in two," he told me; "those who want to fight the war and those who, setting up as a deliberate policy the military caution forced on Daladier by circumstance and chiefly concerned with fighting Russia, have in mind to reverse our alliances and negotiate peace with Germany." Throughout this meeting national defense did not seem to be a live issue. It did not spirit the

---

[4] In April 1938, when the Daladier Cabinet was formed after the Senate's refusal to grant "full powers" to Blum's second Cabinet, the defeated Socialists withdrew sulkily to their tents. On September 13, 1939, during the cabinet reconstruction which followed the declaration of war, the party's executive committee voted non-participation by 18 to 11, partly because it did not get what it thought a fair share of influence, partly because the Cabinet's make-up did not correspond to the Socialist formula for a war government.

Assembly. Two Radical-Socialists, emerging from the most obscure ranks of unknown caucus men, Galimand and Badie, rose to ejaculate their party's rancor at being deprived of the premiership. "Although addressing the Chamber on my own account," said one of them, "what I have to say is concerned with the anxieties of those who consider they are the true majority and insist that they must be treated as such." The other expostulated about "the reckless and dangerous scheming of those who care nothing about human lives and are willing to make them so cheap." Thus discoursed clansmen with sordid minds. Then Fernand Laurent put on the Russo-Italian tune: "In this war our only chance to strike a blow is on Russian territory; that is a matter of simple common sense. To foster our hope let us look at Italy!" And he charged Reynaud, in his capacity of Finance Minister, with having inflated the currency. Reynaud had read the new Cabinet's declaration of policy, which was, in style, reminiscent of Corneille: "We conquer and all is saved; we succumb, and we lose all. . . . The stakes in this total conflict are total stakes." But after those fine words how pitifully he tried to disarm all his critics! He even fulsomely praised the man he loathed: "No one of us has forgotten the painful lessons of the World War. There are blunders we shall never make again. I know how the House feels about it. Often and deservedly it applauded M. Daladier for having been so considerate of our soldiers' lives." And to conciliate the conservatives he spoke of Germany as "helped by Soviet treachery." Léon Blum delivered the only speech worthy of the hour. He dismissed contemptuously all the current talk which had him plotting with the new Premier against the old. He challenged anyone to point out the slightest lapse in the constant support which for the last six months he had given the Cabinet committed to conducting the war. He implored the Radical-Socialists not to break irreparably with the Socialists. But toward the end of his oration an unfortunate reference to the heads of the great industries stirred up in the hearts of many on the Right and Center benches a sense of social insecurity.

A relative of mine in command of a battalion behind the Maginot Line was dining with us before returning to the front. At the mention of Blum both he and his wife became enraged. They proclaimed loudly that it was all thanks to that Jew that we had been thrown into the struggle with Hitler, and they went away excited and angry. I felt as though the debate in the House had suddenly burst into my own study. After forty years the Dreyfus affair had blazed up again, and how vastly more tragic!

Reynaud was saved by only one vote. "The Chamber, approving the statement of ministerial policy and trusting in the Ministry to awaken and lead all the nation's energies to victory . . . proceeds with the business of the day." Out of 424 votes which had been cast, 268 were for the Cabinet and 156 against. However, 111 abstentions had been registered, and the Premier, after what had happened to Daladier, was obliged to consider them as hostile. Three fourths of the Radical-Socialists, despite the ten cabinet posts allotted to their party, had gone against the Cabinet either by their votes or by their abstentions. At ten that night Pierre Laval telephoned his accomplice, General de Chambrun: "They are bound to resign."

Reynaud had not given a good account of himself. He was nervous and fidgety. He had not been able to find the happy phrase which carries off the audience. He had seemed unsure of himself, he whose more usual fault was to be cocksure. He thought he saw the hand of Daladier and a trap everywhere. It fell to Georges Mandel to strike a convincing note of encouragement: "You are up against bitter foes. Don't forget that members like Montigny are fighting to save their skins. But the House will not meet again until April 2. Let's take advantage of the respite given us and go ahead with our work; we shall be judged by what we can get done. If you manage to achieve something, you won't lose a single vote. Rather you will continuously win more."

Reynaud set to work. At the two cabinet meetings held in close succession after the debate in the Chamber—the first on the evening of March 22, the second on the morning of March 23—he called on his Radical-Socialist colleagues for a showdown. Could he possibly believe that they wholeheartedly stood by him? In the voting only thirty-four of their friends and followers had supported the Cabinet. The ten ministers thus challenged to make their position clear withdrew to another room to settle the issue among themselves. By Georges Mandel's watch they remained behind closed doors for thirty-eight minutes. Daladier wanted to quit. He had resigned the premiership on the admission that abstentions should be interpreted as votes against him. What was sauce for the goose was also sauce for the gander. Chautemps, Campinchi, Queuille, and Lamoureux disputed this view. Their strongest argument was that to condemn a cabinet which had renewed the Socialist alliance before even allowing it a chance to prove its worth amounted to refusing collaboration with the Socialists under any circumstances whatever. And it would mean disaster for the party in future elections. The ten decided to stay on, but Reynaud received no assurance of loyal support.

They said they would do what they could. They were in no position to answer for the outcome, the rule of the party being that each member was free to act as he pleased when the Premier had not been selected from its ranks and when members accepting cabinet posts had been given no definite mandate to do so.

For several days after this meeting Daladier continued to wonder whether he should not break away. On the twenty-third, he very nearly called a meeting of the party's parliamentary caucus under pressure from Guy la Chambre, Bonnet, and their friends. He was now cut off from the officials of the Ministry of Foreign Affairs who, all through two long years, had kept him more or less on the straight path. He was left to himself. In his eagerness to oppose Reynaud, he did not seem to mind which ground he was moving to. Indeed, he behaved at times as though he had, all of a sudden, turned an appeaser. Blum's enemy, Paul Faure, who had submitted a proposal for immediate peace with Germany to the Socialist group in the Chamber of Deputies on the very day the Cabinet had been formed, visited him several times. However, notwithstanding Radical-Socialist rancor, the immediate danger threatening Reynaud's Cabinet had been averted.

Reynaud planned to stifle disaffection in his Cabinet through the prestige that would ensue from some quick diplomatic success. What, then, were the problems on the agenda of the Quai d'Orsay and the General Staff which his long-pent-up vitality could hastily ripen and make fruitful? He looked round for them at a meeting of the War Cabinet on March 23. On request, Alexis Léger, secretary-general at the Ministry of Foreign Affairs, had to extemporize a broad survey of all pending business. Pondering over what he heard from him, Reynaud came to the conclusion that this was the time to pull out of the files—where it had lain dormant since December—the draft for a Franco-British treaty to exclude all separate negotiations with the enemy, either for an armistice or for peace. Both Houses had condemned Daladier's apathy. Considerations which in December had compelled Daladier to feel his ground very carefully in his search for closer solidarity between Paris and London no longer had any force.

But as the discussion went on, clever Colonel de Villelume, liaison officer between the Quai d'Orsay, Vincennes, and La Ferté-sous-Jouarre, grasped his lucky hour with great insight. To the delight of the Premier, he propounded an idea still more alluring perhaps than the contemplated treaty with England: a plan for action in Norwegian territorial waters. He served up a neat little speech, brilliant in the breadth of its outlook, which caused Reynaud's ears to prick up. At last Reynaud had to deal with a soldier whose mental horizon went beyond official papers of a technical and negative nature! A war is always lost by the side which cannot bring to bear numerical superiority, explained the colonel. France and England must necessarily avoid finally joining the issue with the Nazis until their resources in men and armaments had been mobilized much further. Meanwhile all they could do was to fall back on economic warfare—that is, to strike at German preparations. What we had so far done in that respect had proved deceptive because only on the sea lanes had we attempted to intercept the raw materials and industrial products which Germany must have to wage war. Out of deference to the susceptibilities of the neutrals, the blockade we had set up to date fell far short of the 1918 precedent. Let us take short cuts![5] Why not obstruct at their source the raw materials used by the Reich? Oil and iron were the fundamentally important instruments of this war, and the Reich had only limited supplies of them. As to oil, there was nothing we could do, since it would take a long time to persuade the British to move on to the Caucasus. There remained Sweden's iron ore and the Norwegian waters through which most of it found its way to Germany. We had already wasted three months looking into the question. The hour had come for us to act on a large scale.

Reynaud asked for a meeting of the Supreme Council to be called immediately. Through Sir Ronald Campbell, British Ambassador in Paris, all was speedily arranged. Four days later the Premier rushed to London. On the twenty-eighth, he did not conceal from Neville Chamberlain, whom he met at luncheon, that, to silence his parliamentary opposition, he must be allowed to score heavily in the diplomatic field. The British Prime Minister had an uneasy conscience. He had a very high opinion of Daladier and felt that his own evasive and dilatory policy with regard to Finland had weakened that Minister's position and possibly brought about his ruin. He had, he felt, deprived France of a capable leader. He was morally bound to help her find another. Winston Churchill frowned upon the suggested undertaking in Norway: he saw nothing but trouble ahead. He disapproved of taking such a jump in the dark. However, he did not insist. Reynaud got almost everything he asked for.

At the Supreme Council meeting, on March 28, Chamberlain not only committed himself to a joint declaration which ruled out any separate

[5] As a matter of fact, in relation to Norway, the Caucasus, and the Black Sea, all such notions had been handled by Gamelin and the General Staff in numerous memoranda.

negotiation for an armistice and for peace—he had always been more or less in favor of making some such agreement—but he also promised that the Franco-British alliance would continue after the end of hostilities and even that it would become the principal instrument for the reconstruction of Europe. He pledged himself to enforcing "positive guarantees" of security against a defeated Germany. The two nations must come to an agreement beforehand so as to be able to discuss adequately any peace proposals reaching them, either through a third power or directly from the enemy—and neutrals should have no voice in the matter. In this way and from the start any possible recrudescence of the 1918–19 visionary theorizing would be avoided. Formerly, the head of the London Cabinet had never been in a mood for alienating to such an extent his freedom of action.[6] He endorsed the formulas hastily drafted by the Ambassador of France, secretary-general of the Quai d'Orsay, who had accompanied Reynaud to London.

As to the forcible measures to be carried out in Norwegian territorial waters, Neville Chamberlain yielded to the arguments which the French had vainly been advancing ever since December. He instructed the Admiralty to lay mine fields along the Norwegian shores, in that "sheltered channel" where the Swedish iron ore could pass undisturbed on its coastwise journey toward Germany and Nazi submarines lurk in safety to attack merchant shipping on the Atlantic route. All through the winter French diplomacy had striven to set the British Navy on that task, either directly, by persuading the Whitehall Admiralty frankly and openly to seize control of Norwegian coastal waters, or indirectly, by the means of the expedition to Finland. When, on February 16, the British boarded and captured the *Altmark*, the French had believed that, with little incitement on their part, the London Cabinet would become entangled in direct action: all it had to do was to follow up the deed of its sailors. But at once Mr. Chamberlain and his colleagues had backed out on the plea that they must not allow Scandinavian resentment to erect a barrier against the plan to send an expeditionary force to Helsinki. Now that the opportunity provided by the Finnish War had vanished, no choice was left: it was a case of making naked force felt in Norwegian waters or of dropping the whole business. Reynaud tipped the scales in favor of direct action.

[6]Under the terms of the Anglo-French financial agreement of December, it had been settled that Interallied solidarity would not end with peace. But this clause had a time limit and did not concern general policy.

The Prime Minister, however, made his acceptance conditional. He said the British public would not understand violence against neutral Norway while our warplanes and our mines still spared the Germans in their homeland. He took this opportunity to put forward again the British plan which Albert Lebrun had blocked a few weeks before. He insisted on mines being laid in the Rhine, where barges plied their trade to and fro as quietly as in the happiest days of peace.[7] Reynaud undertook to win the President of the Republic to that operation. He returned to Paris greatly pleased with himself.

He was immediately and sharply brought face to face with the fact that a French Premier who does not directly control the Ministry of National Defense cannot claim to determine war policies.[8] Daladier, whose hatred toward his successor partook of a physical impulse, made a point of censuring all that had been accomplished in London without him.[9] In his opinion Reynaud had not made the British pay a high enough price for the declaration prohibiting a separate peace. The charge was merely rhetorical, and it could not be made to stick. Besides, Daladier had to realize that this agreement from which he had kept clear in December, on the ground of inopportunity, now suited changed circumstances. But it was within his power to veto Chamberlain's demand that the Rhine be mined as a counterpart for British intervention in Norwegian waters. And he was not slow to blast: "If you comply with the request, you bring the war to a crisis which you are not prepared to meet." Everything that had been settled was thrown once more into the melting pot.

It took Reynaud several days to convince the British Cabinet that it was contrary to all good sense to give up a military plan, recognized as useful, merely because another plan, not immediately related to it, could

[7] See page 47, note 5.

[8] The Law of July 11, 1938 (organization of the nation in time of war), Articles 3, 4, and 5, gave the Premier superior authority in matters concerning "the upkeep of the military forces in personnel and matériel," "the utilization of all national resources," the co-ordination of the three departments of War, Navy, and Air. But the law also had a provision that the Premier "may delegate his power of direction and co-ordination of national defense to a minister who shall assume the title of Minister of National Defense." And, in actual practice, no Minister of National Defense was ever likely to accept the active control of the Premier as defined in the law. Daladier was asserting an independence that, in his place, all others would have claimed.

[9] His excuse for not going to London with Reynaud had been a broken ankle. The clash between Reynaud and Daladier took place at the War Cabinet meeting of March 29. Gamelin, as I have already said, sided with the Premier, and General Georges with the Minister for National Defense. See page 47.

not be simultaneously executed. The letter or diplomatic note in which he expatiated on that theme finally persuaded the British ministers, but meanwhile the document stolen from Gamelin's rooms in a London hotel[10] had probably informed the Germans of the Allies' intentions, and the delay enabled them to profit by the warning.

On the morning of April 8 the British fleet, supported by French destroyers, mined Norway's territorial waters. The very next day brought Germany's smashing return thrust: Denmark and Norway were invaded by the Wehrmacht; Oslo was taken; German ships—having left port three or four days earlier—landed troops at Narvik, Egersund, Trondheim, Stavanger. We were disarrayed. The rulers of the sea (who, unfortunately, did not control the air) had been caught napping in their own domain! French and British ministers met on the afternoon of April 9 to decide how to parry the blow. The public, however, was not disturbed. The official communiqués of March 28 had been keyed to a triumphant tone. Weren't they harbingers of victory? Most people thought that Reynaud had set in motion a sequence of auspicious events. When, on April 4, he received the Executive Committee of the Radical-Socialist group in the Chamber, all was plain sailing for him. He got their support. He put to rout all ill-willed moguls among them. And on April 13—earlier than London had dared hope—British warships forced their way into the narrow neck of Narvik fiord.

For two weeks Reynaud was exultant. He was cheered in the House of Deputies and even in the Senate, where, certainly, he was no favorite. He finally recovered his usual eloquence, an eloquence which had failed him in the initial parliamentary debate on March 22 but had worked wonders on March 28, it was said, behind the closed doors at 10 Downing Street. His voice, crisp and sharp, his firmness in phrasing, stood out in happy contrast to Daladier's far too indecisive manner. Many were those who felt that, in this hour of France's need, a new Clemenceau had at last risen. Reynaud gave the nation a tonic stimulus. The blissful days were to prove short. But, however quickly they went by, it was made plain that a mere semblance of dynamic leadership could attune the French people to its war task and, at a single stroke, heal up the schism that, since 1934, had torn it asunder. The Premier had borne up and steered right onward in accordance with Mandel's exhortations and he had fulfilled the latter's forecast. He had won a position of omnipotence not unlike Daladier's semidictatorship, and he was thought capable of making it pregnant with good results. Daladier's friends began to

[10]See page 48.

spread the rumor that he was getting tired of such a close association with vainglorious Reynaud and that it would not be long before he turned his back on the Cabinet.

2

Reynaud Is No Longer the Man He Was

AT THIS JUNCTURE OF THE WAR, where, in retrospect, the seeds of terrible developments seem to have been lodged, we must break from our story and take Reynaud's measure. Did he really give promise of becoming a second Clemenceau? Was not our judgment misled by a keen desire to see the statesman of a heroic age reborn in some one of the French cabinet ministers?

It cannot be gainsaid that Reynaud's mind is alert, lively, brilliant; by comparison, most public men of our time look of an inferior caliber. Reynaud is endowed with the kind of intelligence which many deem more powerful than perhaps it really is. He has a very special gift for molding the most abstract concepts into striking formulas which everyone can understand. He is unequaled at summing up his thoughts in a few words which seize hold of one's memory. In controversy he clings to the point at issue and strips the problem of every superfluous, casual element that should have no bearing upon the decision. He is a past master at the Voltairian art of clarification. And his clear ideas hold up under analysis—which cannot always be said of Voltaire's. They are not only clear but also "distinct," the characteristic mark of a good intellect.

Between 1930 and 1940 this cerebral mechanism turned out some remarkably sane products. Alone, or almost alone, he preached—as early as 1932-33—that it was folly to keep the franc at its gold content of 1926 when the level of world prices had, since 1929, dropped 50 or even seventy-five per cent or more for certain raw materials—and when England and the United States had, successively, lowered their cost of production by means of devaluation, not to speak of the systematic flexibility of the British currency. If, in 1933-34, Reynaud had been Premier instead of Daladier, or Minister of Finance instead of Georges Bonnet, he would not have been guilty of that fatal error of financial and economic management wherein history needs must find one of the most genuine causes of the division of the country into a "Right" and a "Left" hostile to each other and irreconcilable. He would not have sacrificed the growth of the national income to a narrow and old-fashioned idea of balancing the budget. He would have known that such a balance was unattainable and even fatal as long as the nation's economic body had not been put under careful treatment and had not begun to recuperate. He would not have put the cart before the horse, as all the others stubbornly did. For many years his attention had been riveted on the excellent remedies which were finally applied, during his tenure at the Treasury, between November 1938 and March 1940.[1] He had kept on vindicating them, in a long succession of speeches, against a crowd of ignorant critics.

Reynaud's methods as Minister of Finance thwarted and crossed the benighted orthodoxy of the old Bank of France as well as the new dispensation of the Popular Front. Similarly, in opposition to the army chiefs Pétain, Weygand, Gamelin, and Georges, he tried to break new ground. He recognized and brought out the character of modern warfare. A glance through his books, *Young Men, What Kind of France Do You Wish For?* and *The French Military Problem*,[2] testifies to his innovating spirit. He felt very keenly that a deep renovation was overdue in all aspects of national life. He dreamed of rescuing France from bourgeois stagnation. Laval's miserable foreign policy had no sharper and more pertinent critic: his indictment thereof on December 27, 1935,[3] includes almost everything worth saying. In the same way he exposed the backsliding of Pierre-Etienne Flandin on March 7, 1936, while there was still time to minimize some of its consequences. Courageously he had come forward for an understanding with Russia. One could not help but be moved at seeing him from year to year ever wholly devoted to the task of pointing out what would best serve the public interests, ever scornful of party ties and indifferent to party interests. He exposed in turn the errors of the conservatives and those of the Socialists. He good-humoredly put up with unpopularity and never pandered to any group whatever. More important still, pontiffs, augurs, and pundits did not impress him, even if gathered in colleges, even if called Bank of France

[1]Despite mistakes in details, traceable to Bouthillier.

[2]April 1936 and May 1937.

[3]There we come across this phrase: "Among all great nations, France alone is endangered in her very existence."

or General Staff. With greater justification perhaps than Lamartine, he could have boasted that "his seat was on the ceiling."[4]

However, by April 1940, that critical hour in Reynaud's destiny, weak spots could be detected. Two or three of his intimates (who, however, did not speak until later) were not deceived in their judgment.

As Premier, he was too prone to syllogize for the determination of his policy. He offered a perfect example of the "reasoner who overdoes it," or, in French words, of *"raison raisonnante."* By this I mean that the "geometrical mind" in him was only slightly tempered with intuition, flair, instinctive discernment, those qualities of the intellect which, in their silent workings, impel the reflective process toward the right action. Moreover, he was too much taken up by amusements, by those endless Paris lunches and dinners where a cabinet minister is expected to make an exhibition of himself and feels bound to shine before fools and knaves. No time was left for meditation, for thinking in solitude. Yet, less than all others, a logical mind cannot do without such concentration and respite lest it fall into superficiality. Reynaud was forever clarifying what passed through his head in haphazard conversations with Peter and Paul. Poincaré, Clemenceau, Millerand, Briand hardly ever went out. Reynaud was always out. His way of living condemned him to be perpetually on the hop, skip, and jump.

A man accustomed to thinking aloud as he wrangles with an interlocutor instinctively wants to have the last word. He cannot be content to look to future events for self-vindication. It is not enough for him to be ultimately right; he hardly tolerates, even if only for a moment, to be outwardly wrong. But political speculation and anticipation of the future, to be solid and of lasting value, must necessarily keep clear of current opinion, be directed toward long-range verification, and remain unaffected from day to day by negative facts and circumstances. In the years of his great struggles Reynaud had the requisite patience. The exercise of power now made it a necessity for him to receive the hourly approbation of politicians. The test of the premiership found him wanting in serenity, even in stability. Ever anxious to make the most of his short stature, standing aggressively on high heels, he had always been arrogant. Much had been forgiven him because of the soundness of his doctrine. In the service of a good cause, his slightly irritating quest for telling phrases and paradoxes (a sure way, sometimes, to get into pit-

---

[4] At the general elections of 1936, in the second electoral district of Paris, he was squeezed in between a Communist and a Fascist candidate, the latter sponsored by Laval. He was returned by a scanty majority of twenty-seven votes.

falls) had been overlooked.[5] But an unsteady man does not merit such indulgence.

In the last two years Reynaud had deeply changed. His will power, strained to the extreme and feverishly excited, was often wasted and lost in contradictory moves. He made up his mind too easily on the spur of the occasion.[6] We are all too apt to believe that men change little, that they are to be reckoned with as fixed quantities. We expect to find them at sixty or sixty-five such as we knew them ten or twenty years earlier. An illusion belied by experience. "As do fruits, so men's talents have their season." This aphorism applies to Reynaud as forcibly as it does to Gamelin.

In the past Reynaud had been remarkably fortunate in the selection of his advisers. He had picked de Gaulle for military affairs and a far-sighted and scrupulously honest banker for financial and economic problems. These choices were probably due more to unusual luck than to unerring judgment. At any rate, from the time of his return to office in 1938, he fell a prey to whoever happened to be near him, whether on account of his administrative functions or otherwise. Three treasury officials, Marcel Bouthillier, Dominique Leca, and Gilbert Devaux, got hold of him and did not let him go, even when Reynaud was promoted from the Treasury to the premiership and to the Ministry of Foreign Affairs. These strange characters, in spite of their minor positions, weighed heavily on Reynaud's destiny and on the destiny of France.

One fine day Bouthillier, with an engineering degree from the School of Arts and Manufactures, turned his back on industrial plants to become an "Inspector of Finance." He was enamored of monetary "orthodoxy" in the old-fashioned sense. He placed the rules of the gold standard in the same category as the laws of nature. He was a bad economist and made that fact abundantly clear as the right-hand man of Germain Martin, the Finance Minister in the Doumergue Cabinet. Official business absorbed him completely. A violin and a boat he kept at the Island of Ré were the only modes of relaxation he was known to indulge in. But, under an ascetic exterior, he nourished a headlong am-

---

[5] About 1928 (I don't remember the exact year) I heard Reynaud declare at a dinner table that the Germans would not attempt again to revise their eastern boundaries. I note this only to show that his strong convictions in 1935 and 1940 had come on top of some illusions and did not perhaps have unshakable foundations. Reynaud's mind was soft under a hard surface of words.

[6] When he became Minister of Finance in November 1938 he put his program before the nation over the radio. But ten minutes before the appointed time he did not know whether he would maintain tax exemption on government securities or do away with it.

bition and a great talent for intrigue. Totalitarian notions had already begun to prey upon him.

Leca was a Corsican by birth. He had won top honors for rhetoric and philosophy in the open competition among French state schools. He would, within an hour, improvise a speech for Léon Blum when the latter was Minister of the Treasury, a speech faithfully reflecting the personality of the Socialist leader in its most delicate shades and implications. To do as much and with equal ease for Reynaud was not a problem for him. Temperamentally he was a *condottiere*. Devaux was the son of Caillaux's physician: attached to Leca as was Pylades to Orestes, he had truly mastered his craft. He was intelligent but of a sly and underhand disposition.

Here a strange tale begins. In the spring of 1938 the three pals foresaw that Reynaud would, before long, be transferred from the Department of Justice to the Treasury, and they lay in wait for him. They arranged to be introduced by some subordinate. They played upon his belief in devaluation (at a time when the devaluation of the franc no longer served any purpose), proposed to him some inordinate scheme, and captured his confidence. On the very day Reynaud took office they managed to get one of themselves (Bouthillier) appointed secretary-general to the Ministry of Finance and another (Leca) chief of the Minister's personal secretariat. This gave the triumvirate powers so ubiquitous as to parallel those of the Minister himself. The decree had been made ready. But, as it happened, the *Journal Officiel* was not being published the following morning. Delay was dangerous. It took Leca no time at all to overcome that obstacle. He called up the head of the Government Printing Office and, speaking in the name of the Minister, gave the order to start the presses rolling. But this was not all. It suddenly dawned upon the plotters that the post of secretary-general to the Ministry of Finance had been created long ago and was actually filled by a colleague of theirs. The man, it is true, had been so completely inactive he had allowed his domain to dwindle and disappear under the bureaucratic brambles to such an extent that nobody ever took any notice of him. But he was there. In the middle of the night Leca asked Devaux to get rid of him. The old fellow was awakened "in the name of the Minister," and with the excuse of "urgent affairs of state." Out of respect for the supreme power which was to be made manifest in his house, he dressed and put on collar and tie. He was requested to resign. But what did they have to offer in return? They could not do better than to avail themselves of a chaffing remark of M. Pierre Fournier, the governor of the Bank of

France, which, alert as they were to all possibilities of preferment, they had carefully pigeonholed in the lobes of their brains. "Since I create credit in my capacity as head of the bank of issue," the governor had said, "I should not be the one to distribute it as principal manager of the fund out of which loans are made to public contractors." Why, then, not make a separate and independent post out of this fund's management? The victim, however, grumbled at this proposal. He came around as soon as he heard that his salary would be doubled: 250,000 francs instead of 125,000. Thus did M. Bouthillier get hold of the coveted prize.[7]

The intrigues which Leca and Devaux wove around Reynaud would supply material for a light comedy. They saw to it that no one could visit him or telephone except through them or under their supervision. One afternoon they found a personal friend of Reynaud in his office; unknown to them, he had accompanied the Minister back from lunch. They had the simplicity, or the effrontery, to ask him by what door he had managed to get in.

In May 1940, when Reynaud moved from the Quai d'Orsay to the War Ministry (while continuing to superintend foreign policy from above), a room next to his was allocated to the head of his diplomatic secretariat. Our friends were alarmed at such proximity: it afforded the diplomat altogether too great an opportunity to watch closely the source of favors and honors. Leca and Devaux at once corrected this intolerable state of affairs. They dispatched the custodian of buildings to the intruder to tell him that poisonous emanations had been discovered and that he must pitch camp somewhere else. Leca and Devaux immediately made the vacated quarter into their own and shamelessly bragged of the clever trick they had successfully played.

It was unheard of that two inspectors of finance should break loose from their own ministry to take part in the direction of French diplomacy. Georges Bonnet, in his aversion for the officials of the Quai d'Orsay, upholders of traditional French policy, had thought of smothering them under a wave of treasury men. The latter, in the administrative hierarchy, set themselves up as the rivals of the diplomats. Their special training leads them to observe international problems under a narrow angle, to take into account only the play of material interests, to ignore emotional elements, to consider continuity in foreign policy as

---

[7] In his capacity as secretary-general, Bouthillier became, in practice, a vice-minister. But in order to be even surer of asserting his omnipotence, he took over the key department of the Ministry of Finance, the *"mouvement général des fonds."* He shifted the official hitherto in charge, Jacques Rueff, to a subgovernorship of the Bank of France and replaced him with a mere deputy, the Hitlerian Barnaud. See page 236.

unimaginative and old-fashioned. Money handlers and bankers are accustomed to base their calculations on the "economic man"—that is, on man possessed with the search for immediate comfort, for "butter," as Goering would put it. Few and far between are those who, when they leave the countinghouse for a chancellery, understand that a different keyboard comes under their hands, that henceforward they are up against forces which can be truly appraised only over the span of long generations. In France, Rouvier and Caillaux were representative of that school of financiers who think a nation can choose its policy with the freedom of a customer hefting a necklace in a jeweler's shop. The moment he assumed the premiership, March 22, 1940, Reynaud, through weakness toward minor associates who, for sixteen months, had cared for him as they would for a milch cow, allowed the innovation from which, in spite of everything, Bonnet had held back to come to pass. Leca and Devaux had no scruples; with the young, predatory enthusiasm of their early thirties, they were impatient to conquer Paris.[8]

In his private life, however, Reynaud was the prisoner of another and even more dangerous group—Countess de Portes and her friends. Born Hélène Rebuffel, she was a native of Marseilles, the daughter of a big public-works contractor. I first met her some fifteen years ago, in Geneva, at that time of the year that medley of politicians and society people who gravitated around the Assembly of the League of Nations called the "season." Her magic could not be easily perceived. She was a close friend of Mme. Reynaud, but soon became the husband's mistress. Her own marriage, around 1930, caused only a temporary break. In the end the two women fiercely clashed around their victim, and those who realized that the affair had long blossomed by mutual consent could only wonder at that belated explosion. From morning till night the two furies spied on and pursued each other. This quarrel became a public performance. If he went out with one, Reynaud had to fear that the other would suddenly pop up. In 1938 he moved to bachelor quarters on the

---

[8]The Mannheimer incident is equally significant of the casual way in which Reynaud recruited his associates. Mannheimer, a foolhardy speculator, was head of the Mendelsohn Bank, which had moved from Berlin to Amsterdam. In the summer of 1939 he convinced Reynaud that French credit could be improved by manipulations on the stock market. A loan was floated in Holland and in Switzerland, at a lower rate of interest than that yielded by earlier loans at their current quotation in New York or by French loans of guaranteed gold value. As things turned out, the French state suffered no losses from the transaction. But the association with Mannheimer did not improve its credit, and the banker had been promised counteradvantages which, in the great turmoil of the war, never came to light. Mannheimer was shorn of his wealth. He died suddenly. Although he had been in poor health, most people believed that he had committed suicide.

Place du Palais-Bourbon and decided, really against his will, to ask for a divorce. He induced Georges Bonnet, who was then Minister of Justice, to publish a decree whereby the delays which the existing legislation interposed between separation and remarriage were shortened. He had made up his mind; there was no going back. His paramour's influence steadily increased.

Nonetheless Reynaud continued to be persecuted and harassed. For instance, he had been invited with Mme. de Portes to attend a diplomatic reception. Mme. Reynaud forced an entry into the drawing room while her rival chided such impudence in tones loud enough to be heard by a good many people. As Reynaud was building up his Cabinet, one of his colleagues confided to me his anxiety about a private life which denied him all rest.

Mme. de Portes had gathered around her one of those "smart sets" we grew used to seeing in the Paris spotlight between the two wars. It consisted of derelict members of the old aristocracy who needed political power to satisfy their ambitions or their curiosity or to repair the fortunes that had been wrecked in financial upheavals, of a few English and Americans notorious at once for the refinement of their style of living and for their cynical outlook, of some popular specimens drawn from what it is convenient to describe as the "fellowship of the insiders"—the odd two thousand financiers, academicians, writers, diplomats, journalists, civil servants, members of Parliament, who felt they held the top jobs by virtue of reciprocal good will and an exchange of favors, determined to treat each other well and to conform to the rules of mutual assistance far removed from any bothersome convictions.

Formerly, Paris society never opened its doors to the politicians of the Third Republic. Its interests were narrow, and it held itself open to ridicule for its futile and fossilized outlook. The republican politicians themselves, with political credos still unblunted, stood on their provincial alignment. Politics and society kept their distance. That remoteness was preferable to a nondescript blending wherein all was confused and debased. Georges Mandel told me how Daladier, in a fit of rage, at the time of the ministerial crisis, dubbed Reynaud a "Parisien" as he tried to express his contempt of the man who had lost his earthy roots. This naïve epithet fitted quite well. The former deputy from the Basses-Alpes, whom the electoral district of the Stock Exchange had picked up and returned to the Chamber after he had been outvoted in his home constituency, prided himself on being a fashionable man. He was sixty-two years old. He tried hard to keep young: dyed his hair, bicycled furiously week ends and holidays, took sun baths. The professor of physical culture was a frequent visitor at his house. And let us include in the picture the cocksure vanity of a statesman globe-trotter, always ready, at a moment's notice, to jump into a plane in order to settle overnight some problem of British or American relations. Reynaud's life was all fits and starts. Early in 1940 a common friend said to me: "I am fond of him. But with what strange women he has surrounded himself! What a rotten set!"

3

Norway, Belgium, the Problem of Gamelin. Frustrated Expectations

TOWARD THE MIDDLE OF APRIL, thanks to the fall of Narvik and what seemed to be the success of the Norwegian venture, Daladier's obstructive rancor, Radical-Socialist maneuvers, and senatorial ill-humor receded into the past. At secret meetings of the Senate, held on April 16, 17, 18, and of the Chamber of Deputies, on the nineteenth, Reynaud gained the upper hand all along the line. The Chamber of Deputies unanimously voted a motion of confidence to the government, sixteen members abstaining and thirteen being absent. In the Senate the Premier's enemies had intended to demand an explanation of the Cabinet's make-up. Particularly they could not swallow the inclusion of the Socialists. Reynaud refused to take up any problem of internal policy, saying that it was unbecoming to do so while battle was raging in the north. He insisted that the essential question of the conduct of the war must be discussed exclusively. In order to cut short any machinations by Laval and suchlike, he followed M. Jeanneney's advice not to press for a vote of confidence. He received its equivalent, however, in the form of applause so enthusiastic as to surge into a regular ovation.[1]

[1]Moreover, it is worthy of note that before the Senate Foreign Affairs Committee on April 20 he played up the pro-Italian mania of certain senators. He did not conceal the fact that he had refused to join England in her protest against the abuse leveled in the Italian press at the Western Powers. He added that France was always ready to adjust her differences with Italy. At an earlier meeting of the Cabinet he had even said that, to recognize Italy's legitimate ambitions, some declaration might be published. This was quite a departure from his earlier views. He had climbed down considerably.

Now, on what program would his dynamic personality spend itself? He did not have to look round for it. Events unrolled it before him.

First of all he must see to it that British and French forces held fast to central Norway; that, for this purpose, Anglo-French naval superiority be exploited to the full. In brief, the Germans should be prevented from consolidating themselves in the fiords of the western coast, where British inertia gave them a chance to take a foothold.

Then, since the invasion of Denmark and Norway had completely torn to shreds the legal fictions of neutrality, since no government could any longer even pretend to find in international law a bulwark to its independence, the time had come for nations who held key positions on the map deliberately to join the Western democracies with which, whatever these nations might say, their interest was inseparably bound up. In the London discussions of March 28 all present had denounced the "double standard" of neutrality. Thereafter Chamberlain and Churchill publicly had emphasized more than once how intolerable it was that neutrals allowed Germany to make a mockery of the law of nations while at the same time they required England and France to respect it. The Western Powers would no longer admit two different sets of weights and measures. The action undertaken in Norway was to be considered merely as a particular application of this new decision of principle. Now it was Belgium's turn to reconsider her policy. She could no longer persist in an equivocal attitude, which benefited only Germany.

Finally, Gamelin had to be relieved of supreme command. The Premier saw him as little more than a military senior clerk, with none of the sacred fire in his breast. The campaign in Norway was additional evidence for the soundness of his opinion.

Such is the program which forced itself upon Reynaud's attention in the third or fourth week of his premiership. What did he make of it? Very soon, through the reverses suffered at Trondheim, bitter disappointment came from Norway. The British Admiralty was prepared to force an entry into the fiord, as urged by Admiral Sir Roger Keyes. April 25 had been the day set for this action, and whatever troops disembarked, belatedly enough, north and south, around Aandalsnes and around Namsos, were intended only to divert the enemy from the spot singled out for the principal body to land and to attack. But, to everybody's surprise, these forces sent to keep the mass of the German Army busy seemed to advance without much opposition. This caused the military leaders in London to upset the plans they had concerted with the Navy. On the seventeenth, they decided to reverse their operations, making primary that which had been planned as secondary.

Very soon the strategists had to regret that change in their dispositions. They found it impossible, with improvised landing facilities and under the fire of superior aviation, to unload from the ships the heavy matériel required to face the Germans. Trondheim was the only port along this coast that had proper if limited equipment. It was there that the British Command should have tried to gain a first grip. The Admiralty was still ready to carry out the original plan.[2] But the Imperial General Staff now felt that the adventure had become too dangerous, that, to have a chance of success, the air must first be wrested from the enemy. In short, the Imperial General Staff admitted itself incapable of saving central Norway and called for evacuation.

If we read the bitter debate which took place in both Houses of Parliament on May 8,[3] the wretched way in which things had been managed becomes only too apparent. French and British vied with each other in recriminations. Intervention in Norway should never have been thought of as restricted to the extreme north. Nor should it have been deemed an enterprise of strictly limited responsibility. It was essential from the very beginning that a net be thrown over the whole string of Norwegian ports, not only Narvik, but also Bergen, Trondheim, and Skavanger. There is nothing to disprove that on April 8 and 9 the British Navy might not even have reached Oslo. The British military leaders waited until the Germans had taken roots in the south before taking serious notice of central Norway. Improvisation brought disaster. Even at Narvik, the objective which they had set themselves to carry following the Supreme Council of March 28, the enemy had been left free to get ahead of them, and it was only on the second attempt that they fulfilled their purpose. The London ministers were not heart and soul in the undertaking. On March 28, when giving in to Reynaud's pressure for action, they had thought above all of strengthening his position in the French Parliament. During his visit to Paris, on April 4 and 5, Churchill was still shaking his head over the prospects of the Norwegian campaign.[4] Today, as we turn back to the military commentators of the

---

[2] The "Admiralty has never withdrawn its offer." (W. Churchill, House of Commons, May 8, 1940.)

[3] Chamberlain did not survive it as Prime Minister.

[4] Daladier, immovable in his calculated aloofness, refused to be present at the dinner given in honor of the First Lord of the Admiralty.

period, how striking is the comparatively little heed paid to the aerial side of the whole business!

The British decision to recall the English and French troops fighting north and south of Trondheim brought forth an instant and bitter protest from Reynaud. One might almost say an inordinate protest. On April 24 or 25, unknown to the officials of the Foreign Affairs Ministry, he sent to the British Prime Minister a letter which would certainly have rendered Franco-British co-operation even more painful than it already was, had not Mr. Chamberlain unexpectedly ceased to be the Head of the Government. Reynaud haughtily lectured Mr. Chamberlain on his conduct of the war. Whoever, he said, could not take upon himself to form a broad view of the whole range of the conflict had better not try his hand at it. Without swift action the campaign was sure to be lost. He stated that crushing the German batteries whose fire swept the neck of the Trondheim fiord was worth the sacrifice of a cruiser. He complained that no unity of command existed in the north. He declared that the Paris Government did not contemplate recalling its troops. Even granting that Reynaud stood on solid ground, that, at the end of the third week in April, the two Allies were still in position to achieve some useful results on the Norwegian coast, nothing could be worse than the general tone of the letter. Darlan himself would have been hard put to it to supply and support a separate expeditionary corps with French ships only. At the meeting of the Supreme Council held in London, on April 27, Reynaud came down from his high horse. But he and his companions returned to France downcast and appalled.

As to Reynaud's second task, winning neutrals, it began most unauspiciously. Belgium felt less than ever like playing a heroic role. In the Supreme Council hastily called together in London on April 9 (to take stock of the new state of affairs created by the inrush of German troops into Denmark and Norway), the decision was arrived at to kill two birds with one stone and to urge upon the Brussels Government the abandonment of its alleged policy of "neutrality and independence." In other terms, Belgium was requested to re-enter the alliance of the two great Western Powers and open up her territory to Gamelin's armies. In all logic the Council should have added that Belgium's refusal would automatically cancel the declaration of April 1937, by which the two great nations guaranteed the integrity of the Belgian realm without reciprocity. A valid excuse could easily be found for such an eventual repudiation. It was enough to represent that King Leopold and his ministers had not complied with the terms upon which the above-mentioned declaration had been made conditional: living up to the Covenant of the League of Nations and building up national defense. Such a maneuver would not probably have made a deep impression upon a bigoted monarch[5] imbued with authoritarian notions and surrounded, to boot, by people won over to Germany. But in the half-baked form in which it was finally presented, and shorn of all reference to Franco-British obligations, the demands of Reynaud and Chamberlain could only serve to make the king and his ministers hide their ostrich heads still deeper in self-illusion. The secretary-general of the Quai d'Orsay (who did not attend the seventh Supreme Council) clearly pointed this out when M. Corbin, the French Ambassador to London, called up to ask that necessary instructions be telegraphed at once to his colleague in Brussels, M. Bargeton. M. Alexis Léger did not carry out this request until the Premier returned to Paris and ordered it done.

Belgian irritation steamed up and grew to anger when, in public speeches, Lord Halifax and Mr. Churchill[6] strictured the little kingdom on account of its faintheartedness and its inconsistencies. The Brussels Cabinet went to the length of issuing a communiqué to tell all concerned that it would not budge from its settled policy. Reynaud, however, dropped the matter. He was very soon to change his views about Belgium.

Here, in Reynaud's tragic career, we come to a remarkable turning point. Colonel de Villelume became his confidential military adviser instead of Colonel de Gaulle, whom he had singled out at first for the secretary-generalship of the War Committee and then promptly sent back to his tank unit under the entreaties of Mme. de Portes and Daladier.[7] And Villelume behaved as a prophet of disaster.

For ten years or more Villelume had been detailed to the Ministry of Foreign Affairs. At the outset his job was to clarify for the Quai d'Orsay complicated technical problems arising from all Geneva plans of armament limitations. But these problems had long lost all current importance and he still clung to his desk. He had taken a fancy to his new job, half diplomatic, half military. He gave up all idea of promotion. His business was to keep the diplomats near him informed of what was

[5]On January 16, when he received Gamelin's "ultimatum," Leopold III, it appears, had fallen back on silence as a subterfuge. He had left it up to M. Spaak, Minister of Foreign Affairs, to initiate the final rejection.

[6]April 10 and 11.

[7]Reynaud was embarrassed at having to go back on his word. He begged General Bineau, who, up to December, was "major general" (chief of the general staff), to persuade General de Gaulle to leave of his own accord.

going on in the General Staff, of army gossip. He disliked Gamelin, exposed his crooked schemings, accused him of double-dealing in the recent negotiations with the British, etc. As we have seen, on March 23 his ideas had predominated at a meeting of the War Cabinet. On March 27, in the plane which brought them to London, all present watched with curiosity his long talk with Reynaud. It was not new to them that he enjoyed the latter's favor. The Prime Minister, on taking over the Quai d'Orsay, five days before, would have appointed him to the coveted post of *chef de cabinet* (chief private secretary) except for the surprise and disapproval that spread among all officials. But his hold on the chief was now manifest. Henceforth he would have his say in the intimate circle. Toward Mme. de Portes he was assiduous, attentive. One day he excused himself from an official appointment on the ground of being expected at her house. Withal, he was at times frightened at the reverberations created by his advice, and he kept insisting that he had no influence.

When Reynaud was Minister of Finance he had from time to time glanced at the way the rearmament program was being carried out, and the accounts he gave of what he had been able to see were far from pleasant. How could he reconcile his sorrowful awareness of the Army's manifold deficits and of the delays in our war production with his boldly proclaimed determination to accelerate the tempo of military operations?[8]

Colonel de Villelume somewhat lessened the underlying contradiction. Toward the end of April the Premier let fall a disillusioned remark about the plans for an eventual action in Belgium. Therefore let us dismiss from our minds all idea that admonitory or prompting words on his part had something to do with Gamelin's crazy venture of May 10. He had bowed before the British decision to abandon central Norway, and before Belgium's stubborn passivity he bowed once more. He owned that the Allied armies would run great risks in an offensive across the Low Countries. Within five weeks his militant mood had cooled off.[9]

[8]A few days before the invasion of Belgium, Reynaud sanctioned the British bombing of oil stores in Germany. But he stipulated that it should be done only after the Germans had penetrated into Belgian territory. See page 46 and note 3.

[9]Military documents included in the archives of the French General Staff that fell into German hands at La Charité-sur-Loire and, subsequently, were published in Berlin, have made it known that the whole problem of Belgium came up for discussion before the War Committee in April 1940. Gamelin and Darlan, with Daladier's support, sponsored the long-prepared plan for a counteroffensive. Reynaud sounded a note of warning and then gave way. From the eleventh to the twenty-second of April the armies under Corap and Huntziger were

But he was resolved to discard Gamelin, and this, in itself, is another reason why he should be cleared of all personal responsibility for the crucial military decision of May 10. He had stormed at Gamelin after the Supreme Council of April 9, where he had had to reckon with the tangible fact that the French and English General Staffs did not have on hand, on the night of the German invasion of Norway, whatever was necessary for an immediate counterstroke, for such a counterstroke as Darlan had suggested from the outset, on the twenty-eighth of March.[10] In action this war-school general was exposed and found wanting. Anxiously Reynaud looked round for the leader who was best suited to take his place. He searched for a military genius as Diogenes searched for a good man.

Reynaud had to put up with the sorry truth. From the list of general officers no name stood out beyond debate. The poor opinion Reynaud had conceived of the High Command took in Georges as well as the generalissimo. Giraud and Huntziger[11] were put forward by some as possible choices, but unconvincingly. Would not expediency recommend that he should turn to the chiefs of the last generation and call in Weygand, with Pétain to warrant the change through being made once more the principal "military adviser" to the government?

Pétain happened to be in Paris. Like all the other ambassadors and like Weygand, he had been summoned by the new Prime Minister, who was keen to review with them the whole field of international affairs. He was tired of his Spanish Embassy. In September, on Laval's advice, he had refused to become minister without portfolio. Daladier's offer, however, had stirred in him a desire to be at the seat of government. Ever since December an array of politicians (Piétri, Lémery, etc.) had passed through his Madrid palace and urged him to get closer to the center of power. In February he asked to be recalled, and Daladier, who remembered rather unpleasantly Pétain's reactions to his proposal of the late summer and who was keeping a watchful eye on him, experienced some difficulty in persuading him to stay at his post.[12] Shortly afterward, however, the restless Pétain came surreptitiously to the capital. He dined with a well-known politician at the house of a half-Jewish

---

put on the "alert." "Alert" No. 1 lasted from the eleventh to the fourteenth, and "alert" No. 2 from the fourteenth to the twenty-second.

[10] See page 48.

[11] Gamelin considered Huntziger to be best qualified as his successor, if successor he was to have.

[12] See page 349.

couple, protégés of his. Fearful lest this meeting might be talked about, he took pains to let all concerned know that it had been only fortuitous. He then returned to Madrid, and now he was back again.

As Marshal of France, in active service until his last breath, at least in theory, he wanted to be entrusted with some task not related to the conduct of military operation or even to the general supervision of the war in any executive sense. He felt that to take charge of the morale of the troops would fit him excellently. Had he not earned a great triumph in 1917 when it fell to him to bolster up the armies which General Nivelle had left adrift, on the verge of mutiny? In any case, he would get into the War Committee, and perhaps he might preside over it.[18]

These wishes tallied with Reynaud's personal calculation—with the marshal at his side to outweigh day by day the influence of the Minister for National Defense and do away with the generalissimo. Reynaud had duly noted that, against him, Daladier and Gamelin nearly always joined hands and that, when it came to a showdown, Darlan and Vuillemin backed them. Reynaud, still worried over the vote of March 22, complacently thought that he could add the marshal to his party and use to his own benefit the prestige of the "Hero of Verdun." But was he not aware that since the autumn Laval had made of Pétain a docile tool for his own intrigues? Surely he was. Mme. de Portes's idle talk showed that he had nothing to learn on that subject. The truth is that he had an unfaltering faith in his magic power to win over to his cause even those most predisposed against him. And in Reynaud's intimate circle all put their shoulders to the wheel, for they were attracted rather than repelled by Laval's and Pétain's own ideas about winding up the war.

The Prime Minister, therefore, pressed the marshal to leave Madrid for good and to enter at once governmental councils in whatever capacity best suited him, either as a minister or in some post of authority outside the Cabinet. Before committing himself to Reynaud the marshal sought approval from Daladier. With an eye to the future, he wanted to ward off all possible criticism on this Minister's part. Then, too, he had no confidence whatever in Reynaud. Had not the man just betrayed the Conservatives again? Had he not brought the Socialists back into office? So Pétain went on from the Quai d'Orsay to the Ministry of War. But there, far from receiving the least encouragement, he was vehemently begged not to quit his embassy. "Leave Madrid now!" exclaimed the Minister of National Defense. "Don't think of it! Why, your real job is only beginning. We are perhaps working toward the supreme crisis of

[18] It is doubtful that the Law of July 11, 1938, permitted this.

the war. The greatest service you could render France would be to prevent Spain from joining Germany in the struggle!"

Where, then, lay the duty which the old soldier seemingly would have someone else assign him? Upset at the result of his own initiative, and realizing that to override such unqualified advice as the Minister for National Defense had given him required that he find some other surety besides Reynaud, he hesitated, discussed the matter with several personages of whose testimony he might someday, if necessary, avail himself for his justification. He decided that his last resort would be to unburden himself of his difficulty to the President of the Republic. If only the decision which he dared not take himself could be the outcome of a cabinet deliberation, he would always be able to say afterward, assuming that things turned badly in Spain, "All I did was to obey my orders, like a good soldier!" He soon resumed his post.[14]

The trust of the army experts was not with Weygand, but the man in the street thought highly of his talent for strategy. Moreover, he was favored by the French Academy, the *Revue des Deux Mondes,* the "drawing rooms," conservative society. On his brow lingered the glow of Foch's glory. Whatever happened, no one in the general public would ever reproach the Head of the Government for having appointed him. Politically, both choices—of the marshal and the general—were "safe." And Reynaud could not forget Briand's ill fortune. To replace Joffre, with whom he was determined to part, he had taken upon himself to select military talent where he thought he found it and had chosen Nivelle.

The problem of Gamelin was put before the War Committee on April 12, three days after his inglorious appearance in the Supreme Council. Reynaud blamed the generalissimo for the slowness with which French troops were moving to Norway and asked for his head. Daladier turned aside the blow: the fault, if fault there was, should be laid at the door of the Navy.[15]

On May 8 the Premier returned to the question in a private conference with his colleague—the first the two men ever had since the formation of the Cabinet. Reynaud later maintained that the Minister of National Defense didn't react too unfavorably to his suggestions and that they found themselves in substantial accord concerning Gamelin's mistakes, whereby their respective Scandinavian projects had been impaired.

---

[14]It was at this juncture that Marshal Pétain paid M. Léger the visit referred to on pages 246–47.

[15]See page 46.

Daladier's hesitation, however—nothing more can be conceded to Reynaud—lasted but a very short while. On the very next day he was at loggerheads with the Premier: in the midst of a cabinet meeting they hurled threats of resignation to each other's faces.[16] How could Daladier have controlled himself? In the past he also had felt meekly inclined to put another chief at the head of the French Armies. And since he had not taken that drastic step, he owed it to his own reputation to censure his more audacious successor. He could not, by his ready approval, admit his own timidity. Before all his colleagues he denied having in the least acquiesced—even conditionally—to Reynaud's arguments. He pleaded that Gamelin had not been at fault between March 28 and April 9 and never had a hand directly in the scattering of the troops assembled in February for the purpose of the expedition to Finland. Furthermore, he, Daladier, was ready to study the matter without the slightest prejudice: the whole trouble was to find a better chief than Gamelin. All in all, Daladier was, in reality, not so far from Reynaud. After the cabinet meeting Leca and Devaux exclaimed: "Whatever happens, Gamelin is done for!"[17] But the angry clash between the two political leaders was quite independent of the object of their disagreement. Reynaud went straight to the Elysée and acquainted the President of the Republic with the resignation of this Cabinet. The fact was to be kept secret for five days. The country was not to hear of it until a new ministry had stepped in.

M. Albert Lebrun obtained Reynaud's promise that he still make

---

[16]Campinchi, Naval Minister, and, behind Campinchi, Darlan, supported Daladier. Heaven knows that the "Admiral of the Fleet" had on every occasion crossed the generalissimo. But he did not consider Reynaud a good bet.

[17]Anatole de Monzie, in his recently published reminiscences, confirms the opinion of Reynaud's two close associates: "May 9. Urgent summons to a cabinet meeting. No one knows why, but there is an overtone of solemnity in this Council Chamber of the Quai d'Orsay. Reynaud sits down in front of mountainous files, which men of his household have neatly lined up on the big table. The diminutive Prime Minister smiles his conqueror's quiet smile . . . 'Gentlemen, I must speak to you about the state of the High Command.' And we are treated to a detailed, documented recital of his relations with Gamelin. An indictment rather than a recital. The bill of particulars drags on, page after page, for everything has been recorded for posterity. Reynaud thumps his chest as though posterity were part of the audience. Still and all, his case is meaty, well-ordered, and, in the absence of refutation, overwhelming. . . . Someone lights a cigarette. 'Please be good enough not to smoke; my throat is sore.' Indeed, the tenor's voice is out of sorts. To clinch his argument, he must tax all his energy. The cigarette is put out; no one stirs. Lamoureux whispers in my ear: 'He is being done to death.' Yes, it was a speech before the gallows, a speech that lasted more than an hour. Then Reynaud closed the file and spoke no more. Silence. At that moment the French Army, morally, no longer had a leader." Indeed, Reynaud's indictment of Gamelin lasted two hours fifteen minutes.

another attempt at coming to terms with Daladier. The President of the Republic also sent for the Minister for National Defense and told him plainly that, should he remain obdurate, neither he nor his rival would again take office. And toward the evening he directed a confidential messenger to sound out M. Herriot, who, however, merely repeated what he had said so often before: "As long as the Italian threat weighs down on us, it would be very ill considered for me to assume ministerial responsibilities."

Reynaud kept on raving and shouting that Daladier had tampered with everything he wanted to undertake. On the morning of May 10 the thunderbolt struck. The Germans had invaded the Low Countries. At once discord was cut short and, out of mere decency, the two had to embrace at Herriot's urging. They embraced, but no love was lost.

4

Enter Pétain and Weygand

DURING THE NIGHT OF MAY 15-16 the abyss opened before Reynaud. Often when the day's work was over he would go with Mme. de Portes to La Celle-Saint-Cloud, where they had been lent a remodeled porter's lodge hidden amid extensive grounds. A few hundred yards away, in the château of the estate, which was a large, ugly, and comfortable establishment overlooking rows of ancient trees extending down to the Seine, Daladier and Mme. de Crussol spent their week ends when time was too short for them to go as far as the forest of Rambouillet. The year before, Mme. de Portes had deliberately sought out this proximity, since she then still wished to mend her friendship with the marquise. But even in these peaceful surroundings the two couples never met. Occasionally an automobile would stealthily drive up during the night. It would come to a stop at a prudent distance from the entrance gate. A man would emerge, a man intent upon not being seen. He would move rapidly along the edges of the roadway, avoiding open spaces. Under Mme. de Crussol's window he would whistle softly. She would come downstairs. He would speak to her in subdued tones, then he would quickly disappear through the shrubbery. This was no Leander, no faithful go-between, no gallant devotee of romance. It was merely Serruys, who could not wait to talk over the governmental problem of the hour, to learn some state secret or confide one of his own.

Reynaud was in this secluded spot at the time Gamelin realized that his whole military scheme was collapsing and told Daladier that he doubted whether he could stop the progress of the German armored division if it should try to reach Paris the next day. It was no easy matter to convey this news to the Prime Minister. He sheltered himself for refreshment and recreation; he bolted his door against all serious business and hid behind a protective barrier of peremptory instructions. He spent the evening of the fifteenth at La Celle-Saint-Cloud, and he often revisited it during the days that followed. A lady who enjoyed the hospitality of this little house remarked: "I was astounded at the carefree spirit and conversation which were the rule within its walls. Anxiety never crossed the threshold." Yet it was in this very place that Reynaud suddenly awakened to his cruel destiny: that France was in his charge at a moment of unparalleled disaster.

An eyewitness has described to me the meeting with Winston Churchill, who rushed to Paris by plane the moment he heard the bad news. It took place twenty-four hours later, when everyone's mental distress had already lessened. "The French Premier and the Minister for National Defense were both seated, facing each other, in the study of the Place du Palais-Bourbon apartment. Daladier was all hunched up, burdened with the weight of poignant sorrow; Reynaud held his head erect. He was silent and looked like some broken mechanical toy. The British Prime Minister paced up and down the room, urging them on: 'Don't be discouraged. Did you ever suppose that we should be able to win without first suffering the worst possible reverses?' And he went on giving advice and telling them what he would do if he were in their position. The very flow of his words seemed to bolster him up, and more and more his tone sounded like an injunction. I felt acutely uncomfortable."

As far as Reynaud was concerned, Gamelin's fate was sealed. He had led his armies to disaster. Let him yield the command to an abler man. This time Daladier could only submit. Politically he was shattered, close to death. His friends had left him. Nothing stood in the way of the Prime Minister's will. On May 18 Marshal Pétain, to whom an urgent summons had been sent, was made vice-premier, and twenty-four hours later Weygand became commander in chief.[1] Henceforward Reynaud was in

---

[1] Reynaud's telegrams summoning Pétain and Weygand to Paris were sent by 9 A.M. on the sixteenth of May.

constant touch with them, having moved to the Ministry of War and turned over the Ministry of Foreign Affairs to Daladier. This had not come to pass without the latter's protests; they lasted for four tempestuous hours before he agreed to leave the Rue St. Dominique, and the change was effected only on Reynaud appealing to the President of the Republic.

On May 7 or 8, to appoint the two veterans was to follow the line of least resistance, of minimum responsibilities. But ten days afterward there was a cogent reason for pushing these men into the foreground. Their names, linked to the memories of 1916 and 1918, gave comfort to the French people, lifted them from the depths of their first anguish. Reynaud, who had stood alone for so long, maligned by so many, felt that to arouse a powerful surge of national defense throughout the nation, among soldiers and civilians, nothing else would have the same value as the patronage of those symbols of French strength and glory.

And, indeed, their presence at once produced a great improvement in morale. The return to France of the commander in chief in the Levant caused a wave of optimism. Now everything would be different, since the conduct of operations had been taken from Gamelin and given to leaders of proven competence. The idle talk of a barber in Bordeaux, on the evening of June 14, will never fade from my memory: "I am not a bit worried. Weygand has some trick of his own up his sleeve which he will show the Germans in due time."

But did Reynaud sincerely believe that an octogenarian and a septuagenarian whose shrinking military efficiency was fairly well symbolized by the tiny sword which French academicians wear in public ceremonies could stem the tide? That is another matter. On leaving the War Committee which met on April 3, at which Weygand rambled along on the subject of the Balkans, the Prime Minister had exclaimed: "Little did I know him. Now I have his measure." And as for Pétain, it was surely not the preface which the marshal had written for General Chauvineau's *Is Invasion Still Possible?*[2] that could win Reynaud's admiration. In the third week of May, if the conduct of the war had been entrusted to younger generals with more modern ideas, not encumbered by the stifling precedents of 1914–18, to commanders who understood more thoroughly the implications of the new weapons and tactics used by the Germans, to men more intimately acquainted with the checkerboard and capable of making lightning decisions, would success have been achieved where the two elders, recalled to duty after long years of retirement,

[2]See page 12 and Appendix 1.

stumbled and failed? The equivalent of such generals as d'Aurelle de Paladines, Chanzy, Faidherbe—whom the Government of National Defense, in 1870-71, was able to single out from among the lesser posts of command—could it be found? There is no use wasting time over such speculations. This much at least can be said: between May 19 and June 9, the day on which the French land forces were finally broken as a coherent system, not even one maneuver based on a skillful appraisal of the enemy's strategy can be credited to Weygand. In 1870-71 the successful engagements at Orléans, Mans, Bapaume were not followed up. But, at any rate, they gave evidence of a vigorous leadership. In May–June 1940 nothing of the sort interrupted the monotony of our defeats.

So the only advantage gained was an improvement in morale. An improvement, however, subject to a dangerous lien, not only military but political as well. Henceforward Pétain, simply by threatening to resign, could hold the government at his mercy. Did Reynaud consciously and deliberately agree to the price he was paying? Did he realize that, in case things went badly, he had taken on a man who would become his master? I hesitate to answer these questions in the negative. Remember his likeness to a broken toy on the evening of the sixteenth, at the interview with Winston Churchill. He had not yet entirely yielded to despair, but from that date on the thought of defeat was often with him, and little by little he accustomed himself to face it. As far as those appalling friends of his are concerned, those friends who had been relentless in their effort to put the marshal to the fore, it cannot even be said that they needed to become familiarized with the worst. The moment the Army began to break they saw an opportunity to get back to work on those plans for the reconstruction of France and Europe which the declaration of war on Germany, in September 1939, seemingly had thrown into the discard. From the fourteenth of May on, rumors of hopeless defeat kept emanating from the Premier's personal staff.

The two old soldiers would be precautionary umbrellas for Reynaud's use. If the skies were to clear, they would serve as well as anybody else to win for Reynaud the gratitude of his countrymen. But if there were to be a storm, they would be of unique service. At any rate, on the eighteenth and nineteenth, when they set to the task, passionate considerations of internal policy preyed on their minds.

Two disturbing hints can be produced in evidence of this. On May 17 one of my friends was conversing with Reynaud's assistant chief of staff at Beirut. The general himself was about to leave for Paris. "He believes," said this officer, "that the war is lost, and that reasonable conditions for an armistice should be accepted." But the second symptom is even more relevant. On the day he reported at the Prime Minister's offices in Paris, Weygand was greeted by Baudouin, the major-domo of the place. They did not know each other. They had a brief talk. That same evening Baudouin gave free rein to his enthusiasm. He was under a spell. "Why did we never meet before? What great things we could have done!" The reader, after he has once seen Baudouin at work, will look back with uneasiness to that effusive admiration.

Whatever the intentions of Pétain and Weygand appeared to be on the surface, the seeds of submission had been planted already deep in their hearts. They felt an impulse toward counterrevolution, the counterrevolution which was to come into being on June 16. There is no necessity to question their patriotism. But, after all, patriotism is not something manufactured by mass production. It is not to be found, always the same, always unchanged in every breast. It is a rational conception, but it is also—and principally—instinct. When a decision has to be reached as to what can or cannot be done in the face of an attacking enemy, chiefs who are deeply convinced that for one hundred and fifty years their country has been ruled by a despicable ideal, and through all those years has carried with it the principle of its own ruin, will not always be so bold as others who love the France of the Revolution and the France of the Monarchy alike.

I feel obliged thus to record my doubts, my suspicions. I cannot afford to shut my eyes to many troublesome signs. Having said so much, I shall not make of Pétain's and Weygand's pessimistic prejudice, of Reynaud's periodical fits of discouragement, a main key to the history of the last four weeks of the French Republic. I shall try rather to deal with events as they come within my range of vision.

Never in the course of his career had Reynaud been Minister of National Defense. With long intervals, he had successively headed the Department of Colonial Affairs, the Treasury, the Department of Justice, and again the Treasury. During Reynaud's brief two months as Prime Minister, Daladier had forbidden his interference in questions of national defense. He has therefore nothing to do with the primary causes of the catastrophe.

The conference with Mr. Winston Churchill, on May 16, was the first time that he had to deal directly with the problems of the battlefield in the homeland. The period of his own military responsibility began then. Under the circumstances it was the duty of the Head of the Government to insist upon the dispatch of bombers and fighter planes from the English home defenses to the north of France, to the neck of the German pocket. On the day before, Gamelin had requested the Imperial Staff in London to dispatch ten squadrons of fighters.[3]

Reynaud, at his meeting with the British Prime Minister, insisted that combat planes of every variety be transferred from London to Flanders.[4] The French Premier did not obtain what he wanted. Relatively few units were detached from the home command of the British Air Force, and these, like the planes which made up the "striking force," were more often sent to operate over the highways, the railroads, the ports, and the ammunition dumps of the Rhineland and the Ruhr than over the countryside of the Meuse and the Somme. Winston Churchill hated to weaken the defenses of his capital and to use the planes which he did yield in homeopathic doses for raids immediately linked to actual fighting, a mode of action much more costly than any other carried on at a great distance behind the lines. "Forty per cent in losses as against three or four!" he once remarked. If your object is to try to restore a river in flood to its natural banks, you might as well attack its sources and tributaries a few hundred kilometers upstream.

Thus the appeal made for English air support came to very little. Contrariwise, the reshuffling of the High Command must be regarded, in retrospect, as a critical point in French history. By his appointment of the two old burgraves Reynaud set in motion a far-reaching sequence of causes and effects. We shall no longer be able to distinguish between the acts of the Prime Minister and the acts of the commander in chief, as we did between those of Daladier and those of Gamelin. Henceforth the general conduct of the war, properly the function of the Prime Minister, is confused with its operational conduct, the proper function of the commander in chief. The fate of France was at stake in the Battle of Flanders, then in the Battle of France; and the sands ran out quickly.

[3]British air forces in France included: an air corps under the command of Lord Gort (air component); a "striking force," independent of Gort's command, based in the region of Rheims. The "air component" had some 120 fighter planes and a small number of reconnaissance bombers. I do not know the size of the "striking force." M. Jean Labusquière, who was Huntziger's secretary, says that it included five hundred bombers (*Vérité sur les Combattants*). On May 14 Air Marshal Barratt, in command of this force, got hold of three squadrons of fighter planes for immediate use at Sedan. These had just been received by Gort to take the place of seventy-eight units lost in the first days of combat. According to M. Labusquière, the Germans had started their aerial campaign on May 10 with fifteen hundred fighters and thirty-five hundred bombers, of which five hundred were Stukas. According to the same author, 710 French pursuit planes and ninety-six bombers (of which twenty-six were of modern design) went into action.

[4]Gamelin called again on London for air support on the sixteenth and seventeenth. British sources have it that his demand was fulfilled on or about May 20.

Everything else became negligible. Political problems were then inextricably woven into what happened to pass on the battlefields. Whoever disposed of the armed forces controlled politics, unless the civilian power be served by a will of iron. In her defeat France found the *de facto* technical dictator whom she had lacked when preparing for the great ordeal.

Thus Weygand, in command of the armies, had to ask himself whether the Battle of France should be considered as the last act of national resistance or rather—since the odds were mostly adverse on the home soil—as a struggle intended to be integrated into the wider conflict between Germany and the Anglo-Saxon world, which ought, therefore, to be conducted not as an end in itself, but as a means, with the fixed notion of passing over to the democratic powers (taken as a whole) the possibilities of eventual victory, however remote. Assuming the worst possible interpretation of events, Weygand had to ask himself whether the French Army, defeated along the Meuse, must be led after the fashion of a rear guard in retreat, which sacrifices itself in order to protect the main body of strength, or rather as the principal and ultimate body. Reynaud, invested with political authority, was alone qualified to settle those momentous questions. But, unavoidably, the vicissitudes of the struggle told upon him. Truly, to a great extent, the man in command of our soldiers dictated the policy. The decisions which Weygand was in position to reach and enforce by himself were such as to very nearly bind the civilian power hand and foot. When armies are not fighting, politics overrule strategy, create facts which no General Staff can afford to overlook. But when a critical military campaign is in progress, the doings of a General Staff become the dominant factor.

Very soon—on May 25 and 29—the Prime Minister and commander in chief seemingly no longer saw eye to eye as to the issue: prosecution of the war versus the armistice. But the attitudes they took were provisional, conditional. Fourteen more days would elapse before thesis and antithesis clashed together at Briare and at Tours. Meanwhile all sorts of events, on the field of battle and elsewhere, worked together to shape the diverging positions taken up by the generalissimo and the Prime Minister respectively. The bitter quarrel between Weygand and the British General Staff was one of them.

5

Weygand the Temporizer. The Quarrel with the British and the End of the "Unified Command"

THE VERY MOMENT he left the plane which brought him back from Beirut, Weygand was confronted with the problem of the "pocket."

We have already seen that the Germans pierced a hole through the lines of the 2nd and 9th armies on May 14 and 15. On the sixteenth, when he took over the command of the 9th Army from Corap, Giraud still had some organized units under him, between Maubeuge and Hirson.[1] But south of Hirson, from the upper Oise to the Aisne, soldiers and civilians were in full flight. The enemy hurled its armored and motorized divisions through the breach. A column of light tanks advanced as far as the outskirts of Laon. It was this advance, as we have seen, which overwhelmed Gamelin and the government. On the evening of the seventeenth, other armored units crossed the Oise, pushing forward along the road to Péronne and St. Quentin. This city fell to them on the eighteenth and nineteenth. Simultaneously, the region of Amiens was penetrated by the enemy and, in the north, moving along a parallel line, a column advanced beyond Valenciennes. A map found on a prisoner indicated that the Germans, turning away from Paris, would rush through to the sea in order to cut off Billotte's group of armies, to sever from the Anglo-French military machine one third of its effectives and matériel. On May 20, Amiens and Abbeville were seized and Arras itself was by-passed to the south. The Anglo-French forces were locked in Belgium by dint of aggressive action, and they were gradually being surrounded from the south. On the twenty-first, they were driven from the region of Cambrai, on the northern flank of the "pocket." On the twenty-second, the invader reached the Channel at St. Valéry-en-Caux, on the opposite side. Thereupon he flung armored contingents toward Boulogne and Calais in order to complete his operation of encirclement. By the twenty-fourth, he was to occupy the coast as far

[1] By May 20 the 9th Army no longer existed as an organized force. Its remnants were allocated to the 1st Army. Giraud was taken prisoner by the Germans on the nineteenth.

as Gravelines. With the aid of troops sent from England, Boulogne would hold out until the twenty-fifth and Calais until the twenty-seventh. Then Dunkirk would be isolated. Such was the course of the blitzkrieg.

But on the nineteenth, there was still fluidity everywhere. At first glance the German advance seemed to defy all the rules set up by the masters of warfare: it even seemed to defy common sense. The body of troops which it sought to besiege in the north must have numbered 600,000 or 700,000 men. And in the south, from that part of the Argonne where the 2nd Army held on, all the way to the Oise and the Somme, fresh reserves were being put in the line. The German armored divisions spread on two hundred kilometers toward the west, open to attack from all sides. Often mere motorcycle troops or cars armed with machine guns took possession of hamlets and small towns. Motorized infantry followed the tanks at a great distance—as much as one hundred and twenty-five kilometers, sometimes more. How did Weygand fail to get the better of this stream while it was still shallow? Why did he not stanch the wound opened by the blitzkrieg? Its lips were a mere forty kilometers apart, between Arras and Péronne, on May 21 and even on May 22. His initial blunder was to have hesitated for three or four days before coming to a shaky decision. His very apologists give us the date; he finally established his strategy in consultation with General Georges on May 23. May 23, four long days after his appointment— which he had accepted, moreover, after twelve hours of reflection and after foregoing the forty-eight-hour delay he had asked for making up his mind. On the twentieth, when instant and heroic initiative was required, he brought to a halt the action already under way and substituted for it nothing of his own.

What action was there in progress? As early as the fifteenth, Gamelin, Georges, and Billotte had moved to stop the gap. But they were too long content with half measures. Their first idea was to launch against the enemy's flank from the Sambre, toward the southeast, all the armored or motorized cavalry they could manage to reassemble. The second and third light mechanized divisions, which had gone through bitter fighting before Gimbloux on the thirteenth, were acting as support for the 1st Army, which needed them badly. The 1st Armored Division had suffered heavy losses at Philippeville on the fifteenth. The 2nd Armored Division was guarding over the Oise, and the third was included in the hard-pressed 2nd Army.[2] The first light mechanized division (7th Army)

[2]In the absence of a well-defined doctrine regarding tank tactics, the tendency was to make armored units subservient to the immediate requirements of infantry. Foot troops in

was perhaps available more or less. Out of all this elaborate plan, a plan perhaps not followed up with great energy and retarded by secondary considerations, there resulted only an attack of de Gaulle's units (4th Armored Division) on the seventeenth, in the Laon region, executed with spirit but limited in scope.

When this action, which was the most direct and the boldest of all conceivable moves, miscarried there was nothing left to do but wait for the arrival of reserves. Those which were available to Gamelin, on the tenth of May (some seven divisions of infantry plus the three armored divisions), somewhere to the rear of the 1st, 9th, and 2nd armies, had been sucked into the battle. On the seventeenth he decided to recall the 7th Army from the delta of the Scheldt.[8] The shift did not actually begin until the eighteenth, and the newly assigned positions around the Oise were not approached until the nineteenth, unfortunately too late to prevent the Germans from seizing bridgeheads along the Somme. Again a fatal delay.

Meanwhile a certain number of divisions, which later would constitute the 10th Army (massed to the left of the 7th), had been withdrawn from the second group of armies, which manned the Maginot Line, and from the third group, under the command of General Besson (Belfort "gap"), which guarded the Swiss frontier, and, in case of necessity, were instructed to back General Olry's weak contingents in the Alps. These troops arrived very slowly. This is just one more indication of the shilly-shallying of the higher command and the paucity of military transport.

Nevertheless, the new disposition of our forces between the Meuse and the Oise was taking shape by the nineteenth. The 2nd Army, the hinge army, still retained its vigor. To its left the 6th Army was drawn alongside the Aisne River and the Ailette Canal. Its commander, Touchon, who had been placed in charge of all strategical reserves—to be gathered in an emergency—at first exerted himself in a sort of vacuum. But on the sixteenth, six divisions were already in position and

retreat were afraid of being outdistanced by advancing Germans. They clamored for protection by mechanized cavalry. In that way the forty tank battalions were used instead of being grouped in independent divisions. And the general tendency was to scatter even those divisions and battalions (see Appendix 4, page 595).

[8]Lord Gort says that this order was given as early as May 15. But, if he must be believed, how can the abnormally long time spent in execution be accounted for? According to Weygand, four divisions of the 7th Army (out of eight) were still "entraining" on May 22! Either Gort or Weygand is wrong in stating the date. Moreover, it must have been a very hard job to extricate the 7th Army from the northern battle front. The rash leadership of General Giraud comes in for a good deal of criticism.

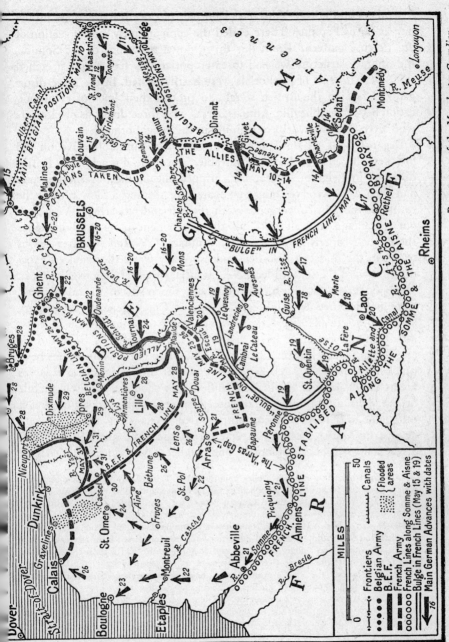

German advance through Belgium and northern France

By courtesy of the *Manchester Guardian*

five others on the way. Four days later part of the 7th Army filled up the line as far as Péronne. There ended the comparatively strong section of our defense pattern.[4] From this town, down the valley of the Somme, the military structure we had to extemporize was feeble and stretched thin. Detachments of territorials were hastily posted. In the same disorganized fashion the British sought to protect their lines of communication between Abbeville, Amiens, Arras with three divisions of pioneers who were building works or training in this neighborhood.

Regardless of all this, on the nineteenth a counteroffensive on the "pocket" became at least conceivable, since the French and British divisions in Belgium had, at last, gripped the Scheldt. A short respite had been won. Reserves might be spared for striking a blow toward the south, possibly in convergence with the 7th and 6th armies. Was it to our advantage to wait until all the component parts on both sides should be properly arrayed and co-ordinated? Wasn't it better for us to act in the midst of disorder, and especially while the armored expedition toward the sea still lacked substantial support? Billotte and Gort, who pondered this question throughout the night of the nineteenth, were not inclined to think so. Yet one of Gort's general conclusions, as it appears in his dispatches, is tantamount to an admission that the attack should not have been deferred. "By joint attacks from the air and of mechanized forces," he wrote, "the tempo of operations has been quickened to such a pitch as to make almost useless whatever reserves are at the disposal of the defense, unless they should be entirely mobile or already in a position to intervene." This comes close to saying that if our game was to be the concentration of reserves, all the odds were against us. Under the most diverse forms, the same question had endlessly harassed both diplomats and soldiers ever since Munich: for

---

[4] On May 19 the 7th and 6th armies composed the Third Army Group, a designation which, until that time, had been applied to the divisions stationed at the extreme right of our defense system, in upper Alsace. General Besson, who commanded the old Third Army Group in the east, also commanded the new Third Army Group in the west. Toward the end of May the Third Army Group, from the sea to the neighborhood of the Maginot Line, included: the 10th, 7th, 6th, 2nd and 4th armies, the last transferred from the Saar to give greater strength to the "hinge." Since the 2nd and 4th armies had a special task of their own to perform (to resist the German movement of envelopment across the Champagne plain), they became the Fourth Army Group, under Huntziger's command, their sector stretching from the mountain of Rheims to the Maginot fortifications.

The Third Army Group was broken asunder in the battles of June 7 and 8. At that time the 7th Army, separated from the 10th, which was itself cut in two, joined forces with the Army of Paris under General Héring. When it was decided to make Paris "an open city" the 7th Army, the Army of Paris, and fragments of the 6th Army retired to the Loire and the Massif Central under Besson's command.

whom was time working? On the nineteenth, once more, it was working against us. On that day, perhaps, we could not achieve much. But the day after, we would achieve even less.

The British Cabinet was convinced of this. On the morning of the twentieth, it sent Sir Edmund Ironside to Gort's headquarters in order to urge immediate movement toward Amiens and to stimulate Georges as well as Leopold. Gort pointed out that he could not at the same time carry on rear-guard action along the Scheldt, protect his flanks, and drive toward the southeast. His lines of communication and his supply depots at Amiens and Abbeville had gone up in smoke. How could he feed the battle? At the very best, two divisions and a few unattached units might be set aside for the enterprise. He allowed himself to be impressed, but he restricted the whole scheme to a thrust south of Arras. Such an undertaking, he remarked, should have the effect of setting the French Army in motion, of giving it heart. As he saw it, the Army Group of the North, comparable to a beleaguered garrison, could attempt no more than a sortie, and the main blow must be struck from elsewhere. Still, having said so much, he yielded. Billotte was won over to the project: the 1st Army would lend its help.[5] Is it in that juncture that Ironside shook him by the shoulders? A conference was to have taken place that evening to arrange details. But Billotte never appeared. Why? Weygand, who was to wait until the twenty-third before he notified the British that he had taken command,[6] had ordered the head of the First Army Group to stay in his quarters. The very most he would agree to was that General Prioux should contribute his mechanized cavalry, but on condition that use of it should be sparing.

The naked fact was that Weygand did not wish to throw himself blindly into this venture. He did not yet see his way clearly enough, and he looked down upon all the planning of Gort and Ironside. He overruled the arrangements of the general in command of the First Army Group. He even reproached him with having made any promise. So the British were to be alone in their fight around Arras on the twenty-first, except for the limited assistance of Prioux. The generalissimo wanted to survey the prospective battlefield and, in person, ascertain all aspects of the problem he had to solve. Why couldn't he commit Georges, whom he trusted, and the thousand professors of La Ferté-sous-Jouarre

[5] In the aggregate no more than five or six divisions were to participate, the cavalry probably not included.

[6] Nevertheless Churchill and Reynaud attended a session of the Supreme War Council held at his general headquarters on the twenty-second.

to the task of providing him with a complete description of the chess-board?

He drew up the plan of battle with Billotte on the twenty-first, held back King Leopold III, who already played a lone hand, spent the whole of the twenty-second and twenty-third in perfecting his disposi-tions and in gathering together his tools. Everyone would share in the attack: the sailors on the seaside, the 10th Army in the south, the 7th Army in the southeast, the 6th Army in the east, and the 1st Army and the British divisions in the north, while the Belgians would remain where they were and act as a covering force. In a session of the Supreme Council, on the twenty-second, Weygand gave an oversimplified out-line of the contemplated operation.[7] On paper everything fitted in won-derfully and was most logically tabulated. But the parts of so burden-some a machine required days and days to be put together, whereas speed was the prerequisite of success. Actually none of the staffwork seemed to be translated into concrete deeds. British officers were there to tell that they had failed to locate such and such divisions in places where, according to Weygand, they ought to have been found. Then, too, Georges's general order: "Let all the forces available in the east be shifted toward the west and the armies echeloned from the Oise to Montmédy screen and protect them," was not issued until the twenty-second.

Weygand returned from his trip on the twenty-second, via Cher-bourg, departed once more, came back, defined his tactics in a note of the twenty-fourth and, on the same day, had them endorsed afresh by Reynaud and Churchill—not a very difficult matter to settle, indeed, since Churchill was hourly protesting against delay. However, as early as the twenty-third, the opportunity had passed—slight as it was—and Weygand bestirred himself in vain. It would never return. Every time he believed he could set the mechanism moving some piece would totter, making necessary a readjustment of the whole. At the most, a few circumscribed actions would be launched. Indeed, Lord Gort as-serts that he never received an authentic version of Weygand's plan. All that he knew of it came from the dispatches of his own government.[8]

[7] On May 24 Churchill complained about lack of instructions and co-ordination. In his answer Reynaud disclosed that Weygand was in touch with the Belgians and professed to communicate, through them, with Blanchard and Gort. But why that indirect contact? Why didn't he meet Gort on the twenty-first?

[8] "The plan had no substance at all. Nothing had been verified, nothing worked out, nothing co-ordinated. Never was a British general called to participate in a more nebulous or unpromising operation." (Lord Gort.)

Just as in Gamelin's day, he was left without orders or instructions—with the added difficulty that Billotte, seriously injured on the evening of the twenty-first, when his automobile collided with a truck, was replaced by Blanchard, whose appointment was never notified and for whom the authority to co-ordinate, conferred on the commander of the First Army Group, on the twelfth, was never requested.[9]

Within one hundred hours the disaster of the Meuse had spread tremendously. It would have been better if the scheme worked out by Ironside, Gort, and Billotte had been approved on the twentieth and put into effect. Now it was too late.

For one thing, the Germans established bridgeheads at Abbeville, Picquigny, Amiens, and Péronne, and, on the twenty-third and the twenty-fourth, held them against the assaults of the 10th and 7th armies. For another, the British Expeditionary Force was more and more pressingly hemmed in by the Nazis. The spearhead of the blitzkrieg, which showed up on the shore of the Channel between the Somme and Boulogne, was disconcerting to the Imperial Staff in London, and when Winston Churchill telephoned Reynaud on the twenty-third, he did not conceal his bewilderment.[10] On the twenty-first, Gort had been compelled

[9] See Lord Gort's dispatches.

[10] Subsequently, Weygand used this telephone call of Churchill's to bolster his case. According to him, the Prime Minister found in the arrival of German tanks on the Channel a pretext for withdrawing from all joint attempts at cutting off the "pocket." Following out this argument, he held that the retreats of the British which had occurred or were supposed to have occurred on the twenty-fourth, in the Arras and Le Havre areas, were deliberate infringements of the orders given by him. Here is Weygand's story as M. Charles Reibel put it on record three weeks later. "A double maneuver was planned since it was necessary for both lips of the wound, some sixty kilometers apart, to be brought together before the bulk of the German troops should have arrived. The south-north movement had made headway with difficulty because we were short of troops below the Somme and because the Germans had larded this whole region with mines. Nevertheless, our troops, at the cost of heavy losses, had been able almost completely to clear the left bank of the Somme and to hold their position there. The north-south movement had worked out more easily: the progress of our northern armies, numerically much more important, had been rapid, and there remained only thirty kilometers to cover before joining when suddenly, on the morning of the twenty-fourth, the five British divisions which made up the right wing changed direction under the orders of their chief and moved off toward the northwest. Delay ensued with fatal consequences: it allowed the German infantry divisions, which were hastily being brought up in trucks, to arrive on the ground and firmly establish themselves. Everything was lost!" (*Why and How It Was Decided to Ask for an Armistice: June 10-17,* by Charles Reibel.) The most authoritative of British sources, among others Lord Gort, whose dispatches on this delicate subject are quite explicit, find in this tale only a falsification of the facts.

Here are the accusations leveled against the French Command: (1) It left the British Army without orders and instructions. General Ironside had a painful discussion on this subject with General Billotte, and Mr. Churchill complained to Reynaud on the twenty-

to hastily set up a defensive front from the northwest of Valenciennes
to Gravelines, over 120 kilometers. The very same day he had decided,
in consultation with Billotte, to retire his troops from the Scheldt to
the Lys and from there to the fortified lines on the French frontier—the
sector from which he had moved forward on May 10. Both commanders recognized that resistance along the Scheldt could not continue for
more than twenty-four hours. The withdrawal toward the Lys took
place on the twenty-third and twenty-fourth. Through the whole length
of the front the British Army was hard pressed. The enemy held the initiative. How could it have been torn from him? Meanwhile Leopold
became more and more uncertain. On the twenty-first, at the meeting in
Ypres, where the details of the retreat were arranged, his promise to take
back his troops to the Yser was not given to Billotte without manifest
reluctance. He was on the brink of branching off toward independent
action. If he should not move in the direction of Nieuport, a serious

---

fourth. When General Blanchard replaced Billotte the same inertia continued. (2) The retreat
of the English troops toward the Lys was settled at a conference held as early as May 21,
with Billotte and Leopold III participating. Weygand could therefore not have been taken
unawares by this movement. (3) The attack planned for the twenty-sixth was countermanded with Blanchard's agreement. (4) On May twenty-sixth, Paul Reynaud went to
London. Winston Churchill, who had attended the ceremony of intercession for France,
in Westminster Abbey, met him at the Admiralty. They agreed to convey to Gort and
Weygand orders which would put a stop to all action at cross purposes. They were both
convinced that the armies of the north had no recourse except retreat to the coast. Having
read the note which Reynaud had prepared for the French generalissimo, General Ironside
objected. The substance of his remark was that the note seemed to imply that in the past
the British Army had not obeyed the orders given it. It could not have disobeyed a leadership which did not assert itself. Certainly a historic document should not contain falsehood,
perpetuate assertions which were not true. Reynaud offered no objections. (5) On several
occasions the British liaison officer assigned to General Weygand sent London incorrect
information on operations. For instance, on the evening of the twenty-third he announced
that the French Army was in the suburbs of Amiens. "Good news!" cried a member of the
Cabinet. "Yes indeed, if it is true!" replied Ironside. The news proved to be false. Had it
been given out in order to spur Gort's troops into an offensive? Gort maintains that on the
twenty-fourth Churchill and Reynaud still considered the Weygand plan possible of execution on the basis of information of this sort supplied by the generalissimo. Eden's dispatch,
which Gort quotes in support of this affirmation, speaks of the capture of Péronne, Albert,
and Amiens by the 7th Army. (6) Finally, it is pointed out by the British that around May
28–29 the Imperial General Staff questioned whether the British divisions could be evacuated
in mass through Dunkirk. "We'll be doing well if fifteen or twenty thousand men are saved,"
said one of Winston Churchill's colleagues to him. Thus the London General Staff must
not be pictured as being exclusively anxious to call back its troops from Flanders in order
to transport them to the other side of the Channel. It dared not count upon the solution
which, ultimately, stood the test. To say that the thoughts of the British ministers and
military chiefs, on the twenty-fourth and twenty-fifth, were entirely occupied with plans
for evacuation is a distortion of history, in the light of what followed. The authority given
Gort on the twenty-eighth, of surrendering whenever he judged he could no longer inflict
losses on the enemy, settles the matter.

threat would arise on the British left flank; an empty space eighty kilometers wide would have to be filled at any cost.

So it was not at all surprising that on May 23 Gort's reserves (the two divisions which had been fighting around Arras forty-eight hours earlier) could not follow the French 1st Army, which sought to clear a strip from Douai to Cambrai as a preliminary to the main maneuver. These two divisions themselves had to keep on fighting on the Scarpe. Nevertheless, Gort tried, under the spur of the British War Office, to carry out Weygand's plan—the plan which had never been communicated to him. On the twenty-fourth, he arranged with Blanchard to launch an attack on the twenty-sixth, with four French divisions, four British divisions, and Prioux's cavalry. But on the twenty-fifth, both generals, together with Sir John Dill, the new chief of the Imperial Staff, who had put in an appearance, agreed to countermand this movement. They had become convinced that from the Somme, the Oise, and the Aisne no force could move forth and meet halfway troops starting from the north. And the Belgians were weakening in the Courtrai region, which might leave the English flank exposed from the north. Leopold was to surrender on the twenty-seventh at midnight, leaving Gort only one hour to solve a terrible problem. The last hand was played and we were finished. The Franco-British armies in Flanders were cornered. And in the south what had been a mere foray of German tanks had become a firmly articulated army.

As early as the evening of the twenty-fourth, Weygand had given Blanchard complete liberty of movement. And, simultaneously, the communiqué of French General Headquarters announced that "it had not been possible to re-establish a continuous front line."

So Weygand admitted that the plan carefully worked out between the twenty-first and the twenty-third had missed fire, and that the whole battle which aimed at drawing together the lips of the wound had been lost even before it was joined. And he wanted this reverse to be made known in spectacular fashion, his intention being to manipulate the story and make it the substance of his personal propaganda against the British. On the twenty-fifth, in the War Committee, he uttered words of discouragement. It was his first formal warning to Reynaud.

Weygand now planned for Dunkirk, Calais, Boulogne, to be set up as a huge entrenched camp, with enough nuisance value to distract the enemy while the Aisne-Oise-Somme front was being built up. The British General Staff co-operated in putting this scheme into effect. What else could it do? But a new fact must be noted. The British Staff had lost confidence in the French Army. In the rank and file ran this phrase: "We no longer have the soldiers of the Marne and of Verdun fighting at our side." Their unlimited, touching faith in the martial virtues of the French people was on the wane. Weygand had not erased the deep disillusionment caused by Gamelin, and in London it was even suspected that he had not seriously tried to free the First Army Group from the German ring: that, in Flanders, he had meant only to follow tactics of attrition; that he had preferred to await the decision on the river Somme. His hesitation, his passive attitude between May 19 and 23, seemed explicable only on this assumption—an assumption granted, moreover, by certain people in Paris. On the evening of the twenty-fifth Anthony Eden, Secretary of State for War, sent a telegram to Gort: "All my information indicates that for the French offensive from the Somme a sufficient force will not be assembled . . . If this should be the case, you will be confronted with a state of affairs in which the safety of the British Expeditionary Force must be your foremost care." This dispatch did not merely signify that from thenceforth Dunkirk would be an evacuation point: it sounded the death knell of the unified command.

On May 26 the perimeter of this hastily built entrenched camp within which the French and the British were to be enclosed was a little more than two hundred kilometers in extent. This was too wide a front for the effectives at the disposal of Gort and Blanchard. Within three days they had to tighten their lines by more than half. Thus the entrenched area shrank into something like a fortress: twenty-four kilometers wide and sixteen deep. On May twenty-eighth, ten thousand officers and soldiers had already put to sea, thanks to an incredible mobilization of small boats and pleasure craft of every conceivable size from the whole British coast line, and thanks to a vigorous air defensive which held off the German bombers whose projectiles might have forced the stronghold to capitulate. But almost at once it became evident that the French and the British armies were no longer of one mind in the struggle, that they were directed toward different ends. Resistance to the bitter end was Weygand's motto, resistance behind lines which not only covered Dunkirk but the other Channel ports. Every day spent in fighting added to the respite needed by the French Army in order to prepare its defense along the Somme and the Aisne. The price could not be too high; let it be paid. But the British did not see things from the same point of view. Perhaps London would be struck before Paris. Surely it was no longer reasonable to involve English divisions in Weygand's strategical plans, which after all were very shaky. The urgent task was to save English troops. Later on they would come back to the aid of their allies if there was yet time, if the German lightning spared the British territory.

Weygand must have learned of this decision of Churchill's and Sir John Dill's from Reynaud, who went to London on the twenty-sixth. Yet he gave no indication of knowing it. He acted as though the event took him unawares. At the conference held at Cassel on the twenty-seventh to arrange for the parceling out of the shortened front, General Koeltz, assistant chief of staff (aide-major général), was seated beside Blanchard. With the generalissimo's instructions in his hand, he still insisted upon a counteroffensive. He futilely urged Blanchard and Fagalde[11] to recapture Calais. On the twenty-eighth, Blanchard informed Gort that he had been enjoined to form a "bridgehead," that he had not been authorized to pay any heed to an eventual evacuation. On the same day Weygand once more protested to the English commander in chief: "It is essential to strike hard . . ." On the next day, the twenty-ninth, Abrial, the "Admiral of the North," in chief command at Dunkirk, displayed wonderment and proved argumentative. Gort must send him one of the English generals so that he could see with his own eyes the orders received from London.

Upon this basic controversy other subsidiary quarrels were to pile up. The French Navy did nothing whatever to rescue French troops from the Dunkirk area, which obviously was to become smaller and smaller as its garrison was constantly diminishing in numbers. Yet French soldiers by tens of thousands were waiting on the beaches. Not for a moment did they suppose that they would not be transported to the other side of the Channel with their British comrades. And the French Command, which had refused to have anything to do with an evacuation, was quick to claim equality in shipping space. Gort provisionally allocated to it two ships and a beach. In Paris, on May 31 and June 1, Winston Churchill yielded to Weygand's request for even shares. Even this did not put an end to the quarrels.

The British Cabinet had decided that the commander in chief of the Expeditionary Force would leave Dunkirk and would transmit his command to one of his army-corps commanders at the moment when the effectives still on the spot should be less than three divisions. On the evening of the thirty-first, there remained scarcely twenty thousand British troops in the neighborhood of the city. There was nothing left for Gort to do except depart. Lieutenant General Harold Alexander, as-

[11]In command of the 16th Army Corps, which had fought with the Belgians and, up to the end, was to cover the British embarkation.

signed to continue the fight, would himself embark on June 2, after having assured himself that no one of his men was left behind. In both cases Weygand protested against what he chose to regard as derelictions of duty. And more than one painful incident has been passed over.

On the twenty-seventh, the 60th Division (one of the two divisions of the 7th Army, fighting with the Belgians) pushed into the narrowing enclave with horse-drawn supply trains, contrary to British rulings. As a result the roads became even more jammed. British anger exploded when it was later discovered that the horses were abandoned on the beach with no one to take care of them and without even having been released from their picket lines. The English sporting spirit can never be downed.

On the twenty-eighth, Gort and Blanchard had words over General Prioux, commander of the mechanized cavalry, which was stalled somewhere between Béthune and Lille: he insisted that his troops were worn out and incapable of going a step further. The Dunkirk nightmare did not end until June 3: by that day 224,000 British and 112,000 "allied" troops (the latter almost all French) had been saved from death or from capture. But this bad dream left behind it a sad trail of military, political, and psychological effects.

The unified command had broken down. Weygand was disregarded both when he pressed the British to overlook the wheeling movement of the German armored forces along the shore of the Channel (May 23) and to persevere in the scheme of operations toward Bapaume, when he stressed the necessity of a counterattack to relieve the Belgians on May 27. In the end, what he had to say was not even taken seriously. He discredited himself by admonitions which were not related to reality and in which it was hard to see anything more than an attempt to save his face before posterity. Henceforward the Supreme Council and conferences of French and British ministers would try as best they might to re-establish unity of action. It was no more than a shadow. As far as the English were concerned, the Battle of Flanders was over, and the Battle of France meant little to them beyond a postponement of the Battle of England. Indeed, it never occurred to them to cease fighting at the side of their allies. They believed, or wished to believe, even as late as June 12 or 13, that Weygand could halt the invader. Their 51st Infantry Division, posted in the Saar ever since March and unable to rejoin the Expeditionary Force in Belgium, proceeded into Normandy and fought with the 10th Army. Also the Pioneers and a tank division which arrived in France too late to be able to reach the zone where Gort was in action. On May 26 and 31, on June 1, 8, 11, and 13, Churchill and Dill were to give promise after promise, except regarding the air forces, which they did not wish to take from their island. And they gave these promises with every intention of living up to them. But all the while they took their own counsel.

The most lasting legacy of Dunkirk was the animosity which obtained, at least temporarily, between the French and the British. The former sacrificed themselves, particularly between May 30 and June 3, to protect an embarkation in which they participated in an important but still inferior proportion. The latter, flowing back toward their threatened homeland, parted with their comrades on the field of battle. To many Frenchmen such was the whole picture. They overlooked the rest. The reader can easily imagine the details with which that picture was elaborated. All the more tragic did these details grow in the legends which always spread like a forest fire whenever hundreds of thousands are at close grip with death. But, between Dill and Weygand, there were no unpleasant clashes, no disputes.[12] At the Supreme Council of May 31 and June 1 all went on harmoniously. "The French commander in chief," a witness told me, "did not even need to finish his sentences. Instantaneously the English commander showed by a gesture that he perceived what his colleague was driving at." But the two men no longer had the same immediate worries. Between them, personally, it was only later that differences of opinion would prevail, and these differences were given expression by third parties: "If the British Army had obeyed General Weygand, the pocket could have been closed," Baudouin, Minister of Foreign Affairs, announced to the press on July 5. On the seventh an official British communiqué replied that Weygand made his arrangements too late.[13] Four or five days after the armistice Weygand, in his

---

[12]Any more than there were between Winston Churchill, Dill, and Reynaud. On May 31 or June 1, Churchill begged Weygand to vent his grievances; the French general avoided the issue.

[13]"The English Command agreed to counterattack on May 21, and, in fact, it did counterattack, whereas the French held back. The British Army was forced to retire on May 23, since the Germans had appeared upon its right flank and threatened to encircle it completely. Nevertheless the Command agreed, on May 24, to carry out the Weygand plan of simultaneous attack against the Germans at once in the north and in the south, and Generals Gort and Blanchard [General Billotte in the meantime had suffered an automobile accident] set the twenty-sixth as the date for beginning this operation. But on the following day, May 25, the Belgians were routed, leaving unprotected the British left flank and making necessary a further withdrawal of the British troops who were supporting the Belgian front. . . . The plan devised by General Weygand was excellent, but it came too late. The disaster took place quite independently of events happening between the twenty-third and the twenty-sixth of May, and for it General Weygand is in no sense responsible. It resulted

capacity as Minister for National Defense, sent out a number of telegrams to the High Commissioner in Beirut, to the French Minister in Cairo, etc.—certainly a most extraordinary procedure—to sum up his grievances. Weygand's accusations and complaints had grown sharper and sharper after the defeat on the Somme and on the Aisne, when the question of a separate armistice became more acute and he asked for the secession from England. One cannot help forming the impression that he deliberately picked a quarrel.

6

Weygand's Strategy

IN ITS BROADEST OUTLINE, such was the course of the battle between May 19 and June 3. But the case of Weygand, the strategist, needs further elucidation.

On May 20, Weygand countermanded the operation to destroy the "pocket" on which Billotte and Gort had agreed, in order that he might work it out in his own way, with better prospects of success, he believed, since as little as possible would be left to chance. From all these preparations, however, no action of any importance ever resulted. Why? Was it that Weygand, although being heart and soul in the undertaking, had to contend with insuperable obstacles because he had deceived himself as to the rate of speed of the German advance to the sea and as to the rapidity with which the Germans consolidated themselves? Or did he neglect the opportunities which came within his grasp because he had in mind another plan, the plan which was to materialize in the Battle of the Somme? Or, to re-echo an opinion held by some, was he hunting two hares at the same time? We cannot come to any final conclusion until the day when a Commission of Inquiry will have investigated the case, but the most probable answer seems to be that the scheme destined to lead him to the Battle of the Somme dominated his mind. The operations which developed in the north served his purpose mainly because

from mistaken arrangements made by General Gamelin." Communiqué of the British Ministry of Information reproduced in *Chronology of Failure* (The Last Days of the French Republic), by Hamilton Fish Armstrong. In July 1940 the British took care not to give offense to Weygand. But one year later Lord Gort spoke bluntly.

he expected them to keep the enemy busy and hinder him from massing southward. Thus he was likely to consider an entrenched camp built around Dunkirk of greater help than the attack on the "pocket."[1]

Between May 20 and 24, to all outward appearances, he followed the example set by Pétain, who, on March 24, 1918, refused to safeguard the liaison with the British Army on the claim that he could not move his reserves from the Champagne front where they eventually would protect Paris against an enemy drive. For twenty long years Weygand had denounced Pétain's pettiness and bad judgment in this earlier juncture wherefrom Foch rose to glory. Foch had determined to use every available means to prevent the French and British from becoming separated from each other and losing the war. The ironic god of battles confronted Weygand with the same network of dilemmas which once had overcome Pétain.

He did not have the courage to boldly pursue the war of movement which had been unleashed on May 10. He was not sure enough that his reputation would be spared in the turmoil. He hid behind academic formulas. He set forth in quest of a doubtful compromise between a war of movement and a war of position. He failed to be a man of single purpose. In the innumerable instructions given his army commanders[2] he sought shelter against the criticism of posterity. What he wanted to do was to execute a correct *kriegspiel* rather than a maneuver instinct with life. He made no attempt to jostle the bold German armored vanguard lest his own forces be thereby disarrayed. He did not seek to create any effect of confusion, lacking all confidence that he could match his adversary in facing the unforeseen. He arranged the placement and movement of his troops so that they would fit every hypothesis; he fashioned a mixture of every possible solution at the price of scattering his resources. Certain aspects of his battle alignment seem to have merely symbolic value, to indicate intentions rather than positive action. It was as though he were saying, "If I had more men, this is what I would do!" He was not bold enough to choose between various modes of action. And Fortune did not give so much as a hint of one of her smiles. Nobody will be presumptuous enough to say that success was within his reach. But he did not try to get hold of it, and in the circumstances of the moment, no matter how desperate the attempt, it ought to have been made.

[1] He told the Supreme War Council, on May 22, that the Germans would have to resume old-fashioned warfare before long and to part with their newfangled methods.

[2] In *Sept Jours* (October–December 1940) M. Henry Bidou enumerates and quotes them.

I have already spoken of his interview with General Georges on May 23, when some principles were laid down for the conduct of the campaign. The two leaders could count only upon effectives which were inferior to those of Germany in quality even more than in quantity. They had under serious discussion an extraordinary piece of strategy: to withdraw from the fortified region and mass the whole of the French Army, every bit of transportable matériel, in the west, with Paris inserted within the sphere of this operation. As against this drastic sacrifice, the abandonment of the eastern area, the defense of metropolitan France seemed likely to be considerably prolonged and the armies in the north might then have a chance of reuniting with the others. At any rate, in case of defeat, evacuation would be possible toward England and France's overseas possessions. The other alternative of energetic strategy —to make of the fortified region France's final redoubt—did not hold forth comparable prospects, since it involved, from the outset, the loss of Paris, of seventy per cent of the war industries, and offered no means of egress. It was merely a blind alley leading to final capitulation.

Men resolved not to consider defeat on French home soil as the end of the war and complete disaster, men convinced that, on the scale of modern war, the Mediterranean was the equivalent of what the Marne once had been, would probably have set their choice upon the former of these two formulas. General de Gaulle told me, in July 1940, that this would have been the best line to take. Weygand and Georges, however, forswore any such grandiose reshuffling and resigned themselves to fighting where they were—that is, with a thin string of troops stretched out from the fortified zone toward the west along the Aisne, the Ailette, the Oise, and the Somme. Such is the interpretation to be put on Georges's general orders of the twenty-second, which were confirmed the following day. Nowhere would there be anything like a normal density of troops. And from one end to the other of this front the battle was to be waged "without thought of retreat," to be on a level with Gamelin's instructions to the troops in Belgium.

Within this framework the action of cutting through the pocket sometimes assumed the importance of the principal operation; at other times it sank to a subordinate place. Anyhow, at the outset Weygand did not want to have anything to do with a clean hammer blow struck from north to south. He preferred to set up a vise, a pair of jaws. He held back the Blanchard army group (including the British) until the 10th and 7th armies on the Somme and on the Oise could participate in the chewing. This lower jaw, however, was never able to move upward.

Meanwhile he satisfied himself with words, or else he used them to delude others. "The Germans will certainly be lucky if they get themselves out of the fix they are in!" he exclaimed on the twenty-second, fresh from his inspection tour, to Darlan, who met him at the railroad station. And on the twenty-third he again said to General Doumenc that the German armored forces would die of starvation in their "pocket."[3]

I somewhat doubt Weygand's sincerity because the daily reports transmitted to the Ministry of Foreign Affairs made it amply clear from the beginning that to prepare for the Battle of the Somme was his first care, that he looked upon everything else as a legacy from Gamelin and as the particular business of the British. Did he hope that the principal German attack would be aimed at London and that he would thus be given time to organize his battlefield between the Somme, the Oise, and the Seine? But, on the assumption that he was honest, that he really entertained the plan he talked about, his calculations were far from faultless. At least he was mistaken as to the possibility of co-ordinating two movements, one from the north and the other from the south, against the Germans, who were established in a middle position, outflanking Blanchard's army group in the west. About the twenty-fourth Weygand appears to have been converted to the idea of a unilateral movement, working from the north toward the south. Then he tried to reawaken British faith in the hammer blow which he himself had countermanded on the twentieth. He no longer found them inclined to advance. For all such goings on there is but one proper adjective—trifling.

In this Battle of the Somme, the Oise, and the Aisne, which, with the armies of the north surrounded, evacuated, or lost, seemed to be the last hope, what were the chances of success? From the sea to Montmédy (the end of the Maginot Line), for some 360 kilometers, the following forces were stationed along the river system: forty-five infantry divisions, three armored divisions, three cavalry motorized divisions. However, a number of these infantry divisions were not yet at full strength, even on June 1, and half a score of them, described as "light" (an appellation dating back to the Norwegian expedition), included only two infantry regiments and two groups of artillery. The semiofficial account of the campaign, published in *Le Temps* on November 17, 1940, emphasizes that the 2nd and 3rd armored divisions possessed a total of only 130 tanks, and the three cavalry divisions had in all only forty armored cars.

---

[3] He told Baudouin (probably on the twenty-third): "Within four days either I shall be Marshal of France or we shall have to request an armistice!" General Georges made similar remarks.

But those figures are unreliable: clearly a case is being made for the High Command. General de Gaulle maintains that toward the end of May a thousand tanks could still have been gathered. Moreover, in the same document, no mention whatever is made of the air forces. In the Battle of the Somme they were scarce.[4] Still, while it developed, British officers did record the presence of roughly one thousand airplanes in North Africa and in Syria, among them many of the Curtiss design which had not yet been unpacked. It has been computed that on the Somme and the canal of the Ailette a division occupied an average of fifteen kilometers, and from the Ailette to the Argonne, twelve kilometers, not counting reserves: some fifteen divisions of infantry, the armored corps, the cavalry. Surely there was no ground for great expectations in all this. Here were scanty tools with which to stop some eighty or ninety German divisions plus ten armored divisions carefully restored to their original strength of May 10.

But we come across Weygand's great idea. It pleased him to think that he had introduced new tactics into the French Army, that he had replaced its rigid linear resistance—the rule up to that moment—by a resistance in depth, invested with elasticity. For fifteen days, between May 24 and June 7 or 8, his technical staffs (that is, Georges's) defined the new method of warfare in a long series of general instructions and memoranda, either signed by the generalissimo or by the commander of the armies of the north and the northeast. Behind the main line was to be woven a vast network of centers of resistance, of "closed groups," of points of support, all equipped with anti-tank and anti-aircraft guns, with "75s" commanding "axes of penetration." Villages, thickets, farmhouses— these were as many fortresses, some powerful, others of inferior strength, all well supplied and further elaborated by means of barricades, mines, etc. If necessary, outside the zone of hostilities, civilian volunteers, under the direction of officers, would hold them. Any artillery unit not already enclosed within one of these redoubts was immediately to fit one up for its own use. Along the battle front men crouching in holes would let airplanes and tanks pass by, watching for a favorable moment to engage the enemy. Units outflanked by armored corps were to roll up into a ball, like a hedgehog, grasping at every possibility of counterattack. It would make little difference if neighboring units should have given

[4] On May 22, Mr. Churchill promised Weygand that all bombers and fighters available on the Continent would be shifted from long-distance raids to the battlefields. On May 30, Weygand complained about the slender air forces left in France, three squadrons of fighters, and on June 3 asked for ten more to be sent. Planes based on airfields in England participated in the struggle but, because of the distance, with curtailed flying time.

way: no one was to worry about the continuity of the line of battle. In the second zone of defense the "closed groups" would carry out the same instructions. The assault of the tanks would gradually lose its momentum in the meshwork and become scattered. And the reserve divisions would be called up to relieve the tiny fortresses and to set free garrisons which had been surrounded. The Germans would be caught in the texture. They would fall like flies in gossamer. Men must vie with the enemy in audacity, cunning, ingenuity, counterinfiltrate when the Nazis infiltrated, show "aggressiveness."

How pathetic was this High Command, so slow in the past to spell out the lessons given by the invader, when it endeavored to overturn completely, to reform from top to bottom, within two weeks, the tactical teachings pounded into a whole generation of officers and soldiers— when it pretended to believe that the master player could be beaten at his own game!

Did Weygand really believe in what he was doing? Was he merely bestirring himself that honor might be saved, as he would say in Cangey on June 11, or did he see victory at the end of his toil? The memorandum which Weygand sent Reynaud on May 29, the day after Leopold's defection and the moment when he had to cross off his books the entrenched enclave around Dunkirk, makes us face the question and even answer it negatively. In that note he elaborated upon his warning of the twenty-fifth and underlined it; he asserted that France was throwing her last stake on the Somme, Oise, and Aisne.[5] If the battle went against her, if the positions which the French troops had received orders to hold unto death should crumble under the impact of the Nazis, France would have no recourse but to lay down her arms. She would then no longer be able to do anything useful to stem the invasion. It was the generalissimo's duty to suggest that, without further delay, the British Government be informed of the irretrievable consequences of such a defeat.[6]

What an amazing state of mind was this general's, working along with the picture of an impending stampede continuously before his eyes. Certainly there were all too many reasons, on May 29, to look with discouragement at the immediate future. But, however despairing the realization of French military weakness, it should not have eliminated

[5]Henri Bidou, loc. cit. Meanwhile, on May 27, Weygand had, for the first time, attended a ministerial council and expressed himself in terms which must have approximated the wording of the memorandum.

[6]In a sitting of the War Committee held at about the same date, Pétain insisted that such a communication to the London Cabinet had better be passed over. The gist of what he said was that there are circumstances in which one must think only of oneself.

from Weygand's vision the strategic rear which, in truth, spread out behind his own picayune "meshwork," the true strategic rear immeasurably more important: an untouched Navy, the French Empire, a fighting England, and the United States which could not watch the destruction of the two Western Powers and the unlimited triumph of the National Socialist Revolution without throwing its own resources into the balance. The man who wrote that May 29 memorandum should have been instantly dismissed, for a High Command which despairs of national salvation must itself vanish.

And, from the British point of view, what sort of light does this memorandum cast upon Weygand? He daily and ceaselessly asked for planes, arms, reinforcements; he begged our Allies to remain on French soil. At the May 31 meeting of the French and British Premiers he backed up Reynaud's plea that, in the embarkation at Dunkirk, French troops should have their turn. And all this with the idea, perhaps even with near certainty, that the outcome would be nothing less than surrender! Thus he truly believed that England was fated to the same ruin as France and did not scruple to involve her in a suicide pact.

Paul Reynaud merely rejected Weygand's opinion.[7] A memorandum like the one forwarded on the twenty-ninth would never have reached Clemenceau without its author suffering the consequences. But the 1940 Premier was the prisoner of Weygand and Pétain, the captive of their spirit of defeat. On May 26 the chief of the marshal's secretariat, Raphael Alibert, later to be Minister of Justice, told anyone who wished to listen to him: "If within three days connection has not been re-established with the Dunkirk army, there is no use arguing about it—we are done for."

On June 5 the ordeal began. The Germans attacked from the sea to the confluence of the Ailette Canal and the Aisne. Their offensive broke forth from the Péronne bridgehead with special vigor. From that spot armored divisions moved on. Others crossed the Somme west of Amiens. The French line was bent but did not give way. Next day, in this neighborhood, the 51st English Infantry Division yielded ground, spread out as it was along twenty-four kilometers. With difficulty it pulled itself together along the Bresle. On the seventh, the Somme front was dislocated. Tanks poured through a fifteen-kilometer breach. They headed for Rouen. The 10th Army, on the left of the line, was cut in two, and three divisions were hurled to the west, toward St. Valéry-en-Caux, while the remainder fell back in the direction of Pontoise. On the eighth,

---

[7] He declared later on, when he was in jail, that he had instructed Weygand to make of Brittany a redoubt, to prepare the last perimeter of defense.

the eastern sector tottered; passage was forced across the Aisne above Soissons.

On the ninth, the Seine was hit at Vernon and Rouen, and as early as the eleventh bridgeheads were rigged up on the opposite shore. The 7th Army had been forced back toward Paris and the 6th toward Rheims, on the tenth and the eleventh. Further, to the east, as early as on the ninth, the enemy was in possession of the Rethel bridgehead on the Aisne. The 4th Army, which had been moved from the Saar as reenforcement for the 6th and the 2nd, had to fall in line with the former. The Nazis rushed into Champagne. Even the 2nd Army itself, an immovable rampart ever since May 15, was shaken in the Argonne region. The hours of its proud resistance were numbered. The Paris area was being hemmed in from east and west. On the eleventh, some thirty divisions at the most could be formed out of the crucible into which forty-five had been hurled six days before. The Maginot Line was left in the hands of twenty-odd divisions, all "fortress" or second reserve, fit only for positional warfare. On the twelfth the order for general retreat was issued. In the military government of Paris, General Dentz superseded General Héring, to whom an army had been allocated to fight ahead of the city. The capital was to be declared an "open city." All dams went down.

The "new" tactics had been no more successful than the old. We are told that the "closed groups" held out heroically, but that the reserves, whose task it was to relieve them, turned out to be far too weak. Some critics blame the general disposition of the forces. General de Gaulle finds fault with Weygand for not having massed his troops on the left, where the enemy could be expected to land its hardest blow. Instead of uniting the thousand tanks he still had into one "imperial guard" and spending them massively, he sprinkled them around. On May 26, General Altmayer of the 10th Army would have frittered away the 4th Armored Division south of Amiens—forgetful of what had happened to the 2nd, along the Oise, on the sixteenth—if the commander of the former (de Gaulle) had not brought him to his senses.

In brief, such is the military catastrophe which befell us three weeks after the rout on the Meuse. Weygand will have to account for it. Of course I don't claim to have avoided every error of fact and interpretation. That story cannot be definitively told until official records have been searched and, to supplement them (since it is to be feared that they may be sadly incomplete and may boil down to mere personal records), until the evidence of men invested with military or political functions has been heard and studied. Subject to what future inquiries bring forth and on the strength of what is at present known, it appears that Weygand lost the Somme-Oise-Aisne battle without having believed that it could succeed, even though he began by sacrificing to that battle all chances of rejoining the armies in the north.

He was always a chief of staff, the private secretary to Marshal Foch, the executant of Foch's orders. The victor of 1918 was wont to tell how, during the early weeks of the last war, his choice had fallen on Weygand. "He was in charge of a cavalry regiment at Nancy, headquarters of the 20th Army Corps, which I commanded. I summoned him, and at once sent him away: intuitively, I had felt that he was of a human structure very different from mine. Then I began asking myself why he repelled me. It was because our natures, our temperaments were poles apart. But perhaps he would contribute a useful complement. I had need of a man who would be meticulous and solicitous of details, in the German manner. And no association was ever happier. I always found him impeccable."

There we probably find the key to the mystery. Foch had been dead for eleven years, and the Weygand machine, somewhat slowed down indeed by the years, continued to roll along. But he was nothing more than a great executant; he had neither the brains nor the imaginative push nor, above all, the heart of a true leader. An idea which was truly his own he seldom had; but he had a capacity for devotion to the ideas of another man, and he prosecuted them in all their implications, even when he did not assent. He was of Pétain's breed, an excellent army and army-group commander, but a generalissimo without scope and without faith.

Before everything else both are (or were) learned staff officers—methodical, careful, precise. Their deficiency lay in their belief that the outcome of a battle inevitably springs from the relative strengths of the material forces involved; that man's spirit, struggling against the dead weight of numbers, is like a bird strayed into a cellar, which can find its way out only by a miracle. Both could well have appropriated a saying attributed to Colonel de Villelume before the crisis: "Why not throw down our hands, once the score can be foreseen? Why insist on playing the game out?" Amid the St. Gond marshes in August 1914, around Amiens in October of the same year, at Doullens on March 26, 1918, and on many other occasions, Foch, Weygand's master, proved physically incapable of despair and rebelled against cold calculations. He was convinced that, side by side with cannon, machine guns, hand grenades, human beings counted on battlefields—human beings, with all their unpredictable reactions—and that for this reason alone the sheer weight of masses of steel possessed no inexorable power.

The assertion will be heard that in May–June 1940 Foch would not have achieved more than Weygand. We can't tell, but we feel sure that he was not the man to hesitate in an emergency. He would have handled things differently. This is the way doubt is instilled.

7

The Tardy Evacuation of Paris and Governmental Disorder

REYNAUD let Weygand manage operations in his own way. The idea of the armistice gripped harder and harder on the mind of the generalissimo; Reynaud allowed him to lead the campaign and yet make its prosecution conditional upon nothing short of a miracle. Each morning he received him at about eleven; these daily reports gradually corroded his will. General de Gaulle was not to leave his 4th Armored Division to become Under Secretary of State for War until June 5. Had he been sent to the War Ministry a week earlier, he could perhaps have recaptured his former influence over the Premier. He could have encouraged him to rid himself of the warrior who no longer wished to fight. The hangers-on kept a close watch, and it would not have been an easy job to sweep them aside. Still, it was then, and not on June 12 at Tours, that an ardent appeal might have struck home. The fact that on June 5 Reynaud wanted to make de Gaulle Minister of War and did actually appoint him to an under secretaryship of state, despite Weygand and to Mme. de Portes's fury, showed that he was anxious not to swerve from his line.

All through the Battle of France the Prime Minister had remained inert. And his inertia was not confined to military matters. It accounts for an error fraught with great political and even military consequences, an error which contributed its full share toward pushing France into the worst possible fate. He kept the government and its most important administrative departments in Paris until June 10. Thereby he caused the executive power to break up. From the fifth to the tenth of June the French Army had been wrecked. On the tenth came the turn of the government.

The cabinet members and their staffs and secretariats moved to Tours and surrounding districts on June 10, when German armored units were prowling thirty or forty kilometers from the capital, three days before the arrival of German troops in the suburbs, four days before their march down the Champs Elysées. Carried out in the midst of disaster, the transfer of the seat of government necessarily brought in its wake confusion of all men and things—incipient administrative paralysis. Moreover, the road to Tours was not closed to fleeing civilians, which made public authority even more helter-skelter. Local officials allowed the hordes moving down from Belgium, from the capital, from the regions of the West and the North to pile up in that tiny city. Those who went through Tours on June 12, 13, and 14 will never forget what they saw there of the hideous countenance of anguish, panic, confusion. In the whirlwind ministers lost too often every vestige of self-control, poise, and balance. To make things worse, they were scattered around in the châteaux of Touraine and neighboring provinces—the President of the Republic at Cangey, the Premier at Chissay, other cabinet members and their retinue at Langeais, Azay-le-Rideau, Ligneuil, etc., one of them even being assigned quarters at Royan on the Gironde. Their comings and goings by automobile, to supplement hastily improvised telephone service, widened already manifest rifts between them.[1]

From the very first hours of the war, in September 1939, it was expected that Paris would be bombed. The readying of an alternative capital on which to fall back had, therefore, been foreseen and evacuation started.[2] A number of ministerial services indeed—the more cumber-

---

[1] Toward May 15 the civil authorities were the first to give the signal for civilian evacuation. They feared a repetition of the 1914 "atrocities." Soon enough the military consequences of these mass migrations became obvious, and the Army Command tried hard to ward them off. Seemingly, the civil authorities did not follow suit. At a gathering of ministers at Cangey, on June 11, someone suggested urging the French people to stay wherever they were, which brought forth that retort: "How on earth can we order others not to do what we have done ourselves?" No one pushed the matter further. But even if a decision had been arrived at, wouldn't it have remained a dead letter? On May 22, at a meeting of a Supreme War Council, Weygand had pressed Reynaud and Churchill to stop the influx of Belgians and other refugees. He wanted the frontier to be closed and the refugees compelled to keep off the highroads except at certain hours of the day and to encamp in open fields, etc.

[2] This was required by the Law of July 11, 1938 (Title 3, Article 59): "The seat of executive power and of the two houses of legislature can be transferred outside Paris at the time

some and furthest removed from the management of the war—henceforth were left in the area of the Loire. The many and complex problems related to a full governmental exodus should then have been properly studied and solved without delay. But there followed the *de facto* armistice, and execution was deferred indefinitely. The June 10 removal was altogether slapdash and under no one's responsibility.

Why was the moment of departure put off beyond May 24? At that date the government, by means of a communiqué already cited, let it be known that the left wing of the French Army, gambled in the Belgian venture, could not be welded once more to its main body, and that a battle of the Somme and Aisne would shortly succeed the struggle in Flanders. On May 16, General Héring, military governor of Paris, had entreated the government to get away. Heed should have been paid to the warning. And what about Weygand? On the nineteenth, when he accepted the high command, he had asked that the defense of Paris should not be required of him as an obligation to be fulfilled at all cost, that the whole question should be considered entirely from the point of view of strategy. This demand might have implied that, under certain circumstances, the presence of the government would be a nuisance and that it had better clear out. But a governmental migration southward connoted resistance to the bitter end in the Paris zone rather than its surrendering. And Weygand, with his inclination toward seeking an armistice, was alive to that natural inference. He said that the government must not budge. "Were the Germans to enter into Paris, the government was under the moral obligation to receive them."

Paul Reynaud and Georges Mandel, Minister of the Interior, dissented from Weygand about fundamentals but they feared lest, out of an abandoned Paris, some uprising would burst forth: perhaps even, under the leadership of Laval or someone like him—a "Commune" intent upon treating with the enemy, and plotting against the legal government.[3]

---

of mobilization, or under the circumstances foreseen under Article I of the present law. The government shall determine at a cabinet meeting, and after consultation with the presidents of the Senate and of the Chamber of Deputies, the date and the place of transfer. Necessary preparations shall be made in peacetime."

[3]Cf. A. de Monzie, *Ci-devant:* "Took lunch with Frossard, Bonnafous, Berthelot. I indicated my desire to remain behind.—No, don't stay in Paris; you will be accused of communicating with the enemy.—Still, if occupation there must be, someone will have to talk with the occupant?—Not you, when only a moment before you were a member of the Government.—And I agree that once the Government is gone, the fact of staying behind is a disavowal. As things are, I have the right to despise Paul Reynaud, but it is not yet wise for me to disavow him." Thus, to remain in Paris, in the opinion of Weygand, Monzie, and many others, was to prepare to negotiate.

The time limit was thus unduly put off. Reynaud only made up his mind on the night of June 7, but held his decision in abeyance; he did not inform his colleagues until the evening of the ninth, at the cabinet meeting to which were read the dispatches of François-Poncet announcing Ciano's final refusal of the French proposals: "Our line of action is settled; even an offer of Tunisia would not change our minds." The Premier did not at once win his point, although he disclosed the content of a strange letter of Weygand curtly giving notice that the time had come for the government to depart if they regarded it their duty not to remain under enemy occupation. Those who had been selected to go first (because they were not directly concerned with national defense) were shy of what people might say and insisted that all should set forth simultaneously. Finally, on the morning of the tenth, the War Cabinet[4] cut the matter short. At five in the afternoon the ministers yielded: they must all set out by midnight.

Thus only three days elapsed between the evacuation of the government and the coming of the Germans. The members of the Cabinet could easily enough have been harassed on their journey by the armored cavalry. How little had they pondered over Bossuet's dictum: "A bishop never runs!" Already, on June 8, General Headquarters had slipped from La Ferté-sous-Jouarre to Briare, a small town in the department of the Loire. The commander in chief and the General Staff thus found the government in front of them, in the northern part of the zone which separated them from the enemy—a preposterous reversal. This unheard-of state of affairs did not last long, but the mere fact that it ever existed at all was enough to betray the extent of civil and military disorder. Since the government had postponed its removal from Paris until June 10, why did it not simply forego its halt at Tours—which at best could be but a station of the cross—and at one stroke continue all the way to Bordeaux?

The only explanation is that Reynaud harbored the dream that Brittany would afford a fairly durable refuge for a portion of the Army and the government. He paid no attention to Weygand's exclaiming before the War Cabinet on the tenth: "The retreat is not in the direction of Brittany!" This was no minor and secondary mistake. Executive deliberations would have been weightier and more sharp-cut if they had unfolded themselves in a spot less directly threatened than Tours. Wan-

[4]Paul Reynaud, Pétain, Campinchi (Navy), Eynac (Air), Marin, Chautemps, vice-premiers; Baudouin, Under Secretary of State for Foreign Affairs; Mandel, Minister of the Interior; Monnet, Minister for Blockade.

dering ministers seemed like puppets buffeted in the wind. Among them, how could one fail to believe that all hope was unwarranted?

Now we enter upon the crucial phase of Reynaud's government of France. Normally, war is the inexorable judge of statesmen. It uncovers the true worth of their achievement in the defense of the nation—that fundamental public interest. If defeat comes, the statesman who, up till then, was held guiltless, but has no greatness of soul to exhibit and fails to seize at every straw to save his country, faces an even more terrible court. Reynaud failed before that ultimate judgment seat.

His unsteady and even devious behavior (an abyss was widening between his words and his deeds), the selection of his ministers and advisers, the subserviency which he all too often showed to unworthy hangers-on profoundly affected the fate of France, of England, of every land in deadly combat with the totalitarian idea. Gamelin and Daladier will have to answer for the military rout; Reynaud must, to a large extent, answer for the capitulation of France. It flowed out of his "concessions" to his surroundings if not of his own will. The conclusion of separate armistices with Germany and Italy (June 22 and 24), in violation of the March 28 agreement; the refusal to carry on the war in North Africa, to undertake, while yet there was time, all suitable preparations and to throw the French fleet into the balance on the English side; the break with the London Government and the conflict at Mers-el-Kebir; the establishment of a quasi-fascist dictatorship co-operating with the Nazi Empire; the blow which endangered all over the world the cause of free peoples so indissolubly linked to French independence: this terrible chain of catastrophes had its origin in a minister who, from day to day, let men and events whittle him away and, in the end, had no fortitude to show but in speechmaking.

He never ceased to proclaim his devotion to the British alliance, nor did he entertain even a fleeting or partial illusion as to what a Nazi and a Fascist triumph would bring upon his country, upon Europe, upon the world. He was not one of those men who thought an "arrangement" with Germany was either possible or tolerable. But had his convictions been the opposite of what they were, he would not have acted differently. Our national history knows no sadder chapter. During the first two weeks of June the ugly deeds, concealed to most, which Reynaud had been piling up for two months burst forth in the daylight. Perhaps they would have done no overwhelming harm had the Army held firm; with its collapse they took on a formidable aspect.

8

Right-Hand Man Baudouin. Reynaud's Secret Council

The starting point for the Reynaud of the surrender, the Reynaud whom we had not detected under the formal attire and trappings of the statesman, must be set a fairly long time back, during the latter days of March. On the thirty-first the newspapers announced that Paul Baudouin, president of the Bank of Indo-China, had been made secretary-general of the War Cabinet and of the Economic Committee, Under Secretary of State to the presidency of the Council: in other terms, his job was to see to it that cabinet decisions should be properly prepared, co-ordinated, and executed.

The "War Cabinet," made up of several ministers more directly concerned than the rest with the conduct of military affairs, and the Economic Committee, including members of the Cabinet whose activities involved finance, production, national equipment, foreign trade, etc., hardly lived up to Reynaud's praiseworthy plan to make all agencies work to the same end, to overcome the evil effects accruing to water-tight administrative compartments. Reform was badly needed, but it did not take root. From the attempt at enforcing it, Paul Baudouin, therefore, derived no truly effective authority. But the other function with which he was entrusted (the undersecretaryship of state) continuously gained in importance. He took pains to sweep aside the notable men who, under the original plan, were supposed to assist him: Colonel de Gaulle for military affairs, M. Baumgartner for finances and economics, M. Robert Coulondre for foreign policy. He wielded absolute control. Thus Reynaud gave authority over the most important matters of state to a man with whom, throughout the years and even in recent weeks, he had not had a single idea in common. Baudouin's powers never ceased to grow. He became a real deputy to the Premier, the relative insignificance of his title notwithstanding. And the tree spread forth its branches on all sides.

During 1938–39 I kept myself "posted" on the ideas which Baudouin expressed in private regarding foreign policy. Hatred of democracy and representative government; optimistic exegesis of fascist and even National Socialist doctrines in their impact on international politics—such were his ever-recurring feelings and leitmotives. Through the totalitarian movement, Baudouin would have it, the Italian and German commonwealths were seeking to recapture the heroic leadership of their yesteryears. Far from taking umbrage, he thought, the French could do no better than borrow from their example. He was convinced that concessions granted the dictators by the two great "have" powers would appease in their hearts any impulse to use the tools of war. On the horizon he saw the shadow of that European Union which he thought (and most financiers thought alike) was bound to come because by definition it satisfied the material interests of the greatest mass. National independence for all was a scandal in his eyes; he was of the opinion that the smaller states should yield to the stronger some share of their economic sovereignty. In his judgment the wisest course for France to follow was to settle back into the quiet and well-heeled ease of Holland and Belgium, free as they were of major responsibilities on the Continent and endowed with rich colonial empires. Seemingly, he had never realized that the Low Countries owed their security, liberty, and prosperity to the French Army and to the British fleet, and that once these two forces were eliminated and an end was made of the existing balance of power, the position of a second-rate nation in Europe would no longer be held attractive. And to fuse together all those notions, there burned in him the hatred of England. In April, Sir Ronald Campbell, the British Ambassador, said to me: "What a sinister man! Every time I go into his office he cannot help grinning."

Oddly enough, the second husband of Baudouin's grandmother was Maurice Rouvier, the 1905 Premier who dreamed of coming to an agreement directly with Germany on the Morocco question, who dismissed Delcassé, the founder of the Entente Cordiale, the true promoter of the Anglo-Russian Treaty of 1907, the creator of the coalition which confronted Germany in 1914. Thus some other link than political inheritance obtained between Baudouin and the individual who said to Paul Cambon, France's great Ambassador to London, on the occasion of his bringing back Lord Lansdowne's offer of alliance: "I beg of you, don't bother me with it again. Nothing could embarrass me more."[1]

---

[1] At the ministerial council which ended with Delcassé's resignation, June 6, 1905, Paul Cambon and Camille Barrère (then French Ambassador to Rome) were present and, in after years, were wont to quote Rouvier's phrase.

And be it remembered that Rouvier had not escaped unscathed in the Panama scandal.

For the last several years Father Gillet, superior-general of the Dominicans and admirer of Mussolini, had bestowed his blessings upon Baudouin, who did what he could to deserve them in his monthly publication known only to a very restricted public: *La Tradition Vivante*. Many a passage from his pen gave witness to a mysticism which jarred on the mind when one thought that it came from the president of that Bank of Indo-China whose sharp practices a judgment of the Seine Tribunal of Commerce had exposed in 1935.² But before he began dancing attendance on the great white-frocked friar, Baudouin had profited by intimate association with what was dubbed the Republic of the "insiders" and with the plutocracy. No sooner had he won a post as a treasury official, through competitive examination, than he showed impatience to rise quickly to the top of the bureaucracy. A big businessman of the last generation, M. Tinardon, chairman of the board of directors of the Say sugar refineries, who treated him as though he were his own son, had him recommended by Léon Blum to the protection of Etienne Clémentel, the incompetent Finance Minister of the first Herriot Cabinet. The ambitious young civil servant became a member of that politician's secretariat. He was still at the Treasury when Joseph Caillaux held office in 1925. Caillaux fondled him, called him by his first name. He introduced him to Thion de la Chaume, his own intimate friend and the all-powerful master of the Bank of Indo-China. Baudouin was in his early thirties. He was a made man.

From 1931–32 on, the general estimate of Paul Baudouin was that he ranked among our best financial experts, although people in the know considered him lightweight and superficial. Several Prime Ministers wished to give him the Ministry of Finance, and in 1937 Léon Blum, who dreaded the ill effects of his social experiments upon the currency and national economy, thought of him for the governorship of the Bank of France. But Baudouin preferred to bide his time and under the Popular Front agreed only to become, with M. Charles Rist, a kind of independent adviser at the disposal of the government. His job was to quiet the qualms of the capitalist world. Powerless to bring about changes in the labor legislation, the two "experts" submitted a public

²In relation to facts concerning the Bank of Indo-China and the Société Spéciale Financière, which dated back to October 1934. In the French edition of that book the name of M. Charles Lévy was linked to those facts. A judgment of the Paris Court of Appeal of January 9, 1939, states that the connection of M. Charles Lévy with the Société Spéciale Financière was severed in May–June 1934.

letter of resignation. In this there was nothing which was not praise-worthy.[3]

But, having kicked over the traces of his past as a spoiled child of the Republic, the banker sprang into the open as an extreme conservative, a conservative in the bad sense of the word, and this in the France of 1938. Then he indulged in those activities which were to make him the chosen Foreign Minister of the government of Bordeaux and Vichy. The Bank of Indo-China—among several others—subsidized press campaigns against Czechoslovakia, awaiting the day when France's other allies, Poland and England, might, in turn, serve as their targets.

Needless to say, Georges Bonnet was a favorite with that brand of money-makers. In February 1939, while Minister of Foreign Affairs, he entrusted Baudouin with secretly sounding out the Duce on a proposed settlement of Franco-Italian differences:[4] two Suez Canal dictatorates to be allocated to Italy; what amounted to the delivery of Jibuti and of the railroad to Addis Ababa; the extension, from thirty to fifty years, of Italian privileges in Tunisia—privileges conferred for ten years in 1896, but which, continuously renewed, had made the fascist colony in that land a state within the state.[5] Mussolini, as was to be expected, pricked the bubble by demanding that the status of his compatriots in Tunisia be confirmed without any time limit. It was the inevitable retort of a blackmailer who sees his victim timidly sidling up. Bonnet and his emissary befooled themselves into thinking that they could keep all this quiet. Baudouin sat on the board of the Jibuti saltworks. As such he had to report to Rome periodically. Wasn't it an easy matter for him to hide the negotiations carried on at the Chigi Palace behind the screen of his own interests?[6] The diplomatic errand, however, was quickly

---

[3]In April 1940, Léon Blum had not yet seen through Baudouin. He was still infatuated with him. When he learned of Reynaud's choice he exclaimed: "Our civilian dynamics will be Baudouin and our military dynamics Gaulle!"

[4]The dispute worsened considerably after the Roman Chamber of Deputies demonstrated against France in the presence of M. François-Poncet, our Ambassador, who had only just taken his post (November 30, 1938) and after Count Ciano's repudiation, early in December, of the Mussolini-Laval arrangements of January 7, 1935. Baudouin said that the Duke of Aosta, Viceroy of Abyssinia, prompted him to go to Rome through M. Rousset-Bert, director of the French railroad in Abyssinia. Baudouin boasted that Daladier had approved of the trip, a boast denied by the Minister's closest advisers.

[5]Under the terms of the Mussolini-Laval arrangements, these privileges were gradually to diminish until their total disappearance after thirty years.

[6]The first time he went to Rome with political designs on the brain, I am told that Baudouin had Father Gillet as an escort. The latter introduced him to Cardinal Pacelli. His claims to deep spirituality were taken seriously by the papal Secretary of State. At the request of the government, the Bank of Indo-China had long been interested in the French

in the wind: among the businessmen who rubbed shoulders with Baudouin were patriots who kept him under careful scrutiny. And this time he gossiped unguardedly. His doings leaked out in the newspapers. Not only had the permanent officials of the Ministry of Foreign Affairs got from their chief no inkling of what was on: they had been misled. We were treated to an unusual show: the Ambassador to Berlin, M. Coulondre, repeating the denials of his Minister in an official communiqué and having to put up with Von Ribbentrop's sneers because the German knew better.[7]

In March 1940, therefore, Paul Baudouin's demeanor in international affairs was very clearly defined. He was Reynaud's open antagonist, even though both men moved in the same social circles. Journalists on his pay roll had insulted the new Premier. Still Reynaud made this glib coxcomb his closest associate. To everyone's wonder, he had named another banker, who had vigorously and publicly opposed his policies, Commander of the Legion of Honor. But Baudouin became his confidant.[8]

Abyssinian railway and the Jibuti saltworks, the latter enterprise more or less closely connected with the Franco-Italian salt company, whose president was highly placed in fascist hierarchy.

[7]Fernand de Brinon happened to be in Berlin on one of his confidential missions: he had informed Von Ribbentrop. No trace of this episode is to be found in the *Yellow Book*, December 1939. The general secretary to the Ministry of Foreign Affairs did not learn the truth from Bonnet until two months later. Coulondre never dealt with the matter in any telegram or report since he came to Paris on February 10, 1939, to tell Lebrun and Daladier what had passed between Von Ribbentrop and himself.

[8]The most complete published statement of Baudouin's ideas is to be found in an article entitled "Les Données du Problème Français" ("Basic Aspects of the French Problem"), which appeared in the *Revue de Paris* for February 1, 1938. "The West has betrayed its mission by shunning reality. Man has lost all feeling for the natural rhythms to which he ever remains subject. Our sensitiveness makes apparent a state of fatigue which the present-day techniques of psychophysiology enable us to measure. The tendency toward shrillness in the sounds of music, which has been continuous for several centuries, is one of the most clear-cut proofs of this. Man is getting the habit of a sequence of emotions cultivated in a vacuum. . . . Hence his often shattered equilibrium and the utterance he gives to exaggerated feelings. His natural leanings are weakened . . ." "Faith in its own destiny seems to have quit Europe. The civilization of the United States—in the main materialist—has nothing to offer which can assuage her pain. . . . For the reconstruction of Europe we need a young and undisturbed vision, rid of that distrust which today embitters international relations. . . . We must boldly face realities. . . . The new Germany and the new Italy demand their place in the sun. . . . Obsessive fear has led our country to subordinate its external policy to alliances which are often merely causes of weakness and the products of a dangerous sentimentalism. Let us do away with that fear." The theme of Latin solidarity rings very high: "It is consoling to think that after so many attempts upon its soul, our country still remains, right at the center of the threatened West, permeated with the sense of that community which, despite appearances, ever makes its mark upon events as upon souls." In the *Tradition Vivante* articles, published during the war, Baudouin some-

What could be made of that riddle? I asked one of Mme. de Portes's and the Prime Minister's friends to luncheon. She was perfectly frank about it. "Hélène forced him to appoint Baudouin. She is about to marry Reynaud. Rome has just annulled her marriage. She wants her new husband to part, once for all, with the men and the ideas which, until now, have cut him off from good society. She wants to knock down the hurdles. That is only a beginning. She deeply longs for respectability."

I had always looked upon Mme. de Portes as a person of no consequence. I believed that her ability to cast a spell over the Minister had long since vanished. She seemed to me the very picture of a mistress who clings to the shadow of the past. Shortly before Munich she had dumfounded me at Reynaud's own dinner table by an abrupt and silly comment on the fast-developing crisis. She foretold a settlement and boldly declared: "We are going to have a wonderful opportunity to reconstruct Europe."[9] I don't recall my answer, but it was such that I never saw the lady again and that, at some ulterior date, she forbade Reynaud to ever receive me. All in all my surprise stemmed from a profound ignorance, which was not dispelled until much later. This woman was far from being a person of no consequence. Her rule over Reynaud did not stop at public affairs, and, strangely enough, it had kept on increasing in the last two years. With fashionable friends around her, she had created for him a style of life hardly suited to his age, but which was to his liking. Thus, as time went on, her influence did not wane; it grew. And this also must be said. From 1936 on, Reynaud became the friend of certain bankers who, like Baudouin, had long assailed his policy and still openly detracted it.

Among them Gabriel Leroy-Ladurie[10] deserves to be singled out. He

---

what soft-pedaled these sets of ideas. The explanation is that he believed in victory. (For instance, he wrote in "Monthly Message" No. 10 that what mattered most was not to repeat the [mistakes] of 1918.) He admitted that the Atlantic group will consist of France and England and "at least balance in weight central Europe" under German leadership. Nonetheless, under the surface he had scarcely changed, and he hoped, in internal affairs, for a "strong executive, curtailing democracy."

[9]In this Mme. de Portes was quoting Baudouin. But had she fallen into a snare set by Ribbentrop or by some of his creatures? I shall not linger over his hypothesis since I know of no fact which would seem to confirm it. While suffering from tuberculosis of the bones, Mme. de Portes spent nearly eight months in Vienna, under the care of a specialist who gained great influence over her. Mme. de Portes, to say the least, was predatory. Reynaud visited her in Vienna more than once. At some date in 1937 he stopped in Berlin and had a long talk with Dr. Goebbels, explaining to the latter, so he said, that Germany, in her own interest, ought not to make war on Russia.

[10]Brother of Jacques Leroy-Ladurie, an exponent of agrarian fascism who served as Minister of Agriculture for a few months, on the resumption of office by Laval in April 1942.

was assistant manager of the Worms commercial firm interested in coal trade, the shipping business, and, since 1932, in banking. This man had first been entrusted with a branch of the French-Polish Bank in Cracow. He was repeatedly invited to visit Germany. He was lost in admiration for the "Hitler Youth" and its rigorous discipline. He purveyed ready cash to our embryo fascists. In various capacities the Worms pay roll included Barnaud (general manager), Pucheu, Guérard, Marion—all of whom were later to participate in the Bordeaux and Vichy usurpations. To all, Georges Bonnet was counselor and friend, and Baudouin, intellectual guide.[11] One may well wonder what on earth can have been Marion's function in a countinghouse—Marion, a former official of the Comintern who had for several years lived in Moscow. Indeed, he was the link with Doriot and his gangs. As for Pucheu, he had a hand in the undertakings of the Cagoulards, a rabble trained to "direct action" which we shall meet later on.[12] At this same crossroads of business and politics Marcel Boussac, a textile magnate not particularly well thought of by his competitors and a friend of Pierre-Etienne Flandin, was active distributing funds, the most competent of observers tells me. "Huge sums have flown out of these two pay offices."

To anyone aware of this state of affairs, Baudouin's appointment was not in the least surprising. Few of us, however, pried into the underground ramifications of money and public life. In Paris I never heard more than a casual mention of the names Leroy-Ladurie and Boussac, and I was blind to their significance. The Prime Minister had only recently taken the president of the Bank of Indo-China under his wing. Toward the end of 1935 one of my friends was present when they were introduced to each other at a luncheon table. Baudouin pandered to the promoter of monetary devaluation. He gave it as his opinion that the long-delayed measure would soon prove necessary and that the franc should be tied to the dollar rather than to the pound. But he backed out at once when Reynaud remarked that our currency and the British had their frame of reference within the same economic whole. The statesman whom Baudouin had set out to charm was not sparing in his criticism. "What a clown!" he exclaimed. In the autumn of 1939 one of Baudouin's friends begged the Minister, through an intermediary, to

[11]Baudouin and Barnaud had gone together through the Ecole Polytechnique before becoming treasury officials.

[12]While he was Minister of Justice, Reynaud informed me, in September 1938, that he could no longer proceed against the Cagoulards. "We couldn't find any evidence." In the light of what we know today, how can we avoid having our suspicions?

find employment for so great a talent. Reynaud was bewildered: "Tell your friend to stop joking at my expense!" A few months later, against himself, he became a party to the joke.

Bouthillier, Leca, Devaux, Villelume, Baudouin, Mme. de Portes—what a conversation piece! Such was the cabal which governed France at the most terrible turning point in her history. Almost every evening it assembled in the small apartment on the Place du Palais Bourbon which Reynaud had been occupying since he had moved out of his home in the Faubourg St. Honoré. Often the discussions lasted until two in the morning. The most noisome praises were heaped upon Reynaud. Remarks were bandied about his "genius." He swallowed it all without batting an eyelash. At the Ministry of Foreign Affairs all these creatures felt that they were exposed to the constant watchfulness of the permanent officials. And to them watchfulness meant ill will, for their consciences were uneasy. From the very outset Alexis Léger, of ambassadorial rank and secretary-general of the Ministry of Foreign Affairs since 1931, had kept his distance. He had made it perfectly clear that he had no intention of handling matters of importance except in private conference with the Premier. This high official had the best reason in the world to refuse to treat any confidential subject in the presence of the Minister's friends. In the end Reynaud had to send them about their business whenever his highest-ranking assistant entered the room. Naturally their dislike for the secretary-general thereby worsened.

Mme. de Portes, who could not restrain herself from prowling all through the building, when she did not boldly burst into the Minister's own suite of offices,[13] drew upon herself the attention of everyone by a vulgar and silly performance. During the alarms of May 16, amazed at the strange spectacle which was taking place in the courtyard of the Foreign Affairs Ministry—files, bundles of papers, all the records being cast pell-mell into blazing fires—she repeatedly screamed out of a window contiguous to the Minister's private office: "Who the hell told you to do that?" Her language was coarse and indecent. "Why, the Minister himself," guilelessly replied the housekeeper clerk, with the officials of the Political Department around him. She had thought of discredit-

---

[13] At times she even played the part of private secretary. Reynaud once or twice passed along to her people entrusted with the discussion of rather important special matters. "I have not time to talk with you. You will report to her." She listened and nodded approval, but her interlocutor was not sure that she understood what it was all about. On at least two occasions she attempted to use her influence to effect changes in governmental policies settled by the Ministry of Blockade and by the officials in charge of Commercial Relations at the Ministry of Foreign Affairs.

ing Alexis Léger. She did not know that, on the personal responsibility and the formal instructions of the secretary-general, the various staffs had systematically delayed the carrying out of the measure. They had finally yielded only to the orders of direct messengers from the Minister and after Léger had telephoned him and received direct instructions in the presence of the political director and the chief officials of the Political Department.[14] This rank piece of folly became the talk of the town. At the Place du Palais Bourbon, Hélène de Portes and her fellow intruders felt themselves secure. There they could concern themselves unguardedly with things that were none of their business.[15] In this privacy they needed to have no fear of the reproach which was implicit in the very presence, however silent and discreet, of men who were doing their duty.

While dealing with the Norwegian expedition I have already spoken of the ill-conceived letter which Paul Reynaud sent to Neville Chamberlain. It was drafted in the precious inner circle. An untimely telegram addressed to Mussolini issued from the same source on April 22. The day before, Hitler's birthday, the Duce had made public his words of greeting on the occasion: He had expressed his desire for the triumph of German arms. In the greatest secrecy, as far as the secretary-

[14]So great was the impatience of Reynaud and his people that fire was not quick enough to suit their haste; they had even conceived the idea of throwing some portion of the documents into the Seine. Thus were destroyed the records of the last twenty years. Nevertheless, the most important records, stowed away in an armored vault, were preserved on May 16. However, in the depth of disaster, M. Charvériat, political director, had them shipped to Morocco and they were thrown overboard as the skipper, after escaping from an air attack, found himself confronted with a submarine. By means of the duplicate kept in embassies and legations abroad, and of the files in current use in the European section which the official in charge took away with him, the gap will be filled, but only in parts.

In connection with this funeral pyre at the Ministry of Foreign Affairs, mention should be made of the at least partial scattering of the General Staff's records when, at the approach of the Germans, it hurried away first from Briare and then from Vichy in great disorder. There is reason to believe that the list of some two thousand persons working in foreign countries for the section of Military Intelligence disappeared. The diplomatic files of Gamelin and other bundles fell into German hands at La Charité-sur-Loire, the train on which they were being carried having been abandoned under bombardment. (Cf. Ribbentrop's indictment against Greece on April 5, 1941.) In his dispatches Gort tells of the loss of part of the BEF records. In 1859 Napoleon III took care to have the archives of the expeditionary force to Italy thoroughly destroyed so that posterity should not cavil at his strategy. Yet the truth came out.

[15]That same day, May 16, Mme. de Portes earned herself a dressing-down at the Place du Palais Bourbon. She had used no discretion whatever in preparing her departure; trunks cluttered the entrance hall and even overflowed into the stairway.

general was concerned, Reynaud took his pen in hand and, doubtless with the able help of Leca, the winner of competitive examinations, severely lectured the "neutral" for his flagrant transgression. In the past, to have treated Mussolini with firmness and not to have remained apathetic to his bombastic explosions would certainly have served rather than injured France's interests. Fascist impudence was endlessly nourished by our surrenders, by the obvious fright which the most violent of the dictator's blusterings aroused in us. But on April 22, 1940, it was already much too late for us to change our tone. By then we could only continue the benign attitude which had become habitual in our relations with Rome.

To do an about-face at the very moment when France was already locked in a death struggle with Germany was merely to give notice that once the crisis was over we would insist upon a pitiless squaring of accounts; it was to spur to a showdown those who wanted it; it was to disarm everyone in the councils of the Italian Government who might still advise against irrevocable action. Taking umbrage at so critical an hour —and in what language!—at Mussolini's attitude toward the Führer created for the Duce a risk of which he was well aware—that of being held in suspicion by the Germans. It impelled him to provide against Nazi ire. At once he ran for cover. He made still more definite his inclination toward belligerence, which was already obvious since the Brenner Pass meeting on March 18.

Through Reynaud's ineptitude the worst came nearer to the crystallization point. The Italian Ambassador to Paris, M. Guariglia, in constant and trusting contact with the secretary-general of the Ministry of Foreign Affairs, had sought sincerely and not without skill to link his efforts with those of our own Ministry of Foreign Affairs in order to uphold from day to day, and even from hour to hour, the unstable Franco-Italian equilibrium. About April 27 or 28 the Duce's Ambassador, in conversation with Alexis Léger, referred to the exchange of telegrams between Reynaud and Mussolini, which he assumed must have been known to the secretary-general. He betrayed his dismay and, for the first time, confessed that he no longer had any confidence in the resources of diplomacy, which until that moment both had been using for all they were worth.[16]

---

[16]Guariglia believed his country's political orientation very dangerous. He saw clearly that the anti-French and anti-British reflexes induced by Mussolini were leading straight to war and that his country would suffer thereby. He had faith in France's military strength.

The general tenor of the Duce's reply to Reynaud was: it is none of your business to judge what the German-Italian system of alliance shall mean to me. But his own psychological reaction, deep within himself, was more violent than the political: on the man-to-man level, he emphatically denied that Reynaud had any right whatever to express himself as he had. The strange point is that, on April 20, Reynaud had discussed Italian affairs in a true spirit of appeasement before the Senate Committee on Foreign Affairs. More or less opportunely, he had proffered an offer of negotiation.[17] Doubtless his real aim had been to calm and to conciliate his opponents in the Senate, Henri Bérenger among others, who were as thoroughly prejudiced as Laval himself when it came to Italy. But the fact remains: he had started by using kid gloves; then, forty-eight hours later, he had put on a pair of brass knuckles.[18]

Reynaud erred alike in his dealings with Franco. In the case of the Spanish regime, as with Italy, French policy had sinned through weakness and flabbiness, but here again the beginning of the spring of 1940 was certainly no time for a sudden reversal. I have no idea by what tactlessness either of manner or matter Reynaud, during that month of April, succeeded in arousing the resentment of the Madrid dictator. But I do know that the deepest personal enmity was expressed in a note transmitted by the Duke of Alba to Lord Halifax or Mr. Neville Chamberlain. Franco gave assurance therein that he did not wish to undertake anything which would be against the interests of England; he went so far as to say that his army would fire upon any forces in foreign uniform which might appear in Spain, but added that a similar consideration toward France was out of the question so long as M. Paul Reynaud headed the Cabinet. To make that remark even more stinging he added that, with Daladier or Herriot, he could still try to apply to

Like his chief, Count Ciano, he thought us stronger than we were and he was fearful of a German victory. He kept on saying: "Don't do anything which would serve us as an excuse. Don't set the reflexes in motion." Laval did not strike him as being the man destined to reconcile France and Italy; he recognized in him no special ability along that line and granted him no monopoly. He had not been deluded by superficial classification of men and programs so common in Paris society. At first his job had been a stiff one: few people accepted or returned his invitations. Later on our easy-going capital opened its doors to him.

[17]And let us repeat that at one of his first cabinet meetings, toward the end of March, he had announced his intention to publish a statement the purpose of which would be to "recognize Italy's legitimate aspirations." "Italy's legitimate aspirations! What on earth does that mean?" was Georges Mandel's comment.

[18]Later on he administered another dose of gentle treatment. See page 271, note 10, the note relative to M. Laurent, secretary-general of the Bank of Indo-China and head of the purchasing commission in Italy.

France the policy which he personally wanted to use to the advantage of the British Government. Informed of what had been said in London, the Premier did not turn a hair.[19]

It is astounding that Baudouin, whose complaisance toward the totalitarians verged on complicity, should have let things go astray in such a manner. But what limits are there to the knavery of so unbridled an opportunist? As for Leca and Devaux, they always acted like menials and henchmen. The picture to bear in mind, then, is of a Reynaud working off his vaunted energy in all directions at the same time, like a rifle whose trigger won't stay cocked, of a Reynaud no longer master of himself or kept on an even keel by the permanent officials. The latter frequently are accused of stifling, of diluting the personality and the brilliant schemes of their Minister. But there are only two alternatives: either a Minister is up to his job, in which case the cautionary arguments of the officials surrounding him will not stop him, or he is incompetent, shaky, sketchy, prone to listen to bad advice, inclined to make serious decisions too quickly—or perhaps he has no strength of will or leans in the wrong direction, and then the duty of the officials who stand near him is to save him from himself.

9

Alexis Léger's Dismissal. Ministerial Dualism. The End of Daladier

THE PALAIS BOURBON CLIQUE finally established its power on May 19, when Alexis Léger, secretary-general of the Ministry of Foreign Affairs, was dismissed in the most summary and insulting manner. This high official had directed French policy ever since the retirement of Philippe Berthelot, in November 1931, and he had unquestionably risen above his function. Beginning with the autumn of 1935, I called on him regularly,

[19]Reynaud had treated the Spanish Ambassador in Paris as of no account. Lequerica was ruffled; did he fan the flame of the caudillo's wrath? However that may be, during that period most Spanish requests were granted (the unconditional return of the Bank of Spain gold, a levy on our wheat supplies, etc.), and not a single one of our counterdemands met with favor in Madrid.

except during those rather numerous intervals when I publicly opposed his Minister. His course of action, as I saw it, conformed to the interests of our country. To safeguard, strengthen, and develop cooperation with Great Britain, to maintain the Polish and Czech alliances, to help Russia break loose from her Rapallo commitments to Germany, to make out of the League of Nations, against the hour of peril, a military and economic association in the wake of the Western Powers: such was his program, and at every turn I found him firmly anchored in it. Neither during the Italian-Abyssinian War of 1935-36 nor during the reoccupation of the Rhineland by the Reichswehr, on March 7, 1936, did he lose his bearings. I can still hear him exclaiming in April: "We have lost Central Europe and we have lost the peace!" All that he said evinced that sense of France's dignity which marks out every great servant of the state. Why was this man of absolute moral and intellectual integrity constantly the focal point of public controversy? Laval, Flandin, and Bonnet, those hardy perennial dissidents of French traditional policy—that is, of the set of principles best calculated to consolidate the independence and greatness of the nation—always found him the stumbling block to their ugliest schemes.

Contrary to the indictment which is now going the rounds, Alexis Léger never took upon himself the right to cause his own views to prevail over those men, whatever they may have wished, whatever they may have done. As an executive agent at the service of the state, he had thought it one of the duties of his position ever to enlighten them, come what might, on the consequences of whatever they contemplated doing, to spare them no analysis and no warning, to dispel their illusions, to point out their errors—always with the understanding that he would then loyally accede to the instructions for which they alone were accountable to the Cabinet as a whole and to Parliament. Every one of them was free to break him, to move him away from the Ministry, to transfer him to some embassy or other, or, simplest of all, to give him orders which they could rest assured would never be tampered with. It would have been better for Léger, if not for the common weal, had they had that much pluck. But they no more dared change our chief diplomatic official than they had dared change the generalissimo of the Army. They hated to commit themselves openly.

In October 1934, when Doumergue, on Tardieu's advice, had the tragic idea of putting Laval at the Quai d'Orsay, Laval called to his side M. Léon Noël, our Minister to Czechoslovakia, a former prefect who, in 1931, had already served as his assistant and who was a man of un-

certain strength.[1] He alleged the necessity of having a friend show him
the ropes. He did not continue the experiment very long. After two
weeks our diplomat was back in his Prague legation. Flandin and Bonnet did not even attempt to imitate Laval's fruitless gesture. Nevertheless, it was their duty to remove Léger if they were doubtful of his good
judgment. The truth of the matter is that they were overawed by his
powers of reasoning, that they were incapable of matching him in
debate, of refuting his arguments. Their own sketchy notions could
scarcely stand up against that considered picture of international affairs
which he daily prepared for them; their scattered and shallow interpretation of the past crumbled away before the organic and deep reaches of
this man who, for eight or nine years, had taken part in every deliberation, in every overture, in every act of French diplomacy. Jealous of his
professional skill, of his ready strength in persuading them, they chose
to make him the scapegoat of their mistakes, to set him up as being a
permanent excuse for their failures, to whisper against him as that
threadbare and mangy fellow who was the source of all the harm. Out
loud or in writing, they bestowed upon him little but praise and bedecked him with the greatest honors. Georges Bonnet carried this two-
faced attitude to absurdity.

It is paradoxical that Laval, Flandin, Bonnet should have put up with
Léger whereas Reynaud dismissed him. Of all the men who had administered our foreign policy through nine long years, none had been
more thoroughly of the same mind as the secretary-general before taking
office. With Reynaud in control, Léger could and did flatter himself that
he would no longer have to waste his energies on harassing pleas for and
proofs of basic principles. It has been said that the two differed greatly
in intellectual temperament. Reynaud leaped from premises to conclusion. His sentences were lively, pointed, short, and quick in their
rhythm. Léger went deeper, paid more attention to detail, let his
thoughts roll forth in vast swells of words. Inevitably two such different
styles would clash. Such is the explanation one most often hears. It does
not suffice. The Minister and the permanent official had known each

[1]Promoted to the Warsaw Embassy, he never was bold enough, in his official correspondence, to put down what he thought of Colonel Beck. Even verbally, and when the occasion
required it, he refrained from any judgment on the Polish leader in the Minister's presence.
To have done so would have been too greatly to commit himself. Unofficially, he made up
for this caution in his conversation with other men, but never to any useful purpose. In
June 1940, M. Léon Noël headed the French armistice delegation to Rethondes. In July he
was the first delegate general of the Vichy Government to Paris and performed his mission,
let it be said in all fairness to him, with firmness and dignity. He asked for his recall after
seven days.

other for years; moreover, their moral parting of the ways did not occur until May 13 or 14. Only then did Léger learn that Reynaud's lickspittles were taking advantage of our first reverses, talked recklessly about "winding up the war," and that their influence was in the ascendant. That should have been the moment to hold back the Prime Minister, to watch over him, to sit close to him, to set him straight. But Léger's pride was wounded to the quick. He scorned the thought of contrivance. Icily he locked himself up in his daily tasks. Mme. de Portes and her faction, having the field to themselves, set to work to tear down French policy.[2] The preliminary work had begun on March 30 with Baudouin's appearance in office. Now the eager hands of a crew of new men reached for the reins of power.

They clawed at the secretary-general because, they alleged, he was a faithful retainer of the Left. It is true that the papers of the Right had always reviled Léger. Not only during the days of Briand, whom he had seconded as chief of secretariat, but also after the Minister's death, during the time when French policy, disencumbered of the Locarno ideology, sought to recruit every possible ally in order to forestall external danger. Particularly, the politicians who blamed Reynaud for letting the Socialists into the government pretended to see in the secretary-general merely the head diplomat of the Popular Front. They forgot that, as a permanent fixture of our diplomacy throughout successive commotions in internal politics, it had been his lot to make his help available, with the same effacement, to governments of the Center Right and National Union as well as of the Extreme Left. They forgot that during the Popular Front regime he had been the target in Parliament for the attacks of the Communists.

This reputation was unfair. For instance, in the initial months of 1935 Léger saw in the contemplated treaty with Russia only a wedge to be driven between that country and Germany. Earlier, under Paul-Boncour

---

[2]About that time, on a Sunday, presumably May 19, a communication from the President of the United States reached the American Embassy in Paris. In compliance with Reynaud's former demand, Mr. Roosevelt agreed to hand over some one hundred aircraft—the very planes which today are still stranded at La Martinique and falling to pieces. And he asked that an aircraft carrier be sent to load them. Eventually the *Béarn* was detailed for that mission.

But Mr. William Bullitt, who had to deliver the message from Washington, had a hard time with Mme. de Portes. As he called Reynaud on the telephone and demanded to be received on an urgent matter of state, she argued that Reynaud was ill and could not see him. In vain did Mr. Bullitt try to see Reynaud alone. She insisted on being present and kept on clamoring that no aircraft carrier ought to sail. It took Reynaud some time to overrule her.

and Barthou, both eager to break up the German-Russian connection which dated back to 1922, he was rather shy at directly linking up France with the Soviet Union, politically and militarily. Stubbornly—and longer than was proper—he stuck to the scheme for a regional pact which, supposedly, would bring together Russia, Germany, Poland, Czechoslovakia, and the Baltic countries. It is worth noting that in May 1935 Laval went to Moscow against the advice of the permanent staff.

As far as Spain is concerned, the personal contribution of the secretary-general is well known. He worked out the "non-intervention" formulas not because he was blind to the danger they involved, but because it devolved upon him to ward off the risk of a break with Neville Chamberlain and his conservative friends—a serious and actual threat. To Blum's obvious displeasure (the French Premier had gone with him to London—July 20, 1936—to continue the negotiations made necessary by the ebbing back of the German armed forces to the Rhineland) Alexis Léger did not hide his alarm at the repercussions of Franco's rebellion on Anglo-French friendship. The story is told that in the hall of 10 Downing Street, before coming to the door where the British Prime Minister awaited his guests, the secretary-general deliberately and at length halted the Premier in front of a bust of Disraeli. This was intended to give the Englishmen present a reassuring look into the mind of their visitor.

But even supposing that the charges leveled at Alexis Léger by the friends of totalitarianism could be substantiated, it was truly unbecoming in Reynaud's mistress to set herself up as an authority on Russia, Spain, and communism. After the Popular Front elections Léger, in private conversation, had warned that lady's friend against the expectations he then freely held that the followers of Maurice Thorez might prompt a renewal of French nationalism comparable to German National Socialism. Said the secretary-general: "Don't look to them for making genuine patriots of workers and peasants."

Before the Chamber of Deputies, on May 16, in the account he gave of the defeat of Sedan, Paul Reynaud remarked: "We may be led to take steps which, yesterday, would have seemed revolutionary. We may perhaps have to change methods and men." That hint was aimed not only at the commander in chief, but also at the secretary-general of the Ministry of Foreign Affairs. Léger was laid on the altar of sacrifice even before Gamelin. In the public eye he was made subject to the most hateful of suspicions. Quite apart from any feelings of justice or humanity, even a shred of political wisdom should have prevented the Minister from weakening in any way the moral authority of the man whom he was assigning to the embassy most important at that moment—Washington.

It later became known that two days earlier, in the first excitement caused by the realization of impending danger, Baudouin had talked at length on reversing our alliances, had again taken up his pet notion of an agreement with Germany and Italy—a notion he had temporarily shelved during the war.[3] With his own eye already on the Ministry of Foreign Affairs, he insisted that, to all intents and purposes, a secretary-general less firmly rooted in the tradition of the English entente should be appointed. Mme. de Portes at once fell in with this idea: "Léger's scalp," she was heard to say, "will win us seventy-two votes from the Right!" After all, both of them and their retinue of friends had schemed to this end for a long time. About April 15 Georges Mandel had conveyed that warning to Reynaud: "You can't throw the secretary-general overboard without injury to your whole policy." Anatole de Monzie, on principle and relentlessly, was the bitter enemy of this man who came across all his diplomatic pranks. While Bonnet was Minister for Foreign Affairs he one day sent the secretary-general to see the Premier and to enlighten him on some pressing business. Monzie was unaware of it and shouted to Bonnet over the telephone: "The traitor is now closeted with Daladier!" At another time he confronted Daladier with an ultimatum: "You will have to choose between him and me!"

In the past such gusts of wind had never uprooted the great trees of the forest. But now they were reinforced by the fear of military disaster. Reynaud tottered in the gale. Before shifting Daladier from the Ministry of National Defense to that of Foreign Affairs he toyed with the thought of giving this latter post to Marshal Pétain or Chautemps, ever keeping it in the back of his head that he could turn to one of these men if the civilian head of our armed forces should refuse to move. And, oddly enough, he had been heard to make this reservation regarding Pétain: "Unfortunately, if he were there, Léger would remain the master of the Quai d'Orsay!" He knew that the marshal had called on the secretary-general in April and of the long private conversation which had ensued.[4] Then his confidential friends had been perturbed to learn that the

---

[3] It was at this moment that he exclaimed: "We picked the wrong allies!"

[4] In a quandary as to whether he should retain his Madrid ambassadorship or become a member of the War Committee, the marshal had visited M. Léger before approaching the President of the Republic. See page 193 and note 14.

marshal was overcoming his prejudices and showering words of praise which spread all over Paris about the secretary-general.

On Saturday, May 18, at seven o'clock in the evening, Paul Reynaud, Marshal Pétain, and Daladier (who at midnight was to become Minister of Foreign Affairs) were returning together from La Ferté-sous-Jouarre, where they had conferred with General Georges. Shortly before eight, Daladier asked Léger by telephone to come for a chat at the Rue St. Dominique. The secretary-general was used to ministers about to take office and anxious to get a preliminary summary of pending business. He found his future chief as friendly and confiding as of old, but with his mind full of the most desperate forecasts gleaned at General Headquarters and only too prone to pour out his sadness and his pessimism. Daladier's mood was such that he could talk only of the terrible turn the battle had taken. At the present juncture of events he had no more faith in military than in diplomatic action. He wondered whether he was not mistaken in staying in the Cabinet. "There was nothing else for me to do, but you will not see me very long under your roof." Then suddenly, as though it were an altogether incidental remark: "By the way, you know, Reynaud would like to send you to the United States!"

Léger at once replied that the offer of the Washington Embassy, if Reynaud ever made it, would be no more than a smoke screen. It would have but one object: to deprive him of his post, to dismiss him. "I would never lend myself to such a piece of hypocrisy. I would never go abroad with an impaired name. If I have been at fault, I should be retired from active duty. If I am adequately filling my job, it is not in the heat of battle and at such a moment that I should properly be assigned away from the center of things. In any case I don't want a consolation prize; I have a right to be given the full meed of injustice!" "I knew you'd feel that way," said Daladier, who was visibly moved. "But the matter is not yet settled. I shall have time to see it coming, and I'll take it up again with Reynaud. In the meanwhile, don't do anything; don't pay any attention to what I have told you, no attention whatever. Indeed, let's leave it that I have said nothing." With this, after a brief exchange of views on the European layout, the conversation came to an end.

The secretary-general was not unduly astonished at the vague threat of which the Minister had informed him. He had grown quite accustomed to such jolts; they shook him no more than some slight tremor would disturb the people of a country where earthquakes are of periodical occurrence. He went back to work.

Scarcely was he seated at his desk next morning when his principal colleagues crowded into the room. They were obviously upset. "What is the matter? Has St. Quentin been lost? Keep calm! Such is the ebb and flow of warfare." One of the officials read aloud a decree which had appeared that very morning in the *Journal Officiel:* "M. Charles-Roux, Ambassador to the Vatican, is appointed secretary-general of the Ministry of Foreign Affairs, replacing M. Alexis Léger, who has been assigned to other duties." "Is that so? Don't forget that we are at a turning point in history. Don't let yourselves be affected in your feelings toward the Minister!" Léger continued laying out everybody's task for the day. He proposed to get an explanation from the Premier later on.

Léger met Reynaud before the morning was over. The Minister effusively greeted his former friend: "I was impatient to tell you the great news. I have decided to entrust you with our Washington Embassy. Only the United States can save us, and that by at once declaring war. That miracle must be wrought before the end of the Battle of Flanders, and you are the only man equipped to do it." "If you are really serious in what you suggest, why have you deliberately made it impossible for me to accept?" "What do you mean?" "For such an unprecedented mission, my reputation would have to be beyond even a whisper of question, and you have already undermined it. Granting that your intention had been to send me to America (and I readily admit that, in the present juncture, duty bids us all to serve where we can be of the greatest use), a very different procedure should have been followed. I should, first, have been consulted on the best way to initiate the undertaking. Once you had convinced me that I was the man best qualified to succeed—something which I do not believe—you should have set the Cabinet to hold a formal deliberation, as the law requires, both by virtue of my rank as Ambassador and of my position as secretary-general; you should have submitted my name to Washington for its approval and then have had a decree appointing me signed at a cabinet meeting. You should have waited until it was published before naming my successor. By reversing the process—that is, by beginning with my removal from the general secretariat, you have in fact fired me. That is the brutal truth. The public realizes this clearly enough. Early this very morning an unfavorable explanation of the change will have been cabled to the various chancelleries, including the American State Department. Is that the way to give me that maximum authority which is most certainly required for a negotiation which, to fulfill your purpose, must not—the word is your own—fall short of a miracle?"

Reynaud was abashed. He allowed that the whole thing had been badly managed and deplored it. "But," he added, "it is still possible to put it to rights by skillful presentation in the press and by special diplomatic padding for which I make myself responsible." Léger insisted that Reynaud's ill will was a harsh fact which could not be concealed. Reynaud demurred to it: "On my honor, never until seven o'clock yesterday evening did it for one instant occur to me that I might have to do without you here. Then, as I was coming back from Georges's headquarters, with despair in my heart, I saw but one salvation, an immediate plea to the United States, and had no hope of anyone's attempting it but yourself. We must go straight to Roosevelt, prove to him that America cannot afford to let the struggle in Europe repeat the experience of the Horatii and Curiatii. You alone are resourceful enough to succeed. The chances are very slight, I know, but even if there were only one in a hundred, it would be worth trying, and you are the man to try it."

After disclaiming the praises which the Premier then showered upon him, Alexis Léger retorted that, even without hope, he would not shirk the thankless assignment. Still, he would have to feel that he was the man best suited for the job, and once again he denied it. His moral authority had been impugned, and there was no way to give it back to him intact. Moreover, he would enjoy no particular advantage in Washington. He had never been there before for any length of time. If he had any special competence, it was in the appraisal for the government of the probabilities of achievement implicit in any given diplomatic mission. In this case he was bound to advise against himself. Circumstances were too critical to allow some men to consult their own convenience, others to plot to their hearts' content. Did the government really mean to try out something new in Washington? If so, it had best turn to someone well known politically, someone highly representative of our national life, someone whose name would at once sound familiar on the other side of the Atlantic, someone like Herriot, for instance: "No, no. Not a politician! The government will never choose anyone but a career diplomat." "All right, then select a diplomat whose credit is unimpaired —Robert Coulondre, who is still in the limelight abroad because of the *Yellow Book,* or else Charles-Roux, whom you are making my successor." Reynaud's reply consisted of strictures on the one and reservations about the other.

Out of patience with this farcical performance, Léger reiterated his refusal of the Washington Embassy. He was through speaking to the cabinet minister; now he spoke to the man himself. "This is the last time we can talk privately. Hitherto we have been frank with each other, as became friends. Why dodge the truth? You have made up your mind to get rid of me. It would be more worthy of you if you were freely to admit the reasons. I know perfectly well how embarrassing politically a collaborator can be who, for ten years, has been the butt of criticism, always left unprotected, given the present lowering in public life, in the face of attacks by deputies and senators and of popular lack of understanding. Have I put my finger on it?" "No. There has never been any need for me to speak in your defense, and you know very well that, otherwise, I should most certainly have done so." "Well, have you ever felt any grievance against me on grounds of policy—either in its formulation or its execution?" "Never." "And as an administrative official?" "I have always had complete confidence in you. Why, only yesterday, while I was preparing to send a message to Roosevelt, it was enough for me to hear that you thought it ill advised. I did not even send for you: I gave up the idea." "And what about the machinations of those intimate friends of yours, the machinations which I have always tried to overlook?" "I know what you have in mind; I know only too well. You are quite right; they have been doing their utmost. Please, do honor me enough to believe that they never made the least impression on me."

Unfortunately, Reynaud was playing fast and loose with the truth. He had spent the whole of the preceding evening in his private office, listening to Hélène de Portes's strident ragings with her friends in support. Thus the illegal decree whereby, without the least trace of consultation with the Cabinet, the general secretariat changed hands was extracted from him before midnight—that is, before the termination of his powers as Minister of Foreign Affairs. Furthermore, and contrary to his description of events, he had telephoned Charles-Roux as early as the seventeenth—the day before the trip to La Ferté-sous-Jouarre—to make sure of the latter's acceptance of the post. Charles-Roux reached Paris on the twenty-first. On the twenty-second, Léger took leave of Daladier, who, now that he was Minister for Foreign Affairs, should never have inertly treated the dismissal of his principal adviser as an accomplished fact. Daladier realized that the nation's anger had been aroused. He was now so far spent that he did not even put on a show, did not even pretend to be firm. When he said good-by to the man who, for so long a time, had been his helper and who, forgetful of his own fate, strove finally to buck him up, to urge him to action, Daladier gave utterance to his profound weariness, his lack of faith in himself, his discouragement: "Something in me is broken. I'll be following you within a very few days."

Alexis Léger's removal perhaps marks the crucial hour in the political evolution of France at war. Had he been in office ten days later, Weygand would have found someone to stand up against him when he dared give it as his opinion that there should be a separate armistice, and did this even before the beginning of the Battle of the Somme. When one considers how unsure the ministers were of themselves at Tours and at Bordeaux, how only a few cabinet votes tipped the scales in favor of surrender, then, in retrospect, the dismissal of this high official does indeed seem a fatal parting of the ways.

Léger's successor, François Charles-Roux, a diplomat cast in the classic mold and above reproach, an efficient assistant for M. Camille Barrère, our Ambassador to Italy up till 1924, had since 1917 been the butt of Caillaux's resentment because, with great courage, he had made known this politician's underhanded doings in Italy. Consequently his career had been choked up in minor posts. He had been out of touch with the English-speaking world for twenty-six years, and only rather vague ideas about it lingered in his mind.[5] In addition, he was by temperament a conservative, with a taste for a settled and decorous hierarchy of values. He had hardly been seen in Paris between 1935 and 1940. He was thus in no position to unravel the tangles of the counterrevolutionary gang. I remember trying to set him straight about Baudouin: his attitude was that of a man who preferred not to be enlightened. He was nearing the retirement age; that was what had made him acceptable in certain quarters; it was not by accident that he had been singled out for this promotion. In the diplomatic sphere the Prime Minister's wobbling would no longer be either watched or restrained.

It is all too obvious. The team of Reynaud (full-fledged ministers as well as personal advisers) had become, ever since April 1, more and more divided into two groups, irreconcilable both as to their natural bent and their ideas. There were the men committed to the closest of alliances with England, to a war carried on with indomitable resolution even under the most terrible setbacks. And there were those in varying degree convinced that "France had picked the wrong allies," and who, therefore, were inclined to make use of military disaster for the purpose of overturning the policy.

We have just taken stock of Reynaud's immediate henchmen. Once all independent diplomats had been subdued, their influence began to

[5]He seems to have approved Reynaud's pleas to President Roosevelt. "As a matter of fact, the United States pushed us into the war. Now we have every right to call its bluff." Such was the purport, if not the actual wording, of his comment on the matter.

expand. In successive reshufflings of the Cabinet—May 10, May 18—the split in government councils became more open. It burst forth for all to see in the reconstruction of June 5. This was to have a heavy sequel. Only eleven days later it was a divided, a double-faced ministry which was called upon to settle the fate of France by a majority vote. Reynaud's inner circle that practically selected certain of the new ministers knew exactly what it was up to.

On May 10 two men were given portfolios—M. Louis Marin, a tried and true patriot,[6] and M. Ybarnegaray, at Reynaud's request nominated over the telephone by Colonel de la Rocque, a lightheaded fellow and boon companion who faithfully reflected his leader's crackpot notions. On May 18, Mandel became Minister of the Interior and at once proceeded to remove from office the prefects, subprefects, and chiefs of police who had fled before the enemy, to hunt out traitors, spies, hirelings of the press. It was then, for instance, that the restrictive measures which Daladier had never been able to bring himself to take were enforced against the owners and editors of *Je Suis Partout*. But offsetting this Jacobin—we now know it all too well—Marshal Pétain was given office, with the title of vice-premier, a title already held by Chautemps. He made the way ready for the most dubious of elements. In vain was Mandel energetic; in vain did his management contrast strikingly with the slackness of his predecessor at the Ministry of the Interior, M. Henri Roy. All this was far from compensating for Pétain's baneful influence.

And why had Léon Baréty been made Minister of Commerce to replace Louis Rollin, who in turn took Mandel's post as Minister for Colonies? Was not Reynaud aware that, in fundamentals, Baréty was anything but trustworthy?

On June 5, Sarraut (Education), Anatole de Monzie (Public Works), Lamoureux (Finance), Marcel Héraud (Public Health), were replaced respectively by Delbos, Frossard, Bouthillier, Georges Pernot, and Jean Prouvost, the last succeeding the same Frossard at the Ministry of Information. Moreover, Baudouin became Under Secretary of State for Foreign Affairs (retaining his previous functions), and Charles de Gaulle became Under Secretary of State for War. But the salient fact

---

[6]Despite this he had shared some of the misconceptions of the times. I remember a resolution passed under his leadership by the "Republican Federation" to the effect that France should not go to war unless its territory was invaded. This amounted to our cutting ourselves off from all our allies, including the British Empire. Unless I am mistaken, this resolution had been drawn up under the impact of the Abyssinian crisis. But M. Louis Marin has behaved under the Vichy regime with such admirable firmness that it seems most ungrateful to dig such episodes out of the past.

was Daladier's removal from the Quai d'Orsay, the curt dismissal of the hapless former "dictator." What a hodgepodge!

The departure of Lamoureux, the man guilty of having said to the governor of the Bank of France, as something self-evident, "When we shall have lost the war . . . ," the disappearance of Anatole de Monzie, the lawyer-businessman who was always involved in some Mussolinian intrigue, Delbos's return to office, and the appointments of Pernot and de Gaulle—all this might be taken to indicate the Premier's will to resist and carry on the war. On the other hand, the partiality shown for Bouthillier, Jean Prouvost, and above all Baudouin, who was thenceforth to be master at the Ministry of Affairs, with only an occasional glance from a Reynaud entirely taken up with the Ministry of National Defense; this and Sarraut's dismissal (at the demand of Marshal Pétain) —Sarraut, who was undeniably a patriot, though somewhat weak when it came to action—indicated that the officially followed policy was split wide open from within.

Since April, since Baudouin's first appearance, Reynaud's friends had endlessly asked him for some explanation, had ceaselessly besieged him in their warnings. Each time cabinet changes were made, such admonitions were renewed. Each time his answer was the same. He had no party behind him. He was a lone wolf and therefore obliged to take advantage of what brains and support were to be found even in the most dissimilar groups. He could not forget the awful free-for-all fight of March 22, when his parliamentary existence hung by the thread of a single vote. He thought it adroit to entice men of ability away from his opponents. Moreover, he knew himself to be possessed of enough intellectual independence, and to be sufficiently judicious with a firm hold on the whole lot of ministers, to succeed in picking and choosing from what came from them that which suited him and in casting aside that which did not. He let slip this amazing remark about Leca: "It gives me physical pleasure to hear him talk!" After May 18 he reduced his critics to silence with a cut-and-dried answer: the national peril wipes out all old quarrels and makes compulsory the union of all Frenchmen! Baudouin is no longer Baudouin. He has ceased to be the man he was.

We must pause for a few moments over the passing away of Daladier. Of course he fell of his own weight. Reynaud, even had he wished to, would not have been able to save him. Nonetheless, he stood for resistance to the bitter end. Whatever political ascendancy he might have retained had been vanishing very fast throughout the last three weeks. To balance the Cabinet by calling in a Radical-Socialist or a Socialist of national stature was urgently needed. The Prime Minister did not awaken to that necessity.

Twenty-six days had gone by since Reynaud's and Daladier's mutual hatred had been on the verge of breaking the whole Cabinet to pieces. Now Reynaud was rid of his rival. Good riddance, he thought—and how foolishly! Daladier, as president of the Radical-Socialist party, had kept that party in line with the war, or at least had curbed the opposition within its ranks. As military defeat after military defeat struck at him he was counted for less and less by his followers. The bonds were loosed; every pretense of discipline disappeared. The Radical-Socialists became a mere mass of terrified molecules. Very soon many of them shifted over to the partisans of surrender.

Such was the tragic disintegration of the man who for two years had made the law. At the May 15 cabinet meeting the sinister words which made Reynaud shiver had fallen from his lips: "Gentlemen, the French Infantry is no longer what it was in 1914." We have heard his sighing. As he saw the parliamentary storm gathering against his colleague, Reynaud did not bestir himself. For the process of elimination to run its full course, he did not have to exert himself. At first he exiled into the Ministry of Foreign Affairs the Minister who was focusing the wrath of everyone. Here Daladier, surrounded by an indifferently manned secretariat, let everything slide and, indeed, kept aloof from visitors. The only business which drew any spark from him was the negotiation whereby we, as a forlorn resort, tried to restrain Italy.

But public opinion was not satisfied with this loss of rank. It screamed for vengeance. On May 27 the presidents of the Senate and the Chamber of Deputies, Jeanneney and Herriot, called upon the President of the Republic to inform him that the management of foreign affairs should be in other hands. Parliamentary committees began to grow impatient. Henri Bérenger intimated to Reynaud, in the name of the Senate Foreign Affairs Committee, that his colleagues no longer were willing to have dealings with the man who was responsible for the public misfortune. In the House the Committee on the Army, spurred on by its chairman, Miellet, a good friend in happier days, hurled stones at the tottering statesman. On June 4, Mme. de Crussol sent Serruys to reconnoiter. He learned that Léon Blum approved the removal of Daladier. At the meeting of June 5, Reynaud asked all his ministers to write out their resignations. They complied. Feeling the ax at his neck, the victim called to witness his honesty, his integrity: "I have looked my sons in the eyes and I knew that I need reproach myself of nothing." And he muttered a halfhearted apology: "If you look back to the state of affairs before 1936, you cannot deny that since then France has been given arms to defend herself." Reynaud's was a cruel answer: "The honesty and integrity of M. Daladier are not at stake." And he tore up the letters of resignation of those whom he wished to continue in office.

Daladier immediately left for Vaucluse, like a wounded animal seeking its hole. He had the bad taste to take a parting shot: "Still and all it must not be forgotten that blood did not begin to flow until Reynaud went into power." Chichery, leader of the Radical-Socialist parliamentary caucus, accepted a portfolio in order to make it clear that the party disowned the man who for more than a decade had been its chief.

Thereafter, as could easily be foreseen, the scales quickly tipped toward Pétain, Weygand, Baudouin, Bouthillier, with Chautemps throwing his weight about, as was his custom—Chautemps, the only first-rank leader of the Radical-Socialists who remained in the Cabinet.

Reynaud had been stung by Mme. de Portes into loading and overloading the wrong side of the balance. To just keep it even, not more, was for him a tremendous problem. Through Marshal Pétain, with whom he had been intimate for years, Laval now was fast becoming a power in the government to which he did not belong. The marshal had even gone so far in early June as to recommend that this leader of the fifth column be entrusted with the conduct of foreign affairs. Suggesting to Reynaud that he turn French diplomacy over to Laval's care—what a portent! On June 5 the favorite son of Auvergne again tried to win M. Lebrun's support for his own obsession—buying off fascist Italy, whatever the price. Reynaud, who now found himself possessed of all the major cabinet posts, the premiership, foreign affairs, national defense, was even more hedged, as far as his effective authority went, than he had been when he railed at a hostile and vindictive Daladier sulking at the War Ministry. Already Reynaud knew that the burden of a war to the finish would crush him. His public utterances did not change. On the radio he hammered away, ever calling for victory in spite of everything. His voice, telling us of disaster after disaster, each time introduced by a few bars of the "Marseillaise," itself more and more frayed, will haunt millions of Frenchmen to their dying day. It tried so hard to be firm and bold yet sounded no more convincing than a gambler's. It was, somehow, no longer sincere. In spite of all his fine talk, Reynaud in his heart was already beaten. His confidence was something mechanical, something artificial; it could deceive no one. When he branded with infamy Leopold III, King of the Belgians, on May 28, when he pleaded so urgently with President Roosevelt on June 10, we could not shake off the feeling that all he sought was a pretext to give up the whole business.

10

The Dilemma Finally Faced: Either Carry on the Fight with the Fleet and the Empire or Sue for a Separate Armistice. The Partisans of the Armistice, Those of Resistance

BY THE EVENING OF JUNE 7, at the latest, it could not escape Reynaud that the Battle of France, called also the Battle of the Rivers, had been lost. Without more ado, inexorably, he was being caught on the horns of this dilemma: either he must seek a separate armistice or continue the struggle. But to continue the struggle meant that the seat of government had to be shifted to North Africa. On metropolitan territory, the French military system, bound up with the Maginot Line now outflanked on the west, could neither hold fast where it was nor, precariously moved back with the loss of all fixed matériel, could it be firmly resettled along the Loire and in the Jura. Doubtless, if Weygand, at the outset of his command, had had the bulk of our armies shifted westward, Brittany might have been built into a temporary "redoubt," substantial enough to cover an evacuation on a large scale, provided that British air forces be brought into action. But, as we have seen, the plans of the generalissimo were laid after a different fashion. Now Brittany was quickly passing out of the picture, with Reynaud unaware of the change.

Did he discuss those alternatives with Winston Churchill? There is some evidence that he did, and as early as May 26, but not very seriously. On May 27 he commissioned Chautemps to make arrangements for the removal of the French Government to London and, two days later, spoke to Weygand about retreating to Brittany. Anyhow, notwithstanding his heroic incantations, he hardly attempted to channel defeat in a direction which would allow for any recovery. Indeed, he did not lay eyes on his British colleague between the Supreme Council session of May 31 and

June 1 and the meeting at Briare on June 11. Everything was left to improvisation and chance. All mischief-makers had the time of their life.

In London the Cabinet and the Imperial Staff, the moment they determined not to risk Lord Gort's expeditionary force in any further operation under Weygand, the moment they considered that an attempt at invasion of the British Isles was impending, raised the question of what they could still do if England were struck to the heart. Their decision was quickly taken: "We shall never surrender," said Winston Churchill in the House of Commons on June 4. "And even if, which I do not believe for a moment, this island or a large part of it were subjugated and starving, then our empire beyond the seas, armed and guarded by the British fleet, would carry on the struggle until, in God's good time, the New World, with all its power and might, steps forth to the rescue and the liberation of the Old." In all this, France was not left out of account. In case new reverses should be met between the Aisne and the Somme, the British ministers thought that the French Government would withdraw to the west with whatever Weygand could save of his divisions and that it would then somewhere seek protection from the sea. "It would be best for it to establish itself in London," Duff Cooper said to me in Paris on June 3. He added: "Paul Reynaud has assured our Prime Minister that, if necessary, he would quit continental France."[1] On June 10, in his first message to President Roosevelt,[2] Reynaud used the sort of language which the English cabinet member had led me to expect. "We will fight before Paris, we will fight behind Paris; in order to carry on, we will shut ourselves up in one of our provinces, and, if we are driven out, we will take our stand to keep up the fight in North Africa or even in our possessions across the Atlantic." Both speeches, therefore, converged to the same point. But whereas the words of the British Premier fitted his acts, the words of his French colleague were no more than vibrations in the atmosphere. Their concord was merely verbal. It sprung from no deep understanding.

At the most the subject was only casually broached between them on

---

[1] A Supreme Council meeting had been held at Paris on May 31 and June 1. The British Ambassador in Paris expressed himself to me in the same terms as Duff Cooper.

[2] Reynaud's first appeal to Mr. Roosevelt was on June 5: telephoning from his apartment on the Place du Palais Bourbon, he asked the President to send a thousand airplanes. On June 10 there was another telephone conversation, followed by a message I am quoting. Finally, on the fourteenth, there was a "new and final" appeal to the President, transmitted through Mr. Drexel Biddle. Reynaud had announced that he intended to make this plea in a speech broadcast the evening before at eleven thirty. (Cf. Hamilton Fish Armstrong, *Chronology of Failure.*)

May 26 and again on May 31 or June 1. On objections submitted by Georges Mandel, Reynaud scrapped the plan providing for temporary refuge in London and did not have it replaced by another. He was not at all sure of himself, and Churchill thought it more useful to bolster up his colleague by a show of conventional optimism. He feared to dishearten him by conjuring up the worst hypothesis. Here we find the British Prime Minister unaware of a great opportunity. Reynaud, as we all know today, was a weak man. He had made no protest against Weygand's memorandum of May 29 whereby, to all intents and purposes, a separate armistice had been brought into the picture. Churchill, had he taken Reynaud in hand before the rout spread out, might well have rescued him from the generalissimo's pressure. But he preferred to let events unfold, assuming that the French Minister's patriotism would plead as good a case as he could have pleaded himself. Needless to say, he had no inkling of what Weygand reared in his heart. His was a fatal misreading of circumstances. As we shall see, he persisted in it until the Bordeaux days. Some phrases Reynaud had uttered in London, on May 26, should have roused him to vigilant statesmanship. On that occasion the French Minister had stated that he was going to appeal to the President of the United States, also try to prevent an Italian declaration of war, but that if he had no success either in Washington or in Rome, he could not answer for what might happen. Both the Prime Minister and Lord Halifax had been struck by the dire forebodings which obsessed him. "How deeply he is shaken!" one of them exclaimed.[3]

Thus, except for a few passing words, the British ministers do not seem to have raised the fundamental question. But did Reynaud himself ever have even the least, the most humble impulse, between June 7 and 10, to direct Weygand toward the North African solution, to start discussing exhaustively with him his memorandum of the twenty-ninth?

[3]Be it recalled that on May 25 Weygand already had breathed pessimism into Reynaud. On May 27, for a second time, I was dragged out of bed to listen, at second hand, to an account of Mme. de Portes's morning prattle. She asserted that Reynaud had discussed with Churchill the necessity of a "separate armistice" with Germany. I do not believe that at that time he went any further than what one of the British statesmen present told me. Another point is worth noting. Perhaps the British Cabinet did not understand until June 11–13 the extent of the French defeat. On June 7, Lord Lloyd, Secretary of State for Colonies, informed Sir Ronald Campbell that he was coming to Paris to talk with the principal French politicians. The Ambassador pointed out that the moment was not propitious. Lloyd arrived in Paris all the same, on the eighth, and was astounded to find how closely danger threatened. He spent the night in the country and the next morning left from Châteaudun.

All indications are negative. North Africa was not mentioned in ministerial discussions before the government had arrived in Tours. In another note, which reached Reynaud on June 10, the generalissimo gave an edge to his former warning. "Our defensive lines can be broken through at any moment. Then the disintegration of our armies could only be a matter of time." Reynaud showed little or no reaction. At the meeting of the War Cabinet on the tenth, he remained silent when the supreme commander of the armies described as fantastic the idea of a "redoubt" in Brittany. He did not point out that, at any rate, action could be taken beyond the Mediterranean. In short, and despite his message of June 10 to Roosevelt, Reynaud suffered Weygand to manage all things, military and political, as he wished; he suffered him to determine in advance the decisions of the executive by the arrangements he made, and to presume that there would be a separate armistice.

Now the fact had become plain: Reynaud relinquished to him the conduct of the war as a whole in addition to the conduct of operations. And the generalissimo sank deeper and deeper in the belief that England was done for and that the disastrous campaign must be ended at the earliest moment. By losing no time we should forestall, among other catastrophic developments, Italy's entrance into the war. Let us not endeavor to remove soldiers and arms overseas to meet halfway the victory that, supposedly, might come to us in after years from the outside world. For everyone to stand fast where he was constituted a better motto! Thus, all the more speedily, the Cabinet would have to come to terms with the enemy, and such was the major requirement. In the same spirit, Weygand had wanted the government to remain in Paris.

There is no other possible way to explain his refusal of General Prételat's suggestion, made on May 26[4] for the first time. This general officer (in command of the Army Group of the East, No. 2) insisted on withdrawing his troops from the zone of fortifications. Why had he to wait until the order for a general retreat was given on the twelfth, when, at last, the commander in chief willy-nilly issued it? At Vichy, Weygand has been greatly blamed for being so obstinate in his insistence upon immobility. On that count he alone is answerable, say his enemies, for some two or three hundred thousand additional prisoners today in German hands. By his own fault three French armies so belatedly attempted to get out of the Maginot trap that their sally, for most units, terminated in German camps.

On his way to Tours on June 11, Reynaud stopped at Briare, where

[4] Paul Allard, *Les Journées Pathétiques de la Guerre.*

General Headquarters had been established. Weygand told him in conference that our defeat was total and that the whole country would lie open to invasion unless an armistice was concluded. Instinctively, the Minister rebelled at the thought. General Georges was called in to give his opinion, and, word for word, the subordinate repeated what his chief had already said. It was agreed that the Cabinet would be made cognizant of the matter in the presence of the generalissimo.

But now the story runs up against a rather singular circumstance. Winston Churchill, Anthony Eden, Secretary for War, and Sir John Dill had flown to Briare at Reynaud's call; they did not start back to London until the morning of the twelfth. Nevertheless, it does not seem that Reynaud plainly informed them of the fateful words he had just heard. There is only one explanation possible for this reticence. With growing urgency he was begging for their help in men and matériel: had he imparted to them the emphatic recommendation of the man who led our armies, he would have been precluding all British reinforcements.[5] He

[5] At Briare a heated controversy burst out between the British ministers, Weygand and Georges. Charles Reibel, in *Pourquoi et Comment Fut Décidée la Demande d'Armistice?* says it occurred at the meeting held at Tours on June 13. Reibel uses dates loosely. He believes, for instance, that the French commitment against a separate peace was only a few days old! At Briare our military leaders demanded help, as they had never failed to do in every conversation and at every meeting of the Supreme Council throughout the preceding weeks. They remonstrated loudly when Churchill flatly declared that for the time being he could not let them have more than three divisions with seventy-two pieces of artillery, but that in October twenty-five divisions would be at their disposal. "That's like prattling about rain to a traveler lost in the Sahara," snapped Reynaud.

As for air support, the British Prime Minister would not part with a single plane. The generalissimo insisted that a few fighters be detached from the English home defenses "in order to ease the burden of the French infantry and spare it the terrible feeling of having been abandoned in the face of the enemy's planes." He was dashing his head against a stone. Churchill's rejoinders involved nothing which should have surprised military men in daily contact with representatives of the Imperial General Staff and, therefore, completely informed as to what the British had available. It is difficult for us not to be surprised at their surprise. On June 10, General de Gaulle, back from London, must have discussed the question before the War Committee.

What Weygand and Georges were really doing was to intrude upon Reynaud's function and to prepare the British Cabinet for an armistice concluded by France. "But, General," said Churchill, "we both of us know from our experience in the last war how situations which look desperate are followed by sudden and victorious recoveries." To which Weygand replied, "Doubtless you have in mind the break through the British front in the spring of 1918. May I remind you that we at once sent twenty-five divisions to your assistance, then fifteen more, and that we still had ten in reserve? Today all my reserves consist of one regiment, and early tomorrow that also will be thrown into the fray. This afternoon we are sending in our last tanks; they are freshly delivered from the factory and have not yet even been broken in." That recital of facts fits in with Weygand's testimony before the investigating judges at Riom, on August 26, 1940, which unfortunately has come to me only in fragments. "Churchill thoroughly understood that the request for an armistice could,

did not do more than hint that, however hateful to him, the armistice might be forced upon his acceptance.

But on the morning of the twelfth, when they returned to England, did Churchill and his associates know that the very next day Paris would be proclaimed an "open city," that is, abandoned to the Germans; that General Héring's army, expressly assembled to defend the capital, would receive the order to withdraw; that the new military governor, General Dentz, would be left practically alone in his headquarters at the Invalides, General Dentz, whose eagerness to fight was not to become apparent, in Syria, until a much later date? These were crucial data which would have made it possible for them to judge how quickly the area of German invasion was spreading out. When he left Paris, on the evening of the tenth, Sir Ronald Campbell never dreamed that there would be no battle of Paris. And General Héring was even more firmly convinced of it than the British Ambassador.[6]

To give up Paris without fighting for it: this was a formidable deed. In 1870–71 it was because the capital city had put up a heroic resistance that the war had dragged on so long in the provinces. But, then, was Paris to undergo martyrdom? For the sake of gaining time, of collecting more troops in North Africa, were the people of France to suffer through those monuments, those stones interlaced with history which, to them, are the very body of the nation raised to spirituality? The discussion which took place is still for us a closed book. Obviously the heart was not in it.

The issue of the armistice was raised and the first collision between the leaders of the Army, Pétain, Weygand, and the ministerial body occurred during a council held in the evening of June 12, at Cangey, the seat of the President of the Republic. The wranglings which then broke loose went on almost continuously, either with everyone present or only

---

in the immediate future, become an irresistible necessity, so much so that he expressed the earnest hope to be heard once more before a final decision was made. He wanted to be warned if the worst came to the worst, and declared himself ready to return to France without an hour's delay."

[6]On this subject the evidence is conflicting. In his message of June 10 to Mr. Roosevelt, Reynaud had said: "We will fight before Paris, we will fight behind Paris, etc. . . ." "But what about fighting inside Paris?" asked Mr. William Bullitt. Reynaud's answer was that all military authorities deemed this impossible.

The truth is that Reynaud had changed his mind. His idea, at the time he thought of taking the whole government to London, was to stage a spectacular battle of Paris. Thus a heroic sacrifice would be the closing scene of the struggle on French metropolitan territory, and, with military glory on their brows, the ministers would find it easier to throw the empire in the conflict.

a handful of individuals, until the night of the sixteenth, but for one single interruption, on the fourteenth, to allow for flight to Bordeaux. Discussion degenerated into an uproar. It did not proceed methodically from one point to another, but writhed, coiled, and uncoiled like a snake, in keeping with the stirred feelings and passions of these hundred-odd men called upon to take terrifying responsibilities—some thirty-five ministers or under secretaries of state and their attendants. Some of those men have made their experience public, have reworded their speeches after the event, more or less faithfully. Questionable summaries have appeared. As you compare reminiscences, notes, and reports, you quickly discover that any attempt to reconstruct the debate would lead merely to writing history after the manner of Livy, to collecting more or less fictional rhetoric. We already know the attitude of each of the participants. Likewise we know the schemings and plottings which molded policy and brought about, within a mere hundred hours, the abandonment of the struggle. It is possible to strike a balance day by day with reasonable assurance. Phrases whose authenticity is unmistakable emerge from the hurly-burly. But it is best not even to attempt any closely knit and literal account.

At Reynaud's request, Weygand opened the great debate. He called to mind the legacy which Gamelin had left him: the lines along the Meuse shattered, a breach opened between the Sambre and the Aisne where the 9th Army had almost completely melted away. Between Arras and Amiens, through Bapaume, he had tried to bring together the armies of the northwest and those of the center. He had not succeeded. General Gort did not carry out his orders. It had never been possible to make up for this setback. The battle which began on June 5 had been undertaken to save our honor rather than in the hope of victory: fifty-five French and two British divisions had tried their strength against 104 German divisions. And then Weygand minutely described the vicissitudes of what was for him the ultimate test, with emphatic reference to the newly prescribed tactics.

Now all was lost. Paris was threatened. He could do nothing to turn that threat aside. The Germans had already reached the left bank of the Seine, at Les Andelys. Although it was cut into pieces, the French Army still retained a certain cohesion. Each unit fighting a retreating action knew the direction it was supposed to take; discipline was still maintained. But our divisions were rapidly dwindling away. Most were now reduced to a few battalions. The soldiers were worn out. Within a few days, or even a few hours, the last links might snap and it would be every man for himself. Should we have to put up with bands scouring the countryside, with little local governments set up after the Soviet model? "I do not want France to run the danger of falling into the anarchy which follows a military defeat." And what about the honor of the Army if the rout developed in full? "As a soldier it breaks my heart to say it, but we can no longer put off asking for an armistice." Weygand was ready to humble himself. Twenty-two years before he had stood by Marshal Foch when the glorious armistice was signed. Tomorrow he would in person meet the German victor and receive notification of his terms. Then the generalissimo rapidly pointed out the causes of the defeat. "The country fell asleep behind the Maginot fortifications. We leaned on them too heavily. The Army did its duty, but matériel was lacking. We never had any air force. Anyone who would think to deny it is a liar."[7]

Such was Weygand's statement of the situation. He confirmed it in a letter to Reynaud. Marshal Pétain, whose voice until then had seldom ever been heard at cabinet meetings, seconded the proposal for an armistice. He had nodded approval the whole time Weygand spoke.

The military chiefs could see that three ministers out of every four turned in loathing from what they proposed. Campinchi, Delbos, even though they expected altogether too much from the barrages which could still be erected in the path of the invader along the Loire, the Garonne, and in Brittany (the "redoubt" in Brittany loomed very large in the debate), did not fail to point out that the fleet and the African Empire remained centers of resistance which the enemy could not penetrate and that we had no right to look upon the Franco-British agreement of March 28 (excluding a separate peace) as a mere scrap of paper. Louis Marin could not restrain his indignation. Reynaud, summing up the argument, insisted that we must be faithful to our pledged word. He declared that France would remain in the war. There is more. General de Gaulle has it that this same evening Weygand was formally instructed to prepare for continuing the campaign in North Africa.

Those were truly admirable words but, unfortunately, with very few deeds to back them up. On June 12, the Premier repeatedly failed to live up to his high intentions! In the first instance, why didn't he, on his own

[7]The reference to the honor of the Army and to Weygand's proposal to lead the armistice delegation excepted, these sentences are quoted in *Sept Jours* by M. Jean Prouvost, then serving as Minister for Information. And they are found also in Weygand's testimony before the Riom Court. Among others, this deserves being reproduced in full: "Were disorders to spread throughout the Army and the population, he [Weygand] would consider the usefulness of the armistice as being already lost. Then the harm would have been done."

authority, reject Weygand's demand for an armistice? Why did he submit it to a ministerial council specially convened for the occasion, introduce Weygand into the council room and, in practice, confer upon
him the status of a regular cabinet member? At the end of the debate it
would have been only in order that Reynaud should force out of the
commander in chief the admission that the Cabinet had decided against
the request of the High Command and that it was not open to anyone
to question the course of action which an overwhelming majority had
approved. Instead of taking that firm stand, Reynaud allowed the commander in chief to assume the attitude and the manner of speech of a
factious leader revolting against the governmental authority. Weygand
had an ingrained contempt for all parliamentarians. He must have felt,
from the outset, that Reynaud would never dare join the issue, that, with
impunity, he could at will bully the civilian power. In Reynaud that lack
of moral strength is even less to be excused because Weygand, carried
away by his impetuous speech, had not only shown his political bias
throughout but had stumbled into an outrageous lie. In his eagerness
to vividly describe the impending danger of revolution, he volunteered
the information that Maurice Thorez, the leader of the French Communists, had taken over the President's palace in Paris, that the Communists had seized the capital. Mandel, who had just been talking on
the telephone with Langeron, the prefect of police, challenged that assertion. "Do you doubt my word?" asked the generalissimo. "No, but I
do not doubt Langeron's either." Whereupon the Minister of the Interior again called the prefect. "The Germans are at Pantin and Aubervilliers," the official reported. "The city is calm. They will take possession tomorrow." On the part of Weygand such a passionate exhibition
of partisanship called for a stern rebuke. Reynaud let it pass unnoticed.
He understood fully that the political regime could not survive the
disaster of which Weygand gave notice, that as between the two possible explanations for what was about to happen, the bungling of the
military men or the bungling of the politicians, public opinion, until it
was more fully informed, would take sides against the politicians and
would not, for a while, sweep both up with the same broom. Chautemps had remarked to him some days earlier, referring to Pétain and
Weygand: "You are no longer strong enough to put yourself in direct
opposition to those two popular soldiers." He was only too prone to
think that Chautemps had spoken the truth. He credited Weygand
with a determination of purpose which this general did not probably
possess. He came to believe that only by having him placed under ar

rest could he stop his efforts to obtain an armistice. The mere thought that, short of that bold step, all further resistance to Hitler was doomed made him painfully aware of his helplessness. Consequently, at the very moment he expressed the decision of the Cabinet to continue in the war and eventually go to North Africa, he left his government at the mercy of the peace faction.

The peace faction was not yet on its feet. Those who belonged to it were loath to commit themselves to open support of the general and the marshal, except Baudouin and Jean Prouvost, Minister for Information, one of the new recruits of June 5. An owner of spinning mills at Roubaix, Prouvost had sharpened his wits in Paris after the last war by the acquisition of *Paris-Midi* and then of *Paris-Soir,* a minor daily which he had expanded into a newspaper of large circulation and equally large photographs. Pretentious and illiterate as he was, British hosts had offended him a few months earlier by seating him at an official banquet in a place which he did not consider worthy of his dignity. He showed them that wounded self-esteem could recoup itself with a vengeance. Such was the breed of men Reynaud had enlisted to help him carry on the war! This fellow prides himself on having first injected into the Cabinet debate the fateful phrase which, shortly afterward, Pétain was to use and abuse: "I refuse to become an *émigré!"* On the twelfth, he alone spoke in support of the two military leaders.

However, the vicious stroke which was to undo·Reynaud's proud concluding statement that France would remain in the struggle was not concocted by the simple-minded Prouvost, but by Camille Chautemps.

The impassioned outbursts of Weygand had scared Chautemps. More than ever he was convinced that the military leader, apparently brimful of energy, would have his way in everything and that it could not be helped. The Cabinet, he thought, must reach an agreement with him. To directly counteract the High Command might bring about the disruption of the civilian power and add possibilities of civil war to the horrors of the German invasion. Chautemps did not try by sheer weight to force a passage for his weak policy. His manner is stealthy, insinuating, conciliatory, ambiguous. He is skillful at creating the illusion that fire and water can mix. He threw in a formula—seemingly modest enough and somewhat humoring the policy of resistance— which, in the end, toppled Reynaud, unsteady on his legs, down the toboggan slide. He suggested that Mr. Churchill be asked to return to Tours on the following day, attend a ministerial council, and discuss with the French ministers all the problems arising from Weygand's request, armistice and peace among others. Outwardly his proposal seemed harmless. But there was a sequel to the proposal, and we have it from another minister. Until that day, he says, Chautemps had refrained from expressing any very definite opinion. He began by disagreeing with the thesis Weygand had expounded and declared that, were an armistice to be concluded, the French people would not understand. Then he harped on the urgency of bringing Churchill within the discussion. But the decisive moment was this. The meeting had already been adjourned, and informal talk went on between groups of ministers. Reynaud and Pétain still sat near each other, whispering. Chautemps, with Frossard and Ybarnegaray and others near him, those very men who, three days later, came boldly forward for the armistice, was waiting for the private conversation to end. To Reynaud, who at last rose from his chair, he said: "I have your promise that the question will be put to Churchill?" "Which question?" interjected Louis Marin, who was on the lookout. "Oh," answered Reynaud, "Chautemps wants me to examine with Churchill what would happen between France and England if we were compelled to sue for an armistice. . . . It will do our British friends some good. Perhaps I shall wrest from them the planes they have so steadfastly refused to send." Louis Marin was beside himself with anger. Chautemps took exception to the violent speech Marin had flung at Weygand's face.

Chautemps' device aimed at blunting that part of the majority argument which dwelt upon our national honor rather than upon our highest national interest. In the debate national honor had perhaps been put to greater use than national interest, because it was easier to handle and cut short all technical controversies with the generals concerning England's chances of survival once continental France was occupied, etc. Let it be granted that national honor precluded France from applying for an armistice. Well, to approach London and ask for leave to do it could not be called sinning against national honor. Reynaud was worn out, caught short, disgruntled. He acceded to Chautemps' move, which soothed the military chieftains and spared the Council painful feeling of irremediable discord.

From the day Daladier was shoved back into his native department Camille Chautemps had been the undisputed leader of the Radical-Socialists in the Cabinet. Within the party itself, and when he deigned to take the trouble, Edouard Herriot, a man of broader human scope, sensitive to the ground swell of national feeling, capable of poetic eloquence by nature, had a far greater authority. But he had no taste for intrigue, and he took things easily. Both the presidency of the House, which had been his for four years, and the mayoralty of Lyons, his personal kingdom for some thirty-five years, which he visited every two or three weeks, kept him too far removed from the political turmoil. To this his intellectual labors and historical research also contributed. He disliked being bothered. A sentimental Pantagruel, he went his way with a misplaced confidence in his astuteness. The ardent patriot was stirred in him to his depths; he would have been incapable of scheming and bargaining in the hour of misfortune. Chautemps, on the contrary, went on performing his natural function of compromiser, the function which periodically, all through his career, had secured a place for him among front-rank politicians. It has been explained that in French politics the Radical-Socialist party swung from right to left and from left to right, as a pendulum. It fed on compromises. Thus, within the party, differences had to be settled continuously. There Chautemps, a born arranger of disputes, tried and perfected his hand. Soon, on the national level, he became the artist called in at intervals to adjust rival courses of action. It had become a second nature·with him. Even on the brink of the precipice he could no more be kept from bargaining for middle terms than an apple tree from bearing apples. It was truly terrible that, standing as he did for the political party most representative of the average man and with the greatest number of office-holders in its midst, he should give his support to those who had been defeated in battle. In his person the Masonic Republic gracefully resigned. Pétain and Weygand could have the floor.

But did he realize what he was doing? Maybe he did not. Years afterward, as he had to put up with the fact that the shameful separate armistices with Germany and Italy were the direct outcome of the initiative he took on June 12 and renewed on June 15 and 16, he started arguing that he never intended to bring them about. At times he said that he wanted only to temporarily conciliate Weygand, to ward off the fury of the general, to confront him with a statesman (Churchill) well able to stand up to him, and, at other times, that the armistice, as he saw it, was not to materialize until a friendly bargain had been struck with England, a bargain providing for the shift of the French fleet to British ports. He chooses to overlook or to forget that no armistice could have been conceded by Hitler to a French government which had thrown overboard all maritime power. There was no middle way between the kind of armistice which took shape on June 22 and the prosecution of the war. Any treaty of armistice was bound to separate France from

England, unless, of course, England should decide to share in the French surrender.

The most that can be said in order to condone Chautemps' responsibility is that he had never been familiar with international problems. Eighteen times he had served as a cabinet minister and four times he had held the premiership for a few days or a few weeks or a few months. He had lost three brothers in the war of 1914–18—one of them, Félix Chautemps, a promising young man already in Parliament. Yet the course of European history between the two conflicts had remained for him a book carelessly read. Herriot and Daladier were steeped in literature, in human letters. Chautemps was an attorney chiefly concerned in the keyboard of electoral interests. To make headway in politics, he had selected the easy path. The scion of a household of Savoyard politicians (toward 1893 one of them had landed in the Ministry for Colonies, thanks to Masonic influence), he had grown up in the lodges.

He is gifted with a quick intelligence and speaks with polished facility. If it devolved upon him to answer a question from the House, bureaucrats did not have to prepare elaborate memoranda or plow through the files for him. It was sufficient that an official orally explained the matter. He would then present it to the members, expressed in terms readily understood by all, but invariably with a conclusion which wavered between affirmative and negative, which was neatly on the fence. I recall a cabinet statement with which he was entrusted in Daladier's absence, toward January 1940, to the effect that the government did not intend to sever relations with Moscow. His presentation was as slippery as an eel. If some accident of the ministerial merry-go-round had planted this man in the Quai d'Orsay, the Republic would have been gifted with an abler and more honest Georges Bonnet.

Circumspect as he was, Chautemps had his fingers and more than his fingers burned during his 1933 premiership. It was he who had let the Stavisky scandal drag on and gradually stir up the populace of the capital. Whatever he might say, his brother-in-law, Pressard, the Paris public prosecutor, was theoretically responsible for the numerous postponements of trial granted to Stavisky for five years by judges whom it had been his official duty to enlighten. Chautemps pretended that he thought the problem was essentially one for the courts and that the government had no business meddling with it. He was reviled, driven from office, accused of being an assassin by the wolf pack of the Right, and, like Daladier, he found asylum in the Popular Front. The careers of both followed parallel curves, but that of Chautemps had the smaller radius. He missed the redeeming feature of Daladier: an intuitive patriotism which, sooner or later, asserted itself above all other considerations.

Chautemps always favored every possible "appeasement." At the time of the reoccupation of the Rhineland by the Reichswehr, although he was not one of those with whom the decision did rest, he discouraged any forcible action. In 1938, a few months before the surrender at Munich, he had an answer for those who said: "We would not be in such a pass if we had been firmer on March 7, 1936." This answer was: "Never for an instant shall I regret my conduct on that day." He was no friend of Laval, but when he himself was Popular Front Premier, in 1937–38, he once astounded people by saying at a luncheon party that he was not opposed to Laval's policy and had the courage to admit it. In those tragic days of June 1940 (was it at Tours or at Bordeaux?—I am not certain), as one of my friends tried to show him that the country's independence hung upon our continuing the war, he quickly replied: "But every hour of my life I have been against war." "And you are still against war while Germany occupies our soil?" "I am always against war."

From June 12 on, Weygand spent more and more time at the seat of the government. He was present at every ministerial council. He made it his main business to see to it that the ministers should fall in line with his recommendations. He played a political rather than a military role. What was his outlook and what was the outlook of Pétain?

Weygand never liked Foch's rival, never spared him his criticism or his most acid comments. But he had foreseen as early as 1934 (I find an entry on this subject in my diary under date of November 4) that if the French Army ever succumbed in war, Pétain would be the Hindenburg of France. He had plainly told him so at the time.[8] No wonder that, in the spring of 1940, he should have been the first to recognize that the old marshal, the popular hero of 1916–17, generally considered free of all responsibility for the catastrophe, alone remained standing above the ruin and the spoils of all the rest. Thus does his farsightedness match Laval's, who, during his 1935 ministry, was always gambling on this white-haired Cid's last foray and, ever since the autumn, had been busily at work adjusting the wires which kept the warrior upright in his saddle. Weygand took care to control his tongue and go out of his way to be nice. "He asks me to lunch so that he keeps abreast of what is going on," he

[8] See page 328.

said toward the end of May, "and it adds the last straw to my weariness, but I cannot afford not to do it." Pétain would be the master, and Weygand, forgetting twenty-two years of embittered relationship, would be the loyal servant.[9] Moreover, he had the satisfaction of noting that everything he said easily turned into gospel truth for the marshal-vice-premier.

They united in the hatred of England, which began to tell on Weygand. Pétain himself had at all times been poisoned with Anglophobia. But whence sprang this mania in Weygand? Between the two wars all the ministers of Downing Street, whether in or out of office, had shown him favor. They had transferred to him their sincere attachment for Foch. In 1923, while he ruled in Syria, the British High Commissioner in Egypt had complained to the Foreign Office about some points of his policy. Lord Curzon annotated the report: "When a man like General Weygand is in question, it is not fitting to prefer charges lightly." In 1924 the Foreign Office, which had little respect for M. de Saint-Aulaire, advised Ramsay MacDonald to suggest the general's appointment to the London Embassy. The Socialist Prime Minister at once acquiesced. No practical step was ever taken. But the very fact that Weygand's name was even considered is evidence of quite exceptional confidence.

Weygand's turning against France's ally had its roots in that burning aversion for the Left, the Socialists, the Free Masons, democracy, parliamentary institutions, which became a frenzy after his retirement in January 1935. Nonetheless, every word he said until May 1940 had shown him to be without the least illusion concerning the inexorable nature of the war and Hitler's cold determination, were he to win, not to stop short with the destruction of the French Army but to go further, to break France up, physically and morally. On April 3, at that meeting of the War Committee where he aired the plan for a Balkan offensive to which I have already alluded, he asserted, with every appearance of flaming conviction, that Germany was a power to which one could give no quarter, that everything should be staked in order to beat her down. He gave a list of typical Nazi cruelties: "Girls from respectable families shipped from Poland to Germany and forced to become prostitutes." With such beasts, how could you stop halfway?

The bitterness of defeat and of wounded vanity turned against England the former chief of staff of Foch, who was not only a marshal of France but a British marshal as well. He sensed that sooner or later

[9]About Pétain's personal relations with Weygand see pages 328–31.

Frenchmen would study his campaign and say to him: "You behaved as though you had no faith in victory. Why then, on May 19, did you accept Reynaud's offer?" More and more acrimoniously he kept repeating that until May 24 we still had had a chance of winning the war, that the British ministers and military leaders had paralyzed the French Army. I have already called attention to the telegrams addressed to the French representatives at Cairo, Beirut, etc., in which he drew up, in whole or in part, his indictment of London. It not only involved the abortive offensive against the "pocket," Lord Gort's five divisions, which, he asserted, had suddenly retreated on the morning of May 24, but also the French division, which had been cut off from the remainder of the 10th Army and made prisoner at Le Havre while the two British divisions that had fought by its side were hastily shipped to England. "I do not censure the English," he wrote, "for having fired upon Frenchmen [this probably referred to some clash between British troops and French military police], but for having prevented our retrieving ourselves on the battlefield."

And he had yet another grievance. When he accepted the supreme command on May 19, Weygand asserted that he could cope with the legacy of Gamelin provided French diplomacy warded off Italy's coming into the fray. At London, on May 26, and at Paris, on May 31, Churchill, much against his will, gave approval for the overture which Reynaud wished, as a last resort, to make to the Fascist Government. British intrigue, Weygand argued in his telegrams, prevented Mussolini from clinching a deal with us. We offered him Tunisia, Jibuti, fifteen billion francs. He spurned our gift because he knew that England would find a way to spoil it. Mr. Churchill must bear the responsibility for the rejection of our offer.[10]

---

[10]What I was told about the terms of the French offer of early June in no way conforms to Weygand's claims. France's eventual concessions were not listed in detail. We only went so far as to inform Rome that they would be very large. It should be pointed out that M. Charles-Roux, secretary-general at the Ministry of Foreign Affairs, opposed the sending of a text which had doubtless been drawn by Baudouin, Leca, and Devaux and which he considered prejudicial to the dignity of France. Did Weygand's story refer to the unofficial negotiations supposedly begun in Italy by M. Laurent, Baudouin's colleague in the Bank of Indo-China, who, since the autumn of 1939, was at the head of our Purchasing Commission in the peninsula? A silly business indeed. On the one hand, M. Laurent bought the products of Italian heavy industry, even including training planes, and paid for them partly with gold currencies, partly with raw materials, thus furnishing Italy some means whereby to arm herself. By January, French orders had already reached a total of 2,400,000,-000 francs. On the other hand, as an amateur diplomat, did he try to satisfy Mussolini's ambition? In March 1940 after the Brenner Pass meeting, the Fascist Government notified Paris that it no longer wished to continue deliveries by its metallurgic works. Then Baudouin

All these were mere assertions, thoughtlessly circulated. From personal experience I unhappily know that General Weygand, when what he believed to be his interest was at stake, could do violence to the truth.[11] During those fateful June weeks so intense was his passion against his country's ally that he broke with Lord Lloyd, his warm friend for many years, in the most invidious manner. The two men met at Bordeaux on June 17. Unforgivable words were exchanged. "There is nothing left of him but a stunted and evil-tempered little old man," the Secretary of State for Colonies told me. "I will never speak to him again. The fellow I talked to the other day resembles in nothing the man I once admired."[12] As he rang the charges on perfidious Albion, Weygand, apparently, came naturally into the language of some squireen from the depths of rural France. He sank to the level of *Gringoire,* a sheet belonging to his friend Horace de Carbuccia, which, in the autumn of 1940, published an article proving that the British attitude toward France had been governed, all through the centuries since the fourteenth, by a desire to avenge the death of Jacques Molé, Grand Master of the Knights Templar, supposedly the ancestors of Free Masonry.

It now served his vanity to announce that, once France had withdrawn from the war, England would not long hold out; that she would perish; that, in any case, it was ridiculous to believe her capable of turning the Nazi tide and freeing a vanquished France from her shackles. England was nothing more than a navy and an air force. "Neither one nor the other can reconquer a country; they can only complete its destruction."[13] Our ally would not save herself and would not save us. Weygand felt obliged to affirm this, for to admit the opposite would amount to justifying implicitly—at least in part—the May 24 decision of the Imperial Staff: to await the enemy within the English ramparts and no longer on the outer slopes of the moat. It is a fact that after June 11, and perhaps even before, Marshal Pétain and General Weygand never tired of telling Reynaud: England will soon lie utterly prostrate, like France. Neither her Navy, nor her coastal defense, nor her industry, nor

---

and Laurent may have endeavored to start a negotiation. Baudouin stood close to Weygand, after May 19, and found him most congenial. He probably kept on disparaging the British Cabinet in the general's presence. But all this is, to a great extent, guesswork.

[11]See pages 343–44.

[12]M. Camille Barrère, France's Ambassador to Rome, had been intimate with Weygand ever since the days of the San Remo and Lausanne conferences (1920, 1922); he was also a friend of Lloyd's. In 1937–38 he was wont to remark: "What has come over Weygand? He's no longer the same man."

[13]Weygand used that phrase in conversation with M. Reibel on June 14 (loc. cit.).

her Merchant Marine will survive the great variety of attacks launched from the French coast line. Let us disentangle ourselves from her as quickly as possible. Let us cut the last ties. What we would risk in battle—our fleet and our colonies—would not ease her lot and, at the same stroke, would make ours worse. We may reasonably expect that the Nazi conqueror has his eye particularly on England, since she holds so many of the keys to world domination, that he will look upon a France divorced from the British Empire as a second-rate power which the all-embracing German Reich need not bother about and can afford to treat generously.

Was this reasoning entirely Pétain's and Weygand's invention? At the Bordeaux Prefecture, on the evening of June 14, I was chatting with one of these rare diplomats from the Quai d'Orsay (they could be counted on the fingers of one hand) who stood for a separate peace. Said he, "We are far from being at the end of our rope. The Army no longer holds firm, but we still possess 'potentials' in the gold reserve, in the Navy, in the Empire. It remains to be seen whether we shall have the courage to tear them from England's tentacles, and, by using them, to obtain good terms with Germany. The cards we still command are far from negligible." I thought I must be listening to Laval, who, at the same hour, wherever he might be, was surely expatiating on the same themes. All those men feigned to ignore that resources handed to Hitler or not brought into action against him necessarily resulted in an increase of his material strength and, in some degree, of his demands.

Pétain, Weygand, and their followers abounded in other silly notions which benumbed their feelings to the German danger. They did not realize that the enslavement of their country, enslavement in body and soul, would follow the armistice they advocated. They naïvely conceived that the triumphant Germans of 1940 would not go beyond their terms of 1871. They deceived themselves into believing that France's trial, however cruel, could not last long and that she would merely have to slough off two or three provinces in order to be released from her enemy's grasp and resume her independent life. They did not size up the crushing millstone which the National Socialist Revolution had set rolling from one end of Europe to the other. They understood the new political universe no better than they did the new military universe.

To cap the climax, they faintly believed that the High Command of the Wehrmacht felt united with the French Command by a bond, fastened above the clash of battle, a sort of spiritual fraternity, an ennoblement which the sword confers, or should confer, on those whose profession it is to wield it. Recall for an instant Velasquez' painting, The Surrender of Bréda. Note the respect and deference with which the conqueror greets the conquered. When they thought of an armistice Pétain and Weygand took for granted that they would be received in this noble style. A hard-fighting knight is betrayed by fortune. He is forced to deliver his arms, to humble himself. The chivalrous victor lifts him up and comforts him. For the victor cannot forget that both he and his vanquished foe have dedicated themselves, each in his own country, to something which transcends mere material interest. Even though a frontier may separate them, they are both the salt of civilization. Before the last war Paul Bourget once wrote that the Vatican, the House of Lords, the French Academy, and the German Great General Staff constituted the true foundations of European society. Notions of this brand still loitered in the brains of French military men. And it must be recalled that in 1918 Marshal Foch was suspected of having been moved by this same sentimentality when he wished to spare the Germans an invasion of their fatherland.

Pétain, like Weygand and so many other army chiefs, had spent most of his life in garrison towns, far from great public affairs. Then, for the last twenty-five years, both had stood near the center of events and had been given an opportunity to learn something of them. We can see clearly that this opportunity was largely missed. Their first and very narrow intellectual training never broadened. One had the narrow mental environment of a small bourgeois and the other, by marriage, of a squireen. Both remained prisoners of all the prejudices of their class.

Finally, the idea of national redemption had imprinted itself upon the brain and vocabulary of the general and perhaps of the marshal also. For a full century and a half France had been lost, wandering in a maze of democracy, atheism, Marxism. Through defeat the conservative tradition would be renewed, cleansed of all defilement. In suffering, France would redeem herself. This was no peddling profit. Taking a wide view, might one not prefer this to victory won share and share alike with the Anglo-Saxon world, to the social upheavals it would bring in its train, with the generals as first victims?

After the war of 1870–71 a vote of the National Assembly had dedicated France to the Sacred Heart and had provided that the Montmartre basilica should be erected. The elected rulers of France had bowed before the divine wrath and cried out, "Lord, how terrible is thy right hand, yet it deals forth justice!" Here was the same refrain, but on how much vaster a scale! The expiatory basilica, this time, would be France herself, her revolutionary devil driven out by dire and bitter humiliation. Weygand struck up Baudouin's tune, and Pétain, at any rate, thought the whipping healthy.

Of all the men who, on June 12, by instinct or by judgment, withstood Weygand's argument and that incipient impulse toward the "National Revolution" which went with it, Georges Mandel, Minister of the Interior since May 18 and Colonial Minister up to that date, was the most daring, the most resolute, the most resourceful. His quarters were at the Tours Prefecture, at the very heart of the political scrimmage. He was not one to miss a meeting of ministers, as did Frossard and a number of others who were in such a daze that they mistook Candé[14] for Cangey. He was never caught off his guard. Together with Jeanneney, president of the Senate, and Herriot, president of the House, he was, in the France of 1940, the only public man on hand responsive to the Jacobin tradition of 1793. And he kept immune from the despair which made helpless men of Jeanneney and Herriot.

He had entered politics at the dawn of the century through the narrowest and humblest of doors. He was the son of a Jewish tailor from the Sentier district of Paris, the haunt of small shopkeepers, behind the Stock Exchange. His family name was Rothschild, which he abandoned in favor of his mother's. His great ambition had been to serve Georges Clemenceau, who was then editor in chief of *L'Aurore,* who wrangled with the Dreyfus case, and had not yet served in any ministerial capacity. Clemenceau jested him as Francis I did Triboulet. The great man came to power in 1906; for three years Mandel was his factotum among politicians. The lobbies of the Senate and the House became his bailiwick: there he knew about everything and everybody that was worth knowing.

In 1917, after three years of war, Clemenceau resumed the premiership and the legendary era of Father Victory began. Now the accessory helper of ten years before was entrusted with the then needed complement of military operations in the field: forceful internal repression. Mandel was in effect Minister of the Interior; the incumbent, Jules Pams, faithfully obeyed his orders. The *Bonnet Rouge* crowd, the Caillaux, the Malvys, all those who were after a "negotiated" peace with Germany soon learned it to their sorrow. At the time he taught himself to play the part of Saint-Just, the implacable commissioner of the 1793 National Convention. In a way he could be as tricky as Laval. He knew how to take advantage of the legislators' personal weaknesses.

[14]The château of Candé had won fame because of the marriage there of the Duke of Windsor. Hence the confusion.

After all, if you set your heart on your goal, you must set your heart on the means. In the fashion of most politicians, he looked at events through parliamentary glasses. The House and the Senate were to him what the tiny area of the king's study was to Cardinal de Richelieu. But he was bold and courageous and tested all things by a trenchant and clear-cut conception of the national interest. He was domineering and had a keen sense of the majesty of the state. It was a most amusing sight to watch him give his orders to some bureaucrat, loftily wave aside routine objections, and conclude with sadistic pleasure: "Tomorrow, at six, you will report to me what you have done!"

By an astounding exercise of his will, this little man who looked like a hunchback and was a cartoonist's delight—long, pale face, prominent nose, stiff high collar of the 1900 pattern—made himself into an incisive speaker. In his earlier days his tone of solemnity and his over-complacent quotations from Guizot had provoked smiles. Gradually he managed to impress the House. He was feared because of his detective's instinct, because of his carefully kept records, because of his deadly accurate memory. He alone had penetrated each man's personal history from beginning to end; he alone never forgot how anyone had voted or who had been a turncoat. It was best not to pick any quarrel with him. He knew exactly how to pile up the inconsistencies of any man who thwarted him, to let it be understood by a word that he was well aware of all sorts of shady business, but that he would not go into it, that he, for once, would be a good fellow.

When, occasionally, since 1935, I called at his office, I found him ever unshakable in his understanding of what the totalitarian adventure signified. Perhaps he flattered himself too long that he could immobilize Laval, whom he had hired in 1917–18 to spy on the *Bonnet Rouge* riff-raff. But he could not forget that he owed his first ministerial appointment to Laval and to Laval's predecessor, Flandin.

During the Abyssinian War, during the negotiations with Moscow, his influence was always in the right direction. On March 7, 1936, in contrast to the flabbiness of most of his colleagues, he protested long and loud about the reoccupation of the Rhineland. All through the war he was constantly criticizing Gamelin, Georges, Daladier. "Those men don't want to fight!" "Someday the Maginot Line will be broken through," he told me in December. But he did not foresee more than a terrible episode from which our heroic determination would emerge victorious. In April we shared our anxiety over Reynaud. "Perhaps the fate of France will be on your shoulders." He made no reply. In military matters his adviser was General Bührer, inspector of colonial troops, a member of the Superior War Council with the rank of commander of an army. Bührer was busily promoting a plan intended to forestall the German offensive in Belgium by an attack on the Siegfried Line which specially trained colonial divisions would launch. The general enjoyed Daladier's friendship, but he had no luck in bringing together the Minister for Colonies and the Premier.

Mandel did not belong to any political group and, more often than not, played a lone hand. Of a conservative bent, the Rightists disgusted him with conservatism. And as for the men of the Left, although of a more humane disposition, he saw them unfailingly ruin everything they touched. In this I merely paraphrase his own words. "His courage is naked impudence," was the constant cry of those who opposed his Jacobin spirit, "sheer mimicry, a cheap imitation of Clemenceau." To this there is but one answer: "You say that his face was only a mask. Very well. When did he ever, once, lay aside that mask to ease himself of this burden of pretense?"

Mandel found support in Jeanneney, president of the Senate, and Herriot, president of the House, over whom, of recent years, he had won real influence. Both of them were angered at what they heard about Pétain and Weygand. But the president of the Senate was no more combative than Herriot. However ardent his patriotism as an old-time republican, however unequivocal his judgments, he had no taste for going out of his seclusion and convincing others. He had been in a Cabinet only once, and then as under secretary to the presidency of the Council under Clemenceau's 1917 premiership, when his job was to catch traitors. He was a man of sturdy convictions, but he had little confidence in the legislative body which showed him its respect by re-electing him annually to the chair. "I speak the same language as about thirty senators at the most!" He was aged and ailing. Both these dignitaries of the regime had the ear of the President of the Republic.

But Reynaud, Reynaud alone, was at the hub of events. Methodically, Mandel urged him on, heartened him. He fought against a powerful opponent. Mme. de Portes, installed at the Château de Chassey, with Baudouin close at hand, kept on the watch. The whole night was hers to undo what the Minister of the Interior had accomplished. Ministers leaving the council room often found her standing at the door. Whereto could Mandel look for help? General de Gaulle held strong views about Weygand and imparted them to the Premier. But he had gone to seek reinforcements in London on June 8. He would return there on the fourteenth in order, at least, to make ready the transfer of the French Government to North Africa. At the seat of government he was but a fleeting shadow. Only one man remained who could pry Reynaud loose from the company of treason, fear, folly. That man was Winston Churchill.

II

Tours: *June 13. The Last Franco-British Conference. Reynaud Swerves from His Official Policy for the First Time*

ON JUNE 13 Reynaud carried out the decision arrived at by the Cabinet the night before. By telephone he had asked Winston Churchill to return at once to the banks of the Loire, and the Prime Minister landed by noon at the Tours airport. From Sir Ronald Campbell, the British Ambassador, he already knew of the ministerial debate, of Weygand's request for a "separate armistice," and of Chautemps' proposal. Lord Halifax and Lord Beaverbrook came with Churchill. Sir Alexander Cadogan, permanent Under Secretary of State at the Foreign Office, and Major General Sir Hastings Ismay were also in the party.

Reynaud moved most cautiously all through the introductory part of his short address. He made reference to what he had said on May 26 and 31. At the first of these meetings with the British ministers he never concealed the fact that, if Italy could not be stopped short in her preparations for war or if the United States could not be induced to intervene, France might perhaps have to stop fighting. At the second meeting, behind his brave words, his anxiety, much quickened by Weygand's note two days previously, was clearly visible. Now Reynaud appropriated to himself the warning of the generalissimo, only making it slightly conditional, very slightly indeed. The Fascist Government had declared war three days earlier. The French people would resist unfalteringly if they could see light at the end of the tunnel. But, in the darkness, there seemed to be not even a glint. The only source of light was Mr. Roosevelt. America must declare herself outspokenly against Nazi Germany, must enter into the conflict. The Premier would address a third and last plea to the White House. "If the answer is not in conformity with our wishes, I shall request you to relieve France of her commitment of March 28."

Lord Halifax, as soon as he saw the direction Reynaud's brief speech was taking, scribbled on a piece of paper, "I hope that we shall not answer any conjectural question." He took this means of reminding Churchill (a reminder which was probably unnecessary) of the fundamental rule of British diplomacy: As far as possible, never anticipate events in assuming new commitments or giving up treaty rights. The Prime Minister's reply was to the point: "We fully realize France's sufferings. They are ours. We thoroughly understand that circumstances may occur where France would have to lay down her arms. But to ask the British Government to relieve France, without any further delay, of her obligations is a different question. We cannot do better than wait for Mr. Roosevelt's answer. Once it has been received, a full discussion will follow."[1]

A long silence ensued. What more was there to say? Mr. Churchill asked to be permitted to take counsel privately with his advisers and colleagues. The handful of Englishmen went out into the garden of the Prefecture. Should they at once press Reynaud to define the kind of armistice he had in mind? Would it be in accordance with the Dutch precedent? Would it imply the French Government's moving to London, to Algiers, and the continuation of the alliance, or would it mean the submission of all Frenchmen, at home and abroad? There is good reason to believe that this question was debated. The majority was of the opinion that to go into this matter would be to give Reynaud grounds for assuming that his request had virtually been accepted, that he could consider himself freed of his bond without any British stipulations having been stated. "Make him promise not to come to a decision without first having seen you again," someone suggested. Churchill took

---

[1] In jail, as he reconstructed the past, Reynaud had a different tale to tell. Mr. Winston Churchill, he said, was carried away by a generous impulse, and his utterance, had it been made known to the ministerial council, would have sounded there as an authorization given France to get out of the war as best she could. However, Reynaud passes over in silence his petition to the British ministers. He boasts that he never weakened one single minute in his opposition to the separate armistice. It is impossible to take very seriously a testimony flatly and minutely contradicted on the British side. As to Chautemps, he maintains that Reynaud, in his meeting with Churchill, did embark upon a course of action entirely at variance with the ministerial decision of the night before (the outcome of Chautemps' proposal). Moreover, the Cabinet was ignorant of Reynaud's intention to appeal once more to President Roosevelt.

up the idea. They returned indoors. Confronted with his visitors' at least provisional refusal, Reynaud did not press the subject any further. It was agreed that as soon as Mr. Roosevelt's expected telegram should make possible a thoroughgoing examination of the issue, all would meet again. The place chosen for this purpose was a town on the coast of Brittany, south of Brest, probably Nantes (my informer could not remember), the date not being fixed. In the meantime the question of a separate armistice was to remain in abeyance.

The Prime Minister had one request to make: that the three or four hundred German pilots then confined in French prison camps be at once transferred to England. General de Gaulle jotted down a few words to make sure that it would be done. As they left the room the visitors found themselves face to face with Jeanneney, Herriot, Mandel, and one or two others. Mr. Churchill repeated what he had said to the Premier: "France's sufferings are ours. . . ." Herriot spoke, his voice strained with feeling: "France owes it to herself to resist in the midst of disaster, to stay at your side." His own eloquent tears provoked the tears of everyone. None hid his sorrow. Some moving phrases came from Jeanneney also.

In these June 13 proceedings two puzzles come forward which we cannot afford to overlook.

Why was the problem of the continuance of the war by the French fleet and empire not frankly broached? Mr. Churchill and his associates had learned from Sir Ronald Campbell and then from Reynaud the advice, or rather the injunctions, hurled forth the day before by Weygand and Pétain at the cabinet meeting, their pressing demands for an immediate cessation of hostilities. Reynaud's beating about the bush could not conceal from them that he was not insensible—to say the least—to the generalissimo's and the marshal's pressure. They were able to appreciate how much weaker and more faltering he had become since the London conversations nineteen days earlier. "He is utterly played out," observed Lord Beaverbrook. They were struck by his oft-repeated metaphor of a tunnel without a ray of light in its darkness. This same image was a commonplace of Baudouin, who had run across the Englishmen at a restaurant before the meeting and had sat down at their table. Then, Baudouin had contrived, with an appalling description of the defeat, to attune them to the scheme for an armistice. "We understood," said one of them, "whence came the wind that was blowing Reynaud along." And yet Winston Churchill made no attempt to find out what was in Reynaud's heart! He remained just as reticent as he had been on May

31–June 1! I certainly do not wish to seem to criticize him, for it is all too easy to be wise after the event. The Prime Minister was well aware of Baudouin's activities, but had heard very little about Mme. de Portes's intrigues and those of the rest of the inner circle. He had no idea of their importance and relied on the Premier's strength of purpose. If only he had known that, at the very moment they were in conference, Hélène de Portes, worried over what was going on, tried to get into the entrance hall of the Prefecture, to override the orders of the sentinel and the officer in command, was roughly used by them, and begged Baudouin to rescue the Head of the Government from British clutches! With no possibility to penetrate those lower strata of French affairs Mr. Churchill thought it more expedient, once again, to trust Reynaud's better nature. He may well have feared lest to search Reynaud out on the spot, to endeavor to find out by hard questioning what he still concealed even from himself, might perhaps cause the obvious cracks in his policy to widen and deepen. Churchill was also deceived as to the momentum of the invasion. He and his companions saw an orderly withdrawal where there was in fact a rout. And didn't they dread to have to state their terms apart from all regular consultations with their military and naval advisers? Was it not wiser to have everything cleared up prudently and with insight at the conference in Brittany? There was no danger in waiting.

Alas, Churchill and Reynaud were never to meet again. The Englishman had had his last chance to grab the Frenchman by the shoulders, to breathe into him his own dynamic spirit, to save him from being ruled by a woman. Most of the French ministers still thought of fighting on to the end. If Reynaud had appeared before the Council that very evening with a Franco-British agreement of the sort to be produced three or four days later at Bordeaux, with an agreement already put in shape and his personal acceptance of it signified to Churchill, the advocates of surrender would have been discomfited.

The other puzzle concerns Reynaud. At the last cabinet meeting he had taken his stand against Pétain's and Weygand's request. To all appearances he had still very much in mind the plan for a governmental and military retreat toward North Africa. Yet in Churchill's presence he did not dispel all doubts as to the sort of surrender he contemplated! He gave no inkling whether he did or didn't mean to follow the Dutch example! He actually kept his own counsel. What a strange behavior!

Worse still, by his appeal to Roosevelt he played into the hands of the partisans of a separate armistice. What did he expect from this step?

He knew that the President could, at the most, turn over to him two or three hundred aircraft if he saw his way to part with all the existing matériel. Three days earlier, on the telephone, the American chief executive probably had not minced words, and surely Mr. Bullitt must have supplied him with further details. When he brought the United States into the argument, Reynaud could only have been revolving rather confused purposes in his mind. First, the call to the American President would temporarily halt Weygand's peace drive; it would earn Reynaud two or three days' respite in which to prepare his course of action. Then (ruling out all question of immediate American help) Reynaud might hope that, by such a dramatic gesture, France's distress would be brought home to the United States and help to kill its neutrality. Any move on its part savoring of eventual intervention in the conflict would counter the arguments of our military sages that England was a marked victim for the Nazi conquerors. But the former advantage, a respite, the only one of which he could be reasonably sure, carried with it a terrible price. Roosevelt's admission of his own helplessness, which Reynaud must surely have foreseen, was bound to bring about a psychological shock exceedingly helpful to the supporters of the armistice policy. They might have had to back out a moment, but only to get a better start. Thus would Reynaud hasten the very thing which he made much of wishing to avert.

To judge Reynaud, particularly in the pangs of a supreme crisis, I know very well that a great deal must be laid to his lack of discernment. Since May 18 he had been obsessed with the idea that the supineness of the United States in the face of what he called "the absurd combat between the Horatii and Curiatii brothers" was against all common sense. And he was one of those men convinced that, in diplomacy, sound logic is sure to carry the day. However, plead for him as you will, the worst interpretation of Reynaud's behavior cannot be dismissed. He was willing to pay this terrible price implicit in the message to Mr. Roosevelt because he sought to save face before acceding to the marshal's and the general's advice. He needed an excuse to turn round. America supplied it.

Of course the former fighting man was not altogether dead within him. We shall see him bestir himself from time to time. But he was merely a shadow of his former self. Mme. de Portes's and Baudouin's slave had come out the winner. If there was any case of split personality, the two halves were not equal. Is it possible to cite a single case of Reynaud's quarreling seriously with Weygand and Pétain? Of his threatening to oust them? If any quarrel ever broke out in private, the secret was well kept. And here is what clinches the matter. Having decided upon the risky business of consulting Mr. Roosevelt, the very least he should have done, had there remained in him any trace of a desire not to bow before defeat, was to have shrouded his pleading in secrecy and then to have revealed the refusal of his entreaties with the utmost circumspection. He acted in exactly the opposite way, betraying none of that prudence which would have been instinctive in a man resolved to carry on the fight. Immediately, on the evening of the thirteenth, he informed the French people by radio of the message which only the next morning, still clad in his Chinese pajamas, he was to pass on to Mr. Drexel Biddle, at the Château de Chassey. Let us leave it at this. Reynaud's maneuvering was intended for internal consumption rather than conceived as a serious attempt to change the face of the war. He was telling the country: soon we shall be at our wits' end. His recourse to Washington can have no other meaning.

The Franco-British discussion at Tours reacted powerfully on the French cabinet ministers who, at the Château de Cangey, were anxiously awaiting the Premier's return. They expected Winston Churchill to take part in their deliberation by the side of Reynaud, to wrangle about Chautemps' proposal for relieving France of her March commitment. When they did not see him they were keenly disappointed. Chautemps was at a loss to understand Churchill's absence. "How inconsiderate of him!" he bitterly remarked. As though the Prime Minister, confronted with a conjectural request—one which changed nothing, until further notice, in the functioning of France's war machine—would hasten to confirm that request, give it body and substance, by plunging with thirty-five people into a full-dress debate![2]

At the meeting the ambiguity of Reynaud's conduct, the outcome of this conjectural scheme for an armistice, became only too apparent to everyone. On the one hand, he announced that resistance went on and that he had given Churchill a formal assurance to that effect. In that spirit the Council invited him to utter on the radio a great *sursum corda*: "Let us lift up our hearts!" It was mentioned again that Weygand would have to remodel what was left of his "strategy" and assemble as many troops as possible in Brittany. On the other hand, Reynaud told his colleagues of Churchill's words of affection for France, and

---

[2]Reynaud asserts that he contrived to keep Winston Churchill away from the ministerial council. He feared lest Churchill's compassionate oratory should smooth the way toward the "separate armistice," make it easier and thus swell the number of Ministers who insisted upon ceasing all resistance.

at once the Baudouins, the Prouvosts, understood them as a tacit acceptance of our request. The plea to the White House which, until then, had not been revealed to the Cabinet also served to strengthen most of those present in the opinion that the movement toward capitulation was already under way. "Let us not expect anything from the United States!" exclaimed Chautemps. Nor was this pessimism discouraged—rather the contrary—by Reynaud's explanation of his call to Mr. Roosevelt: if America yielded, it would change the fortunes of the war. Wasn't it as much as an admission that if America were adamant, the war was lost? Moreover, the problem of the French fleet was stated, elaborated. A fixed determination to negotiate an armistice would not have begun to take effect differently.[3]

Pétain, Weygand, and their partisans were still outnumbered. Once more it was up to Reynaud to drive out the whole intrigue. But he left both sides at loose ends. Consequently the majority frittered away, Weygand broke out into new remonstrances, and governmental perplexities increased. Rivière, a socialist Minister of Pensions, wept silently. The day's open defections consisted of Laurent Eynac, of Ybarnegaray, and Bouthillier, Reynaud's intimate and favorite. According to the Minister of Finance, Reynaud had no business to tell Winston Churchill that the Council was determined to proceed further with the war; no formal governmental pronouncement could be quoted about it. He asked that the question of the armistice be decided·at once, with each man taking sides on his own responsibility. "It is impossible to go on fighting; it is also impossible for the government to leave France. You can't carry off the land, the cradles, and the graves."

Weygand could not afford to leave the problem of the armistice pending. Delaying actions had not been planned far ahead by his general staff. Once the great battle begun on June 5 had been lost, everything else seemed negligible to him. Hence the June 12 orders for a general retreat had been extemporized. The troops retreated at the rate of fifty or sixty kilometers a day, and units did not keep together. Officers and soldiers were tired out. They collapsed from weariness and lack of sleep. Whole divisions were now reduced to two or three battalions, with two or three 75s as their only artillery. Weygand had withdrawn the Army of Paris

---

[3]That same evening Sir Ronald Campbell learned the trend of the ministerial discussion: surrendering the fleet to the Germans had been described as a shameful act. He did not find much comfort in such talk. The question of the fleet had been raised by Mr. William Bullitt, in the days before the battle of the Somme. Later on the French fleet was never absent from Mr. Drexel Biddle's preoccupations. The offer to have it sheltered in American ports was put forward all the more eagerly as the prospects of British resistance darkened.

from the firing line. Had he, at least, ordered the destruction of the military supplies which were almost ready for delivery in the factories of the capital's outskirts, especially the swarm of Somua tanks which were to be available in September? It preyed more and more on his mind that he must cover his mistakes by cutting short that sequence of deadly facts which he felt moving on as an inexorable indictment against him.

The Council's decision to set the remnants of the French armies toward Brittany infuriated him. He accused all and sundry of plotting behind his back. He paced the floor shouting that the sight of these ranters prepared to go on fighting with the lives of others was unbearable. He repeated that neither France nor even England had a chance to survive except by coming to terms with the Reich. How could one be sure that within a few years British and Americans would outmatch Germans in the air, with Germany's greater productive capacity reinforced by the output of French factories? And would the French people agree to being abandoned by the government? Must it not be assumed that in the midst of ruin, misery, and death, with the Army utterly wiped out, Soviets would sprout forth from the earth?

In that utterance of Weygand flamed up the whole political theory behind the armistice, behind the National Revolution, the Bordeaux and Vichy governments. It rested on the assumption that Frenchmen were incapable of reacting to the invader like the Dutch or the Norwegians, not to mention the Poles and the Belgians. Nothing but despair was to be expected from them.

The ministers expected to leave for Quimper on the following morning. During the night Reynaud sent word to them that Bordeaux was to be their goal. From that moment all the men who insisted on the continuation of the war looked in the direction of Algiers. General de Gaulle prepared to go to London forthwith, as already arranged. There he would investigate ways and means of transporting men and matériel to Africa on the largest possible scale.

A new protagonist appeared upon the scene—panic. To be precise, we must recognize that this panic had a character of its own, far removed from its etymological sense. Between June 12 and 15 no terror was visible in Touraine and further south. Long lines of automobiles glided down the roads. When they came to the entrances of a town, drivers waited patiently until the whole column could move on. There was very little excitement, and between people whose cars were stuck in traffic jams, with only a few inches between them, there was very little

conversation. Rather were they in a mood for silence. But what little
they did say showed the illusions they harbored. Freshly toppled from
an established security and happiness, they had no conception of the
catastrophe which befell them. They believed that the Germans would
be halted somewhere on the lines of the Seine, the Marne, or even the
Loire, that the old-style, long-drawn-out war of position would begin
anew, or else that an easy and not too harsh peace, of the sort Pétain
and Weygand contemplated, would be patched up. By fleeing toward
the center and the south of France, they sought shelter from the horrors
which Polish, Dutch, Belgian narratives conjured up before their eyes
and which, moreover, had not been erased from their own memories of
1914. But they did not understand that even if they escaped the invader,
they would not escape slavery; that invasion and temporary slavery were,
indeed, inevitable, but that permanent slavery was not, and that to
accept it so as to get some relief from the circumstances of the moment
would be the absurd and unforgivable crime. They thought of their
worldly goods. They wrangled with petty problems of their own. How
many of them perceived that all worldly possessions meant very little if
the country was not to be free?

On my way from the Department of Corrèze I passed through Poitiers
on the thirteenth. The small town was overflowing with people. But a
crowd at the races would not have seemed very much different. Here
was Count Clauzel, our former Ambassador to Berne. He had come to
rent a house in the countryside. There he would quietly await the end
of the thunderstorm. With him was General Raguenau, who had been
deputy chief of staff of the Army and, in 1918, I believe, a principal
liaison officer for the American Expeditionary Forces. This gentleman
obstinately averred that the whole war doctrine of our military chiefs
had been vindicated by events. What good was it to argue? At La Palice,
on the fourteenth, a shipowner on whom I called suspected me of being
out of my senses when I warned him that in continental France every
line of defense would yield and that we should have to take up the
struggle afresh on the seas and, beyond them, in the French Empire. My
experience with another shipowner, in Bordeaux, on the fifteenth, was
the same. I took luncheon at a small hotel by the seaside in the Vendée
region. Some fifty people were there, blissfully loafing through their
holidays. The man in the street, or even in the market place, was blind
to reality. He counted off the toll of the enemy's conquests: Paris,
Rouen, Rennes, Rheims, Châlons, Nevers, Clamecy, Vesoul. It would

soon include Riom, Tournon, Rochefort. How many centuries was it since foreign soldiery had last been seen there? He was submissive to his misfortunes, and he did not try to take a rational view of them.

Someone should have cried out to these men and women in flight; someone should have told them that each of them had a duty—to sit tight in his own home, on his own soil, at his own task; for his part, to preserve the shape of France throughout the cruel days when the enemy would strain to wound it and twist it. Someone should have told them that here was a sort of resistance fit to match that of the soldiers, the sailors, the militant men of all descriptions who were bound in duty to go across the seas. What had been lost within the nation's narrow boundaries would be won again in the larger compass of the continents.

But no voice was heard to put the matter in that light. Up to the very last minute foolish hopes were raised. But a little effort would have been enough to awaken the French people to a full realization of what was needed for their redress and their victory. They would have understood their patriotic duty. The very air they breathed would thereby have been changed. On the instant, the government would have pulled itself together. On June 14, as Reynaud sped along toward Bordeaux, his car came to a stop and he was recognized. He was apprehensive of the reaction of the crowd, but men shouted out (they were from Alsace): "Don't give up! We'll get them yet!" And all broke into cheers because they still thought of him as a rock.

His traveling companion that day was an official who wished with all his heart that the feigned wisdom of the military men would not intimidate the government. He knew all too well that a Nazi conquest would be merciless. He kept his conversation with the Premier centered on North Africa. "You must be the Gambetta of 1940!" Reynaud was startled at this sudden allusion to the Tribune of the People. His imagination set to work. "Yes," he said, "in 1871, France was prostrate despite Gambetta. But the tradition of revenge emerged from his outwardly ineffectual exertions and counted for much in the victory of 1918!" Throughout the rest of the trip the Minister seemed once more serene and resolute.

The inarticulate mass of the refugees reverberated upon the government, now tongue-tied, now talking casually. Little by little it dawned upon the ministers that to snatch from the enemy's grasp (not, alas, from his control!) the broadest possible area of the homeland was to fulfill the prime need of all, to satisfy the universal longing. The psychology of those in flight tended to shape governmental policy. The inhabitants of such towns and villages as were yet far distant from the invader, seeing the pitiful horde strung out along the roads, contributed their share to the dead weight of pressure. Would they too be swept away in this tidal wave of humanity?

On Sunday, June 16, the parish priest in a small village of my acquaintance quoted the cry of despair from the gospel narrative of the tempest on the Sea of Tiberius: "Master, we perish!" Everyone listened in helpless amazement. No, all was not lost, but no one had enlightened the priest or his congregation. And the prayer of the man who still had his own roof over his head was, "Lord, may the Germans never get this far!"

It was at Tours, and later at Bordeaux, and in the government, that I saw true panic, shameful panic. Here were lack of faith, despair, pointlessly fluttering about, utter want of stanch purpose and method among the men who were supposed to rule France and also among the politicians, diplomats, journalists whose trade it was to follow events day by day. Not that all men, good and bad, should be lumped together. But a mere handful of bad men sufficed to make the rest ineffectual.

I arrived at Tours during the evening of the thirteenth. I must not even consider chasing over the countryside in search of friends. Would I be let back into the city once I went outside it? By chance, and without any attempt on my part to see anyone in particular, here is what crossed my path. Herriot's lamentations to the journalists: "My friends, oh, my poor friends! Let us stick together, just as closely as we can. . . ." The conventional attitude of a few remaining English journalists: "Everything isn't as bad as the fifth column makes it out to be. . . . All you have to do is to keep a cool head on your shoulders. . . ." Personal warnings from several high officials of the Ministry of Foreign Affairs: "Reynaud will soon be done away with. This very minute you should be getting ready to leave the country. Don't take any chances with a regime subject to Laval, Pétain, and the Germans!" I went into the first restaurant which I came across. A former Minister and the representative of a foreign country had met Reynaud two hours earlier. They still had faith in the firmness of his resolution, and my doubts on the subject annoyed them. In spite of their desire to deceive themselves, they wavered under the sundry scraps of news which, from time to time, leaked out of the ministerial châteaux and outstripped their own.

A government which is truly imperturbable and which knows what it is going to do is hedged in radiance. An all-pervading energy emanates from it. Such was the case with Clemenceau in 1918, with Winston Churchill in July–October 1940. But the confused Reynaud-Pétain-Weygand-Chautemps administration had no more fluid than a corpse.

In this picture must be included the French Army, whose general retreat, begun on the twelfth, was degenerating into a rout. How endure such a sight unless one has a heart encased in brazen armor? And the ministers were not thrice-girded.

The retreat had not been planned. The High Command had not believed that it would have to withstand the enemy for so long a time. It had thought that the sluice gates of invasion would have been closed more quickly. It was caught short, like some supply corps ready to feed a regiment which all of a sudden has an army on its hands. The High Command's one design was to prevent bodies of troops from scattering and stampeding during the three or four days which must yet elapse before the Cabinet could be won over to an armistice. The very idea of managing things so as to gather at several points along the coast, either Mediterranean or Atlantic, a nucleus of effectives to be shipped out to the Empire was utterly repellent to the leading generals. On the twelfth or the thirteenth Weygand protested against a decision of Reynaud's ordering to Morocco the first contingent of the 1940 class. He made much of a remark falsely attributed to General Noguès, to the effect that at that season of the year young men there died like flies. As though, with the nation in its throes, ordinary considerations of hygiene were of compelling importance! The generalissimo's only concern was to keep enough compact units to protect public order. Such a strategy of social conservatism did, in fact, help the Germans to bag still more prisoners.

It is a story of agony and dissolution. The 10th Army, which on June 5 held the line of the Somme and had promptly fallen into several fractions, had lost one of its divisions at Le Havre. The whole force was finally separated from the armies of the center on June 12 and 13. On the fourteenth, the Germans reached Dreux. Weak mechanized units were stretched toward Chartres and Châteaudun as a covering force for the main body of troops. They were stretched too thin, and from the seventeenth on, enemy tanks penetrated the whole area. They overran Cotentin and Brittany. The staff of the 10th Army was made prisoner at Rennes. General de Fornel de la Laurencie's 3rd Corps and a few cavalry outfits alone were able to fall back on Nantes.

The 6th, 2nd, and 4th armies, the central plate of the French shield, spread out from the Aisne and the Ailette to the Maginot Line: they were driven from their positions on June 8 and 9. Rethel was lost. On the twelfth and thirteenth, the Germans burst around both sides of the Mountain of Rheims. The 6th Army, bent back on the Montmirail-Cézanne-Romilly axis, was soon split up. The 4th was outflanked by tanks which rushed for Châlons-sur-Marne and Vitry-le-François, and the 2nd was pushed to the Ornain, which the enemy had already crossed on the fourteenth. The three armies no longer constituted a coherent whole. The Germans moved forward at their leisure from Troyes toward Nevers and from Chaumont to Besançon. They reached Clamecy and Vesoul on the fifteenth, Besançon on the sixteenth. The seventeenth, they were at Pontarlier, on the Swiss frontier. Around these cities they had only Territorials to deal with.

Under General Héring's command, the Army of Paris and the 7th Army (the latter violently cut off from the 10th and the 6th armies, with which it made up Group No. 3) awaited the invader behind the Oise and, on June 11, seemed in a position to hold him in check.[4] But on the thirteenth, the High Command's will-to-an-armistice and (supplying strategic justification) the loss of the Mountain of Rheims led to the proclamation which made Paris an "open city." General Besson, who had been in command of the 3rd Group of Armies, now broken up, took over these forces, which were not to be put to the test for which they had been assembled. No longer were they at the disposal of the military government of the capital, assigned to a new commander, Dentz, with the mandate to surrender. General Besson moved his troops back to the Loire. But the German assault hit this river west of Orléans on the eighteenth, and the stream was crossed at Nantes on the nineteenth, then, on the twentieth, at Saumur and east of Tours. The left wing of the 7th Army was lopped off on the lower part of the Cher River. The remainder was threatened on both flanks. On one side, Montluçon and Riom were taken on the twentieth and, on the other, Thouars and Cholet. German spearheads touched Rochefort and Royan on the twenty-second and twenty-third, Tournon on the twenty-fourth.

Army Group No. 2 (General Prételat) was made up of some fifteen fortress and second-reserve divisions intermingled with excellent Polish units. It was no more in contact with the armies of the center, and after the seventeenth it even was shut out from a possible retreat toward the south. Garrisons were left in the Maginot fortifications which would still be fighting fiercely four days after the armistice. French and German delegates of the Wiesbaden Commission had to hurry up and give them, on the spot, notice of the order to cease firing. Group No. 2 was

---

[4]According to the semiofficial account in *Le Temps*.

enclosed in a cage which grew smaller from day to day: to the south, in the Vosges, the 8th Army (General Laure); to the north, from Commercy to Sarrebourg, the 3rd (General Condé) and the fifth (General Bourret). The 8th attempted a break-through toward Besançon, and a portion of it, despite harrying by two thousand tanks, took refuge in Switzerland. The 5th was authorized to surrender on the twenty-second. The 3rd dispersed.

As for the six or seven divisions posted against the Italians in the Alps, their task was simple enough until the eighteenth. Then they were attacked from the rear by the Germans, who, on the nineteenth, crossed the Rhône over the bridges at Lyons and, later, at Culoz, and who forced their way to the farther bank of the Isère at Voreppe.

This rapid summary omits what is really the essential. Those units, fleeing like partridges before a crowd of beaters, were nothing more than dismembered skeletons. On the twenty-fourth, the four armies which had been drawn back to the center of France numbered hardly sixty-five thousand combatants, and on the twenty-second, Army Group No. 2, some ten thousand men.[5] On the seventeenth, every center of population having more than twenty thousand inhabitants had been declared an open city. Such places fell without resistance. This was as much as to admit that there was to be no more systematic and continuous fighting. It is impossible to conceive of a retreat in greater contrast to the orders issued to the Red Army in the summer of 1941: yield to the enemy nothing but scorched earth. In France, obviously, those Russian tactics could not have had the effectiveness which is theirs where the space available for a retreat is practically unlimited. But by the fifteenth of June anything like general-staff leadership was hardly visible.[6] At points thought to be easy to defend, local actions broke out which bore no relation to one another. All plugs, all stoppers popped in rapid succession like champagne corks. On the twenty-third, the Germans did not deem it worth their while to press their prey any closer. We lost touch with the enemy. The crushing of our military machine had a

[5] Semiofficial account published in *Le Temps*. It is quite possible that the figures were made worse than the reality.

[6] Nonetheless, huge destruction was inflicted by the enemy or voluntarily accomplished: thirty-five hundred works of public utility were destroyed, including twenty-five hundred bridges. Railways suffered, perhaps, more than the rest, with tracks breached in sixteen hundred different spots, rails torn up on a total of two hundred kilometers, five hundred bridges wrecked, and twenty-eight tunnels caved in. Canals and rivers were made unserviceable for water traffic on a stretch of fifty-two hundred kilometers. Burned-out houses and public buildings must also be added to the list. Whether an exhaustive survey has been made is not known.

physical effect on the government. It made that distant prospect of salvation which, despite everything, still hung over the horizon seem even more remote.[7]

12

Bordeaux: June 15. Reynaud's Second Great Deviation of Policy. The Note Sent to the London Cabinet

THE MINISTERIAL CARAVAN arrived at Bordeaux on June 14, toward the end of the day. Reynaud conferred with the British Ambassador. He informed him that General de Gaulle was in London to arrange for the transport of men, weapons, ammunition, and supplies to North Africa. The first ships had put to sea. The operation was conceived on a larger scale than at Dunkirk. England was requested to lend extraordinary assistance. To my knowledge, this was the first time the subject was officially discussed between London and Paris. Was Reynaud then to be Gambetta reincarnate?

On the morning of June 15, Reynaud held another conversation with Sir Ronald Campbell. The latter cabled the Foreign Office that the plan in Bordeaux was to set up two governments—one to go to North Africa, the other to stay in France. A little later he completed his report: he had just received "very satisfactory" assurances with regard to the fleet. The head of the French Cabinet had told him that, "it will never be turned over to the Germans." He was surprised that things were moving so quickly. The task he had set himself to perform above all others was to have the French warships removed from territorial waters, beyond the reach of an armistice negotiation. He thought he was close

---

[7]For the six weeks of fighting which ended with the armistices of June 22 and 24, French losses were as follows: 100,000 killed (an approximate figure; 80,000 of these had been accounted for on February 15, 1941), and about 1,800,000 prisoners. As to wounded, no definite figure can be quoted. According to the records of the German 15th Armored Division (33rd Division of Infantry at the time of the battle of France) which the British seized in Libya, the German High Command ordered its troops to take as many prisoners as possible. Lately higher casualty figures have been quoted.

to his aim; instead he should have been on his guard. Did not those very assurances imply that the policy of North Africa still trembled in the balance, that the alternative policy of the separate armistice was still running strong? Lebrun, Jeanneney, Herriot, and all the ministers who could not despair of their country took the African outcome as settled. But Laval also had arrived in Bordeaux. After leaving Paris he had gone to his stronghold at Châteldon, some thirty kilometers from Vichy. From Tours his friends in or around the government had called him to the rescue.

Adrien Marquet was mayor of Bordeaux. Seven years earlier he had broken with the Socialist party. He was one of those who were exasperated with Léon Blum's finespun intellect. He had a yearning desire for office and a belief that in the social shufflings brought about by fascism and Nazism the beginnings of a wave which would roll far into the future could be discerned. Hitler! Mussolini! You set us free from the dry scholasticism of our Marxist professors! Such could have been Marquet's cry—and Déat's as well. Conceited, vulgar, astute, the mayor of Bordeaux was a past master at demagoguery. The first time he ran for municipal office this mountebank was opposed by local big business. In the end he won it over. The Bordeaux royalists, always fairly numerous, came to realize that this formerly despised rabble-rouser was a first-rate enemy of the Republic.

At Tours and at Bordeaux, Jeanneney and Herriot either made a serious mistake of omission or else suffered a serious setback, I am not sure which. They failed to gather together one hundred or one hundred and fifty patriot members of Parliament to back the advice which they were giving the Premier and the Cabinet. Perhaps they thought that the departure for Algiers, seemingly close at hand, made this effort unnecessary. What they lacked either the wisdom or the ability to accomplish, Pierre Laval, with Marquet's help, effected against them. With open arms the mayor welcomed, indoctrinated, entertained the wandering deputies and senators, gave them the run of his City Hall.[1] Laval's first care was to get in touch with Marshal Pétain, Baudouin, and the

---

[1] In *Ci-devant,* A. de Monzie has the following entry for June 17: "This Town Hall where some ten, fifteen, twenty of us legislators are lodging, as though in some emigrants' hotel, presents an extraordinary picture well worth description. Some few are able to get in deep enough to see Marquet, the local Caesar; most have simply transformed these Bordeaux lobbies into the "Pas Perdus" of the Palais Bourbon. From without we are swarmed by the notorious, by celebrities of every brand: the cast of characters of a society picture taken in Deauville, but all rumpled, suddenly grown old, as though a whirlwind had tattered their make-up. . . ."

other like-minded ministers, and also with Lequerica, the Spanish Ambassador, his friend and intimate, through whom, perhaps as early as May 25, he had attempted to approach the Germans. He did not doubt that this show would be his. He went to see the President of the Republic and tried to bamboozle him. The marshal-vice-premier and the commander in chief at last had at their side a bold and astute politician who would know very well how to make a clean sweep of all old-fashioned politics.

Two governments, one which should operate in the overseas empire, the other to remain in France, Campbell had cabled. In all probability such was the correct solution of the problem with which Reynaud had to grapple. Had it been acted upon, Weygand would have surrendered to the Germans after the same fashion as General Winkelman, commander in chief of the Dutch Army, on the fourteenth of May.[2] The President of the Republic and at least a few of the ministers would have crossed to the other side of the Mediterranean to seek the freedom of action and the independence without which their duties could become only a superior means of national enslavement ready to the enemy's hand. In the autumn of 1918, when Germany was crumbling, President Ebert and the generals of the Reichswehr similarly split their functions. With this difference: the sea did not lie between the invader and any part of German territory. All the vanquished could do was to exploit the cracks in the victorious coalition by diplomatic maneuvering and to upset the would-be rebuilders of Europe with all sorts of occult military raids and undertakings in the outer reaches of Germanism, from the Baltikum to Upper Silesia, where the social structure was half ruined. Then did politicians and diplomats set to work in Berlin and audacious officers sally forth to do mischief on the periphery of the Reich. But, after all, the game was not promising except in the diplomatic field. How much more potentially fruitful the governmental split upon which defeated France could fall back at will! Reynaud's political intelligence was too great not to be attracted. But when it came to carrying out the project, Reynaud still did not have the requisite steadfastness.

Until now Pétain behaved like the generalissimo's shadow. He had done little more than repeat Weygand's long diatribes briefly and in an undertone. However, he had known all the time that by a mere gesture

[2]Winkelman's order to cease firing, at the end of the afternoon of the fourteenth, excluded Zeeland, the southwestern province which was cut off from communication with the rest of the country and where British troops had landed on the twelfth. And it was specifically stated that the order did not apply to the Navy, which would continue to defend the Dutch colonies in both hemispheres. (Hamilton Fish Armstrong, *Chronology of Failure*.)

of resigning he could bring the politicians toppling, stultify their words and actions. On the morning of June 15 he formally requested that a cabinet meeting should be called for the afternoon, and he notified Reynaud that he would raise the question of the armistice, would insist upon an immediate decision.[3] Once again Weygand's old argument for the immediate negotiation of an armistice was rehashed.

Reynaud rejected it in peremptory terms. He was not only under obligation to await a reply from Mr. Roosevelt, but also to confer with Mr. Churchill. He had committed himself to that procedure two days earlier, and he could not get out of it. As to the policy at stake, he reasserted that a retreat to the African Empire opened up the only possibility of survival. The discussion threatened to become embittered. He spoke of giving up the premiership and was taken to task by the President of the Republic. It was then that Chautemps suggested the "compromise" whereby he nullified and perverted the scheme for dividing the executive which, that very morning, Reynaud had imparted to the British Ambassador—the compromise that, in the same way as the Tours formula, was to cause the Head of the Government to swerve still further from his purpose.

Why would it not be a good thing, he asked, to find out the terms of an armistice, and even of peace, through the intermediary of a great international authority, the Pope, or, better, the President of the United States? Should the German conditions prove unacceptable, the government would become again a united body and be all the better able to require of the nation the more heroic course—unlimited occupation of the homeland and the removal of the government to Africa. Once transplanted to Algiers, the President of the Republic and his Cabinet would

[3]Before the meeting Reynaud received Weygand and did what he could to make him endorse the halving of the government. Under the plan the generalissimo was expected to stop the fighting of his own movement, without any preliminary understanding with the Germans, without a formal armistice being concluded, exactly as Winkelman had done. And since Weygand had repeated, day after day, that nobody in the Cabinet cared at all about relieving the troops of this terrible ordeal, Reynaud argued that the Dutch precedent, if followed, would bring relief much quicker than an armistice negotiation ever could. But Weygand, in his hate for the republican institutions, retorted that if it was possible for a queen, for a dynasty, to leave metropolitan territory, a republican regime, built on such moving foundations that one hundred cabinets had passed on the stage within seventy years, could not afford to do so. "As to surrendering in imitation of Winkelman," said Weygand, "never shall I put the flag to such a shame." Reynaud asserts that he succeeded in persuading Pétain for a brief moment, during the ministerial council of June 15, through laying stress upon the suffering of the rank and file. So much so that Pétain left the room in order to remonstrate with Weygand. But, adds Reynaud, the remonstrating came from Weygand, and the old man turned tail.

no longer be at Hitler's mercy. In their negotiations with him they would have the advantage of relative independence. The fleet would go to English waters if an armistice came in force.

Then why not cross the Mediterranean and negotiate afterward? The reply was that, before going any further, the proof of the conqueror's unreasonableness must be made clear to the nation. If this were not done, the French people would become indignant and would disown the "runaways." Moreover, if it were cleverly managed, the overture could in no way prejudice what might be done later. Several ministers objected: "Once your arm is in the toils, do you think you can pull it free at will?" And was it so difficult to guess at Germany's demands? The men who thus showed their common sense were Monnet, Louis Marin, Rio, Delbos.

Louis Oscar Frossard, Minister of Public Works, who, on the evening of June 13, at Tours, had urged his colleagues to rally around Reynaud's leadership and leave all controversies in suspense as long as the answer of President Roosevelt was not at hand, followed in the steps of Chautemps. Still another Marxist converted to social conservatism! During World War I, his heart had been with the Zimmerwald and Kienthal agitators. In 1920 he had campaigned for the union of the Second and Third internationals.[4] For several years now he had been of the middle class, of the bourgeoisie, and here he was betraying the Republic and his country. A low-grade schoolteacher, a deputy, a journalist: a clever fellow but too much of a trickster. Reynaud had given him office, in the tradition of the parliamentary game, because, on March 22, he had been one of those who had successfully assailed Daladier.

The Premier could feel that the majority of the Cabinet was drifting away from him. He no longer stuck to the premiership and seemingly wanted to be rid of it.

Did he seek immediate release? We know that already several of his sayings had been understood to point in that direction. There is more. He declared that the government which applied for an armistice would have to do without him.[5] Did he represent that, from the point of view

---

[4]At Socialist party meetings, when critics of Frossard, who had become too moderate for their taste, recalled to him his Soviet zeal of 1920, he would say in his own defense: "In those days I was a mere youth of twenty." "Unless I am mistaken," Marx Dormoy would reply, "your age at that date was fully thirty."

[5]On the other hand, discussing the problem of the fleet with Sir Ronald Campbell, either on June 15 or on June 16, he was fearful of German and Italian naval reprisals if the French fleet sailed for British ports. He even said that Italy might then seize Tunisia with her ships!

of those who favored a separate armistice, the very first step, logically, should be to leave for Africa, since this guaranteed freedom to the parleys, and that it was absurd, under the pretext of having to spare public opinion, deliberately to give up such an advantage? Did he explain that a fettered diplomacy couldn't fare better than a fettered army? Very likely he did, but I have no positive information. On this question Reynaud had the right and the opportunity to be inflexible, to break cleanly with the opposition. Who, then, would have dared reply that, even for two or three days, it might be better for us to talk with Hitler bound hand and foot? Anyhow, the ulterior motives implicit in Chautemps' suggestion would have been laid bare. Nevertheless, Reynaud yielded to the proposal of the "conciliator." "Gentlemen, let us be united!" cried the Head of the State in a firm voice. A vote was taken. There was no further disagreement. The decision was unanimous.[6] Sir Ronald Campbell was called to the Premier's office and the following note (here given in substance, not verbatim) was handed to him: the Cabinet has decided that the government will not be able to leave French soil until the terms of the armistice have been ascertained to be unacceptable. The Cabinet has no doubt of what will be the result, but believes it wise to prove to public opinion that it is impossible to nego-

[6]Many wished, later on, to find extenuating circumstances for their failings at Bordeaux. They explained: (1) that the plan of moving to Africa could not be carried out on June 15, that preparations should have been begun a week earlier; (2) that the German command would not have hesitated to throw its troops across Spain, the Strait of Gibraltar, and Spanish Morocco, on the heels of the fleeing government, and that the Nazi invasion would at once have extended to the French Empire.

It does not seem that this objection was ever raised by anyone at Bordeaux, either military or civilian. It is a fallacious objection and, besides, it came up as an afterthought. The British and French held absolute control of the sea, and Spain was at their mercy. The government of General Franco would not have courted disaster through taking risks on the side of Germany: its rather timorous policy in the last three years is witness for it.

Besides, Germany, even if faced by a French Empire arming against her, would nevertheless have had to attend to more important undertakings—the assault on England, in the first place. She would not have postponed what was rightly regarded as the principal operation for the sake of devoting herself to a byplay. And the Bordeaux men who foretold that within three weeks England would get it in the neck certainly did not think otherwise. It must be added that in Spain and Portugal, swarming with German agents, no preparation of any kind was noticed.

But if the struggle was not to continue overseas, could not the French fleet, at least, keep on fighting by the side of the British squadrons? The question of the empire and the question of the Navy were separable, and the latter did not give rise to the same objection as the former. However, there is no evidence to show that, from among those who opposed the prosecution of the war in Africa, a single voice was heard to consistently suggest joining the French fleet with the British. Thus their bad faith is unmasked. Indeed, they did not want France to remain in the war, and still less did they care to find out whether there was any possibility for her to do so.

tiate honorably. If England will agree to the French Government's request for an armistice, the head of the Cabinet is authorized to state that the surrender of the fleet shall be deemed an unacceptable demand.[7]

This note makes it perfectly clear that Pétain, Weygand, and their followers had won the upper hand, that Reynaud was no longer able even to stand by the procedure agreed upon at Tours. This procedure had been ambiguous enough: in spite of everything, it bound him not to reach any decision until he should have once more seen Churchill. But so forgetful of their promise to the British Premier were Reynaud himself and other drafters of the document that they gave notice of a *decision* (the word is used) to take another step and, this time, a fatal one toward capitulation. How futile, on their part, to depict the actual request for an armistice as merely a stratagem intended to reconcile the High Command with the Cabinet and to stiffen the morale of the French people! Let us not question the sincerity of the men who invented the formula—and the reasons for doubting their sincerity are all too compelling: it must perforce be recognized that this tremendous action, the request for an armistice, was in itself a primary fact, a fact outclassing all others, certain to have unreckonable consequences, far beyond the intentions which had inspired its proposal. Nor was this all. A fairly explicit threat of blackmail was conveyed to that very London Government to which a promise had been given that nothing would be done without previous consultation. In case it refused the proffered deal, Reynaud and his colleagues, in their own words, might look upon the surrendering of the fleet as an acceptable German condition.

Thus far had Reynaud traveled before taking stock of the telegram of refusal from the President of the United States, which, as I have pointed out, could lend only an almost irresistible impetus to the argument of the military leaders. Reynaud was not only going back on his commitment of March 28; he was betraying his personal pledge of June 13 and, moreover, trying to bully the ally he was leaving in the lurch. How sudden and repulsive an about-face in policy was manifest in these brief sentences forwarded to London through Sir Ronald! The first few words referred to the Reynaud-Campbell interview of that same morning, to the removal of the government and war to the bitter end; the last few words foreboded submission to the will of Hitler and even

---

[7]M. Chautemps maintains that this version of the note is unknown to him, that at any rate the note was not delivered to Sir Ronald Campbell until June 16 (a Sunday) and that the important part of the ministerial discussion took place on the morning of that day. Authoritative British sources contradict his testimony.

possible enmity toward England. Conceive a master cheat, brooding upon the same ideas as Baudouin, but keen to change craftily, to attune the end he has in mind with the Jacobin ardor he had until then seemed to show: both at Bordeaux and at Tours would he not have behaved as Reynaud did? Is the hypothesis by which I prefer to stand—that of a man who had lost faith, whom his mistress, Baudouin, and Weygand pulled down each time he, from long habit, sprang up anew—any more pleasing?

The British Cabinet wasted no time over empty recriminations. It did not dispute the Premier's extraordinary performance of the June 13 agreement. Right away it informed him of the terms under which it would be willing to annul the March 28 commitment. The French fleet must be sent to British ports, "pending negotiations." What was the precise meaning of this rather vague expression? In due time Sir Ronald Campbell gave it this interpretation: the ships were to be in British ports before and during the negotiation of a separate armistice. Needless to say, they would not return to French waters if the parleys succeeded, but the Ambassador had no business to clear up that point.

Two days earlier the French Cabinet, as it pondered on the winding up of the Anglo-French alliance in case hostilities were to cease, had hit upon the formula: "The Navy will never be turned over to Germany." And the British Ambassador, when he learned of it on the fifteenth, before the cabinet meeting, seems to have expressed satisfaction. But Mr. Churchill and his colleagues immediately drew the conclusion that a French Government which had accepted an armistice could be nothing more than a slave, that its wishes toward and contracts with all states other than Germany would be valueless, and that there was no conceivable guarantee against the French fleet's eventually being turned over to the enemy except its being at anchor in British waters. One need not have been a seer to predict that only such surety could be thought sufficient by the Admiralty and that it would never permit an enormous naval force to go bobbing about on the ocean checkerboard—a force little less than one third the entire British Navy, capable of bringing about the ruin of the empire if the totalitarian nations should succeed in gaining control over it, directly or indirectly.

The Downing Street ministers believed themselves entitled to think that the France of Reynaud or even of Pétain, overwhelmed into surrender and laying down its arms even overseas, would nevertheless long for an English victory in the future, would never dream of falling in with the Nazis' "New Order," and would instinctively make use of her last free breath to fortify the eventual liberator. From the point of view of the French national interest, their reasoning was beyond challenge. Unfortunately, our military leaders and their ministerial associates, as I have pointed out, fancied that they could soothe and propitiate Hitler by offering him, along with a request for an armistice, their refusal to pile the French fleet into the English pan of the scales, or even to allow it to be laid up in United States ports. To their eyes the British Empire was already prostrate.

The British Cabinet's answer to Reynaud was embodied in two notes. They were not received in Bordeaux until the afternoon of June 16.

13

Bordeaux: June 16. The Scheme for a Franco-British Union and Reynaud's Resignation. His Appointment to Washington

EARLY ON JUNE 16, Reynaud called the ministers together to inform them of the reply of the President of the United States to his appeal of the fourteenth. Mr. Roosevelt's attitude was in keeping with all expectations: material aid on as broad a scale as possible, but no military commitments, since they could be entered into only—and he emphasized this point—with the approval of Congress. It could not be otherwise: the construction placed by several ministers upon Mr. Roosevelt's statement was that it justified the Cabinet in its decision, the previous day, to obtain London's release from the pledge of March 28. It foretold the end of British as well as French resistance.

Marshal Pétain rose. This time he had in hand a letter of resignation, intended as a weapon which he had no doubt would make Reynaud yield. He broke away from his usual reticence. The sentences he uttered might as well have been spoken by Laval.[1] Let us have no more delays for which France will pay dearly. No more talk of emigration (as though

---

[1] As a matter of fact, M. Henri Queuille, the Minister of Supplies, had some reason to believe that Laval and Marquet contributed to the drafting of the letter. (See the French language newspaper *France*, June 8, 1943.)

North Africa were an alien land!). No more chasing after the fancy that France can be rescued from her defeat by action from without. The country can rise up again only through its own strength. It behooves the government to set the example, to strike its roots in French soil, amid the French people, to share its common sufferings. The marshal's intervention meant that the hours of Reynaud's premiership were numbered. Those who had made up their mind to follow the old man came out into the open. With difficulty Reynaud persuaded Pétain to withhold his letter of resignation and wait for the British reply to the French note of the preceding night. Besides, he had not yet thought of doing away with the Tours arrangements to the extent of canceling his trip to Brittany.

General de Gaulle was still in London. He had fulfilled the task which Reynaud had entrusted to him three days earlier. The Interallied administrative agencies, particularly the one concerned with the Merchant Marine, had set themselves to the job of removing from continental France, to Algeria, Morocco, and Tunisia, everything that could be found useful for the prosecution of the war. From Bayonne, from numerous Mediterranean ports, between Toulon and the Spanish frontier, hundreds and hundreds of ships of all sizes were to sail. But the French note of the fifteenth, with its most disturbing reference to an armistice so out of tune with the Tours agreement, alarmed the Prime Minister and the French Under Secretary of State for National Defense. They anxiously wondered how the Bordeaux Government would react to the British and the American answers, both of them forwarded almost simultaneously and tumbling over those ministers who seemed to have been shattered by defeat. Reynaud had said: "I see no light at the end of the tunnel." Why should England not try to provide this light which could not come from America? Whence was born the suggestion of an Anglo-French union.

I have not been able to find out who invented it and currycombed it into favor. Perhaps some Interallied agency official of a Geneva turn of mind, accustomed to make free with the idea of national sovereignty, wont to indulge in far-reaching novelties which, more often than not, it must be admitted, failed to evince any sure political judgment. Anyhow, the scheme was a happy one under the circumstances, well suited to the extraordinary needs of the hour. "The union" of France and England was to be "indissoluble." A constitution was to provide for the management of national defense, diplomacy, financial and economic policy, by means of joint governmental bodies. "Every French citizen will at once enjoy British citizenship, and every British subject, French citizenship. For the duration of hostilities, there will be but one single War Cabinet, directing the forces of the two nations. The two Parliaments will be formally associated, costs of reconstruction shared equally. . . . And thus we shall conquer . . . " Those last words bear Churchill's stamp. A magnificent dream, worthy of this high-souled statesman, deeply attached to France—not only to the France of his own day, but to that score and a half of generations of Frenchmen who, ever since the twelfth century, through so long a series of contacts, hostile or friendly, have shared in molding the history of his own country and today, as seen in retrospect, seem to have been mellowed by the passage of time and turned into familiar figures. From this dazzling project he expected three advantages to accrue.

The first was its psychological effect. The bitterness of invasion might be lessened in French hearts. The German tide could sweep over all of continental France; the people would suffer as those whom the German inrush submerged in the northern and eastern regions from 1914 to 1918 had suffered, yet not to the same degree as Poles, Dutchmen, Belgians, Norwegians, fated to look beyond their lost frontiers for nothing more than exile—exile among friends, it is true, but, for all that, exile. Humiliation would be less intense, hope better founded. Let the French and the British nations intertwine their roots: a Frenchman who sets foot on the shore at Dover; Southampton, Plymouth, Cardiff, or Bristol will not feel himself a refugee, but endowed with the same right to talk about the common weal as though he himself had sprung from English soil.

In London, French ministers were to hold a privileged position beyond the reach of the Belgian, Dutch, Norwegian, Polish, Yugoslav, Greek governments. They would match their British colleagues by bringing their weight to bear upon the management of the war. To start with, even one of them, perhaps, might become the Prime Minister of the Anglo-French community. In defiance of the common enemy, with both people being on an equal footing, something comparable to their feudal enlacing in the eleventh and twelfth centuries was in prospect. We must not think in terms merely of a sham construction, of a dose of tonic, of a psychological treatment, of a moral cure. The proposal was ambitiously conceived. Who could claim that England intended to avail herself of France's rich inheritance to buy off Germany and save her own skin since, despite the invasion, Frenchmen would still hold in their hands France's destiny, and not in the servile Vichy sense?

In the more distant future the eighty-eight million Anglo-French, backed up by an empire of 575,000,000 souls, should be better able to maintain order on the Continent than they had been by means of the intermittent harmony which, for one hundred years, went by the name of "entente cordiale." No so-called "realist" statesman could insist that the rest of Europe must either bow before German numerical preponderance or else wander into megalomaniac delusions. This one third of mankind would act as an irresistible lodestone for the United States. Its magnetic effect should be noticeable even in the near future. American isolationism would melt away.

We do not have to separate what was visionary from what was realistic in this scheme. At the moment, in the struggle and for the purposes of the struggle, it was pregnant with a positive policy, and nothing else mattered. All necessary adjustments would be brought in later. For the Act of Union to stand justified it was enough that a closer co-ordination of the two countries than was possible under the classic arrangements of an alliance should follow.

General de Gaulle twice called Reynaud on the telephone: first in the morning and then in the afternoon of June 16. He implored him to do nothing final until he had once more seen Churchill, whom a cruiser was, that very night, to deliver on the French coast. And he briefly outlined the plan of amalgamation which the British Ambassador was shortly to present. The Premier was astounded. "Are you sure of what you are saying?" "Certainly. I am talking from Mr. Churchill's office. He is right here and would like to speak to you. . . ."

The London proposal reached Sir Ronald Campbell at the very minute he was handing on to Reynaud the British answer to the French note of the day before about the armistice. Both agreed that the answer had better be "reserved" until the French ministers had settled the preliminary issue suddenly raised by Churchill, the Union of Great Britain and France.

At five o'clock the Cabinet reassembled. Reynaud did not immediately inform it of the amazing British suggestion. He deemed it good tactics to announce at the start that in the opinion of the London Cabinet the step contemplated by the French ministers on the previous night—to apply to the Pope or to President Roosevelt for a rapid investigation of armistice or even peace terms—was not consonant with French interest and French honor. Reynaud did not submit the text of the British notes Campbell and himself had agreed to differ so as to clear the way for the so-called "Union" proposal. He did not disclose that those British notes amounted to a conditional acceptance of the French demand. He tampered with the truth. His diagnosis was probably that the ministers, with a British refusal ringing in their ears, would not dare push further their quest for an armistice, that, having lost all hope of British acquiescence, they would be all the more inclined to favorably consider the newfangled idea of Mr. Winston Churchill.

Reynaud proved wrong in his forecast of ministerial reactions. The alleged summary rejection of the French note was resented by a majority of his colleagues. Therefore he utterly failed to impress his audience when he sprang upon it the grandiose plan. He succeeded only in irritating Pétain and his group. To them England was doomed. Of what help would it be to France to grasp the hand stretched out to her? By choice, a drowning man does not seize hold of another. On the part of the British what was nothing more than an astute political maneuvering could not resolve the inexorable military problem. This is how their minds worked.

Needless to say, more than one of those gentlemen asked himself how he might make out in so extraordinary a federation. The "Republic of the backslappers" and its easygoing manner certainly could not survive in the merger. Nor could our style of Free Masonry. Nor the "Counterrevolutionary party" (to use the appellation current in the 1789–94 period), which lived in the hope of tearing down the Republic and, to borrow Maurras' mode of speech, felt that General Monk was on the way: how could it fare under the wings of England, indissolubly bound up with Parliament and democracy? Nor Marshal Pétain, whose faintheartedness of March 24, 1918, the British had never forgotten. Nor General Weygand, who for three weeks had made it a practice to blame them for his own reverses. Think of it! All the politicians who knew how to jabber away in English would certainly have the best of it. What thoughts must have crossed Laval's mind when he heard of Churchill's "trick"! And Darlan's—the Admiral of the Fleet—who at once foresaw himself perpetually a subordinate. Leaving all these more personal objections to one side, it must be granted that Churchill's scheme could not but deeply disturb little bourgeois stay-at-homes, who read the curve of events in most petty fashion and, from time immemorial, had been smitten with a complex of social inferiority at the sight of the aristocratic forms still kept up across the Channel.

There was no debate worth that name. A few absurd remarks passed. "I would not have my country become a Dominion!" shouted Ybarnegaray. A carping Minister believed he had detected in Churchill's proposal a definite intention to grant the French an "empire citizenship," with rights inferior to those enjoyed by citizens of the United Kingdom —in short, to reproduce the inequality which, rather late under the Caesars, subsisted between Romans and provincials. Perfidious Albion! It must be true! Chautemps declared that he did not want to be changed into a British subject, that the proposal, besides raising numberless problems, was irrelevant to the single issue set before the Cabinet—to keep on with the war or withdraw from it. Thus did he bring back the controversy to the very point from which it had moved twenty-four hours before, when, in the Cabinet, the contending factions had temporarily reconciled their differences by asking for the price at which Great Britain would allow the French request. Chautemps, who had initiated that "middle solution" (while seeing it as a decisive progress toward the cessation of hostilities), now boldly spoke out. He pressed Reynaud to sweep aside British objections and go ahead. At the same time, since he must always compromise, at least in form, to be true to his own native disposition, Chautemps attempted to explain that France was sure to gain by negotiating an armistice. Assuming that German conditions proved unacceptable, she would become capable of firmer resistance with all her people united behind the Cabinet, with the rift between the military command and the political power mended at last. It was at this stage of the discussion that Mandel broke in and said that under the circumstances Chautemps' thesis was little more than a farce. The Minister of the Interior having pointedly added that certain of his colleagues were determined to make peace, whatever it might cost France, Chautemps burst forth in a tirade: "I won't allow you to say that there are here present both brave men and cowards. We all are men with hearts, who suffer deep within ourselves the national tragedy. My dear friend Laurens, a deputy from Loir-et-Cher, was killed at Blois, where two hundred civilian victims have been accounted for.[2] The French people are caught like rabbits driven into a hutch. The crowds of fugitives on the highways make a target for German bombs too horrible to think about. Words cannot describe such useless, unprecedented slaughter." Chautemps was putting it correctly. On the one hand the town, the village, the electoral district, the department, the évacués, the highway, the stricken friend. On the other, the independence of one's country, which could still be preserved by the most cruel sacrifice, but by a sacrifice events were to prove no more arduous than the tortures of surrender.

[2] At Blois civilian casualties reached a much higher figure.

The vote was taken informally, loosely, since it was clear that a majority of ministers supported the Radical-Socialist leader.[3] There were thirteen ministers in favor of his proposal and eleven against. Reynaud should never have regarded that decision as final.

To the knowledge of the ministerial council, Reynaud had given his word to Churchill that no step would be taken for the armistice as long as they had not met again. Why did he, for the second time, break his pledge? Why did he let go? Why did he humble himself before a narrow majority of ministers who had no right to judge him and exercise the function of a scattered Parliament? Why didn't he call back the British Ambassador, have him formally deliver the "suspended" British notes and submit them in full and at once to an extraordinary council, Jeanneney and Herriot included? Why didn't he make his own the Chautemps proposal, with the capital addition that forthwith the French fleet would be ordered to join the British fleet? Was he frightened by Pétain, by Weygand, by the whole gang of politicians behind them— Laval and others? Truly, standing against Pétain backed by twelve members of the government, could have led far, very far. A government of the armistice had been in the making for twenty-four hours, and the marshal had with him a full list of ministers—"all unreservedly devoted to the new policy," boasted an old henchman of his, General Brécard. Only Mandel could have been daring enough to lock up the partisans of surrender.[4]

[3]This accounts for the fact that various figures have been given. Here is the most probable tabulation of the ministers' votes:

For the proposal of Chautemps:	Against:
Marshal Pétain ⎱ Vice-Premiers. Chautemps ⎰	Paul Reynaud, Premier, Minister for National Defense and Foreign Affairs.
Ybarnegaray, Minister of State.	Louis Marin, Minister of State.
Eynac, Air.	Campinchi, Navy.
Bouthillier, Finances.	Dautry, Armaments.
Baréty, Commerce.	Sérol, Justice.
Tellier, Agriculture.	Mandel, Interior.
Frossard, Public Works.	Delbos, National Education.
Prouvost, Information and Propaganda.	Monnet, Blockade.
Rivière, Pensions.	Rio, Merchant Marine.
Pomaret, Interior.	Pernot, Family and Public Health.
Julien, Post Office and Telegraphs.	Rollin, Colonies.
Chichery.	

Two of the ministers must have abstained or been counted absent, among them Queuille, Minister of Supplies.

[4]M. Camille Chautemps contends that the whole responsibility of the armistice, under the form it took on June 22, and of the break with England, falls upon Reynaud because the latter deliberately gave a false version of the British notes, did not acquaint the

Poor unfortunate Premier! Be it said again that he had long been shaken in his faith. He convinced himself he had done enough to vindicate his public attitude of other days. He had avoided losing face too blatantly. One of his colleagues who held fast against Pétain to the very end laid bare the whole truth, exclaiming, when the discussion was over, "At last we are free!"

But in freeing himself Reynaud held his head high: "Only a minority of the Cabinet shares my point of view. I cannot see myself as the man commissioned to ask England to release France from her commitment. Perhaps someday you will have need of him who built his whole policy upon the Franco-British friendship and alliance." Proud words indeed, but from a man who could ill afford to be proud.[5]

The news was immediately telegraphed to London. Winston Churchill and Sir Alexander Cadogan were already seated in their railway compartment. The train was about to leave. They went back home.

I was waiting for the end of the ministerial council in a Bordeaux café with some friends from the Ministry of Foreign Affairs. We had little doubt of the outcome and the inevitable acts of the successor government. All the shameful deeds which were to cram the records of Bordeaux and Vichy seemed as clear-cut to our eyes as though they belonged to the past, not to the future. Nevertheless, had we been totally unprepared, the news could not have struck us more to heart. "You had better leave the country," said one of those present. "Yesterday, again, Baudouin asked us over the telephone not to give any exit visas. As though he were already the boss and wanted to stock the woods in advance for Hitler's shooting party!"[6]

The dignified piece of oratory with which Reynaud adorned his relinquishment of office was unfortunately not his last political gesture. He was yet to step down a sorry slope.

He spent the evening with his intimates—Mme. de Portes, Colonel de Villelume, Leca, Devaux. But the family circle was not complete. From

ministerial council with the terms laid down in Downing Street. "I should have willingly handed over the fleet," he explains. "I always had that move in mind." But to carry his point Chautemps must give proof that Pétain and Weygand could have been won to a course of action most likely to anger Hitler and rule out all possibilities of armistice. He always described both as powerful enough to impose their will and determined to secure an armistice at any cost and without delay. And there is no other key to his own conduct.

[5]According to Chautemps, Reynaud did not resign forthwith. All agreed to meet again at 9 P.M. By then Reynaud was found closeted with Pétain, to whom the premiership had passed.

[6]Baudouin was still Under Secretary of State for Foreign Affairs and nothing more. Reynaud's immediate subordinates had no orders to take from him.

being Under Secretary of State, Baudouin had been promoted to the
Ministry of Foreign Affairs, in spite of Laval, who had laid claim to this
office and had scorned the portfolio of justice. Baudouin was now moving in the political stratosphere, directly by the marshal's side; he was
soon to become a brazen censor of his fallen chief. Despite the triumph
of her good friend, whose interests she had so tenaciously served, Mme.
de Portes was not pleased with the world. Reynaud's response to her
promptings had been poor. On learning the substance of the Churchill
proposal, she had in vain slipped onto the desk of the Premier a note
paper on which were scribbled these words: "I hope you will not be an
Isabel of Bavaria." But the ghost of Charles VI's queen had not impressed the Premier. He had actually commended the Act of Union!
And here he was, once more a plain citizen, though still a member of
a dispersed Parliament. She was overflowing with reproaches. She
sighed: "You alone in the government could hold off the Anglo-Saxon
world!"

From her he did not get more rest than in his days of influence. To an
official who, a few days later, complained at a nasty turn he had suffered
at her hands, Reynaud simply said, "What a mettlesome woman!" He
had in his pocket the list of the new Cabinet. In a half-jeering tone he
asked Villelume, "Would you like to know the name of the new Minister of War? It is Colson." General Colson, chief of staff of the Army
(outside the war zone), was the colonel's pet antipathy.

General de Gaulle came in. He had left Winston Churchill only a
few hours earlier. He deemed it wise to take charge of Reynaud at Bordeaux and escort him to the Breton port where the Franco-British conference was to take place. He listened to the idle tattle of this distraught
and perplexed crowd. He scrutinized this woman whom he had come to
believe capable of the worst machinations against France. And he
thought very little of Georges Mandel's opinion that within a few days
the negotiation of the armistice would get the better of Pétain, that
French policy would swing back to what it had been. Silently he left the
room. He was to fly back to London the next day.

Mme. de Portes busied herself trying to pick up a few fragments out
of the wreckage. She had always hoped that Reynaud might perform
his political somersault in time and himself undertake to organize
the "New Order." He had not shifted quickly enough. Captive of a
policy too explicitly and firmly laid down, and only withdrawing from
it by halves, he could not be the man at the helm who causes the ship
to veer abruptly. Yet she felt that he ought at least to have secured for

himself a share in the new Cabinet. Sheltered by the prestige of the marshal, it would have been easy for him to grow a new skin..It was up to him to adapt himself to the circumstances of the time and, very soon, to sidle over toward "continental" ideas. In fact he had let Pétain hand over to Chautemps the vice-premiership which, following the rules of ministerial rotation established in recent years, should have been his.[7] For the Reynaud-Hélène de Portes tandem there was only one last hope —the Washington Embassy. Mme. de Portes had seemed to have this ultimate resource in mind as early as May, when she packed her children off to the United States.

On June 17 or 18 the retired Premier was offered the American post. But he was not yet ready to accept it. Did this mean that he wished to stand firm in the logic of his past? Of a past he thought he had washed clean of so many mistakes by lifting up his head at the eleventh hour and which he hoped nobody would question? Or did he clearly realize that, after so many proud utterances, he could not decently justify in Washington the break with England and all that was to follow in its wake? Or had Georges Mandel, who could not rid himself of his habit of looking at the world through parliamentary glasses, inoculated him with his own illusory faith in the sharp reaction of French politicians against what might transpire at the armistice parleys, and in a consequent political reversal? None of these hypotheses, in any case, corresponded with reality for more than a fleeting moment. Reynaud was sheer flotsam in the ocean drift.

Probably on June 20 or 21—I have not been able to determine the date more accurately—Reynaud telegraphed Winston Churchill. In the name of their friendship he begged him to rest satisfied with Pétain's and Darlan's word concerning the fleet, to resign himself to its remaining in French waters, and to accept as sufficient guarantee the marshal's and the admiral's keen sense of honor. In substance he was endorsing the formula which Hitler and his advisers were only too eager to include in the terms of the armistice. Churchill made no reply. He was overheard saying: "This is the third time he has betrayed me."

On June 22, Reynaud agreed to have the American Government sounded out on his appointment to Washington.[8] A shocking recantation. He was now willing to make a try at convincing Mr. Franklin Roosevelt, Mr. Cordell Hull, and the people of the United States that German

---

[7]Talking about the past, in 1941, Reynaud declared that on June 16 he had been asked to become vice-premier.

[8]The telegram to M. de Saint-Quentin was sent in the evening of June 22.

triumph and British ruin were facts which had to be lóoked in the face. He who prided himself on being the soul of national defense, the "fighting spirit of France," as the British Prime Minister would put it in the House of Commons on June 25, was ready to back up in America the doings of Laval, the fast-emerging vice-premier or, rather, dictator. A kind Providence spared him this shame.

But at a very heavy price indeed. On June 23, M. de Saint-Quentin received from the Ministry of Foreign Affairs the dispatch requesting him to ask the American Government's assent to the appointment of his successor. He had to postpone until the next day (a Monday) his call upon the Secretary of State, going no further, on Sunday, than unofficially informing the Under Secretary, Mr. Sumner Welles. Meanwhile his instructions were canceled. On the morning of the same Sunday, M. de la Baume, French Ambassador to Madrid, had just informed Baudouin and Bouthillier of an extraordinary find by the Spanish police. In the luggage of Messers. Leca and Devaux, the two handy men whom the future Ambassador had sent on ahead to America, nineteen million francs had been discovered in various forms—gold, French currency, American dollars, securities. There were also jewels, minutes of recent discussions in the Supreme Council, technical documents on methods for destroying the Rumanian oil wells, on blocking the channels of the Danube—in short, the files which, of late weeks, had accumulated around the Premier's desk. Secret state papers of sufficient importance to make the Ambassador exclaim, "Here is enough to hang a man!" Leca had been appointed assistant financial attaché in Washington, and Devaux had been mandated to wind up the business of the French economic commission in the United States. The two officials thought they were safe with their diplomatic passports. Instead of heading straight for Lisbon, they had gone via Madrid, irresistibly attracted by the Velasquez paintings to be seen in that city. They aroused the suspicions of their hotelkeeper by their clumsy precautions. These grabbers of political spoil, these would-be rulers of Paris, got themselves caught like the merest greenhorns. Nor was that enough for them. They at once wrote to Reynaud to tell him of their bad luck. For his own sake he must ward off the blow; the whole business must be hushed up as quickly as possible. They topped their misadventure with a touch of supreme impertinence: they sought to deny M. de la Baume any right to examine this letter, which they could forward only by means of the diplomatic pouch. They did not overawe the Ambassador. Despite the threats at which Hélène de Portes' friends were so proficient, M. de la Baume did much more than unseal the note. He had it photographed, and prints were sent on to enough of the ministers (including the marshal himself) to forestall any complicity by silence. Indeed, before he had even taken up his new post, Reynaud was dismissed by his former subordinate.

This abortive diplomatic mission, of which most people in France have never heard, laid bare before the American Government the former Premier's apostasy. So great was Washington's faith in Reynaud, in the sincerity of his public statements, that he was believed to be beyond the reach of any idea which did not tally with those attributed to him and, consequently, incapable of coming to terms with the government of the armistice, much less of entering its service. In reply to a private telegram of the former Premier, sent the day after his resignation, President Roosevelt, in the most generous language, had personally expressed sympathy for the unfortunate champion of French resistance.

Today Reynaud dares assert that his appointment to Washington originated in governmental initiative and that beforehand he never was aware of it. But such an excuse will not do. Before the Madrid surprise was sprung upon him he had found time to visit Mr. Drexel Biddle, Ambassador to Poland, and, in Bordeaux, the acting substitute for Mr. William Bullitt, who did not move out of Paris until July. Reynaud wanted the Ambassador to make things easy for him in Washington on arrival, and to win his interlocutor he categorically declared that "he enjoyed the confidence of the marshal and saw eye to eye with him." Once again, in his answer to Mr. Biddle, the President mentioned French resistance. Anyone who fostered it would be welcome.

On June 28, Mme. de Portes was killed in an automobile on the road to Ste. Maxime, where Reynaud had a house. Brakes were applied too suddenly, a pile of trunks collapsed, and she was struck in the neck. Reynaud came out of the accident half scalped. On July 12 he took his seat in the National Assembly at Vichy, his head wrapped in bandages, and we do not find his name either among the eighty of the opposition or among those who abstained from voting. Probably on account of his physical condition, he was one of the few who were excused. However, a member of the Chamber of Deputies who was on the spot bears witness that, with the shadow of Laval's jail already cast upon him and in the hope of warding it off, he advocated support of the Cabinet among the Socialists who had belonged to his Cabinet. Not openly, but surreptitiously, he strove for Pétain, for Laval, for the enslavement to Germany. We are through with Reynaud. He has resigned from his own self-respect. Later on, in jail, he will collect himself, dispute Weygand's strategy and politics, flatter Pétain and scoff at him in turn, attempt to speak and to act in consonance with what he was supposed to be in the great days, with that image of him still lingering in the memory of the French people, from whom his terrible record has been concealed.

BOOK TWO

Pétain

SECTION I: PÉTAIN AND THE COUNTERREVOLUTIONARY MOVEMENT

INTRODUCTION

In the night of june 16, Pétain became head of the Cabinet. Then began the most shameful chapter in French history. Nothing in the long annals of our past can compare with it. In the disaster of 1870–71, in the bloody convulsions of the Commune, the French people did not lose the sense of its own dignity. Indeed, one need only glance over the minutes of the National Assembly of that time to see that it was dignified and in the grand manner, according to all the standards of elected assemblies. The Revolution of 1789 tore at the very soul of the French people, but, with its Napoleonic sequel, it remains our national epic. The Wars of Religion in the sixteenth century and the Fronde in the seventeenth reflected, above all, an overflowing vitality. There French aristocracy ceased to exist as a political force, and the loss was doubtless a great one. But at the same time arts and letters soared toward the perfection of classical antiquity. We must go back to the initial decades of the fifteenth century, to the reign of Charles VI, "the insane," to find a distress that can compare with that of today—our homeland under foreign yoke, and French factions making pacts with the conqueror.

Yet the parallel is more apparent than real. An undeveloped organism cannot feel as intensely as an adult. Five hundred years ago the component elements of our nation were scattered, and Jeanne d'Arc's true miracle was to make France conscious of herself. Moreover, with both invader and invaded steeped in feudalism and Christianity, conquest could cause no abrupt changes. For three whole centuries Guyenne owed allegiance to the crown of England, and during the second half of the fifteenth century Bordeaux rebelled because it would not shift fealty and yield to the rule of the men from the north. Let us delve even deeper into the past. For France's present disruption, both material and moral, the nearest equivalent is found in the fifth century. Can we be satisfied even with it? Those who watched "Romania" break up felt what we feel today, or rather what we would feel if we despaired of the United Nations. The death throes of the empire of the Caesars, however, lasted more than two hundred years, whereas an ax has crashed upon us. Invasions filtered through imperceptibly before they battered the walls of the eternal city and submerged it. It can even be argued that, between conquerors and conquered, the Church acted as a coalescent for which we have no equivalent today.

The fact that passes understanding is that Frenchmen should have been found, on June 16, 1940, to wish passionately for an armistice which meant the end of national independence; that, in their haste to sue for that armistice, they utterly overlooked the great resources still available for continuing the fight; that they should have seen in the agreements signed with Germany and Italy the means to enforce their own power at home; that, grasping at long last an opportunity to overwhelm the Republic and to cast our country into a fascist mold, they should have looked to the enemy as to a friend.

To pretend that the France of 1940, like the Germany of 1918, was compelled to imitate her conqueror's institutions in order to humor him is a poor excuse. That counterfeit of democracy, the Weimar Republic, in which Germany sought to clothe herself, was in essence merely play-acting, a sham, a preparation for revenge. The "National Revolution" of Bordeaux and Vichy, on the other hand, is the work of sincere imitators, staking their own lot on the success and the permanence of their imitation. For them the armistice was not what it had been for the Germans, an inevitable outcome to be borne in a spirit of resistance, an outcome not lacking in promise, thanks to the quarrels among the victors, but rather the means—the means attained by deceit—toward a supreme end, reshaping their country from its foundations.

As we look back at the staggering events which followed each other in such swift succession during the latter days of June 1940, we see boldly outlined against the light, as though upon some rocky crest lording it over the countryside, two figures crowned with oak leaves—Pétain and Weygand. They alone, the supposedly faultless masters of the art of war, gave the final push. At first Weygand, commander in chief of the Army, exerted himself the most, but later he faded away into Pétain's shadow.

Moral catastrophe, unconditional surrender, abandonment of arms, deliberate humiliation of the spirit cannot be accounted for if one considers these two men alone, however big they loom up in the sky. But behind them, on the far slope of the hill, stands a mighty faction which has been gathering its forces since 1934. These are the people who, in 1936, prevented France from bringing the Nazi dictatorship to terms while she was yet the stronger of the two. These are the people who were willing to accept Adolf Hitler's hegemony over all Europe rather than chance a conflict which might unleash a social upheaval. They hailed as victories for peace the annexation of Austria, the military reoccupation of the Rhineland, the coming of the Germans and the Italians in Spain, the dismemberment and then the incorporation of Czechoslovakia into the Reich. For all they cared, Poland and Russia could have been handed over to the Nazi conqueror.

They had no patience with anyone telling them that Hitler's aggression was not to be held off by limited concessions, that once the Nazi beast was let loose conflict became inevitable and more and more unequal the longer it was postponed, since the armament of a regimented and mobilized country must constantly exceed ours. They dared pretend not to grasp the portents of the time. Indeed, a total French withdrawal, a complete submission to the demands of the Führer would have introduced a conquest in disguise, an elaborate camouflage: this enabled them to quibble and to picture as consistent with the nation's survival something which was not.

The truth is that this faction had for six years been quite ready to barter with French independence. It gave it away all the more easily on June 16, 1940, for having been willing to trade it off the preceding September 3—if not earlier. The great achievement of the cabal lay in securing Pétain and Weygand as its leaders. Then there sprang forth from the earth a conspiracy which hitherto had only here and there broken the surface and which, but for the military defeat, would merely have kept shifting about in the dark. And without this brazen gang, Pétain, even relying on Weygand's help, would never have carried through so complicated and so far-reaching a job. He had not the audacity.

To get at the root of the facts which crowd upon each other after June 16, to understand their implications, we need to ascertain the precise contribution of each set of men involved. We need to understand how military leaders of unquestioned patriotism came to join with politicians who long since had dealt with their country as if they were its receivers in bankruptcy. We have seen what the two army chieftains did after their appearance on the scene May 18. We must now have a closer look at them, take their measure in the past, and see where they stood in the counterrevolutionary medley.

My narrative can no longer be subject to the unity of time and place. It broadens and branches out. I must describe the current of events downstream and upstream, beyond Gamelin, Daladier, Reynaud, and also before them. The tale of our military disaster is more or less self-contained. The military and political mistakes made in 1939 and 1940 were of such immediate impact that I have been able provisionally to leave aside the long chain of antecedents, or at least to indicate their influence only by passing allusions or references. But all these prior happenings lay with their full weight on the period which opens up on Pétain's premiership. The Nazi sorcerer forces his way, and as though by a stroke of his wand, it may be said that the hatreds, the rancors, the habits of mind, the falsehoods, the schemes for personal profit, seemingly buried in bygone years, surge back to life. Far more than the men actually on the stage, they are the true signers of the separate armistice. The counterrevolution—beyond compare sadder than defeat—can be grasped only by making a fairly detailed cross section of Republican France.

I

Pétain's Counterrevolutionary Inclination. His Military Record—the Legend and the Truth. His Belated Association with Weygand

MY OWN MEETINGS with Marshal Pétain have been relatively few. We crossed together on the *Lafayette* in 1931; we had two or three hours' conversation on a railway train in the spring of 1933; I have not seen him since. The impression I still have is of a man no longer at the hub of public affairs and who followed them from afar, amateurishly. In the course of our last conversation he was good enough to express his approval of the direction taken by my daily comments on foreign affairs in the *Echo de Paris*. "My praise is worth more than you might think," he added. "I have only recently come to agree with your ideas." What were these ideas? To me, as clear as daylight, Pan-Germanism lay at the root of the European problem, and I had never conceived that events could be interpreted in any other frame of reference. I am sorry now that I did not ask the marshal what was the point of view he had so tardily abandoned. Had the illusion of the League, of Locarno, of the Disarmament Conference told upon him as upon so many others? I rather think so. Besides, he talked to me about anti-aircraft defense and, above all, about his property at Villeneuve-Loubet, in the Var Department. On this subject he was inexhaustible. Ten years earlier he could have sold his land for 800,000 francs; he would surely never again have such a stroke of luck. To cap his misfortune, his steward was cheating him, and so he had limited yearly disbursements to eight thousand francs. "That will make the fellow come to heel!" The old man loved his acres, but he loved his money even more.

On the marshal's score I cannot pass any personal judgment. I shall limit myself to reporting what I heard many times from Marshal Foch, General Weygand, General de Castelnau, and that common friend and intimate of them all who wrote a remarkable book, *La Crise du Commandement Unique: Le Conflit Clemenceau, Foch, Haig et Pétain* (*The Crisis of the Single Command: The Clemenceau, Foch, Haig, Pétain Quarrel*), published in 1931 and so hastily removed from the shelves of the booksellers, so little noticed in the press that it can almost be described as having altogether vanished. Here is the verdict of those four authorities: "Pétain is an executive of conspicuous merit, preparing his operations with the greatest care and thrifty of shedding blood when he carries them out, but major ultimate responsibilities lie beyond his scope."

In the restricted circle of military experts Pétain first rose to notoriety while he held the infantry professorship at the War College, about 1908. In our country infantry tactics, as defined over the course of the twenty preceding years (more and more rigidly as the battlefields of 1870 were lost from sight), rested on the idea that the foot soldier is the kingpin in the fight, that by his movements backward and forward he determines its rhythm and outcome. The artillery is his servant. At his orders its job is to wipe out obstacles which cannot be overcome with his small arms. A skirmish line is stretched out. It alternately fires and moves forward. The reserves come up as needed and gradually fill the gaps. The problem is to gather together the greatest mass of man power at the enemy's weakest point. Then is launched the decisive attack—the assault.

Such tactics linked up with the strategy of the offensive to the bitter end extolled by Colonel de Grandmaison and his friends. Pétain, first in his lectures, then in the field at the head of a brigade, a division, and, by October 1914, an army corps, was its everlasting critic. The regulations said: "The artillery does not prepare attacks; it supports them." He answered: "The artillery conquers; the infantry occupies." Again, the regulations said: "A brave and well-led infantry can seize trenches defended by the enemy." He replied: "The defensive is fire power which causes the enemy to stop; the offensive is fire power which moves forward." All this amounted to reversing the relationship set up between the infantry and the artillery, to seeing to it that the foot soldier should not advance blindly and that the gunner should not strike out like a deaf man. How could the foot soldier point out to the artilleryman the obstacles whose destruction might help his own progress, the artilleryman being willing to shoot only when he knew what he was about? The solution of the problem was the barrage, a running fire which preceded the troops. And toward 1916 the putting in service of the automatic rifle (a weapon invented ten years earlier but neglected by the theorists of the offensive) enabled the infantry to distribute its fire according to plan. Between infantry and artillery there came into being a division of labor much better wrought than that whose main feature was an expensive barrage fire.

This whole recasting of ideas was not Pétain's doing, and only the war, that ultimate teacher, brought to fruit principles which were later universally acknowledged. But Pétain was one of the outstanding advocates of the doctrine due to win the day. It is an odd thing to have to record that at the beginning of the last war he figured as the head of a new school, not unlike General de Gaulle in our time. Near Arras, in May 1915, his army corps was the first seriously to shake the enemy in his field fortifications. Yet before the conflict he had been out of favor with the General Staff of the period. He had been retired as a colonel. So he also had been hit because he was too much in the right and perhaps worried the mandarins. Hence a trace of bitterness and rancor from which he, in all likelihood, did not altogether free himself until he was crowned with the sad honors of Vichy. Thereafter the war which had exalted his abilities equally shed light upon his limitations. How impartially it settles men's accounts!

On February 25, 1916, General de Castelnau, chief of General Staff, assigned Pétain and his 2nd Army to the sector of Verdun, which had been attacked four days earlier, in accordance with General von Falkenhayn's plan to deal France a knockout blow.[1] The ground was contested step by step on both sides of the Meuse, and five months later, July 20, the French stormed the German lines and turned the tide. But it should be noted that the all-important and risky decision—the decision not to withdraw from the right bank of the river, to avoid a recession which would infallibly have led to the loss of the fortress—was taken on the morning of the twenty-fifth by General de Castelnau. "From the very moment when Joffre and Castelnau decided that the right bank would be defended, the role of the general (that is, of the strategist) came to an end. . . . The Battle of Verdun was merely a struggle between soldiers; it could have been led by a detail of technically well-instructed staff officers."[2] And it must be added that, in April, General Joffre thought it necessary to remove Pétain from the sector, to promote him to the command of the Army Group, because he found him inclined to order that very retreat against which the High Command had set its head two months earlier.[3] He replaced him with Nivelle on May 1. Thus Pétain is more a tactician than strategist. At Verdun the strategists were Joffre and Castelnau.

Jules Cambon said of Pétain: "He belongs to Marshal de Castellane's breed, who succeeded in bringing under control the troops of the Restoration, made up of the wreckage of Napoleon's Grande Armée." On May 15, 1917, he was made commander in chief after General Nivelle's rash and bloody offensive had taken the heart out of the troops, leaving them no expectation except that of being slaughtered in vain

[1] "I chose Pétain because, having been formerly in command of the 2nd Army, I particularly valued its staff." (Castelnau.)

[2] General X, *Le Problème du Commandement Unique.*

[3] Marshal Joffre says it flatly in his *Memoirs:* "At this juncture a new commander of the Army Group had to be appointed. Thus occurred an opportunity to acknowledge his merits by a promotion and to get him away from Verdun, which seemed to me necessary . . . During a round of inspection which I made at Pétain's headquarters, in July 1916, I was struck by his pessimism, and the impression was shortly afterward confirmed by others. As early as June, Foch's firmness during his visit to headquarters had calmed the excessive fears aroused by Pétain, whose confidence in the length of time resistance could continue at Verdun was very limited."

attacks against trenches and barbed wires. Pétain was able to cure them of their despair and temper them once more for the struggle. It was the moment of the Czarist Army's incipient disintegration. The first whispers of Bolshevism circulated among the fighting men. The Russian contingents stationed along the French lines had their Soviets, in which participation in the April 16 offensive was determined by majority vote. Between May 20 and June 10 there were "collective refusals of obedience," which, in encampments behind the lines, veered toward rebellion. By means of a firmness allayed with mercy, Pétain re-established discipline.[4] In 1922, Ludendorff asserted that this was the equivalent of a victory. Lined up for inspection, the men were moved by the sad and almost compassionate expression with which this general of magnificent stature looked at them. He refrained from all large-scale undertakings; he approved only of local actions. They were successful. What a contrast to Nivelle's bragging and lightheadedness! The French Army recovered itself. And perhaps it is no paradox to say that the fundamental pessimism of their chief was what managed this cure. The bravura of a Mangin, the abruptness of a Foch would never have served, would have aroused the indignation of the suffering mass. In any case, let us bear in mind Pétain's pessimistic cast. It is a constant in his make-up. At the very time he was reawakening faith and the spirit of sacrifice, his words addressed to a group of officers at Nancy disgusted Maurice Barrès: "There is nothing for it but to make peace."

Before long he was put to the test which sifts out the greater men, leaving behind those who merely have ability. Let us see how he met it.

In November 1917 the Italian Army was routed at Caporetto. Lenin and his associates had seized power. Our General Staff reckoned that before the end of the winter the German command could concentrate some two hundred divisions in the west. Pétain and Haig, commander in chief of the British Expeditionary Force, had only ninety-nine and fifty-five respectively. Even adding the twelve Belgian, four American, and two Portuguese divisions, we were still inferior in effectives. But the worst of it was that France and England were short of recruits to the point where they could not make good the losses of their existing units; twenty French divisions were to be done away with between April and December, and a like number of English divisions after November. What was to be done? Pétain said that we should be satisfied to hold

[4] In all, there were only about one hundred and fifty death sentences and only twenty-three executions (Painlevé, *Comment J'ai Choisi Foch et Pétain*).

down the gains of the German offensive whenever it might come and, for the rest, rely upon minor counterattacks. He added that, before accepting battle, we ought to wait until the American Army was in position: eighteen divisions were to arrive from the United States in July, and these merely the head of the tide. Foch would have none of this procrastination, since it was all too likely to leave us open to the enemy's blows before our friends from across the Atlantic were at hand. His January 1, 1918, plan of operations provided for a "counteroffensive of extrication" to be followed by an "offensive aimed at deciding the issue." But to put this into effect he demanded unity of command, a novelty praised by Pétain, when it seemed likely to devolve upon him, but with which he would have nothing to do when Foch was in line for it. Pétain contended that his understanding with Haig concerning loans of troops made the reform superfluous.[5] Two irreconcilable doctrines were set against each other: one calling for action designed to produce a showdown, under the direction of a single chief, and the other for a defensive battle with agreements for mutual assistance between two generals.

The German attack began at five in the morning on March 21, 1918, between the Scarpe and the Oise, exactly as the general staffs had foreseen for months. Yet here is the bewildering fact. The 3rd and 5th British armies (Byng and Gough), engaged by forty-seven German divisions with twenty-seven in reserve, numbered but twenty-one divisions. And the greater part of the British reserves (sixteen out of eighteen divisions) had been stationed north of the Somme, while the French reserves (thirty-nine divisions) were massed in Champagne and from the Argonne to Switzerland. In other terms, Haig was concerned above all to protect the Channel ports, and Pétain, the region of Paris. Each put it up to the other to take on the full force of the assault. One was waging a war in the English interest, and the other, a war in the French interest. Neither one nor the other looked to the common interest for inspiration. And those wonderful agreements for mutual help, which Pétain had puffed up (in words) for the purpose of dissuading

---

[5] Pétain snubbed General Dufieux, chief of the Bureau of Operations, who had prepared a memorandum on the unity of command, and he got rid of General Debeney, major general, also won over to the change. Incidentally, a timid attempt at putting the unity of command in force was made on February 1 and 2; then the French and British governments decided that general reserves should be set up, with Foch in charge of them. It was a device to introduce him stealthily into the supreme leadership. He requested thirty divisions. Haig and Pétain did such a good job that the whole scheme blew up on March 14.

Haig from the scheme for unity of command, had shrunk into a memorandum of modest scope, stuffed with reservations, which, in practice, was to shrivel further.

On the night of March 21–22, Haig requested Pétain to furnish three divisions; on the evening of the twenty-second, three more; and then, on the valid argument that Ludendorff was massing his whole attack on the British Expeditionary Force and seeking to flank it on the south, separate it from the French, and hurl it back to the sea, Haig insisted that Gough's army be relieved along a forty-kilometer stretch, from the Oise to the Somme. With his sixty divisions he then would keep up the fight between Arras and Péronne. Pétain was horrified. In effect he was being asked to hurl twenty divisions into the fray; he could not spare them because he judged that the principal thrust would be leveled against him in Champagne and that the movement begun March 21 was no more than a diversion in the enemy's plan. He added six divisions to his loan of the day before, and he suggested that General Fayolle be put in charge of the fighting in the sector south of Péronne. But he would not hear of relieving the British completely.

The two men met at Dury on the afternoon of the twenty-third and parted without having come to an understanding. On the twenty-fourth the defeat of Gough's army was worsened. Without further ado, Pétain concluded that the English were lost and made arrangements accordingly. Toward eight in the evening he issued orders to his three army-group commanders, Fayolle, Franchet d'Esperey, and Castelnau. They said in essence: "Above all, hold firmly the general framework of the French armies; particularly, do not allow the group of reserve armies to be cut off from the remainder of our forces. Then, if possible, remain in contact with the British forces. In battle, lead accordingly." Twice in this document Pétain used this formula: when he spoke of the 1st Army, which was to hook on to the "British right if the latter continues to keep hold"; when he spoke of the cavalry, which by reconnoitering was to "cover the left of the group of reserve armies (its main task) and to seek to maintain communication with the British right (its subsidiary task)." This wording clearly indicated that Haig was to be left to his fate and that Pétain was not willing to take a chance in Champagne for the sake of supporting him.

Simultaneously, Foch, in a letter to Clemenceau, sketched out an exactly opposite plan. "However valiant these forces [the British] may be, their numerical inferiority to the German mass requires the setting up of a French mass, held in reserve in the region northeast of Amiens, with an eye to warding off the unforeseen and, if necessary, to counter-attacking the German offensive." Everyone knows the end of the tale. In despair, and suspecting Pétain of the direst scheming, Haig called to France Sir Henry Wilson, chief of the Imperial General Staff. The British Cabinet dispatched Lord Milner, Secretary for War. At the Doullens conference, March 26, Pétain gave up his obstinate refusal of the preceding days, but "by his coldness of manner, by his pessimism, everyone understood that he would never find the troops needed for salvation."[6]

Foch, who had cried out, "Let's die with our boots on, let Pétain die, let Haig die, then we'll stop the Boche!" was commissioned to "co-ordinate" the movements of the armies. Pétain completely reversed the orders that had been given forty-eight hours earlier. His own adjutant general had not waited for this about-face to set the reserves in motion. In four days the hole was stopped. "The blindness of the commander in chief almost led to defeat," concludes General X.[7]

[6]General X, loc. cit.

[7]In his *Memoirs,* Marshal Foch tells the same story as General X, and on some points he adds to it. Thus we are informed that when he learned of Pétain's orders, issued on the evening of March 24, Haig, on the twenty-fifth, directed the British Army to "beat a slow retreat, keeping the ports of the Pas-de-Calais covered. . . . As against one single German battle, the Allies were fighting two distinct battles—a British battle for the ports and a French battle for Paris. These battles were to continue apart and drift away from each other. Thereby the Allied commanders could not but widen the gap between their armies, which was exactly what the Germans wanted most. The gap might have widened beyond repair and we would have been on the road to sure defeat." On March 25, Poincaré wrote ("Au Service de la France"): "Clemenceau rates Pétain for his extremely pessimistic remarks. He [Pétain] dared say that if we were beaten, we should have the British to thank first." Then, again, on the twenty-sixth: "Clemenceau took me aside and said: 'Pétain's pessimism is unbearable.' Just think! I would not dare repeat to anyone but yourself what he told me. The Germans are going to get the best of us. Now, should any general speak or even think that way?" Clemenceau relates ("Grandeurs et Misères d'une Victoire") how on the twenty-sixth, at Doullens, people were fearfully asking each other in the courtyard of the Town Hall, "Will the Germans capture Doullens?" Pétain broke the silence by pointing to Haig and exclaiming: "That man will be forced to surrender right in the midst of battle, and we'll be lucky if we don't suffer the same fate." "Such words, coming from the lips of an expert," remarks Clemenceau, "were not of a sort to bolster up the confidence which we wished at all costs to maintain." In *The Navy* (August 1940), Marshal Sir Archibald Mont-gomery-Massingberd, who was present at the Doullens meeting, wrote, "Never was a general given such a dressing down in public as Pétain got from Foch on that occasion." A memorandum of the proceedings was drawn up by Lord Milner after the Doullens gathering. It was published toward the end of the war and, so far as I remember, confirms that body of evidence.

In 1923, Pétain induced General Debeney, then his immediate subordinate, to come to his defense. Debeney wrote a memorandum in which he drew upon his recollections as head of the 1st Army. These were necessarily very fragmentary and inadequate, since he had no knowledge of what had been passing between the commanders above him. This document

Foch and Weygand needed no urging to plunge into their recollections, the latter extracting manuscript notes from his desk drawers the better to substantiate his story. And even after this month of March 1918 they very frequently had to rebuke Pétain. Forcibly they took away from him his chief of staff, Anthoine, whose ingrained pessimism was aggravated by his chief's.[8] In September 1918, when the "offensive aimed at deciding the issue" was in full swing (and how successfully)— later on Ludendorff was to confess that he had seen defeat looming as early as August 8—General Pétain begged the Allies' generalissimo to put a stop to the campaign until spring. For the month of November, which was to bring forth a victorious armistice, he could foresee only the busy routine of setting up winter quarters. "Just as we had to put a checkrein on Mangin," Foch used to say, "so we had to give Pétain the spurs." And Weygand would add this. On November 21, 1918, all the leaders of the Army were present at the Metz Place d'Armes to witness the conferring of the marshal's baton on the chief of the French Army: "during the ceremony Destiker[9] and I kept whispering to each other, 'And to think that we have shoved him to such an eminence by untiringly kicking his buttocks!'"

An army which has hammered through to victory will at once begin to decay. I have no idea who is the author of that pithy maxim, but it fits perfectly what took place in the France of 1919. Toward 1930 the booksellers displayed an anonymous volume entitled *Feu l'Armée Française*. (*The French Army, Deceased*). An ominous title which must have haunted many minds in May and June 1940. It told no more than the truth. It is safe to say that for some twelve years, until about 1935, the French military system was utterly down at the heel.

Marshal Pétain, appointed commander in chief designate in case of

---

was inserted by General Laure, Pétain's man Friday, in his volume, *Le Commandement en Chef des Armées Françaises du 15 Mars 1917 à l'Armistice*. Debeney again discussed the subject in his book, *La Guerre et les Hommes*. Debeney, extremely cautious, and Laure, much bolder, argue around the relevant point. They make no mention of the March 24 orders.

[8]In October 1914, Foch had already caused Anthoine's removal from Castelnau's staff. "And here I ran into the fellow again, this time with Pétain!" (From my diary.) Twice in the spring and summer of 1918 the inveterate pessimism of Pétain clashed with Foch's masterful strategy. On May 30 and 31, under the impact of the check suffered at the Chemin des Dames, Pétain arranged for the abandonment of Nancy, Verdun, etc. He even advised the government to get out of Paris. On July 15, unduly disturbed by a German advance west of Reims, he started canceling all preparations for the counteroffensive Foch was nonetheless to launch triumphantly on July 18.

[9]General Destiker ranked next to Weygand in the personal staff of Marshal Foch. A second-rate man.

war, vice-president of the Superior War Council, and, from February 18, 1922, inspector general of the Army, together with General Debeney, who had become chief of General Staff after General Buat's death in 1923, should have kept an eye on the staunchness of our defenses.[10] He did not perform this highest of all duties.

In the highly conservative House which Clemenceau succeeded in having elected in 1919, the "Horizon Blue House," out of the forty-four members of the Committee on Military Affairs, no less than thirty were army officers, ten regulars, and twenty reservists. These well-intentioned men behaved like demagogues. And far from tightening the reins, it seemed as though the High Command sometimes encouraged what was going on, or at least tolerated it in silence. The Superior War Council was reorganized in January 1920, and the Superior Council for National Defense in February 1921. Their tone was one of weak acquiescence. But, after all, Pétain alone was in control, Foch being engrossed in his function of military adviser to the Allied and Associated Powers. From the outset Pétain must bear the blame for the Army's decay. Pétain and Debeney had ceased to take their profession very seriously. Surely a great war would not again disturb their own lifetime.

The demobilization decree was promulgated on December 28, 1919. Only three classes were to stay on with the colors. True enough, these consisted of men tried in battle and led by proven officers. They scattered along the Rhine, in Upper Silesia, in Schleswig, at Memel, in Syria, Morocco, in the Ruhr. At first everything went well enough. But with the passage of two new laws governing military service—that of April 1, 1923, enacting eighteen months' training in place of the three years in effect since 1913, and that of March 28, 1928, still further reducing the period to twelve months—our effectives fast vanished. They were barely sufficient to man the necessary overseas garrisons. Worse still, the peacetime strength of the French home establishment was cut from forty-five to thirty-two divisions and then from thirty-two to twenty, and in numbers the regiments were reduced in proportion. All this meant

---

[10]At Pétain's wish the functions of the vice-president of the Superior War Council and those of the chief of General Staff, which Joffre had united in himself by virtue of the decrees of July 28, 1911, were split. "A disastrous division of authority," in Weygand's judgment. Following Foch's suggestion, he saw Pétain and asked him not to let a dual High Command, acknowledged dangerous before 1914, become the rule once more. "Do you actually think that I'll tie myself down to waiting upon the Minister each day for his signature?" replied the marshal. The Weygand-Gamelin quarrel of 1931–35 resulted from this state of affairs. The two decrees of January 18, 1935, re-established the unity of command and bestowed it upon Gamelin. Weygand never tired of saying, "To have agreed to such a division of authority was the greatest mistake of my life." Cf. page 23.

that the change cut very deep. In future the regiment of the standing army could no longer serve as a matrix, at the time of mobilization, for two other regiments, reserves, and Territorials. The permanent forces were too small to yield a combatant army by means of any sort of internal inflation. We had to institute a system of "centers of mobilization." The regiment was reshaped into a military school, into a huge boardinghouse, every six months disgorging half its occupants and taking in a new batch to replace them. All *esprit de corps* vanished. The regulars no longer set the tone. In substance France had an army of second reserves, interlarded with regular or professional elements, unable to produce a steady annual flow of competent NCOs. It could no longer supply the *"couverture"*—that is, the troops singled out long in advance which at the shortest possible notice must be in position to stave off an attack while the bulk of the military system is being mobilized and assembled. Such wide gaps could only be stopped or concealed by makeshifts. It is not putting it too strongly to say that, given such an organization, behind the *"couverture"* the peacetime setup disappeared at the moment of mobilization. Three weeks later a wartime army arose in its place, an inexperienced herd ready to become an ordered battle line only after at least six months' strenuous effort.

Toward 1926–29 no one any longer denied that all military vigor had been lost in that demagogic shuffle. The Minister of War, M. Painlevé, in February 1926, admitted that "the Army is shot through with deep uneasiness. Commissioned and uncommissioned officers are depressed and grasp at every opportunity to quit the service. The pick of our youth spurns our military schools." And the best Painlevé could do was trust to a miracle. "If, tomorrow, our country were in danger, the shock would pull the Army together, as it would the whole country, and none would be found wanting." While he was still Minister of War, in September 1928, on the anniversary of the Battle of the Marne, he repeated much the same phrase. Such was the destruction that had come to pass.

Can the faintest sign be detected that Pétain tried to swim against the tide? Alas, no. In a public address at Béthune, on September 25, 1919, he heralded the one-year military service. In the disarmament race he himself fired the starter's gun! When called upon to consider the two proposals which were to become law in 1923 and 1928, in accord with the Superior War Council he stated the conditions prerequisite to his agreement. They were: the enlistment of 106,000 professional soldiers to serve as a nursery for NCOs; the provision of 15,000 military employ-

ees, 30,000 civilian employees, 15,000 mobile guards—in order to free the
soldiers from jobs having nothing to do with military training. Reservists should without fail be called back for periodical instruction. After
1923 and 1928 these conditions were met only in a very limited way.
Reservists, above all, were left peacefully at home. The marshal knew
not how to be obdurate. He paid no serious heed to the increases in pay
so desperately needed after the monetary crisis of 1924–26. He was content with inadequate readjustments.

Moreover, he let the General Staff become hidebound. The High
Command, so wide awake between 1914 and 1918, lost all keenness of
spirit. The rich store of experience on which it had fed through days of
battle began to grow rigid and obsolete. It forgot the last lessons taught
by the great trial—the lessons of the tank and the airplane. Aviation
was turned over to an independent Air Ministry, a natural prey for
businessmen and lobbyists. Pétain and Debeney washed their hands of it.
The short campaign against Abd-el-Krim, directed by Pétain in person
(1926), is a fair example of the general torpor.[11] Mosquitoes were chased
with steam hammers. On the other hand—and mainly to the advantage of its members who were commanders of armies—the Superior
War Council approved the extension of age limits by ministerial decrees, from sixty-two to sixty-five for generals in charge of divisions or
bigger units and to sixty-eight for the commander in chief. These army
commanders would, henceforth, be mere humble petitioners before
the Cabinet. Finally, the Law of January 14, 1930, provided that continuous fortifications should be built from the Rhine to Longuyon.[12]
Indeed, the French people could rest in peace. It was well protected.
All this Pétain either willed, suffered, or allowed to pass.

But in 1929, when Foch died, a new phase began. Two years later, at
seventy-five, Pétain was to leave the active command. General Debeney
was close to the age limit. The marshal had to choose both an assistant

---

[11]Here was another opportunity for Pétain to show his pessimism. He was so doubtful
of being able to crush Abd-el-Krim that armistice parleys began at Oudjda. An agreement
was about to be signed when Colonel Corap captured the disaffected chieftain by surprise.
We later paid dearly for this feat of Corap's, since he was rewarded beyond his abilities.

[12]The outcome of protracted studies and discussions which began in the Superior War
Council as early as 1925. A complete scheme could never be worked out. On May 28 and
June 4, 1932, the Superior Council by a narrow margin (one single vote) rejected a plan
for the permanent fortification of the northern region, beyond Longuyon-Montmédy. On
June 14, 1934, Pétain, as Minister of War, requested and obtained 292,000,000 francs to
weld the Lorraine front with the northern front; however, he left to his successors the task
of defining what the "northern front" would be and even of carrying out the works he
had contemplated for the region beyond Montmédy.

and a successor. He hit upon General Maurin. The very suggestion raised a hurricane of protest. The general had brains and the reputation of being a distinguished artilleryman.[13] But during the most trying months of the last war he had been among those who easily reconciled themselves to the thought of defeat. "That pig Maurin!" General de Castelnau was wont to exclaim. That nickname, borrowed from one of Maupassant's short stories ("Ce Cochon de Maurin"), had gained currency among staff officers. The marshal was disgruntled and tried to work out a compromise. Maurin would be made head of the General Staff but in case of war would immediately give way to Weygand, the opposition candidate. "I insisted that I should be free to stick my nose into anything I wanted to in peacetime, not wishing to take on responsibility without equivalent authority. Maurin yielded, was servile to my every demand. Happily the two-headed monster was abandoned. Pétain certainly knows how to make unintelligible decisions." I reproduce Weygand's very words. He got the appointment.[14] And he became commander in chief in 1931.

Thus Pétain and Weygand were, for the first time, hitched to the same cart. But after so much sarcasm and criticism how could Weygand shift from the marshal he revered to the one he had so long treated with contempt? The answer is that he had come to the conclusion that Foch's inevitable successor in the esteem and respect of the French people would be the great warrior who outlived him. Therefore he was taking care to capitalize this ascending power. As freely as ever he went on flaying the commander in chief of March 24, 1918. But in Pétain's presence he kept his inner feeling well hidden. I find in my diary, under date of November 3, 1934, that when he advised the marshal not to continue as Minister of War in the Flandin Cabinet, he used the following argument: "You represent a reserve strength. Perhaps, someday, you will be the Hindenburg of France. You mustn't risk your prestige in Parliament." What an astonishing foresight! The commander in chief Weygand dimly presaged military defeat and counterrevolution! Did he

---

[13]His book, which he published toward 1938 under the title *La Guerre Moderne* (*Modern Warfare*) and which he described as "his last will and testament," is perhaps the best of all the second-rate military literature of the day. The picture he paints of the course of future battles remains convincing enough, despite his skimpy notions on tanks and planes. Should anti-tank weapons be better perfected and the air forces involved approximately equal in strength, one might be inclined to think that he was close to reality.

[14]From 1925, when Herriot deprived him of the high commissionership in Syria because he was not a true "republican," to 1929, when Pétain made him his assistant, Weygand served as head of the school for higher military studies, dubbed "the school for the marshals of tomorrow!"

so deeply despair of his own country? At any rate, his solicitude for the old man can be understood.

Yet heaven knows how they quarreled! They worked side by side from 1929 to 1931, then once more after February 1934, when the marshal accepted from M. Gaston Doumergue the portfolio of national defense, and later on, in 1935–36, for at that time both of them, though without any active function to perform, still had some influence over the High Command. Weygand was thoroughly aware of the Army's frightful weakness. With his own flaming logic he pleaded the case for a military reawakening. He tried to do the best he could with the system at his disposal, based as it was on twelve months' service. Despite everybody and everything, even despite the law itself, he created regiments. But mere palliatives no longer sufficed. What was needed was to pour first men and then matériel into the emaciated skeleton. The "hollow years" would soon be upon us. The "twelve months" must be done away with. I have noted down the limpid and convincing statement he made at my home for some friends who had come to listen to him. Unfortunately his all-absorbing advocacy of this one indispensable reform distracted his attention from the mechanized army and the war doctrine of Major de Gaulle.[15] "Professional soldiers would be expensive, very expensive," he pronounced. "If Parliament let us have them, it would in turn refuse us an increase in the length of time to be spent in military training by our young men. We mustn't strain the French budget to the breaking point. Then, too, this professional army would not be ready for five years, as even its proponents admit. Think of it! Five years! War will come long before that! And what a fertile breeding ground for communists those gangs of mechanics would be!"

As between the marshal-minister and the inspector general, disagreement did not stem from this novel concept, which appealed to neither, but rather from the contemplated increase of the term of service. Weygand had hoped that once he became a member of the Cabinet, Pétain, running things with a high hand, would promptly settle the matter. He was soon disillusioned. In vain did the Superior War Council, at an informal meeting on May 11, 1934, unanimously record its approval of the reform; the Minister, as frightened before Parliament as though he owed his mandate to an election, would not ratify it. On July 4, at a

[15] Set forth by General Baratier (*Le Temps*, September 4, 1934) in a way that tears the veil from the future. The general was reviewing de Gaulle's book, which had just come out, *Vers l'Armée de Métier* (*Toward a Professional Army*). It is likely that the Germans did little more than adopt the French reformer's conclusions regarding the elements embodied in an army of assault.

meeting of the Senate Military Affairs Committee, his "pretense" was to hold on to the framework of the one-year law. "Short of events requiring exceptional measures for our safety, we shall not look to extended military service." The "hollow years" of 1935–39 were drawing near. Confronted with the National Socialist Revolution, his solution was like Daladier's! Thus, in 1934, all the young men of twenty-one were not called. A pool was made of those left in civilian life to be spread over the lean seasons.

On October 10, with Weygand's reproaches ringing in his ears, Pétain tried halfheartedly to find a compromise. French youth would spend fifteen months in barracks. "That silly idea must have come to you from Gamelin or Guinand,"[16] was the commander in chief's brusque comment. Belatedly, on November 3, Pétain summoned Weygand and, of his own accord, announced that he would give his support to the whole reform.

But it was rather late in the day. When at last Pétain gathered enough courage to speak he was just clearing out of the War Office and his cabinet career was over for the present. Of what help could he be? He did not even refrain from further mischief. After Flandin had asked him to name his own successor, and Gamelin, his selectee (who was to become commander in chief a few weeks hence), had refused the offer, the marshal did not object to General Maurin being chosen on Piétri's suggestion.[17] It is easy to imagine Weygand's vexation. In 1933, Maurin, together with Gamelin and Carence, had voted against him on the Superior Council over the great question of the "hollow years," then in its initial stage, and he was not the man to forget it. In his very first speech Maurin made reference to Pétain's decision early that summer, feigning ignorance of the marshal's later reversal. Everything had to be started anew. It took Hitler's gesture, unilaterally abolishing the military clauses of the Versailles Treaty (March 16, 1935), to convert Maurin, and, behind Maurin, Flandin. Even so they did not dare put the two-year measure in force by a permanent and specific law; instead they sought to achieve their purpose as though something dangerous or shameful was being contrived by means of a permissive clause discov-

[16]About Guinand see page 118.

[17]In June 1935, M. Bouisson offered the War Ministry to General Georges, then reputed to be a forceful soldier. Marshal Pétain, who had accepted Maurin seven months earlier, was against this choice, since he felt it would shut out his own influence. Maurin, as Minister for War, made Pétain a member of the Supreme Council for National Defense and of the "High Committee" whose task was to co-ordinate the requirements of National Defense (November 14).

ered in the Army Recruitment Law of March 28, 1928.[18] Weygand had
relinquished his command on January 21. He could not restrain himself. He dashed off to see Pétain. "Is national defense going to be affected by governmental fluctuations?" In very low spirits, the marshal
answered, "I'll see. Perhaps I can do something. But neither you nor I
understand politics!" As he related that conversation Weygand added,
"I showed the marshal every respect. But more than any other man he
is responsible for the present condition of the Army."[19] On March 24
the whole business was still dragging on. Maurin had succeeded in dividing the Superior War Council.[20] He and Flandin asked the "grand
old man" to arbitrate. Pétain told them that there was no urgency, that
there were no proper accommodations for large numbers of effectives,
that to keep calm was the first requirement, etc. To keep calm! He himself had made it difficult for anyone to remain serene by the article he
had written for the March 15, 1935, *Revue des Deux Mondes*.

The article amounted to self-indictment. Pétain described the "giant's
stride" taken by German military power in 1934. He set down the German Army's peace establishment of 580,000 men as against our meager
covering forces, scattered over twelve hundred kilometers, from Dunkirk to Nice. He conjured up "the lightning offensive, the sudden attack by tanks and airplanes."[21] He thought that Germany, upon mo-

[18]Article 40: "When circumstances require it, the Government may keep with the colors
temporarily that portion of a class which has served a full year. The Government is to
inform both Houses of this decision if they are in session, and within a week if they
are in recess." However, Flandin had drawn up a bill as early as March 11.

[19]From my diary; March 18 conversation with Weygand.

[20]I find in my diary, under date of December 18, 1934: "X takes luncheon with General
Maurin. The latter is quite literally frightened out of his wits at German rearmament. Said
he, 'If war comes, we shall have an eighty per cent chance of being beaten.' However, in the
sitting of the Chamber of Deputies, on November 23, Maurin dared to say: 'I shall be seriously concerned in the question of national defense but, to the best of my effort, not tragically concerned, and I should like others to behave accordingly. . . . And this I want to
make known forthwith: all necessary orders have been given out to make sure that the
intemperate zeal of some military elements will not jeopardize a peace which we value
above everything.' What demagoguery!"

[21]In conformity to the views expressed by General von Seeckt in his book *National Defense*,
dated 1930. "Modern strategy will aim at forcing a decision by means of well-selected
mobile forces kept ready to strike before the enemy has set in motion its masses of armed
men, etc." It was to parry that eventual flow, as described by the German general, that
Pétain and Weygand resolved to have the Maginot fortifications permanently occupied in
strength. Moreover, a system of local mobilization was devised whereby reservists living close
by ("frontaliers") could be speedily assembled. Fortress regiments were organized, of
course, against a corresponding reduction in numbers of mobile and fast-maneuvering
infantry.

bilization, could assemble eighty-five to one hundred divisions. He wrote that she "scorns mystical notions of disarmament," that the "opprobrium which acts of violence call forth in the world leaves her cold," that "she respects power exclusively and that she would resign herself to peaceful policy only under the threat of forces gathered to hold her in check." But at the War Ministry, one year earlier, what had been done by Pétain to ward off the danger, to make good the consequences of his own neglect as commander in chief? On his own admission, almost nothing. On June 1934 he had persuaded the Parliament to vote 1,275 million francs for building fortifications, but half of this amount had been set aside to balance former unauthorized expenditures. In 1934–35 the watchword was deflation, retrenchment. In September 1934 the government had laid down the principle that the military appropriations in the preceding budget would merely be repeated.[22] Pétain had complied with it. In March 1935 he deplored the weakness of the reserve divisions. But in 1934 had he even gone so far as to carry out the law for the periodical training of reservists? No, it was not carried out, for the sake of economy, he avowed to his readers. In 1934 he had but imperfectly and haphazardly given effect to small-scale measures: adding a third regiment to certain infantry divisions, expanding frontier divisions to nine battalions, strengthening light divisions, etc. Late in 1934 and 1935 he seems to have known better and recommended the two-year military service. But we have seen that, his article hardly off the presses, he again weakened on that capital point. And the tale ends there.

However, in the note of April 17, 1934, to the British Government, Doumergue had asserted that national defense was to be the prime consideration and that no more disarmament proposals ought to stand in the way. In practice he had slammed the door on the Geneva conference. And he was right: the recovery of the French Army could not

---

[22]In accordance with Pétain's estimates in 1934, 5,689 million francs were appropriated for army expenditures in 1935—257 million less than the 1934 figures, which, besides, Pétain had reduced in April, cutting down fabrications of matériel by one third (two hundred million). In 1933 over six billion had been spent. At first Pétain had applied for 6,696 million. But the Finance Minister countered his demand with the plea that a resilient Treasury ought to be numbered among the requirements of national defense and he did not insist. Outside the budgetary accounts, Pétain secured eight hundred million for war matériel (see Chamber of Deputies sitting of November 23, 1934). Under Pétain the amounts granted outside the budgetary law, on special account, didn't equal those made available to his predecessor and to his successors. From 1936, when the government of the Popular Front was formed and submitted a fourteen-billion-dollar program, no limit was, in practice, set to appropriations except by capacity of industrial production. Be it noted, however, that in the sittings of June 14 and 16, 1934, Léon Blum and Daladier thought the governmental program unduly large.

be postponed. France could not afford to waste time. But, having sent the conference packing, Pétain and his colleagues sank back in their easy chairs.[23] From month to month Pétain knew fairly well what was going on in Germany, and here is all he could find to say in his one and only speech before the Chamber of Deputies, June 15: "By voting this money, [the 1,275 million] you will make it plain to the world that France, far from fostering any aggressive designs, pursues but one end: to provide for her safety!" Only a few days before, the marshal had disclosed to the House Committee on military affairs the extent of Hitler's preparations, a first installment of the article he would publish in the *Revue des Deux Mondes!* One can almost hear the sheep sententiously asserting that it does not dream of attacking the wolf.

This narrative is incomplete, but at least it serves the purpose of unmasking facts which are known only to a handful of people. It shows us the chasm separating Marshal Pétain's real achievement from that attributed to him in the popular imagination. But why, then, was he hailed as the "hero of Verdun"?

To the average man the heroic Battle of Verdun, stretched over so many months—that most wholesale of blood sacrifices suffered by the French people—became, with the passage of years, the very epitome of the whole 1914–18 war. In this grueling ordeal there was no brilliant strategic stroke, no lightning inspiration to excite imagination. A great multitude, hovering for months on end between death and life, repeatedly decimated, stopped the enemy by some sort of herd steadfastness. In this disciplined flock men seemed interchangeable, as though they were no more than ciphers. With only rare exceptions, there was nothing to evoke the type of combat that lent luster to the arms of a Bayard, a Gaston de Foix. From this wearisome and singsong epic sprang the cult of the unknown soldier, and the unknown soldier was like hundreds of thousands of other soldiers. He was the mass-production hero. He was chosen as from a lottery of coffins. But the people's soul, however great its response to a leveling liturgy, craved something more. The victory of Verdun—though the masses were conscious of its immense significance—would have lost some of its awe-inspiring power, had it not taken on some distinct human shape, had it not been all aglow with the will, the intelligence, the wisdom of a great leader. Enshrining the unknown soldier called for enshrining that leader.

Thus was built the legend of Pétain. The reflexes of the crowd produced it. What a difference with the fame of Joffre and Foch, which

[23]Laval constantly expressed his disapproval of the April 17, 1934, note.

scrutiny and time could but enhance! The Pétain legend is like a fountain which collects in one single stream a host of rivulets and channels them into an artificial head.

2

Pétain's Counterrevolutionary Inclination. The Link with Laval. His Readiness To Sell France's Allies. His Embassy to Franco

IT WAS THE YEAR 1935. Pétain was seventy-nine. His career was over, notwithstanding the fact that on account of his rank he was still theoretically in active service and sat on the Superior Council for National Defense. Active service! As a military man he had let go ten years before. Ever since 1929 Weygand had striven to make up for the extremely adverse balance sheet resulting from his management, and the generalissimo's slackness had been well dissembled. But those who were close to the man could not be deceived. Precisely because it seemed drained of all real vitality, this wonderful carrion attracted all the buzzards of politics. They pounced upon it to house their most sinister machinations. Think of having at your disposal the legend of Verdun, ready to camouflage anything! A valuable monopoly.

Ever since Pétain came into the Vichy kingdom he has been widely depicted as a monarchist, a Cagoulard, a Catholic, a devout man of long standing. I do not believe that these tags are supported by facts. In any case, he can only fairly recently have turned a practicing Catholic. When he was over sixty he married a divorced woman. It is not likely to have been a church wedding. At least so another great military man used to say, who was not given to joking about such matters. As for the Cagoule, its tentacles reached Pétain's personal staff and into Franchet d'Esperey's,[1] but no specific evidence has yet come forward to show that the

---

[1]Through Major Lacanau-Loustau, an eccentric, and Colonel Groussard, respectively. Pétain was rather fond of this Lacanau-Loustau, commander of the Antibes battalion of Chasseurs Alpins, an outfit of which he himself had been in charge. It was while Pétain was stationed at this garrison that he bought his Villeneuve-Loubet property, which was close at

present head of the French State had been personally involved. I do not believe that before 1934 he had any lasting political connection.

In 1916–18 the marshal had been notable for treating Ministers, senators, and deputies with a certain reserve, when so many general staffs eagerly wined and dined them. Military men are wont to denounce the intrigues of politicians. In the last war they themselves quickly displayed that they knew how to maneuver elsewhere than on the field of battle. But in those days Pétain's dignified behavior was a matter of comment and particularly attracted Painlevé, the Minister of War, who preferred him over Foch for commander in chief when a successor had to be chosen for Nivelle.[2] Afterward, on every occasion, he paid great deference to the ministerial office, whoever might be the incumbent. We have seen how hesitant and even perturbed he was in April 1940, when listening to an opinion expressed by Daladier which did not at all suit his ambition of the moment. While Léon Blum was Premier, Pétain never trespassed against a proper courtesy. Certain little peasant slynesses, indeed, are a part of the record; such, for instance, was the buttering up of Clemenceau in his extreme old age—Clemenceau, then the enemy of Foch and Weygand—to insure honorable mention for himself in the *Memoirs,* which were on the eve of publication, and to escape from the sharp words they might be expected to contain. It was not until February 1934, the date of his appointment to the War Ministry in

---

hand. It should be recorded that in March 1938, during Blum's second premiership, Lacanau-Loustau circulated among his friends a projected lineup for a Pétain Ministry.

It would seem that General Dufieux also was related to the early Cagoulards.

But the history of the Cagoule is not simple. Care must be taken to distinguish one period from another and also one group from another. At the outset the apparent purpose of the "protection service" organized by Groussard (with the help of the intelligence section of the General Staff) was to correct the deficiencies of the government police in its surveillance of communists throughout the Army. The Popular Front was in power, and the communists were included in the governmental majority. Groussard, his friends, and perhaps his chiefs drew the inference that the official police would surely be thwarted. Therefore they volunteered to set up a new organization. Later on the "protection service" worked in conjunction with the Union of Self-Defense Groups and the Secret Committee for Revolutionary Action, the two genuine Cagoulard societies. Groussard says that, perceiving the presence of numerous German and Italian agents, he and his fellow army officers withdrew. The whole performance is extremely confusing. We must differentiate between (1) the "protection service," (2) the Union of Self-Defense Groups (General Duseigneur), whose sole aim, it seems, was, if occasion required, to suppress a communist uprising, and (3) the Secret Committee for Revolutionary Action, which was making ready to seize power. Yet Duseigneur purchased his arms from the third group. Cf. page 432.

[2]Foch, who had been in command of the Army Group of the North, had been relieved of his post on December 22, 1916. His brutal and costly hammer blows during the Battle of the Somme (then wrongly appraised as fruitless) were held against him. On May 15, 1917, he was appointed chief of General Staff.

M. Doumergue's government, that Pétain clearly took his stand in French political controversies.

This Ministry of National Union was brought together by the former President of the Republic, hastily summoned from his country home near Toulouse after the bloody outbreaks on the Place de la Concorde. It took upon itself the job of restoring the moral unity of France. Doumergue was an honest man, but of very limited intellectual scope. As a supreme arbitrator between groups and factions, he evinced narrow-mindedness and prejudice, and his awards ceased very soon to pass unchallenged. But this was really pregnant for the future. When forced to forego the undertaking, after an attempt at constitutional reform which was ill conceived and promptly cut short, he turned his power over to Laval and Flandin, in a sort of political testament, utterly mistaking the seeds they bore within them. Laval and Flandin—the two men who above all others ruined France—were the heirs of this obviously well-intentioned if clumsy bonesetter from the Languedoc.

But from the spring of 1934 who was it who, week by week, praised Laval to the skies, hailing in him the long-awaited rejuvenator of French diplomacy? None other than Pétain. Louis Barthou was still alive and headed the Foreign Office with an awareness of the danger, a nerve, and a consistency which, in the eyes of history, might have redeemed the mistakes made in home politics had not assassins in the pay of Mussolini felled the patriot statesman as he sat beside King Alexander of Yugoslavia. The murder took place on October 9. Long before that crime was perpetrated Pétain had started extolling Laval, "the Foreign Minister of tomorrow."

What a godsend for Laval—who endlessly sniped at Barthou's watchwords, the strengthening of old and the making of new alliances, an entente with Russia included—for Laval, who was already ruminating his 1935 appeasement formulas! What a godsend for him to find at the very top of the military pyramid a man more disillusioned than himself! Could he ever have dreamed of such an exalted voucher? He has let slip remarks which are an acknowledgment of his luck. And how he wheedled the old fellow! Plenty of others had their eyes on the prey; he snatched it right from under their noses. Attending Barthou's funeral, the marshal outdid himself on Laval's behalf. The salvation of France required that the Colonial Minister become the Minister for Foreign Affairs! And to vindicate the claims of his candidate he was content to assert: "He is the best, the ablest man we have." He already longed for a Laval premiership.

How was it that Pétain, so careful not to compromise himself, always so measured in the past as to his speech and bearing, now so boldly hurled himself into the factional fight? Here seems to me the most plausible answer. He was cut to the heart by that fear of a social upheaval which in so many a conservative had silenced every feeling of patriotism. The small landowner in him had been aroused to defend his acres. He gave unforgettable proof of the violence then stirring within him at the October 13 ministerial council, which settled the shuffling of portfolios and assigned Laval to the Quai d'Orsay. The meeting was about to adjourn when the marshal asked M. Doumergue's leave to speak: he had some remarks he would like to submit. M. Doumergue pressed him to fully explain his mind. "There remain weak spots in the Cabinet which should be made right," he said. The Minister of Justice, Chéron, an amazing specimen of Norman peasantry, beat his breast: "Are you talking about me?" "Yes," replied Pétain. "The ex-servicemen are behind me, and I declare that your presence here cannot be tolerated." For months the Rightist press had heaped insults on poor old Chéron because he was suspected of shielding the murderers of a Paris magistrate who had investigated the Stavisky affair and whose body had been found on a railroad track.[3] As between cabinet members, here was a nasty row. The accused burst out in pathetic oratory. But he was unwise enough to place his portfolio at the disposal of the Premier, assuming that it would be restored to him. And in this he missed his guess.

Chéron was soon avenged. Those whom he left in power were to be ousted within a few days, and the marshal's petulance hastened their downfall. Pierre-Etienne Flandin, however, when he described the incident to me,[4] underlined this detail. "At the instant when the Minister of Justice threw in his resignation, the marshal, who was seated between Marquet and myself, seemed to falter. We told him to keep quiet: 'Let Chéron go ahead; it does not matter anyway.'" This episode shows what fire can lurk behind Pétain's external placidity. It betrays the frightened bourgeois, the partisan, and the wavering fumbler all at once. But now he was quitting the halls of government. We shall not meet him again, sallying forth into public affairs and far afield from his own military province, until May 1935.

He was at that time sent to Warsaw to represent the French Government at Pilsudski's funeral. Laval, on his way back from Moscow, where he had gone to discuss with Stalin what was to be done with the Franco-

[3] A case of suicide rather than a crime: such is the belief today.

[4] My diary: conversations with Flandin on October 20, 21, 22, 1934.

Soviet treaty signed at the beginning of the month, broke his journey to join the delegation. The two men stayed at the same hotel and spent the evening together in an intimate discussion of French affairs. They gradually settled on two basic themes: a criticism of the existing regime and the difficulties of government under a parliamentary system, the desirability of an authoritarian policy in line with the needs of the hour and the supposed hopes of a certain section of French public opinion. In every way the marshal urged Laval on, encouraged the Minister of Foreign Affairs, the coming Prime Minister, to go ever more boldly forward, confident that it was in the national interest. Let him brush aside the parliamentary opposition. Laval, more cautious and also better aware of all practical limitations, did not dispute the general substance of what Pétain said, but declined to shoulder the burden. In a country so quick to spurn the least suggestion of personal power, what was needed to get rid of Parliament was someone above parties, above political life, and someone who was not elected to serve a mandate and tarred with the brush of faction and cabinet intrigue. Only a man of the marshal's stature, nationally on a higher plane, could command sufficient support throughout the land. Now it was the marshal's turn to beg off. He pointed to his political inexperience and his small aptitude for the tasks of power. Vainly Laval strove to reassure him—it was an undertaking which required nothing more than common sense and which would be far easier for one whose authority rested on an unsullied reputation. Discreetly peppered with mutual compliments and exhortatory discourses, the conversation wound its way to no conclusion. Laval freely informed his friends that, as far as foreign policy was concerned, he had found Pétain to be "the most pacifist of all Frenchmen."

Exactly five years later, within a month, the two of them, working side by side, were to strangle the Republic. It is easy enough to see how it happened that in 1936 Gustave Hervé, formerly an anti-war socialist (doubtfully become a patriot during the last conflict), should have written a pamphlet entitled *We Need Pétain!* (*C'est Pétain qu'il nous faut!*)

Other episodes of this Polish visit deserve notice. The German Führer had delegated Marshal Goering to attend the ceremonies. This was natural enough, since he looked upon Pilsudski and Beck as allies. Just as had been the case with the burial of King Alexander of Yugoslavia,[5] Marshal Pétain's first concern was ostentatiously to indicate, by every

---

[5]Pétain and Goering were closeted together a full hour and a half in a railway carriage between Oplanatz and Belgrade.

possible means, his friendship for his German brother-in-arms. In vain he was advised to let Goering make the first move—which Goering would hardly fail to do, since his instructions doubtless required him to play up to Laval and those surrounding Laval. From the moment of their first meeting, in church, the aged French officer was eager to start the ball rolling. After the absolution everyone present walked in a long procession to the ground where the military parade was to be held. The distance was seven kilometers. Pétain's seventy-nine years rated him a carriage. Hence he had been in his seat on the reviewing stand for some time when the cortege came into sight. Spotting Marshal Goering, he left his place, rushed up, and lavished courtesies upon him. The same performance was repeated at the Cracow banquet, after the last rites in the Wawel. Marshal Pétain was not present at the ensuing conversation between Laval and Germany's number-two man. However, the delegates of all nations of Europe were again surprised at seeing the Marshal of France profusely showering Marshal Goering (who was on his way to meet M. Laval in a private sitting room) with public evidence of an exaggerated friendliness. So many petty gestures which nobody would think of mentioning were there not to be seen in them a tremendous tragedy of history at its source. Are we to recognize in this open good will toward a great dignitary of National Socialism the beginning of a personal infatuation? Or was it rather that Marshal Pétain wished to exhibit on Polish soil his disapproval of the Franco-Russian Pact, on which the signatures were scarcely dry? And in doing this had he not every reason to believe that he was at one with the very signer and seeming promoter of the treaty, Pierre Laval?

Here we must stop short and ask the marshal a few questions. As early as 1934 he had found fault with the foreign policy enforced in the preceding thirteen years—with the Polish alliance of 1921, which was reformulated in 1925, with the Czechoslovak alliance of 1924 and 1925, and with the coping to the structure, the understanding with Russia of May 2, 1935, which, if sincerely fulfilled, would also have implied military solidarity. Because of his backing of Laval, because of the confidence which he endlessly showed him, one may presume that Pétain was even finding fault with the traditional friendship for England, a friendship which the Minister would not hesitate to scrap in the summer and autumn of 1935 in order to help Mussolini in Abyssinia.[6] But had he any

---

[6]Pétain's Anglophobia cannot be ascribed to his experience at Dury and Doullens. Traces of it appear at all times. He tried to prevent the French Army from taking part in the Battle of the Somme (1916) as well as in the Battle of Flanders (1918). In a speech

right to dismiss French policy so cavalierly? Had it been shaped without his knowledge and against his advice, despite his objections? Not in the least. As commander in chief and then Minister of War he had, in common with all the other military leaders, desired that the closest of bonds should link France to Germany's other neighbors. As a cabinet colleague of Louis Barthou, the instigator of the Soviet negotiations, had he not given his approval to everything that was done? A mania for making pacts, delusions of grandeur, says the marshal, blaming the disaster on French diplomacy, like many other generals. Our Army was not big enough to live up to so many obligations.

The truth is that every one of these alliances had been negotiated and concluded under the solicitations of the High Command, which in a number of cases was all for going further than the diplomats.

Thus Marshal Foch, when he went to Poland in 1922 to draw up the military convention assumed in the political agreement of the preceding year, paid little heed to the government's instructions. On the spot he agreed to measures of application which, in fact, stretched the intent of the contract. The Warsaw Cabinet long made use thereof to draw us beyond the political commitments which, in 1925, had been somewhat lessened by the Locarno formulas. Foch's idea (and Marshal Pétain never indicated, in the twenties, that he was of another mind) was that France, looked upon by Germany as her principal foe, would of necessity be attacked on the very day when the hour of revenge and upheaval was struck in Berlin. What we had to fear was not being dragged into war through our duties toward the Slavic states, but rather that they should not come to our support. Doubtless the Reich would so pamper the satellites that it should have to fight on a single western front only. The danger was not that we might be caught in others' toils, but that they might refuse to enter ours. Therefore the mania for making pacts meant, in the judgment of our strategists, the receiving of guarantees far more than the bestowing of them.

Let the reader ponder on this. The General Staff was organizing the Army for the defensive and not for the offensive. Consequently, it expected from our Allies a great deal over and above what it was prepared to give them. Its calculation was that they would divide the German

---

delivered at Meaux on September 9, 1934, in his capacity as Minister of War, to commemorate the Battle of the Marne, here is what he had to say about the British, who stood beside us in battle, and the Italians, who aided us from afar by their neutrality: "The British, whose solidarity with us was intermixed with a sound understanding of their own interests . . . Our Italian *brothers,* quickening a friendship which seems due forever to be the sign of our relationship . . ." How significant is his choice of words!

effort at the outset of hostilities and thus lighten our load. What could the General Staff promise with its concepts of static war and its Maginot setup? Merely that after two or three years the French Army, which Poles, Czechs, and Russians would have helped to save for the first few months, would roll on toward the east, swollen with all the resources of the Anglo-Saxon world, and would liberate an eastern Europe in the meantime submerged under the German tide. According to this notion, the very weakness of the French military system called for the making of alliances. It was essential that the first blows should not fall thick and fast on our covering forces. France wanted to have the little nations' assistance because she felt her own debility. In the so-called mania for making pacts, in the so-called delusions of grandeur was to be found—and we have to admit it—some degree of unconscious cynicism. It is best to leave Don Quixote well out of it. The astonishing thing is that we should have succeeded in enlisting anyone under so disheartening a banner! "Sacrifice yourselves and then seek consolation from the ensuing deluge in the thought that with patience and the passage of time you will be able finally to lift up your head above the flood."[7] But it is outrageous that men in constant touch with the action of the Quai d'Orsay, consulted on every occasion and urging that pact be piled upon pact, should later have cried out against our diplomacy as unbridled and asinine merely because political swindlers had persuaded them: (1) that Hitler did not look upon France as the all-important enemy; (2) that his design for conquest was limited; (3) that we could permanently satisfy his appetite for territory by handing over to him the nations we had gathered into our alliance; (4) that, as a consequence, the pacts we had tucked in our safe were nothing more than devices to destroy our own peace.

Had not the military a right to change their minds? Certainly, but then they had to speak openly and state their reasons. Yet when did any of them ever tell a Premier or a Foreign Minister, "You may consider as null and void our past opinions on the need for a Czech bastion, a Polish diversion, a basic co-operation with the British Empire?" Never, even when they were given a chance to do so. Here is a con-

[7]This is why Frenchmen had no reason to be indignant at the treaties of reinsurance entered into by the Polish, Yugoslav, or Rumanian cabinets. However, they had a right to protest against the dealings of a Beck or a Stoyadinovitch inasmuch as the reinsurance sought from Germany developed into complicity, which was the case with these two ministers. The reinsurances obtained were very ambiguous, and in spite of everything, the system of alliances built by French diplomacy was, at any rate, an obstacle. Beck betrayed Poland as well as France when he plotted against Titulescu in Bucharest—to quote but one example.

vincing instance. On March 15, 1938,[8] the permanent Committee for National Defense held a meeting, with Marshal Pétain and Léon Blum, the Prime Minister, seated face to face, and with Gamelin and the heads of the Navy and the Air Force present. Their discussion dealt with the Spanish War, with the immediate problems it raised for France and with its wide international consequences, reaching even as far as the related threat of European war. The Minister for Foreign Affairs, Paul-Boncour, and the secretary-general of his Ministry, Alexis Léger, spoke at length. The latter called attention to our diplomatic commitments. Over the whole debate hovered the most oppressive questions of the hour—those of resistance to Hitler and Mussolini in Central Europe and south of the Pyrenees. Someday we may have to think of carrying our African troops across the Mediterranean and the Atlantic. And what of the Sudeten squall, contrived in Berlin? Indeed, a few days later a memorandum, approved by Gamelin, would be forwarded to London showing that help could be lent to Czechoslovakia.

You can see how broad was the ground covered. Did Marshal Pétain at any point protest? Make clear that he saw things otherwise? Did he make any reserve, even in detail? No. He never opened his mouth. He approved of everything. Not a word did he utter against the Jew, whom he has jailed, condemned, and abandoned to the Nazis. Yet that same Jew was importunate, repeatedly asked him, seeing that he was silent, "Are you thoroughly in agreement, Marshal? . . . Haven't you any objections to express?" "None whatever, Mr. Prime Minister, none whatever!" And he answered in tones of deferential regard.[9]

The most amazing transformation along these lines was that of Weygand. As inspector general of the Army he had convinced himself from 1932 on that French policy toward the Soviets must be revised. We should take advantage of Stalin's and Hitler's first quarrels to undermine

---

[8]This meeting may have taken place on the sixteenth.

[9]Obviously, Pétain did not speak as he felt and thought. Here is a case in point. During the summer of 1936, Lord Mottistone (Minister for War in 1913, then Sir John Seely) was present at the dedication of the Vimy monument. Pétain invited him to share his railway carriage on the return trip to Paris. "We have a rotten government," said the marshal, "and I want to tell you that the French people won't fight." "What you have just told me is a very serious matter and I shall esteem it my duty to inform my government." "I should think you would repeat it, and when I spoke I was well aware that you should do so." Between 1936 and 1938, Pétain certainly had not changed his views; he always stood where Anglophobia, counterrevolutionary passion, and defeatism met.

In passing be it said that on his arrival at the Gare du Nord, Pétain was greeted by the cheers of two or three hundred young people whereas Léon Blum alighted from the same train to find himself alone on the platform.

and destroy the Russo-German rapprochement, begun at Rapallo in 1922. In wartime, Germany would then no longer be able to exploit the Russian hinterland; our Czech and Polish allies, our Yugoslav and Rumanian associates would be freed of the heavy threat which weighed upon their rear, and they might even obtain supplies therefrom. It would be possible for us to gain the support of the Turks for the defense of the territorial *status quo*—the Turks, who had been intimately linked to the Kremlin for seven or eight years and who could not enter into any commitment toward a third power without Soviet approval. How could that powerful chain of arguments be seriously refuted?

In the spring of 1934, General Gamelin had come to Geneva to attend the disarmament conference. He accosted me in the entrance hall of the League Palace and impelled me to change my attitude toward Moscow in keeping with the new policy. But what a strange road Weygand traveled! At the beginning of 1933—that is, long before the Ministry of Foreign Affairs had taken any definite step—he wrote a foreign states-man, whom he had always found amenable to his ideas, a regular admonition on the subject. If Poland did not wish to join France in the military alliance with the Soviets forced upon us by the growth of the German Army, so much the worse for her! Then we would get along without her. From October 1932 one of the officers on his staff, Colonel de Lattre de Tassigny, had been endlessly exchanging views with General Wenzof, Russian military attaché in Paris. It should be observed that Weygand (according to the letter which I have already mentioned) used the words *military alliance,* while the more restrained Quai d'Orsay was satisfied with a sort of Eastern Locarno, wherein our freedom of decision would not disappear altogether. The Franco-Russian treaty was signed by Laval on May 2, 1935, who nonetheless did not have it ratified either by decree or by law. Internal controversy over this diplomatic action had broken out several months earlier. All the men whose foremost preoccupation was to preserve the social order damned it.

One day M. Henry Simond, editor of the *Echo de Paris,* said to me, "You led me to believe that Weygand was in favor of the new policy. He is not. His story is that he was never consulted." By way of reply I invited to luncheon M. Simond, Weygand and his wife, M. Titulesco, and two other friends. At my request Titulesco put the question to the general. "When M. Barthou bluntly informed me that we all must get nearer to Russia, I went to you for enlightenment and advice. I could appreciate the reasons for the change, but the road looked steep to me, and I wondered whether the French Cabinet would have enough resolu-

tion to stick to it. I asked you whether the innovation was really necessary. You left me no room for doubt. You replied: 'It is necessary.' Is
this a fair account of what took place?'"

Weygand had no choice. He was on the spot. Reluctantly he mumbled,
"Yes." And Madame Weygand moaned, "What a pity to associate with
such ruffians!" This luncheon took place on April 6, 1935. When, in
March 1936, the Legislature was finally debating the treaty's ratification,
a short note dictated by Weygand was sent around to the newspapers:
contrary to widespread rumors, he had played no part in what had been
done. In the House a more explicit "communiqué" made the rounds.
"General Weygand: in his capacity as Inspector General of the Army,
not consulted; in his capacity as a private citizen, opposed." Could any
lie be more barefaced? If in one of the articles daily published under my
name I had dared to throw that lie in the teeth of one of our great army
leaders, the *Echo de Paris* would have been shaken to its depths. Emile
Buré's *L'Ordre* printed a full account of the luncheon, and M. Alexandre
Varenne, before the vote was taken, read my letter to the House, adding
simply, "It would be cruel to say any more." The next year, however,
when I brought a libel suit against the weekly *Gringoire,* Weygand, who
had in no way protested against my making his reply to Titulescu public,
handed to my opponents the brief "communiqué" which had done
service twelve months before: "In his capacity as Inspector General of
the Army . . . in his capacity as a private citizen . . . "

Events persisted in pushing Pétain and Weygand together whether
they liked it or not. They were shoved into the same political and social
camp. After long lives spent in little garrison towns, when at last they
settled down in Paris they had no old friendships to fall back on there,
no broad circle of acquaintances, because so many years elapsed between
visits. They fell in with ready-made "cliques." I don't clearly perceive
how Pétain wound his way across Parisian society, but my dining almost
every month with Weygand enabled me to catch more than a glimpse
of his own progress, and from what I know about the one, I can draw
conclusions about the other. Weygand was a director of the Suez Company, a preferment never before given to a military man. Both were
members of the French Academy, which, quite apart from literary talent,
traditionally elected to membership the country's most worthy servants.
A fine military achievement, brilliant scientific research, even a notable
engineering feat were thought to be worthy manifestations of the French
spirit, on the same level as prose and poetry. To honor and to brevet
intellectual merit wherever it could be found: what a fine boast! But it

sank to the level of a farce with the French Academy of 1935–40, a miserable body of men, some ten members set apart, one quarter of its number! What prejudice, what trifling, what baseness when public affairs were on the carpet! Enlightenment about it will come to anyone who turns over the file of the *Revue des Deux Mondes*. And what of the drawing rooms these gentlemen haunted, where they hatched out their precious "elections"? Spiritual independence and dignity fared badly there. Such was the narrow sector of Parisian society where Pétain and Weygand were most at home. There the institutions of the Republic and the British Parliament were held to be mere nurseries of bolshevism, and the last rebuff dealt Hitler and Mussolini reproved as a mortal thrust at the foundations of the civilized world. Historians have always expressed astonishment at the "great fear" which swept over the country in July 1789, while the Estates General were deliberating at Versailles. Everywhere was heard the same cry, "The brigands are coming!" And spontaneously men joined together in *"gardes nationales,"* which kept in fetters the dying monarchy and its defenders. Since 1934 the French Conservatives suffered their "great fear." "Revolution will swamp us!" And nowhere did intellectual panic flourish more luxuriantly than among the self-perpetuating second-rate thinkers and artists who, at public functions, wear palm-bedecked cutaways of 1801 style.

In my presence, on March 18, 1935, Weygand delivered himself of the following: "I am in favor of military force, alliances, religion, and I am against Free Masonry."[10] Mind you, unlike Pétain, he approved of alliances. But we have seen in how limited a sense. And on every other subject he could surpass his elder in violence. He was of illegitimate birth. Papers friendly to his star slyly hinted at the Emperor Maximilian for his father. One of them even embroidered the story, adding that, thanks to an escapade of the Duke of Reichstadt, Napoleon himself was among his progenitors. Only this last touch was fanciful: at least everyone who amounted to anything under the Republic believed so. What is beyond question is that he entered St. Cyr under the patronage of King Leopold II of Belgium, that his name was then not Weygand, and that, authorized to serve in the Army with the status of a foreigner, he was naturalized by special favor. Other men might have grown proud of the romantic aura with which such an origin surrounded him. Not Weygand. Our ancestors of the sixteenth or seventeenth centuries, with a healthy lack of conventionalism, would have said guilelessly: "The Habs-

---

[10]He wanted to start an anti-Masonic league. I insisted that the day would come when he might serve his country again, and that he should not fritter away his authority.

burg bastard," and that would have been the end of it for everyone, including the person most intimately concerned. Weygand married the daughter of a brigadier general, and his titled in-laws did not accept him without reluctance. He was humiliated. Instinctively, he could not bear to be wanting in conservative orthodoxy. All too often after 1935-36 his lucid mind, which I had so long admired, could not any more hold the rabid politician in check.

In 1939, because it happened to suit his convenience and the circumstances of the moment, Daladier brought the two overage leaders back into public office. This time they were to have a hand in diplomatic affairs, not as before, incidentally to a military command, but from within, on their being entrusted with definite missions.

In February 1939, Pétain was appointed Ambassador to Madrid. Our relations with Spain were on an uneasy footing. French cabinets, from 1936 on, had not been able to deal effectively with the Germans and Italians in the Iberian Peninsula: for all that, the thanks of Franco were not due to us, and he kept right on seeing our Republic as a foe. How could we go the whole way to meet him and yet avoid humiliation? The wisest thing seemed to be to choose the man who, around 1923, had supposedly known Franco at the center for higher military studies or, in any case, had met him in Morocco about 1926. The marshal had always expressed strong reprobation for the ideas and the personnel of the Barcelona Government. Moreover, he belonged to a quasi-Fascist Academy. Surely all he would need to do was to appear in his dress uniform. The mere power of his presence would do the trick. We could forego all explanations.

The officials of the Ministry of Foreign Affairs had not commended his selection. The installation of a marshal of France in the Madrid Embassy seemed to them a shot above the mark, a departure from what they regarded as the right psychological attitude to be taken toward Franco's Government. In the juncture perhaps it was not a bad idea to call in a soldier, whom social conservatism in all countries could not but bless and praise. But then why not simply turn to Weygand, who, moreover, had the advantage of being more active and much more on his toes intellectually, fit to digest a diplomatic brief and defend it? The preliminary agreement put in shape with Count Jordana by the academician Léon Bérard evidenced what a dim-witted bigwig could do when matters of great import were committed to him. But, while dealing with the Spanish problem, Daladier had to think of national union at home, which was still to come, which he wanted to bolster. As he put it, the employment of Pétain involved no risks and was sure to be endorsed by public opinion. The employment of Weygand would be too harshly criticized in Parliament, where many suspected him as a factious and seditious person.

In the Madrid Embassy, for the last time, we see the marshal in his natural guise, under the full light of day. In Paris, Tours, and Bordeaux, in the shadow of Daladier and Reynaud, throughout the war, we caught sight of him by flashes, shifting about silently, keeping his own counsel, remarkably cautious, showing his hand only at the end of the game, when he thought he did not incur any risk in being bold. Later on, when possessed of unlimited political power, his appearance, his actions, his behavior will be systematically screened from our eyes by discreet attendants and propagandist writers, by the creation of a "myth." Rites will be performed around him. The Madrid interval provides the last chance to examine whatever was left of the great leader in his eighty-fourth year.

Once everything had been settled with the Premier, he took childish glee in repeating over and over again, "Well, well. Here I am an Ambassador! It had never come to my mind that such an offer would crown my career. I am deeply interested." And he scurried about asking rather foolish questions of the officials. But he did not forget to put in a request for a larger expense account. Shortly thereafter his chief military assistants turned up to inform themselves on "essential items." They did not hide their worry: could such old shoulders ever carry so heavy a burden? Where would the marshal find that quickness of decision needed to get through the day's work in a large modern embassy? Confronted with the most trivial of private telegrams, he sometimes took two or three days to draft an answer. His inertia was increased by the stubbornness of old age.

One of the prerogatives of a marshal of France is to have a staff in attendance, even when he does not fulfill any function. Therefore Pétain would take with him to Spain a military household. Would this household domineer in the chancellery? In principle, it was determined that diplomatic tasks would be under the exclusive care of professionals. The Ambassador did not demur and, in view of his inexperience in such matters, asked that a permanent official of first-rate ability be assigned to him. At once one of our best-qualified embassy counselors was removed from his post at Brussels—a post of front-line importance—to serve by the side of the marshal. This choice had first been submitted to him for his personal approval, with a recommendation calculated, it would seem, to please him: "The official suggested is as energetic as he is intelligent; he has verve, sharpness, and enterprise." Pétain, who made a point of seeing him beforehand, expressed complete satisfaction. For two months he swore by this diplomat. But his military suite, restricted to details of etiquette, official ceremonies, and social relations, grew restive. When they had set out for the Caudillo's court they had dreamed of a graver and more exalted role. And so two inimical factions dwelt under the same roof. The military household and the chancellery were at loggerheads.

Franco's welcome was frigid. Our envoy recalled their common past. His remarks fell on deaf ears. He was greatly put out. He was mortified. At an important public ceremony the dictator's attentions were ostentatiously focused on the German Ambassador, and the marshal was left out in the cold. But, as he described the scene, he could not resist the temptation to improve it—a specific failing of many diplomats. He innocently explained: "I felt by the way Franco grasped my hand that he regretted not being able to treat me better."

Weeks went by. Files piled up. The Spaniards showered us with claims to which we yielded without getting anything in return. We handed over the gold of the Bank of Spain earlier deposited with us by the Republican Government. To help feed the Spanish people, we levied on our wheat reserves, overruling the objections of the Minister of Agriculture. But what became of our own requests—for instance, Darlan's protests against the illegal help given German submarines in peninsular waters? Deliberately the marshal let them pass into oblivion. "I am here," he kept repeating, "to create a good atmosphere." His diplomatic counselor, under the stimulus of the Ministry of Foreign Affairs in Paris, impressed the marshal with the necessity of intervening, of saying something, and finally both together went to call on General Franco. The interview dragged on without the subject being broached. Finally the counselor himself had to say what his chief preferred to skip over. Thenceforth the confidential assistant became *persona non grata*. He was relegated to routine business, which he would transact with the officials of the Ministry of State. The Ambassador had no further desire to be accompanied and supervised. Needless to say, the Spanish officials guessed what had occurred and were quick to take advantage. So also did the military household, which eagerly clutched its hour of vengeance. Very soon, and without the knowledge of the man concerned—which meant without even officially assuming administrative responsibility— the Ambassador wrote a personal letter to the Under Secretary of State

for Foreign Affairs, secretly requesting his counselor's recall in terms
bound to be injurious to his reputation.

Meanwhile internal politics wove their threads around the Ambassador. The Embassy was moved to Hendaye for the summer. Here, on
the edge of Spain, between Biarritz and San Sebastian, and closely linked
to Madrid society, dwelt adherents of the *Action Française,* passionately
devoted to the Spanish Nationalists and sure that in France events
would unfold as they had beyond the Pyrenees, that Pétain would
"restore order" in the Franco manner. All these makers of parallels
gyrated around the old man; his talk reflected theirs (war had already
begun), and the counselor had to give warning. In the autumn the
Piétris and the Lémerys and others flocked to San Sebastian (or
Madrid).[11] They were coming to seek out the dictator of their choice.
In February 1940, five months after he had refused the portfolio of
Minister of State which Daladier held forth to him at Herriot's request,
the marshal gave way under increasing pressure from his visitors and
applied for a release from his duties. Daladier did not want him back
home under any circumstances. He contrived this little piece of deceit.
A pompous letter, full of rhetorical flourishes, was dispatched to the
Ambassador by return diplomatic pouch. It extolled the services he had
performed, the happy outcome of his mission, the even more crucial job
still to be done. Clio, the Muse, working in the choicest marble or
bronze, could not have laid it on thicker. Sweet vanity puffed up the
recipient. Almost with reverence he would extract the parchmentlike
document from his upper drawer and show it to a favored visitor. But as
spring approached, deep down within him, the old fellow was disillusioned about Spanish affairs. The only reason his counselor had become
unbearable was that the man's very presence amounted to a judgment
and a reproach. On many an occasion the marshal had already hinted
that he would never have consented to serve in Spain had he first been
shown the text of the Jordana-Bérard preliminary agreement. Toward
the end of his ambassadorship he quite openly told people in Paris that
"we must change our tone with the Spaniards, get tough with them."
Nevertheless, repeating his Warsaw and Cracow gestures, at three
separate encounters with the German Ambassador he had shown attentions which were scandalously out of place. At eighty and more one
cannot get rid of the "old man."

[11]One day the marshal showed his associates a list of a tentative Pétain Cabinet. Apart
from Laval and Lémery, it was composed entirely of military men and important civil
servants.

Simultaneously, Weygand was taking his diplomatic fling. As with Pétain, governmental convenience made him an Ambassador. The son of Pahlevi, shah of Persia, was to be married to an Egyptian princess, and that potentate was preparing a magnificent wedding. An English prince and a high German dignitary were to be among the guests. So he begged the French Government to send as its representative an important political figure, preferably M. Herriot. M. Daladier was all the more anxious to please him because our relations with Persia had been severed as the outcome of a silly quarrel sprung from some jokes in a magazine. However, elections were to be held for the presidency of the Republic, and Edouard Herriot, as president of the Chamber of Deputies, could not leave Paris. Nor, at such a juncture, could any but a minor political personage be withdrawn from our national life. And the shah was extremely touchy. Several cabinet meetings were held without the Minister of Foreign Affairs being able to settle the question. Finally it was referred to the officials of the Ministry of Foreign Affairs, who, at the eleventh hour, fell back upon Weygand. Thus, all unwittingly, they put him in line for other more important duties. In Iran he would receive new instructions, requiring him to stop at Ankara, there to negotiate our military treaty with Turkey. Once again this designation suited the convenience of the government, for it would have been difficult to spare from the Superior War Council any military man of sufficient stature to meet Marshal Cakmak on equal terms. Moreover, the Turkish Government would find it less embarrassing to receive an envoy who happened already to be in the Near East than some man sent specially and directly from Paris and therefore offering the Germans a better motive to complain.

Weygand was not soon to be freed of Eastern affairs. They led to his taking charge, in Beirut, of the Mediterranean Army after having been involved—for similar reasons of public facility, but also because of an increasing revival of his personal reputation—in a whole string of supplementary and unforeseen assignments along his return journey through the Balkans. The Bucharest, Athens, and Belgrade governments scarcely dared stir under Germany's watchful eye. They shied away from the least hint of any intention to join with the Western Powers eventually. We wished to prepare their minds for the future, to lure them into military consultations. General Mittelhauser, in charge of central and southeastern Europe on the General Staff (he had long served as head of our mission to Prague), would ordinarily have been given the job by virtue of his special qualification. But to send him would have been to let the cat out of the bag, and for that reason he would not have been welcomed in any of the three capitals. Again, the most discreet procedure was to take advantage of the route our envoy extraordinary must take in any case. As it turned out, he was not able to make a serious approach to the problem he was determined to raise and, naturally, he blamed our diplomacy for it. He was always only too prone to cavil at its agents. With all that he began to build up within himself the dream of a hundred Balkan divisions to be hurled into the fight against Germany. Back in Paris he brought into play his abilities at salesmanship; to the great indignation of Gamelin's circle, which cursed the Ministry of Foreign Affairs, he took over Mittelhauser's long-standing position. Asiatic and Balkan matters had swept him back into the center of the governmental and military stage.

Gradually the two chieftains have reunited. They have been thrown into the cast of a strange consulate. People who had seen the "Hero of Verdun" at close quarters during the last several years feared, on June 16, 1940, that he would crumple under the weight of the state affairs. But near him they saw Weygand, full of nervous energy, bustling, a ready speaker. They complacently imagined that a transfusion of strength might occur and they took heart.

3

Monetary Crises Split the Nation. Léon Blum

WE CAN NOW WRITE with perfect assurance that Pétain and Weygand were no match for the test which awaited them. It has been, and it will be, alleged, on their behalf, that, in May–June 1940, they were caught short, burdened with unlooked-for responsibilities, shattered by defeat, prevented from giving the best that was in them. But we have traveled back along a span of five, ten, twenty years and found that in peacetime, when unharried in thought and action, they had not been very different from what they were during France's bitterest days.

Since the last war Pétain's intellectual faculties slumbered. His assets consisted of peasant greed, deep political passions, and the legend of Verdun. Weygand had long been thought of as a second Foch by keen-minded judges who believed they recognized in him the solid element in the marshal's talent. On the eve of the hostilities his recent record proved him to be of no great moral stature and well below the standard with which his interlocutors, impressed by his peremptory manner, had often credited him. His conception of French interests was constantly warped by his obsession of "conservative orthodoxy," by his fear of what others might say. He published a few second-rate compilations (a biography of Turenne, a history of the French Army) which kept him away from steady professional work. He fully deserved to be dubbed a *Revue des Deux Mondes* general. Like Reynaud, Weygand is a small man, as small as the clique around him. There is no rich human fund in him upon which he can draw. I shall always recall a dinner with Prince Paul (not yet regent of Yugoslavia) at which the general was present. I disliked the obsequious way he bowed to the prince. I still had faith in him, but for the first time his personality grated on me.

Pétain's and Weygand's intrinsic merit and the events they set in motion offer a striking contrast. Truly, these men are effects far more than they are causes. They served as a blind for counterrevolutionary forces, long held in check by the great majority of Frenchmen, and now, at last, put in a position of dominance by military defeat. One is reminded of that statue of Father Nile with children swarming all over him. Father Nile represents Pétain, but to make the symbolism accurate the old man should be less huge and his offspring sturdier and more numerous.

The names of Pétain and Weygand, linked with the name of Laval, will go down in history as bywords for the counterrevolution of 1940. Flandin and Bonnet also will be bywords, not counting the small fry. But Laval stands foremost. He was the true master of the hour. Four years and five months earlier, power had slipped from his grasp. Yet the plotting that undermined Reynaud and got the best of his patriotism, the cabinet upset of June 16, 1940, the separate armistice of the twenty-second, the betrayal of our allies are branded with his name, although he was still away from office. They are branded with his name as conspicuously as the attempts to declare war on Great Britain, the dictatorial constitution, and the increasing help to Germany which, subsequently, were the outcome of his ministerial activity.

Observed from day to day during the years when Europe was still teetering between peace and war, when France wavered between humiliation and resistance, his whole conduct, hidden as it was under a thick coating of systematic lies and double-faced utterances, might not

look consciously criminal. What he did in 1934–35, for instance, if taken
without reference to the future, may still be construed in such a manner
as to make everyone think that he was merely blind to the implications
of his own acts. In October and November 1934—the first two months of
his tenure at the Quai d'Orsay—even though I watched him closely, I
felt I should not altogether condemn him, so cleverly was he able to
dissemble and mislead. But in 1940, as soon as the German victory had
been won, he tore off the mask and openly spoke his mind. His furious
conviction, his passionate outbursts disclosed that, in his heart of hearts,
he had always considered armed resistance to Germany as a greater evil
than the loss of our national independence. Before, an onlooker might
have been deceived by the waves which, on the surface, played in various
directions: in June–July 1940 anyone could see that the undercurrent had
never changed.

Laval's devilish skill was to avail himself of the crisis in French society
—most probably a passing crisis—to enlist the men, to create the moral
atmosphere needed for a policy of surrender. Because of him a considerable fraction of the liberal bourgeoisie—for fifty years the backbone of
the Republic—behaved in the homeland in the same way as, at the time
of the French Revolution, those Royalists who fled beyond the frontier
to fight their own country. Because of him an "internal emigration"
came into being. Seeds of counterrevolution would have existed in
France even without Laval. They would have sprouted out anyway. But
then they would have withered quickly. Out of scattered, confused, and
unstable elements Laval molded a solid body of public opinion and the
shock troops of the new order. In a France calmly going about her
ancient and appointed task he could have hoped for no more than a
minor cabinet post; he needed a total upheaval of society to forge ahead.
Only through revolution can politicians of such low instincts take command and maintain themselves in power. Laval is the man who thought
that France would solve her problems by voluntarily relinquishing her
rank among nations. To have conditioned to that change both propertied
men and socialists, by promising the former confirmed possession of
their wealth and the latter peace everlasting, is Laval's unique achievement.

Such ideas could tempt his daring and cunning only because the
nation had been deeply split. The opportunity that passed within his
reach was not unlike the one which Catiline (not to mention the great
war lords of that time) tried to grasp during the last century of the
Roman Republic, when the political and social fabric suffered from an

endless sequel of cumulative alterations. Throughout the ages the healthiest communities must at times weather storms during which they either transform their customs and institutions or founder. To that mighty stroke of the wings which can carry them to the heights there is no alternative but utter downfall. Out of France's vicissitudes between 1920 and 1940 we must select some groups of facts, record general trends needed for an understanding of the Laval-Pétain-Weygand set. The counterrevolutionaries hurl in the Republic's teeth the history of its last twenty years as their justification. There is but one reply—to hurl the truth back at them.

The 1918 victory gave France a conditional supremacy over Europe. She had been bled white more than any other nation. The joint enterprise had been guided by Foch, one of her military leaders. The spiritual radiance of Paris, so continuously felt throughout the nineteenth century, added to the glory of her arms. But France could exercise effective power only on two conditions. She must keep at her side England and the United States, her allies and indispensable associates; she must also find within herself some vestige of that dynamism which had left its mark on Europe between 1789 and 1848. Unhappily, France had lost her dynamism.

French society in the nineteenth and the first part of the twentieth centuries bore the stamp of the bourgeoisie. It was far removed from what it had been one hundred and two hundred years earlier. The French people had remained fundamentally the same. But in public affairs, in the management of the state, those whom the old regime dubbed *"roturiers"* had come to the fore, and this sufficed to change the face of the country.

What is "the Third Estate"? Everything. What has it been until now? Nothing. What does it want to be? Something. Thus wrote Sieyès in his famous pamphlet of 1788. The French bourgeoisie began to call the tune in the reign of Louis Philippe, and toward 1880, under the Third Republic, it felt that it was indeed everything. The men whose main stimulus was to make money, whether they belonged to the professional classes, practiced a handicraft, or earned a livelihood in trade or in manufacture, big or small, had outstripped those who did not need to strive so avidly for personal gain, the rank of their birth being a sufficient source of honors and riches. The spirit of business displaced that of public service, the old sentiments rooted in religion, knighthood, and devotion to the king.

The usages and customs which tied the average Frenchman to some

corporative or family group had disappeared. "No man is under obligation to leave the paternal estate undivided." This principle of the
Napoleonic Code had freed property from joint family control, while
the provisions of the Rights of Man—equality of all before the law, public offices accessible to everyone, subject only to merit and ability—
had freed individuals from stereotyped social hierarchy. Only in the
United States, removed as it was from the Greco-Latin tradition, had
individuals been so completely free from feudal and monarchical bonds.

We are tempted to smile today at the political simplicity, at the
castles in the air built by the apostles of liberty after 1789. All the same,
in the heroic period, they were the nation's life breath and motive force.
They even put their seal upon the European continent. But afterward,
in their settled days, the very different seal they impressed upon their
own country proved more lasting.

One of Louis-Philippe's ministers coined the watchword "Enrich yourselves!" So well did it reflect the temper of his time and of the time that
followed that the resurrection of the imperial regime under Napoleon
III made it still more powerful. Those generations of Frenchmen are
characterized by an avid desire to preserve or to increase their worldly
possessions; a hatred for risk; a liking for contractual obligations to
secure the future; an eagerness to hold public office, either through
election or competitive examination—not so much because of any ambition to serve the general welfare as because of a wish for established
position, for respectability often coupled with the basest servility; a horror of war, inasmuch as it threatens to exact its blood toll from large
groups of the population; an impatience with governmental regulations.
As early as 1869, Ernest Renan, candidate for election to the Chamber
of Deputies in the Seine-et-Marne Department, was shocked by the all-
pervasive materialism. So also was Prevost-Paradol, after similar contact
with the electorate. They both deplored that the self-abnegation of the
ancestors was fading away among their contemporaries. The old sentiments, once supremely expressed in the orders of chivalry, in the crusades, in the Cluniac Benedictines, in the royal institution as it existed in
France, were fast receding.

The sun shone bright on this new society. For the French people as
a whole, during a full century, government bonds, mortgages, rents, all
forms of property remained extraordinarily stable. The purchasing
power of money kept on an amazingly even keel in this community
largely formed by peasants. Our grandparents' lives basked in deep tranquillity, shattered though they were by two terrible alarms—the social sedi-

tion of 1848 and the war of 1870-71 with its by-product, the Commune. The 1848 revolution proves that if the occasion arises, the "bourgeois," fearful for his possessions, readily turns to a dictator for safety, and we should never make light of that lesson. The war of 1870, which brought forth a rebirth of patriotism and an awareness of the need for sacrifice, reminded the French people that no person had a right to say: I shall not live dangerously. Most of them awakened to a better sense of collective discipline. This feeling greatly benefited the 1875 Republic and inspired its successful foreign policy prior to 1914.

On the eve of World War I the snug bourgeois edifice began to show cracks. Small farmers, small manufacturers, small merchants constituted the political and economic backbone of the country. With us large banking and industrial concerns put in a rather late appearance, and then on a smaller scale than elsewhere. Narrowness of outlook was dominant, and it was not the special failing of any single class, not even of the Radical-Socialists, with all their reputation for being hidebound. From top to bottom, and as much among adherents of the Right as of the Left, pettiness was all too much the rule. The business pioneer with broad views, the economic empire builder of the Anglo-Saxon or German variety, was the rare exception.

It is simple enough to describe the economic system in force before 1914. Agriculture was sheltered by higher and higher tariffs. Wheat was still grown on the most thankless soil at production costs out of all proportion to those in the New World and eastern Europe. Industry was willing to put up with the many handicaps inherent to this rural policy on condition that the home and colonial markets be set apart as its own reserve. Each party to this arrangement believed that it worked to its own advantage. The farmer could go on tilling his land as had his forebears; the manufacturer was protected against foreign competition and did not need to improve his machinery or seek new outlets abroad; the craftsman could continue to scorn mass production to his heart's content. But, in the long run, this meant that great opportunities for profit were lost. France's wealth was growing more slowly than that of competing countries. Her population, the largest in Europe in 1789, failed to increase despite a reduced death rate. This amounts to saying that the average age was higher in France than elsewhere, that there were fewer young and more elderly people. Too many countrysides were becoming depopulated. Nation of perennial bachelors and only sons—such was the title of a book published in 1896. The enforced equal division of estates among the testator's children, the forbidding by law of the free disposal of one's property were partly responsible. Caution, fearfulness, timid husbanding of capital assets: France was a nation of small people.

Middle-class France was redeemed in a sense by certain constant features of our race: strongly marked individual temperaments, a preference for highly skilled and quality work, a horror of regimentation bordering on defiance of authority, an aptitude for expressing oneself in the arts. The nineteenth century was a magnificent triumph for the spirit, and that alone is enough to dispose of any theory of decadence. Dislike for conformity can be a sign of boundless egoism. However, coupled with the diversity of our regional traditions, it makes for the peculiar charm of our people. Men are less like each other than elsewhere. The pencil of Daumier, the satire of Flaubert and Mirbeau should not make us forget that extraordinary variety of human types. What remains today of the ludicrous bourgeois they have exposed to everlasting derision? Joseph Prudhomme and M. Homais have only a scattering of descendants. True, other ridiculous figures may have entered the scene, but on the whole there has been a freeing of the spirit, less formalism in manners, greater refinement and sincerity. The old bourgeois house smelled musty: the windows are being opened wide. Fragonard would have found himself at home in the Paris of the twentieth century. The trouble is that the modern world is dead set against the political and economic casualness which sprang from the way of life of the average Frenchman. And the average Frenchman was aware of the threat. What made France so appealing to the foreigner was a source of weakness.

In England, in Germany, in the United States, mass production began at the turn of the century. The 1914–18 war hastened its tempo. Everywhere economic and financial power became more and more concentrated, and governmental action impinged more and more upon private affairs. Among the belligerent nations the state, in order to carry on the fight, assumed an abnormal share of authority which was not to be easily discarded. Taxes and controls multiplied; administrative machinery increased in complexity; the free play of supply and demand was interfered with. On levels where, of old, the administration had no impact on the individual, social discipline became essential.

Moreover, it was only natural that the working classes should, in the course of time, become aware that their civil and political liberty must be a means rather than an end; that the aim of social reforms must be to protect their living standards from the fluctuations of the market. On the morrow of World War I the impending clash between state socialism and freedom was already apparent. The French community could not keep aloof from such universal trends. It was clear that it would have to come to terms. By the Versailles Treaty the iron of Lorraine and the potash of Alsace were merged in the wealth of the nation; factories expanded or were modernized on "reparations" at the expense of either the French or the German treasuries; large- and medium-size businesses doubled in number.

The little fellow, however, was still the kingpin. But, on the one hand, his elbowroom had shrunk. Much more than before, he had to reckon with the state, whose parasites and creditors swarmed about: officials, pensioners of all descriptions, owners of government securities. He hated paying his good money into the public coffers; he waxed eloquent over the interference of the bureaucrats. For all that, he was the very first to cry out for protection against ruinous price changes. In certain fields the free market was done away with or severely curtailed. Public authorities handled so huge a volume of funds, yielded by taxes, borrowing, and social legislation, that they controlled credit. On the other hand, the industrial proletariat, which had kept pace with the growth of big business, laid claim, in the form of wages, to an ever-growing share of the national income while, at the same time, the national income did not, year after year, increase steadily.

The middle-class Frenchman became afraid of this twofold tendency, of the vise in which he was being caught. A Lady Bountiful state managed by the trade-unions: what an infernal device! The French Revolution had turned labor into a commodity, subject to the hazards of industry and commerce. Gracchus Babeuf and the "Society of Equals" got nowhere under the Convention, and the Directory threw them to the guillotine. When the Russian Revolution revived such repellent ghosts the Frenchmen of 1920 behaved more or less like their ancestors of 1793 and 1796. The "rights of man" no longer seemed so attractive now that the social revolution strove to appropriate them. The main election poster of the "National Block" in the 1919 campaign portrayed a Bolshevik with a knife clutched between his teeth. The bourgeois gazed at it and did not smile. Indeed, and despite the German defeat, they thought the world was in a bad way.

Inner transformation was called for at the very moment when France's international role was broadening. Who could shoulder this dual task?

France has no established governing class—that is, a portion of the community able to judge matters loftily and from a long-range point of view, above the passions of the moment, immediate advantage, or minor concerns. The nobility became politically emasculated in the seventeenth century. The upper middle class (*grande bourgeoisie*) never acquired any real stability or breadth of outlook. Terrified by the Commune, the rural electorate swamped the 1871 National Assembly with men from those two classes. But the "notables" they elected were unable to fit themselves into the representative system. They did not bridge the gap opened in 1789.

How different they proved themselves to be from those English aristocrats who asserted their oligarchical liberties in the thirteenth century, widened them gradually into parliamentary and popular freedom, succeeded in healing the schism of 1688, and kept right on happily meeting the test of universal suffrage. The horizon of our own "notables" was, in its way, just as narrow as that of the little fellows.

During the first forty years of its existence the Third Republic has been served by a liberal bourgeoisie deeply devoted to republican institutions, of great political culture, drawing from the history of the last hundred years the lessons it taught for governing the French people. The Ferrys, Cambons, Barrères, Ribots, Jusserands, Delcassés, Poincarés, and a host of others were of such origin. Seemingly, the breed was dying out by 1920. Or rather such men no longer went into politics.

What were the springs of action powerful enough to bring the French together in an emergency, to tear them free of their individualism and supply them with the equivalent of collective discipline? Religion? The Catholic Church sided against the Revolution because of the civil constitution of the clergy. Only some three decades ago did it withdraw from this negative attitude, and it is striking that a religious revival closely followed almost at once. But in the nineteenth century the Church, with all its magnificent merits, with its missionaries, its teachers who made the Mediterranean a French lake for the second time in history, did not seriously count as a positive factor in home politics. Its hierarchy, to all intents chosen by the state, lacked intellectual distinction.

The call of national defense? Certainly. But here a qualification is in order. The call of national defense had evoked a tremendous response in the 1792 crusade for the "rights of man." This link with revolutionary France gave French patriotism a peculiar flavor; it had become Jacobinism, a sullen determination to fight for freedom. Surely one might have foreseen that it would suffer from any weakening of the French people's faith in their Republic. Above all we must remember the 1,317,000 dead of 1914–18. France lost one third of its young men between the ages of twenty and thirty—the most enterprising, the best suited to meet the new circumstances. In the mourning which they left behind them, and in the pervasive uneasiness, the joy of victory and the full realization of what had to be done to permanently secure its results were lost.

The spirit of enterprise? Full scope was given to it overseas, and a fine colonial empire bears witness to it. But at home it was no more than half awake. Once again, in the twenties, the average Frenchman was distrustful of himself and of his kind. He feared the future.

It was at this point that fatal monetary mistakes worsened the social changes already under way, while, under the encouragement and pressure of the United States and Great Britain, our traditional diplomacy swerved from the strong line it had instinctively tried to follow in German affairs and no longer resisted the popular demand for a minimum of exertion in foreign policy. France was drifting toward moral disintegration.

To pay the expenses of war and to finance the reconstruction which followed in its wake, the easiest method, the method most immediately pleasing to the haves and the have-nots, was chosen. Not only were existing taxes but slowly increased; no real severity was exercised in collecting them. The "closed circuit" technique had not yet been invented. Bank-note circulation and credit accounts in the banks, which flowed in swelling volume from chronic budgetary deficit, were inadequately reabsorbed by short- or long-term borrowing. The means of payment thus made available to the public grew more rapidly than the stocks of consumers' goods, with soaring prices as the result.

When, in March 1919, the French Treasury was cut off from the sterling and dollar credits allotted to it during the war, and when it had to balance its excess of imports by shipping gold abroad, the franc began its decline on the international money market. At first this decline was fairly slight, but it became much steeper as soon as private capital, fearing ever greater depreciation, fled to London or New York. An end was not put to the crisis until 1926, when the franc was stabilized at a rate of 125 to the pound sterling and 25 to the dollar, after having sunk to a level twice as low. The cut in the gold value of our currency, then, was no less than 80 per cent. And to calculate the real loss, it should be remembered that since 1913 the purchasing power of gold itself had diminished. To a large extent France paid for the war through monetary inflation.

This monetary collapse did not mean that all Frenchmen, taken as a body, were the poorer. Quite the contrary. For many these were prosperous days. The devastated regions sucked up labor, materials, manufactured articles. Since the exchange value of the franc on the international market had fallen off more quickly than had its purchasing power at home, more goods could be bought with francs than with other currencies. Industry and commerce were in a flush of expansion. Those who depended on fixed incomes—derived from investments or government salaries—suffered; the rest of the community did very well. Thus took place a shifting of wealth within the social structure. Some had less than formerly; others, far more. Observing the fortunes made by others within a few years or even months, all those whose revenues and remunerations could not move from the old levels whined and protested. Old families in the provinces, unfamiliar with the mysteries of finance, guided in their investments by dunces, fools, or sharpers, never were able to repair their fortunes.

Above all, civil servants were hard hit. Their stipends (niggardly at best) were doubled by M. Poincaré; to restore their former standard of living, these should have been quintupled. Proportionately, the higher ranks fared worse than the lower. Thereby our whole administrative framework was debased. To measure the harm done, one would have to know intimately the workings of those tiny family budgets, calculated to the last penny. Loss of social position, necessity of getting along without a cook or a maid—such middle-class tragedies were deeply resented. The ablest of the government employees found a haven in private business. I remember the case of a certain general, whose name is mentioned in this book, who spent three or four years in a banking house, had a run of bad luck, and, duly scorned, returned to his army command. Applicants for government jobs diminished both in number and in quality. The Army, in which the pay had always been very low, took an even worse beating than did the other branches.

Henceforth political discontent became rampant. The Radical-Socialists were its target, especially M. Herriot, Premier after the May 1924 elections, head of what was then called the "Cartel of the Left." And no wonder, since the currency had crashed to the bottom under their management. Unquestionably, their amateurish talk, which was not free of demagoguery, proved harmful, although they hardly did more than to precipitate an inevitable process. But monetary and economic problems lay outside the range of the common man, at any rate in France. He is crassly ignorant and impervious to sound reasoning when it comes to such matters.[1] No fair appreciation of the facts can come from him.

[1] As an astounding example of the general ignorance, one could single out the case of Henri Chéron, 1929–30 Minister of Finance. For years he had to report to the Senate, as the mouthpiece of its Finance Committee, about the budget: appropriations and expenditures,

To crown it all, a majority became convinced, irrespective of party classifications, that in April 1925 Herriot had had the statement of the Bank of France tampered with so as to conceal the issuance of bank notes in excess of the legal limit. Looking back, the accusation sounds ludicrous. Edouard Herriot's main error was merely to take too seriously the advice of an incompetent governor of the Bank of France, M. Robineau, and of an equally incompetent secretary-general, M. Aupetit, and to put his confidence in the conservative financiers of the day. In the face of a floating debt of some one hundred billion francs, these would-be experts wished at all costs to preserve the rule, today outmoded, whereby the sum total of bank notes could not be increased without a new agreement between the bank and the government—that is, without a new law. The outcome was certain: those who held t' floating and short-term debt saw their chance of repayment lessened in proportion to any increase in bank-note circulation. The bank notes handed out to those who rushed in to redeem their securities aroused the anxiety of patriotic citizens who refrained from getting their money back. As between National Defense Bonds and bank notes, the distinction was imaginary, since the former could be discounted on demand. Both were, in fact, valid instruments of payment.

Jean Parmentier, leading treasury official, a man of broad and courageous intelligence, tried in vain to prove to the Premier that these bonds should be paid in full upon maturity, and that the legal limit for issuing new money should be automatically expanded to admit of all reimbursements. In vain did he plead for what he called the "single ceiling." All the orthodox economists rose in arms against him. The day came when the legal limit was exceeded, and Herriot was branded a counterfeiter. He resigned with everyone cursing him. This was the first of the monetary dramas. It made the devaluation successfully carried out by Poincaré in 1926–1928 look like the price paid for political dishonesty.

The next phase in our monetary vicissitudes was attended by much more serious consequences. Poincaré saved the franc. However, stabilizing it at the rate of 125, he undervalued it in relation to the dollar and the pound sterling. He went too far in the reduction of its gold content. French production costs became the lowest in the world. As they

---

even in their most minute details, held no secrets for him. But when he stepped up into the Finance Ministry he actually asked where the bank notes with which taxpayers settled their obligations were kept and if sufficient safeguards had been taken in New York to protect the French gold deposited in the Federal Reserve Bank against gangsters and their forays. This detail was supplied to me by Pierre-Etienne Flandin, who succeeded this hoary Norman peasant at the Treasury. And I could name a Premier whose notions were similarly childish.

gradually adjusted themselves to costs in other countries, thanks to the interplay of trade and exchange, the latter fell down vertically. We had come to the great economic earthquake of 1929–32.

Early in 1931 it was our country's turn to pay more for its manufacture of goods than did its foreign competitors. Suddenly, in September 1931, the British Treasury decided to lower the gold content of the pound by 40 per cent, and in March 1933 Mr. Roosevelt's administration dealt likewise with the dollar. For this British and American monetary policy the case was overwhelming. Raw material prices had sunk by two thirds or even three quarters at a time when the price of processed goods, hooked in wages, fell by comparison only one third or one quarter. This unequal deflation of prices brought about the so-called "spiral movement," the ruin of the one set of producers being constantly worsened by that of the other. Indeed, because of the difference between price levels, the two types of products could no longer be traded against each other. The Anglo-American devaluation cut down industrial costs and raised the purchasing power of raw-material producers.

As regards France, the important consideration was not to determine whether London or Washington Treasury experts were right or wrong, whether the experiment in a "flexible currency" carried out in England did or did not commend itself. The brutal fact, the essential fact, was that French production costs were henceforth lifted 66 per cent in relation to those of the other nations. At once exports and the tourist trade withered. Industrialists and merchants had to put up with shrunken turnovers. Capital moved abroad, on its owners' correct forecast that, sooner or later, devaluation, after the Anglo-American pattern, would force itself upon us. In 1931 the Bank of France had in its vaults six thousand tons of gold; in April 1938 it was to have scarcely two thousand left. Between these two dates the loss was continuous. It has been calculated that in 1935, under Laval, the national income—the sum total of individual earnings—was no more than half what it had been under Poincaré seven years earlier. And government taxation took away half of it as against one third in 1928 and one quarter in 1914. Between 1926 and 1930 France had enjoyed the lowest operating and interest charges in the world. Between 1933 and 1937 the whole setup was turned upside down; we manufactured and borrowed at greater cost than anyone else.

Meanwhile Moderate and Radical-Socialist cabinets succeeded one another. None of them condescended to understand that the only possible remedy was to put the franc in line with the gold value of the pound and the dollar. All wasted their ingenuity on trying to re-establish an

equilibrium between internal and external prices by cutting down salaries, wages, and government expenditure, by assessing new taxes, by
setting up higher tariff walls, by enforcing additional "quotas." They
would not see that, through deflation, they only increased the havoc.
Obstinately they clung to the ancient teaching of liberal economics, to
the classic doctrine of the gold standard. As though the political and
economic world had not budged! As though the raising of the discount
rate made it possible for the bank of issue to woo back or stop short
capital funds in flight to other lands! As though a man with francs to
his account, seeing on the other side of the Atlantic 100-per-cent profits,
would be discouraged by the prospect of having to pay 6 per cent on the
sums he borrowed! As though the French State could close its eyes to
whatever might happen in industry and await the automatic return of
good times as a result of the excess of bad! Almost alone in all the world
our nation stuck to this procedure, whereas, if it were to be successful,
a general adherence to it was necessary. The Flandins, the Lavals, the
Germain Martins, the Georges Bonnets stood idly by while the French
economic body wasted away. Did they not have behind them unchal-
lengeable authorities—most of the regents (directors) of the Bank of
France, private bankers, the bulk of treasury officials?

Next to the Army General Staff and the French Academy, here was
another closed corporation worthy of indictment, another government
service which, by co-optation, had become self-perpetuating. Blaming the
1870–71 defeat on an insufficient political training among Frenchmen
and on the frivolous mood of the Second Empire, Hippolyte Taine,
Albert Sorel, and other prominent figures had founded the Ecole des
Sciences Politiques. As I looked over the programs listing the various
subjects taught in this institution I was often amazed at the number of
degree-spangled pedants who now replaced the founders. The majority
of treasury officials were recruited from this school. Vanity of examinations and competitions! These fellows were not chosen because of their
intrinsic merit, the strength of their personality, or their fine character,
but merely because of the supposed orthodoxy of their views, their
powers of mimicry, their connections, their position in Parisian society,
among the two or three thousand persons who held the big jobs, set the
fashion, handed out favors, and made the law. The High Command,
the Institut de France, the Treasury—to this list we must add several
more trained flea circuses! The Bank of France, the membership of the
Stock Exchange, big business—all deserve to have their names written
on this roll. Among others, one might single out the metallurgist and

coal-owner committees (Comité des Forges and Comité des Houil-lières), the general confederation of producers, with crews of academic camp followers, devotedly in their pay.[2]

Here, in brief, is the typical career of a treasury official in good stand-ing with the ruling clique; assistant director of the "Mouvement des Fonds," the key department in the Treasury, by the time he was thirty-two years old, director at thirty-seven, assistant governor of the Bank of France at forty-two, director or manager of some large bank or con-cern at forty-five. At first he would have to live on the meager salaries doled out by the state to its servants with, as a solace, speedy promotions in the Legion of Honor. Then, having spent a few years at the apex of the hierarchy, he would drop his administrative job and get into big money. Inspectors of finance (treasury officials) and great businessmen were one huge family, and that connection could not be called a very healthy one.

Instinctively, the French people abhorred devaluation. Having suffered it in 1926, they thought it defied common sense to call it in again. Why submit anew to a surgical operation when it had already been tried and had effected no lasting cure? The question was being considered in such naïve terms. If the prejudices of the majority of the owning classes were to be overcome, it was indispensable that the "elite"—that is, our intellec-tual and professional leaders—should be unanimous. Yet those leaders adopted as their own the most flabby reasonings of the man in the street. They would not admit that there was nothing in common between the monetary readjustment necessitated by the collapse of prices all over the world and the devaluation of 1926 made necessary by the inflationary policy of the preceding decade. They refused to see that from 1929 on-ward the Poincaré devaluation had been nullified up to a point by the general lowering of price levels and that the franc could buy in 1933 as much as one half of what it bought in 1914, one half and not one fifth.

In 1933 one of the treasury officials who held a top-rank post in the Bank of France was given the task of inciting a newspaper campaign against the innovations of the British Treasury and of Mr. Roosevelt's New Deal. Here, perhaps, we put our finger on one of the basic causes of France's catastrophe. Representative institutions can function pass-ably only if the "elites" of the nation are there to supply intellectual leadership at the polls. By "elites" I mean the men who spend a lifetime investigating problems of public policy (financial, military, diplomatic),

---

[2]This was a new breed in public life—the college professor or scholar turned an economist and businessman! François Poncet, Lucien Romier, Eugène Miraux, Pierre Pucheu, etc.

whose work transcends all party and sectional interests. Intellectual leadership means that those men must be bent on finding out correct solutions regardless of their eventual consequences upon those party and sectional interests. Whenever such intellectual leadership is lacking or insufficient, whenever the bonds of personal friendship or the sordid calculations of the great and powerful have long interfered with the fair recruiting of the "elites"—General Staff of the Army, diplomatic service, treasury officials, Institut de France, influential circles in finance, industry—whenever no enlightened, if restricted, nucleus of public opinion is at work, outside party lines, to influence politicians and leaven the multitude, the government and the people, in the long run, will conform to the description in the Bible of the "blind leading the blind." Between 1931 and 1936 the financial community, an oligarchy of officials, bankers, money dealers, company directors, most of them having risen to eminent positions less by their own merit than by biased co-optation, inheritance, or, in the case of stockbrokers, by purchase of their offices,[3] have cast France upon the rocks. This is where the wrongheaded "experts" have brought the country.

During the 1924–28 period those who enjoyed fixed incomes suffered from the currency devaluation. After 1932 much the same people—government employees, ex-servicemen, those who lived on returns from their securities—profited by the lowering of price levels. Their gains, on that account, much more than balanced their losses—the reductions of salaries and pensions, the new taxation of securities enforced by law decrees. But such is the mood of the general public that it deeply resents all tampering with the nominal amount of salaries, pensions, or incomes. It cannot be brought to calculate in terms of purchasing power.

And now, for the first time, industry was hit: producers—that is, employers, as well as labor—were not spared. The former ceased to derive profits from their business and were fearful for their investments. The latter thought themselves lucky if they had to put up with merely fractional wage cuts. Confronted with bitter unrest on all sides, cabinet after cabinet wore itself out in futile attempts to balance the budget by ever stiffer levies on a shrinking national income—a procedure equivalent to trying to square the circle. But whereas the Right, with its "direct-action" satellites, who were just then appearing on the scene,

[3] Among the "co-opted" should be listed the names of some of the highest servants of the state: generals, ambassadors, whose pensions no longer allowed them to keep up their former scale of living and who succeeded in getting themselves appointed to boards of directors despite their obvious lack of capacity. Some of them, involved in illegal manipulations during the 1932–38 crisis, were haled before the courts.

blamed the Left (in the juncture it meant the Radical-Socialists) for the public distress, the Left cried out against the "Fascist conspiracy" and the "two hundred families" who were supposed to rule all movements of capital funds, who controlled banking and industrial monopolies. Weren't corporation directorates as firmly held by them as had been feudal tenures? Nor was the Left wrong. That two hundred or four hundred or eight hundred families should have preponderance in a nation's economy is natural enough. The disgrace is that such an oligarchy should be without merit and breed incompetence.

As a retort to the bloody riots of February 6, 1934, a twenty-four-hour general strike was called for six days later. On July 14, 1935, the Popular Front was organized, in the form of an electoral and parliamentary alliance between the Radical-Socialists, the Socialists, and the Communists. And once the general elections of April 26 and May 3, 1936,[4] had been won, a veritable popular revolution broke out on May 25. The working classes acted without the least ill temper. All they wanted to do was to "buck up" Léon Blum, forestall any weakening on his part in this moment of triumph. He, as head of the Socialist party, which had won the largest number of seats in the House, was the Prime Minister designate. He took office on June 4. By the end of that month 12,142 sit-down strikes, involving 1,830,938 strikers, were on record. The terror in the Conservative camp can readily be imagined!

And now the mistakes of the Left were to be piled upon those of the orthodox financiers and of the ministers they had advised. In the official residence of the Prime Minister the employers, represented by the Gen-

[4]Here was the line-up in the House then elected:

Communists: 72 seats as against 10 in the 1932–36 legislature.
Dissident Communists: 10 as against 11.
Socialists (French section of the Second International): 146 as against 97.
Radical-Socialists: 116 as against 159.
Independent-Socialists (two groups): 37 as against 67.
Independent-Radicals: 31 as against 66.
Left Republicans: 84 as against 99.
Popular Democrats (Catholics): 23 as against 23.
Republican Democratic Union: 88 as against 77.
Conservatives: 11 as against 6.

Thus the Popular Front, strictly speaking (Socialists of the Second International, Radical-Socialists, Communists), had 334 seats in a house of 618. Moreover, it had the more or less regular support of 37 Independent-Socialists and 10 Dissident Communists. But throughout the country it had not obtained a clear majority: Second International Socialists, 1,887,000; Communists, 1,453,000; Radical-Socialists, 1,401,000 out of a total of 9,800,000. When the election figures were placed before M. Lebrun, on the evening of May 3, he exclaimed: "How could they do anything like that to me!"

eral Confederation of Producers, etc., came to terms with the C.G.T. (General Confederation of Labor), speaking for labor. They agreed upon the principle of collective bargaining, upon election of shop delegates who were to apprise management of all workers' grievances, and upon an immediate increase in wages (June 7). Concurrently the Cabinet laid before Parliament a whole series of bills which embodied the provisions of this settlement and, in addition, prescribed the forty-hour week and vacations with pay, nationalized the armament industry, reformed the Bank of France, and set up a wheat board. Thus an entire social code was made law within a few weeks. It was justified to a very large extent. One of my friends, sitting on the employers' side all through the meetings under Léon Blum, told me of his surprise when some C.G.T. members were able to refer, without being contradicted, to weekly wages of seventy-five francs paid to women in factories working for national defense at the very outskirts of Paris. But the arrangements made for war industry were fraught with danger.[5] Some clauses inserted in the standard collective contracts to which both parties had to conform seriously cut down the management's freedom of action in order to protect "militant" union men from being fired by way of reprisal. Above all else, in the Europe of 1936, with German preparations already in full swing, the forty-hour week was nothing short of a catastrophe. This introduces into the picture the personal responsibility of Léon Blum.

The Law of June 21, 1936, put the forty-hour week in force for all workers and employees in industrial and commercial enterprises. Trade by trade, and industry by industry, the decrees issued in ministerial councils determined how, in each instance, the law was to be applied. The reformers believed that the industrial equipment had been renewed in 1919 when the forty-eight-hour week was made compulsory, that it still was up to date and would help maintain the volume of production. They thought that the increase in the purchasing power of the masses would swell the demand for consumers' goods and that the unemployed would go back on the payroll. But their expectations failed to materialize. Owners showed no desire to invest fresh capital, to "rationalize" their methods of operation, to run new risks. They were swayed by the fear of losses rather than the hope of profit.[6] The hourly average

[5]Law of August 11, 1936. Blum should not have failed to take into account the warning which came to him from the General Staff, at the end of June, in the form of a memorandum. In the nationalized factories many of the shop delegates were Communists.

[6]The Popular Front Cabinet could not feel entitled to strike at the roots of the existing social order. For we must remember that the Radical-Socialists, included in the majority, were the conservatives of the Left. Said Blum, "We shall try to bring forth out of capitalism

workman's output went down 10 per cent. Industrial output remained at approximately the same low ebb. Yet the October 1 devaluation of the franc (suffered rather than desired by Léon Blum, who was fearful of the widespread public prejudice against it) should have effectively primed the pump: for the first time in five years French production costs were approximately on a level with those in other countries. In the autumn of 1938 they had sunk 20 per cent below. Why, then, did we stay at the low-water mark? In vain did orders come in; the factories were in no position to fill them. In both management and labor there were too many shirkers.

Most unfortunately, the forty hours were portioned out to five out of the week's seven days. Saturday became a second Sunday. For forty-eight hours plants were shut down tight. And there were not enough "skilled" workmen to run factories on a two- or three-shift basis. Furthermore, the owners thought it risky to increase personnel, having no assurance of being able to lay them off at will if business again began to lag.[7] As prices rose with manufacturing costs, and the increase in the purchasing power of labor was thus cut down to 10 or 15 per cent, while that of people with fixed incomes actually shrank, surely no one could pretend that a very strong stimulant had been administered to our economy. Between September 1936 and February 1937 a rise in production of 3 to 6 per cent at the most took place. During these same months Holland also devaluated her currency; she enjoyed a 33-per-cent increase. The truth is that no monetary juggling can make up for lack of zeal and for disorder. For more than two years, from the summer of 1936 until Paul Reynaud's decrees of November 12, 1938, everything in France moved very sluggishly.

In the autumn of 1938 French production was 25 per cent lower than in 1930; German production had gone up 30 per cent in the same interval. Blum, who studiously exerted himself at moderation and who, in March 1937, was to proclaim a "breathing spell," admitted the necessity

---

all the reforms it can stand." In fact, he did not keep his word. He forgot that, without the incentive of profits, private enterprise is impossible, and that, shorn of all enterprising spirit, no capitalist regime can survive.

[7]The interference of shop stewards in management's business and, above all, the arbitration methods required by the Law of March 4, 1938, regarding the settlement of industrial disputes, the participation in all collective-bargaining negotiations of the C.G.T., with its irresistible powers of intimidation—all this made the owners feel that they were no longer masters in their own factories, that they had already been subjected to a first dose of expropriation as a prelude to total extinction. Whenever they discharged a workman they had to give proof that his union activities, even if tinged with communism, played no part therein. Many of them just gave up.

to make up for work time lost in one way or the other. The first decree on this subject was dated October 27, 1936. Special "credits" of fifty, sixty, and seventy-five hours could be granted yearly, "in the interests of national safety and defense," but with a wage rate increased 25 per cent. The employers did not even try to take advantage of such measures. Their contracts would no longer have been profitable. And the trade-unions, under Communist influence, occasionally set down the condition that there must be no unemployment in the area where such "credits" were being sought.[8] The "relief measures" were broadened, at the end of 1937, by the second Popular Front Cabinet formed under Chautemps' premiership on June 23; then by Daladier (to whom Parliament had delegated full powers) in April and August 1938, etc. But it was not until Paul Reynaud became Minister of Finance that the whole system was straightened out. He was the first to knock down the "second Sunday"; he did away with all legal restraints on overtime and lowered the rates of pay for it with their burdensome effect on the cost of production. After the final enslavement of Czechoslovakia working hours were increased to sixty in factories working for national defense[9] and to forty-five hours in all others.[10] On September 1, on the eve of war, the sixty-hour week was made the rule everywhere. From statistics prepared by the International Labor Office one learns that, on the average, French labor worked for 45.7 hours a week in 1936, 40.2 hours in 1937, 38.7 hours in 1938, 40.8 in the first half of 1939. With Hitler at close quarters, what a pitiable jump!

Many men, belonging to the most diverse sets of people and schools of thought, stand guilty of this economic anemia which made very nearly impossible any strenuous rebuilding of our military machine. However, to fully one third of the French nation the whole charge must fall upon Léon Blum alone. And at least one of the reasons for it was plain enough. The ill effects of "orthodox" monetary policy were not all understood. Even today people who pride themselves on their financial wisdom will tell you that the 1932–36 deflation policy failed very largely because it was not carried far enough. But when it came to factories which had actually closed doors or to workmen who had seized their

---

[8]On July 11, 1936, Gamelin appealed to Daladier regarding this problem of licit exceptions to the forty-hour week, but with no particular result. From the point of view of national defense, no such exceptions could serve their purpose unless they were spread through the whole network of our industry. The June 20, 1936, law on vacations with pay was applied with equal inelasticity.

[9]Decree law of March 20, 1939.

[10]Decree law of April 21, 1939.

shops in sit-down strikes, you were up against things which almost hit you in the face and were an immediate offense to the eyes and ears. And so, for the vast majority of the owning class, Blum and nobody else was the responsible criminal.

It was under his leadership that the Left, beaten on February 6, 1934, had taken the offensive and got its revenge. The bosses who did not dare put up even a nominal resistance at the famous 1936 meeting in the Premier's offices never fully recovered from their fright. The "revolutionaries" of the Left overawed the opposition in Parliament, a minority in the House, but the majority in the Senate. Most Conservatives sprang to the conclusion that "the dirty Jew had turned France over to the Communists!" A mighty wave of hatred surged up against him. It did not crash down on him, because even the most outspoken were scared. But as you saw it swell, you could easily imagine the power of its impact if people should think that they could strike with impunity. I remember a middle-class housewife saying to me: "I'd love to meet Blum sometime so I could spit in his face!" The Premier's own nephew, a child of nine, asked him, "Haven't they chopped your head off yet?" And then again, two weeks later, "Are you still alive?" By the same token, Herriot, who had withdrawn, it is true, from the political turmoil as President of the House of Deputies, but so deeply, so tenaciously hated in 1925, was more or less forgotten.

Hatred for Blum was to unite all the counterrevolutionary elements, now burning at white heat. When Marshal Pétain became dictator he deliberately associated in the same indictment the Socialist Prime Minister—even though the latter's long tenure of office had ceased twenty-seven months before the beginning of the war—and the military and political leaders of 1939–40. By so doing he laid bare the origins of his own access to power. The fury and the bitterness which Blum stirred up in men's hearts ultimately handed our whole national community over to class consciousness. Laval, Flandin, Bonnet could never have built up their following without Blum's name as a rallying cry against the Republic and against the nation. Never did politicians make use of a more overwhelming bugbear. Blum was the man of Stalin, and Stalin justified Hitler. Actually Blum hated the Communists and their alliance, but who cared to know?

Did Blum deserve this general condemnation? I had only recently met him at the house of the common friend who introduced him to Lord Halifax. Most of the 1920–40 politicians were scarcely pleasant company. Surely no one would ever have thought of entertaining them had not their government position made them temporarily interesting. But here was a man whose conversation was broad and subtle, a man of transparent honesty and charming manners. As a human being, he attracted one's respect and friendship.

His mistakes were heavy. They lose importance only in comparison with the crimes of his enemies. Let us make every allowance for circumstances: he was suddenly brought up short against incipient revolution, barely held under control, and a single misstep could perhaps have set flame to the tinder. The propertied classes were even more overawed than he was at the forces so close to breaking loose. Yet, granting all this, he cannot escape censure. He proved too submissive when confronted with the widespread social commotion unleashed by the mere prospect of his accession to office. The intellectual nobility which underlay everything he said made an impression on the working classes. It is greatly to their credit that they remained faithful so long to a man who could put up only by an obvious effort with the boisterous good fellowship of political gatherings. Could he not have used his moral ascendancy over the strikers to sidetrack those of their claims which were against the national interest? Doubtless his answer would be that the Communists kept stirring the masses and that he could not assuage them. He would point out that their support was nonetheless necessary and that, had he parted with them, the counterrevolution might have overflowed the dam. But there is no doubt that, through social reform clumsily copied from the American New Deal and applied on a massive scale, Blum, for two long years stultified our principal means of economic recovery—currency deflation. In their folly his predecessors had left it to him. He sterilized it. Two whole years lost! And at what a juncture in Europe's history! There is his failure.

When he became Head of the State at the age of sixty-seven he had to rid himself not only of doctrinaire socialism, but of a cumbersome underlying ideology. "My real vocation was to write books," he told a friend in the summer of 1935. I have glanced through his printed works —almost all published before 1914 (he was not elected to the Chamber until 1919). In *New Conversations of Goethe with Eckermann* (*Nouvelles Conversations de Goethe avec Eckermann*) my eye was caught by a passage running somewhat as follows: Humanity should be ruled by men who have the leisure to master the whole of human knowledge, who are endowed with the same synthetic view of the universe as Descartes or Leibnitz. But could anyone today encompass so much? Each pioneer of science slaves away in his own tight little cell and has no time left to look out of the window. Happily we have the critics. Their task is not to add to our knowledge of things visible or invisible. We should not expect from them such labors of the mind. Their job is to grasp and co-ordinate the findings of the research workers and artists scattered everywhere. They weld dispersed fragments together. They are born conductors of states and nations. . . . Thus did Léon Blum conceive the public man. He had to painfully gird himself whenever he felt that action had to be taken. He is the French Pythagoras. He believed that divine numbers rule the world.

He served as "Master of Petitions" in the Council of State—that judicial body which passes upon the technical aspects of proposed legislation and settles all legal differences arising between the State and private citizens. During the 1914-18 war he was chief of secretariat for the Minister of Public Works, a Socialist, Marcel Sembat. Reports drafted by him on cases of administrative law are considered models of their kind. Still, in the midst of hard, practical work, he kept on gazing at the stars, at pure ideas that no human contact can defile. "I don't like him," Marcel Proust once remarked. "He knows nothing of the mysteries of the human heart." He meant that Blum reveled in abstractions and that he did not fathom life to its true depths. He had been a disciple of Jean Jaurès, who was a magnificent force of nature at the rostrum but, according to Albert Thomas, utterly incapable even of taking the right streetcar if left to himself. Blum had spent the midnight hours in his youth in endless talk with Lucien Herr, another Socialist and librarian of the Ecole Normale Supérieure, who left the imprint of his thinking upon a whole generation of intellectuals and who was no better fitted than Blum to withstand the impact of day-to-day life. The story runs that Herr wanted to publish a magazine to expound his doctrine. As he could find no "angel" to back the project, he decided that the thing to do was to play the stock market—scientifically, of course, and after careful weighing of probabilities. He would lower himself to the point of courting Mammon, only to win the weapons wherewith Mammon could be brought low. Needless to say, the speculation went wrong. Blum is of the same breed.

He had a small apartment, furnished without a trace of luxury but in excellent taste, facing the Cathedral of Notre Dame on the Quai de Bourbon in the Isle of St.-Louis.[11] Here was a perfect setting for soli-

[11]Silly tales have been told of Blum's wealth and affluence. He and his three brothers had inherited a ribbon factory which had not been prospering for years. He even had to help

tary meditations and intimate conversations. He could provide a good talk all by himself. Within the orbit of his personality the aesthete, the scholar, the writer, the dilettante, the jurist, the statesman, the socialist shone in turn. Occasionally the prophet of Israel, aroused once by the Dreyfus affair and astir ever since, might break in. And the Greek sophist was always at hand.

For many years Léon Blum's superficial handling of international problems in his daily newspaper articles had disgruntled me. Even as late as 1934 neither he nor his party voted for national-defense appropriations. He was all for disarmament at the very moment when Germany was piecing together her war machine. He had already reversed his policy when I first met him. All the interviews he granted me centered upon diplomatic and military matters, with the single exception of one discussion of monetary problems in July 1936, when I was astounded to find him opposing devaluation. How well I remember his recurring lament: "Once again we've talked about nothing but the Army!" The implication was clear: what miserable times we live in!

I must admit that his mastery of international affairs impressed me. He kept abreast of all the reports of our representatives abroad. I remember his saying about Gamelin: "I'm afraid he is preparing for a 1914 war." General de Gaulle had already been or was shortly to be shown into the Premier's brown-walled study overlooking the Seine. Nor had he any illusions during his term of office on what Hitler was up to. He had fully grasped the meaning of the militarization of the Rhineland. Hitler's style of eloquence, in brutal denial of everything he held dear, contributed to his being speedily brought down to earth. Very likely if a Bismarck or a Bülow had been at the head of the German Government, he would have slumbered on much longer in his old prejudices. His awakening was thorough—very thorough. And he was courageous and patriotic enough not to attempt, for the sake of self-vindication, to formulate his new course in terms borrowed from the past. I have heard of this remark he made: "Only now do I understand the harm done our nation's best interests by the rebuff administered to Poincaré's policy in 1924."

I have already noted that in September 1936 he submitted to Parliament the largest armament budget ever proposed (fourteen billions), which earned him a subdued "well done" from Weygand in the *Revue des*

---

out the two brothers who ran it. Yet a total stranger asked him one day to lend his "famous silver plate" for an exhibition!

Deux Mondes.[12] Unfortunately, what was really needed was not so much appropriating vast sums of money for matériel as getting production lines moving. This matériel remained much too long in the blueprint stage. And, not to revert again to the question of the forty-hour week, the behavior of the Communists in the nationalized armament factories had something to do with the delay.

With the best intentions, Léon Blum miscalculated the timetable. He did not correctly appraise the significance of the fleeting hours. Either he thought war would come much later or else he underestimated the time France would require to catch up with the military strength of her enemy.

4

Laval Minister of Foreign Affairs: A Fatal Bifurcation

WHILE THE FRENCH were very nearly coming to blows over internal affairs, Germany rearmed. She started from what was almost a clean slate. Nor did she await Hitler's revolution of January 30, 1933, to set the ball rolling.

In July 1931, Chancellor Brüning came to Paris. Scarcely had he left Laval's office when I went in to learn what had passed between the two ministers. The Reich was feeling the full impact of the general collapse of world prices; its financial structure was threatened. "I offered the Chancellor the help of our gold reserve," the Premier told me, "on condition that, for ten years, no question as to Germany's eastern frontiers—rather ill protected under the Locarno treaties—should be raised. Brüning's unhesitating answer was that he would be swept out if he gave any such assurance!" The crisis which was shaking the world economy had diametrically different effects on France and Germany. It

---

[12]*Revue des Deux Mondes,* October 15, 1936. France's military position: "The parties hitherto most adverse to military expenditures and sacrifices have united with others to allocate huge credits to the Army and the Navy. Now the way is clear for the performance of a great task."

softened and paralyzed one nation; it hardened the other, attuned it to the fiercest preparations for war.

Hitler strove for dictatorship. The depression not only added to his followers; it set under way a stricter and stricter control over capital funds together with the regimentation of industry. When the Führer finally got the better of old Hindenburg he found already in control a governmental machine with totalitarian tendencies as well as a fully developed war doctrine. His great contribution was to supply the motive power—the one-party system and the compelling program expressed in the words: blood, soil, and *Lebensraum*. It amounted to a supremely explosive version of Pan-Germanism.

By no means was the Führer tempted to imitate the Lavals and the Flandins in their deflationary experiments, or even to borrow from Blum's "breathing spells." He laughed his own gold reserves to scorn. These had fallen, according to the published balance sheet of the Reichsbank, to less than one hundred million marks. What did it matter? He had resolved to apply his people's toil and wealth to the building up of Germany's military might. Within a few years the least attempt to hide ownership of foreign funds was to be made punishable by death. He reduced all civilian consumption to the utmost. In short he invested both the Reich's labor and working capital in the war effort. The currency degenerated into a mere system of chips and tokens. He aroused the populace to a frenzy of hatred against the 1918 victors and continuously fanned the flame.

All this was done at breakneck pace. When Hitler took over the reins of government the Versailles Treaty still stood firm upon its foundations. It is true that in July 1932 reparations had been thrown out of the window at the Lausanne Conference, as a result of the moratorium imposed from without by Mr. Hoover and the long-exerted British pressure. The disarmament clauses had been broken. As early as 1928, in connection with German arms shipped off to Hungary and discovered by Austrian railwaymen in the St. Gothard station, Briand had, in practice, brought to a halt the investigations which normally it would have been the function of the League of Nations' permanent military commission to conduct. He had meekly complied with Scialoja's suggestion that the Council should step in, substitute itself for the military commission, and, of course, bury the case. It was a portentous decision. Never afterward would a French Minister have the courage to lay before the international institution a bill of particulars on German rearmament. But, despite all this, the frontiers then in existence seemed strongly buttressed. The German High Command had not yet got beyond the stage of general planning and preliminary preparations, contrary to the belief of Pétain and Weygand as indicated by their public or private utterances in 1934.

On October 14, 1933, Hitler officially broke with the League of Nations, the Hague World Court, the Disarmament Conference, etc. Could anyone be deceived as to the meaning of this step? It gave notice that threats and blows were to rain fast and furious upon the established international order. According to the Geneva Covenant, no "member state" might be released from membership before fulfilling all its obligations. Was not this the moment to lay bare the facts of Germany's secret rearmament program? Sad to say, both Englishmen and Frenchmen in Mr. Henderson's private sitting room at the "Hôtel de la Paix" were frozen with fear. Hitler had nothing. His opponents could have crushed him, but they shivered and talked nonsense. For nearly six years this silly farce was to be repeated each time the Führer perpetrated a new outrage.

Why did France not make war until September 3, 1939, and then only because England took the lead? The German military machine achieved full strength only in 1938–39. In the autumn of 1939 Hitler still needed eight months to perfect his armored divisions. Why would the Paris Government not hear of a preventive war when Poland suggested it in 1933, knowing full well that her suggestion would be refused and thereby paving the way for her change of policy in a German direction? Why didn't our government have the courage, with England's support, to stop Mussolini short in 1935, to strike a blow which might have brought down the other dictator also? Why did it permit Germany to re-establish her armies along the Rhine in 1936? Why, four months later, did it allow the two totalitarian states something like a free hand in Spain, forgetting what had been a fundamental French policy since the days of Francis I and Charles V? Later, in 1937 and 1938, our military superiority was on the wane and there was no obvious choice of the most opportune or of the least inopportune moment. But why had we suffered so long in silence, stood with folded arms while the balance of military power was reversed? Between 1933 and 1936 Germany was weak, yet at a glance one could see that she was making herself ready for battle. Why, then, let the peril grow to formidable size? It is a scandal that in the closing days of August 1939 France should have had to make the choice between war and the loss of her independence as a nation. Probably the 1914 war was inevitable, given the then existing distribution of material power. But of all the wars ever inflicted upon us, that which at last broke out in 1939–40 could the most easily have been forestalled while it was hatching, say in 1936–37.

The explanation of this dire and stupid performance lies in the doings and characters of Pierre Laval, Pierre-Etienne Flandin, and Georges Bonnet. These three men made use of all the elements they found around them—the confusion of the French people caused by internal upheavals, their being split into two hostile factions, the worries of the well-to-do huddled over their fortunes, the resentment of the industrialists, the passionate desire of the newly rich to hang onto their quick-gotten gains of the 1920–30 era, the poverty of the working classes, the hatred of war and the war weariness which sprang from the slaughter of the preceding generation. They concocted a policy which amounted to a total submission to the National Socialist and Fascist dictatorships.

They were helped by the constantly decaying Franco-British Entente Cordiale, by the hostile feelings which the London and Washington governments, from 1919 on, constantly displayed at what it pleased them to call "French imperialism." To hear the bankers of the "City" and of Wall Street talk, you might easily have supposed that France, by her refusal to reduce her Army to the dimensions of a mere police force, stood in the way of a permanent continental peace. In a famous epigram Lord Tyrrell neatly summed up this tragic folly: "It was our trifling error to take the Germans for Englishmen and the French for Germans!"

It was against all reason and common sense. Four great empires had fallen: the Germany of the Hohenzollerns, the Austria-Hungary of the Hapsburgs, the Russia of the Romanovs, the Turkey of the sultans. Upon their ruins jerry-built national states were painfully groping for stability. And British and American statesmen failed to understand that these newly redeemed countries, these freshly won liberties could not survive and be turned into permanent structures unless they were manfully bolstered up against the eagerness of the vanquished for revenge. Today everyone can see that France, a middle-class nation, quite apart from the question of her numerical and territorial status, has little natural gift for imperial domination, and that she was going against her natural bent in trying to consolidate the fluid materials let loose by the destruction of the great imperial fabrics. She now lies prostrate. Look at her; compare her to her conqueror. Do you see any—even remote—resemblance on the score of brutal expansion?

The names of Louis XIV and Napoleon are sometimes flung in our faces. Those monarchs betoken a passing exuberance of French power. The great emperor's unstable conquests, like the swollen torrents of some desert river which overnight becomes a flood of waters, only to shrink back again into a shallow brooklet, resulted from the coexistence of an extraordinary military and political genius and of a very special and fugitive dynamic impulse largely accounted for by the discovery and monopoly of the democratic idea. Here is nothing which can bear comparison with the organic imperialism of the German mass, born of geography and history (and all the harder to check for that reason), arising from the juxtaposition of industrious, disciplined German peoples and of great Slav hordes with their shaky national shapes, ruled for the most part by foreign masters and wont to attract the Western conqueror as the clay does the potter. This simile holds good to this point and no further, for the Germans never fulfilled what they call their historic mission during those centuries when they seemingly had everything their own way in the borderlands of the East. They subdued, absorbed, or destroyed the national states of Prague and Warsaw. For generations they held a controlling position at St. Petersburg. But only to find out, during the nineteenth and early twentieth centuries, that the passion for independence had grown all the more eager and stubborn in the hearts of so many direct and indirect subjects, that the minute the Hapsburg or Hohenzollern master began to reel, Lazarus came forth from his vault.

It has always surprised me that the word "Pan-Germanism," which points to the main cause of European instability in the last half century, never became truly current in the vocabularies of English and American students of politics. Take as an instance the *Memoirs* of Lord Grey of Fallodon, British Foreign Secretary from December 1905 to December 1916—eleven years. Not once will you come across the term. And yet in September 1908, with the annexation of Bosnia and Herzegovina, there began that war which has lasted thirty-six years to date and which now encompasses the whole world. In all there were two unequal intervals of superficial peace, totaling twenty-seven years—six years before the first war and twenty-one between the defeat of William II and Hitler's cataclysm. Despite the peaceable relations maintained by the chancelleries during these two periods, the truth is that, deep down, the fight never ceased.

France's duty, in the early twenties, was to put a stop to it once and for all and, for that purpose, to take full advantage of the victory of the "Allied and Associated Powers." Under Millerand and Poincaré she bent her back to the task, but it was a task not to her liking. In the past, to safeguard her interests, all she needed was to play a game of balance with three or four other great powers. But from now on, with Russia being either hostile or playing a lone hand, and with England governed more often than not by dreamers and amateurs, France's job was to weld the small states, however unsecurely established, into a coalition eventually able to keep in restraint a resurgent Germany, in the hope that, sooner or later, London would join. The Anglo-Saxon world, yearning to reopen its former channels of foreign trade, to reconstruct what it called its own "devastated areas," taxed its ingenuity to dishearten us. To recover her prewar markets, England more or less unwittingly worked for the re-emergence of prewar political Europe. She strove to bring about a "balance of power."

We have already seen how the new Radical-Socialist leaders were of all men the worst equipped to properly understand what had to be done. The average Frenchman was congenitally reluctant to assume so many responsibilities, to sustain such expenditures, effort, realism. He voted against Poincaré in the 1924 elections. How much more pleasant to look at was the sort of international parliament which obtained in Geneva! There the French senators and deputies included in governmental delegations to the League of Nations found themselves in familiar surroundings. How much more pleasant the prospects of everlasting peace implied by the Covenant, the Locarno treaties (which amounted to England acting the praetor without lictors, axes, or rods), the Kellogg-Briand Pact, the blissful ease of the Dawes and Young plans! For comfort's sake alone, the French people acquiesced in the policy of convenience whose triple motto was "disarmament, arbitration, security." Moreover, Frenchmen would say, since the British and Americans had abjured all policy based on force, had our nation sufficient strength, by itself alone, to enforce any such policy? In the spring of 1929, only a few months before he was returned to office, Ramsay MacDonald, at the invitation of an Anglo-German society, spoke in the Chamber of the Reichstag. He offered his listeners a pathetic assurance: England would never unsheathe her sword in defense of the Versailles Treaty. In the front row of seats, immediately beneath the speaker, sat the counselor of the British Embassy, with tears in his eyes. How could anyone doubt what the British course would be in an emergency?

Between 1931 and 1935, French diplomacy had to reckon with the possibility of an Anglo-German agreement on the reduction of armaments. On June 18, 1935, Sir John Simon's last official act at the Foreign

Office was to conclude a naval convention with Berlin, of which the Paris Government had no knowledge until the last moment and against which its objections were of no avail.[1] Nevertheless, on February 2, only four months earlier, frightened at the National Socialist Government's break with Geneva, the Paris and London cabinets had worked out a joint plan of peace consolidation which was submitted to the Führer. Since Hitler's only reply had been to incorporate into the Reichswehr, on March 9, air forces which Germany was forbidden to possess, to proclaim, on March 16, his will to rearm, in infringement of the Versailles Treaty, and to order universal military training, they should, at least, have stuck together. Sir John Simon's behavior, in the juncture, was paralleled by that of Laval a few months later.[2] With some shadow of reason, the French Minister could claim that in the Abyssinian affair he was paying back our friends in their own coin. Meanwhile, between 1924 and 1929, British and American capital, drawn by high interest rates, had poured into the German economy, making possible a complete renovation of industrial equipment—the equivalent, according to the commission of experts set up at Basle, to twenty-five billion marks, as against less than fifteen billion paid in reparations. What a wealth of arguments made available to those who were urging France to pull in her horns!

When Laval took over the Ministry of Foreign Affairs, on October 13, 1934, the French were not only divided among themselves, which practically gave him at the outset a free hand for gradually parting with a policy of resistance; an added factor was that no deeply rooted diplomatic tradition held sway to keep him within bounds. Ever since Her-

---

[1] And afterward Paris knew only a portion of what had been agreed. Even when the negotiations were completed Sir Robert Vansittart had to admit to M. Corbin that he was not at liberty to inform him of the naval building program allowed to Germany. Berlin had exacted a promise of secrecy.

[2] During the course of the London discussions (January 30–February 2) between Mac-Donald, Simon, Flandin, and Laval, someone inquired, "Supposing Germany were to reject our settlement, what would we do then?" "If we are to think that, under such circumstances, the scheme is null and void," observed Sir Robert Vansittart, "then it would have been better that we had never met at all." French and German armaments were the main issue. Somewhat earlier, in October 1933, after Germany had cleared out of the League of Nations, a Franco-British plan similar to that of February 1935 had been thrown overboard by the British Cabinet, which was frightened at the very idea of arousing the Reich Chancellor's irritation. It had preferred to negotiate separately with Berlin, which provoked France's refusal, on April 17, 1934, of the dangerous compromise Hitler was not unwilling to concede. Speaking in Geneva, Barthou, in substance, said to Sir John Simon: "Don't do it again!" Baldwin took offense at his words. When Barthou went to London in July 1934, to talk over the eventual treaty with Russia, Baldwin's first gesture was to refuse an invitation to dine with the French Minister. In January 1935, Flandin and Laval, both bitter critics of the April 17 note, tried to bring things back where they stood before.

riot's term at the Quai d'Orsay in 1924 and since that of Briand (who followed Herriot in 1925), the fundamental impulse of our diplomacy—to counter any power which sought to win hegemony over Europe by a coalition strong enough to ward it off—had seriously given way to the shortsighted opportunism practiced in Geneva. The Four Power Treaty of June 16, 1933, proposed by Mussolini, the contemplated foundation of what was dubbed the "sausage makers' club" (because the smaller countries were seemingly to be tossed to Germany as propitiatory victims), was but one of our surrenders. A futile surrender, indeed: it was enough that the advantages to be granted to Germany should be made to depend upon the conclusion of bargaining agreements and the observation of normal diplomatic procedure for the Führer to scorn our gift. From 1924 to 1934, under pressure from London and Washington, the decay of French diplomacy kept step with the decay of our Army. Here lies the very heavy share of responsibility to be borne by England and America for the separate armistice, the French counterrevolution, and Pétain's accession to power.

Of course, by the time Doumergue placed Barthou's mantle on Laval's shoulders, the London and Washington governments no longer viewed European affairs with the eyes of Mr. MacDonald, Sir John Simon, or Herbert Hoover. They were beginning to see that the French Army was their own first line of defense and that they had more to fear from its debility than from its strength.

As early as the spring of 1933 Mr. Norman Davis declared in Geneva that the United States would no longer insist upon the principle of the freedom of the seas, a shibboleth which had allowed England to shirk implementing her duties against an eventual aggressor as defined under the Covenant of the League of Nations. Already there were unmistakable portents of Mr. Roosevelt's clarity of vision, courage, great foresight. Already, in March 1933, I could hardly believe my ears when, in Washington, Mr. William Bullitt told me: "If you don't destroy German armaments, even at the cost of going to war, France is lost!" In July 1934, Mr. Baldwin assured Barthou that, in case of war, England might be expected to take her place by France's side. However slow it was in coming, one could have seen that reversal. And, to the experienced observer, Simon's incongruous about-face, in the spring of 1935, partook of the nature of an accident which hardly affects the ulterior course of affairs. Indeed, in the days after June 18, so keen was the uneasiness caused in London by the French reaction to the naval treaty that an immediate tightening of the bonds between Great Britain and

France was deemed possible by M. Corbin. But the French Ambassador had no authority to follow up any overture.

It was only natural that Laval, having passed through that experience, should owe the London Cabinet a grudge. But he never ought to have overlooked the fact that British interests and ours stood together and that we had no choice as to policy. And when Mr. Baldwin, Sir Samuel Hoare, and Mr. Anthony Eden, dislodged from their worthless international schemes by Italy's inrush into Abyssinia, held out their hands to us and, in return for French co-operation in the Mediterranean, proposed, on September 24, 1935, to seriously discuss the problem of the demilitarized Rhineland; when, early in October, the countries represented at Geneva backed up the two Western Powers in order to punish the fascist outrage against the law of nations, we really could not afford to hesitate. We should have made capital use of our grievances, not to justify a refusal, but to exact full measure. Never had we dared hope that the League of Nations might engender a coalition. Yet, on the Geneva stage, in the twinkling of an eye, a coalition was drawing together against a feeble and isolated Italy. Louis Barthou, who had devoted all the eight months of his tenure of office in 1934 to winding up the Disarmament Conference, the impediment which delayed France's military reorganization, to separating Russia from Germany, to bringing England back to her senses, would have looked upon the Abyssinian adventure as a godsend. But Barthou was no longer there. The revolver which Mussolini had loaded was well aimed: Barthou had been struck down. Laval, the arbiter of our foreign relations, not only did not bother to exploit a state of affairs so favorable to the long-awaited cementing of the French continental system, he set himself to destroy its loose constituent parts which it was his duty to piece together.[3] At a luncheon given for Wickham Steed on April 8, 1940, at the Foreign Policy Center in the Rue de Varenne, Henri Moysset, a Pétain Minister in 1941, singled out one of Laval's friends and cried in scorn, "The High Court! The High Court!" He did not exaggerate.

What was the guilt of Laval in 1934–35? Briefly this: Mussolini's complicity in the Marseilles assassination could easily be traced. He was not yet tied up to Hitler; relations between them had been strained by the bloody business at the Vienna Ball Platz. He was the protector and the host of Dollfuss. If I am not mistaken, Frau Dollfuss was visiting him on

---

[3] At a luncheon given at the British Embassy in Paris (about December 6, 1935) in honor of Sir Samuel Hoare, with Gamelin and Weygand among the guests, Laval was heard to exclaim, "To hell with the League of Nations, and especially with its officials!"

the very day when the Austrian chancellor was put to death. The Duce was loathed by the Little Entente and the Balkan Entente; for six years he had unceasingly called for a revision of frontiers. He was cut off from everyone. At last, was not this the time to shove him aside and do away with him? Laval thought otherwise. He hindered and obstructed the action taken in Geneva by Yugoslavia with the support of the Little Entente. He likewise stifled the trial of the murderers in the Aix-en-Provence Assize Court, forcing Queen Marie to forego her right to be a party to the proceedings and silencing the lawyer she had retained, Paul-Boncour. His one idea was to earn the despot's gratitude.

Heedless of all warnings, he insisted on going to Rome, and the famous French-Italian agreements were signed on January 7, 1935. A great day for him, he obviously thought! He prided himself on having committed the Duce to the maintenance of Austrian independence and on having enlisted him against Germany, especially for the supervision of her armaments.[4] But there was a flaw in the arrangement. To score his success—his specious success—Laval had not dared insist on the fulfillment of a prerequisite condition, without which the contract bade fair to be worthless—the squaring of long-standing accounts between Italy and Yugoslavia. His advisers had repeatedly explained to him that the key to a true understanding with Rome was there and not elsewhere. Who could deny that Italy would not be able to uphold Austria so long as her right flank was exposed to an attack by Yugoslavia? Who could forget that in July 1934, when Mussolini planned to pour his troops over the Brenner to avenge Dollfuss, King Alexander I had put him on notice that, in such an event, his own army would at once move into Austria? With an inimical Yugoslavia threatening her north of the Adriatic, Italy was not in position to ever move against Germany. All Laval had in his pocket was a scrap of paper. Did he mind so much? He had his own idea about Mussolini's usefulness in German affairs.

The fact not much to be doubted is that Laval, to make a start, handed over Abyssinia to the Fascist dictator. Mussolini says so himself in the correspondence already mentioned,[5] as does General de Bono,[6] who, on January 8, took ship at Naples for Eritrea, just as though he had

[4]By 1935 the Disarmament Conference had shrunk to a mere shadow. The plan under consideration was to submit to Germany a table of European armaments, on which all would have agreed beforehand, and to summon her to abide by it. Such was the object of the February conference in London, already alluded to. It was the sequel of the meeting at Rome.

[5]See pages 158-59.

[6]In a book on the Abyssinian war which he published in 1936.

waited until Laval signed the blank check. The French Minister has tried to wriggle out of this by insisting that he never did anything in violation of existing treaties. This is true of his official acts. But the two men had several private talks, one on January 7 at the Venezia Palace, the others in quiet corners while officials were ironing out details. And their respective testimonies as to what they said to each other during these several asides do not coincide. At any rate, in Geneva, Laval tampered with the enforcement of Article 16 of the Covenant against the Italian aggressor. As French delegate, his proper concern was to bring Article 16 to bear as promptly and energetically as possible, so that it might later be applied against Germany. Actually Laval slackened, enervated, impeded sanctions. Endlessly he protested against the mobilization of the Home Fleet, pleading that this left the Geneva Council uncommitted, since it was carried out solely on British initiative. He rejected Titulescu's theory that the League's Covenant permitted and even encouraged an automatic and instant reaction against the aggressor on the part of each member state. When the uncompromising language of the British obliged him to promise the use of French naval and air bases on the Mediterranean should the Fascists unleash the dogs of war (October 26), he instructed his military negotiators to whittle this forcibly obtained concession down to nothing.[7] And, at the very moment that he gave an impression of joining in the use of economic restraints, he was arranging with Rome to dull their edges. He was against broadening the rather feeble blockade to include petroleum. Sir Samuel Hoare, upon his arrival in Paris at the beginning of December, consulted with two French friends who hailed from utterly different schools of thought. Both agreed that Laval would betray him if ever England and Italy came to blows. Here was surely the meaning underlying Mr. Baldwin's remarks in the House of Commons, "If my lips were not sealed . . ." On December 7 the foreign secretary could see no way out except to yield to Laval's terms. And all these contrivances took place when Hitler was manifestly preparing to reoccupy the Rhineland, when the closest collaboration with London was imperatively needed. But Laval had already made up his mind about the remilitarization of the Rhine. Secretly, and against the advice of the permanent staff of the Quai d'Orsay, he received Ribbentrop in December. He fostered meet-

[7]On December 28, 1935, Commander Auphan, whom Darlan appointed to command the French fleet in 1941, told me: "Between the October 26 undertaking and its fulfillment, we always interpose lengthy intervals supposedly needed for our mobilization." On October 31, Auphan had been even more explicit: "We are ordered to make a policy of lying. Let's say outright yes or no. Let's not keep saying yes, only to go back on our word afterward."

ings between French and German veterans—and among the leaders of the French contingent there were several men of ill repute. He sent Montigny to Berlin.

He would have none of Turkey's advances and didn't mince words about it. The government of Ankara belonged to the Balkan alliance and wanted to have a pact of diplomatic solidarity with France similar to those we had entered into with Yugoslavia and Rumania. "You can win over the Turks with a slice of bread," Nicholas Titulescu kept telling Laval. "Later on the price will be much higher." It was Laval's belief that to retain our allies and to win new associates was to throw the gauntlet at Italy and Germany. On April 7, 1939, the day after the Italians marched into Albania, M. Saracoglou was to say to the French Ambassador, "It is M. Laval we have to thank for what has happened."

In Rome, when coming to an agreement with Mussolini over Austria, Laval had ridden roughshod over the Little Entente and the Balkan Entente. For the allies and friends who had built up those two systems with our encouragement, vital interests were at stake: they were practically told they had better obtain from Mussolini, their archenemy, whatever guarantee they could. And at Stresa, in April 1935, without even giving a thought to these associates of ours, Laval freed Hungary of the military clauses of the Trianon Treaty. But in this case he soon had to retrace his steps.

It had been understood that, in conformity with the Covenant, the Geneva powers would mutually indemnify one another for any economic losses arising from the application of Article 16 to Italy. Scornfully, Laval offered to add eleven horses to French imports from Yugoslavia.

At Warsaw, Belgrade, Bucharest, he treated as foes all those who wished to base their nation's policy on an understanding with France. He loathed Titulescu's extraordinary clarity of vision and utter frankness. In Colonel Beck he saw a man after his own heart. Nor was he unaware of what sort of fellow this colonel had shown himself to be,[8] or of what he had in mind for the future. In December 1935, Marshal Smigly-Rydz and General Sosnkowski, inspector general of the Army, were doing their best to obtain Beck's removal in the interests of the friendship with France. Laval rescued the threatened politician by sending a clean bill of health to Warsaw.

---

[8] As Minister of War in 1923, Barthou ordered Beck, then military attaché to the Polish Embassy, to be expelled from French territory. The General Staff, tipped off by the Czechs, had sent a decoy to see the colonel. Beck pocketed the bank notes offered him as a reward for turning over documents relating to the French Army.

After endless wavering the Minister, on May 2, 1935, signed the treaty with Russia, negotiations for which had been begun by Paul-Boncour and Barthou. Going a long way beyond the idea which the Quai d'Orsay had in mind—an eastern Locarno encumbered with checks and balances —Laval had pushed on to a bilateral agreement, to an alliance.

Laval, indeed, had taken care to immerse it in the phraseology of the Geneva Covenant, and, therefore, possibilities of evasion were numerous. But definite obligations were there, and apparently Laval took them so seriously that a fortnight later, in a telegram sent to Flandin from Moscow, he mentioned joint studies by the two general staffs among the points discussed with Stalin. With all that, before leaving the Soviet capital he tried to arrange a brief interview with Hitler on his way home, and as early as July 3 he passed the word to newspapermen that they should start campaigning against the U.S.S.R.: "It has not taken it long to betray us!" He postponed indefinitely any ratification of the instrument he had signed. It looked as if he had come to terms with Russia only to be able to make a better bargain with the Führer.[9]

It is open to anyone to judge for himself what survived of France's authority, of her ability to keep or to win friends or allies after such a series of misdeeds, on the very eve of the German reflux into the Rhineland.

How did Laval dig out of his mind and his heart this policy against all reason, a policy for which you can find no equivalent in all the ages of our history? The man is a depraved peasant. In him the harsh meanness of the tiller of the soil, who busies himself with increasing his acres, has been perverted into the lust for money and the means of satisfying that lust—political power. He was first elected to the Chamber of Deputies in June 1914; throughout the last war he set himself up as a Socialist of the Kienthal and Zimmerwald school. In the secret sitting, on June 1, 1917, he expatiated on the military mutinies of the previous weeks and threatened the Ribot Cabinet with an uprising of soldiers and workers

[9] On November 29, 1935, Gamelin waxed indignant over Laval's utterances concerning negotiations with Germany at a meeting of the Permanent National Defense Committee held five days earlier. "I couldn't sleep a wink. . . . He is betraying the Soviets!" But the trickster had outsmarted himself. One episode of the Stalin-Laval conversations was heavy with consequences. Stalin had expressed a hope that the French Army would be strengthened; Laval replied that French Communists had long done all they could to thwart our national defense. Since Stalin himself condemned their behavior, Laval got him to make a public statement. Had it not been for this statement, the Popular Front of July 14, 1935, would never have been possible. The Communists having reversed themselves on the question of the military budget, the abyss which had held Radical-Socialists and Socialists apart from the Communists was bridged over. Laval must often have regretted this Moscow achievement.

if peace was not shortly made. Six months later he was perfectly willing to serve as Clemenceau's agent, receiving his hire from the secret funds for his sly work, sniffing around the revolutionary gang. In his law practice he sold the political pull at his disposal. His hoard grew fatter. From a dingy apartment on the Boulevard St. Martin he moved to the Champs Elysées. He had sources of income other than the bar—and the bar, as we have seen, included, in his case, all sorts of shady dealings. Pierre-Etienne Flandin once described to me one of Laval's transactions; it involved by turns a banker, a newspaper (*Le Lyon Républicain*), and M. Raymond Pâtenotre, whose ambition centered upon an under secretaryship of state. It paid a profit of two millions, whereas, but for the under secretaryship thrown into the bargain, a loss of three millions would have had to be written off. Ministerial influence had turned the scale. In 1934, Flandin set his colleague's fortune at some forty million francs. *Nouveau riche* in his beliefs, his instincts, his feelings, he could not but translate them into political action. He had worked it all out: in the May 1936 elections he would sweep the country with the cry that a Franco-German settlement must be reached and the currency's gold content retained, despite everybody and everything. He kept repeating: "No decree of mine will ever mobilize the Army or devaluate the franc." And he quite literally meant what he said.

Of all men he was the least prepared to understand Hitler's dynamic power. About Europe, England, Germany, Italy—not to mention countries at greater distances—he knew nothing. While he was staying in Rome, in January 1935, he asked François Charles-Roux, before going to the Vatican, "What's the Pope's name?" The Ambassador mistakenly assumed that the pontiff's family name was what he wanted. Not at all. He simply didn't know that Pius XI was the head of the Church. What is more, he could not get rid of the impression that Pius was the direct successor of Leo XIII.

Laval thought that the Duce would be satisfied with the gifts he bore him, that he could deal with the dictator as he was wont to do with some corrupt journalists or legislators. His ingrained pandering to the lower instincts of men made of him the Robert Walpole of the rabble. The worst was that such practice warped his whole outlook on the world.

By contrast, he loved his home, was devoted to his wife—a prudent, shrewd woman with plenty of common sense, except in diplomacy— and his daughter, who was a lady of fashion and knew how to make advantageous friendships.[10] Able, bold, strong-willed, with a taste for unlimited power, true Asiatic cunning, and a sense of police methods in the spheres of government, such was Laval as I saw him.[11] My acquaintance with him dates back to 1931, the time of his first premiership. He impressed me by his blunt, direct, unadorned manner of speech. He bore the appearance of one who tried to evolve a practical policy, impervious to established doctrines and current formulas. He must not have thought too ill of our acquaintanceship, since he telephoned me on November 13, 1934, a half hour after he had moved again into the Foreign Office. For nearly a whole month on end I tried to fathom his mind, since I did not wish to criticize him unfairly. On December 10, I broke with him after a semipublic controversy at which he let slip disturbing words, and in deference to some whose duties enabled them to keep a close watch.[12]

[10]She is René de Chambrun's wife. All credit is due to the head of the family, the marquis, a patriot, imbued with the liberal tradition, courageous. But the two brothers—the general and the ambassador—played shabby parts during the last period of the Republic. The general, in command of a sector around Fez in 1925, was to blame for the spreading of Abd-el-Krim's rebellion—if Weygand is to be believed. The latter added that, despite this blot on his record, Chambrun succeeded in getting himself appointed commander of the division at Tunis and then of the army corps at Bordeaux, so large was his following, both Left and Right, among members of Parliament. He exerted himself to be given the command of an army in time of war, but Weygand put a stop to that, and for this General de Chambrun tried all the more strenuously to worm himself into Pétain's favor. He could not do without a highly placed military protector. As for Charles de Chambrun, our Ambassador to Rome, the officials at the Quai d'Orsay regarded him as the hireling of Laval. Fawning upon every breed of politician, he dared tell Léon Blum that Mussolini was delighted when the Popular Front took office. Blum, out of all patience, had him recalled. There is some ground for the belief that Charles de Chambrun was not entirely unconnected with the difficulties raised in Rome over the credentials of M. de Saint-Quentin, his successor. In these credentials the imperial title assumed by the King of Italy had been purposely ignored. General de Chambrun's shadow would seem to loom large at the source of Pétain's connection with Laval. The general is José Laval's father-in-law.

[11]Here is a specimen of Laval's parliamentary machinations. Toward the end of December 1935, having to steer his course through a dangerous debate in the House, and feeling doubtful about the issue, he himself made and had others make threats against Chautemps in relation to the Stavisky scandal. Laval held Chautemps to account for the votes of some wavering Radical-Socialist deputies. The state's attorney, Fernand Roux, worked a hostile reference to Chautemps into his indictment.

[12]By "breaking" with Laval I mean that I did not want further appointments. To perform my work I relied on what I could find of his deeds and words in the day-to-day reports of my assistant. Let it be said, incidentally, that he tried to buy this friend, a well-informed and diligent man who repulsed him to his own loss. "Breaking" with Laval also meant that I no longer accepted without careful checking any information or statements which originated from him. He thereupon flew into a rage. From the prefect of police came the warning that, upon Laval's instructions, I was being shadowed. I nonetheless was able to go on describing diplomatic events and Laval's political management. I later learned that, toward

5

Flandin and Bonnet. Bonnet's Ruthless Sabotaging of the Policy of Resistance to Germany Results in Its Being Carried Out under the Worst Possible Conditions

FLANDIN AND BONNET finally made it impossible for France to follow a strong, reasoned, foresighted policy. They handed our country over to the mercies of Hitler and Mussolini. They set it tossing on the waves. Different from Laval though they were, they completed his work.

Flandin is what people often describe as a "grand bourgeois," the equivalent of these "new men" trained in business and politics, who, in the Roman Republic, superseded the old nobility. He belongs to a family which basked in the sunshine of public honors. His father, once attorney-general in Algiers and then a senator, was appointed by Clemenceau as resident general in Tunis in reward for services rendered at the "Haute Cour" trial of L. J. Malvy, the Minister charged with dereliction of duty in wartime.[1] He was first cousin of the two Ribières, one of them a treasury official, the other, Master of Petitions in the Council of State and Poincaré's chief of secretariat during that great man's last years in office. A "grand bourgeois"! He was more than six feet tall and was astoundingly bold in harmonizing his profession as a lawyer, his useful-

---

the middle of December 1934, Laval countenanced the negotiation of a press, or "moral disarmament" pact with Germany. Dr. Aschmann, head of the Press Department at the Wilhelmstrasse, came to Paris. The officials of the Quai d'Orsay pointed out to him how out of tune with French political circumstances were his plans. Ribbentrop and Von Lersner put in an appearance either shortly before or after him, the former calling upon Laval unbeknown to the permanent staff. Brinon announced in *Le Matin* the impending arrival of Rudolf Hess. Plainly, Laval had very special reasons for being impatient with all peepers.

On November 3, 1935, shortly after I had published an article which disclosed Beck's 1923 misadventure, Laval, without the approval of the Cabinet, issued a decree extending to Prime Ministers and Foreign Ministers the protection afforded by press laws to the heads of foreign states.

[1] When Malvy received a full pardon in 1925 he came back to the Chamber of Deputies. Flandin apologized to him for his own father's action.

ness to financial and commercial corporations, and his parliamentary and cabinet position. Attacked in the Chamber for having retained his connection with the Compagnie Aeropostale even after he had become a Minister, he defended himself with complete cynicism. He hardly took the trouble to refute the charges. He haughtily cast analogous accusations upon those who had sought to run him down. His fellow deputies refused to make an issue of it.

Flandin's style of public speaking was frigid and disdainful. In debate he affected the manner of the businessman who has no time to waste on sheer oratory. I never ceased to be amazed at the effect wrought on Parliament by his numerous financial discourses, a pretentious display of technical pronouncements which could catch only the unwary. This remark of Flandin's brother, a well-known physician, which was reported to me, sounds like final judgment: "I can testify that ever since he entered politics—and he was pretty young when he did—he has never bothered to read a serious book." In short, Flandin was a fraud. Between 1931 and 1937 he put on "English" airs, to use a current expression. To the average run of deputies Flandin was a fellow "who had his personal laundry done in London," was very well connected there, had explored the secrets of Downing Street. Even Pierre Laval was so impressed by what seemed to be his Premier's sure foothold in England that when he went with him to MacDonald's and Baldwin's capital, toward the end of January 1935, he refused to take any evening clothes; he was determined not to accept invitations from a society in which, alongside so egregious a "gentleman," he would surely suffer from a feeling of inferiority. The fact is that, in London, Flandin had access to only one private house, and it is questionable whether his status there was one of friendship or mere acquaintance. In any case, he would go to England once a year for the hunting season, dressed up like some Tartarin familiar with the tailors of Savile Row. Of English political and social personages Flandin knew only those whom he met at the dinner table of his single British friend—apart from Becky Sharp, whose acquaintance we made at the Elysée and whose intrigues influenced him, at times, beyond reason.

With Georges Bonnet we are back among the limbs of the law. Laval was dextrous, tenacious, quick to act. Flandin had self-possession and audacity bordering on effrontery. But, looking back, my only recollection of Georges Bonnet is the long, sharp profile. I feel as if I had never looked him in the face. And morally I can see him only in an oblique position, moving slantingly between the most contradictory ideas. Whatever he might be saying, his personality was such as to leave no doubt of his congenital inaptitude to follow any line except that of least resistance. He was industrious and hard-working. Georges Mandel used to tell me that he was a born lobbyist and, as a deputy, had few equals in the art of keeping the favors of his constituency by patient attention to detail. Like Léon Blum, he had served in the "Council of State." Hence his real knowledge of the law and the management of public affairs, a knowledge which, in his case, did not make for statesmanship but for mere trickery. He had neither Flandin's loudmouthed if fleeting convictions nor the specious realism which gave consistency to Laval's career. He was rather a weak imitation of Chautemps, like him a Radical-Socialist of conservative leanings, but endowed with a veneer of doctrinal orthodoxy picked up in the Masonic lodges. Behind the screen of his day-to-day contrivances he was so fainthearted that he could be caught in the act of flagrant lying. One may form an idea of his duplicity from this fact alone: on April 7, 1938, he accepted the portfolio of foreign affairs from Daladier with a firm promise that he would follow, as regards Czechoslovakia, a policy repellent to his own convictions.

Pierre-Etienne Flandin is the Minister who lost the Rhine, who did not avail himself of the rights which the Rhineland Pact of Locarno conferred on France and of the residue of military superiority we still retained to deal Hitler's regime a blow from which it might not have recovered. He allowed the new Reichswehr to reoccupy its old strategic springboards. The defections among our allies and associates, already begun during Laval's term of office, became under him even more open and precipitate. The legacies of Laval's mismanagement were tragic. However, a few moments of courage could still have salvaged the Versailles Treaty! According to the best-informed German sources, we should not even have had to translate our words into acts. All the mistakes of the past could have been redeemed without striking a blow. Had some divinely wise power been ruling France and had it stuck to the principle of the economy of means, it might have waited until March 7, 1936, before taking a decisive stand but, on that day, would have forced the issue.

That evening everything was quickly settled at an informal political and military council hastily gathered in Flandin's office at the Quai d'Orsay. Prime Minister Sarraut, General Maurin (War), Piétri (Navy), Déat (Air), Mandel (Colonies), were there; also General Gamelin, Admiral Durand Viel, and Alexis Léger. The last of these had just had a long talk with Gamelin and found him ready to assume the military responsibility implicit in firm action—the seizure of the Saar district. Flandin accurately stated the case and the drastic initiative for which it called. But the ministers in charge of our armed forces, over the heads of their general staffs, at once took exception to his proposal. They cudgeled their wits to throw spokes in the wheels. "Suppose," said Maurin, "we were to mobilize the troops and nothing happened: how embarrassing to have to keep these men under the colors! Look at the British in the Mediterranean! They don't know what to do with their Home Fleet, at battle strength since September!" Piétri pleaded that the decision suggested was dangerous, that it might lead to war, that peaceful methods were still very far from having been exhausted. Déat, who arrived late, had less to say than the others, for the trend was already patent.[2] Flandin took note of the disagreement and, without so much as turning a hair, drew the conclusion that the matter had better be dropped. At the full sitting of the Cabinet the Minister of Foreign Affairs was to assume the same attitude of personal unconcern. At the very last minute, before his chief left to attend the meeting, Léger once more implored him not to give in or let his colleagues disapprove of the needed counterstroke, for the secretary-general knew all too well what would be the consequences of backing down, both for France and for Europe. "Don't worry. I am going to renew my 'recommendation.'" Then, glancing ironically at the permanent official, he added, "Aren't you afraid they will lose their nerve?" "Ultimately, all depends on the Minister of Foreign Affairs," Alexis Léger replied. In the end Sarraut and Mandel found themselves alone in their advocacy of resistance.[3]

Subsequently, Flandin boasted that he had won for France a compensating advantage, canceling out the fresh strength yielded to Nazi military might: this was the alliance with England, which came off in November and December, after being worked out at the conference held in London during the greater part of March. But, considering the

[2]In the April–May 1936 elections Déat was a Popular Front candidate in a Paris constituency. At the first ballot (where no absolute majority was secured by anyone), he was outdistanced by his Communist competitors. Unwilling to abide by the rule of the Popular Front, he insisted on standing for the second ballot. He was defeated. No choice was left him but to break with the Popular Front. Later on he was elected at Angoulême on an anti-Communist platform. Thus his pro-German feelings are explained by a rebuff at the polls.

[3]Sarraut has been much criticized for an expression which he used in a radio speech, Strasbourg falling within the range of German guns if the Rhineland ceased to be "demilitarized." It was taken from one of François-Poncet's dispatches, and the wording, requested of the permanent staff at the Quai d'Orsay, had been seen by the Foreign Minister before being submitted to the Premier.

formal obligations which England had assumed under the Locarno Pact, Flandin should have been able to cast this alliance into stronger metal. He should not have freed Great Britain, out of hand, from her specific commitment to apply economic sanctions. So far as I know, the conference of March 1936 was the only international discussion in which the secretary-general of the Foreign Ministry was not asked to participate, and this omission cannot have been unintentional.[4] In the various instruments signed on March 19 the tie-up with London was made subject to such a maze of procedure that we had to concede a good deal to British policy in order to render it effective. We paid for it in August by accepting "non-intervention" in Spain, and, in October, by postponing indefinitely—that is, rejecting—the Soviet offer to Léon Blum for immediate joint study of Czechoslovak defense problems. Besides, Flandin himself put so little trust in the nucleus of alliance he had secured from the British Cabinet that, stopping in Berlin on his return from Copenhagen early in 1938,[5] he divested himself of his London-made raiment and entered the ranks of the totalitarians. He took his new stand with less shame than Laval and Bonnet. He was the least dangerous of the triumvirate because of his clumsiness, but he was the most brazen.

The problem which faced Bonnet when he took office in April 1938 was no longer the same one that had taxed the wit of his predecessors. The time had passed when France could jostle Germany and compel her to lie low. The Reich had closed its western borders against our pressure with field fortifications, and its army was no longer weaker than ours. All internal liens placed upon its sovereignty in 1919 had snapped one after the other: reparations, disarmament, the demilitarized zone in the Rhineland. The Reich was about to blast away the territorial clauses. In March 1938, Hitler took the first step in his conquest of eastern Europe by the annexation of Austria. Every sign pointed to the forthcoming thrust against Czechoslovakia. In order to fulfill our commitments to this ally, were we willing to chance a war which might take on the dimensions of the 1914 conflict? Or should we permit the Nazi Empire to swallow the Slav states, one by one?

There can be no dispute about it: we should only too quickly choose the latter alternative were we sure of being able, thereafter, to protect our own national independence. But where was the serious student of

---

[4] Albert Sarraut, alarmed at current reports, telephoned Flandin in London to urge upon him a harder course. He was informed that the Minister could not be reached.

[5] I cannot check that date. Flandin's journey and conversion may have taken place earlier.

European affairs who dared deny that the German power, once it was entrenched along the lower Danube and the Vistula, must bid for European hegemony? Who dared affirm that, under National Socialist ascendancy, France could hold intact its territorial inheritance, its colonies, and its freedom? The National Socialist Revolution worked its way not only by external aggression but by boring from within. Hitler had a way of towering over his victims even before the onslaught was launched and of impairing them spiritually and materially.

Then the German Italian link had to be reckoned with—the Steel Pact of May 22, 1939. If it wanted peace, the French Government had not only to put up with the Führer's continental hegemony but also to carve Mussolini's spoils out of its own colonial and even home possessions. There was no middle course. This infernal dilemma had to be met: either to serve in bondage with moral and material impairment of all we held dear or to resist and incur terrible risks.

In such circumstances how was it possible to define our policy in rational terms? Since we lived perforce with the vision of an impending test of arms, the tightening of our bonds with England and Russia was a primordial duty.[6] The Soviets were under obligation to come with us to Czechoslovakia's assistance. But England's pledge of alliance stopped short of our frontiers. We could not afford to cry out, "So far and no further!" to a conquering Germany until we had succeeded in bringing our two allies together, and we needed a respite for doing so. That set a first limit to our freedom of initiative.

There was a second limit, in an opposite direction. We could not, without upsetting the system of collective resistance which we had established, belie too openly or drastically our commitments toward Prague. Thus, if Germany moved first, all refusal on our part to take up the challenge would entail for us a grievous loss.

Finally, this consideration had to be constantly borne in mind. Hitler was not the man to let us procrastinate and thus increase our military strength. The Berlin dictator would not allow the headway he had gained over us to be lessened.[7] It was altogether fitting that we should

---

[6] Be it noted—it is of major import—that the application of the Russo-Czechoslovak Treaty, signed on May 16, fourteen days after the Franco-Russian one, was made contingent upon the application of the latter, in consequence of Litvinoff's request to Beneš. The Soviet Government did not leave anything to chance. France must already have been at war before it joined.

[7] Robert Coulondre, French Ambassador in Berlin, telegraphed Georges Bonnet on March 19, 1939: "The danger [that of Germany acting in the west] could even be increased by the mere fact of our speeding up or intensifying our armament production. . . . We must

angle for time to weld our alliances together. But we should not delude ourselves into believing that, by delaying the issue, we might add to the number and to the efficiency of our weapons as compared to those of our enemy. On the contrary, when it came to armaments, time worked against us. Indeed, the delays we tried to purchase were to be paid in terms of greater military inferiority. To sum up, there was only one hope of staving off the conflict. France, England, and Russia in association—if they could get together quickly enough—might succeed in frightening Hitler, in making him participate in a European settlement.[8] Whatever the viewpoint from which the issue was examined, this conclusion was inescapable: without prompt co-operation with England and Russia peace was a forlorn hope.

Such a courageous policy had to be followed up to the end, and no shilly-shallying could be indulged in if France was to weather the storm. It was one of the sorriest strokes of luck that Georges Bonnet, thanks to the hazards of ministerial bargaining, should have been the man singled out to implement it. He could give it no more than he had in him: an inborn taste for double-dealing, the resources and the weakness of duplicity. And even that must be qualified. His duplicity was divorced from all strong purposes. It sprang from fear; it was hesitant and groping.

In the months and years after our defeat Bonnet has never varied in the explanation of his purpose as Minister of Foreign Affairs, and therefore most people today believe that from the outset he wished to yield

---

produce with redoubled energy but as secretly as possible." Gamelin often stressed the same point. Even Bonnet made it his own, on August 23, 1939, at the meeting of the Military Council called to appraise the consequences of the German-Soviet treaty. He asked "whether it was better to be true to our obligations or else to reconsider our attitude and take advantage of the ensuing breathing spell to build up our military strength—weighing the fact that France then risked being attacked in her turn, after a lapse of perhaps only a few months." (General Decamp's account.)

[8] Robert Coulondre telegraphed on June 1, 1939: "The Führer has asked Generals Keitel, his chief of staff, and Von Brauchitsch, commander in chief of the land forces, whether, under present conditions, a conflict would turn out in Germany's favor. Both made a distinction based on whether or not Russia stayed out of the fight. Supposing that she did, General Keitel replied, 'Yes'; but General von Brauchitsch (whose opinion carries more weight) answered, 'Probably.' Both said pointblank that if Germany had to fight Russia as well, she would have small chance of winning the war. . . . The opinion obtains [at the Wilhelmstrasse] that Herr Hitler will gamble on war if he does not have to face Russia, but that, on the contrary, if he knows he must deal with that country, he will pull in his horns rather than run the risk of seeing himself, his party, and his country lose." Even before Robert Coulondre put these words on paper a highly placed German diplomat implored one of his French friends: "Get busy and sign up with the Russians! It's the only way to avert war. And I speak as a German patriot!"

to the dictators and never dared seriously impede them. But the story of his diplomacy is far more complicated.

Unable as he was to make up his own mind and to keep steadfastly to his resolve, he most often carried on two games simultaneously, one above board and the other below it. Of course he never sincerely stood for resistance, but neither did he unflinchingly stand for submission. The *Yellow Book* published in December 1939[9] presents him to posterity in an almost irreproachable light, according to the tenets of French diplomatic tradition. By contrast, an unbroken succession of incidents, reported by the most reliable authorities, lays bare the undermining work which he pursued under cover of the official policy. He kept on wrecking or unsettling with one hand whatever he did with the other. The French people of 1940–42, stunned by the German triumph, were only too prone to think that, in 1938–39, peace was worth buying at a very great price, even at the cost of our sovereignty. For that reason, in Vichy and in Paris, publicly and privately, Bonnet has always extolled the subterranean aspect of his activity, although taking care not to disclose it indiscriminately.[10] "There," he said, "lay the unity, the reality of my diplomacy." Such assertions are only empty pretenses. The documents printed in the *Yellow Book* involve him to the hilt in all the steps officially taken by the French Government or on its behalf. He would have us believe now that the pledges he gave to resistance were a mere subterfuge, that he did not want them to bear any other result but to enable him to remain in office and proceed further with his secret manipulations. But the facts are there, and he cannot erase them from his record: on September 3 he personally declared war on Germany, and for ten days after that event he clung like a leech to the Ministry of Foreign Affairs. Can a declaration of war be called a subterfuge? To anyone who pins him down on the record, his plea, then, must inevitably amount to this: "I carried out to the point of declaring war the strong

---

[9]The *Yellow Book* does not give out the whole truth about Bonnet. Charles Rochat, director of political affairs, was detailed for selecting in consultation with Bonnet the telegrams which had better be left aside. To placate Bonnet was not the only motive. It was in the general interest that French diplomacy should not be exhibited on the market place with all its scars. In all probability Herr von Ribbentrop did not wait until the end of June 1939 to remind Bonnet that the Franco-German declaration of December 6, 1938 (as they agreed to interpret it), implied the abandonment of eastern Europe by France. But Bonnet did not see his way to contradict the German Foreign Minister for many months. Therefore all reference to the question, prior to the end of June, has been suppressed.

[10]The pamphlet published under the name of Philippe Henriot (a deputy for the Gironde department whom Laval promoted to the Ministry of Information in January 1944), *Comment Mourut la Paix*, has been pieced together by Bonnet.

policy for which I had no use because I wanted the better to discomfit and halt it." Bonnet's case ends on sheer absurdity.

Specifically, Bonnet cannot escape indictment on three counts:

First, he exercised all his ingenuity to destroy our alliances, the only brake we could apply to Hitler's progress.

At the very start of the Czechoslovak crisis in 1938 we must note the London Conference of April 27–29, when Daladier and Bonnet tried to reach an understanding with Downing Street on a joint line of action. It was by harping on the theme of France bound in "honor" to support her ally that the Premier pried Mr. Chamberlain loose from his leanings toward non-intervention, which he had actually repudiated in the House of Commons on March 24, but to which he had meanwhile largely reverted. "Yes, Honor!" the Prime Minister repeated sadly. Honor! The word rung in Bonnet's ears as he listened without batting an eye. A sorry joke when you think of what was to happen! On May 20 the conflict between the Sudeten Germans (with Hitler behind them) and the Prague Government broke out. A false alarm. Germany was still short of the mark in her preparations, and Sir Nevile Henderson, at Berlin, used threatening language which perhaps went further than his instructions—as weak men are apt to do. However, on September 12, at the Nürnberg Congress, Hitler thundered out that the Bohemian blood brothers had a right to return to their German fatherland. It was up to France to say that she supported Beneš.

Meanwhile Bonnet, to put the advocates of resistance out of countenance, eagerly explained to everybody the numerous reasons why we should not bestir ourselves. Our air force was in a bad way. The Siegfried Line had to be reckoned with: General Gamelin could not outflank it since M. Janson, Belgian Foreign Minister, had just refused to allow us eventual passage through his country. Poland's course was more ambiguous than ever: Colonel Beck had not even concealed that his country would mobilize against Russia if the Soviets made any gesture toward helping the Czechs, and we had not been able to win assurances of free transit for Russian matériel. Marshal Smigly Rydz asserted that he had no recollection of the promises we had secured from him in return for the September 6, 1936, Rambouillet agreement (regarding the rearmament of his country); he went so far as to say that if the partition of Czechoslovakia was in the offing, no one would be surprised at Poland seizing what was hers in the Teschen area. Russia, Bonnet added, wants war between the Western Powers and Germany, but she will be careful to take no part in it. He did not whisper a single word concerning either the conference on policy, or the meeting of the League Council, or the staff consultations suggested by Litvinoff (who in Geneva, on September 11, had urged action, in similar terms, on Bonnet and Lord de la Warr), or the arrival in Prague of a Red Army general assigned to reconnoiter airfields.[11] As to England, our Minister stopped at nothing in his efforts to persuade the government that we could in no way rely on her. He was greatly helped in his treachery by the personal views of the British Ambassador, Sir Eric Phipps. One day Bonnet even dared tell some callers of an altogether disconcerting "British note." Later he was obliged to admit that it was no more than a summary, written by himself, of a conversation with Phipps.

Bonnet sought to make use of Belgians, Poles, Russians, British, and Czechs, to plant the seeds of doubt in French minds, and afterward he thought to make use of the French to frighten the rulers in Prague.

He kept saying that Beneš and Hodža did not want to fight and, at the bottom of their hearts, hoped that by declaring our unwillingness to intervene, through a *non possumus* as to our treaty obligations, by ostensibly building under their very feet a bridge to capitulation, we French would enable them to keep face before their own people. Beneš and Hodža were resigned to losing the Sudetenland, he argued, but they felt helpless as long as their fellow citizens kept faith in French assistance. To help those two statesmen the best thing to do was to discourage those fellow citizens.

To bolster his argument, Bonnet produced a telegram from M. de Lacroix, our Minister to Prague, dated September 20. The truth was that Bonnet had convinced Hodža of France's resolve to keep aloof and that Hodža in turn had tried to convince Beneš of it. But, true to type, Bonnet had avoided recording in any note or other official document what he had, time and again, so emphatically said in conversation. Beneš wanted to force him to do so. Not because he was determined to avoid throwing his country into the war, but because of his fear that France might leave Czechoslovakia in the lurch. He insisted that France's default must not come stealthily but be made tangible for his whole nation. At the same time he calculated that insistence upon a written statement would arouse Bonnet's opponents in the Paris Cabinet. This

[11]M. Litvinoff sent word to Beneš that if war ensued Soviet Russia would stand by Czechoslovakia, whatever the Western Powers might do. But Beneš did nothing to ascertain the extent of the eventual Russian support. Failing Franco-British help, he was not prepared to go to war.

explains what passed between Paris and Prague on September 20, including the telegram freely quoted by Bonnet, later, to exculpate himself. The Minister held off committing himself in any way except verbally. To nail him down to his responsibility, M. de Lacroix insisted upon Bonnet dictating at once over the telephone the political statement requested by Beneš. Only lately has it been made known that Bonnet had Mistler with him that evening.

Such was Bonnet's method of strengthening our treaty bonds at a critical juncture. One can easily figure what sort of dispatches the ambassadors of England (Eric Phipps, a little man frozen with fear at the very name of Hitler), Russia, Poland, the United States, Italy, and Germany sent home after visiting the Quai d'Orsay. Hitler could rest undisturbed. France would not fight.

The surprising thing is not that governments both friendly and hostile should have become convinced of Bonnet's weakness, but that it should have taken them so long and that, mindful especially of Daladier's utterances, they should still occasionally have believed France capable of action. How furious was Bonnet when, on September 27, four days after the Godesberg ultimatum and twenty-four hours after the second Anglo-French meeting in London, Daladier was able to read aloud in support of his own firmer policy Chamberlain's second message, which Sir Horace Wilson was handing Hitler on that very day: "If France, in the fulfillment of her obligations, is actively drawn into war, England will feel obliged to support her." At the cabinet meeting the two men clashed violently over this formula. Bonnet's rage increased during the evening, when he learned of the Foreign Office's communiqué: if France went to war, she would be assisted by England and Russia.[12] Bonnet pretended it was a forgery. In the same breath he branded as a lie the Reuter dispatch stating that on September 28, at 2 P.M., the Reich would decree a general mobilization. Bonnet had set himself up as Hitler's beater, the man to rouse and drive the game. He did not wish our political alliances and associations to give the despot the least worry or the German leader's brutality to become apparent to the French before they had given way.

The second count in the indictment against the Minister is that he turned the Munich Conference into a boundless diplomatic disaster. His daily remarks, made in his private office at the Quai d'Orsay or at some dinner table, were passed on to Berlin by the German Ambassador,

---

[12]The Foreign Office, in a second communiqué, and Daladier, before the Chamber of Deputies, confirmed the authenticity of this document.

Count Welzeck. I have already pointed out that at this time Keitel and Brauchitsch did not deem it wise to go to war. But Bonnet, unaware, waved a red flag in front of the bull. It is quite likely that the bellicose declamations at Nürnberg were, in this sense, the creation of our own Foreign Minister.

Indeed, Chamberlain's trip to Berchtesgaden was planned on September 13, in an effort to stop the dangerous interchange between the dictator and this weakling, an interchange carried on through the intermediary of the German Ambassador. But the remedy, in the end, proved worse than the disease.

Thus was taken, unwillingly, the first step toward the surrender of the Sudetenland. The men who sponsored it, who brought in Chamberlain so as to sidetrack Bonnet, explain that Daladier, when he put Chamberlain on the move, did not contemplate that Hitler should benefit by any territorial change except through an international procedure designed to hold in check and regulate the German onrush. So much so that Hitler, to get rid of the international procedure, hurled his Godesberg ultimatum which Chamberlain (who proved to be a feeble negotiator) could not get the cabinet meeting of September 24 to accept.[18] So much so that the clash seemed to draw nearer and nearer.

On the twenty-eighth, all the odds were that Czechoslovakia would be invaded that very evening or the next day. At 10 A.M. the untiringly reiterated British proposal for a conference whose ultimate purpose was, indeed, to make of the little republic a Switzerland or a Belgium propped up by international guarantees was repeated for the third or fourth time. Spurred on by the secretary-general, Daladier and Bonnet decided that François-Poncet, French Ambassador in Berlin, should at once renew that British proposal with a slight variation in form and substance. The fate of our country hung upon what was going to happen. French ministers must not, before posterity, place themselves in the position of having taken as final for themselves also the refusal meted out, not to a representative of France, but to Sir Nevile Henderson and, earlier, to Sir Horace Wilson and Chamberlain himself. Poncet did not appear to understand the object of this French overture, which to him looked like asking for a rebuff. But upon explicit instructions he went to the Chancellery. At quarter past eleven he was received in audience. Shortly afterward he telephoned: "What a surprise! The Führer talked

---

[18]In that discussion, I am told, Lord Halifax parted with Chamberlain for the first time. In that discussion, also, Chamberlain's famous phrase came on record: "I know that Hitler will not only keep his word but prove better than his word."

to me in an altogether different tone from that he used with my British colleague. 'I cannot say no to your suggestion,' he told me. 'I will give you a written answer this afternoon!' " That answer, instead of the note which had been announced, was the invitation to Munich.

What, then, had happened? We have since learned the truth. Otto Abetz and another personal envoy, whose opinion carried more weight with Hitler than did that of Welzeck, had sent word from Paris that Daladier would not give in, that partial mobilization, ordered on the twenty-sixth, was actually in process, that the clockworks were already in motion, and that things were slipping toward war. Hitler was convinced and yielded. Mussolini also intervened, but, above everything else, it had begun to dawn upon Hitler that perhaps Bonnet's voice did not predominate in French ministerial councils.

At Munich it fell to the Premier and to Alexis Léger, who accompanied him, to stand by the principle of a Czechoslovakia assured of an independent life and international protection within straitened boundaries. On paper they won two important concessions: a delegate from Prague would sit on the Berlin Committee of Ambassadors, which was to map out the new frontiers, and the strict ethnical rule that all populations of German race belonged to Germany might be departed from in order to safeguard Czechoslovakia's national defense and economic existence.

On September 29, while the stiff argument with Hitler and Mussolini continued late into the night, Bonnet, at his Quai d'Orsay office, grew impatient of this slow pace. He telephoned and had others telephone. His newpapers were standing by, ready to speak out. Caillaux was holding up an article which would be printed and arouse a storm if the delay lasted too long. The conference came to an end. The Munich protocols more or less agreed with our requirements. But when the moment came to enforce them, what had been won was jeopardized by the weakness of the British and French representatives on the Berlin Committee. The Germans and Italians, following the lead of the Nazi High Command, rebelled against the decisions arrived at in Munich, threatened to go back to the Führer and reopen the whole question. Nevile Henderson talked directly by telephone with Mr. Chamberlain, and François-Poncet with Bonnet.[14] Both were encouraged to give way. Soon there remained nothing of Czechoslovakia but a truncated and subjugated body. That this small republic should barter its French and Russian alliances for a status like Switzerland's might be called an in-

[14]See page 4, note 5.

telligible bargain, one safeguarding, at any rate, France's dignity. But to cast our ally into the abyss was shameful beyond description.

Daladier's policy in the juncture is hard to defend. He really opened the floodgates of German conquest when, for the sake of overruling Bonnet, he advised Chamberlain to travel to Berchtesgaden and, in that manner, assumed responsibility for the first meeting of the British Prime Minister with the Führer on September 15. Afterward how could we expect to dam the torrent? But the ensuing moral catastrophe redounded to the guilt of Bonnet—of Bonnet, who had re-entered the negotiation with a vengeance. Upon the conclusion of the Munich Agreement the Franco-British guarantee of Czechoslovakia's new frontiers had automatically become effective. Immediately, as we have seen, Bonnet cast to the winds France's signed obligation. Thus we were stripped for the future of all diplomatic defense. Who could ever again trust our pledged word?

The Russians quickly drew their own conclusions: the Third Republic's promises of help no longer had any value for anyone. The Franco-Soviet Treaty of May 2, 1935, had no more substance than a scrap of paper. Neither on September 15, when Chamberlain left for Berchtesgaden, nor on the twenty-second, when he went to Godesberg, nor on the twenty-eighth, when the British and French proposed their conference, had the Russians been notified in time—they who were allies or at least associates.[15]

The abiding, the mystic faith in "Munich" so widely instilled by Bonnet, the belief in a sure prospect of peace attested before the public by his journalists, was a fraud. It was a fraud because the public was never told that some precarious peace could be had only if France, once for all, turned her back on eastern Europe—and this was a deadly policy.

All the camouflage used at the time won't blind us to the fact that Bonnet and also Chamberlain had settled on that policy. There can be no other possible meaning to the Franco-German declaration of December 6 —the promise of mutual consultation between the Paris and Berlin governments—as well as to the Anglo-German stipulations of September 30, which served as model for it. The ink was hardly dry on the Munich Agreement when Bonnet and Chamberlain had consigned it to wrack and ruin, insofar as it forbade Germany any isolated initiative in Czechoslovakia. Bonnet, at any rate, was not naïve enough to think that hence-

---

[15]In contrast, it is worth noticing that Hitler insisted on the participation of Russia in the conference suggested by Mussolini at the eleventh hour on August 31, 1939. Yet he had merely concluded with Moscow a pact of non-aggression!

forward the Führer would act with greater moderation in Bohemia and in the eastern reaches of our continent than he had during October. The brutal inrush of German troops into Czechoslovakia had failed to alienate Chamberlain from his September 30 understanding with Hitler or to prevent Bonnet from signing that of December 6. Could anyone suppose that Bonnet and Chamberlain, having meekly condoned the mutilation of Czechoslovakia, were resolved to interfere with her being put to death?

The fact is that, after Ribbentrop left Paris, Bonnet, by deft underhand wirepulling, succeeded in having the Foreign Affairs Committee of the Senate vote a request for the abrogation of the alliances with Poland and Russia. He took it upon himself personally to study the matter during the Christmas holidays and allowed it to drop only when he had satisfied himself that these treaties were so full of loopholes that in practice we could get out of them at will. But had he pledged himself to the German Minister for Foreign Affairs? Both men have repeatedly given the lie to each other. Certainly one of them speaks against the truth. Which one of them? In presence of third persons Bonnet said nothing at the Quai d'Orsay which altered France's official position. He even permitted Alexis Léger to remind the Nazi Minister that since the question of the Czechoslovak minorities had been settled, on November 1, by the Vienna arbitration, the time had come for Germany and Italy to carry out their promises and add their guarantees of Czechoslovakia's boundaries to those of the Western Powers. But he did have two private conversations with his visitor—one at the Hotel Crillon and the other at the Louvre Museum, where he offered to serve as guide. To this day nobody has unraveled the riddle of that privacy.

To appraise the damage done we need only consider our respective positions on September 15 and on December 6, at the starting point and at the culmination of the so-called Munich policy. In December, France no longer had a single sure ally at her side. Czechoslovakia was moribund; Colonel Beck's pro-Germanism still held Poland in its grip; Russia, it is true, had not explicitly given up the 1935 treaty with France, but, according to one of her leaders, this was solely in the vague hope that the now empty shell might somehow scare off the Germans. In London a member of Parliament exclaimed, "It is not wise to go tiger hunting with the French!" England, despite the insults which Italy lavished on the Western Powers, thought it opportune to carry out the Mediterranean convention drawn up with Count Ciano in April and left in suspense!

We come now to the third major accusation. Bonnet, having cast our alliances overboard, drifted toward war without winning them back.

In spite of his own acts and his own convictions, in spite of himself, Bonnet returned, little by little, to our traditional policy. He set about thwarting the Central Empire and its aspirations to hegemony. Coulondre faithfully tried to abide by the new understanding with Berlin. But on December 15, nine days after the famous declaration of Paris, he reported Germany's plans for expansion, and kept it up, week after week, there being no lack of data.[16] Did Bonnet stop him? No. The Ambassador went right ahead. On February 4 he was instructed to insist upon the overdue guarantee of Czechoslovak frontiers. We got a refusal and took it rather badly. There followed on March 15 the forcible entry of the Reichswehr into Czechoslovakia. Two days later the Wilhelmstrasse was presented with our protest. Coulondre sent word on March 16: "From now on, Hitler is launched upon the conquest of Europe." As early as March 27 it became apparent that the tip of the German lance was pointed at Poland. On March 31, Mr. Chamberlain, finally opening his eyes to Hitler's formidable scheme and scrapping the Munich outlook, announced that if Poland were threatened in what she thought to be her "vital interests," England would come to her support with all her might, a formula repeated with certain limitations by M. Daladier on April 12.[17] Bonnet followed the tide. He went on to negotiate with Warsaw for the extension of the Franco-Polish Treaty of 1921, so that it might measure up to the British commitment.[18] It is true that he connived in London against the Anglo-Polish agreement, but officially he conformed to the British line.

How did Bonnet reconcile this new policy with his acts of the preceding autumn? It would be idle to ask him. Mr. Chamberlain and Lord Halifax, who knew him well by this time, behaved as though he did not exist. Thus French diplomacy was in no position to correct London's major mistake: relegating Russia to the background, not dealing with

[16]"The first part of Hitler's program—the integration of the Deutschtum within the Reich —is now fully achieved; the hour of the Lebensraum has struck." (December 15.)

[17]The British Cabinet had granted that Poland should be the sole judge of what constituted her vital interest. The Franco-Polish Treaty of 1921 stopped somewhat short of this.

[18]To cap the climax, in the months after the armistice Bonnet accused General Gamelin of having confronted him with a Franco-Polish military agreement, signed without his knowledge. In fact, Gamelin had been given instructions to work out a new convention to correspond with the new political treaty. He brought it to completion without having ascertained the stage reached in the Paris-Warsaw conversations. However, by an exchange of letters with the Polish War Minister, he made it clear that the military arrangement was necessarily subordinate to the political and could have no independent effect.

her until after contracts had been made with Warsaw and Bucharest, then lowering her to the level of a mere supply depot for Poles and Rumanians to draw upon at their best convenience, without even promising her a genuine alliance. Now that we have seen the might of the Red Army displayed in battle, we cannot help wondering what the cabinet ministers of that day made of their brains. If Russia were to furnish arms, she would draw Hitler's enmity and would suffer the repercussions of Polish reverses. Yet she was not to be allowed to move her soldiers outside her own boundaries. What a fantastic notion! It had to be abandoned, and at last the Soviet Union was offered the full status of an ally. But even in this ulterior stage of the negotiations there were still many unwarranted restrictions. The two western nations had agreed to guarantee Lithuania, Latvia, and Esthonia, which are the very outworks of the Russian fort. They promised that Germany would not be permitted to invade these countries. But when Stalin asked to be allowed to protect himself, if necessary, against what he called "indirect aggression" (fascist revolutions breaking out in these tiny lands), his claim was considered excessive. The exclamation of Molotov has been recorded by a British diplomat: "You want us to fight with you, and you deprive us of the means to defend ourselves!"

Generally speaking, to quote the judgment of a participant, it can be said that up until May 3 (when Litvinoff, Peoples' Commissar for Foreign Affairs, was dismissed) Russia was eager to make a treaty whereas England and France did not much more than toy with the idea. After that date the position was reversed. The two Western Powers now wanted results while Russia held back or rather increased her demands.[19] Bonnet indulged throughout in a game of meddlesome outbidding. No sooner would the British submit a formula to the Russians than he hastened to put forward another, and endlessly the whole matter was reopened. In June, however, he took fright. Was he alarmed at the possibility of a Russo-German rapprochement, to which his attention was called from Berlin and even from Washington? He strove hard to rebuild the Russian alliance at the eleventh hour, an alliance which he had constantly undermined before and after Munich. In a private message to London he laid stress on the necessity of complying with Molotov's requests. A fortnight later he solemnly warned Count Welzeck and, through him, Von Ribbentrop: "It is my duty to make it perfectly clear that any undertaking, no matter of what sort, which, by tending to change the *status quo* at Danzig might arouse Poland's armed resistance,

[19]As late as the fourteenth or the fifteenth of June, Russia submitted a set of proposals.

would call into play the Franco-Polish treaty and would compel France to come immediately to Poland's assistance."[20]

His firmness came too late. What had been lost was not to be retrieved. On August 23, Russia finally showed her hand, probably after having received territorial offers from Berlin on or about the fifteenth—if we are to credit not only her own rulers but also an Ambassador who was rather close to events. Half our diplomatic structure crumbled away at the crucial moment. Bonnet shares with others the responsibility for what happened, but his is the larger share. He was set on preventing war, and he succeeded only in destroying the one means whereby war might perhaps have been averted, the means which, in any case, opened a road to victory.

Today, naturally enough, but with a singleness of purpose which ill matches his own past, Bonnet furiously seeks to prove that, had it not been for the contriving of Daladier and of his own permanent officials, he would have saved the peace, either through a direct German-Polish conversation on August 31 or, even later, through Mussolini's arbitration. There is no other way for him to seek refuge from his countrymen's charges and reprisals. But the *Yellow Book* slams the door on both allegations.

What of a direct German-Polish conversation? "I shall not agree to it," said Hitler on August 29, "without previous assurance that the Polish Government will submit to my will." He set a time limit, August 31. On March 15 he had dealt no differently with President Hacha. To the British Ambassador, during the night of August 30-31, Von Ribbentrop read rapidly and unintelligibly the list of Germany's terms, only to say that the time limit had already been passed. On the thirty-first, at London's request, the Polish Ambassador was received by Von Ribbentrop toward seven in the evening; he said that at any instant a letter would arrive from his government accepting "direct contact." But within twelve hours the Reichswehr moved into Poland. Thus the Führer was never willing to publish his demands until it was too late to consider them.

What of Mussolini's arbitration, or rather the conference which Ciano suggested to Bonnet on August 31 at 1 P.M., to take place on September 5? In the morning of September 1, Bonnet himself, personally carrying out the Cabinet's decisions, set up two prerequisites: the participation of the Warsaw Government and full discussion of all the problems which might endanger peace. But what about the concomitant Nazi onslaught?

[20] July 1, 1939.

On September 2, at 5.20 P.M., Lord Halifax, acting in the spirit of the alliance with Poland, added a third condition: the German troops shall retreat.[21] At 9 P.M., Bonnet informed Count Ciano that his government was of the same mind. That ended the matter. There is no use going further, said Ciano in substance; actually, all he had tried to do was to localize the German-Polish war, to cut Poland off from the nations which had promised her their assistance.

What are we to think of a Minister of Foreign Affairs who, not having the courage to resign, and being unable to disavow publicly the official decision which he had reached in common with the government, later and in secret held as morally responsible a permanent official who, of course, did not have access to ministerial councils? An executive agent's responsibility goes no further than the faithful discharge of his instructions, and in the *Yellow Book* Bonnet himself proves that he allowed no one else to carry out the government's policy in which he had himself concurred. A careful timetable of what he did during the three fateful days—August 31, September 1 and 2—clearly establishes that, from beginning to end, from hour to hour, of his own will, he himself and he alone had the whole sequence of events in hand, starting with Count Ciano's proposal telephoned to him by M. François-Poncet, our Ambassador to Rome, and at once laid before the Cabinet, and ending with the final transmittal to the Italian Minister of the French Government's ultimate answer, together with all the intervening calls to Halifax, Ciano, and the principal French ambassadors concerned. The truth is that Bonnet, at the Ministry of Foreign Affairs, handled the whole business. To him alone everything was communicated or made known. He looked into everything; he made everything ready; he proposed, he discussed, he accepted everything. The performance was entirely his own, and the secretary-general never had a chance to participate. The newspapermen to whom, on September 2, in his wily manner, Bonnet hinted at the part supposedly played by Léger knew quite well, like everyone else at the Quai d'Orsay, that for more than two days, from the early afternoon of August 31 to the evening of September 2, the Minister had purposely seen very little of his principal assistant (thus cut off from all firsthand information) and for some thirty hours had kept out of contact with him.

When, on the evening of September 2, Bonnet at last called in the secretary-general to bring him up to date, all had been compassed al-

---

[21]That third condition had indeed been put forward by the French ministerial council in the morning of September 1. But in his telephone message to our Ambassador in Rome, Bonnet deliberately passed it over.

ready, with Léger left out and denied any opportunity to give his chief even the most trifling advice. Bonnet inveighs against Léger for having described to him the Italian offer of a conference as a "snare to catch the unwary." As though, by expressing that opinion on August 31, around 12 A.M., Léger had made it impossible for Bonnet, Daladier, and the other ministers to form an independent judgment! As though he had trespassed with his prejudice upon the sanctuary of their conscience! As though he had worsened whatever prospect of peace might still exist by appraising accurately the move of the fascist Government! But, indeed, the Italian proposal was still unknown to Léger when he uttered the warning against the "snare to catch the unwary." The second bureau of the General Staff (military intelligence) had for ten days informed the Quai d'Orsay that it was in the making, and Léger took it for granted that it would not fail to turn up at the proper moment. Of all necessity, therefore, he must have spoken in general terms.

Bonnet was able, all along, to act according to his own light. He became hysterical in the afternoon of the thirty-first when he realized that the Italian suggestion was not likely to be taken at its face value by Daladier and the Cabinet. He mendaciously quoted the French Ambassador in London. Corbin had told him, he said, that the British Government approved of Ciano's plan in principle, an assertion which Corbin stoutly denied, shortly afterward, in a direct call to Daladier. Unabashed, Bonnet challenged the Premier's right to communicate with ambassadors and officials under him except through his channel, a restriction which the Premier impatiently rejected. As he began scribbling a note all present believed that he was about to quit. No fear! His telephonic conversations, recorded in his own hand, show that, notwithstanding the continuation of the old double-dealing, he toed, at all decisive moments, the line drawn by the government. And Léger was not there to compel him to do it.

Given all this, at what time is it possible to find the secretary-general steering the ship? Certainly not during the three crucial days, any more than during the preceding weeks, humming with exceptional diplomatic activity, when important telegrams were delivered straight to the Minister's office and often were even secretly withheld for his own private information; when all telegrams of instructions were signed by the Minister's own hand; when the leading foreign ambassadors were summoned and received directly, and without third parties present, by the Minister; when our own envoys abroad were questioned or instructed on the telephone directly by the Minister; when even foreign cabinet members were themselves reached on the telephone directly by the Minister; when, finally, the press was greeted and kept informed by the Minister himself, in his private office.

The truth is that today, in order to lighten the burden of his official responsibility, Bonnet is piling one bad excuse upon another. He alleges that in cabinet meeting after cabinet meeting he opposed Daladier—yet was unwilling to resign and thereby forego further opportunities to influence his chief's policy. He alleges that the British Government dragged him in spite of himself toward a declaration of war and forced his will by confronting him "with an accomplished fact," as is evidenced by the five hours' interval which elapsed in Berlin between the maturing of the ultimata presented by Henderson and by Coulondre respectively.[22] But then what was the use of his remaining in office? He cannot disclaim his share in the break. And when he had the audacity, on September 2, to tell the newspapermen that "in every way" Léger and others made it impossible to stave off the struggle, he spoke with his tongue in his cheek. At the bottom, when he notified the Germans on July 1 that any undertaking against Danzig would align France with Poland, he himself, of his own free will, drew up an undated declaration of war.

On August 22, apprised of the forthcoming signature of the Russo-German Pact, Bonnet asked for a meeting at the War Ministry of the various ministers of national defense and the leading military men, in order to find out whether "the Army, the Navy, and the Air Force were, or were not, in condition to honor the commitments provided in our treaty of alliance" with Warsaw. The minutes of this August 23 session, drawn up by General Decamp, record the universal feeling: "France has no choice." Bonnet himself confessed to the examining magistrates at Riom (July 7, 1941) that "he was not aware of the extent of unpreparedness in our national defense," and that "from the August 23 meeting he kept a very clear impression that no consideration drawn from our military potentialities was of a sort to affect our external policy." This definitively clinches the matter.

[22]This five-hour interval arose from the fact that Chamberlain, who had had to face the wrath of the House of Commons on September 2, advanced, with Paris's consent, the time fixed for the declaration of war while Gamelin was not willing to forsake even so short a respite.

6

The Counterrevolutionary Crowd

SUCH WAS THE SUCCESSION of faulty and cowardly deeds which issued in war and defeat. Under ordinary circumstances a great public revulsion should have cut short and swept away Laval, Flandin, Bonnet, and all their works. But if the diplomatic acts of these three ministers often aroused alarms, protests, outcries, they also in like degree united the counterrevolutionary minority. A majority will often split over the platform of its choice while a militant minority will become still more consolidated. Even under the Popular Front government, this minority spoke loudly and authoritatively about foreign affairs. It numbered in its ranks a large section of the "elite," whose function should be to foresee and to warn. However strong-minded he may be, any minister in charge of the Quai d'Orsay is bound to feel embarrassed and disturbed when he finds the Institut de France among the censors of his policy. And the Popular Front Minister of Foreign Affairs, Yvon Delbos, was no man of iron.

The counterrevolutionaries were a motley and confused lot. Among them could be found many leaders, each with a rank and file of his own. They were apt to flock to employers' associations and to a handful of big banks. Perhaps the easiest way to sort out and describe the strongest and most active elements in that crowd is to stand at Laval's side and see what passes by. For, once again, a good deal revolved around him.

In his political career Laval had associated with many parties from the extreme Left to the Right, and several ministerial departments had been committed to his care. Everywhere he had left behind him both clients and spies. He lived with them on a footing of mutual assistance. "Laval's man!" That tag, so often heard, was sometimes attached to a Socialist, sometimes to a conservative. We might do worse here than resurrect the term of abuse once commonly applied to the friends of the Duke of Orleans during his profligate regency—the "Roués."

In France, as elsewhere, fascism spread across the different political strata. Let us not make any mistake about it: fascism was not the monopoly of the Right. Such men as Paul Faure and René Brunet (Socialists), Belin (General Confederation of Labor), Communists of the Giton variety, the leaders of the Postal Employees' and Teachers' Unions, all at least wished Laval well when they did not actively busy themselves in his behalf. We have already come across his Radical-Socialist accomplices. Although they were no friends of his, the old-fashioned "antiwar" Socialists (Marcel Pivert, etc.) joined in his game from the outside. When Léon Blum was Premier with the Popular Front in full blast, restraints were applied against him which originated from within his own party and which furthered the enterprises of his avowed enemies.

Better than anyone else, Laval knew how to use the press. Most of the papers yielded without a struggle. After all, this was not a very difficult achievement. A mere score of men dominated the field in France, and they were none too hard to bring to heel.

At the hub of the wheel the Havas Agency handed out advertising contracts. And not merely advertising contracts, but the bounty of such gentry whose reputations needed currycombing. Havas enjoyed a kind of *de facto* monopoly. Should some rival agency grow threateningly big—the Agence Radio, for example—it would at once be bought in. The major Paris and provincial newspapers—some ten at most—got the lion's share. The rest plotted and scuffled to get larger cuts. By temperament the two leading lights in this firm, Léon Rénier and Pierre Guimier, were servile and conniving. A phone call would go out of their offices between six and eight in the evening. That was enough. Some piece of news embarrassing to a particular minister or to a certain financial interest would next morning be passed over in silence by the great dailies. Usually an unofficial denial, a hint of dreadful consequences to come were quite enough to bring those who had dared open their mouths back into line. But what did it matter, after all, if a few isolated journalists did speak out? The tens of thousands of readers whom they kept posted were insignificant in comparison to the millions led astray. Fully seventy out of one hundred Frenchmen never knew that Italian planes sent to the assistance of the Spanish generals crashed near Oran at the end of July 1936; that the acts of piracy in the Mediterranean, denounced by the Nyon Conference (September 1937), were chargeable to Italians; that German aviators bombed Guernica.

Facts which might arouse the nation to its peril were stifled. But anything which could turn Frenchmen against Russia, against the "Marxists," against England herself, and also make them look favorably upon the dictators, was hammered home. Bunau-Varilla's *Le Matin,* in November 1933, published Fernand de Brinon's famous article playing up Hitler with sentimental flourishes.[1] In February 1936 the Führer, through the channel of Bertrand de Jouvenel, was given the opportunity to explain his policy to the readers of Jean Prouvost's *Paris Midi.* The military reoccupation of the Rhineland was to follow within a few days: as far as propaganda could go, it was a remarkable performance. The Quai d'Orsay had only succeeded in delaying the publication of the article by a week. For years on end the *Petit Parisien* upheld Mussolini against all comers: one of its owners, Pierre Dupuy, had dreams of becoming Ambassador to Rome. The *Journal,* fallen from Letellier's to Guimier's control (Guimier, whom Léon Blum very properly caused to be thrown out of the Agence Havas), endlessly found excuses for the shift of France's allies or associates toward Germany and Italy, be it under the leadership of Beck, Stoyadinovitch, Charles II, or Leopold III. In *L'Intransigeant,* and later in *Le Jour,* Léon Bailby and his successor, Fernand Laurent, harped on pro-Mussolinian and anti-Soviet themes. In *Le Temps* the foreign-policy daily editorial was entrusted to Roland de Marès. Jacques Chastenet[2] was delighted with the services of this

---

[1] Fernand de Brinon had first contributed to the *Journal des Débats,* under the management of M. Etienne de Nalèche, who was a friend of his family and a gentleman. Until about 1931, Brinon attracted no attention whatever. He was more or less in step with his fellow journalists. I recall Nalèche joking over his adaptability: "He goes to Berlin and sends me an article to rejoice all good Germans. He travels back via Geneva, and what I get smacks of the Genevan faith."

Brinon was a second-rate writer endowed with a keen sense of intrigue. He worked for a paper which, all through the nineteenth century, had championed liberalism and gained fame by enlisting the greatest literary and political talents. The honor of having what one wrote published side by side with contributions from members of the Institut de France was thought to be the best part of the salary. Brinon had social ambitions, and he insinuated himself into a few great houses, but his purse was light and he had to strive continually to make both ends meet. He even tried to make money by playing the races. Only toward 1937 was he to achieve a certain financial independence by his marriage to a "non-Aryan." He never tried to woo fortune with his pen alone. He was on the lookout for a political patron. Thus, in turn, he fawned upon Tardieu (1929–32), Daladier (1933), Laval. He finally sunk his hooks into the latter, who in 1935 considered making him an Ambassador to Warsaw (that is, to Colonel Beck), but desisted for fear of the outcry that would have greeted such an appointment. Meanwhile Brinon had met Ribbentrop and Abetz, and from 1932, at the latest, his relations with them were intimate. It was during that year that I called Tardieu's attention to this acquaintanceship. At first he was rather surprised, and then said, "Now I begin to understand a few things!" He had suddenly thought of Octave Homberg's trip to Berlin. This former diplomat, turned banker (and for a while a very opulent one), had found all doors in the German capital open to him and, when Tardieu asked why, had replied, "Brinon gave me some letters of introduction."

[2] As Secretary of Embassy, he served with Tirard, High Commissioner for the Rhineland. Like Tirard, Max Hermant, and other advocates of "Rhenish separatism," he went into

hard-working Belgian who indulged in noncommittal platitudes, never came forward with an opinion of his own and when great events were in process gladly turned over his column to him. Then all of a sudden a mind that would admit of nothing but our coming to terms with the totalitarians shone at the top of the front page and waxed eloquent. The political articles in the *Revue des Deux Mondes* signed "René Pinon" evidenced the shortsightedness and levity of which an honest man, in his efforts to break open all doors leading to the French Academy, became capable. I have already spoken of Jean Prouvost; his *Paris-Soir* was a kind of crude newsreel. From a technical point of view it was remarkably well run by Pierre Latzareff, but its publishers never dared risk following a line even faintly consistent. They were perfectly happy to print alternate articles by Flandin and Léon Blum. They conformed to every trend that a spirit of businesslike pessimism could discern among the two million readers. After Munich they raised a fund to buy Mr. Chamberlain a country house, which he refused. They hired brilliant journalists as well as a few men of ill repute. Of what use was the paper's financial independence?

In years gone by these papers had been at the beck and call of Millerand, Poincaré, Briand. They had acclaimed the seizure of the Ruhr, the League of Nations, the Locarno treaties, the Kellogg Pact. Now they sheepishly trooped behind Laval and his cronies. What did they care for the lead they had tried to give the country three, five, ten years earlier? Besides, they were careful not to commit themselves too definitely. They sinned by omission as much as by commission. In a well-handled prop-

---

business around 1924. He became deputy director of the Union des Mines Bank, but, together with the director, was relieved of his post as a result of heavy losses incurred by this institution on the New York stock market in 1929–30. When the Coal Owners' Association (Comité des Houillières) bought *Le Temps* on equal shares with the Comité des Forges (Count de Fels being thrown in between the two on an inferior footing), Chastenet became editor in chief of the paper. No one can suspect that the huge economic corporations which owned *Le Temps* were bribed or hired. But they were unable to keep their house in order and make all their contributors and editors conform to decent standards. The head of the Comité des Houillières and the true guiding spirit of *Le Temps* was M. de Peyerimhoff de Fontenelle, formerly Master of Petitions in the Council of State, a conceited and skeptical man. I myself have seen a letter written on behalf of *Le Temps* to a notorious Italian agent. It dealt with an advertising contract concerning tourism which involved the paltry sum of seventy thousand francs. "Don't ask me to change our Rome correspondent," said the signatory. "As it is, I expurgate his dispatches." *Le Temps's* other editor in chief was Emile Mireaux, a man who had left a university career to serve the Comité des Forges and manage its subsidiary publication, the wearisome and bulky *Bulletin d'Information Economique,* with headquarters on the Boulevard St. Germain, a true museum of day-to-day partisanship and aberrations. He was later Pétain's Minister of Public Instruction.

aganda program silence is golden; it is worth just as much as argument. Several times Georges Bonnet tried to bribe *L'Europe Nouvelle,* of which I was editor in chief. Five hundred thousand francs would have been readily handed out to the owner in return for merely discarding one of our contributors whose satiric shafts pestered the Minister.

Alongside the pens with tips of felt there were those that scratched shrilly. The weeklies *Candide, Gringoire,* and *Je Suis Partout* might just as well have been gotten out by Goebbels or Starace. Henri Béraud's article, "Must England Be Reduced to Slavery?" ("Faut-Il Réduire l'Angleterre en Esclavage?" October 1935), will go down to posterity as the masterpiece of this sort of writing. The Germans had it distributed in London by the thousands. Bundles of copies shipped to Egypt had to be stopped in transit because of the complaint of the British Embassy.

Je Suis Partout carried the prize. It systematically flouted France's friends and extolled her enemies. Roosevelt is "of Jewish extraction,"[3] "the century's most conspicuous noodlehead," "he wants to start a war so as to re-establish Jewish power and deliver the world to Bolshevism." Beneš is "a scoundrel," Titulescu, the "congenital idiot bred in chancelleries." "If we are at war's threshold, we owe it in some small measure to Mr. Winston Churchill." Only the camp followers of the dictators were praised. Thus we were told that Léon Degrelle had no taste for Hitler. "No one thinks so, not even the journalists in the pay of Moscow." "Franco's victory is perhaps the dawn of a new policy in France." "All of us in France—apart, of course, from the Marxists—have praised the Duce's achievement in Italy, and with admiration we have watched this achievement extend into Tunisia; we have seen the rough and uncouth Sicilians little by little become aware of human dignity, awake to an ideal, their fatherland, and seek to make themselves worthy of it." "Despite his affectation of violence, despite his thriving in a glare of publicity, Goering is a sensitive soul." Alsace-Lorraine "for forty-eight years has escaped the systematic bestialization of the French people, the result of which is the Radical party." "Tunisia is a Jewish colony." "North Africa is a Jewish kingdom." "We must swear to destroy the democratic world of Versailles." "Above all let us not prate of the humiliation and defeat of France. At Munich no one has been vanquished except Moscow."

---

[3] All my quotations are taken from the articles written for *L'Europe Nouvelle* by M. Georges Bidault, which appeared in June 1939. In each case M. Bidault supplied references. One of the first of Georges Mandel's acts, May 19, 1940, when he was made Minister of the Interior, was to order the arrest of Charles Lesca, the director of *Je Suis Partout.*

We can properly bring this brief account to a close with a few sentences written by M. Thierry Maulnier, not indeed for *Je Suis Partout,* but for a monthly named *Combat* (November 1938). They tell the whole story. "These parties [of the Right] felt that if war should come, not only would the disaster be boundless, not only the defeat and laying waste of France be within the range of possibility, but, even more, that Germany's defeat would mean the crumbling away of those authoritarian regimes which are our principal bulwark against communist revolution and perhaps also the instant bolshevizing of Europe. In other words, a French defeat would indeed have been a French defeat, while a French victory would have been less a victory for France than for the principles quite rightly regarded as leading straight to France's ruin, and to the ruin of civilization itself. It is to be regretted that the men and the parties who shared in that train of thought did not, most of them, say as much, for there was nothing improper in their doing so. Indeed, in my judgment, this was one of the chief and well-founded, if not the best-founded, reasons for not going to war in September 1938." A French victory, then, would only have filled our author with disgust.

In this tidal wave of insane words, how tell where fanaticism ends and knavery begins? The boundary line is hard to draw. Most newspaper owners were a crude, an uneducated lot, not even politically intelligent. They were businessmen who traded articles and news. They might have made money cooking food or selling postcards just as easily. Bunau-Varilla was the strong man among them. In their collection of documents concerning the origin of the 1914 war the Germans included a telegram from Herr von Flotow, their chargé d'affaires in Paris. Therein it appears that on June 6, 1905, twenty-four hours after Delcassé's forced resignation, Bunau-Varilla prided himself on being able to name that statesman's successor and requested the diplomat to indicate a person on whom Berlin would look favorably. "Given the *Matin's* influence . . . its advocacy in this matter would undoubtedly have the desired result." Bunau-Varilla had not approached Von Flotow directly: he had sent his man Friday, M. Cavelier de Cuverville, which made it easy for him to deny the episode when it was made public in France.[4] He convinced no one. "Cavelier de Cuverville," M. Barrère said to me, "was Bunau-Varilla."

Our press satraps piled up handsome fortunes. Prudently, they stayed

---

[4] The weekly *Lumière* for December 21, 1935, printed it. Flotow's dispatch is to be found in Volume 20 of the German documents. It is numbered 6,853.

behind the scenes.⁵ The more audacious predatory raids on public and private pocketbooks were carried out by a sprinkling of editors and contributors, commonly credited with the friendship of ministers, with a hold on their favors, and by the business managers of more humble, and thereby all the more daring, sheets⁶—for such shaky enterprises could not always pick and choose.

The smallest fry of all were the journalists attached to the various ministerial departments. At the Quai d'Orsay they were given their little envelopes monthly. This practice was started by Gilbert Peycelon, Briand's factotum. Those who received their tiny stipends were treated as officeholders, and themselves felt that they were part of the bureaucracy. They were "leg men," from day to day dutifully reporting official truth; nor did they differ much from their colleagues in all other lands, who do the same job without getting a cut from the public purse. And this must be said: Everywhere men were found who did turn their backs on the fleshpots. Laval lost the day to certain editors of the Agence Havas, whom he wished to corrupt and make subservient to a writer of his choice, entrusted with the task of preparing a daily political bulletin. When Tardieu was straightening up his desk on the day of his departure from the Ministry of the Interior, he scoffed at a young fellow who handed him back his money.

The worst evil wrought by Laval and the rest of them was their allowing German and Italian agents to prostitute the French press.⁷ During the Paris Conference in 1919, Orlando once invoked French public opinion in Clemenceau's presence as supporting his country's claims. Without saying a word, our Premier opened a file and produced the list of Rome's hirelings. During the years 1935-40 the various French governments knew perfectly well what money was being handed out. There

---

⁵In recent decades the corruption of the French press may be traced to Adrien Hébrard, head of *Le Temps* until about 1914. In a resounding speech before the Chamber of Deputies, Jean Jaurès disclosed Hébrard's doings in relation to the Carthusian monks and the liquor produced by them, the chartreuse, of which they had been dispossessed. That sprightly Parisian was the first to smile.

⁶M. Barthou, Minister for Foreign Affairs in 1934, told me that a journalist who directed a starveling paper (a man since risen high in the firmament of the Paris Nazi press) received as much as seventy thousand francs a month from the Quai d'Orsay. As for the major contributors I refer to, the venality of one of them at least was notorious. His demands for money were publicly scored by Primo de Rivera and before the Budget Committee of the Hungarian Legislature.

⁷Charles Corbin, our Ambassador in London, received so many complaints on this subject from the Foreign Office that he ended by refusing to discuss it. But in private conversation he could not escape.

was no need of wading through the police prefect's reports to know roughly what went on. At the German Embassy those unfriendly to the Nazi regime did not think it amiss to talk, and a Venetian nobleman, tongue loosened by champagne, would now and then recite his "good deeds" for the week. In my diary I have put down this ludicrous anecdote, late in 1935. A member of the French Academy (one of those who now lauds the National Revolution) asked for two railway passes to Rome, where he was to represent his august institution at some public ceremony. The best he could get was a 70 per cent rebate on the Italian railroads. In the Eternal City he made a great fuss to secure refunding of the balance. Back in Paris, he finally was paid 620 francs. He was keen to recover his parlor-car expenses as well—750 francs more. But he did not work hard enough at it. His claim was dismissed. Later on this novelist went to Berlin and came back with a book friendly to the new Germany.

How would it have been possible for Laval to deal drastically with Otto Abetz, the fountainhead of German subsidies, the Paris representative of the National party's Foreign Affairs Bureau, the private domain of Joachim von Ribbentrop, and from February 1938, when that gentleman was made Minister of Foreign Affairs, his unofficial delegate? Abetz was closely connected with Fernand de Brinon, Jean Luchaire, Bertrand de Jouvenel, Georges Suarez—the hack foursome so dear to Laval's heart. These adventurers had long since staked their all on a victorious Germany,[8] and their press campaigns, scattered in papers of every complexion, conformed punctually to German and Italian leitmotivs. On the very eve—or just before the eve—of his removal from Paris, required by Daladier at the eleventh hour (July 1, 1939),[9] Abetz was still an honored guest at the hospitable board of Horace de Carbuccia, who edited *Gringoire,* and Bertrand de Jouvenel attended the dinner.

In November 1934, Abetz helped found the "Comité France-Allemagne,"[10] which he was still urging to carry on its task in April 1939,

---

[8] Jean Luchaire's secretary is now Frau Abetz. I hear that, under the rule of Vichy, Jouvenel has kept silent.

[9] Toward the end of June 1939 the editor in chief of a provincial newspaper informed Daladier that he had had a visit from an agent of Ribbentrop full of mysterious hints: writers of tremendous influence were going to deflect France from the Polish business, etc. This time Otto Abetz had to go packing.

[10] On the morrow of Locarno, German and French big business (metallurgists, coal owners, etc.) had put the same label on a committee of their own. But they gave it up on the assumption of office by Hitler. The Marquis de Vogüe, president of the Suez Board of Directors, headed the French group.

after the annexation of Czechoslovakia, refuting the argument of those who felt that it had best close shop. In 1934–35 his good offices led to the ex-servicemen's organizations of both countries fraternizing in several congresses, replete with the most vulgar sentimentality and with all the most fetching tricks of stagecraft—a stirring telephone speech by Hitler and, in at least one case, a bugler blowing the "Cease Fire" of the armistice.

In these German junkets the veterans of Right and Left vied to outdo each other. Jean Goy and Monnier had an audience with Hitler in Berlin on November 3, 1934, and their rival Pichot went there twice, in August and in December. In June 1935, Albert Delsuc had his turn—the secretary-general of the Federation des Blessés du Poumon (the organization of veterans who had been gassed or had other pulmonary injuries). Delegation after delegation followed in the wake of these chieftains. "Oh, there was nothing faked about the emotional surge which carried these men into each other's arms [the German and French veterans]," wrote Delsuc in *Le Matin* for June 28.[11]

What fertility of invention, what resourcefulness! Abetz started the "Left Bank" club to guarantee full houses to lecturers who might come from the other side of the Rhine. One evening, to honor him, the staff of "Left Bank" enthusiastically broke out into a recital of Nazi songs. Would any one of you enjoy taking a trip in Germany? Slip Abetz a word and the invitation will be forthcoming: you will be put up in the hotels run by the Brown House. Would any one of you enjoy seeing the Führer's triumph at the Nuremberg Congress? It's Abetz's job to sort out the "guests." Why not publish your books across the Rhine and draw a generous advance on your royalties? Just call on this obliging fellow: at least a score of writers—members of the Academy and others—have already learned the ropes. Abetz is a "man of good will."

Look at the trail he blazed through Parisian society, where men like Melchior de Polignac, who knew and employed Ribbentrop in his champagne business, had opened the doors for him.[12] Personally, I never had

[11]On his return from one of these trips a certain deputy reported to an important Jewish concern that the Germans had spoken of appropriating three hundred millions for anti-Semitic propaganda by the ex-servicemen. That interesting piece of information brought him a handsome reward.

[12]Shortly before the banquet given the German Minister of Foreign Affairs on the occasion of the Franco-German declaration of December 6, 1938, Melchior de Polignac telephoned M. Lozé, Chief of Protocol, to ask that his champagne should not be forgotten. Did it not deserve the place of honor?

Here is a sample of Abetz's humor. He was spending the evening in the home of a young attaché at the French Embassy in Berlin, M. Bertrand. The other guests were M. Max

the luck to run into the man himself, but only too well did I know the human material that it was his business to shape in the Nazi interest. Whoever was even faintly aware of the danger threatening France had to decide for himself, when attending parties, whether he would passively listen to the most revolting conversation or become involved in intensely disagreeable verbal rows. In July 1936 I was dining at the Spanish Embassy, on the invitation of Señor de Cardenas. The sit-down strikes were in full swing. On my right a lady who bore one of France's proudest names cried out: "Things would have gone much further had not Hitler, thank Heaven, sent emissaries to stop them short." The Führer, champion of social order, shielding France with his mighty arm! Could one conjure up a more ludicrous vision? This stupid woman, daughter of a family of big industrialists, however, accepted the Nazi providence as a fact and could not understand why she could not openly gloat over it. Another time, at supper, Count de T. opened the conversation with the remark: "I have invested a part of my fortune in Italy—a sound country as long as Mussolini is in control." There were four of us sitting at a single small table. The lady of the house had to come over to stop our quarreling. Today the invader has taken possession of Countess B.'s village, she who dared say, "I'd rather have Germans than Communists wandering over my grounds!" Unhappily, she is no longer in this vale of tears to witness the fulfillment of her wish. Don't let anyone think that such sort of talk went by unchallenged. One day I saw with my own eyes the summary removal of an unknown young woman who went around to marriage receptions, after Munich, getting people to "sign Mr. Chamberlain's golden book."

Outside the capital, in the provinces, the chatter of little people who claim themselves of noble birth was merely a less polished reproduction of what was being heard in Paris. Toward 1938 one of them confessed to me that the *Protocols of the Elders of Zion* was his favorite bedside book. The *Protocols of Zion!* A White Russian forgery explaining the whole world's agony by a conspiracy of the leaders of Israel! To these rustics Franco was the great white hope of Christian civilization. He outshone Hitler and Mussolini.

In this whirlwind of folly what had become of the *honnête homme,*

Hermant (formerly a promoter of "Rhenish Separatism," now a political adviser to insurance companies) and the Socialist deputies, Déat, Montagnon, Coste. M. Hermant railed at the scheme for a Franco-Soviet treaty. Then, by accident, the conversation veered to the young leaders of S.A. and S.S. troops who were slaughtered in June 1934. "German youth always sprouts up again," said Abetz. And he added: "How unfortunate that Frau von Schleicher's photograph was never reproduced in the French press! What an ugly woman!"

the ideal of manhood in seventeenth-century France, the man of sound general culture, free of professional bias, who is supposed to be the repository of his country's wisdom, common sense, refinement, and style? What had become of this fine flower, which never failed to bloom, so we were told from time immemorial, in the hothouses of the Institut de France, French Academy, Academy of Moral and Political Sciences? We can single out the names of a few brave individuals who strove against the tide: Henri Bergson, François Mauriac, Louis Gillet, Georges Duhamel, the Duc de Broglie. To this tiny band may be added a few who exercised more prudence, reserved judgment or were neutral: among them, Marcel Prévost, the Duc de la Force, Valéry, the egregious poet, and also Maurice Paléologue, the official whom, in the Quai d'Orsay of 1898–1905, Théophile Delcassé entrusted with the confidential part of his work. But why did not that last representative of France's successful diplomacy before 1914 rank with the courageous and the foresighted? The sorry truth is that Paléologue was dominated and held in leash by that great Minister's opponent and predecessor, Gabriel Hanotaux, an Anglophobe, an embittered man, whom he had to thank for his election to the Academy. These few apart, there was nothing left but fascists and half-fascists. Admiral Lacaze, an acrimonious old fellow who assumed to represent the Navy in this select circle, announced one day that it would be easy to bring Mussolini back in tow; we had only to yield him equality in sea power at the Disarmament Conference! I reported this to M. Camille Barrère, under whom the admiral had once served as naval attaché in Rome. This sailor without a ship hounded me with his fury. In the French Academy fascist Italy was a power. Joseph de Pesquidoux was elected on a letter of recommendation from Marshal Badoglio to Marshal Pétain.

In all elections André Chaumeix pulled the wires. He is typical of a certain breed turned out by the Ecole Normale Supérieure—of the man who builds nothing of his own upon the foundation of classical literature he acquired by the toil of his youth, but rehashes it over and over again with his mind fast asleep. He was, he still is, editor in chief of the *Revue des Deux Mondes* and of the *Journal des Débats*. For twenty years the same article has regularly flowed out of his pen: an elegantly phrased diatribe against the politicians of the Left. He never stooped to a serious discussion of facts. Did he know much about them? He was the brilliant diner-out. He repeated what he heard, touching it up with a witticism, a quotation, an anecdote. Surely that was enough! A piece he wrote on Masaryk's death impressed itself on my mind because it was so much in character. Whether you revered or hated the creator of Czechoslovakia, his romantic career, full of abrupt changes, which ran its course through the most exciting days of Europe's drama, could scarcely be severed from strongly marked political ideas. Chaumeix passed Masaryk's convictions over in silence; they might have frightened his readers. The bust he modeled was so soft and vague in its outlines that any name could have been carved on its base. Chaumeix took orders from the Comité des Forges and, initiating the two marshals into the mysteries of the Institut, of the drawing rooms, and of Parliament, acted as the keeper of their conscience.

Abel Bonnard, Pierre Benoit, Louis Bertrand formed the hard Hitlerian core. In 1936 the last of these was Ribbentrop's guest at Nürnberg. A young woman who is today Frau Abetz's secretary described what happened. The old enthusiast was possessed of the desire to get an answer to an agonizing question: in the designation "National Socialist" should the chief stress be put on the first or second word? He kept asking his Nazi host with true perseverance, "Supposing I owned a house in your country. Would it belong wholly to me? Would not some superior right of the state encroach upon the capital value and the income?" Ribbentrop knew exactly how to temper his reply. Bertrand sighed with relief. "At last I am reassured! The regime is more national than socialist!" Two members of our petty nobility, a worthy pair, the d'E——, gaped with admiration at this heartening exegesis.

In that medley, hatred of England was perhaps the most constant element. Of England as well as of Russia. Why? If it were not for England, no one need trouble about the Soviets. Her system of democratic government, wholesome, sound, paying good and regular dividends, proves attractive to other peoples. But, as far as foreigners are concerned, England, mother of Parliaments, can be compared to a lawny slope which gently leads to a bolshevik hell. Poor fools! Little did they understand that popular government across the Channel was nothing but a deceitful appearance. Little did they see that a small and stubborn oligarchy remained in control, that hidden contrivances kept the masses in their proper place. So they copied the outward show, the sham frontage, and left out the inimitable reality it concealed. In their striving to transplant British liberalism, they slipped all too easily into radicalism, then socialism, then communism. And, beyond peradventure, the London aristocrats deliberately baited the snare. Was not their money behind every revolution? Whence came the pamphlets to bespatter Marie Antoinette with mud? People clamored against German and Italian money which they saw at work everywhere. Did they so readily forget that flood of sovereigns dubbed "St. George's Cavalry"? Here was the wall of reasoning on which to chalk such scurrilities as Henri Béraud's, mentioned a few pages back.

In 1938 Léon Blum went to London and was hospitably entertained there by Neville Chamberlain, Lord Halifax, Lord Cranborne. For him intimate dinner parties were given; he could chat freely and informally. Not more than pomp and ceremony had been imparted to others. Rumors of this welcome trickled through to Paris. Society men and women at once complained to the British Embassy of what they regarded as a conspiracy against France or at least an affront.

During the autumn of 1935, in the very midst of the Abyssinian crisis, the daughter of an English diplomat was invited to luncheon at a golf club. "How I pity you for being English!" one of the guests told her. His host requested him to leave.

With Laval in office, this was the period when the prefect of police had to take the precaution of keeping Sir George Clerk and his staff under guard. In like fashion *carabinieri* surrounded the Farnese Palace at Rome. Nonetheless, subordinates of the British Embassy freely plotted with Parisian smart sets against those who wanted to see the Western Powers once more hold their heads high. A great many people at the Foreign Office censured them severely. For all that, they were left undisturbed.

As he thought of perpetuating himself in the premiership, Laval had plans of his own for internal as well as for external affairs. He never stopped calculating round this set of problems: how to win the parliamentary elections of May 1936, fell the Popular Front, assemble men of every political and social background and set up an authoritarian cabinet under the aegis of Pétain? He never publicly proclaimed any such program. However, he occasionally let himself go as far as to say this out loud to some of his visitors, as though he wanted to test their reaction. A conversation which was repeated to me on October 27, 1935, a few minutes after it had taken place, takes off the lid.

Laval: I have a mind to gather my party together.

X: What party may that be?

Laval: The Anti-Capitalist party. The men of the Left have never dared do anything. They have never laid a finger on the insurance companies, the trusts, the power monopoly. In senatorial elections they have accepted contributions from the Paris Electric Light Company.[13] The

[13]Comptoir Parisien de l'Electricité.

campaigns of the Popular Front are subsidized by the big interests, who thus try to protect themselves. The various direct-action groups include a number of anti-capitalist elements. From among these a party could be recruited. And that is my party. The platform would be simple; internally, a few steps taken against plutocrats; externally, a Franco-German rapprochement. Such a movement could gain formidable momentum. The French people does not take kindly to the idea of international commitments. It will only accept obligations which redound to its own advantage. It is uncapable of reciprocity. I regret that this should be true, but we must allow for it. Here is the watchword! A Franco-German understanding as against alliances—that chain of alliances which will drag us into war! I myself believe in the co-operation of the Western nations, England, France, Germany, Italy.

X: But that is going back to the Four Power Pact!

Laval: And why not? All I know about Hitler is that he looks upon my doings with great sympathy. In this country an agreement with Germany would be more popular than one with Italy. The French people do not like Benito Mussolini. What public opinion evinces today is not friendship for Italy but a dislike for England. The countryside still cherishes Napoleon's fame. To the peasant England is always the emperor's wicked executioner.

By his control over the purse strings Laval had for four or five years held in line leagues and groups of direct action, all born of widespread discontent: the Patriots League, under Taittinger, a Paris deputy of Bonapartist background; the Croix de Feu, under Colonel de la Rocque, etc. At the time when Laval coveted Doumergue's succession André Tardieu had warned him (November 1934): "Surely you don't think you can run the country with all that bunch against you!" He had answered with a grin: "I have been Colonial Minister—Taittinger won't wiggle. As for La Rocque, the Ministry of Interior takes care of him; we will have him well in hand." By the side of Taittinger and La Rocque, Doriot comes in for special mention. Doriot, a working man who graduated at the Comintern and had grown to be a fierce mob orator, was deputy from the Seine and mayor of St. Denis. An ardent Communist, excoriated in both lower and upper Houses for being a partisan of Abd-el-Krim, he had turned against Moscow and for this reason was backed by manufacturers and bankers. Taittinger, La Rocque, and Doriot: these ringleaders were permanently in touch with the Head of the Government. At will Laval applied correctives to what they did. On July 7, 1935, the Croix de Feu and the National Volunteers of the Lille-Roubaix-Tourcoing neighborhood held a meeting at Mouveaux. La Rocque inveighed against "rotten parliamentarism," boldly used the expression, "When we seize power . . ." Through the Agence Havas, Laval got these words toned down: "Degenerate parliamentarism . . . when our ideas come to power . . ." He was the boss; he could have his own way in everything.

Leaguers and ex-servicemen—those whose chiefs gladly ate Hitler's bread—were the means whereby Laval's legislative and journalistic following stretched out into the streets and highways.

Here, indeed, were the fields from which to harvest a new party. And it was incipient fascism. The Popular Front, already aware of its own might, challenged Laval to defend the Republic. Our sly fox preferred not to come to a showdown. The peasants were becoming alarmed at those regional meetings of the Croix de Feu on the grounds of some château, with their hundreds of automobiles dashing over the country-side. So in the Chamber of Deputies he staged a love feast of national reconciliation, at which Ybarnegaray, La Rocque's principal lieutenant, was on hand to aver that the Croix de Feu had no designs upon the regime and that they would dissolve. Laval quickly turned this seem-ingly voluntary gesture into an obligation incumbent upon all similar groups (December 1935). Was he trying to form a great coalition of these elements now set free from their various allegiances and subject only to himself?

In November, Brinon had been sent to Berlin, where an inclination to seek an agreement with England rather than with France had become apparent. Understandable enough on the eve of the military reoccupa-tion of the Rhineland, this trend bothered Laval. Nonetheless, the Pre-mier's presumptuous policy was beginning to raise its head at home and abroad. It came all too soon. On January 23, 1936, the Cabinet lost a vote of confidence in the House. That was a memorable day. What might Laval not have undertaken as the elections drew near? But he was not even given enough time to unfurl his flag. Ministerial power was sud-denly wrested from his grasp. The authoritarian reform, the master stroke which he had thought to accomplish smoothly and peaceably, re-ceded into the future. From February 1936 all he could do against his opponents, henceforward entrenched in office, was to plot and propa-gandize. The Popular Front had won the first round.

Twenty years before, Laval had entered public life as a revolutionary socialist. Now he was joining forces with those who had never felt com-fortable in a France dedicated to the "rights of man." In his thirst for revenge he made it his business to exploit the moral fissure in the French soul, the aftermath of the 1789 revolution.

Two Frances which lost no love on each other have lived side by side for one century and a half. The seamless garment of the nation has never been thoroughly rewoven. Whatever mending was attempted never amounted to more than patchy and ill-sewn darns. Under varying battle flags—those of the king, of the Church, of the Bonaparte pretender, and even of some general on horseback—strong minorities always fought against the Republican idea, against parliamentary democracy, neutrality of the state in religious matters, social reform, loud in their boasts that they were going to drive the rascal politicians out and replace them with a clean, resolute, and national government. They can be seen tirelessly at work in general election after general election: 1877, 1881, 1885, 1889, 1893, 1898. In 1885, had it not been for Rouvier's boldness, had it not been for the money he profusely spent, they would have won the day in spite of their own disunity. They were brought to the ground only under the impact of the Dreyfus case (1898–1902), when they staked whatever moral and political conceptions they stood for on the guilt of a Jewish army officer who was being tried for treason, on what should have been considered merely a question of fact. They floundered on the Republican rock, much more unyielding than their own makeshift association.

But these minorities did not falter in their patriotic loyalty. At least, since the War of 1870, the nation's single-mindedness against threats from abroad was on every occasion made amply clear. In 1814–15 there had been Frenchmen who were so devoted to the old regime, who so hated the Revolution and its Napoleonic sequel that they willingly and even enthusiastically greeted foreign sovereigns while their country's territorial heritage was in jeopardy. That breed seemed to have died out.

In 1914, Albert de Mun and Maurice Barrès, writing for the conservative readers of the *Echo de Paris,* were, with Clemenceau, the Tyrtei, the martial poets of the Republic. In those days our national defense found lukewarmness and skepticism among those who belonged to the extreme Left. In 1934, 1935, 1936, alas, the picture was reversed. We were carried more than a century backward. The *"émigrés de l'intérieur,"* the men who, in the homeland, behaved as though they had passed to the other side of the frontier the better to fight their country, rose from the past. The old discord and strife was with us again. Embittered against established institutions, it is not so sure that many did not look with indifference at an eventual military disaster, that they did not harbor the feelings of those Royalists who cheered Wellington at Bordeaux,[14] Alexander of Russia and Frederick William of Prussia at the Porte St.-Denis.

Whether he liked it or not, Charles Maurras pulled in the same direction as Laval and found himself among his men[15]—Charles Maurras, who, throughout the early years of the twentieth century, labored to restore some intellectual dignity to the French monarchical tradition; Charles Maurras, headstrong, obstinate, deaf, a closed mind and a truly Moorish fanaticism. The first time I went to call on Paul Cambon—a day that will never fade from my memory—that great statesman was reading one of Maurras' books, *Kiel or Tangiers*. "I've never seen anything so silly," were the first words he spoke. The pamphleteer explained that the French Republic had a choice between two policies—co-operation with Germany or co-operation with England. Either one could be fruitful, but whether it turned toward the east or toward the west, the Republic, with her bungling diplomacy, would spoil everything. As time went on Maurras found it increasingly difficult to place the British and the German worlds on the same level, from the point of view of French interests. He perforce had to discriminate between them. But, notwithstanding that change, he never rid himself of his deeply rooted aversion to British political empiricism, an empiricism which, from decade to decade, gave the lie to his own rigid doctrine. Moreover, as he always had a tendency to reproduce seventeenth-century solutions, held by him as unsurpassed models of what an ordered Europe ought to be, he was convinced that German particularism and Hapsburg Austria were buttresses Europe could not afford to be without. I very much doubt that he ever properly understood the German problem in its terms of today.

He is impervious to any events which do not fit in with his theories. He proclaims himself a positivist and yet allows facts no primacy. His brain works like Procrustes' bed. He compels both men and things to lie down, and what extends beyond he mercilessly slashes and cuts off. He never tired of hurling accusations against Captain Dreyfus. Colonel Henry's forgery? Much ado about nothing! Decisive evidence was lacking to condemn the criminal. It existed, but diplomatic considerations kept it locked up in the archives. That generous officer, Henry, produced the needed symbol and paid for it with his life. Maurras reminds us of

[14]Lynch, who was mayor of Bordeaux and became a count under the Restoration, annually held a public banquet to commemorate Wellington's entrance into his city.

[15]As a matter of fact, Laval was in direct contact with the *Action Française* as early as 1935.

St. Simeon Stylites. He never comes down off his column except to get bricks, year by year, to build it higher and a little further from reality.

This must be kept in mind. As he defined it, royal authority for Frenchmen will be an authority "by birth"—that is, as little open to discussion as membership in their own families, and arousing in them the same depth of feeling as before 1789. Think of Rabaut St. Etienne, deputy from Nîmes to the States General, who fainted away when the ushers cried out, "The King!" What Maurras hopes for is a return of that sentimental surge and atavistic attachment. And, for ruling men, wonderful tools they must be. The trouble is that they are no longer there. How shall we get them back? Maurras is not to be caught short. A preliminary dictatorship will cleanse the French soul of the devils who have possessed it. And then the old monarchy of ours is bound to come into its own. Very well, but this prerequisite deflects from the presumably patriarchal regime of our dynasty. To begin with, at any rate, we are not being led back to ancient institutions, but to a variety of fascism, and indeed Mussolini has occasionally set himself up as a disciple of Maurras —something which this French royalist repaid by condoning the crimes of the Duce.

Toward the end of his *Enquiry into the Monarchy* (1924 edition) Maurras arrives at the conclusion that, to set aside Republican institutions, brutal force must be resorted to, and he raises the question of how the blow can be struck home. Our champion of royalty is thereby led to speculate on the subject of military defeat. Certainly he does not wish for it. He would stop short of nothing to forestall it. "He will try to halt the train before the dread catastrophe." But since invasion is part of the Third Republic's inescapable fate, he loudly asserts that his duty is "to prevent all those evils which *are sure to come* from bringing death upon us. . . . Is there any reason I should shy off the thought that, one day, the internal enemy may be overwhelmed by the consequences of his own mistakes or crimes and that we could take advantage of a moment of stupor to get rid of him?" A moment of stupor! Could there have been a better prophetic description of the moment at Bordeaux? The meaning is clear: a Battle of Sedan would be a relay to Divine Right. And the whole train of ideas comes into full light. Mussolini and Hitler (above all Mussolini) have contributed to the spread of the Neo-Royalist movement for years, both by their practice and by their teaching, which gainsaid democracy's claim to inevitability. Their triumphal arms are fated to finally dispose of this alleged dogma, the almost universal faith of the West.

Once more the gash of 1793 and of 1814 was reopened in the French soul, but slit by more cunning scalpels than Maurras could employ. His true role has been to keep alive the old inclination toward national schism, to tear at the scar during the period when it was healing. He prevented anything which might have resembled a constitutional Right from maturing. But in 1934-40, as soon as a counterrevolutionary aggression got under way, Laval's gross demagoguery was more likely to win the day over Maurras', for the Maurras doctrine was attractive to a restricted public only, to those who, in the breaking up of the traditional social hierarchy, felt neither the courage nor the strength to hold fast to their own personalities, who feared that they would be overwhelmed by the leveling wave. Maurras reconciled conservative elements which up until that time had been inimical to each other. But, even collected together, those could not, numerically, be very impressive. They could hardly be a match for the formidable mass movement Laval planned to launch. Anyhow, national disaster was to both men a crossroad. There they met.

I cannot think of the throes of the *Echo de Paris* during this upheaval of our political foundations without a tightening of my heartstrings. This newspaper catered, above all, to the conservative and Catholic public, army and navy officers' families. Quite frankly, that section of French society did not particularly attract me. I did not have such people in mind when I wrote. "The widow of an officer killed in action in 1914 whose son is at the St. Cyr Military Academy"—a current saying had it that such was the typical reader. I had sworn to myself that I would set forth international events precisely and fully and would take men's measures impartially, regardless of all party lines. As narrow-minded conservatives in no way appealed to me, I gave little heed to them. And I must pay my editor, M. Henry Simond, that tribute: he always left me completely free. Never did he in any way give me orders; much less did he offer suggestions or advice. Which goes to show that even under the Havas monopoly islets of independence could still exist. Only once did it happen that M. Simond said to me, in connection with a Rumanian loan from which the Banque de Paris et des Pays Bas had made excessive profit: "You have twice said your say; now, please, don't rub it in!" With impunity I attacked François-Marsal, Millerand's lightheaded Finance Minister, the guiding star of "right-thinking bankers"; criticized Poincaré on Rhenish particularism and the agreement with the Turks—greatly to the annoyance of this statesman whom, moreover, I liked and respected. My good-tempered employer never said me nay.

However, starting in August 1935, with England and Italy at grips, everything turned sour overnight. Assuredly, Henry Simond did not undertake to change my point of view; he knew that to do so would have been to waste his time. But he begged me to water my judgments. Simultaneously Laval's personal campaign against me was at its height. I limited myself to recording the facts and explaining them, to contrasting my description of European affairs with his. But on this much I stood pat. "The general feeling of our readers is against you," the editor in chief would sigh. "You are probably in the right, as against the Premier. But remember the fate of the *Figaro*. It also told the truth when it pleaded in Dreyfus' favor. All the same, it wrecked itself in the process. And it never recaptured its former vogue." Henry Simond, already a very sick man, tried to placate the "officer's widow with a son at St. Cyr" by encouraging staff writers who had until then dabbled in internal affairs to tackle foreign policy. I feel compelled to broach that painful business: I cannot pretend to have forgotten it. Ahead of my articles, which always held to the same political line, were the offerings of these writers who were regularly kept in hand by Laval. For several months they cried out against the "Russian betrayal,"[16] heaped abuse on the Negus, whom they called the "rat of rats," and screamed from the rooftops that we must "uphold Mussolini in everything, everywhere and to every purpose." This last contribution, a blank check for Mussolini, was sent in from Rome and was shelved during M. Simond's absence. In the same spirit Herriot, public enemy number one, was held up to general scorn.[17] On March 9, 1936, the foolish pen warned that the "Popular Front was dragging France into war" to pull Moscow's chestnuts out of the fire. It was not until March 19 that he began to reverse the tune: "Patriots! Beware!" But conversion was not more than an interlude. Let the public subscription undertaken a few months later to buy a sword of honor for Colonel Moscardo, the intrepid defender of Toledo's Military School, stand witness for that. And also the plea for Chiappe's election, the defense of the Cagoulards toward the end of 1937. A whole-

[16]This outburst began on June 29 and 30. To my knowledge the conversations with Laval took place on June 24 or 25, and again on July 5. To ingratiate the *Echo de Paris* with its readers Henry Simond was weak enough to publish articles by Gabriel Hanotaux. Yet the *Echo de Paris* had, for years, been the mouthpiece of Théophile Delcassé, whom Hanotaux hated tenaciously.

[17]Articles of November 5, 6, 7, 8. On November 2 the Popular Front had staged a "Franco-Soviet friendship" day at Lyons.

hearted change of face was not to come until later. Between 1935 and 1938 the *Echo de Paris* failed in the task which it had so magnificently fulfilled since 1905; as far as it was concerned, it led French conservatives astray.

The coming into office of the Popular Front Cabinet, on June 4, 1936, determined as it was to oppose Laval in everything, fed the fury of the pro-fascist press. During the first fortnight of January 1937 I stated in the *Echo de Paris* that the Germans were making ready to enter Morocco. My articles were based upon dispatches from General Noguès, High Commissioner at Rabat, from M. Vaux St. Cyr, Consul General at Cologne, and upon the serious warning conveyed to the German Ambassador by the secretary-general of our Ministry of Foreign Affairs. The weekly *Gringoire* commissioned Georges Suarez to insult me in its columns: I had invented that piece of news out of whole cloth in order to precipitate war between France and Germany. I sued that sheet for libel in the Seine criminal court. M. Delbos, Minister of Foreign Affairs, wrote a letter stating that all I had said reflected the truth, as it stood on record in the archives.[18] Come what might, Horace de Carbuccia insisted on parading a string of witnesses whose shamelessness has become today a blatant scandal: Fernand de Brinon, Bertrand de Jouvenel, Edouard Pfeifer, Gaston Bergery, Paul Marion, Eugène Frot,[19] most of them now bedecked with honors either in Paris or in Vichy. I am really proud of having been chosen by those men as their common target. The court awarded me damages of thirty thousand francs (an amount rarely exceeded in cases of that sort) and, besides, imposed a fine. The defendants did not dare lodge an appeal. Pfeifer and Marion (himself a former official of the Comintern) argued that I had been hostile to Russia until 1934, during the years when she had been peace-loving, but that I had turned friendly to her as soon as her warlike mood had become obvious. According to these gentry, then, the proper thing to do had been to praise the Soviets when they were bound to Germany by the Treaty of Rapallo and to revile them after they began turning toward the Western Powers!

But those difficulties of mine are only of anecdotal value. The im-

[18]The detailed information used in my article was communicated to the Foreign Office by the French Ambassador in London on January 8, 1937, and Mr. Anthony Eden passed it on to the House of Commons on January 19. Strangely enough, Mr. Eden's speech escaped my notice at that time.

[19]Daladier's Minister of the Interior on February 6, 1934, who, by the arrangements he made, was largely responsible for the bloodshed on that day, and who subsequently apostatized from the Left.

portant fact was that the government itself was being pushed around and frightened by the fascist rabble. Already we had gone beyond the stage of mere verbal attacks in the press and scurrilous libels. Preparations for "direct action" were discovered: they pointed to an impending resort to force. In the autumn of 1937 the goings on of the Cagoulards, the "Secret Committee for Revolutionary Action" were bared. They were made into a laughingstock. M. Moytessié, the public-spirited official who was then at the head of the Sûreté Générale, however, took them seriously and explained to me why he felt disturbed. Six or seven thousand men (to speak only of the Paris area), armed by Italy and organized into brigades, regiments, battalions, with a general staff divided into its four classical component bureaus—here was perhaps no very weighty subversive tool. But, in the midst of mass rioting after the February 6, 1934 pattern, their plan to have squads of killers creep up onto certain ministries over rooftops and through gutters was not so foolish. Somehow the Nazi invasion of the Austrian chancellor's residence could be re-enacted. The Cagoulards are stained with the blood of several murders. The assassination of the Rosselli brothers had shown what they could do at Mussolini's behest. Marx Dormoy did not remain in charge of the Ministry of the Interior long enough to have the crimes of the Cagoulards thoroughly investigated, and I am afraid that his successors, including Paul Reynaud as Minister of Justice, deliberately cut the proceedings short. About the Cagoulards see page 334, note 1.

It was a far cry from Colonel de la Rocque to Eugène Deloncle. The colonel was a pompous fool. By mobilizing his "Leaguers" three or four times a year against the "communist uprising" which each time was surely going to "break out this very night," he finally became tiresome to all. In vain would these nocturnal forays end with merry feasting, at which old friends of the World War enjoyed being together again: boredom and a sense of futility pervaded the whole venture more and more. In contrast, Deloncle, an engineer, a methodical man and a visionary who had dreamed all his life of becoming the twentieth-century Bonaparte of our internal affairs, was not beyond dealing nasty blows. One may wonder whether, in December 1935, Laval's purpose, when he dissolved all the "Leagues," was not to open the field to new and unknown promoters of political and social upheaval. Thanks to the step he took, the truly militant were released from timid and passive leadership, in which they themselves had lost faith. Now revolutionary agitators who meant business were, at last, supplied with rank and file.

In foreign affairs the Laval party and its henchmen prevented Blum, Delbos, and their ministerial colleagues from redeeming what, under their predecessors, had already been more than imperiled. It will perhaps suffice to relate an incident which Señor de Cardenas, the Spanish Ambassador, was at no pains to hide. Toward the end of July 1936 this diplomat, although an ardent royalist, still represented the Republican Government of Madrid in Paris. Before resigning he apparently wanted to be sure that the rebellion would not peter out. He had, therefore, to comply with instructions received from Madrid and ask Léon Blum for warplanes. The Premier at once received him at the Hotel Matignon and, without a shadow of hesitation, granted his demand. "Good! I'll give orders right away!" The Ambassador's vexation and anxiety can easily be imagined. Were the Spanish generals then, despite the fascist air forces that had rushed to their help, to suffer defeat at the hands of the French Popular Front and, what was worse, on his own entreaty? Cardenas frantically looked for a monkey wrench to throw in the wheels, a monkey wrench which would still not belie him in his role of loyal agent. A telephone call came to his rescue. "Would you mind waiting a few minutes in the garden?" asked the Prime Minister. "This is urgent business and I can't put it off." Señor de Cardenas did not wait to hear the request a second time, but scurried off to the garden. Shortly afterward he returned with this bright suggestion: "On behalf of my government, allow me to thank you for your willingness to lend assistance. But would it not be wiser to consult Madrid as to the types of planes best fitted to the task?" "How right you are! Let me hear at once what you find out!" The Ambassador dashed to the British Embassy, where he had friends. They agreed immediately to unleash the French Rightist press. Its howls rose to high heaven. Sir George Clerk, Phipps's predecessor, did not mince his words, and some of his staff terrified drawing rooms and editorial offices. "England would repudiate the March 19 agreement, wash her hands of a France now openly turned revolutionary!" Léon Blum and Yvon Delbos, his Minister of Foreign Affairs, fearful of losing the British alliance, were cast headlong into the so-called "non-intervention" arrangement. Thus they backed down before what was to be an Italo-German monopoly of waging war in Spain. Naturally the French system of collective security was all the more discredited throughout Europe. How could a government impotent to hold off its adversaries from the immediate approaches to its own territory hope to maintain peace over the whole continent? From 1936 to 1938, from Laval's and Flandin's departure to Bonnet's arrival, the Popular Front did not rebuild our diplomacy from its ruins.

Hastily probed, such were the inner recesses of the counterrevolution in 1935-37. The reader should not jump to the conclusion that it was irresistible. Far from it. In election tourneys the counterrevolutionaries were unhorsed more often than not. They bit the dust in May 1936, and, in all probability, no better luck would have visited them in future contests. And, mind you, they never went to the polls with their program of direct action made public to the electors; it was garbed in the dress of democratic orthodoxy. They mixed with moderates and conservatives of the old patriotic type. Newspapers, society people, drawing rooms, the academies, bolstered as they were by "Leagues" and leaders of ex-servicemen associations, doubtlessly contributed to molding the most vocal section of public opinion, but they did not dominate the silent bulk of the citizenry.

In 1938, however, the harm they had done was considerable. Laval, Flandin, Bonnet, in the prosecution of their policy, had been spared that revulsion of public feeling which, normally, should have stopped them. And the "average" Frenchman had been cheated of that matchless tonic which consists of the unanimous voice of the people in the hour of the nation's danger.

Once war was declared, no trace of all these conspiracies could be seen in the open. The fascist sectarians would only stealthily creep out of their underground shelters. We have watched them slinking along the margins of Daladier's and Reynaud's stories. Before the first flash of defeat they masked their cravings, they concealed their true natures, they walked warily—above all others, the marshal. Then a Premier and a commander in chief worthy of the duties entrusted to them could with no great trouble have lastingly reduced to impotence the few thousand-odd persons around whom an amorphous and fickle rabble from time to time took the shape of a party. But amid the disaster Pétain and Laval seized power and gagged both Republicans and patriots: forthwith the faction pulled itself together in broad daylight. Never had it been so numerous. And the union with Germany, which it had not been able to consummate on the morrow of Munich, all hope of which seemed to have vanished with the declaration of war on September 3, 1939—that union, events brought within its reach.

SECTION II: THE DICTATORSHIP OF PÉTAIN

I

Duplicity of Pétain, Baudouin, Darlan during the Armistice Negotiation

PÉTAIN BECAME PREMIER on June 16 at about ten in the evening. The ministers who made up the Cabinet might well have been selected with a view primarily to getting a majority vote in the Chamber of Deputies and in the Senate. The marshal's determination to rule with a high and firm hand was not yet apparent.

Unusual names were comparatively few: Generals Weygand, Colson, Pujo, and Admiral Darlan (men who were at that time supposedly above politics), Frémicourt, president of the Court of Cassation, Albert Rivaud, a Sorbonne professor, supposedly pro-German, who was soon to get out of a bad job. The rest of the ministers were taken over from Reynaud's government, and we have already seen that he had based his choice on an exercise of the broadest parliamentary convenience. Baudouin, Bouthillier, Ybarnegaray, by reason of their ideas and their connections, naturally landed at Pétain's side. But Pomaret and Frossard, Independent Socialists, Rivière and Février, "Marxist" Socialists, Chautemps and Chichery, Radical-Socialists, were typical offsprings of the Third Republic in its decadence. Chautemps, who was confirmed in his office of vice-premier, had been a Minister uninterruptedly for eight years. One could not have found older or shoddier cloth from which to cut a new coat.

Pétain lacked boldness and self-confidence. He trembled at the thought of opposition surging up all around him. He did not dare take more than one faltering step at a time. He dissembled and simulated. He fooled Chautemps. This astute politician thought naïvely that, in the new regime, methods of compromise would still have their place.

In the negotiations of the armistice the duplicity of Pétain and his men is to be seen at its worst.

The first act of the Head of the Government was to summon the Spanish Ambassador, Lequerica. With Madrid as intermediary,[1] the marshal professed himself ready to appoint plenipotentiaries, and he asked Hitler to put a stop to the advance of the German Army and bombing by its air force. That the gang now in control had decided to carry their undertakings through to the bitter end became clear from Pétain's 12.30 P.M. broadcast, June 17. He made public his overture of the preceding night. This amounted to informing the Germans that, come what may, he would lay down French arms, that they could squarely bank upon the fact that their victims would not even try to turn and flee. Our soldiers, throughout the empire as well as at home, were given notice that their sacrifices had come to an end. Whatever remained of stoutness of heart was summarily dismissed. The old man's curt rhetoric echoed from one end of the country to the other as a clarion cry to "cease firing." The Germans kept right on coming and striking, but the French had heard the bugle sounding the armistice. So outrageous was the marshal's blunder, even in the judgment of those who favored surrender, that on the same evening, at nine-thirty, Baudouin sought to undo it: "France will never accept shameful conditions which would mean the end of all liberty for the spirit of her people. . . ."

Now let us glance at the other side of the negotiation, that which concerned our British ally. For four days Pétain, Baudouin, and Darlan went out of their way to have Sir Ronald Campbell, British Ambassador to Bordeaux, and the Downing Street Cabinet believe that they would in all essentials abide by the two notes received from London on June 16. Reynaud and Campbell, as we already know, had agreed to leave these notes in suspense, but upon rejection of Churchill's proposal for a political union of England and France they had become effective.[2]

---

[1]A striking change from the suggestion discussed two days before, in the ministerial council under Reynaud. At that time the United States, and not Spain, was mentioned as the most desirable intermediary. Baudouin's theory, at the outset of the new regime, was that, within the New Order, the Latin nations—France, Italy, Spain—must unite and balance Germany's power. See page 492, note 1.

[2]Campbell confirmed them to Baudouin and Darlan. He also took this precautionary step: he asked Charles-Roux, secretary-general of the Ministry of Foreign Affairs, to have copies of the notes distributed to every minister. Thus all the members of the Cabinet were given direct knowledge of the British Government's position toward the contemplated armistice. It did not prevent Baudouin and Jean Prouvost from issuing to the press a fantastic account of the discussions in Tours of June 13, which cast damaging imputations on British good faith. According to them, Winston Churchill, in agreement with Halifax and Beaverbrook,

The Bordeaux Government was striving hard to give the impression that they wished to keep up resistance.

Here is a transcript of the conversations which passed with Sir Ronald Campbell. On the seventeenth, at one in the morning, Baudouin, Minister of Foreign Affairs, received the Ambassador. He informed him of the change in government and spoke of the overtures which had already been made to Germany. Only an honorable armistice would be accepted. Handing over the fleet must be looked upon as infamatory; under no circumstances would France agree to it.[3] Baudouin merely repeated what Darlan had already found time to tell Campbell. On the same day the British diplomat saw Pétain, who had just delivered his radio harangue to the French people. He thanked him heartily for the reassuring words he had heard during the previous night from the Ministers of the Navy and of Foreign Affairs, but he wished to have them in more precise form. Falling back on the terms set in the note from London the day before, he insisted that the French fleet be sent to English ports without further delay. Without seeming to do so, the marshal side-stepped the principal points at issue. He was asked to act straightway. He dodged the request by a promise, and one none too definite, to act later and in very different fashion. The short dialogue came to this: Pétain: "We should prefer scuttling." Campbell: "But what will the government do if the German demands are inacceptable?" Pétain: "I shall remain on French soil. Very likely a small government will move to North Africa."[4] Campbell: "Indeed it is essential that some of the ministers go there."

Pétain's words, telegraphed to London, revived hope there. Were

had told Reynaud that "if events forced France to demand an armistice from Germany . . . England would not heap blame on her ally in trouble and would understand the situation in which France found herself, much against her will. . . ." But meanwhile, "certain French ministers, notably Georges Mandel, acting without government instructions, intervened with the British Government so that the Churchill, Beaverbrook, Halifax declarations could not be maintained, and so Britain took toward France a much less comprehensive and a more imperative attitude." (Published by Jean Prouvost, High Commissioner for Propaganda, at Bordeaux, June 24.) Cf. Hamilton Fish Armstrong, *Chronology of Failure*, 91–92. In his weekly, *Sept Jours*, Prouvost has enlarged upon that relation.

[3]On the seventeenth, and on several days thereafter, equivalent assurances were to be given to Mr. Anthony Drexel Biddle, who tirelessly urged sending the French ships to American shelters and reminded all concerned of the promises given before to Mr. William Bullitt and to himself. But after Mr. Drexel Biddle had concluded a long talk with Baudouin, on the seventeenth, officials attending the Minister noticed some irritation on his part: "The fleet! That's all the Americans give a damn about in our calamity!"

[4]Chautemps had been picked up to head the "small government." The choice of this weakling show how little reliance should have been put on Pétain's heroic plan.

the marshal and his satellites reverting to the formula which Reynaud had disclosed to the Ambassador on the morning of the fifteenth? That would not be so bad. Mr. Alexander, First Lord of the Admiralty, together with Admiral Sir Dudley Pound hurried off to Bordeaux. On the nineteenth, they were joined by Lord Lloyd, who felt sure he would be able to talk freely and frankly with Weygand. Simultaneously, a plane brought over M. Jean Monnet, head of the Franco-British Co-ordinating Committee, and M. Emmanuel Monicq, financial attaché in London, both entrusted with arranging the details of the sea transport.

On June 18 the Cabinet met at great length. After it adjourned a note was handed to Campbell. Therein it was set forth that the fleet and the Army would carry on the fight until an armistice had been concluded, and that, consequently, French warships could not possibly sail into British waters. The ministers unanimously acknowledged that any suggestion of an agreement to surrender the Navy should be rejected. Rather than yield, France would struggle to the bitter end. Whenever the army on land should find itself forced to capitulate, our squadrons were to be ordered to join Great Britain's. If need arose, they would be scuttled. Darlan used the same language almost word for word in talking with the First Lord of the Admiralty and the First Sea Lord. But with a not unimportant variation: "The fleet will take refuge in the harbors of a friendly power." Unquestionably, Darlan had America in mind. What an inconsistent chatter! At times the views expressed drew close to Churchill's demands and then abruptly they veered away from them. Even the least suspicious observer could have here glimpsed some cunning game.

On the nineteenth, the marshal and his Foreign Minister seemingly cleared up everything for good and all. They verbally informed Campbell and Alexander of the following decision.[5] The President of the Republic, the presiding officers of the Senate and of the Chamber of Deputies were to set forth for North Africa. The Ambassador and the First Lord expressed "great satisfaction." A little later the Ambassador went to call on M. Albert Lebrun. He congratulated with him for the Cabinet's resolve to refuse any dishonorable demand of the enemy and to set up a "small government" overseas. He offered the use of ships for the

[5]On that point I can avail myself of direct evidence. It was on the nineteenth that a governmental decision was reached secretly concerning the departure for Africa of Albert Lebrun and some ministers. The same day the officials on the staff of Baudouin drafted a set of decrees enabling Pétain and the ministers commissioned to assist him in the homeland to deal with internal affairs. Special powers were transferred to them on behalf of the President of the Republic.

transfer. That same evening, and this time with Alexander, he visited Pétain and Baudouin again. The latter volunteered an additional explanation: if, as was most unlikely, the enemy's terms should prove acceptable, the fleet would be scuttled. If not, it would carry on.

All this stopped short of what the Prime Minister wanted, but not perhaps of what he expected. Who could ever have hoped for more from the marshal and his advisers? Alexander and Dudley Pound felt they had done their job. They were unburdened of a great worry. That very night they went back to London, and Lord Lloyd followed them the next day, the twentieth. Everything had been arranged to convey Lebrun, Jeanneney, Herriot, and a handful of ministers to Africa. On the nineteenth, at Darlan's orders, the auxiliary cruiser *Massilia* was placed at the disposal of any members of Parliament who wished to depart. "We've been cheated," cried Campinchi, Reynaud's Minister of the Navy. "They have stolen our policy!"

Yet, in reality, this whole business was intended merely to pull the wool over people's eyes. Here is the bitter truth: the real policy was an unshakable[6] determination to yield to Hitler, provided only that he would leave intact some scrap of our home territory. The only reason Pétain, Baudouin, and Darlan reluctantly fell back for a while upon the plans worked out under Reynaud eight days earlier—the marshal to remain in France like the captain of a sinking ship, a group of his colleagues to organize resistance in Africa—was because the Germans, deaf to the proposals of June 17, were pushing ever further into French soil and taking prisoners by the hundreds of thousands.

Hitler and his counselors could not bring themselves to believe that the French Government would ever include the Empire in an armistice. So they shoved on mercilessly. Would not any respite they granted be used to prepare further resistance? On the nineteenth, the German Army crossed the Loire between Nantes and Tours. That night, Bordeaux was bombed. Almost at the same moment, after sixty hours' wait, a reply to Pétain's appeal was delivered. It consisted merely of an inquiry as to who the plenipotentiaries would be. There was no mention of either place or date for the meeting.

[6] "Unshakable" is the word. On June 17 a Jewish lady friend of Baudouin's had made up her mind to leave for England and came to bid him goodby. He expressed surprise at her sorrow and said to console her: "What a tragedy you make of all things!" Note the way Pétain described the North African policy of resistance in his speeches to the French people on June 23 and 25: "Vain talk and idle plan. . . . The silly dream of a sprinkling of Frenchmen who are ill informed as to how such a struggle could be maintained." In such public utterances he was sincere. When he spoke otherwise he was not.

Shortly afterward, however, faces and hearts at Bordeaux regained their cheerfulness. The news spread that the invasion had reached the high-water mark. How could this be accounted for? It was very simple. The invaders had at last understood, by dint of hard thinking, that the dominant concern of Pétain and his ilk was not national resistance but counterrevolution; that the total occupation of France bade fair to transform them into Dantons and Gambettas—Dantons and Gambettas in spite of themselves—that it was, therefore, in the Nazis' interest to call a halt and grant the Bordeaux counterrevolutionaries something that was conceded to no other conquered government—a formal armistice. If Hitler's generals were to seize all France's departments, one after the other, they would force the marshal, against the grain, to delegate power to a fighting "small government" in Africa. Indeed, that would be helping those who sought to arouse the French Empire. But if they discontinued the forward movement, they could rely on Pétain's complicity to curb these stubborn patriots. They probably did wisely, at the outset, when they put the fear of God into France's new rulers by making them believe that the German Army would stop at nothing. That way they had softened them up. But now they had better take their profits.

Campbell became aware of the changed tone on the late afternoon of June 20.[7] He even specifies the time of the day when the North African

[7]However, as late as June 21, 7.20 A.M., officials of the Ministry of Foreign Affairs still were given the order to hold themselves in readiness to leave immediately by air with Baudouin and Charles-Roux. This order was finally cancelled by 8.30 A.M. That timetable comes to me from an official who had a hand in the preparations made for the governmental transfer to Perpignan and Algiers. I have taken it as the guiding thread all through the maze of conflicting evidence. M. Camille Chautemps' testimony conflicts not only with the data supplied by the said official but also with the corroborating details obtained from authoritative British sources. Therefore I merely place it on record. I have not woven it into the texture of my own narrative.

According to M. Chautemps, it was only in the afternoon of June 19 that the setting up of a separate governmental authority in North Africa was seriously considered by Pétain. Then the President of the Republic summoned Pétain, on the prompting of Herriot and Jeanneney, and warned him that the government could not procrastinate in Bordeaux, exposed to the risk of becoming virtually the prisoner of the advancing German Army. Consequently, in the evening, Pétain, who regarded himself as bound in honor to remain on French soil, asked Chautemps to go to Algiers with Lebrun, Jeanneney, Herriot, and most of the ministers. On the following morning (June 20) the decision tentatively arrived at by Pétain and Chautemps the night before was formally endorsed by a ministerial council where Weygand, Baudouin, Bouthillier, etc., clashed violently with Lebrun, Darlan, Chautemps, and the marshal himself. Chautemps insists on the all-important result achieved at that juncture by his personal action which, for a week, had consistently aimed at detaching Pétain from Weygand. If that solution had been maintained, he explains, national unity would have re-formed around the marshal. France would have continued in the war and been spared the terrible division which was to materialize under the Vichy

stage setting began to totter—5.30 P.M. Stricken with anxiety, he dispatched a note to Baudouin at six in the morning of the twenty-first: the British Government must be consulted before the armistice articles are accepted. "Naturally," Baudouin replied. "We have every intention of doing so." Hourly the Ambassador awaited the promised telephone call. Silence, anguish, and silence. Toward midnight he learned that the draft treaty had been received and that the Cabinet was to discuss it at one o'clock in the morning. So the Minister of Foreign Affairs was not to summon him until after a decision had been reached. He hurried to the offices of the Premier. Too late! Baudouin could not be seen. When François Charles-Roux told him of Hitler's terms, in very broad outline, he violently objected to the article which required the fleet to be disarmed in French ports and, under the authority of a government which could no longer be free, to remain within the Germans' reach. He jotted down the formulas Churchill had used six days earlier, to serve as memorandum. At the same time he considerably weakened them, bearing in mind what Pétain, Baudouin, and Darlan had said to him on the seventeenth, eighteenth, and nineteenth: our warships should be put out of harm's way in English or *American* ports. He insisted that the Cabinet be made cognizant of his note immediately. Then he sat cooling his heels in the outer office.

He was not admitted to the Minister's presence until 3 A.M., the twenty-second. Baudouin read him the naval paragraph and elaborated on it. "That's all that concerns you!" He did not feel entitled to divulge

---

regime. Unfortunately, Laval, on June 21, bullied Lebrun and Pétain. The formal decision reached in the ministerial council on June 20 was not acted upon.

That assertion of M. Chautemps tallies with what I have said concerning the secret governmental decision of June 19. But Chautemps does not pay any heed to what had passed on June 17 and 18 between Pétain and Sir Ronald Campbell. He even denies all knowledge of it. Against him, Sir Ronald Campbell testifies that, long before June 19, Pétain had, at least, paid lip service to the North African scheme. And this main point deserves to be stressed. The North African plan was finally given up on June 21 at 8.30 A.M., hours before Laval bamboozled Lebrun, a scene described in the next chapter. Contrary to M. Chautemps' testimony, Pétain, then, cannot be said to have tenaciously clung to the plan between the nineteenth and the twenty-first. He and some of his ministers seriously thought of it as long as they had reason to doubt the intentions of the German military command. Once they heard that the invasion had been brought to a full stop, they lost interest. As to the influence of Laval over Pétain and his men, it did not break in suddenly on the twenty-first. It was a constant pressure bearing on the old man and his entourage. Laval must be considered an inseparable adjunct of Pétain.

The ministerial deliberation of June 20, which Chautemps describes as the most dramatic and impressive in the whole series of ministerial deliberations he has attended since June 12, was a side show conceded to the pathetic insistence of Lebrun, Herriot, Jeanneney, etc. The decisions which made the policy were taken elsewhere.

the whole of the German document. To sweep aside the objections of the ally he was throwing overboard, he gruffly stopped the conversation and tried to leave the room. But Campbell did not give up. He followed him and tore the paper out of his hands. At eight o'clock the Ambassador called upon the marshal in an ultimate attempt to undo what was so near accomplishment. Pétain feigned surprise. "Your government should harbor no apprehension. We hope the French fleet will be able to get to African ports—Mers-el-Kebir, Casablanca, Dakar. Whatever happens, the Germans won't touch it. It would be scuttled first." Already, in that early phase, African anchorages were being served up as a guarantee! The Armistice was signed at six-fifty that evening. Campbell took his leave. Now that the French Government is obviously under German control, His Majesty's Ambassador could no longer remain at his post. The Germans might arrive at any moment. The Ambassador must return to London. His government will settle its course in accordance with events.[8]

In its dealings with London how can anyone pretend that the Bordeaux Cabinet acted in good faith, how can anyone charge its continual wavering to new facts that compelled it to shift from position to position? Pétain and his colleagues had reiterated assurances that they would not surrender the country lock, stock, and barrel into the hands of the Nazis. Then, confronted with a proposed armistice at least as harsh as the worst they had expected, and perhaps even harsher, they recanted totally, and they sank into boundless submission. To believe their good faith, one should have to assume that the Nazi requirements turned out to be less drastic than they themselves had imagined. And that is impossible.

Once England had declared its will to conquer or die, it went without saying that the Nazi dictator would use the French nation as a springboard from which to jump upon his enemy, that he would outdo all precedents in his demands for disarmament, for military, political, and economic occupation. But had the men of Bordeaux foreseen, from the outset, that two thirds of our country's territory were to be held by Germany? That they would be compelled to supply not the upkeep of a garrison, but, in cold truth, of a huge combatant army, to which they

---

[8]François-Poncet happened to be in the secretary-general's office when Campbell arrived. As the French diplomat rose from his seat Charles-Roux asked him not to leave: "I won't be but a minute!" This forewarning of speedy dismissal hurt Campbell deeply. He keenly felt the pathos of what was taking place, the far-reaching implications of the break.

would have to print four hundred million francs daily—an amount exceeding the needs even of this military horde—and that the surplus accruing from the levy would be used methodically to plunder the country? Had they foreseen, on the sixteenth or seventeenth, that the line separating occupied France from the zone described as "free" would be a moral, political, and administrative barrier substantially uncrossable even for top-flight civil servants and official correspondence, that the nation would be broken into three parts, that the German authorities would tear away from the occupied region the rich northern and eastern frontier departments down to Switzerland, dubbing them the "forbidden area," and, for reasons of their own, would join two of these departments (the Nord and the Pas-de-Calais) to Belgian provinces under the Brussels Kommandantur?[9] Had the men of Bordeaux foreseen, before they made their pact with the Führer, that they should have to hand over such Germans as their executioners might demand "by name," to outrage the right of asylum, to accept the bloody brand marks of dishonor?[10] All the same, without a second thought, although they could

[9] In the late summer of 1940 the department of Moselle, Bas-Rhin, Haut-Rhin, underwent a *de facto* reannexation in the Reich. The occupied zone (including the forbidden area) consisted of forty-nine departments and twenty-three thousand municipalities, with twenty-eight million inhabitants, as against twoscore departments, fourteen thousand municipalities, and fourteen million inhabitants left in the "free zone." Some ten departments were divided between the two zones. "Unoccupied France is the France of uneven land and mountains, often poor, sometimes unfertile, whereas in occupied France are to be found plains and level uplands, broad and verdant valleys, coastal climates, mild and rainy. The first is ill supplied with bread, milk, meat, butter; it has enough potatoes, sheep and goat's milk, cheese, an abundance of fruit and vegetables, great stores of wine and some tobacco. The second produces bread, meat, milk, butter, cheese, potatoes, sugar, which were formerly shipped throughout the length and breadth of the land. However, it lacks fruit, wine, vegetables, tobacco." M. Caziot, Minister of Agriculture under Pétain, has asserted that, from the point of view of foodstuffs, the occupied zone represents more than two thirds of the country's total yield in all essential foodstuffs. (*La France Libre, Chronique de France,* December 16, 1940.)

[10] Article 12: "The French Government is required to hand over upon demand all Germans whom the German Government may specify by name, whether they be in France proper or in French possessions, colonies, protectorates, or territories under mandate." The Italian Armistice was silent on that matter. I have been creditably informed that Marshal Badoglio, head of the Italian delegation, wanted to spare the French this shame. But—and this detail caps all—the French delegates, sticking their necks out in their eagerness to be humiliated, seemed not to understand what he was hinting at during a plenary sitting of both delegations. He adjourned the meeting so as to be able in private to explain more clearly what he had in mind. It goes without saying that, in practice, Mussolini's vengeance lost nothing by Badoglio's gesture. Remember always that, according to the counterrevolutionary notions of the Lavals, Baudouins, Pétains, the refugees were no more than scoundrels guilty of having stirred up the dictators and having helped to draw France into the conflict.

use the Empire and the fleet at least to intimidate their conquerors, they bowed meekly before the torturer's rack that had been set up for their country and accepted unmeasurable slavery.[11]

But, fearful lest England take advantage of the German terms to alarm whatever elements in the population were still capable of indignation and rebellion, they studied day by day how best they might hoodwink Winston Churchill's envoys. I can only repeat: had the German demands been swollen to any conceivable degree of violence or cruelty, the Pétain Cabinet would have acceded so long as they were left some snippet of land where, sheltered not from German control but from the physical presence of the German soldiery, they could give their wonderfully reformed institutions a chance to take root. Their only other proviso was to be supplied with some way of saving face about the navy.

The bad faith of the Pétain government is especially obvious in the arrangements it agreed to regarding the fleet. How could it possibly have deceived itself into believing that Article 8 did not basically contradict the assurances given London and renewed each day for almost a week? To all intents, this government had accepted the essence of the English demand for a material guarantee, however different in detail had been the formulas it proposed: withdrawal of all units to English or American ports; in case of need, scuttling. The solutions held out to Campbell by the Bordeaux Government had had this in common with Churchill's request that it would not be within Hitler's or Pétain's or anyone's power, however much they wanted it, to hurl the French warships into the strife against the former ally. In lieu of this material guarantee, Pétain and his ministers produced Hitler's solemn promise, reinforced by their own, that the French squadrons would be left idle, far from the din of battle, and that there would be no demand for their transfer under the peace treaty. So many words, easily misinterpreted, easily warped by the passage of events. We must never forget that any promise between

[11]It is quite beyond my capacity to define this bondage by quoting chapter and verse: I have not the necessary data. Have the two armistice conventions even been published in full? Were there not secret articles appended to those of which Ronald Campbell snatched a copy? Charles Rochat, who succeeded Charles-Roux as general secretary of the Ministry of Foreign Affairs, answered negatively the anxious queries of his colleagues. But was he free to speak? Moreover, we know very little about the procedural aftermath of the armistice, the series of decisions reached by the Armistice Commission residing at Wiesbaden. We do know, for instance, that, legally, the distribution of all petroleum reserves was entrusted to the German authorities. In one way or another nothing was forgotten. The Gestapo was made free to come and go as it chose all through the "free zone"; it supervised the French police and had under control, not only airports and seaports, but the principal railway centers and post offices, external commerce, etc. Nor were the considerable quantities of war matériel in process of manufacture overlooked.

one natioñ and another always includes an implicit reservation: *sic rebus stantibus,* if circumstances do not change. Heaven knows that the Germans have worked this reservation to death! The two solutions, then— that which Pétain and his ministers had promised and that which they delivered—were not even comparable.[12] Moreover, I have still to hear that any assurance that came from the Bordeaux Government to the British was ever committed to writing.

The scuttling orders which were given to the fleet (at the same time as the conclusion of the armistice), in order to convince the American and British governments that whatever happened there would be left no possibility of Hitler trespassing beyond the terms of the contract, were hardly of a type to set doubts at rest. Inevitably they gave rise to questions which could not be answered with any degree of certainty. Would it, for instance, always prove practicable to carry out these orders at any given moment on unexpectedly short notice? Would there always be

[12]Article 8. "Apart from the portion which shall be left to the French Government for the protection of its interests in its colonial empire, the French war fleet must be assembled in ports later to be designated; it shall there be demobilized and disarmed under German and Italian supervision. The selection of these ports shall be made in accordance with the ships' home bases in peace time. The German Government solemnly states to the French Government that it does not intend to use for its own war purposes the French fleet which will be stationed in ports under German control, with the exception of such units as may be necessary for guarding coasts and raising mines. Moreover, the German Government solemnly states that it does not intend to lay claim to the French fleet when peace is concluded. Apart from that portion of the French fleet (to be determined later) which is to defend French interests in the colonial empire, all warships now away from France are to be brought back to France." Article 9 of the Franco-Italian armistice is more precise with regard to the units which shall escape disarmament: "Exception shall be made of the units the use of which shall be authorized by the German and Italian governments for the protection of French colonial territories." This difference should also be noted: "The Italian Government states that it does not intend to use in *the present war* the units of the French War Fleet placed *under its control* [italics mine]." The German text is weaker. All appearances point to the Germans having made use of the Italian Armistice to stop the gaps in their own instrument or to obtain rights which they themselves had failed to insert therein. For instance, Article 18 of the Italian Armistice reads: "All airports and air installations in the above-designated territories (metropolitan or overseas) shall be placed under Italian or German control." Article 12 of the German Armistice merely says: "The airports and installations of the air forces located in the *non-occupied zone* [italics mine] shall be subject to German or Italian control. It will be licit to require their demolition." In May– June 1941 the German Command was to exercise in Syria the rights defined under this Article 18 of the Italian Armistice.

By Article 9 of the Franco-Italian Armistice, Italy "reserves to itself the right to demand, as guarantee for the fulfillment of the armistice convention, the delivery in whole or in part of infantry and artillery 'collective arms,' of armored cars, tanks, self-propelled and horse-drawn vehicles, ammunition belonging to units engaged or deployed in any manner whatsoever against the Italian armed forces." Thus Italy held a lien on the whole French military establishment in North Africa. Germany took advantage of it to have one thousand five hundred trucks turned over to Marshal Rommel in December 1941–January 1942.

the will to carry them out? Moreover, were there not other sets of instructions issued at the same time, or perhaps later and of a different nature, to be used owing to the circumstances which might arise? Or perhaps had not the scuttling orders simply been drafted in accordance with the rule which is or ought to be observed by a General Staff: prepare and plan appropriate action for every conceivable emergency which may occur?

And, as though to cast doubt upon the value of the whole arrangement, a clause was inserted to the effect that, at the conqueror's discretion, the ships in their various ports might be exempted from the necessity of having to disarm and be kept available for the defense of French overseas possessions! Defense against whom? Certainly not against the Germans, who did grant that privilege, but against the British. The Nazis' underlying scheme became patent.

Both Germans and Italians were engrossed with the same purpose as Pétain: to avoid anything which might impel French sailors and French colonials to take action with British assistance. For the time being, Germans and Italians sought nothing further. This was in all likelihood the only reason why Italy was not allowed to take over either Tunisia, Corsica, or Nice, why she was allowed to occupy only a very few square miles at Mentone and at Lans-le-Bourg. The Germans did not dare believe that, at sea and overseas, French armed forces could be turned against the British. But to all intents and purposes they established as a principle that by rigorously shutting off the French Empire from any possibility of being used for British operations (that is, by rendering military services to Germany) the Bordeaux Government could preserve a few crumbs of moral and imperial power. Thus, between victor and vanquished was planted the seed of collaboration. Darlan threatened with the loss of his navy, which would have meant for him loss of all influence and political power, must have seen the armistice policy in a new light as soon as he learned of the aforesaid articles. As for Laval, ever flitting about in the background, he greeted therein the humble but sure beginning of what he described as a great European policy.

Things were clearing up. In the very midst of disaster, hope, even optimism, flowered among the Bordeaux counterrevolutionaries. The armistice, they kept telling people, must be looked upon only as a temporary settlement since the British Empire must surely have fallen before the end of the summer if not earlier. France might the sooner be freed from her strait jacket the better the grace with which she now wore it. The peace treaty was what really mattered. And the vanquished, ready and willing to join the victor, might perhaps be able to soften his terms. The armistice would not last and it would not sink deep. Its teeth would not have time to scar the flesh of the nation; only lightly would they harrow it. And meanwhile forty whole departments had been spared the German heel. Did millions of Frenchmen ask for more? Once rid of republican institutions, the people will be reborn.

This left one new danger (and anxious minds in Bordeaux were constantly reverting to it) that England and our own patriots might still ruin everything. So let the most handsome promises be heaped into Mr. Churchill's arms. Bounced about from day to day, he will waste precious time, and what is his loss is our gain. Such were Pétain's thoughts, instinctive and deep within him. They had not wavered since that hour toward midnight of June 16 when, crumpled in his armchair, he set to work to halt the invasion. He and his followers tricked London. They swore to heaven that they would accept no dishonorable armistice. By their standards, it is true, no armistice was to be held dishonorable that sublet to them a parcel of French territory. This was what they wanted. This was why Pétain and his men dissembled and pretended throughout these decisive days.

2

How Those Forces Which Seemed Ready To Split Away from Pétain Were Won Over to His Side

THE NEW REGIME relied upon the shock which the French people had undergone, and their dismay, to gain time for entrenching itself. Our people had no means of knowing what had recently taken place, but they knew that the least gesture of revolt, the least sign of disagreement would set the German Army advancing once again. However, even in Bordeaux, there existed men who were determined still to have the government move to Africa and to further this played on the prospects of the slavery which might otherwise be ahead. The Cabinet feared they might succeed in enlisting support among politicians for this aim. A cabal had brought Pétain into power; could not another remove him? Over the radio, on June 18, General de Gaulle cried out to France and the world that a battle had been lost, but that the war would be won. He foretold that the whole world would be set ablaze and that Germany, having gained victory by means of the machine, would ultimately fall by the machine. He called upon officers and soldiers to back him. He denounced the military faction and denied the legitimacy of its new-found power. His speech combined patriotic inspiration with sound foresight and wisdom, and how many of those who listened to him thought they saw at the end of the tunnel that light of which Reynaud had spoken and were comforted!

What might happen if from Algiers, Rabat, Tunis, Lebrun, Jeanneney, Herriot, Mandel were to join their appeals to those of this military leader then at Winston Churchill's side? Would not Pétain's Government fall to pieces?

Invariably, craftiness formed the old marshal's first line of defense. When Chautemps today thinks back over the whole story he must see in their true perspective the attentions which were bestowed on him for some very few days. On June 17, Georges Mandel was arrested for the first time. This was occasioned by an anonymous letter in which a Bordeaux merchant accused him of collecting a store of weapons. It had a strange sequel. The marshal demeaned himself to the point of drafting two letters of apology in succession, his stouthearted opponent having found the first too feeble. In actual fact, but for the deep-rooted indecision of M. Albert Lebrun, the controlling organs of the French Republic—presidency of the Republic, presidency of the Senate, presidency of the Chamber of Deputies—would have been removed to Algiers on the twentieth or else the twenty-first, along with a retinue of legislators.

The air raid on Bordeaux, in the night of the nineteenth, had made plain even to the most credulous what sort of freedom any government which stayed in metropolitan France might expect to have under the Nazis. On June 19, and in the ministerial council held the next morning, Lebrun could believe that the departure for North Africa was a settled matter, that the disconcerted marshal had, once and for all, waived his objections. While Pétain and Baudouin were telling the British that a withdrawal overseas was inevitable, they deceived our late allies regarding the true nature of their own personal desires. But at the same time they disclosed their fear, their intermittent fear of what the morrow might bring. The outcome hung by a thread. With the help of Darlan, Lebrun, Jeanneney, and Herriot might have made secure what they had won (verbally) against Weygand and Baudouin. But Laval, by his own devices, propped up the marshal's shaky authority. On the twenty-first, heading a delegation which included Marquet, Piétri, Georges Bonnet, Portmann, Bergery, he roughly handled and bullied Lebrun.

Jean Montigny has reproduced the scene from Laval's own account. "Why are we here?" Laval asked the President of the Republic. "To talk to you about your intention to leave the country. To adjure you not to carry it out. We shall not consent that the government should go to Africa and by this almost fraudulent shift should prosecute an impossible campaign. The President of the Republic must take with him the seals of state: he, therefore, will take with him the government of France. He alone will make the policy. Now, there is one policy which has been condemned by the government. This is the Reynaud-Churchill policy. Are you going to revert to it by dint of your departure for Africa? Two men alone—General Weygand and Marshal Pétain—are in a position to say whether the war can be continued. If they believe that it is necessary to cease firing, we should all bow to their judgment . . . If you leave your French homeland, you will never set foot on it again. Yes, when it is known that you have left the country at the hour of its greatest distress, there is only one word which will come to all lips: and that word is *deserter* . . . perhaps even a stronger word, *traitor* . . . I say it plainly and I accept all the personal consequences—I will not yield. My friends and I will not accept any such order and we will use our liberty to serve our country."

On the lips of Laval that speech sounded as inevitable as it would have on those of Hacha addressing Beneš, of Quisling remonstrating with King Haakon, of Prince Paul talking sense to King Alexander. Nor did it need such powerful ammunition to fell M. Lebrun.

In September 1940, Marshal Pétain told a visitor: "The National Revolution was successful only because of Laval." It was a hommage well deserved. But why did not Pétain, on the sixteenth, give Laval a post in the Cabinet immediately? The marshal's great concern to make changes gradually, not to be hasty in showing what was in his mind, not to make the British realize the whole truth, supplies the answer. Nevertheless, he kept Laval at hand as a reinforcement.

On the twentieth, under pressure from Laval, the marshal had ordered the ministers not to leave Bordeaux before eight o'clock the next morning. He had sent Hitler a telegram asking him to spare the city until June 30 so that the government, in its discussion of the Armistice, should not feel the desperation of hounded men. On the twenty-first, after Laval's upbraiding of the President of the Republic, the old soldier

probably thought he was rid of the danger of a split in the governmental
structure. Then he learned that Jeanneney and Herriot, on being told
of the terms of the Armistice, had once more stirred up M. Lebrun and
that the African scheme would come up again at the cabinet meeting
of the twenty-third.

The waverings of these three old-time leaders were but one among
many symptoms of the crisis. What French forces remained physically
untouched by the disaster were tending toward a policy breaking away
from the authority of the central government. These forces were the
Navy, North Africa, Syria, the colonies, etc. Ever since the days of the
Capetian kings a call to unity had always been synonymous with a call
to independence. For the first time in the life of our nation the central
government held high the banner of foreign enthrallment. Secession by
all those who either on shipboard or on land could put the sea between
themselves and the Nazis should, it seemed, have followed.

During these first days of counterrevolutionary triumph the activities
of Weygand were extremely influential. In the popular imagination he
was not yet disassociated from the personality and scrupulous honor of
Foch. What I have written about him earlier in these pages was utterly
unknown. Now he took it upon himself to stop the movement toward
England. In the hour of their country's peril all men instinctively grope
their way toward the flag, that is, toward the Army. Weygand commanded the Army. Weygand was the flag. His actions now formed an
abuse of this trust—and one frequently to be repeated.

But could Darlan be relied upon to hold his sailors in line? To say the
least, his perplexities lasted most of the week. He thought only of preserving the fleet, his own special little kingdom. If his warships were to
leave for America or England, or if they were to be scuttled, or if they
were to be disarmed by the Germans, the evil from his point of view
would be equally great. On the whole, he judged that the safest course
was to play Pétain's game. On June 22 he could have sailed with the fleet
if he had so desired. It was an opportunity such as never came within
the reach of any other military leader, but instead he chose to remain
Minister of Marine.

The support of Weygand and Darlan was an element of the marshal's
dictatorship—a necessary element but not in itself sufficient. A political
wirepuller, who should be resourceful, shrewd, and tough, was indispensable. So Pétain could no longer afford to postpone summoning Laval.
Laval alone would know how to check once and for all the counter-
moves of the Parliamentarians. So, on June 23, he was appointed Minister

of State; so also was Marquet, the mayor of Bordeaux. But what if, at the sight of this Minister with the mark of the gallows in his face, the British and our own patriots rose in alarm and Pétain, finally, be the loser? Let them try. Laval will be a match to them all. The government would suffer a greater loss if it had to get along without him. It was out of the question that Pétain should himself administer public affairs. Seated far above, he could only be the deity who alone on very great occasions condescends to act. Certainly no laughable figure such as Raphael Alibert, the Secretary of State attached to the Premier's office, could fill the intervals.[1]

Laval was the soul of the counterrevolutionary faction which, for a week, had been surrounding and maintaining surveillance over the new government and making ready to pounce on the top jobs. Away with hesitation! The National Revolution was under way. These innovators, who had never ceased to treat the country's independence as a perishable merchandise, which should be moved off the shelves before it lost its value, found every way open ahead. They rushed in. Their ambition was to write the last chapter of French history—and that is no exaggeration, if one believes that a France in bondage to foreigners would be no more than a dead body.

The armistice with Germany was signed on June 22 at six-thirty in the evening; the armistice with Italy about forty-eight hours later (June 24 at seven-fifteen). In the grasp of Hitler and Laval our country was shut off from the Atlantic. One could almost see the steel fire curtain falling down. Sir Ronald Campbell, with his counselors and secretaries, left Bordeaux on June 23. Charles Corbin, our Ambassador in London, resigned his office. He was a man of loyalty and good judgment. Having wholeheartedly served the alliance with England, he felt he could not apply a policy which had been suddenly reversed. His intentions were good, but stopped short of the point to which they should have led him.

---

[1] A lawyer, an official of the Council of State who never found a crevice to suit him in Republican society. "The most chickenhearted of Frenchmen," Léon Blum used to tell me. He had sought his fortune in many nooks and crannies, notably in Ernest Mercier's Relèvement Français (French Redemption) movement. This great electrical magnate had for the last fifteen years assumed the task of renovating our political life. He tried with high courage to propagate among the "elites" healthy and vigorous watchwords. But, as we can see, those in his employ were not always well picked. Particularly nasty accusations were directed against Alibert. After his dismissal he took refuge with the *Action Française,* and a stroke of luck admitted him to Pétain's secretariat during the days when the marshal's exalted future was vaguely taking shape. After June 16 he took on the tone of a high-and-mighty judge. He pounded the table with his fist and cried out for vengeance. He denounced the Jews, the Free Masons, the warmongers. He wanted to be the sword of the new government—and he attained this goal. On July 12, Pétain made him Minister of Justice.

He did not dare struggle against the enslaved regime. Subsequently he returned to France. By contrast, his chargé d'affaires, Roger Cambon, who also sent in his resignation on July 4 (on the morrow of Mers-el-Kebir) did not budge from London. The illustrious name he bore could not be tarnished by contact with such infamy.

France could communicate with the Anglo-Saxon world now only through the United States Embassy and Canadian Legation installed at Vichy and through Vichy's Embassy in Washington and Legation in Ottawa. From now on I can no longer make any pretense at describing events in detail, precisely and accurately. What goes on in our native land can only be seen as through a darkened glass. The best I can do is to trace the broad outlines. But from time to time I have met individuals who had, only a few weeks before, chatted with the marshal, with Weygand or Laval. Diplomatic information has filtered through. Occasionally we will be able to look at things more in detail.

Let us focus our attention on the octogenarian now invested with limitless power over the French people. A power exceeding that of Napoleon or of the 1792 "national convention" or Louis XIV or any king we have had, it sprang from despair, from dismay, from a universal or almost universal silence, such as had never previously obtained in the land. The old man had fine blue eyes, a noble carriage, the mien of a hero crowned with wisdom. Yet how far removed was he from the real problems of the hour. He had strength enough for only two or three hours a day. Whatever he might attempt, they would still keep their distance. Let no one expect him to plow through a file of documents, to reach, in some point or other, a conclusion of his own. All he could do was receive reports, listen to what others were willing to tell him, indulge in truisms and platitudes, give utterance to his views of the eternal verities. He had no great power of concentration, and what he had was soon used up. Even when receiving ambassadors in the afternoon, he would suddenly nod and doze. He had no landmarks to guide him through the maze of current day-to-day business. He knew nothing of diplomacy, of our domestic administration, of finance, of economics. In 1939–40, at the Quai d'Orsay, the remarks he made on international events astounded those who heard them. It was difficult to see how in the world it had been possible for him to have spent so much time in responsible tasks and still remain so ignorant and uncultured. For twenty years he had let his brain stagnate. He had hardening of the intellectual arteries. The years weighed more heavily on his intelligence than on his body. Anyone who wanted to make himself understood to the marshal had to reduce everything to its simplest terms and speak childhood adages or maxims in popular clichés. A bird in the hand is worth two in the bush. A thing worth doing is worth doing well. And the famous admonition of the fable: "Work hard, work well; work will never fail you." How one is reminded of Lamartine's revulsion against such tags!

Many of those who went to see him testified that he made a deep impression on them. But, when pressed to repeat what they heard, the most they remember are a few commonplace phrases. The source of their illusion is simple. He let them do the talking. They saw before them his solemn and serene countenance. He sparingly poured forth a few words. It struck them that brevity befitted sovereigns. A certain Ambassador to the Court of St. James's, many years ago, remarked to me that Queen Mary could carry off a ceremony in truly regal style because she had the gift of immobility. Pétain had the same kind of majesty. From his military training he had preserved the physical demeanor of command, the semblance of strong resolve. On June 26, when he heard that Laval was going to share in his vice-premiership, Chautemps belatedly understood the portents of the time and complained to the marshal: "Is this merely a personal distinction you wished to confer on Laval or am I to assume that my services are no longer useful to you?" "Your second alternative is correct," said the old man without a stir.

Now that he had mastery over the government, his reflexes were those of a general officer who bullies his subordinates. Treating the officers around him brusquely had always seemed to him part and parcel of a healthy military tradition. Toward 1938 he remarked to a lady who had expressed the hope that she might see him someday at the head of the state: "I'm not at all sure that the French would enjoy my government. I would manage them all as I would an army." To say all this does not mean that he was moved by some grim purpose, but merely that he could think and act in no other terms than those of his profession. Some of those who burned incense at his shrine have spoken of a strange theory he held. It was that a political chief, like the head of an army, is capable of adequately supervising the work of only three men. One pair of lips to give orders and three pairs of ears to receive them: such should be the rule from top to bottom of the administrative hierarchy. The Army is a perfect society. A generalissimo worth his salt will give no direct orders except to commanders of army groups. The impulse thereby set in motion filters down through generals in command of armies, army corps, divisions, brigades, and so on, until it reaches regiments, battalions, companies, platoons, squads. Transfer this to the political world. The Premier should have dealings only with a tiny group of top-flight ministers, and each of these with the several secretaries of state under him. Thus the orders given out at the apex would by degrees reach down to the base of the administrative pyramid. They would pass from the secretaries-general of the various ministries to the "provincial governors," who held in leash the departmental prefects, from the prefects to the subprefects, and from the subprefects to the cantonal executives and mayors somewhere near the bottom.[2] This structure was naïvely planned. All it could lead to was overlapping and confusing jurisdictions and further complication of an already top-heavy system, an increase in the bureaucracy. The old warrior, grown senile in the service, was trying then to force the political and civil world into a military pattern—and at a time when the latter no longer really possessed any merits worth copying.

If only some wonderful gift of personal magnetism, in the absence of a clearly defined purpose, had permeated these odd innovations, a number of which were in any case stillborn! But once again Foch's judgment of Pétain in 1917-18, when Pétain was in his prime, forces itself on the mind. "A fine executive but a bad commander in chief." All the more true on the political level where he was in strange land.

By nature Pétain shied from ultimate responsibility. He was all too prone to doubt everyone, himself as well as others. Was he then a mere automaton, a mechanical toy wound up in the dim past? There was still very much alive in him the artfulness of the peasant. He was quite capable of playing his little games; he still had plenty of tricks in his bag. He was vain in the extreme, and his vanity had been outraged. Foch had treated him condescendingly, and in 1918 the English had helped in his being forced down a rung on the military ladder. He had his revenge against all those who had humiliated him, and he relished it. Even in that evil day, what a comfort! The possession of power infused him with new vitality. Soon he took on the professional deformity of kings: the wild egoism of the despot was added to that of the old man. Better than anyone, he knew how to drop servants whose usefulness had come to an end or who might embarrass him. And it did not take him long to grasp that he must never associate himself too closely with the

[2]The re-establishment of the old French provinces (if not of provincial governors who, by the end of the old regime, had lost all their importance) was a pet project of the *Action Française*, since the departments, offshoots of the Revolution, had destroyed regional "liberties." No cantonal executive was ever appointed. Of those plans nothing came to maturation except seventeen "regional prefects" invested with extensive powers concerning economic affairs, police, etc. (Laws of April 26 and August 19, 1941.)

doings of his advisers so that he might always feign surprise and instantly dismiss whoever was guilty of having done something that did not work out to his own regal advantage.

Under a constitutional regime every action by the irresponsible sovereign must be approved by a responsible minister. Hence public resentment fastens on the ministers when there is cause for it. At Bordeaux and Vichy everything should have worked out differently, since the ministers were answerable only to Pétain and since his duty was to watch over them night and day. All this, however, was merely theoretical. Pétain, as an absolute ruler, succeeded in retaining the advantages enjoyed by Albert Lebrun. He avoided committing himself before the people. Hardly ever did he say a word, except in private, which might tie him down. Did some governmental decision arouse the ire of the public? He pointed out that the Germans had a noose around his neck and could pull it tight at will. Therefore everyone should have enough faith in him to believe that his heart, if not his actions, represented the tabernacle of a most burning, eager patriotism! And if this was not convincing, it was only because he had been misunderstood or his meaning had been distorted.

For long centuries the fathers of the Church argued over the relation between the Godhead and hypostases—that is, the personal forms He assumes. They ended with one single Godhead in three hypostases. Pétain could stick to no such formula. The number of his hypostases was unlimited, and all at will could be disavowed.

The Laval who set up shop alongside the marshal was as different from the Premier of 1936 as the latter was from the neophyte who, in 1931, was Mr. Hoover's guest at the White House. The Minister who journeyed to America was simple and unassuming. Those who conversed with him found him not without common sense. To Frenchmen heartily weary of Briand's ideology the senator from Auvergne was not distasteful. His intellectual reach was short and he was incredibly ignorant. Yet it did not seem entirely to the bad that for once a man in charge of public business should be set upon seeing the world as it was and not be satisfied with talk. Three years later, little by little, we discovered his double-dealing.

At the end of June 1940 the politician who reascended the stage was steeped in hatred, determined to wipe out his opponents, to get his revenge once and for all, to weld France's destiny to that of Germany. As of yore, he was surpassingly skillful at maneuvering in legislative lobbies. But the vague wish for omnipotence which his meetings with

Mussolini and Stalin may have awakened in him, the leaning toward political gangsterism which showed in certain of his earlier talk and acts, now burst forth in the open. He was to furnish proof that law courts and parliaments can fashion a dictator as effectively as can mass meetings, street fights, communist cells, and military camps. Perhaps they do it even better, for violent measures are particularly fruitful when they are coupled with the art of handling men.

For five whole months, from July to December 1940, Laval methodically carried out a well-planned program which was in strict conformity with the inherent logic of the armistices. Whoever had wanted the armistices must have wanted this program. It followed in their wake as inevitably as one link follows another in a chain. But Laval hurled himself into the task with so much passion, with so much disdain for his own wariness and cunning—the old wellsprings of his strength—that the marshal, unable to endure any such reckless policy, and wounded in his almost kingly pride, finally did away with him. Who could ever have foreseen that the Vergilian line *Sic vos non vobis* could even fleetingly be applied to this insatiable egoist?

Laval's actions at this time fell into four parts: the rallying of the overseas empire to Vichy; the assertion of governmental control over the fleet; the constitutional organization and implementation of the dictatorship; and the attempt at making an alliance with Germany.

The first of these, indeed, was already under way at the time of Laval's appointment. General Noguès, High Commissioner at Rabat, Gabriel Puaux, High Commissioner at Beirut, General Mittelhauser, army commander in Syria, Cayla, governor-general of West Africa, etc., were being brought to heel. On general officers, of course, the advice and urging of Pétain and Weygand had more effect than anything Laval could devise, suspected and scorned as he was. Nevertheless, that Minister's supporting acts were not entirely fruitless.

Apart from Cayla, I know all these servants of the state personally. There can be no question but that their first impulse must have been to fight at England's side. They made no attempt to hide it. Numerous witnesses bear evidence of their bent which, alas, did not prompt them to action.[3] On the seventeenth, eighteenth, nineteenth, they all criticized Bordeaux's folly and wanted to keep aloof from it. By the twentieth and twenty-first they began to waver. Only characters of rare mettle could break with official France, represented as she was by two illustrious

---

[3]There is even a message from Mittelhauser to Sir Archibald Wavell and a ringing reply from the same French military leader to a telegram from the French colony in Cairo.

soldiers. Only strong men could gather enough courage to cut themselves off from the seeming majority of the French people, from all
established hierarchy. "Every last one of you is wrong and I alone am
right." Very few have enough firmness of conscience to be able to utter
that proud admonition. Least of all General Noguès, who was a kind
of military Chautemps, practiced in the devices of politics. Had he not
won from Léon Blum his appointment to the Morocco high commissionership, which since 1925 had been held by a civilian official—a by no
means ordinary achievement, because the Socialist Prime Minister, in
numberless press articles, had argued that generals ought not to be employed outside their profession?

Never lose sight of this truth, applicable to all officials, great and small:
whoever wants above all to hang on to his pension and his honors, come
what may, will try to do so by *not* severing himself from the legal structure to which, willingly or under compulsion, the majority are tied. In
1940, at any rate, it looked the safer course. To rebel was a risky business,
unless the crushing of the Nazis should follow.

Noguès was the senior proconsul with, in the language of strategy, a
key territory under him. All the rest would follow his lead. Everything
was settled when it turned out that the memorandum which Noguès
had sent to Bordeaux, to urge continuance of the struggle, ended, as far
as he personally was concerned, with an evasion. In effect, he told the
government that he would begin weighing the matter afresh and, at the
most, execute the armistice with shame on his face.[4] The threat was un-
impressive. Marcel Peyrouton, resident general in Tunisia, long addicted
to fascist methods, met Noguès and Le Beau, the governor-general of
Algeria in Algiers. He easily overcame Noguès' objections, and Le Beau,
an honest man, had perforce to submit.[5]

Gabriel Puaux had drafted a letter to the British Ambassador in
Egypt. He kept it safe in his pocket. Meanwhile the Bordeaux Government had ascertained, to its intense relief, that an American Ambassador
would remain in residence at Vichy. "How could I suspect a government

---

[4]His reply to Catroux, governor-general of Indo-China, who had congratulated him on
the rumor of his revolt, was: "You are mistaken." Catroux did not dare resist the Japanese
ultimatum of June 16. A word of encouragement from Washington would have put him
right. But, in all likelihood, Washington did not want to risk worsening its relations with
Japan.

[5]On June 22 and 23 the British consuls general in Algiers, Tunis, Rabat were instructed
from London to press Le Beau, Peyrouton, and Noguès to secede from the central government. Some have been at pains to explain that such a "tactless" step had caused a revulsion
of feeling in the three men. I am not impressed by that explanation.

with which the United States continued full diplomatic relations?" said Puaux. From Washington no encouragement whatever reached General de Gaulle, who, with Winston Churchill's backing, had been leader of the Free French ever since June 18. Such was the High Commissioner's excuse. And even Winston Churchill did not feel much concern over what became of Syria and French West Africa.

The battleship *Richelieu* arrived at Dakar on June 23. Her commander, Captain Marzin, attended a meeting at which it was decided to call in British forces. The governor, the commandant of the garrison, and the ranking naval officer were all present. Marzin dashed out to sea; he feared that when our former allies appeared he might lose his freedom of movement. But no English squadron came. Dakar was a fruit ripe for the plucking at any time one wanted it. Why hurry? That was how things were seen at Whitehall. But then Admiral de Laborde and later Rear Admirals Lacroix and Platon[6] were dispatched to check the drift toward England. For the same purpose Weygand found time to visit Beirut about June 25. Three days later the armistice came in force in Syria. None of this was Laval's doing. However, he was soon to show his face.

On the twentieth, aboard the *Massilia,* Daladier, Campinchi, Jean Zay, Viénot, Mendès-France—all former ministers or under secretaries of state, left Bordeaux, accompanied by some fifteen members of Parliament. With official help they set forth to join the government—which they believed to be on the point of going over to Africa. Both Herriot and Jeanneney had made arrangements to depart and only at the last moment realized what the Cabinet really had in mind. The others were not warned. Laval ordered the Casablanca authorities to hold everyone on the ship and afterward assign forced residences to the whole lot. For more than a month the passengers were treated as prisoners while the servile French press denounced their flight and treason to the French people. The flight and treason of men who were determined to flout

---

[6]A zealot of *Action Française.* In prewar days Darlan had to rebuke him because of a Maurras portrait he made a point to exhibit in his cabin. The work of those men was to be completed by Pierre Boisson, who, at the time of the armistice, was governor-general of Equatorial Africa. Until June 23, Boisson displayed a wild determination to resist. He changed all of a sudden on hearing of his promotion to the governor-generalship of West Africa in Dakar (June 25). He assumed his new function on July 23 and twenty-four hours later, in a first telegram to Vichy, pointed out that "in all French circles most wished for the African colonies to side with England . . . The solution of the crisis called for much psychological insight and gradual administrative treatment." Boisson, later on, made himself conspicuous by the cruel treatment meted out in his jails to followers of de Gaulle and officers and men of the British Merchant Navy.

Hitler's power or the power of his satellites, who could not bring themselves to forswear the independence of their own country! At all times it has been judged praiseworthy and meritorious to escape from the enemy's control.

Strangest of all was the story of what happened to Mandel. It is stamped all over with the trademark of Laval. Having learned of Daladier's arrival in Morocco, the London Cabinet sent Alfred Duff Cooper and Lord Gort there to establish contact with him. These two emissaries arrived at Rabat on the evening of the twenty-fifth. At that time the *Massilia* had been lying at anchor for some twelve hours in the Casablanca roadstead. Duff Cooper and Lord Gort tried to reach the British consul by telephone, but came up against official instructions forbidding this. They had an unpleasant talk with M. Morize, secretary-general of the government of Morocco. Not only did the latter tell them that it would be impossible for General Noguès (lingering at Algiers in conference with his colleagues) to receive them: a policeman forbade General Dillon, British liaison officer living at Rabat, to leave his hotel.[7] They did not persist in their endeavor and flew away. Mandel was accused of having been in communication with the British Cabinet and of having shared in a treasonable plot. He was haled before a military court. The officer whose task it was to investigate the case decided to drop it. He was recalled to France before he could even hand in his decision. Military courts were brought into action against others than Mandel. Mendès-France, an air-force lieutenant whose regiment had been transferred to Morocco, was falsely charged with desertion. Later he was brought before the court-martial at Clermont-Ferrand, where the presiding judge was a fanatic, Colonel Perré.

---

[7] "I would rather have received an order to shoot myself," Morize told Duff Cooper. "But, as an official, I have to obey."

The *Massilia*, on June 26, steamed out into the open sea to make all contact impossible. Its political passengers were ordered to take up forced residence on the evening of the twenty-sixth. Later on, in July, long after Mers-el-Kebir, an English destroyer entered the inner harbor of Casablanca, and Daladier had an opportunity to board her. On two separate occasions he failed to reach the appointed place of meeting, either through oversight or hesitancy. The third time he embarked on the lighter hired to carry him off. But while still some eight hundred yards short of the destroyer, the lighthouse focused its searchlights on him and he had to go back to the dock. He was, at the time, only casually watched in one of the city's small hotels. By contrast Mandel, whose courage and dignity were beyond praise, was under constant surveillance.

Dragged back to France, Daladier, until the time of his arrest, lived at a friend's château near Gannat. One of my acquaintances went to see him. "If I am given a secret trial," he said, "I shall not escape. Laval will have me killed. But if the hearings are public, I have no fears. I shall know how to defend myself."

By such preliminary moves Laval prepared the ground for the surrender of Parliament. The people were stirred up against the "refugees," and an especially energetic group, for Daladier and Mandel knew how to make themselves heard, was kept away from the National Assembly which in time was to strike down the Republic.

In the second operation Laval likewise played no part at the outset, but he made great capital of it. I refer to the taking of the fleet under control and to the painful clash at Mers-el-Kebir on July 3. When the British ministers read the terms of the Franco-German Armistice on June 22, their real perplexities began. As to the Navy, could Article 8 of the armistice be taken by them as an acceptable substitute for the material guarantees they had attempted to get from the Bordeaux Government? At first Winston Churchill wanted to think so. Heretofore he had never seen through Darlan's duplicity regarding England, the jealousy which the world's paramount naval power aroused in the admiral. Churchill asked no better than to think him a faithful warrior. But the vastness of what was at stake gave him pause. A careful study of both armistices little by little convinced him the risk could not be overlooked. He wondered whether the provision that the French warships might be spared disarmament and assigned to the defense of the French Empire was not the germ of collaboration. Neither Pétain nor Baudouin nor even the Admiral of the fleet had kept the promises lavished on London's envoys during the preceding days. It sufficed to compare the armistices with the words they had spoken to Campbell. When Duff Cooper and Gort returned, a decision was reached. The French fleet would be called upon either to set sail for British waters with reduced crews, or to join the British squadrons, or to have itself interned in American ports, or to be demilitarized in the French West Indies, or to scuttle itself.

A friendly settlement seemed the most likely outcome. On June 17 the overtures for an armistice, broadcast by the marshal, had come as a great surprise to officers and crews, well aware of France's strength on the ocean. Vice-Admiral Traub, maritime prefect of Brest, had plastered the town with posters describing Pétain's radio speech as a Nazi fabrication. He proclaimed France still to be at war. On the evening of the eighteenth, Darlan and Weygand had given telegraphic orders not to stop the fight. Everyone expected to get instructions to move toward England. The same day two 35,000-ton battleships, the *Richelieu,* which had finished her trials, and the *Jean Bart,* which had not yet started on hers, took to sea on their own initiative, one getting up steam at Brest and the other at St. Nazaire. Their skippers did not want to fall into the German net.

Slowly the underlying significance of things unveiled. Messages from the Ministry of the Navy changed in tone. "Do not continue to carry instructions received from British authorities." "Cease informing British liaison officers of the contents of our dispatches." "Put them ashore." "Stop using Gibraltar as a source of supply." "All merchant ships in British convoys are at once to detach themselves therefrom and make for a French port." Gradually the veering round became more marked. The sailors of the *Richelieu* thought they were bound for Bordeaux to carry away the government. Soon their eyes opened to the harsh fact that African ports had been designated for the disarmament of our various units.

On June 26, Darlan personally undertook to explain to all seamen by radio what had taken place.

And with what guile! A candidate for office addressing electoral meetings would not have selected his words differently.[8] He spoke as though France were still mighty on the seas. He emphasized that the "demobilization" of reservists would be carried out "in humane and socially enlightened fashion." The men let go. The whole drama confused them. It

---

[8]The document is worth reproducing textually. Darlan is in it, large as life. His interpretation of the armistice need not be merely taken as propaganda. It affords a peephole in the negotiations with the enemy.

"No. 3158. (1) I have at hand clauses of the two signed armistices; none of them are dishonorable; our Navy and Air Force should see in the exceptional treatment accorded them a tribute to their conduct and a recognition of their worth. Pay no attention to versions which you will see in the French and in adverse papers; they are likely to be incomplete. You may expect to receive complete texts from me, as well as minutes of verbal discussions which at various points somewhat reduce the severity of the written provisions—minutes brought back by our own delegates, among them Admiral Le Luc.

"(2) Once again and for the last time I repeat that we retain all our warships and naval aircraft, that we are not limited as to the number of naval effectives we may have in active service, and that our opponents have entered a solemn written obligation not to lay a finger on our Navy under the peace treaty. Being defeated, what more could we hope for?

"(3) It is now a question of abiding loyally and with dignity by signed agreements. To act otherwise would be definitely to complete the ruin of our country, already seriously crippled by defeat. To accede to selfish appeals coming from abroad would lead to our home territory's becoming a German province. Our former allies must not be listened to. Let us think as Frenchmen, act as Frenchmen.

"(4) Everyone must await my orders, wherever he is; they will reach you within a few days, as soon as the Armistice Commissions can get to work. These orders will first of all provide for the movements of vessels toward French ports and then for preparing—I stress that word—the demobilization of reservists in a humane and socially enlightened fashion. They will not be thrown into the streets.

"(5) It is forbidden to make use of the transmitting facilities of land radio-telegraph stations, naval and otherwise, in continental France, Corsica, North Africa, the Levant and

lay within their chief's power to sway them in one direction or another.

Unfortunately, an important squadron, lying at anchor at Mers-el-Kebir and including two powerful 26,000-ton battleships, the *Dunkerque* and the *Strasbourg,* an old modernized battleship, the *Bretagne,* some light cruisers, destroyers, and the aircraft carrier *Commandant Teste,* was in Vice-Admiral Gensoul's charge. A few weeks after Munich, Darlan had substituted this second-rater for Vice-Admiral de Laborde, in whom he thought he had discovered a dangerous rival. When Commander Holland, former naval attaché in Paris delivered the ultimatum (he had come on the destroyer *Foxhound*) Gensoul dared not make a decision. For an hour and a half, sweat streaming down his cheeks, the British officer begged him in vain to harken only to France's ultimate interest, at one with Great Britain's: the admiral insisted on asking the Vichy ministers for instructions, and they, with the German ax at their necks, with all radio stations under enemy control, could make but one reply: Refuse Admiral Somerville's proposal.[9] A few days later, at Alexandria, Vice-Admiral Godefroy, with a number of cruisers under his flag, took a very different attitude.

Mers-el-Kebir was the most devastating clash between the French and English. Some thirteen hundred men were killed. Thanks to the ineptitude or the blindness of those who today claim that they fought in the revolutionary spirit of the sailors on board the *Vengeur,* 147 years before, the sacrifice was made at the expense of the nation's independence. Laval the demagogue found himself in a position, at least for a season, to embitter hearts against England. How easy it was to build up the contrast for the man in the street, the ordinary seaman and the soldier,

---

Djibouti until an agreement is reached regarding them with Germany and Italy, a matter of two or three days. Other colonial stations are free to send messages. Continue everywhere to listen, as provided in the L.T. regulations—I repeat, L.T. (Liaison, Transmission)—in order to be sure to catch anything that passes through the air.

"(6) Every command receiving information or orders from me must use its best ingenuity to pass them to other commands, by whatever licit means of transmittal may be available. The anxiety all through the Navy is traceable to insufficient information as to events and decisions reached.

"(7) I appeal to the spirit of discipline wherein lay our strength throughout the conflict. I cannot believe that those who faithfully obeyed me when I had to ask them to die for their country will lack the moral courage to obey when my purpose is to make sure her recovery, however hard it may be at the moment.

"(8) Inform all those under you and acknowledge receipt.

0807/26/6
Admiral of the French Fleet: DARLAN."

[9] It is said that, all the same, a white flag was hoisted for fourteen minutes. The English seem not to have seen it. I am told that, in Vichy, Baudouin did all that he could to bring about the conflict.

between the chivalrous Bordeaux Government, insisting in its armistice that the French warships be not used against the allies of yesterday, forswearing the great material advantages which their surrender must surely have produced, and the hail of bullets received by way of thanks! And it was all the easier because the ultimatum delivered by Commander Holland was never published in France in a complete version. The choices of internment in the United States or withdrawal to the West Indies were carefully deleted. Even Pétain himself was not to hear the truth until six months later, and then from a senator who was one of Laval's retinue.

As early as June 23 the officers and the men of the *Richelieu,* which was heading for Dakar, had resented the "surveillance" of a British cruiser. They bore ill that evidence of distrust. One can understand how they felt after Mers-el-Kebir. Yet on July 9, when British pilots succeeded in hitting the *Richelieu's* screws with a torpedo, the crews of our submarines refused to counterattack. Despite what the raging press kept screaming at them, many understood what went on.[10] Once Pétain showed to one of his visitors a letter which he had received from a peasant in Brittany. That man had lost his son at Mers-el-Kebir but did not complain. He correctly interpreted British motives.

To precipitate the Cabinet into a declaration of war was, however, beyond Laval's reach. Pétain and the rest held him back. But from the events of July 3 he first of all won a propaganda advantage. In future, hatred of England could be freely inculcated. In the second place, the Germans, who had long been in fear lest England might seize the strategical keys to the French Empire, were astounded that Gensoul's squadron had not steamed off in the wake of Somerville's fleet, that it had even returned the fire of our former allies. They began to wonder whether the French naval forces did not deserve their confidence. In a spirit of profound skepticism they had drawn up the clause of the armistice entrusting French sailors with the protection of the Empire against the British. Henceforth they took it seriously. They allowed all units to remain in active duty. In their own interest they could have

[10]It should be noted that at Mers-el-Kebir the air force played no part. Two or three planes daily, during the preceding week or so, had been sneaking off for Gibraltar or England. General Têtu had had all magnetos removed. Seven or eight machines in the end circled around over the fight. They deliberately tried to get in the way of British aircraft but didn't fire at them. One English pilot, however, misunderstood the motion made by a French officer and shot at him. The English plane was knocked out of action. At the armistice General Vuillemin had concentrated what remained of our air force in North Africa.

done worse than stimulate and arouse against London the outraged honor of the conquered. Darlan's more clearly defined tendency toward what, in a few weeks, was to be called "collaboration" can likewise be listed among the positive results of the affray. At first, as indicated already, he had been somewhat lukewarm in his endorsement of the armistice. It is even said that he had radioed messages urging the admirals not to obey his orders if, from their wording, they gathered the impression that he had ceased to be a free agent. He took care to instruct them—so the report goes—to take orders from a substitute, should the necessity arise, in a sequence which he established and which began with the name of Laborde.[11] All this, we know, had been ephemeral. Elated with his appointment to the Ministry of Marine, he had given the Pétain regime a trial. The application of Article 8 in the armistice to his ships was to be the real touchstone for him. Well, the English had fired upon the fleet, his political springboard, and at the same time he did not doubt that he could lastingly command German gratitude. The question was settled once and for all. From then on he was convinced that the Army of the Sea would hold together. Alongside of a land army in ruins, it would enable France to deserve well of the continent's New Order.

3

The Vichy Constitution; Suppression of the Republic and of the Republicans

THE THIRD STAGE in the counterrevolutionary process was nothing less than the establishment of a dictatorship on French soil. It involved the

[11]The Mers-el-Kebir incident persuaded Pétain and Laval that the English would not suffer any hostile undertakings, however slight, on the high seas and the Empire to pass unchallenged, and certainly the lesson, at the very least, thwarted a few of their schemes. The only vessels destroyed in the North African harbor were the old battleship *Bretagne* and the 2,800-ton destroyer *Mogador*. The *Dunkerque* was almost completely repaired within six or seven months. The *Strasbourg* fled. Captain Collinet, who commanded her, was made a rear admiral for his feat. Off Alexandria, British naval pressure was successful: without any bloodshed the old battleship *Lorraine*, three 10,000-ton cruisers, a 6,000-ton cruiser, three 1,500-ton destroyers, and a few submarines were neutralized. In English ports were netted the two old modernized battleships *Paris* and *Courbet*, the 3,000-ton destroyer *Triomphant*, the large submarine *Surcouf*, about ten other submarines, and a dozen other destroyers. There was a scuffle aboard the *Triomphant* and two men were killed.

destruction of the republican regime and the suppression of civil liberties. The "rights of man" were shouted down, special legislation enacted, the police hurled against every shadow of resistance or opposition. This time Laval shared the glory of the deed with no one else. Without this skilled tactician at his side, Pétain might not have thought it possible to throw out M. Lebrun and Parliament; he would have gotten along as best he could in their company.

Laval had little to do, it is true, with the ideology of the new regime. The greatest claim to its authorship lay with Maurras and the *Action Française*. Their followers bustled around the marshal, among them Raphael Alibert, Minister of Justice, who framed the major statutes and ordinances. These men did not have to look for formulas: they had them ready-made. To bring the French nation all the way back to what he called the parting of the ways in French history, to the 1789 "bifurcation," to pull down what had been built thereafter and to erect an entirely different structure: such was the lifelong program of Maurras. Laval thought all this was antiquated ratiocination and scoffed at it.

What did he care! He would have no competitor in the performance of the one task which really mattered: to make a clean sweep of existing parliamentary institutions. He would have boundless power, for Pétain wouldn't try any tricks with him.

The authoritarian regime was defined in the Constitutional Acts of July 11 and 12, 1940. No silly complications, no adornments. Marshal Pétain simply stated that he was assuming the functions of Head of the French State.[1] "The Head of the French State has plenary governmental powers; he names and dismisses ministers and secretaries of state who are responsible solely to him. He exercises legislative power in ministerial council."[2] "If, for any reason whatever, he is prevented from fulfilling the function of the Head of the State, M. Pierre Laval, vice-president of the Council of Ministers, shall by right assume it." "In case the latter shall for any reason whatever be prevented from doing so, he shall in turn be replaced by whomever the Council of Ministers may select by a majority of seven votes."[3] Here, in all their starkness, are the essential arrangements: to Pétain's absolute monarchy no limit was set except a time limit, and this at an uncertain date—such was, at any rate, Laval's interpretation. "The National Assembly fully empowers the Government of the Republic, under the authority and signature of Marshal Pétain, to

[1] Constitutional Act No. 1, July 11, 1940.
[2] Constitutional Act No. 2, July 11, 1940.
[3] Constitutional Act No. 4, July 11, 1940.

promulgate by one or several acts a new constitution for the French State." That text meant—always as Laval chose to read it—that Pétain was invested not only with full executive, legislative and even judiciary power, but, in addition, with constitution-making power. The constitution Pétain was to draw up "shall guarantee the rights of labor, the family, the fatherland. It shall be ratified by the nation and put in force by the Assemblies created pursuant to its provisions."[4] Thus there was to be a constitution on which the country might have its say. All we know, however, about this constitution—put off into the vaguest future—is that it was not to prevent the Head of the State from exercising legislative power in the Cabinet Council, that is, from dispensing with the Assemblies he himself would have called to life, "in time of external tension or of serious internal crisis"[5] and that, under such circumstances, he should wield absolute authority, with the one proviso that he could not "declare war without the consent of the Legislative Assemblies."[6] As for "national ratification," the marshal or his successor would determine the method whereby it was to be secured. At the secret session of the National Assembly (morning of July 10) Laval sidetracked any promises on this subject. Some members attempted to make him declare that there would be a plebiscite. He replied, "No. For, as we have seen, a plebiscite in our country begets an imperial regime, an empire in the Napoleon III sense."[7] Others asked him, "What will happen if the constitution is rejected?" He curtly retorted: "It will take wanton and harebrained men to envisage a constitution which is not consonant with the customs, desires, and will of the country." This explanation left those who listened to him where they were. In truth, neither in the name of the marshal nor in his own

[4]Constitutional Law of July 10, 1940, passed by the National Assembly. It opened the way for the constitutional acts quoted above. It was intended, in a juridical sense, to bridge over the abyss between the old regime and the new.

[5]Constitutional Act No. 2.

[6]Constitutional Act No. 2. Why was this exception to the "imperium" so carefully safeguarded against the day when the constitution shall have been put in force? The device is transparent. One of the counts in the indictment against Daladier was that the declaration of war on Germany was not directly authorized by a special vote of Parliament. The only way in which the two Houses had been called upon to express their views was through the approval of a proposed appropriation of funds. This was pure quibbling. But Laval did not want Daladier to be in a position to retort: "The new constitution is going to grant you precisely that liberty to declare war which you—wrongfully—assert that I abused."

[7]Laval's words are quoted by Jean Montigny in "Toute la Vérité sur un Mois Dramatique de Notre Histoire, 15 Juin–15 Juillet, 1940." Note that the "Empire" used as signifying Napoleon III was the pet antipathy of the *Action Française,* because it extolled the "rights of man" and the sovereignty of the nation as expressed in plebiscites.

(he surely intended to work in his selfish interest) did Laval ever agree to any brake being placed upon governmental omnipotence unless the new motto—Fatherland, Family, Work—can be counted as such a brake. Laval could not permit any limitation, now or ever, to the arbitrary decisions of Marshal Pétain.

He reached the acme of impudence when, having repealed both wholesale and item by item the Constitutional Laws of February 24 and 25 and July 16, 1875[8]—i.e., the Constitution of the Republic—and having removed the words "République Française" from official documents and the façades of public buildings, he boasted that he had not transgressed any law! He had, in fact, carried out a *"coup d'état."* But, he tried to explain how can you describe as a *coup d'état* a governmental step approved by a majority of senators and deputies, gathered in joint session as a National Assembly, in conformity with the 1875 Constitution? That plea of Laval does not make sense. The National Assembly was not free. Under German pressure applied through Laval, it was in no position to reject his proposals. Simply because a majority did not rebel against constraint, the inference is not to be made that the consent it gave was valid. By the same token, yielding one's purse to a burglar would be the equivalent of a gift. Then too, how many members were prevented from coming to Vichy? The passengers of the *Massilia,* at least, were detained in Morocco.[9]

[8]The 1875 Constitutional Laws were done away with as a whole in Constitutional Act No. 2.

Constitutional Act No. 1 annulled Article 2 of the Law of February 25, 1875: "The President of the Republic is elected by an absolute majority of votes in the Senate and Chamber of Deputies, sitting in joint session as the National Assembly. His term of office is seven years. He may be re-elected. . . ."

Constitutional Act No. 3 suppressed Article 1 of the Constitutional Law of July 16, 1875: "The Senate and Chamber of Deputies meet every year on the second Tuesday of January, etc. . . ."

Constitutional Act No. 5 (July 30, 1940) made null and void Article 9 of the Law of February 24 and Article 12 of the Law of July 16, 1875, concerning the erection of the Senate into a Court of Justice to try either the President of the Republic or cabinet ministers, to take cognizance of conspiracies against the safety of the state, definition of procedure, etc.

A queer way of doing things. The deathblow was preceded, accompanied, and followed by partial mutilations.

[9]In secret session (according to a direct testimony) Laval shamelessly told the members of the National Assembly that, if need be, Weygand would sally forth to curb them from his general headquarters in Clermont-Ferrand. He said also that a rich reward was in store for a submissive assembly: the free zone would be extended to include Paris. Moreover, a rumor spread that all members placed on record with an adverse vote could be jailed. M. Badie tried to read out to the Assembly a statement drafted on behalf of the eighty opponents. He was shouted down.

Moreover, constitution-making power cannot be delegated. If this were not true, the sovereignty of the nation would no sooner achieve its most exalted embodiment in the National Assembly—a solemn joint meeting of the Senate and of the Chamber of Deputies provided for under the 1875 Constitution for occasions of exceptional importance— than it would sink without leaving a trace in some act of abdication. In 1866, Thiers denied that the people's right to assert its sovereignty could be waived and allowed to fall in abeyance, even temporarily, as the outcome of a plebiscite; he took as starting point for his reasoning the Imperial Constitution of January 18, 1852—a constitution far more authoritarian than that of 1875. As against Laval, the point is all the more telling.[10]

Finally, it can be maintained that, in his constitutional acts and decrees, the marshal transgressed the Constitutional Law of July 10, and thus went beyond his mandate.[11]

---

[10]Assuming, for the sake of argument, that the constitution-making power could lawfully be delegated, another obstacle stood in the way of Laval: the Constitutional Law of August 14, 1884, which prescribes that the republican form of government must not even be put in question. It did not come within the power of a proxy (Laval, in the juncture) to tamper with that enactment. Contrariwise, notwithstanding common belief, the Law of August 14, 1884, would not have bound an Assembly that set itself to the task. The National Assembly is the highest expression of the nation's sovereignty. The laws it makes do not require the signature of the President of the Republic. No National Assembly past or present has authority to bind the national assemblies of the future. Then the limitations defined in the past which must be honored in the future are those relating to the Assembly's own freedom. The 1871 National Assembly (which framed the Republican Constitution) was very ticklish on this matter. It had been elected only a few weeks before the Commune; it could not erase the Paris outbreaks from its memory.

The Law of February 15, 1872, the so-called Tréveneuc Law, provided that the General Councils in each department should meet at once and choose two delegates to constitute an assembly in whatever place it might be safe from violence, if "the National Assembly, or any which may succeed it, should chance to be illegally dissolved or prevented from meeting." The Laws of August 18 and October 12, 1940, which suspended the departmental and district councils, saved Pétain and Laval from this threat, which, in the circumstances, did not amount to much. No greater courage could be expected from the department councils than from the National Assembly, there being no real difference in membership.

[11]The argument on this point runs as follows. Under the Constitutional Law of July 10, 1940, Pétain was invested with constitution-making power only. Therefore he had the right to work out a constitution but not to enact ordinary laws. In the discharge of his executive function he was not given greater scope than had been imparted to Daladier and Reynaud under the various enabling acts. In addition, the constitutional law he was commissioned to draft could not be held valid until ratified by the nation and put in force by newly elected bodies. On such grounds the constitutional acts and all the legislation promulgated under Pétain's name are worthless. But here is a moot point. Does the wording of the Constitutional Law of July 10, voted by the National Assembly, place the republican form of government above all changes? The case can be argued both ways.

Moreover, the critics of Pétain lay stress on the government's statements published to

But why did Laval prefer the utter destruction of the Republic to the setting up of an authoritarian executive within the framework of the Republican regime? Bonaparte put up with the words: "République Française, Napoléon Empereur" on his gold silver coins. Why did Pétain, spurred on by Laval, exact more?

Before senators and deputies Laval evoked the wrath of the Germans, ready to strike and strike again, whose mailed fist could be held off only by the immediate slaughter of the "Masonic and Jewish Republic."[12] Obviously the Nazis did rely on Pétain's servility to bring them a harvest fully as rich as would be brought by their occupation of the free zone (provided that the saving of effectives made possible by the existence of a puppet government be entered on the ledger). Obviously they would have looked askance even at a bridled and hobbled Republic. The Nazis would have worried lest it might shelter an opposition which might set the marshal to rights. The Nazis wished to spare themselves the repercussions that even a remotely liberal regime at Vichy might have in occupied territory. Let us concede so much to Laval. But all this does not explain why both he and Pétain took such delight in suppressing political and civil liberties. Regardless of what the Germans did or did not demand, these two men forced an unlimited dictatorship upon the National Assembly because they were resolved to use it to their advantage, the one to restore France to her original hierarchical pattern, the other to integrate her into Hitler's order, to thrust her into total alliance with the conqueror. They made no attempt to bargain over the dose of absolutism to be injected into the French political body. For their own purposes they wanted the Republic destroyed, root and branch.

The July 10 National Assembly freely recognized that, under the circumstances, the 1875 Constitution could not remain intact, that a reform was inescapable. On July 9, when the two Chambers were consulted separately on the advisability of constitutional amendments in the form required by the 1875 procedure, there were only three hostile votes in the Chamber of Deputies and one in the Senate. But the next day, once the text of the Constitutional Law had been disclosed, the opposition

---

introduce the constitutional bill and on the additional explanations which came from Laval. A promise can be read into it, they assert, that between the elected assemblies then in existence and those which were to succeed them, all break in continuity would be avoided. But governmental statements and ministerial declarations do not by themselves create a legal obligation.

[12]"If the opposition should carry the day, what would happen tomorrow? You understand what I mean. France, and France alone, would be the sufferer." (Preparatory meeting of deputies, July 8.)

was outspoken. The Taurines-Dormann counterproposal reflected the feeling of the average member. It provided that the Constitutional Laws of 1875 should be suspended until peace was made: that, by decrees having force of law, the marshal should take the steps necessary for the preservation of order, for the life and recovery of the country, for territorial liberation; that he should be given the mandate to work out, "in collaboration with the parliamentary commissions concerned, the new institutions which shall be submitted to the nation's acceptance as soon as circumstances allow of a free discussion." Clearly enough, under this arrangement, the dictatorship would at least be kept under watch. It would be based on expediency and not on principle. Would the Germans have taken exception to such mitigated omnipotence and cried out against it? They were spared the trouble. To cut short the debate, Laval brought out his hidden weapon. It was the letter extracted from Pétain a few days before: "Since it is difficult for me to attend the sessions, I am asking you to serve as my representative. The voting of the bill which the government submits to the National Assembly seems to me necessary to ensure the salvation of our country."

On Laval's advice Pétain had decided to have no direct contact with the two Chambers, even to procure their abdication, thus stressing his determination to rule from beyond the reach of public opinion, or, if necessary, against it. Yet he had said at a public reception, "I do not wish to be either a dictator or a Caesar." But on this matter Laval steered him back onto the right lines if ever there was need to do so.[13] It certainly did not prevent the vice-president of the Council, at the Assembly's secret session, from asserting that everyone could count on him to safeguard the rights of the civil power as against the military! Here was a boasting which for sheer effrontery more than matched Flandin's fervid rhetoric on the theme of money. Money has corrupted everything; money has led us to the present pass. Flandin excoriating the evils of money! The thought cries to high heaven! Juvenal's eternally apt phrase fits perfectly this situation: *"Quis tulerit Gracchos de seditione querentes?"*[14]

---

[13]M. Chautemps, who, on being dismissed from the Cabinet, was entrusted with an official mission to South America (where he never went) and then to Washington, testifies that, on July 9, Pétain said to Laval: "If you fail to carry the constitutional bill through the National Assembly tomorrow, you will have to go." But Chautemps must try to make a case for Pétain.

[14]"A shadow stretched over this land, and over many others. The shadow of money. It is money which has corrupted everything." For tactical considerations Flandin had intended to vote against the constitutional bill. Laval asked him to dinner and made him change his mind.

Eighty Senators and deputies had the courage to pronounce themselves formally against the constitutional bill. Seventeen abstained from voting, thirty "excused themselves," four are recorded as "not having been able to participate," and one hundred forty-nine as "not having participated." Out of a total of 850 legislators (not counting the 72 Communists expelled in 1939), 569, or barely two thirds, supported Pétain and Laval.

The men who stood up against dictatorship belonged to almost all parties, since, at such a juncture, fortitude and conviction mattered much more than political programs. So intimidated was the Assembly, so pervasive the fear which the marshal's chief steward had implanted in it, that, sad to say, no one, not even Léon Blum, worthy, courageous, and directly involved as he was, dared point the finger of scorn at the most obviously absurd of all the arguments in the base indictment leveled against the dying Republic.[15] "The proof," screamed the Minister, "that you were not serving France, but rather the most insane of ideologies, is supplied by a note handed M. Léon Blum in January 1937, by Signor Cerutti, the Italian Ambassador." In it Signor Mussolini explained the meaning of his intervention in Spain. He could not endure the existence of a Bolshevik or semi-Bolshevik government on the shores of the Mediterranean. He could, however, understand France's worry over General Franco's policy. And by his own intercession the Duce would cause General Franco to assure France that his effort was in no sense aimed against her. Such was the proposal Laval reproached Blum for not having eagerly seized, and which he used to expose the ignominy of the Republic. The obvious reply was that Mussolini had, for months, constantly wronged the French national interests by getting grip on the Peninsula and that to make him an intermediary to the *Caudillo* was merely to bolster him up in an attitude damaging to our safety.

Even more relevantly, it might have been pointed out that on January 2, 1937, Neville Chamberlain had entertained similar proposals from the Duce and signed with him a "gentlemen's agreement" regarding nonintervention, only to discover, a few days later, the shameful trickery of which he had been the victim. But on July 10, 1940, with the Germans less than fifty kilometers from Vichy, and all roads open to them, how could the treachery of the dictators be denounced? Blum had to keep his

---

[15] Besides, this passage in Laval's speech before the deputies on July 8, in which he exonerates Germany of aggression, deserves recording: "Since parliamentary democracy wished to enter the ring against Nazism and Fascism, and since it has lost the fight, it must disappear from the face of the earth." These impassioned words welled up from the depths of his soul. No conqueror had to whisper them in Laval's ear.

mouth shut. Shamelessly, Laval could belabor his gagged opponents.[16]

The Vichy laws supplied the tools wherewith to construct a dictatorship. The next job was to annihilate all opposition, not only of those who spoke or acted, but also of those who, through their records, their inclinations, their idiosyncrasies, their interests, were judged likely to speak or to act someday. This included members of Parliament, journalists, faithful servants of our traditional diplomacy, members of department and district councils, mayors, municipal councilors, officials, college professors and teachers, priests and monks finding their inspiration in Pius XI, leaders of the General Confederation of Labor and of unions who would not jump on Laval's band wagon, officers no longer in sympathy with the High Command, Free Masons—indeed, to sum up, all men of independent mood. In the National Revolution there was no room for people whom intellectual and material concerns linked to democracy, nor for those who took pride in remaining unfettered in their views on public affairs.

In the "totalitarian" countries the necessary purge was made possible only through the agency of the "single party"—a few thousand bullies at the outset given the task of frightening and, if necessary, of beating the rest of the population into silence. Pétain and Laval did not need this. They had an advantage which was unique. Never forget it: the Germans were almost within a stone's throw.

The summer and autumn of 1940 were devoted by the Vichy Government to this task of marshaling everyone into line. On July 30 the marshal set up the Supreme Court of Justice, fixed its organization and jurisdiction. It was to judge the "ministers, former ministers, or their immediate subordinates, civilian or military, accused of having betrayed the duties of their trust, by deeds which had influenced the passage from the state of peace to the state of war, before September 4, 1939; those who had made worse the situation thus brought into being"; and also "every person accused of attempts against the public safety and of crimes and

---

[16]Herriot courageously undertook the defense of the *Massilia* "passengers," but abstained from the ballot. The opponents of the bill tried to enlighten him about Laval's true purpose, but could not dispel his illusions. Jeanneney, presiding officer of the National Assembly, who was consequently not entitled to vote, upheld the view that the majority should be calculated according to the legal number of seats—which showed how he felt. Blum voted in the negative. The only other Popular Front leaders who followed suit were Vincent Auriol, Jules Moch, Marius Moutet, Marx Dormoy, Justin Godard, Paul-Boncour, Ramadier, André Philip. It was a weak showing. A few influential Rightists likewise cast adverse votes: Bonnevay, the Marquis de Chambrun, Champetier de Ribes, the Marquis de Moustier. Henri Bérenger, Campinchi, Yvon Delbos, Georges Mandel, Paul Reynaud are recorded as "excused." Albert Sarraut gave his vote to Pétain. Guy la Chambre too.

misdemeanors associated therewith . . . all accomplices and accessories. . . ."[17] "Public prosecution must take place within a limit of ten years after the perpetration of the deeds, even if the latter occurred prior to the promulgation of the present law . . ."[18] By Constitutional Act No. 7, promulgated on January 26, 1941, the marshal appointed himself grand justiciary. It was entirely up to him whether he would take the place of the Supreme Court, inflict unlimited penalties upon ministers and high officials, past or present. Thus the last word would not rest with the judges of his own choosing if their servility fell short of his expectations. The victims he had singled out could not escape.

In September, one after the other, Pierre Cot, Guy la Chambre, Daladier, Gamelin, Reynaud, Mandel were indicted. So likewise Léon Blum, on October 18. Jacomet was to follow much later, on April 21, 1941. So much for the ministers of former days. Not many men were to be hit, but the rest would see and understand.

Under the Law of July 23, 1940, "All Frenchmen who have left French metropolitan territory between May 10 and June 30, 1940, in order to go abroad, without being formally entrusted with an official mission by some competent authority, or without legitimate reason," shall be considered as having willfully shunned the duties and obligations incumbent upon members of the national community. A legitimate reason? It was denied to those who had left their country because they would not admit that the war was over, because they would not abandon all hope of maintaining national independence. All were presumed guilty. In fact, even in cases where men had been urged to go by officials with full ministerial authority behind them, on June 15 and 16, before Pétain came into office, even when they had been provided with documents vouching for their intentions, and even with official papers commissioning them to go abroad on public business in the sense of the law, the penalty was applied and their properties confiscated. The measures taken against the *Massilia* passengers thus became of wider application and more rigorous. Every head that would not bow was stricken. In that special case the National

---

[17]Constitutional Act No. 5 (July 30) and Decree of August 1, regarding the organization, jurisdiction, and procedure of the Supreme Court of Justice.

[18]A Decree of September 24, 1940, added to this list, "The ministers, former ministers, or their immediate subordinates, who within the ten years' time limit have committed acts of speculation or misappropriation of funds, or have betrayed their trust by speculating on the value of the national currency or by making improper use of funds subject to their control." This was done to reach Paul Reynaud and Georges Mandel, neither of whom had ever had charge of the Ministries of War or Foreign Affairs, and who, consequently, could have wriggled through the meshes of the net stretched on July 30 and August 1.

Revolution avenged itself upon a handful of officials, deputies, and journalists who, in recent years, had resisted the rabble in German and Italian pay and had sought to make the French aware of the fate in store for them. In order to please Hitler, the most honorable, most honored Jews, who for nearly a century had been recognized by the highest French society, were included in the list.[19] With the Laws of July 17, August 20, September 3, 5 and 12, the overhaul of the administrative structure was begun and the first political prisons or detention camps were opened. "Officials considered undesirable may be deprived of their posts at any time before October 31, 1940."[20] Such elements, even if French . . . may be removed from all administrative services and from the various public bodies as have shown themselves unworthy of carrying on their callings by their actions or their attitudes." In France or overseas, "individuals dangerous to national defense or public safety may be interned."[21] The Law of August 30, 1940, dissolved secret societies.

The status of the 165,000 French Jews was determined by the Law of October 3, 1940: they were ousted from all public and administrative functions and from the Army; they were forbidden to teach in schools and colleges. As to the press and the cinema, they were temporarily tolerated in inferior positions. In the liberal professions they were to be subjected to *numerus clausus*. The final piece of legislation was promulgated on June 2, 1941. Then they were expelled from many fields of private enterprise. They had to give up banks, real estate, and publishing business.[22] In March 1941, Xavier Vallat, a fanatic, was installed as commissioner for Jewish affairs, only to be succeeded, the following year, by a scoundrel, Darquier de Pellepoix.

A September 24 decree, which was to be executed as a law of the state, set up a court-martial to judge "persons charged with crimes and machinations against the unity and safety of the fatherland." Note the date—September 24; six days earlier General de Gaulle had tried to seize Dakar. Here notice was being served of the uprooting of "Gaullism."

---

[19] Later one name had to be deleted—that of the ingenuous Samaritan who, at his own expense, had enabled the marshal to pay off the mortgage on his Villeneuve-Loubet residence, once contracted to meet the debts of a prodigal stepson.

[20] The time limit was extended to March 31, 1941, by the Law of October 23, 1940.

[21] Law of September 4, 1940. Nothing less than the *lettre de cachet* (arbitrary warrant of imprisonment).

[22] It is worth noting that in the occupied zone the first German ordinances against the Jews were dated October 1 and 24, 1940. Vichy had dashed ahead to make up for lost time and to outdo the Germans. Once again the Law of June 2, 1941, followed on the German ordinance of May 28, 1941.

After several preliminary steps, which were no more than veiled preparations, the Councils of the departments and of the districts were suspended by the Law of October 12. As a corollary, the powers of the prefects had been or were increased on July 29 and October 30.

As for the Senate and the House, they were allowed to fade away with the passage of time. Laval, to put them in a mood for their great abdication, had boldly provided in Constitutional Act No. 3 (July 11) that they would continue to exist until the convocation of the Assemblies foreseen in the Constitutional Law of July 10, 1940. Article 2 of the act, it is true, further prescribed that both Chambers should be adjourned until otherwise instructed and that they could never meet again except upon the direct summons of the Head of the State. Thus the door had been shut but not quite fastened. Of course there was no thought whatever of letting the eight hundred ghosts ever return, but their emoluments continued to be paid. For months on end, until August 1941, when the marshal stopped their pay and sent them packing to Châtel-Guyon, fleeting shadows could be seen gathering around Herriot and Jeanneney on the duly appointed days, determined, come what might, to keep up the fiction. The two Orpheuses sought ever to lead their flocks back to the light of the day. The reduced staff of secretaries they maintained to keep unbroken the parliamentary tradition was finally scattered in the summer of 1942.

The General Confederation of Labor was dissolved on November 9, 1940, and Masonic lodges were closed as early as August 13, 1940.

It is not our purpose to follow in greater detail the exactions of the dictatorial power. From month to month the ordinances to which I have already alluded were to be broadened, deepened, strengthened. What use is there in piling up a list of the official documents? How Pétain and Laval set their governmental machinery in motion has now been indicated, and we can leave it at that. By the end of the first summer all who disagreed with the regime had been forced to cower. No longer was there any effective opposition to the Head of the State and to his right-hand man. One of my friends passing through Toulouse in October was entertained at dinner by Maurice Sarraut, editor and owner of the *Dépêche de Toulouse,* one of the mainstays of the Republic from the beginning of this century. He ventured the opinion that there was no great difference between Pétain and President Hacha of Czechoslovakia. At once Sarraut, in mortal terror, begged him to keep quiet. Even in his own home the walls might have ears! My friend went his way. In a remote village he met a Socialist deputy, by nature an extremely loquacious fellow. The good man would not let him enter this house until he had thoroughly explored all nooks and corners.

There spread through the land swarms of policemen, professional or volunteers (that is, of the stool-pigeon type), flocks of informers, witch-hunters, spies, sycophants with every sort of badge of office: in all, some fifteen varieties of the genus were numbered. With the marshal's *"garde de protection,"* organized by Peyrouton and Colonel Groussard, were linked in each prefecture "bureaus of inquiry and research." The "French Legion" created in the "free zone" under the Law of August 29, 1940, with an eye to absorbing and replacing all the ex-servicemen associations, was, some months later, rendered accessible to anyone willing to join, to all the busybodies of the National Revolution, to all the lickspittles, beggars, job seekers, men down on their luck who needed government favors to eke out a livelihood.[23] This, at last, was the "single party" by means of which the dictatorship sought to consolidate its position. In the background German control commissions moved around about the seaports and airfields of what was called "unoccupied" France and about the principal post offices and the railroad stations. Who could ever restrain them? The Gestapo—visible or invisible—was omnipresent. Such was the network of surveillance which encompassed Frenchmen under Vichy, and as for conditions in the other zone—it is just as well to pass them by in silence.

Looking back to those first three months of the National Revolution, bestrewn as they are with decrees and arbitrary enactments, what, over and above the Republican Constitution, do· we find dragged in the mud? We find the declaration of the rights of man and the citizen, endorsed by Louis XVI on October 5, 1789, and for all essentials incorporated in the civil code: the equality of all before the law, individual liberty; the principles that sovereignty resides in the nation, that no man may be haled before some star chamber,. that laws cannot be retroactive; the guaranteed enjoyment of one's property,. the·non-transference of the guilt of an individual to members of his family—which, of course, means that a condemned man's property shall not be confiscated. France had been pushed back toward the laws of feudalism. But it was not the feudalism of the eighteenth century, well worn and smooth from custom and use, but something altogether more brutal. One may even say

[23]The Legion and the National Volunteers had grown by 1942 into such an unwieldy and mixed multitude that the Vichy Government reversed the policy of expansion and organized independently a nucleus of carefully selected dependable men, the Service d'Ordre de la Légion. Darnand, the French Himmler, and a French replica of·the Nazi SS was the outcome.

that the Law of July 23, 1940, taking away the French citizenship of
those who had departed in order not to suffer direct or indirect subjection to Germany, has no precedent in all our history. It was borrowed
from Nazi and fascist statute books. Until then even the worst criminal
on the steps of the scaffold was still a Frenchman. In true *Action Française* style, by means of an article in the *Revue des Deux Mondes* for
September 15, 1940, and of radio broadcasts on October 11 and 30,
Pétain saw fit to extol the task so wonderfully performed.

Laval had brought the third stage of operation to a happy conclusion.
But the fourth, collaboration with Germany intended to expand into an
open alliance, was a far more ticklish business. It was to baffle him in
spite of all his passion and cunning.

4

The Enforcement of the Armistice Gradually Under-mines Vichy's Power

THE COUNTERREVOLUTION was in full swing. But in that very autumn of
1940, when Pétain and Laval indulged in the belief that an all-round
agreement with Hitler would soon clinch the policy which had be-
witched them since 1935, the handwriting was already flaming on the
wall. Their tyranny was never to be secure; their government was never
to have its hour of ease.

England did not conform to their expectations. Contrary to all the
reckoning of the French Command, she held out against the Nazi invaders. In fact, these calculations of experts can properly be characterized as highly inexpert. Had they understood the problems which had
to be solved for an invasion of the British Isles, had they correctly appraised the Battle of Dunkirk, where the British air force showed what
it could do when fighting close to its bases, Pétain, Weygand, and their
friends would not have decided with such inflexible confidence on Hitler's and Goering's victory. These leaders, who only recently prized so
high a futile defensive creed, erred, in June, by miscalculating England's
chances. Was it wishful thinking?

By the end of October, Hitler had finally lost the battle of the air. The war was to continue endlessly. The armistice could no longer be described as a mere transition toward peace. Obviously, for an indefinite period, it would regulate French relations with Germany, settle the condition of France.

Day by day, to their grief, the French were to discover what lay concealed behind the June convention. Day by day, Laval, like Pétain, had to learn for himself that to persecute and scatter the personnel of the Republic was but the least and easiest part of his task.

The Germans, squeezing "the most beautiful kingdom under Heaven," aroused and fed in the "average" Frenchman a resistance directed immediately against their occupation and, later, against Vichy because of its acquiescence.

In the summer of 1940 this resistance was barely felt. And it took time for the disguised Kommandantur, labeled "National Revolution," to be put in the same class as the Nazi Kommandantur by the mass of our people. But the ever harsher enforcement of the armistice inevitably caused popular feeling to confuse both powers—the one that enslaved and the one that, however much it was itself a slave, helped forge the fetters of bondage.

This confusion did not become really complete until the end of 1941, but it began at once. It did not develop steadily; it had its ups and downs, and it did not affect the marshal in the same way as it did Laval or even Darlan. Yet it kept growing because France's material and moral ruin was growing too. The story of Pétain and his followers can be understood only against the background of the enforcement of the armistice and its painful impact upon the French people.

At first they were surprised at the punctilious behavior of the German Army. Upon their initial contact with the invader many thought that, after all, the counterrevolutionaries were right. But this correct and even courteous demeanor was merely the polished surface of a relentless system, the screen intended to conceal an implacable method.

Not only were the million and a half prisoners in German camps[1]— the better part of the male population between the ages of twenty and forty—cut off from the nation. Compelled to work hard and underfed

---

[1] On May 8, 1942, figures of German origin were published at Vichy, of course with the approval of the censorship. At the end of December 1941 the number of prisoners of war held in German camps was 1,256,681. Prior to this the sailors, the sick, those who had fought in both wars, etc., had been released. Therefore a total of 1,500,000 men seems warranted for the summer of 1940, and in Germany even higher figures have been mentioned.

(their rations were one third less than those of Frenchmen in France), they quickly showed signs of physical decay.[2]

It is estimated that the French population is diminishing at the rate of three hundred fifty thousand souls a year in these armistice years. Besides the absence of one million and a quarter young men, other causes are at work: fewer marriages and births throughout the country, inadequate nourishment, a higher death rate. But the detention of so many of our soldiers ranks first. And it will have a lasting effect, since many of these prisoners, even when repatriated, will never recover physically.

What is more, these slaves, tightly enclosed behind barbed wire, act as distant warders and watchers over their own families by the very fact that they are at the mercy of their enemy. They were hostages from the very beginning, they were permanent hostages. How many French people, to the farthest ends of the world, felt themselves cramped and even paralyzed by that thought? Laval, in all his mouthings on collaboration, never had a stronger argument than that of the prisoners.

No other tribulation moves the French so deeply as the absence of so many of their young men, the cruel treatment inflicted upon them. But their lot was indeed hardly surprising. The same cannot be said of the daily indemnity of twenty million marks (four hundred million francs at the rate of exchange determined by the Germans), which was reduced by a quarter on May 13, 1941. Still less can it be said of the way the indemnity was used—to lay the country bare through organized plunder. In that respect the resourcefulness of the conquerors caught the people unaware.

Between 1919 and 1924 the "Allied and Associated Powers" quarreled over the "scales of payments," over the schemes elaborated in London and in New York to enable the Germans to meet the reparations provided for in the Versailles Treaty without too much discomfort, without a lowering of their standard of living or a tax burden heavier than that imposed on the victors. Thanks to these intellectual acrobatics the folk across the Rhine actually raked in more hard cash than they disbursed.

Hitler and his advisers found the right scheme: grab everything there is to be grabbed. First of all, the forces of occupation used and abused

[2]Lieutenant Colonel Billotte, who returned from Germany in 1941, estimated at nine hundred calories the ration issued to prisoners. A normal ration is supposed to require twenty-five hundred calories. In France average rations are reported to have approximated fifteen hundred calories in 1941, twelve hundred in 1942, and nine hundred in 1943.

the right of requisition. Under this head they seized a great number of ships, a third of all the railway rolling stock, all the stocks of gasoline which had not been destroyed, all the foodstuffs needed for the Army, etc. At the same time they racked their brains how to spend on the spot the enormous sums paid as indemnities. They did not haggle; they gave every man the price he asked. They flooded the country with their "occupation marks," which the Bank of France cashed against its notes. But strive as they would to be lavish with their paper money, buying everything in sight for their military and civilian services, handing out to every one of their hundreds of thousands of soldiers two and a half marks daily as pocket money, acquiring industrial bonds and stocks on a vast scale, spreading wide their largesses among the native population of Morocco, settling like a vast cloud of locusts on every asset owned by the French: in the spring of 1942 eighty billion francs still remained to their credit on the books of the Bank of France.[3] They had been at their wit's end to spend them. Our territory was scraped clean of everything that might be styled consumers' goods. And since, without a *quid pro quo,* the Germans would hand over none of the products of the occupied zone needed by the "free zone," their requisition was extended to the latter as well. Even cargoes from North Africa, Madagascar, and Indo-China were pounced upon, and as much as 80 per cent lifted from a single shipment. The London Ministry of Economic Warfare estimated the value of foodstuffs taken over by the end of 1941 at between twenty-six and forty-four billion francs. As for the raw materials and processed goods laid hold of by the enemy, the same authority fixed the total sum at thirty-five billion francs.

Stripped by all this plundering, our industries could obtain from Germany alone the raw materials they had formerly imported—wool, cotton, copper, tin, oil, coal, leather, hides, rubber, wood, etc., amounting in all to twenty-four billions out of thirty-five spent abroad yearly. So there was nothing for them but to fill Berlin's orders. It is calculated that by the autumn of 1941 these amounted to about thirty billion francs. Thus did Franco-German economic collaboration take shape. The rulers at

[3] To the German seizures must also be added the manufactured goods bought by virtue of the prewar "clearing" agreements, which were resurrected to supply an additional levy. Officially, this merchandise was to have been paid for by German exports. The Bank of France, however, had to turn over twelve billions to the French sellers, and there was no compensation in kind. Here was another source of impoverishment. (On the enforcement of the armistice, cf. Hervé Alphand, economic director of Fighting France, formerly director of commercial treaties, *Situation Financière et Economique de la France,* March 1942.) In the summer of 1942 the sums to the credit of the Germans in the Bank of France abruptly fell very low. They had started building lines of fortifications.

Vichy were allowed to direct the economic life of the country, but only on condition that they made the maximum contribution to the war effort of the Nazi Empire. The economic section of the German military government in Paris posted supervisors at every spot in French civil administration and industry which was of the least concern to it, particularly in the central office for the allocation of raw materials, the key department of the Ministry of Industrial Production. In every one of the thirteen sections a German official was on duty.

It rested on Nazi good will that French industries should continue to operate feebly, at 50 per cent capacity, or come gradually to a full stop. In the main the French industrialist was gradually being turned into a supplier of labor and machinery.[4] He knew very well that, in Hitler's Europe, France was to be brought back to an agricultural pattern of civilization. At an early date removals of factory equipment across the Rhine were reported. In February 1942, according to the Germans, 140,000 French workmen were employed in the Reich.

The French peasant stood pat. No collaboration with German economy for him. He lacked fertilizers, labor, etc. Agricultural production decreased by one fifth or more, thereby falling below the needs of the country. Whatever goods the peasant might have he exchanged as little as possible against paper money, for which he had no use, thus injuring the enemy and his city-dwelling French compatriots alike. Each year it proved a heart-rending job to bridge over the April–June period, when little if anything of the old crop remained in store and the new crop was still to be reaped. It dawned upon the Germans that to exploit the soil of France their own farmers must be imported. They tried the experiment, it appears, on properties whose owners were prisoners in Germany and which therefore were lying fallow.[5]

This rough sketch, summary though it be, enables one to indicate clearly enough the very humble status of the Vichy despots. In the Nazi "order" they were merely the tawdry managers of a nation in misery. What could they do? They could prevent the measly supplies not carried off by the invader from being grabbed by the strongest in a thieves' market; they could divide up scraps of bread and the few hours of available work, regulate exchange of services, find some sort of job for the two million discharged soldiers, resettle in the occupied zone the three million refugees encamped south of the Loire, patch up the

---

[4] I do not refer to that class of factories which had been set apart and catered for the home market. Raw materials were more parsimoniously doled out to them.

[5] According to Radio Berlin, March 6, 1942. Cf. Alphand, loc. cit.

wreckage of war on which sums amounting to one third of the reparations paid after 1918 were to be spent. A wretched job performed by helpless rulers.

Nonetheless, the governmental façade was pretentious in the extreme. Ministers and their toadies damned the economic liberalism of the nineteenth century, railed at modern capitalism. They lauded a controlled economy. It sounded altogether too much like sour grapes. In such times as ours not everyone who wants it can have a free economy! And the control which so stimulated the pride of Pétain's men was, in fact, German control. They bragged of their reforms—the restoration of the peasantry, the prohibition against subdividing small farms, apprenticeship, pensions for superannuated workers, the "family code," the amendment of the inheritance laws in favor of large families, special rewards for marriages and births. So much tinsel borrowed by a band of ragamuffins from a theatrical costumer to cover their nakedness.

Above all, Vichy boasted of having done away with the class struggle by means of the Labor Charter of October 4, 1941. Indeed, the main disposition of the Labor Charter was to merge the old labor unions in "professional families," which employers and employees had to join, and, for the enforcement of all-round discipline, to bring in "social committees," in which the voice of the management was predominant. Government supervision obtained everywhere. This arrangement, it was explained, was only a preliminary. When the whole plan had been worked out, full-fledged "corporations" would come into their own. Corporation or no corporation, fascist labor policy was the model. An instrument of bondage was at hand.

The truth was that the French, rationed since September 1940, did not have enough to eat, that more than 800,000 of them were out of work at the end of 1941 (despite the 1,250,000 prisoners), and that the improvement recorded afterward was sheer illusion. Malnutrition cut down the productivity of labor, which in turn led to less and less well stocked grain bins and warehouses.

The great innovations upon which the Vichy Government prided itself had no life except on paper, or were stage scenery concealing outright subsidies. Even the strictest regulations were often circumvented. The black market laughed at police restrictions, and officially fixed price ceilings were evaded in bargaining between merchant and customer. How could it be otherwise when the daily ration was 40 or 50 per cent less than what is needed for normal energy? There is no subduing an empty stomach. But the majority of Frenchmen could not afford the relative luxury of the black market.

The Secretary of State for Food Supplies, in accordance with the Law of October 13, 1941, had to make inventories of what nutriment was available and to dole this out through a network of commercial operations supervised from end to end, while his colleague, the Secretary of State for Industrial Production, was responsible for distributing all raw materials among processors and elaborating production plans. Both found themselves in the same boat. They could only pass around the leftovers from the German meal, the scraps discarded by National Socialist factories. The Secretary for Industrial Production, surrounded by an impressive array of official bodies, took the easiest way out. He surrendered to the representatives of big business, to those who, between 1930 and 1940, had ruined France's economy and were supreme in the "social committees." In the "organization committees" (some one hundred and fifty in number) are to be found again the men of the Metallurgists Union and of the Coal Owners' Union. Yet they were said to have been scattered at the same time as the leaders of the General Confederation of Labor. Thus did Vichy wipe out the economic feudalism reviled by the marshal!

How Bouthillier boasted of the financial fabric built up after the armistice! During the eighteen months following the capitulation the Treasury disbursed some 450 billion francs, a total greatly in excess of the national income during the same period, and yet the bank notes in circulation—271 billions on February 22, 1942—had increased by only seventy billions since the end of 1939. The country had therefore been spared currency inflation. The franc had fallen into no such bottomless pit as had swallowed the mark in 1923. Groundless complacency. Here was merely another miracle of the "closed monetary circuit," borrowed from the finance ministers of Hitler and Mussolini. And, in a conquered country, it is a fake miracle. Taxes supplied yearly about one hundred billions, which met the normal expenses of the state, of the departments and municipalities. Extraordinary expenditures (public works, relief, etc.) plus the costs of occupation—in all two hundred billions—were covered by advances from the Bank of France or by the issuance of treasury bonds. The problem was to pump away the bank notes and credit balances of individuals by means of short- or long-term loans. This was not very difficult to solve. What could Frenchmen do with their ready funds? There were no goods to be bought. On the stock market gamblers, rather than investors, had a chance. The prices of securities were not freely quoted and they rarely changed hands. Real estate could be sold only with permission from the state. Capital could not be exported. When Germany, on May 13, 1941, granted a reduction of the war indemnity, and then abandoned the limitations which stood in the way of transferring securities and paper money from the occupied to the free zone and to North Africa, she required in return that at every frontier economic controls be set up, after the pattern of those in force on her own territory, and under the direction of a high German official. She was indeed careful to preserve the French monetary tool she had used to exact her levies.

Either Frenchmen took their money to the Treasury or their banks handed it over for them, if they had preferred to leave it on deposit. Bouthillier fooled no one, and Laval scornfully dismissed him in April 1942.

True enough, although prices were more than four times what they had been when the armistice was signed, the monetary system on the surface remained more or less sound. In theory, when hostilities ceased, the currency would be safe. Safe in the same sense as a brake that has never been applied, has even been removed from the vehicle, and, consequently, did not shatter into bits when the wheels were smashed. Consequently, the public debt did not evaporate through a process of inflation. It will remain and weigh very heavily on all productive forces, terribly hampered, besides, by the practical destruction of nearly all the implements of industrial activity. When reconstruction comes it is hard to see how confiscatory measures can be avoided. For the time being, with the shops almost empty, fortunes in ready cash could scarcely benefit their possessors except by giving them access to the black market. But this does not imply that under the marshal's government speculators and profiteers did not abound. Public wrath has branded them already. Vichy might prate about its new "moral order," but our old acquaintances, the vultures among parliamentarians and lawyers, still found that game was plentiful. Never in the past had such a prey as Jewish wealth come within their reach.

Such abstract accounts of the disintegration of the economic structure begin to pulsate with life the minute you reflect upon the human suffering they entail. In the very homeland of good living the search for one's daily pittance is the constant preoccupation, the obsession of men and women alike. "A happy circumstance," as one letter writer put it, "for it sometimes prevents us from thinking!" Sometimes! Many must surely wish they could escape into a purely animal existence and forget the rest. People quickly realized that it is more harrowing to go without the spiritual than the material bread—that spiritual bread which, hardly noticed, comes to every citizen from his own country. Picking themselves up after the stunning blows of May and June, they were eager for that viaticum. They found out the measureless price of what they had lost. They became painfully aware of their own degradation and debasement.

France no longer had a capital, or, more precisely, Paris was forbidden to exercise the functions which a capital performs. Not a single voice, written or spoken, remained free. In occupied territory the papers seemed to retain a certain frankness in manner and in controversy, but for no other reason than that the Nazi power let them enjoy assailing the established government, Pétain and his men. By contrast this false show emphasized both the independence which they lacked and the monotonous obedience to a set of closely knit orders which enhanced the servility of the Vichy sheets. No authentic news regarding the defeat and the surrender, events which remained beyond everyone's comprehension, was ever published. What I have written about Gamelin, Daladier, Reynaud, Weygand, Pétain, Laval, is mostly unknown to the French people. At the outset condemnation was passed wholesale on the worthies of the former regime: none of them would, in August 1940, have been safe from assault on any city street. With the passage of time a sense of discrimination was reawakened in the public. The English and American radio clarified for a wide circle what was going on in the world, but each little knot of Frenchmen, each hamlet, each class of city dweller reacted in a vacuum. Gone was that endless compounding of ideas, of tendencies, which habitually takes place at the center of government. No collective opinion could take on solidity except after a long interval, and in the light of facts so overpowering and weighty as to admit of only one reaction in a French heart.

Not for military reasons alone did the Germans draw lines of demarcation, set up rigid internal frontiers, encourage Breton, Flemish, and Basque separatism. They wanted to split wide open government services, business, families, intellectual groupings, moral and material interests, great and small. This vivisection of French life added to requisitions, legal robbery, rationing, and the National Revolution, spawned antagonisms: cityfolk against peasants, occupied against free zone (their respective populations did not behave in the same way toward the Germans and toward Vichy), workers against employers, poor against rich, popular irritation toward the Army and even, up to a point, against the Church, which was under suspicion of favoring a return to the policy of the throne and the altar.

The Germans had determined that France should be made incapable of ever rising again to her moral stature. Both for our country and for Europe they had in mind major surgical operations. Their first aim was to reduce the national consciousness to an anesthetic state. Their object was not only to wreck France's military vigor, not even to drain from the conquered country that which might help them bring England to her knees and dominate the world. Whatever they attempted for that purpose need not cause any astonishment. What they were seeking was something which went further and deeper. The Nazis acted as though, convinced that the New Order was there to stay, they were bent upon the destruction of France as she had been known all through the centuries, upon recasting her in their own mold, upon truncating her spinal cord. One would think that they planned to squeeze her into the tiny dwelling space allotted to her under their scheme for the remodeling of Europe. To keep repeating that they intended to change her into a community of serfs is to tell only half the truth. They did not want a race of brawny slaves, of gladiators who might revolt under some future Spartacus. Their policy of occupation, whether planned in advance or the result of its cumulative effects, could only produce, if sufficient time was allowed, the physical degeneracy of the French people.

The Vichy dictatorship was never weary of proclaiming that the nation's unity survived in it, that through Pétain and Laval there still existed a nation and a policy. For several weeks many people took these assurances at face value, even though the silent absolutism at Vichy ran so counter to their habits of mind and feeling as to make them feel lost in an uncharted sea. But England's heroism, her confident courage, the exhortatory words of de Gaulle, of Churchill, and, at a greater distance, those of Roosevelt, set them reasoning again. It was seen that hope had been after all possible in June, since, three months later, the British Empire was still holding off the conqueror, since the New World was little by little starting to the rescue. Yet look at the deadly bargain their masters had accepted! What, indeed, could be said for it? Would anybody dare to plead that physical contact with the invader had been spared to fourteen million Frenchmen and that the twenty-eight millions in the occupied zone would suffer more today if Pétain, with special facilities for access to Hitler, were not from time to time to raise his strong right hand in their defense?

This was hollow consolation indeed for the French, who could not imagine any misfortune worse than theirs. In fact, many of them saw little difference between the German boot and Pétain's shoe since they moved back, of their own free will, to their homes north of the Loire. But even were the plea well grounded, it could not withstand the retort that a slight improvement in the condition of the conquered was not worth the price of making that condition permanent nor of adding to Britain's burden, nor even of lengthening the war. Therefore Vichy's apologists, those who shrank from asserting that the consolidation of the New Order was in the best interest of their country, were led to assert—and some of them went so far as to do so—that to have continued war in Africa would have led to consequences disastrous for England herself. Would not the German Army have hurled itself against the French Empire, pushing the Spaniards on as a vanguard?

To dispose of this nonsense, remember that the British fleet, with the help of the French, in June 1940, swept every corner of the Mediterranean, and that the ports of the Peninsula, wide open to allied bombardment, would have been answerable for the wisdom of Franco—of Franco, who was, moreover, as we have seen for four years, little disposed to yield himself body and soul to the Falange, to the vengeance of his people. Moreover, never would the German High Command have been diverted from the task which brooked no delay: the frontal assault on England. And England, with a solid mass of French naval and colonial power behind her, would not have labored under such a terrible sense of isolation in the interim between the armistices of June 1940 and the involvement in the war of Russia and America. But even admitting the whole Vichy case on North Africa, no valid reason can be produced, at any rate, for the abandonment of naval and political resistance.

In the last resort Vichy, in the search for an excuse which sounds plausible to French ears, must fall back on these three leitmotivs. (1) "Sufficient food will come in three months with a German victory and in some years with a British one. The choice is painful. But the nation's independence must be secondary to the survival of the race." (2) "Under a British triumph, France would suffer as much as under a triumphant Hitler. She can still hope for a 'draw,' for a peace ending in a compromise. For her there is no better solution. By means of the separate armistice she has perhaps made that advantageous outcome possible. Wait and see!" (3) "The French people's political revolution is, in any case, a guarantee of future revival."

The advocates of surrender, the Fabre-Luces, Drieu la Rochelles, Paul Morands, Abel Bonnards, and others played endless variations on these themes. They applied to France and paraphrased in a thousand ways Ennius' line, "Conquered Greece tamed her brutal conqueror." In their own immediate neighborhood they could build up an illusion, produce a superficial belief. But these rickety propaganda scaffoldings could not hold. If Germany imposed her hegemony upon the whole world, who would dare suggest that the French race might yet be spared? Did not the armistice foreshadow a permanent policy; nothing less than the destruction of France proclaimed in *Mein Kampf?*

As for the doctrine of the "drawn match," could it amount to anything more than a justification for the military assistance Germany demanded, than a two-faced adherence to Hitler's cause? A "draw" could be nothing less than a disguised defeat for the Anglo-Saxon world. And France, like Russia, like the whole Continent, would be Germany's to exploit. Who then could take Pétain and Laval seriously when they appealed to the theory of a drawn war as their justification for maintaining the "integrity" of the Empire?

Pétain and Laval, in their diminutive capital, lay defenseless, exposed to the most far-reaching German exactions. Being determined never to resist Germany to the bitter end, never to go overseas, they could not but let the German writ have a free run in those outlying possessions which they had prevented from striking out toward freedom. As regards the Empire, the "centralist" policy of Vichy can be accounted for only by the fact that both the marshal and his Minister did not doubt the final triumph of the Führer. "Better the shadow of an Empire than nothing!" The decision reached by the Germans to attack Russia in June 1941 explains why, nevertheless, the African possessions of France were left comparatively alone. The Germans did not have time to make full use of that tool with which Vichy supplied them: a centralized administration extending overseas.

The theme of submission to the worst, on the ground that the glorious National Revolution would compensate all losses, is even less well founded. Who is going to believe that the movement initiated by Pétain and Laval resembled the first transports of Hitler and Mussolini? The fascist and National Socialist revolutionaries, however hateful their acts of violence, breathed the spirit of national pride. They reveled in bruises and beatings. In grandiloquent phrases they promised themselves the mastery of the world. What could a senile marshal and a dishonest politician risen from the sump of the Republic have in common with these gangsters? Hitler, Goering, Goebbels, Heine, Hess, Mussolini, Starace, Grandi, Farinacci were bandits and adventurers; but they were not the dregs of the governing classes which they strove to overthrow. Their brutal vitality was beyond dispute, and around them sprouted up none but new faces. In their fight for power they had ceaselessly denounced the "defeatists" and those who were too anxious to appease the foreigners. A hideous and grotesque rabble, but men of vehement temper.

How could they bear any comparison with them, these ministers and officials who racked their brains to palm off shame as honor, cowardice as courage, pusillanimity and ignorance as wisdom, humiliation as virtue, and wholehearted acceptance of the German victory as moral regeneration? What was the sense of their parades of legionnaires to the blare of trumpets? A funeral procession of penitents or flagellants would have been better suited to the spirit of the hour. And what of those flocks of generals, as self-satisfied as their predecessors might well have been on the morrow of Austerlitz or Jena, who crowded into Vichy to receive a rain of medals?[6] Listen to the soldiers cursing in their barrack rooms or in railway coaches. They jeered at the officers who abandoned them on the field of battle and were now trying to turn them into a glittering professional army, with instructions to wash their hands before meals. "To hell with them! It was not worth their while to flee from the enemy simply in order to push us around like this!" Lend an ear to the echoes reverberating from the "work camps," to which the young men were dragged and set at trifling tasks for eight months because the armistice forbade their induction for military service. Nothing but lies, odious trickery, and—I must repeat—abuse of trust.

In the closing months of 1940 the vague outlines of the indictment against Vichy floated in men's minds, formless, unclear. Then they made a coherent whole; they fitted together, but only for a select few: university men, groups of young officers, prisoners in Germany, a good many trade-unionists, socialists, and Catholics, such socialists as were clear-sighted enough to disown their party officialdom, which was corroded by Laval's and Belin's acid, a crowd of politicians and officials, the lesser clergy and members of religious orders who often failed to imitate the prudence of the prelates. But, whether fragmentary or veiled, criticism of the regime was taking a singular hold upon the workers and the peasants.

Not solid patriotic reasoning, but sentiment and personal interests,

---

[6]Weygand, as Minister of National Defense, had the impudence to propose, in August 1940, that the generals who had been in command of armies should be kept on active duty, without age limit. Pétain put a stop to this insolent challenge.

served the Vichy Government. The renewed fear of a Popular Front; the mystical legend created around the marshal; the naïve belief of the business world that it was, that it would be profitable to co-operate with the invader; the desire to justify the conservative counterrevolution, to prove that democracy was in the wrong; the dread of social leveling; the reluctance to condemn sacrosanct hierarchies which constituted the pillars of society and, above all, the belief in German invincibility. All this was to wane much more quickly in the bottom than in the middle layer of the bourgeoisie, and more quickly in the middle than in the top layer, in the occupied than in the free zone; more rapidly and thoroughly when Laval, rather than the marshal, stood in the foreground.

For over a year Pétain was given the benefit of the doubt. The middle class and even the populace attributed to him all sorts of hidden designs, a desire to dupe the Germans, some complicated kind of machiavellianism. People sought eagerly to endow his words with a veiled significance. For a long while the rumor circulated that he was conniving with General de Gaulle, was the godfather of one of the rebel's children, etc. In short, as far as Pétain was concerned, the run of Frenchmen fought against the evidence for a long time. They could not resign themselves to thinking that a Quisling, a Hacha, a Mussert, a Degrelle could exist among us in the exalted position of a marshal of France. And it was convenient, to say the least, for industrialists dealing with the Germans to claim the marshal as their preceptor in patriotism, to aver that he alone could judge what needed to be done. To determine from month to month the successive stages in the movement of public opinion is out of the question. It did not become finally clear until the end of 1941. By then Pétain's moral status was badly impaired.

Nonetheless, as early as the autumn of 1940, a muffled pressure was brought to bear on Vichy. I would not call it public opinion. The expression "popular sentiment" is more accurate. Public opinion, however loudly and imperatively it expresses itself, can argue and compromise; but popular sentiment, a kind of natural force, is relentless. It came to light in letters opened by the censorship, in the marshal's correspondence, in reports from prefects and the police. It was like the rumble of a rising tide.[7] The revolt of the lowly has its everlasting symbol—the epic of

[7]Sometime in October 1940 the Russian chargé d'affaires in Paris had some dealings with the Vichy delegation concerning the properties of the Baltic States in the French capital. Incidentally, he expressed indignation at Laval's *pourparlers* with Abetz, of which he seemed to have full knowledge: "The whole French nation testifies by its attitude that it cannot be enslaved. The Parisians behave perfectly. In Brittany, the most reactionary of all the provinces, the priests are so many British agents. Be watchful! For in Europe some states

Joan of Arc. The Head of the State and his vice-president of the Council had before them a silent visitor whose disquieting countenance they sought to scrutinize. Their confrontation with the French masses was beginning.

5

Pétain Dismisses Laval

PEACE! Peace! Pétain and Laval certainly never imagined that the armistice would not be promptly followed by a final settlement. If its torture were to be prolonged, the French nation would never forgive them. It would take its vengeance and they knew it. This was their program—release of the prisoners of war, a more generous supply of food, and less administrative constraint in the occupied zone, where Vichy's decrees were ineffective unless approved by the Nazi military authorities—a state of affairs which enabled the invader to exert pressure on the action of the government in the "free" zone. For the fulfillment of that program two rival methods were possible: either petty bargaining from day to day or an over-all treaty which would entail considerable material advantage at the price of France's permanent and acquiescent subjection. The choice lay between the bold game and the timid game. From the very outset Laval was for the bold game which offered the only chance of a handsome dividend. As for the timid game, Brinon said early in July, our pockets would be picked gradually and we should end with nothing.

What if only Hitler were willing to negotiate a basic pact and to put an end to the legal state of war? It is true that France, as she was situated at the center of the conflict, could not hope to become a quiet oasis even under these circumstances. Nevertheless she would have a right to ask her overlord for certain mitigations and favors. Within the New Order she would be promoted to the status of an associate. What was more, if events lent themselves to it, she might re-enter the fray against

have not yet uttered their last word." At about the same time a friend of mine visited several prefects in the free zone. They all told him that from 80 to 90 per cent of the people were pro-British.

her former ally and thus win the gratitude of the Nazi Empire and take precedence over Italy. She would prove her mettle and restore her self-respect. Something Baudouin said after Mers-el-Kebir indicates the moment when a decision hung in the balance: "Our relations with England are now moving on a very different plane."[1]

We have already seen how the Cabinet overruled Laval, on July 5 or 6, by refusing to consider a declaration of war against our former ally. The marshal, whose timidity was a stumbling block to bad and good advisers alike, dared not risk that step. Nonetheless, until the middle of October, it rested with Hitler to make a final over-all arrangement with Vichy. The opportunity lay within his grasp as long as the French military experts thought they could see England prostrate at his feet within the near future. Had the Führer, toward the end of summer or the beginning of autumn,[2] boldly unshackled his victim, had he undertaken to respect the frontiers of France, who can gauge the psychological effects of such a gesture? As it was, Hitler did things by halves and clumsily. In August he was even foolish enough to begin absorbing Alsace-Lorraine within the German Reich in violation of the Armistice, which was merely a cessation of hostilities accompanied by guarantees for the

---

[1]Foreign Minister Baudouin was soon to be reduced to complete impotence as Laval encroached more and more upon the conduct of French diplomacy. Incidentally, Baudouin was no less secretive with his own secretary-general, honest Charles-Roux, than Laval with others. The policy which Baudouin personally wanted to carry out can be seen very clearly in the explanations he gave to a French diplomat who was taking leave after his appointment to a distant post overseas, two or three days after the clash at Mers-el-Kebir. "What happened at Mers-el-Kebir enables us, at last, to turn public opinion against England, to uproot all pro-British prejudices. Thus we shall be in position to co-operate with Italy and Spain, to create within the New Order a Latin bloc, strong enough in the long run to put some curb on German power. But here is what I fear. As long as Churchill, that raving maniac, that alcoholic, remains in office, war will continue, and therefore, with plenty of time before us, we shall have a good chance to succeed in all our planning with Italy and Spain. But were the British to throw Churchill overboard, our prospects would be darkened. Halifax could hardly fail to become Premier. A peace of compromise would soon be in the making between England and Germany. Then great schemes of territorial dismemberment might be considered and France's hour of most deadly danger would strike." Baudouin is personally responsible for not acquainting Pétain with the full terms of the ultimatum Commander Holland delivered to Admiral Gensoul.

[2]When did the men of Vichy realize that the German onslaught on England was doomed to failure? Assuredly it took them more time than the German Command to correctly appraise the check inflicted on the attackers. About September 15, Laval took several German generals to dinner at Maxim's. General von Stretius thanked him and added: "I hope that you will soon be our guest." "I shall be back by October," answered Laval. "I hope that by that date you will be hosts to me in London." The German generals thought that it was a most unpleasant jest on the part of Laval. One of them said as much to members of the Vichy General Delegation to Paris the next day.

victor, but not a permanent settlement. We now know what happened. During the summer of 1940 the men who ruled Germany did not agree about the fate of France. To the High Command schemes of collaboration and association with Vichy were utter nonsense. They pressed strongly for breaking up the country, so much so that Brinon himself hoped for a few weeks England would continue to hold out. He could see no other way of reducing the arrogance of the generals.

It is not easy to follow Vichy's mental processes on foreign policy through the month of October. Authority was divided. Certainly Pétain, Laval, and Baudouin—the latter Minister of Foreign Affairs until the twenty-eighth—did not work hand in glove. Pétain and Baudouin had not the hardihood to follow Laval all the way. In a radio speech on October 10 the marshal said that France was freeing herself from "so-called traditional friendships and enmities." On the twenty-sixth he met Hitler at Montoire. On the thirtieth, again over the radio, he told the French people why he had accepted Hitler's invitation. He announced his policy of "collaboration" and uttered those grave words: "This policy is my own; no one has dictated it to me. . . . Till now a father has been talking to you. From now on it will be a chief." Simultaneously, the defeat suffered by the Nazis in the battle of Britain could no longer be concealed. Everything pointed to a protracted struggle. A formal settlement between France and Germany might involve the French Government in the conflict. Whatever the limits set to French participation, the English would nonetheless bomb French cities by way of reprisal. "We cannot face that danger," said the marshal to Alphonse de Chateaubriant in November.[3] Thus the marshal, having gone halfway with Laval, came to a halt.

I have recorded these two men's meetings and conversations since 1934. The fact is that, less than a month after the *coup d'état,* they parted company morally. One of my friends was surprised to find the marshal hostile to his vice-premier at the end of August. He was invited to dinner at the Sévigné Pavilion and he listened with amazement for the space of almost an hour to long accounts of Laval's pilferings and thefts volunteered by the host. He had known all about them for a long time and could easily have added some details of his own. But why on earth should Pétain take such pleasure in telling the story? Was it possible that he had only recently learned the truth and was now giving vent to his indignation? Recently? Well, hardly.

[3]Who reported the conversation in the weekly *La Gerbe.*

In September my friend paid a visit to Vichy once more. Meanwhile the Cabinet had been reshuffled. All the former parliamentarians had been thrown out of office, but all the functions and honors of Laval had been confirmed. "After what you told me, Marshal, I expected that the man at the top would also be changed." Then it was that Pétain delivered himself of the dictum which I have already quoted: "I can never forget that without him the national revolution would not have come to pass."

The marshal's household was storing up resentment against the Minister, who already thought himself master of the situation and made no bones about it. "He has not yet resigned himself to the limitations of an old man. Some morning he will be found dead in his bed." Among the members of Pétain's inner circle were: General Brécard, army commander, for many years on the retired list and one of the chief's old retainers; General Laure, whom the Germans released in November; du Moulin de Labarthète, a rather colorless treasury official who had worked with Paul Reynaud at the Ministry of the Colonies in 1932 and whom the Ministry of Finances had unceremoniously shipped off to the Madrid Embassy in 1939, happy to be rid of him;[4] B. Menétrel, of the Army Medical Corps, son of a doctor who, in his time, had looked after the marshal's health. Weygand's name should likewise be mentioned. He was not one of the family group but was still hanging about in the outskirts, already an embittered and lonely man. He had been deprived of the Ministry of National Defense in the September cabinet shake-up, and this at the request of the Germans, who knew how hotly he had protested in the Cabinet against the annexation of Alsace-Lorraine. In June he had seemed to be the National Revolution's second-in-command. Still a great figure in the autumn, he was fated to become, one year later, even less than a figurant. A few other names deserve mention: Marcel Peyrouton, Minister of the Interior; Raphael Alibert, Minister of Justice; Henri Massis and René Gillouin, compilers of speeches and articles, private secretaries, official commentators, apologists, the former a fool or a knave, the latter a strayed sheep destined to return to the fold.

Within the counterrevolutionary faction almost all these men were linked with Charles Maurras. Maurras, in that autumn of 1940, was anxiously asking himself whether the wonderful opportunity to restore the dynasty of the "forty kings who made France in a thousand years" might not melt away, whether the demagogue from Auvergne might

[4] Du Moulin de Labarthète parted with the National Revolution at some date in 1942.

not deflect the favorable current toward a personal dictatorship, toward a socially leveling movement like that of Hitler or Mussolini.[5] Was not Laval recruiting renegade ringleaders from the labor unions? As far as Maurras was concerned, the July 10 regime had only one justification— the restoration of the House of Bourbon. He dreamed of a rebirth of the old-time French community, with its professional stratifications, its hierarchical pattern. The workers, hideous human cogs in the industrial machine, would for the most part be eliminated. They would not loom large in a nation of tillers of the soil and skilled artisans. France must recover her soul through agriculture, craftsmanship, and a contrite heart —contrition being strangely prized by this godless "positivist." The rights of men, which all could claim, must give way to special rights and privileges in the original meaning of the word, symbols of a perfect division of labor. From the highest to the lowest, each would have his appointed station. The citizen would be entitled to play a part in the community only by virtue of his special aptitude to perform some particular function, not because he was capable of applying his reason to any public issue. Political assemblies would be replaced by "corporations" voting on matters within their sphere but having no voice whatever when the general interests of the state were at stake. In place of universal suffrage there would be the election by their peers of employers and workmen brought together in common enterprises. France would become a network of consultative bodies with a strictly limited jurisdiction and a beneficent diversity and inequality. Under the spell of authority from above, the country would be a well-ordered hive of activity. Capitalism and Socialism, which fare together like Siamese twins, would no longer exist. Capitalism means great financial, industrial, commercial trusts, involving a systematic drain on private funds, investments on a massive scale, far-reaching international combines. These economic monsters, the hotbeds of governmental chaos, and of class struggle, must be destroyed. The true ideal is the man who owns his domain, who rides his horse over his fields in the early morning light, his chest bare to the winds, directing and supervising his subordinates.

[5]Undoubtedly Pétain had it in mind to restore the throne. When Baudouin, Minister of Foreign Affairs, broke the news of the Duc de Guise's death to him, he reacted with the phrase: "Then it will fall to the Count of Paris to succeed me!"

The Count of Paris went to London in 1941: "Alas," he exclaimed, "all my supporters are in Vichy!" Unfortunately for him, he visited Vichy in the summer of 1942. His personal campaign was to end pitifully in Algiers in the days after Darlan's assassination. In the summer of 1941 and later Mr. Winston Churchill toyed with the idea of a French constitutional monarchy. An emissary from Weygand discussed the question in Lisbon with Sir Ronald Campbell, the British Ambassador.

What a moral cleansing that would mean! The Mediterranean-Atlantic canal would soon be dug, the Trans-Saharan railroad quickly built—those two undertakings so shamefully neglected by the Republic. Such was the canvas which believers in *Action Française* could embroider to their taste. When he was in a confidential mood Weygand would extract from his pocket a paper entitled *How To Run France* (*Commandement de la France*).

Laval sneered at such tomfoolery. "These silly amateurs," he explained to a diplomat, "perhaps think they know how to tear the French away from representative institutions. They are wrong. The French people will not give them up as easily as that. The only way to make it forget them is to administer a stiff dose of Socialism. I have finally come round full circle, I have returned to the faith of my youth. I alone am capable of severing the masses from democracy." His meaning was clear enough. Pétain's gang was perfectly sure that Laval would take advantage of the understanding he was so eager to make with Hitler to set up a totalitarian state.

Thus, in the eyes of those intimately associated with the Head of the State, the negotiations the Minister had in hand seemed to open a broad highway toward a national reformation in direct contradiction to everything they held dear. And they came to fear Laval's conversations with the Germans, his trips to Paris, from which at any moment might issue the thunderbolt which would put an end to all their schemes.

The difference was not merely one of principle; it extended also to method. Laval kept saying: "I know my fellow countrymen loathe my plan for joining the New Order. But that is no reason for my giving it up. The duty of a statesman worthy of the name is to bring about whatever the interest of the country seems to him to demand in the face of all opposition. To my mind the outcome of the war is clear as day. If Germany falls, I shall be hung. But that prospect leaves me cold. It is much too remote."

The marshal was not attuned to any such recklessness. His personal popularity gave him a vast advantage over Laval, and he was proud of it. When he traveled about he was careful to leave his Premier at home. At Toulouse, at Marseilles, standing under floodlights on the balcony of the prefecture, he showed himself to the people with the tricolor clasped on his breast, a sight to bring tears to the eyes. Had Laval's ugly face come into view, it would have spoiled the touching picture. The electric current running through the crowd would have been interrupted.

The marshal took a pride in the National Revolution. It had reached the point, he thought, of winning Frenchmen's hearts. For he took seriously the sententious maxims manufactured in the Gillouin-Massis literary establishment—an unsavory mixture of La Fontaine and Maurras. He recited them with complete sincerity. Hero worship was encouraged by the administration.[6] The leader's portrait was displayed in shop-windows, mounted upon pedestals draped in red, white, and blue. Not even St. Thérèse, lying on her bed of state at Lisieux, called forth deeper devotion. But under this cloud of incense the national saint only pretended to drowse. He listened studiously to what his swarming devotees said and used it to advantage. He had no intention of risking such incomparable glory by embarking upon any rash adventure. He had no intention of scandalizing the faithful. Laval might snap his fingers at prudence: he had nothing to lose and everything to gain. But the marshal could move only in the direction of a German alliance with great circumspection. Many a prefect reported that 90 per cent of his district was pro-British. Here was a warning. Better give the German victory time to sink in. Eventually the French would jump on its band wagon of their own accord.

Pétain wanted to be especially cautious with America. He cared for the Anglo-Saxon world no more than did Laval. Privately he delighted in calling it money-ridden, and, incidentally, Weygand did not differ from him. As far as the marshal was concerned, there was no difference between an English invasion of French soil and a German occupation. Both were equally injurious to the national heritage. But despite all this he seemed to sense that the instinct of the mass of Frenchmen led them to believe that the policy of the United States would determine the outcome of the war, give the British the aid necessary for victory. He was well aware what vast hopes America inspired in the hearts of the patriots. So he made it a point to finesse and he handled President Roosevelt with kid gloves.

No more than his Minister did Pétain think the entry of the United States into the struggle probable or even possible. His Ambassador in Washington, Henry Haye, pointed out to him daily all the weak spots in the military, industrial and social structure of the great republic. Surely the last thing he wished was for the President, by throwing Amer-

---

[6]Gaston Bergery, Ambassador to Moscow, a professional cynic, returning from Russia in June 1941, following upon the rupture of diplomatic relations, managed to have a good-sized portrait of Pétain exposed to the view of all comers in his Pullman parlor! Even in a railway compartment and in Sofia he deemed it useful to perform the rite.

ica into the war, to pull down the melancholy altars erected in his honor and the framework of the national revolution. Early in December, before Laval's dismissal, he bluntly declared to a person of consequence who had broached the subject of Admiral Leahy's appointment as Ambassador: "I see what Mr. Roosevelt is driving at, but don't worry. He will get nowhere with me. He will not make me budge." His visitor objected that the American Chief Executive did not dream of exerting improper influence. Obstinately the marshal repeated, "I know what's in his mind, and he won't get anything out of me." By that he meant that Mr. Roosevelt would get nothing substantial, but he would be pliable enough in making concessions that didn't matter. Toward the end of October he had promised that no military assistance would be given to Germany—a commitment so vague and general that the Department of State tried hard in December to have it clearly defined. He authorized Admiral Robert, High Commissioner for the West Indies, to conclude a preliminary understanding for neutralizing Martinique—warships, planes, gold reserve. He was determined to put on a smile if he could and to say nice things. The French must never be able to reproach him with having estranged the United States. It was better to give America time to estrange herself.

Laval, on the other hand, chafed under the threat of the New World against Germany—a threat which might, if translated into action, arouse the French against the New Order and throw them back into the arms of an England more confident than ever of victory. His own inclination then was to assume a sharp tone with Washington. On October 25, on the eve of the Montoire meeting, a message from President Roosevelt as well as a noble appeal from King George VI reached Vichy. Both Heads of State, fully aware of what was at stake in the discussion between the Führer and the marshal, tried to restrain France's rulers. The debate in the Cabinet which resulted in the afore-mentioned assurance of the marshal to America has come partially to our knowledge. It is so extraordinary that were it not for the unquestionable authority of the informant, one would hesitate to accept its authenticity. Laval, beside himself, declared that Mr. Roosevelt's communication deserved but one answer, a word in two syllables, the coarsest in the French language. "We quite understand what you mean," said Baudouin, Minister of Foreign Affairs, and then Pétain: "You are of the opinion that a point-blank refusal should be cabled to Washington. But the problem is to find an appropriate formula." "No, no circumlocutions! I mean exactly what I say. My son-in-law lives among Americans: I know just how to handle them," and again he uttered the insulting word. Not without justification did the American diplomats, in their memorandum of December 5 or 6—in which, for the first time, Pétain was pressed not to commit himself beyond the obligations of the armistice, a trim formula which was to be of very long service[7]—insert a paragraph aimed specifically at Laval and distinguishing between his deeds and the marshal's.

The conflict, which had been ripening since the summer, burst forth on the evening of December 13. The Minister's dismissal was like some political drama from the sixteenth century. It would have been better staged in the Château of Blois than in the Hôtel du Parc at Vichy, with halberdiers instead of the marshal's "bodyguard"[8] as an escort for a Laval now suddenly fallen from power. We know only Laval's story, which certainly does not lack piquancy.

The marshal asked all the ministers present at the Cabinet to hand in their resignation. He returned them all except Laval's. Then he withdrew to his private office, where Laval followed him, exasperated by the phrase which had been thrown in his face: "You have deceived me."

Pétain: I don't trust you. You are hiding what you are doing from me.

Laval: What do you mean? I have told you everything.

Pétain: Perhaps. But you have never been willing to put it in writing. I have warned you, but you paid no attention.

Laval: I have no time to write. It would have been out of the question for me to dictate a report on so confidential a matter as the negotiation with Germany. And, what is more, I have no confidence in the men around.

Pétain: I should have put any report you made in this safe and I alone would have read it.

Laval: Who has the key of that safe?

Pétain: I always carry it with me.

Laval: Marshal, would you be so kind as to show it me?

Caught short, the marshal was foolish enough to accede. He rummaged in all his pockets, he tapped them from the outside. He could not find the key. And afterward he complained of Laval's impertinence.

Pétain's household, added the discomfited Minister, had supplied their chief with a grievance concocted to further their own ends. If this was

[7] In his conversation with the Vichy Ambassador, Henry Haye, on November 4, Mr. Cordell Hull had already used that formula and discriminated between Pétain and Laval. A memorandum of that conversation drafted by the Secretary of State was published on December 6, 1943, together with President Roosevelt's message to Pétain of October 24 and other state papers concerning the relations with Vichy.

[8] See page 334, note 1.

the case, the household hit the mark. Laval's special talent, when he was handling any thorny business requiring the approval of third parties, lay in proceeding by insinuation. Casual remarks were let drop here and there. Failure to reply was construed as consent in advance which the Minister would then claim after the event. But, if his enterprise failed, he would deny that he had said anything at all. According to M. Jean Montigny, this is exactly how he behaved at Vichy during the first days of July, when he wished to prepare his cabinet colleagues for the overthrow of the constitution. After letting a hint fall from his lips as though by accident, he hastily left the cabinet room, asking to be excused: "Forgive me, but there is an important group of senators waiting for me. . . ."[9] Always an ambiguous approach, a tiny shove instead of a frank and open explanation. By such means had he thought he could launch the treaty with Hitler. "Dust in his eyes!" Pétain would not see through it.

But his scheme was of vast proportions. In some shape or other it involved military collaboration, the use of French bases[10] by the Germans and even of the fleet, after a period of transition marked by the performance of convoy duties; a German promise that France might keep Nice and Corsica and also her overseas possessions, provided that they were utilized in accordance with the needs of the New Order—especially in Africa, the economic complement of Europe. The French flag would still fly along the southern shores of the Mediterranean, but to satisfy Spain's ambitions in Morocco and Italy's in Tunisia, the device of a condominium was contemplated and, of course, ultimate control by Germans, whether open or secret, capped the program. Very little is known about the whole business; we can only discern its general purport. Long afterward it transpired that a subsidiary negotiation between France and Spain followed the main lines of the project worked out, but quickly dropped, by Delcassé, in 1902, when he tried to get the approval of Madrid for the French protectorate over Morocco contemplated at that time. France was, in effect, to appear as a partner of the Reich. In the federal organization of Europe she was probably to be placed on the

[9]In November the marshal had complained that the vice-president of the Council did not keep him posted on conversations with foreign ambassadors and ministers. At about this time one of them mentioned in his reports that M. Charles Rochat, political director at the Ministry of Foreign Affairs, had been present at a conversation he had had with Laval. For once the marshal had forced acceptance of a witness.

[10]The right to occupy Dakar and to use Tunisia territory in transit was to be immediately conceded to the Germans (see page 511 and note 9). Of this, definite evidence has come to us, although some doubt obtains as to the date.

same level as Italy.[11] Some degree of autonomy was to be accorded to her in return for her promise to conduct herself as a faithful subordinate. The French prisoners were to be released in large numbers and the war indemnity lightened.

The deep-rooted rift between Pétain and Laval has already been indicated. But why did the break come on December 13? Twenty-four hours later the ashes of the Duke of Reichstadt were to be carried to the chapel of the Invalides and deposited near Napoleon's grave. The private ceremony, held by torchlight, was to be followed in daytime by a public ceremony. Laval had thought it clever to give the ultimate phase of the parleys this theatrical prelude. Was not bringing the body of the Duke of Reichstadt back to Paris like some powerful gust of wind, rekindling in French hearts their latent hatred of England?[12] Hitler had thought well of this stage setting; he has told how, in order to offer a worthy reception to the marshal, the presidential palace, the Elysée, had been modernized. Engineers from Berlin had replaced the outmoded heating apparatus. The only feature lacking to make the arrangements complete was the presence of France's hero. But the hero felt that his hand would be forced. At the last moment he suddenly decided to keep away.

Common talk had it that a *coup d'état* complementary to that which took place in July was hatched by the Minister—this time against the Head of the State. Once safely installed in Paris or at Trianon, the marshal would not have been able to extricate himself. There he would have languished with much pomp and circumstance but under careful surveillance, to the benefit of Laval, who would really pull the strings. *Coup d'état,* however, is hardly the right word. Two days before the Montoire meeting Laval had met the Führer to plan the mechanics of the interview. In December he did it on a broader and more ambitious scale, wheels within wheels carefully oiled and plenty of room for blackmail. There was no great departure from the precedents created by him, acquiesced in by Pétain.

Laval carried on the exchange of views semisecretly, as was his wont, either in person or with Fernand de Brinon as intermediary—his trusted servant in both good times and bad, and now accredited to Abetz, an old crony. The marshal, bound to "collaboration" in principle ever since

[11]Diplomatic reports had it that Mussolini, vexed at the Montoire meeting, attacked Greece out of hand, so as to prove to the Führer that Italy was not a negligible quantity. But the Italian rout in Greece enabled Hitler to maintain his offer to France.

[12]Cf. what Laval said in 1935 about the people of France, Napoleon and England, page 424. All the more firmly does he cling to his historical notions because they are few and mean.

October 26, was kept vaguely informed by Laval, who was a past master at screening the boldest enterprises behind acts which appeared thoroughly natural and unobjectionable. Anxious to preserve his own position Baudouin sounded the alarm, but to no practical effect. He— or others—had suspected Laval of peculation when the Bor mines in Yugoslavia, the property of a French corporation, were sold to Germany.[13] But the cat was let out of the bag by the Germans themselves. They talked too much. The French have no monopoly on indiscreet gossip. The story goes that Major Fonck, the famous airman of 1914-18, on returning from Berlin, where he had spent a good deal of time with friends of Goering, was able to enlighten some Vichy minister about the tenor of the prospective agreement.[14]

Laval and his circle thought the affair was as good as settled. It was one of their axioms that France could be ruled only from Paris and that the transfer of the government to the banks of the Seine was the indispensable prerequisite for seriously taking things in hand. Once the Hitler-Pétain pact had been sealed, the nation would recover its nervous center and then the dictatorial regime would begin to function with full vigor. At last France would be cast once for all in the National Socialist mold.

The marshal wanted to go back to Paris, but not if he was to be there under the thumb of a Merovingian mayor of the palace. His return to the capital had been guaranteed by the Armistice. On July 11 he had told the French people: "We have asked . . . the German Government to liberate Versailles and the ministries district." On August 13 he reverted to the matter: "The German Government on August 7 informed me that, while standing by the principle of its former acceptance . . . for various technical reasons and so long as certain material conditions continued unfulfilled, it could not permit the transfer. We must then wait a while longer, but I believe I can assure you the delay will be brief. May I add that if you long for my return, I long for it as eagerly as you?" He referred once more to the question on October 10 but afterward omitted it altogether, for he had learned in November that the Vichy diplomatic corps would not be allowed to move with him. How could the Germans have tolerated ambassadors and ministers claiming their traditional immunities in the very heart of a military

---

[13]The shareholders were paid a price about 20 per cent higher than the current market quotations.

[14]Was Pétain's ignorance of Laval's dealings with the Nazis as profound as he professed it to be? Darlan, at any rate, approved of some of the articles in the projected agreement.

zone? Moreover, Pétain had come to fear that Laval, with the help of the French Hitlerite gang—Déat, Doriot, Luchaire, etc.,—and leaning upon the occupation authorities, might cut him off, dominate him, freeze him into an inert figurehead. Besides, was it possible for him to pay Hitler a second visit and still keep free of definite and far-reaching commitments? Laval's mistake was to force the pace. Pétain was shocked into reaction, and his household pulled him back by his coattail.

But can it be said that the marshal and his political lieutenant differed fundamentally, that their quarrel was over more than a question of timing? The fact remains that on October 26, at Montoire, Hitler had offered to leave France in possession of her overseas empire provided that it was used for the benefit of the Nazis against England and, if necessary, against the United States. In general outline, at least, the marshal had accepted that proposal and had tried on the radio to prepare the country to swallow it.

The article, amounting to a regular manifesto, which the marshal published in the September 15 *Revue des Deux Mondes* revealed his doctrinal beliefs. He sought to connect French history with the New Order. He argued that Hitler's concepts of work and wealth were borrowed from the good sense and prudence of our own ancestors. These tillers of the soil, he explained, had no liking for the gold standard or large-scale movements of capital; and he recalled the fable of the plowman and his children. With as much reason he might have maintained that the French of the seventeenth century preferred donkeys and horses to internal-combustion engines. All this was merely the drivel of Pétain's ghost writers.

But the main point is that the old man repeated to one and all that he thought Germany's victory inevitable. At the end of November, he tried to impress this notion upon an ambassador who was leaving for America. Hence, as far as accepting the New Order went, he agreed with Laval. He broke with him only over the tempo of the rapprochement with Hitler's Empire, over the degree of public acceptance which must be obtained beforehand, over the nature and the object of the National Revolution, and, if one may use this figure of speech, over his share in the royalties.

The Germans knew nothing of what was brewing at Vichy. Pétain's stroke was a slap in the face. During the evening of the thirteenth, Otto Abetz called the German Ambassador at Madrid on the telephone. By error he was connected with a line over which Peyrouton was regaling someone with an account of the palace revolution. Abetz spoke up. "I have a right to know all about it!" Three days later he was on his way to Vichy with an escort of armored cars. On December 17 he entered into a long conversation with the marshal and Darlan, and, to begin with, he had the Minister of the Interior's halberdiers withdrawn from Chateldon. Laval, now looking to his own safety, was to go back to Paris as a member of the ambassadorial party. A few moments before his departure he could be seen drinking champagne with German officers. Abetz insisted upon the recall of General de Fornel de la Laurencie,[15] general delegate of the Vichy Government to the Army of Occupation, who, on December 10 or 11, on instructions from Pétain's entourage, had ordered Déat to be put under lock and key.

On December 24, Darlan, vice-president of the Council designate, was granted an audience with Hitler. He came back rather worried. He had upheld Pétain's right to choose his ministers with complete freedom and had drawn upon himself that retort: "The Marshal is free to do what he sees fit, but so am I."[16] On January 18 the Head of the State thought it advisable to humble himself to the extent of receiving in his private railway compartment the unfaithful servant so ignominiously and swiftly discharged. Subsequently Pierre-Etienne Flandin, the new Minister for Foreign Affairs, who had sent our embassies and legations a very harsh telegram on the subject of his predecessor, referring to his "conspiracy" and accusing him of having attempted to relegate the marshal to a purely honorary status, was obliged to announce that Laval would return to office, though not with his previous omnipotence. Finally, in early February, the Vichy Minister of Foreign Affairs sent out word that Laval was to remain where he was—that is, to stay in Paris safely behind the German bayonets.

The Germans, therefore, had resigned themselves to getting along without the French politician best suited to thrust his country into the New Order by reason of his cunning, his ability to maneuver, his conviction that he personally could survive only in case of a German triumph. Foreign diplomats have recorded this utterance of Hitler's: "I have the

---

[15]General de Fornel de la Laurencie was a friend of Weygand. Laval had selected him to conciliate the former generalissimo with whom he was continuously quarreling. The first delegate general was Léon Noël. In fairness it must be said that he behaved courageously. He did not remain general delegate more than a week (July 5–July 13).

[16]At the December 24 meeting Hitler informed Darlan: "The French Government must make up its mind. Laval's appointment as principal minister was none of my business, but I cannot help being concerned at the fact that Laval was thrown out at the very moment he was about to conclude an agreement with Germany."

force on my side, and I'll make them see it. Why worry about anything else?"

All outward signs indicate that after a few weeks of perplexity the Nazis reached an understanding with Darlan on a program of collaboration. In the end they recognized the force of the admiral's argument: take care, Marshal Pétain, because of his prestige among the French, will in the long run prove more useful than the man who is scorned by his fellow countrymen and whom he has thrown aside.

However this may be, those responsible for the management of the Nazi Empire, in January 1941, were faced with a most embarrassing dilemma. On the one hand, in accordance with Pétain's offer, they could choose an empiric method and be content with successive doses of co-operation doled out over many months. The advantage of this policy was to humor the French, to tame them gradually to the conqueror's will. On the other hand, Laval's policy, quick and trenchant, was perhaps the only one to take into account the ultimate reality—the stubbornness of French patriotism. The latter was the more costly of the two. It might compel the Germans to increase their army of occupation. But was not the alternative a snare and a delusion? Our Nazi masters concluded that the experiment urged by Darlan was worth trying. With their consent it lasted for sixteen months and twelve days.

6

Pétain: The Enigma

THE MARSHAL probably never was so popular as at the time of Laval's dismissal. To the great bulk of the French people the fallen politician represented nothing but corruption and betrayal. Squarely facing the issue, the Head of the State had broken Hitler's tool. Those who had steadfastly refused to judge the old man harshly, even on the most glaring evidence, prided themselves on having remained faithful to him. Certainly he had erred, on June 17, when asking the enemy to "seek with us, as between soldiers, after the fight and in an honorable spirit, means to put an end to hostilities." "As between soldiers!" What an absurd illusion! We had simply fallen the prey to the most grasping of conquerors. Again, on June 25, he had misled the country by making it believe that "at least honor was saved." Such a claim was nothing but hypocrisy! It simply was not true that France had fulfilled the demands of honor on June 17. But, in the stubborn and prejudiced opinion of the French, the folly and the shame of surrender involved only Laval. The marshal, like the whole French population, had been his dupe. The sainted leader had suffered in silence. He had waited for his opportunity. He had redeemed himself.

For eight centuries a marshal of France has been the very symbol of military virtue. Under the earliest of the kings he did not merely command armies. He also interpreted the code of chivalry and exercised a moral jurisdiction over men at arms. Later on the marshals' court settled affairs of honor. The accusations of treason or near-treason preferred against Bernadotte, Marmont, Bourmont, Bazaine (this list is not exhaustive) in no way impaired this highest of military dignities. In the eyes of the populace a glorious halo surrounds the marshals of France; it springs not only from each one's individual deeds, but from all the exploits recorded over the ages. Thus the stars which we can locate shine with the added radiance of unmapped, nameless celestial bodies. The whole country was stirred when, on December 16, 1916, Joffre received the baton. No general had been made marshal of France since the time of Napoleon III.

Prévost-Paradol remarked on the dangers of this title in 1869. It accounts for the fact that men who are no more than the shadows of their former selves outlive their day and continue, with the support of the public, to lay claim to the high military offices. The Pétain of Verdun justified this judgment only too thoroughly. The matchless sort of lifelong nobility conferred in France by the marshalship sustained his legend and, in the mind of the majority, added to it a kind of infallibility. For long months the red and gold kepi, the seven stars blazoned on the sleeves, the *Médaille Militaire* hid from the French people what was going on. At the very depth of our woe that sky-blue figure was always pictured in silhouette against a background of battlefields. Only in 1941 did the sentiment of the masses revolt when collective executions began. The revulsion would have been quicker and sharper had Laval remained in the government.

Flights of eloquence and noble laments aimed at depicting as necessary to the country's salvation what was in fact no more than connivance with the victorious Germans and the selfish preservation of the men and institutions of Vichy. Here was already enough to baffle the critical spirit of many, especially among the middle class. But there was more. Pétain's tactics consisted in gradually inducing the French to accept the "inevitable" victory of the Nazis. This victory, however, had still to come to pass. For, having lost the Battle of Britain in the autumn of 1940, the Germans, in 1941, lost the Battle of Russia. As a climax they had to shoulder the burden of war with America, which the French recognized as being far more decisive than Japan's triumphant drive in the Far East. No more in 1941 than in 1940 did Pétain have the audacity to carry his ideas or feelings to their logical conclusion. He still had to bide his time.

Thus the first contrast between his patriotic speeches and his servile behavior was complicated by a further contrast between the marshal's halting and seemingly halfhearted policy and total collaboration with Germany toward which he was moving. Full collaboration was his goal, but he often strove to put the crowd off the scent. At times the panegȳrists of the marshal have, therefore, maintained with some success that whatever help he doled out to the Germans was designed to cheat them, not to make a German victory easier. Such is the dual origin of the Pétain enigma. A thorough investigation of Pétain's past alone could clear it up, but very few people have ever succeeded in dissecting his career.

In 1942, had it not become obvious that the marshal was dominated by the most hateful prejudices? Nonetheless, both in the "free" zone and abroad, those who feared a popular uprising still refused to see him as he was, the leader of a counterrevolution masquerading in the trappings of a leader of armies. The best way to finally dispose of the legend of the blue tunic is to dismember bit by bit the persistent illusion which it generates, to break down one by one the servants of the master and the records of their deeds.

In 1941, as before, Pétain's was not the hand to threaten, to order, to strike. He required always a factotum by his side, and the need persisted when Laval had gone, though, apparently, the office was split in two. The incumbents were Darlan and Weygand. The former held a string of controlling posts: he was vice-president of the Council of Ministers, Minister of the Navy, of Foreign Affairs and, for seven months, of the Interior.[1] The latter, removed from the Cabinet in September, was

---

[1] Flandin was dropped after the Hitler-Darlan agreement. In order to fulfill his commitments, Darlan had to control French diplomacy. That Laval might be appeased, Peyrouton was given the Buenos Aires Embassy. In July 1941, Darlan was to give up the Interior in favor of Pucheu, but in August he became Minister of National Defense.

"General Delegate in Africa," with a commission to co-ordinate the civil authorities and exercise direct power over the armed forces.[2] In the judgment of their fellow countrymen and even of foreign diplomats at Vichy, Darlan and Weygand moved in very different directions. We shall see that, when it came to fundamentals, they did not fall so much apart. They might clash personally, but their politics were closely linked together. This misleading semblance of disagreement was yet another source of confusion in the public mind.

Darlan's Anglophobia has already been mentioned. It was genuine. Did it spring from that absurd scheme for Franco-Italian "parity" which angered the French at the 1930 Naval Conference, where I myself witnessed Darlan in full agitation against it? Was it of older vintage? In any case, it would be a mistake to suppose that his Anglophobia cut deeper with the Admiral of the Fleet than his ambition to be at the top of the ladder. He was one of the greatest opportunists of our generation. Before the war he had been the very prototype of the officer who stops at nothing in order to win promotion and decorations. By masterly maneuvering he won honors no one before him had ever dared covet. Thus, yearning to succeed Admiral Durand-Viel as commander in chief of the Navy, he managed to have his appointment signed six months before the post became vacant. In order to step up a rung in the Legion of Honor—from the collar of a commander to the badge of a grand officer —he did not rest until the governing body of the order broke the rule requiring the minimum of three years to pass before promotion from one grade to another. There is no end to the vile stories told about this tireless climber.[3] After the Armistice he boasted of himself as the great French military leader who was never defeated or even (he never shied from any claim, however immoderate) as the only great Allied leader who had emerged as victor from the fray, for the Lord alone knew where the British fleet would have been had he and his seamen not watched over it. In all justice didn't he deserve a place nothing less than the highest after Pétain himself?

---

[2]The high commissioner at Rabat and the resident general at Tunis continued to take their orders directly from the Ministry of Foreign Affairs, the governor-general of Algeria was still under the Ministry of the Interior, the governor-general of West Africa, under the Colonial Ministry. Later on Weygand, without change of status, was made governor-general of Algeria, succeeding Admiral Abrial, with whom he continually disagreed. M. Chatel, secretary-general of the "General Delegation," then became vice-governor of Algeria, and his former function passed to Admiral Fénard. After Weygand's departure Fénard was entrusted with what remained of the co-ordinator's office, but "co-ordination" vanished.

[3]For more on that subject see page 562.

In June he suffered a nasty rebuff. As Minister of the Navy, he was put under Weygand, then Minister of National Defense. Needless to say, the subordination was purely formal. If, in earlier days, Darlan had stood out against Gamelin, chief of national defense, surely he was not going to dance attendance now on a generalissimo who had been thoroughly drubbed in battle. It was an intolerable scandal, all the same. And it went on, in September, when Huntziger succeeded Weygand. But the Navy had taken charge of the overseas possessions, on the pretext of nailing them fast to the allegiance of Vichy. An admiral, Decoux, governed Indo-China; another, Esteva, Tunisia; still another, Abrial, Algeria. And this was only the beginning of the admirals' regime. Revenge drew near.

Darlan bedecked himself with Laval's spoils. In his place he became—and remained till the day of his death—heir presumptive to the marshal. In the government of the state everything was under his control, including the Minister of National Defense, Huntziger, an able man but of weak character.[4] The tribe of Darlan's sailor friends began to pounce upon the highest civil jobs—the Paris prefecture of police, provincial police superintendencies, departmental prefectures, etc. Even the very head of the "public authority commissioners"—whose duty it was to uncover abuses and make the bureaucrats toe the mark[5]—turned up to be an old walrus, Admiral Gouton. Everyone repeated the witticism of Cardinal Suhard, Archbishop of Paris: "When I die, an admiral will doubtless be the next man to carry the crosier and wear the miter." The Hitler-Darlan conversation of December 24 was to have its sequel on May 12 at Berchtesgaden. It is significant enough that the Führer, on this occasion, conceded to the vice-president of the Council the release of the five or six admirals and of the eleven thousand sailors who were prisoners in Germany. They were set free in two batches. Hitler and

[4] For instance, Huntziger had been the leading military negotiator of our rapprochement with Turkey. On that account he supported the policy of Syrian emancipation. But toward the end of 1938, Georges Bonnet, egged on by Henry Haye and other members of Parliament who did not wish to grant independence to the Nationalist Government at Damascus, raised objections to the treaty which had been drawn up with the latter. He asked Huntziger to change his position. Huntziger at once obeyed. As president of the French Delegation to the Armistice Commission at Wiesbaden, Huntziger evinced great readiness to comply with all German demands. The civilian members of the delegation continuously outvoted him. He was a rabid follower of the *Action Française*.

[5] "To oversee the application of the orders of the central authority, in the spirit of the National Revolution" (Law of August 11, 1941). This new office had a tale to tell: of all French governments, that of Vichy was the worst served and the most frequently betrayed. The seven provincial prefects also watched over the discipline of the state officials.

his advisers had sized up Darlan: a capable seaman, a conceited braggart when he landed on politics, he had the makings of a useful ally. After Mers-el-Kebir all his warships were left under his command. Now the Germans gave him permission to repair completely the *Dunkerque* and the *Richelieu* and to finish building the *Jean Bart*.

In public no one hurled louder insults at England and longed more ardently for a German victory.[6] Still less did he attempt to mince his words in private. On June 4 he told Admiral Leahy, in substance, with the marshal nodding his approval that for seventy years British statesmen had worked tirelessly to arouse France against Germany and to prevent the two countries from reaching an understanding. England's security required that generations of Frenchmen should see in Germany their hereditary enemy. Today France was paying the price for this machiavellianism. She had every right to reverse her policy and to collaborate with the victor. And who could alter the fact that, in any event, eighty million Germans would still confront forty million French?

How can that wild statement be accounted for? The foundations of the New Order were already laid, and Darlan thought them unshakable. There were even those who hinted that he was in the running for one of the most exalted dignities under the new empire, not merely master of Vichy but (who knows?) Admiral of Europe. To be provided with a balanced economy, the continental federation needed Africa, and he was in a position to deliver the goods. He held the ace of trumps. What a royal gift for Hitler! And what a reward for Darlan! He would defy what was left of British sea power. Warships would convoy French merchantmen and prevent their complying with the right of search.[7]

From March on, Darlan's language was so clear cut that no one could profess to ignore what he intended to do with his country. He would jump at the first opportunity to throw the French fleet into the melee. But confronting Darlan there was Weygand.

[6]March 9: statement to American correspondents, with Pétain present: "The British blockade borders on imbecility . . . The Germans have proved themselves more generous and more humane than the English" (regarding food supplies). May 30: "If—what is impossible—there were a British victory, Paris would be reduced to a cemetery. England dragged France into the war. She has always divided in order to rule." In this speech Darlan put himself under Pétain's authority three times. This must be taken only as a sample of many other discourses. To an old friend of his, an admiral, who said that England was sure to win, he rejoined: "You speak like a Gaullist!"

[7]Only on the condition that the right of search would be resisted did the German authorities allow French merchant ships to sail. In fact, the English stopped exercising the right of search against the French Merchant Marine, except when it was known that raw materials were included in cargoes. Even in that case they were rather lenient.

The myth of Weygand, heir to Foch's genius, is as slow to die as the legend of the Hero of Verdun. It stood up under the terrible outcome of the Battle of France. With the coming of autumn, more and more Frenchmen recognized what a mistake it had been not to carry the war over to Africa, and it pleased their fancy to believe that the task entrusted by the marshal to the former commander in chief was secretly to start afresh the plan which had not materialized in June. Of course in official speeches the plan was repudiated and described as a mad venture. But, after all, were not those at the helm bound to throw sand in the eyes of the Nazis? And how could anyone dream that Foch's heir could yield the French Empire to the Germans and Italians, that he would not strive with all his strength to save it? Even in America, Weygand's African mission seemed like a bright patch of blue in a lowering sky: so why wonder at French illusions? How many young men, seeing in Weygand a de Gaulle more powerful than the real one, got away to Africa by all sorts of subterfuges to enlist under his colors! They thought they would reach the world of freedom. All that they did was to get nearer to a concentration camp. And it was not long before they knew the truth. As early as January, Flandin, Minister of Foreign Affairs, suspecting that his portfolio was going to be given to Darlan and wishing to win support from the Germans, permitted them to replace Italians in the disarmament commission provided for Morocco, under the terms of the armistice with Rome.[8] Our military system in Africa had been reinforced till October. In January it began to dilapidate. Noguès protested against Flandin's twisted interpretation of the contract. Weygand gave him no heed. Whatever energy remained in him had been spent a few weeks before, when he remonstrated with Pétain about an order bearing Darlan's signature, which provided for the free passage of Nazi troops across Tunisia and for the installation of a German garrison in Dakar.[9]

As Lord Lloyd was wont to say, Weygand had turned into a stunted little old man. The smart cavalry lieutenant had utterly disappeared. He looked like a retired jockey. He was a bitter and lonely man, distracted with contradictory thoughts and feelings.

He went on blaming the British for the issue of his somber campaign.

[8]Moreover, the Germans sent to Algiers a "Commission de Liaison" which kept watch on the Italians at work in the local commission of disarmament.

[9]Was it the outcome of the Laval-Abetz negotiation in the autumn of 1940? My sources, a general who read the order and an admiral, don't agree. The admiral hesitatingly gives another date: May 1941. Weygand called Laval a dirty coal retailer. To Scapini, who boasted to him of the New Order, he retorted, "Well, I would prefer an English victory!"

As we have seen, he had drawn upon himself the wrath of the Germans, and it may be guessed that actual contact with the French Empire made him aware of the deadly responsibilities he had lightly assumed in preceding months and years, that his guilty conscience then began to speak. All too well he knew that the superintendence of North Africa was given him only as a consolation prize, to make up for his loss of ministerial power, and that Berlin was keeping an eye on him. But he hated everything vaguely resembling the Popular Front just as much as he hated the Germans. Nor had he any delusions concerning the marshal's rancor toward him. If Pétain had forgotten the remote past, would he not have made Weygand the kingpin in his dictatorship? Could he have preferred first Laval and then Darlan? Would it not have been in order for Weygand to be given, in relation with the Head of the State, the same status he had held with the commander in chief in 1929–31, with the Minister of War in 1934, with the Minister of State in May–June 1940? Someone once said that vengeance is a dish to be eaten cold.

Had Weygand to choose between a British victory, bringing in its train a resurrection of the French Republic, and the Nazis' New Order, which way would he jump? I have known him well, and I believe his answer would resemble Pétain's.

Detestation of democracy—which would certainly call him to account; the wounded vanity of a strategist more than once belied in his plans and calculations by the event—that, I fear, is what lay at the bottom of his heart. Was England, through the success of her arms, and de Gaulle too, through the fulfillment of his prophecies, to get the better of him once again? Of the leader of the Free French he was heard to say: "A traitor. A bullet or two through the brain is what he deserves!" He still bore the scars of the pointed shafts aimed at him by the great critic of the General Staff. No wonder that he unleashed the Vichy police on the trail of Mme. de Larminat, wife of a general in the service of the Cross of Lorraine. He forwarded to Vichy a personal letter from a colonel he knew well, denouncing the policy of the Armistice, and the colonel was made to suffer for it. With Weygand a large admixture of mean sentiment is characteristic.

He was sent to Algiers around mid-September—a few weeks after the Cameroon and Equatorial Africa split off from Vichy and a few days before General de Gaulle's abortive attack on Dakar—for the purpose of heading off the disaffection of the military, of the colonists (who, for weeks, before they reverted to fascism, were fearful of losing their property), of the officials faithful to the Republic, of the natives upset over the disappearance of oil, sugar, tea, and cotton goods. The most pressing business was to nip the movement in the bud. Making the round of the garrisons, he did not hesitate to say in harangues delivered to his officers within four walls, "Yesterday's ally will perhaps be to-morrow's." "The last battles, as Marshal Foch used to say, are won with the remnants of armies. . . ." Whoever has an end in view cannot afford to haggle about the means to attain it. Weygand trimmed his words to fit the wishes, needs, and interests of each group he felt it necessary to soothe or conciliate for the moment.

Weygand undertook to buy food supplies from the United States. He had now something to show in the way of hostility to the Germans. In November and December 1940, as already indicated, Laval's policy had suffered by his interference. He informed Pétain and Darlan, when they resumed collaboration in the grand style of the fallen Minister, in May–June 1941, that North Africa should not be open any wider to German emissaries. The unity of French Africa, he explained, would not stand under the test. Seemingly it is because of Weygand that the African Empire was kept out of the fighting begun in Syria against the British. American agents, on their arrival in Algiers (especially Mr. Robert Murphy, counselor to the Vichy Embassy, in December, and a naval officer before him), swallowed deep draughts of the proconsul's talk. In all direct dealings Weygand was careful not to ruffle them, since America was necessary to the tranquillity of his rule. He even went so far as to draw up a list of the airplanes and tanks that might be delivered to him. "Once they have arrived, I'll shift over to the United States and England!" Weygand's requirements were enormous; on the face of it, Washington could not deflect so much matériel from the Battle of Britain. But Weygand's suggestion produced the desired effect.[10]

The formula which Weygand was to reiterate publicly for months on end—namely that he meant to defend North Africa against any invader, whoever he might be—was considered the height of adroitness by all who, having heard what he said in private, thought they had actually understood the riddle thrown out to the multitude. Weygand, they believed, was too clever, too patriotic not to discriminate between the British, bent on liberation, and the Germans bent on enslavement, or to forget that he owed to the British fleet alone what little freedom he had. Certainly he must use ambiguous language before the crowd: the enemy

---

[10]In July–August 1940 Darlan had already hit upon this method of attracting American sympathy. He then told American diplomats, "Give me thousands of tanks and planes; I'll fight all the way to the Cape of Good Hope!" A magnificent piece of bluff.

was everywhere on the watch. But those in the general's confidence need not be disturbed by such trifles.

Washington's envoy must have congratulated himself on being firmly established in Weygand's confidence when police reports describing the comings and goings of German officers were communicated to him. He was a man of Irish descent, a Catholic, an old friend of Henry Haye. Occasionally he went so far as to make innocent gibes at the English. This furnished a cozy little common ground which, in addition to the general's verbal stratagems, gave warmth to their conversations. All the same, Weygand judged the United States to be as much a materialistic country as Great Britain. He used this expression to an official who paid him a call in January 1941.

From time to time Weygand sounded a note which ought to have undeceived everyone. On June 23, 1941, he exclaimed at Casablanca, addressing a gathering of legionnaires: "Believe me, our duty cannot possibly lie on the side of our former ally." But those who were determined to keep on trusting him through thick and thin refused to understand: "Don't you see," they argued, "that the battle in Syria drags on? The general is morally obliged to throw a stone at England occasionally. Let's not condemn him out of hand for words imposed by circumstances." They were still prating on that theme on August 31, when Weygand endorsed the great fascist speech Pétain had delivered on the twelfth.

Let us assume that Weygand dreamed of a draw, whereby France, her Empire, and, above all, her National Revolution would survive as between an England and a Germany equally exhausted and negotiating a peace. Let us assume that it seemed wise to him to avoid a clash with Germany, so that the territories entrusted to his care might arrive at this historic juncture without having undergone too great a disturbance. That would be the most charitable interpretation we could put on his behavior. Anyhow, whatever it may have been, the dream of Weygand led nowhere because it never impelled him to independent action. He himself settled the debate by the words: "I am too old to become a rebel." About November 1940 he had said that he would not carry out Laval's orders (and indeed it is worth repeating that his objections proved a real hindrance to Laval's bargaining with Berlin). In 1941 he did not evince any greater pliability to Darlan's behests. But what did it matter in the long run, since he never failed to say that an order from Pétain would be law for him?[11] Everyone knew or ought to have known that

[11] Notably in the presence of Admiral Leahy, in March 1941.

the marshal would bow to Hitler's ultimatum rather than sacrifice the political edifice erected at Vichy, rather than allow the German occupation of the entire home territory, rather than withdraw to Africa. No more than the marshal, therefore, would Weygand, of his own free will, ever rally to the cause of the United Nations while still in peril. Nothing less than their overwhelming victory was required to force his hand.[12]

But this must always be remembered: whenever the French grew indignant at Darlan's behavior, they comforted themselves with the thought that, sooner or later, Weygand would put things right. Weygand was their hope. For a long while Washington and even London saw in him a future candidate for the leadership of the Fighting French. Entwined with the enigma of Pétain, and still further complicating it, making the confusion of the French nation and its friends worse confounded, there lay the enigma of Weygand.

The apparent contrast between Darlan and Weygand is not an isolated fact in the Vichy hierarchy. From top to bottom we find, at every level, individuals differing among themselves both in their opinions and their inclinations. By their very coexistence, however, they made it easy for the marshal to mislead the French, the British, and the Americans, and even at times the Germans, as to his real intentions.

The ministers and high officials whom he used to rule the country fall into three categories. Those who had acted in the past as German agents and had staked their very lives upon the subjection of France. Misguided experts and industrialists, honest enough, but turned totalitarian because of their social conservatism. And, last, men who had proved that they were not lacking in patriotism, but who enlisted in the counterrevolution either through ambition long thwarted, or infirmity of character, or cowardice.

Heading the list of those of the first type is the name of Fernand de Brinon. Installed in Paris with the title of French Ambassador, he handled the political relations between Vichy and Berlin with Abetz, himself Ambassador of the Reich. Brinon had wormed his way back to the

---

[12]As to the real attitude of Weygand, the most impressive piece of evidence we know comes from a personality who, formerly, had filled a prominent position in the French diplomatic service and who went to Algiers, in the spring of 1941, for the definite purpose of exacting from the general a promise that he would eventually help an Anglo-American landing in North Africa. For years he had been on friendly terms with Weygand and commanded the latter's confidence. Weygand's answer thoroughly disappointed him.

The key to the riddle of Weygand is perhaps to be found in this warning of the Egyptian doctor who looked after him in Syria, a warning given to a British general in July 1940: "Don't be mistaken about it. In spite of his relatively youthful appearance, Weygand is, in a sense, a very old man: all his will power is gone."

former capital at first unofficially, then as a delegate of the vice-president of the Council—that is, Laval, to whom he had sold his soul in 1935. The general delegate of the French Government in Occupied Territory, General de Fornel de la Laurencie, ranked above him. But, having thrown out the master, Pétain retained the servant. He recalled Fornel, replaced him by a second-rate general, and allowed Brinon to take the first place by giving him the highest diplomatic rank.[13]

The boast of Vichy is to have restored "moral order." Brinon supplies a very good test to weigh the sincerity of Vichy's claims. Knowing the tricks and manipulations of Laval thoroughly, freely accusing him of being a traitor and a thief, reproaching him with having used even the negotiations with Germany as a means of financial profit, how in the world could Pétain have ignored or pretended to ignore all the facts of which his intimate household had been aware for years regarding the "French Ambassador" in Paris? This creature played fast and loose with the "moral order." Here is a petty detail, but one which reveals a good deal. On the official list of Vichy officials figured his mistress, who had been a stenographer for one of the newspapers to which he contributed, with this charming description: "Chief of Private Secretariat." Her influence in Paris under the Nazis proved how openly they both flaunted their relationship. Why should Brinon have cared? It was he who, in the interest of Vichy, kept watch over the Doriot, Déat, Luchaire, Deloncle gang. And his heaven-sent friendship with Abetz must be borne in mind too. Brinon had weapons ready for use. He had helped Pétain and Darlan over a difficult transition after Laval's departure. The marshal was under an obligation to him.

Jacques Benoist-Méchin, a liberated prisoner of war who became Secretary of State to the presidency of the Council in June 1941, attended to Franco-German problems at Vichy. He was in direct competition with the "Ambassador," and the two loathed each other. They were the twin children of Hitler and the counterrevolution, even though Brinon considered it a loss of dignity to have been given such a mate. Both careers are strikingly symmetrical. The title of Baron of the Second Empire, which Benoist-Méchin scorned to use, corresponded to the more dubious count's coronet sported by Brinon. Both were timeserving scribblers and

---

[13]The most devastating affront to which Brinon was ever subjected came from General de Fornel. The general decided to hand over his functions with full solemnity. One after the other he introduced his staff, drawn up in line, to Brinon. However, when Brinon started to shake Fornel's hand, that officer hastily drew back and exclaimed, "Oh no! I will not shake the hand of a traitor!" At Vichy, on December 13, the decision had been reached to place Brinon under arrest.

gave themselves the airs of men about town. To eke out their existence during those always arid days before they received their monthly stipends, Brinon frequented the race course while his counterpart dealt in antiques.

At first employed on odd jobs by Bonapartist organizations, then peddling his German translations to anyone who would pay him a pittance, Benoist-Méchin finally became secretary to the correspondent of the *Frankfort Gazette,* Friedrich Sieburg, who, notwithstanding his show of liberalism, was a Nazi spy burrowing about in Parisian society.[14] From those beginnings, very similar to Brinon's, his rise proceeded. On Abetz's suggestion and with the help of the German General Staff, he wrote a history of the Reichswehr, intended to intimidate the French people, and for their consumption he rewrote *Mein Kampf.* In the summer of 1940 these advance scouts of the German conquest resumed their work which had been interrupted the year before, and were pushed into high administrative posts by their patrons from across the Rhine.

On the roster of truly infamous Vichy personnel these names appear also: Marion, Secretary of Information; Pucheu, Secretary of State for Industrial Production and Minister of the Interior after July 1941; Scapini, delegate to the Wiesbaden Armistice Commission in charge of prisoners of war, but spending most of his time in Berlin; Belin, Minister of Labor. The latter was one of those Marxists who have no use whatever for either civil, political, or national liberty in their program, one of those union manipulators inclined to think that dictatorship more than any other system of government can satisfy working-class demands. None of these men possessed any qualities to recommend them to the marshal's favor. Marion was just a piece of communist wreckage.

Pucheu had been the paymaster of Doriot's followers and of the Cagoulards on behalf of the Worms Bank. He had the reputation of a brutal man who did not stop at bloodshed. Scapini, blinded in the last war, was thoroughly dissipated.

Barnaud and Lehideux, the latter a son-in-law of Louis Renault, the big manufacturer and the paragon of fascism, were more respectable characters on the surface, but they also stamped the regime with Hitler's trademark. Barnaud, with his mystical tendencies, recalls Baudouin. Here too we find treasury officials and prominent members of the "Metallurgists" and "Coal Owners" associations, the mainsprings of collaboration.

[14]During an interval Benoist-Méchin had been employed and discharged by William Randolph Hearst's International News Service.

Disgusted with all this scum and factional intrigue, one may turn to Lucien Romier and Henry Moysset with a sense of relief. They were as unlike Abetz's clique as possible. In ministerial discussions the marshal looked to them for wisdom. Once Laval had been thrown out and his dangerous imitation of National Socialism discarded, the former was put in charge of the "National Council's" consultative commission, which sought in vain to draw up the promised constitution, while the latter headed the Committee on Trade Unions Organization, which gave birth to the Labor Charter.

Lucien Romier, editor in chief of the *Figaro,* a graduate of the Ecole des Chartes, a former student at the French School in Rome, addicted to the study of the sixteenth century in France and in Italy, had taken a national line in his newspaper articles. It is true that he had done it with so much caution, with so much care not to commit himself, that his picture of events was like some high-altitude aerial photograph. But even though he was unwilling to examine things too closely, lest he unwittingly take sides on controversial or polemical questions; even though his seeming high-mindedness was in fact no more than abject fear, still his intentions remained honest. What on earth induced him to get into such company? In 1926, Herriot, under whom he had studied, offered him the Treasury in an ill-fated attempt to form a cabinet. Was Romier so disappointed that he felt impelled to revenge himself fifteen years later? As for Henry Moysset, his story is even more astonishing. I have known him for thirty years or more. He had ceaselessly investigated Pan-Germanism and inveighed against it. In 1938 he paid me a compliment which I appreciated. In the process of writing a history of French foreign policy he had taken the trouble to reread my articles in the *Echo de Paris* since 1918. He told me that they supplied him with a guiding thread through the intricate maze of events and that he agreed with their main purport. On April 8, 1939, at a luncheon given in honor of Wickham Steed, he exclaimed to a senator friend of Laval who was seated opposite him: "When will that trial for treason come up?" Moysset, a historian who never completed the books he began,[15] had never been able to choose once for all between the study of the past and a political career.

An indefatigable talker, in 1917–18 he won the friendship of Georges Leygues, then Minister of the Navy, who, spurred on by his new friend,

---

[15]Unless I am mistaken, he published only one book: *L'Esprit public en Allemagne vingt ans après Bismarck* (about 1910). He had in hand: an economic history of the French nation, a history of the Revolution of 1848, some study I only vaguely remember on an Italian diplomat of the sixteenth century, and the history of French foreign policy since Versailles. He will probably never hatch out these eggs.

cast envious eyes on the Ministry of Foreign Affairs and the premiership, two offices he held in 1919–20. The experiment was a pitiable failure, and Moysset had to start afresh. This time he followed in the footsteps of André Tardieu, a better track. It did not lead him very far. However, while he was at the Ministry of the Navy, he had taken up with Darlan, a practiced navigator in government offices. He rendered him the same services as to Georges Leygues: he tried to teach him the rudiments of diplomacy. But that he, the Republican patriot, should have escorted Darlan into counterrevolution, under the protection of the Nazis, passes all belief! Why did he not quietly retreat to a book-lined study in his native Aveyron, where his lack of purpose would not have done any harm?

And so, side by side with Darlan, infatuated with "collaboration," there was Weygand, who wavered and talked in conundrums. Side by side with Brinon, Benoist-Méchin, and other servants of Abetz there were, with their round clerical faces, Romier and Moysset, whom no one had previously accused of tenderness toward Germany, whom no scandal had ever touched. The catalogue of "decent people" might be extended. There was Charles Rochat, for instance, political director of the Quai d'Orsay under the Republic, who deserves to be mentioned among them. But we need do no more than notice a few typical examples. Looking upon this ill-assorted flock, how could Frenchmen, devoted to the commonweal and aware of the country's peril, fail to be puzzled? The enigma of Pétain derived strength from the presence of so many ministers and officials so dissimilar in their origins, political creeds, and moral value. It was not easy to trace the internal transformation of the best of them. It could be done only after having weighed and judged them for a period of years. But what did it matter, after all? The "best" ones were only minor characters in the drama. Even if they may have succeeded, from time to time, in attenuating the policy of the regime, that policy still remained a crime against the country's independence.

Here are the installments in terms of military collaboration paid to Hitler, or rather to the Axis, since Japan also benefited by them.

First we have the supplies allegedly provided to Rommel's army in Libya during the early weeks of 1941. To the best of my knowledge it has never been possible to verify British suspicions and suppositions on that point. The Admiralty, amazed that so many tanks and trucks could have escaped the vigilance of its fleet, has always thought that German and Italian transports crept along the Tunisian coast and even that there were among them vessels flying the French flag. The Admiralty has also wondered whether, in order to shorten the sea passage, war matériel was not carried over the highways of the protectorate. The champions of Vichy have denied the accusation and have described it as groundless.[16] They have likewise pointed out—and here is the important point—that the relations between Vichy and Germany were governed not only by the terms of the Armistice, but also when these terms were irrelevant, by the rules of neutrality as prescribed by international law. Pétain, Darlan, and their followers thus felt able to claim that no one should consider himself injured if German vessels passed through territorial waters under French jurisdiction, or even if they put in at French ports, for not more than twenty-four hours. This was the principle which they were careful to establish.

No occupied country is morally entitled to claim neutral status since the belligerent whose boot is on its neck will make it work one-sidedly.[17] But even supposing that the Vichy crowd were forced by Berlin to invoke international law and to apply it (to the extent that it furthered Nazi interests) their spiteful revolt against the British blockade, a blockade which was in accord with international law as only recently France herself interpreted it, made it clear that they were, at heart, in the totalitarian camp.

Far more serious than this episode, half buried in obscurity, was the transformation of the African Army into a body of troops upon which the rulers at Vichy could rely for the prosecution of their collaborationist policy. Weygand never attempted to use the measure of independence which geography and the English Navy allotted him in order to prevent Pétain, Darlan, etc., from sending to Algiers, Morocco, and Tunisia, in ever-growing numbers, officers of all ranks imbued with the principles of the National Revolution and determined to fight British and Americans rather than the Nazis. Weygand, in his detestation of the Gaullist movement, in his rancor toward England, remained passive or perhaps did not even refrain from giving encouragement, while officers whom Vichy suspected of lukewarmness or enmity were sent home and replaced by "reliable" men, sometimes chosen from the retired list. Many were

---

[16]The order from Darlan to Weygand, of which I have heard recently (see page 511), may perhaps be quoted as evidence against Vichy.

[17]On February 21, 1942, a German submarine made port at Martinique, unloading a sick sailor and going back to sea before the twenty-four-hour period was over. Vichy asserted its neutrality when war broke out between America and Germany. Strictly speaking, Vichy was within its rights when it gave refuge to the submarine. Yet Washington, which had congratulated itself on the "declaration of neutrality," declined to accept the consequences.

placed in custody. Gradually the African Army was brought into step with the aged marshal. Thus came into being the force which opened fire on American soldiers in November 1942 and was within an ace of causing a catastrophe.

Meanwhile, by March 1941, following upon Flandin's decision concerning the disarmament commission,[18] sixty-five Germans (thirty-five of them officers) had already taken up residence in Morocco, and in April one hundred thirty more came to swell the first contingent. Very soon Weygand had barely at his disposal 100,000 soldiers plus 20,000 auxiliaries instead of the 170,000 men he had found with the colors on his arrival. There was in Algeria and Morocco enough matériel to equip some eighteen divisions in the old style. What part of it the Commission of Disarmament allowed the French Army to retain must have varied with the vicissitudes of collaboration. But the matériel confiscated by Germans and Italians was not destroyed. It was merely kept in special depots. The French Army could snatch it in an emergency. Obviously the Germans felt that the servants of "National Revolution" could be safely trusted. On the day of the landing that calculation nearly came true.

Here is the most serious case of all—Syria.

At the end of April, Yugoslavia and then Greece fell before the German onslaught. The surrender of the Yugoslav Army took place on April 18 and of the Greek Army on the twenty-third. Crete was to be overwhelmed on June 2. Ever since March the Germans and Italians had been driving the British troops back toward the Egyptian frontier. Rachid Ali had started a rebellion in Iraq. Vichy was convinced that within a few weeks the British would have lost Palestine and Egypt, would be attacked in Iraq, and would have no alternative but to withdraw to India. "What is going to happen? I'll tell you," Pétain told Admiral Leahy on May 14. "There will soon be no British Empire in the Mediterranean." The minute England was at bay and wounded the marshal and Darlan became emboldened. "The sooner the war ends the better," said Darlan on June 1. At last the decision was drawing near. It had been expected daily all through August and September 1940, when the Germans were credited with the ability to take the Channel in their stride. The Montoire conversations were thus to have a sequel. But Hitler was at Berchtesgaden. It was a long journey for an old man. The Admiral of the Fleet made the trip.

The meeting with the Führer was granted only under conditions laid

[18]See page 511 and note 8.

522   *The Gravediggers of France*

down by Rudolf Hess in Paris early in May.[19] Syria, at that time, loomed very large in the strategic picture, and Germany wished to use it as an air base. Moreover, she required that the arms left behind by the three divisions of the former Army of the Levant which had long since gone home, should be turned over to her. The armistice merely gave Germany and Italy control over the airfields. As between their control and their use there was a vast difference. No less a difference existed between the confiscation of arms[20] and their delivery to yesterday's enemy, to be used against yesterday's ally. Darlan cheerfully passed over the legal points behind a curtain of lies.

The staff of the Ministry of Foreign Affairs were not informed of the arrangement. Guérard, a treasury official and former tool of the Worms Bank as well as head of Baudouin's secretariat, reached Beirut by plane, together with certain German officers, in order to convey to General Dentz, the High Commissioner, the orders of the vice-president of the Council. What followed revealed clearly enough the zeal of this military leader who signed the capitulation of Paris. A single instance will suffice. On May 12 he sent to the Iraq frontier a company of Tunisian sharpshooters. He seemed to be protecting Syrian territory against possible raids by Rachid Ali. This scrupulous concern for neutrality might indeed be regarded as laudable. But under cover of supplying this small unit, on May 12, 25, and 28 he sent three trainloads of matériel, amounting in all to some seven hundred tons, which included two batteries of 75s, one battery of 105s, trucks, aviation gasoline, etc. The Turkish railroad commissioner, who was in residence at Aleppo, did not see through the trick and gave the requisite permit. It had been arranged that engines would be sent from Mosul to move this French equipment. They were late. They failed to appear at Tell Kotchak on May 13, the appointed day. Dentz, however, did not want his connivance to be fruitless. He ordered some officers of the Engineers (despite their protests) to take the supply trains into Iraq. He thus forced French soldiers to become active combatants against British. Not for an instant did he hesitate, for time was pressing and Rachid Ali was almost encircled. In the end his little arsenal fell into British hands. Dentz had the impudence to demand that it be returned to him.

Never was the agreement between Vichy and Berlin, the voluntary

---

[19]Approximately one week before his landing in Scotland.

[20]In theory France still retained the ownership of those armaments and could not lose it unless she violated the armistice. In order to overcome this difficulty, Vichy agreed to sell them.

participation of Vichy in a strangling alliance with Germany, so close to fulfillment as in the month of May 1941. The Nazi demands not only covered Syria, but for the third time, at least, the air and sea bases of Africa as well as the fleet, under pretext of using it for patrol and convoy purposes. While Darlan was at Berchtesgaden (May 12), Pétain lingered on the Riviera to avoid answering Leahy's questions, to escape explaining what was beyond explanation—the breaking of his pledged word. Then, on the fifteenth, Pétain addressed the French people in the peremptory language of a commanding officer. "It is none of your business to judge what I do. You have only to obey me."[21] In October–November 1940 the victory of Britain's air force had freed France from the consequences of the Montoire interview. Hitler's sudden decision to destroy the Red Army and to abandon his prey in Syria and Iraq spared us the dishonor of the agreement made by Darlan with the Führer.

Absorbed in eastern Europe, where he was to launch his attack on June 22, Hitler lost interest in Syria. His machinations in Iraq had failed. He let things take care of themselves. Withdrawing his air force, he left the task of driving back the Free French and the British to the Vichy troops. The Nazis, as astounded by Dentz's behavior as they had formerly been by Gensoul's resistance at Mers-el-Kebir, congratulated themselves on having tried the Pétain experiment. The marshal gave them a kind of right wing to cover their armies invading Russia—Russia which, with its Red Army, was going to save not only Syria but North Africa from the Germans. Frenchmen were killing each other. It was almost too good to be true.

The Axis did not gain possession of Syria, but Indo-China fell into its lap in July 1941. Obviously there was no chance of defending that colony. Vichy tried to put the blame on Washington because in the autumn of 1940 the United States refused to sell war matériel to the military envoy of the Hanoï governor-general. But how could the Washington Government have deflected to Indo-China planes badly needed by the British or have upset priorities long since established? Was the advice forwarded to Vichy that, in the circumstances, it had better seek for a compromise? However, Vichy's error was in thinking that this colony should be amicably handed over to the Japanese, that any sign of resistance and even of protest would only make its fate worse.[22] During the

---

[21]Pétain did not convince Admiral Le Duc, who had charge of the Ministry of the Navy on Darlan's behalf. Le Duc asked to pass into the naval reserve.

[22]It should be admitted that at the time of the Japanese ultimatum of June 16, 1940 (establishment of Japan's control over the Yünnan railroad), and of the sudden invasion

summer of 1940, Baudouin had expressed some absurd views on the subject of the Far East. It was he who signed the September treaty which placed the Tonkin airfields at the disposal of the invaders and permitted them to maintain there a garrison of six thousand men—with every facility for freedom of passage and the dispatch of reliefs, which in fact nullified the limitations on their numbers. The interests of the Bank of Indo-China must, by then, have been made secure. Baudouin thought that French sovereignty was something that could be put in cold storage and brought out again someday, fresh and undamaged. In January 1941, Darlan, with as little wisdom, accepted the arbitration of Tokyo between Indo-China and Siam. The result was the seizure of the western provinces of Laos and Camboge. The deathblow was struck on July 29, 1941. The military privileges which had been extended to Japan in Tonkin were extended to the whole of the Indo-Chinese Union, and all restrictions were lifted.[23] In effect, this French colony had been incorporated in the Japanese Empire, including 200,000 tons of merchant shipping, which the Japanese seized in February 1942. Admiral Decoux, who put his name to this disgraceful transaction, was one of Darlan's followers, honest but fainthearted. Some years previously Admiral Godefroy, then in command of a cruiser squadron, had submitted a report on three 10,000-ton cruisers recently commissioned under his flag. This report was far from pleasing the builders and designers of vessels of that type, including Darlan. They called upon Decoux, who was in command of a similar squadron, to give his opinion. He obediently wrote the exact opposite of what had been said by his colleague.

This deliberate abdication, this complicity in the attack against Singapore, which took the shape of a formal treaty with Japan for the joint defense of the colony, cries shame upon us, in Asia. At any cost we should have steered clear of such a pact, if only to avoid providing the Germans with a precedent by which they at once sought to profit in North Africa.[24]

Relying as they did upon a German triumph in the west, where we still held our positions in Morocco, Algeria, and Tunisia, Pétain and his ministers were still more logically bound to bank upon an Axis triumph

---

of northern Tonkin in September 1940, by Japanese troops from Kouang-si, the local authorities were neither firm nor wise. They opened the breach.

[23]Through its diplomatic representatives Vichy fostered belief in a numerical limit of eighty thousand men. But, according to those who have read it, the July 29 agreement speaks of "unlimited" effectives.

[24]And this takes no account of the declaration of neutrality made to China in the summer of 1940, utterly at odds with the treaty of July 1941 (joint defense of Indo-China).

in the Far East, where we had nothing to fight with. What they did not understand was that a moral token of resistance might in the future strengthen our cause. But they thought only of the New Order.

In this rough outline of the positive help given to the Axis empires, the next chapter takes us back to Africa. Weygand was recalled from his Algiers headquarters on November 17. Two days later he was relieved of his African command. This sacrifice was offered to the Germans, as Vichy explained, with the idea that in return they would postpone their other demands—namely, the handing over of naval and air bases. The truth is perhaps much more unkind to the regime.

Some people have interpreted the incident in such fashion as to justify the hopes placed in the ex-generalissimo. The Germans expected no good of him, they explained, since his dismissal seemed to them comparable in importance to all the rest of their program, which they accordingly agreed to postpone. Today we know what actually happened. Weygand may indeed have showed by his attitude that he would not be easily persuaded to draw upon his meager reserves of transport to furnish the trucks demanded by Rommel, who was preparing to withstand the assault of Auchinleck's columns in Libya. Doubtless, also, as in the days of the Syrian war, he urged the danger of possible defection among the officers and civil servants under his orders. It may even be granted that after having put up with him for more than a year the Nazis could not have believed that a generalissimo in the Foch tradition would remain permanently servile. They may well have feared a change of temper on his part, and may therefore have wished to get him out of the way along with other generals and high officials reputed to have character and ability.[25] But, however true this may be, Weygand himself told his friends that the Germans had issued no ultimatum and that it was Darlan who, anxious that no one should keep an eye on the machinations he had started at Berchtesgaden, called for his dismissal.[26] To set him thinking of retirement, Weygand had been shown during the

[25]Emmanuel Monicq, secretary-general of the High Commissariat at Rabat, former financial attaché at London and Washington, and General de Lattre de Tassigny, military commander at Tunis, were sent back home long before Weygand. General Beynet, in command at Algiers, was appointed to the Armistice Commission in Wiesbaden. He was replaced by General Koeltz, Georges's former adjutant general. Moreover, Noguès' powers, in his capacity as commandant of Moroccan troops, were turned over to General Alphonse Juin, released from the fortress of Königstein. Noguès, as a military commander, had passed into the reserve on reaching the age limit. In November, Juin inherited from Weygand the commandership in chief of the Army of Africa.

[26]Weygand asserted also that he was given the option to continue as governor-general of Algeria. If that is true, the Germans had nothing to do with his dismissal.

Syrian campaign a letter from Abetz to someone or other, and later a memorandum from General von Stuelpnagel ("the assassin of Paris," Weygand called him), demanding his head from Benoist-Méchin—"that fool or traitor." In order to wear him down and exhaust his patience, Vichy constantly summoned him to conferences, in June, in August, in November, Lucien Romier, on Pétain's and Darlan's instructions, tried to persuade him. General Huntziger, with the same end in view, perhaps sought to find him at fault in his organization of the coastal defenses. Weygand went to Pétain, who held an informal council to receive him. He was determined to have it out and declared: "I have no desire to remain in charge without the approval of the government." He awaited its approval in vain. No voice was raised. It was quite clear that all that was left for him to do was to resign.

So Weygand went back to the Riviera to resume the writing of his memoirs and reconcile them with his recently acquired devotion to the marshal. Those who had seen in him a source of great strength were completely mistaken. His feet were not solidly enough planted on French soil to allow him ever to break with those in command of the army, his real family. But now that he was stripped of his "proconsulate," he freely indulged in verbal fireworks against Vichy. Visiting shops in Cannes, he could be heard to exclaim, on the slightest provocation: "The Germans are lost!"

However weak the barrier which went down with Weygand, wheat, oil, and all sorts of supplies, if not, indeed, weapons, flowed afterward to Rommel's assistance. Vichy did not trouble to conceal its hand. French merchant vessels were chartered to the Germans. Everything was transshipped and loaded on trucks at Tunis—gasoline, flour, etc. And those trucks—some fifteen hundred of them, one third borrowed from North Africa—were never returned. Of course, according to the official theory, all this was strictly in accordance with the armistice. Finally, at the beginning of February 1942, the battleship *Dunkerque* sailed quietly off for Toulon, in defiance of the written promise given by Pétain to Admiral Leahy ten months earlier.[27] One of the excuses alleged was

[27] In March 1941, London learned that the *Dunkerque* was about to leave African waters. The American Ambassador at Vichy, at the request of the British, pressed the marshal for an explanation. Feigned or real, the latter expressed surprise. He knew nothing about the orders given the *Dunkerque*. Nobody ever told him anything! Darlan was summoned. It was merely a matter of petty routine, he alleged, and certainly nothing worth troubling the marshal about. In Admiral Leahy's presence Pétain telephoned to Mers-el-Kebir to countermand all arrangements made, and to give signal proof of his good will he, of his own accord, drew up and signed the afore-mentioned promise. By February 1942, anyone could see the value of the marshal's commitments. In Pétain's name, Darlan maintained that

that the *Dunkerque,* which was badly damaged during the engagement at Mers-el-Kebir, could only be partially repaired in that port. But the reassembling of the French fleet in home waters necessarily worked to Germany's advantage, unless we are to suppose that the Nazis, who, under the Armistice, could forbid any movement of warships which did not suit them, did not mind being cheated, a somewhat extravagant supposition.

Such is the record of military collaboration with the Nazis which can be charged against Pétain and Darlan. The whole story is crystal clear. What is to be found on the other side of the ledger? What acts can be credited to the Head of the State and his henchmen in which may be detected a genuine will to further the cause of independence and liberty as soon as opportunity offered or from which can be inferred the slightest wish for a German defeat regardless of the consequences on the Vichy institutions? The agreements entered into with the United States and the slowing up of collaboration with Hitler after the St. Florentin meeting on December 1, 1941, are often quoted as cases in point. On careful examination, those facts do not yield any evidence which friends of Vichy can find to their liking.

In the understandings reached by the ministers of Pétain with the Washington Government they profess to see something like a turn of the wheel on a course toward the west. If they think this they either deceive themselves or are trying to deceive others.

The principal agreement was concluded at Vichy on March 9, 1941, by means of an exchange of letters between Leahy and Darlan, but was held in abeyance for more than four months while details were ironed out and the Syrian campaign went on. It related to supplying North Africa with food, fuel, and clothing.[28] Its terms were simple enough.

---

there had been a misdeal, that in return for the immobilization of the *Dunkerque,* the Vichy government thought it had obtained assurance both of food from America and of the British abandonment of the right of search. Once undeceived, the aged chieftain no longer considered himself bound. Now whether Pétain, in March and April 1941, knew or was ignorant of the decision arrived at regarding the *Dunkerque,* the fact remains that time after time, according to the direct knowledge of foreign diplomats in Vichy, Darlan did not keep the marshal informed. The moment a question was put to the latter his most frequent reaction was to send for the admiral.

[28]Despite everything said to the contrary, this negotiation was set in motion by the British. Conversations had begun in Madrid at the beginning of November 1940. The High Commissariat of Morocco was anxious to barter its phosphates for Spanish supplies. But Spain had little to spare. England made available to the Spaniards escudo credits in Lisbon to the amount of two thirds of their obligations. Throughout the discussions the English looked to a lifting of the blockade as far as Morocco was concerned, in return for being allowed to organize a system of controls. In January the Americans became involved and,

As against the sale of American supplies in moderate quantities (six vessels, two of them tankers, were assigned for this purpose), the Vichy Government not only renewed its months-old pledge not to exceed its commitments under the armistice in its dealings with the Germans, but also agreed that some twenty American observers should be posted throughout the French African Empire, including Dakar, to make certain that neither the goods shipped through Casablanca nor even analogous products should find their way to the French mainland. From Algiers, where he lived close to Weygand, Mr. Robert Murphy, counselor of the United States Embassy at Vichy, supervised the whole operation. We are at the heart of the question. By means of such an interchange of amenities, did Pétain really sacrifice his counterrevolutionary policy to the higher interest of not cutting himself off from Washington and of anchoring the nation's hopes on America?

Here are the advantages which the United States believed it had secured. By making available the oil, the sugar, tea, and cotton goods needed by the natives, America not only forestalled the disorders which Germany might put forward as an excuse for intervening to maintain order, but also prevented the discrediting of French authority. Thanks to American action it would stand firmer and stronger, better able eventually to concentrate upon resistance against the Nazis. In the second place, American goods, in spite of everything done by Vichy-minded officials to hide their origin, spread the gospel of liberty among the masses of the people. They served as constant reminder that the forces of freedom were on the march. Finally, through the observers whose reports Mr. Murphy collected in his clearing office, the United States gained a most useful insight into the heart of the great French possession. The value of such secret intercourse was to become apparent when the military might of the United Nations overflowed into French Africa. And that was not all. By signing the supply agreement, American diplomacy had, as it were, put a bridle on the Vichy Government. The minute it fell short of fulfilling its promises the six vessels would suspend their sailings and remain at their moorings in the New World. Thus the bit was drawn taut and the unruly horse held in check. Then, when he

---

as a matter of convenience, finally replaced the British. They had previously gone as far as to exchange views with delegates from Rabat at Vichy and Washington—as early as August 1940 traces of a talk which the American Minister at Tangiers had with M. Emmanuel Monicq, secretary-general at Rabat, can be found. However, those preliminaries were rather vague. The text of the final agreement was worked out in Rabat, at M. Monicq's residence, by Mr. Murphy and M. Léon Marchal, Moroccan director of commercial negotiations. on February 27, 1941.

seemed more manageable and gave assurances of good behavior, the reins could be slackened and he could move forward again. In other words, shipments of supplies could be resumed. As the optimistic inter- preters of the United States African policy saw it, Pétain, indeed, was lending a hand in establishing a kind of American protectorate over North Africa—incomplete, tenuous, hidden, disguised, but of real effi- cacy nevertheless. Pétain would think it worth while to reduce his complaisance to German demands if he had reason to fear the cessation of American supplies.

That was the case of the optimists in the United States. But to confirm our skepticism it need only be remembered that at any moment the Germans could have upset the whole system if they thought the ar- rangement likely to do them harm. During the summer of 1942 they still tolerated the presence of Mr. Murphy and his staff. Why were they so long-suffering? Their patience was not without an object. They believed that in this bargain a Vichy wedded to "collaboration" had got the better of Washington. And but for the successful Russian resistance they might have proved right.

Pétain and his crowd availed themselves of the North African agree- ment to indoctrinate the French people. They were thus able to chide the discontented and the impatient: "If America, the friend and ally of England, does not turn her back upon us, surely the action of the Government cannot be so reprehensible!" Further than that, the American observers and their chiefs, who naturally wanted to acquit themselves with honor for the enterprise which they had undertaken, took full credit for anything which seemed to give substance to their hopes. Sometimes—as was only humane—they were apt to forgive Pétain and Weygand what was unforgivable and regularly to allow them the benefit of the doubt. Frequent stoppages of supplies occurred: on Weygand's departure, when the help given Rommel came out into the open, after Laval's return in April 1942. But these stoppages were al- ways followed by resumptions after a few weeks' interval—which meant that a host of pledges of good conduct had been given, which had ap- parently been accepted as satisfactory. By this means the potential rebels in North Africa were disconcerted, those rebels whom Weygand had taken seriously[29]—not to mention the people in France proper whose feelings were hostile to Vichy. Pétain and Darlan, deliberately bent on collaboration and doing their best to carry the French people along with

[29]In the autumn of 1942, North African concentration camps had many thousands of inmates—De Gaullists, Communists, Jews, and political refugees.

them, could point to American indulgence as an argument in their favor. Through public statements (especially in May and August 1941) President Roosevelt, Secretary Hull, and Mr. Sumner Welles strove to counteract this propaganda. But Pétain and Darlan were in a position to tell the French that actions spoke louder than words.

For all that, was Vichy really affected, even to the smallest degree, by the active presence of the United States in the French Empire—a harbinger of vast developments? So long as the power of Vichy still stood firm on the feeble foundations of 1940, so long as the Germans left the forty departments assigned to Pétain inviolate, not the faintest intention of moving in the American direction was apparent. As for the old marshal, he might just as well have been turned into a wooden statue of the kind that celebrated Hindenburg's glory in 1917-18. He would not have been more completely inert. The Washington diplomats were well aware of this. They never dared ask him what he proposed to do if the Germans tried to make him move beyond the provisions of the armistice and used force to compel him. Yet the question would have been entirely in order, since he had given his promise not to go beyond the terms of June 1940. Meanwhile the government surrounding the marshal started to organize the defense of North Africa against the "Anglo-Saxons," in all seriousness, and the outcome was to prove that it did not take its task lightly. So deeply convinced of Vichy's inflexible determination to resist were leaders like Noguès and Boisson, both of anti-German bias if left to themselves, that, in their talks with Washington's envoys, those opportunists went no further than fine words. Even the assurance voiced by Americans in Vichy and Algiers that the United States was not necessarily hostile to the National Revolution fell on deaf ears. When the actual test came every man of importance was found on the wrong side. The German dreadnought, tossing about in the gale, had to run foul of the Vichy hulk, and to cause great leaks to spring: only then did the rats—and not so many of them after all—swim wildly off to safety and finally clamber aboard the American ship, as they would have climbed on to anything to save their skins. Let it be granted that American diplomacy was well advised to prepare itself for the reception of these rodents and that from them it gained for the armies landing on November 8, 1942, more than it could have obtained from lesser reliance on the good will of Vichy and from a much freer recourse to espionage and fifth-column methods coupled with the stirring up of patriotic elements. Let it be granted that the price paid elsewhere by the Fighting French—or which had to be paid later in the form of fresh strength given to all the forces represented by Vichy—was not found too heavy. One is nevertheless bound to conclude that as long as Pétain and his whole retinue could keep in countenance their dealings with the United States over North Africa betrayed no desire whatever to join hands in the end with the Western Powers against the Nazi conqueror. The action of the United States has been brought in here only as a touchstone of Pétain's motives.

In the same way we cannot be grateful to Vichy for the *modus vivendi* arrived at in November 1940, by Admiral Robert and Admiral Greenslade, in command at Puerto Rico. The Germans themselves had to recognize that it was unavoidable. Had the United States not been conceded a modest measure of neutralization in Martinique, it would have had to take over the island. Surveillance by patrols, the immobilization of the French warships, of the *Béarn's* planes, and of the gold reserve, as against the shipment of supplies, with American military observers in key places, constituted the minimum conditions with which the Washington Government could possibly be satisfied. Once it was itself at war it had to tighten its control; later on it even sought to extend it.[30] From the outset Robert, the petty tyrant of Fort-de-France, tried to bind his co-signatory in return to guaranteeing the institutions and personnel of the dictatorship in all the French possessions of the Western Hemisphere. The counterrevolution would thus have been safeguarded against the Gaullist liberation on the threshold of America, a paradoxical state of affairs. Toward the end of December 1941 it was at least overthrown at St. Pierre and Miquelon.

In no part of the French Empire, therefore, do we find any Vichy policy betokening the least intention—even as a matter of precaution— to look to America for salvation. Some concessions were indeed grudgingly made in cases of prime necessity, which were admitted as such by the Wiesbaden Armistice Commission. Mendacious appearances were sold to the Washington Government at a good price, and all Frenchmen, at home or abroad, who were fighting against Germany or her vassals, paid the penalty.

To no greater extent than those narrowly circumscribed agreements with Washington did Vichy's hesitation to intensify collaboration with Germany, observable during the weeks which followed the meeting between Goering, Pétain, and Darlan at St. Florentin, on December 1, 1941, or the renewal, two weeks later, of the promises which Admiral

---

[30]Upon the landing of American troops in North Africa and the German inrush in the "free zone," American control was made absolute.

Leahy had secured during the course of a year, or the declaration of neutrality issued after the entry of the United States into the war, deserve to be called real symptoms of a change of heart toward the Western democracies.

The St. Florentin, like the Montoire meeting, was the natural outcome of a decision reached during the spring and summer to merge once for all the National Revolution of Vichy with the Nazi upheaval. But in 1941, as in 1940, the autumn brought with it military changes sufficiently striking to intimidate the marshal and his advisers. In 1940 the failure of the German assault on England had given them pause. In 1941 the victorious resistance of the Red Army and the entry of the United States into the war produced the same effect. Had Hitler formulated his policy toward France more rapidly and intelligently in 1940, and had the Montoire conversation taken place three weeks earlier, the course of events would very likely have been different. So too in 1941, if Nazi diplomacy had not procrastinated and had yielded more quickly to Pétain's request for an audience.

Early in November, according to diplomatic evidence, the Head of the State and his ministers assumed that Moscow would be evacuated and that the Soviet Union would collapse. Soon any opportunity to deal with Hitler under favorable conditions would be lost, they sighed, using the same language as that of Laval twelve months before. The Führer would have no further need of France and would not decently reward her for joining the New Order which he was now finally to establish. In the solemn assembly of all Europe soon to be convoked, we could expect nothing better than to take the seats assigned to us. Such was the talk that went the rounds. The men who engaged in it had but one desire—to come to terms for good.

However, not only did the Soviet capital hold firm, but Japan's declaration of war plunged America into the struggle. The Führer had other fish to fry than those of Vichy, Madrid, Casablanca, Algiers, Dakar. Once again his grand plan for European federation sank into the background. He did not go personally to St. Florentin, but merely sent Goering as his delegate. The French awakened to the tremendous vicissitudes in the course of the war which were impending. The reverses inflicted upon the Nazi armies on the frozen steppes offered dazzling evidence that the Colossus was not invincible. And America's entrance into the war meant that England was sure to win. It must be said to the credit of the French nation that it didn't wait for the oppressor to shake and totter before it held up its head. After the terrible happenings in Syria, citizens rose in revolt against the will to total collaboration which Pétain and Darlan displayed in August. They got the better of the marshal's gang. They are our martyrs. In 1940, when Pétain was drifting toward Germany, he had not been arrested by the valor and the unlooked-for survival of England alone. His dispute with Laval concerning internal reform had also blocked his path. In 1941 the blood of the hostages held the old man back. It operated in the same manner as the prowess of the Red Army, the stubborn heroism of the British, the first American battles. So firm was the faith of the French people in the sons of Washington that Japanese victories were overlooked.

Thus it was not of his own will that the marshal, during the first weeks of December, turned his back on a comprehensive pact with the Nazi Empire, and, as far as collaboration was concerned, continued a "gradualist," after the pattern of the payments by installment made in Syria, in Indo-China, and in North Africa.

Some foreign diplomats wished to believe that each of those installments had been exacted by threats, by violent exertion of German pressure, that the Vichy Government did not want to do what it did, and that it yielded grudgingly. So they contributed in keeping alive the enigma of Pétain, which has been cleared up in the balance sheet of assets and liabilities drawn up above. They argued that, at each crack of the whip, the beast of burden never moved more than a single stride forward. All that is needed to prick that bubble is to put on record the letter of resignation submitted to the Head of the State in June 1941, by Jules Basdevant, Minister Plenipotentiary, professor of international law at the University of Paris, successor to Fromageot and Louis Renaud as director of the Legal Department of the Ministry of Foreign Affairs. Basdevant had resumed his post in October 1940, at the request of Baudouin, Foreign Minister, and Jacques Chevalier, Minister of Education, in the belief that France would scrupulously fulfill the terms of the armistice, but would deem it a point of honor not to give any military assistance to a state with which peace had not yet been negotiated. "I hold respect for law and a sense of honor to be among those moral forces which France cannot renounce." Basdevant was obliged to admit that official interpretations had transformed what should have been only supervision and control into the unlimited use of French resources for the benefit of the conqueror. He could see no reason why the Germans, relying upon what had happened in Syria, might not at any moment use the Vichy airport for military purposes or fly their planes over the whole of French territory at home and overseas, thereby making all of it a zone of operations. He denounced the public utterances of Darlan, in which France's position was described as though the armistice agreement in no way defined it, as though the surrender had been unconditional and Germany's good pleasure had a free rein. The provisions of the armistice might be harsh, he concluded; but the obligations which they imposed were, after all, not unlimited. It was a matter of our honor not to go further than we must.

Against Darlan's wishes, Basdevant refused to resort to legal tricks in order to satisfy Nazi demands or to squeeze them into the framework of the armistice terms in violation of their letter. An official whose duty was to guard against every demand beyond the letter of the agreement had clearly become convinced that his government expected him to help the Germans to push forward their machinery of conquest. So he left rather than act as legal adviser in the interest of collaboration. But what are we to think of his employers? If they had been determined upon resistance, they would have cried out at the tiniest comma shifted by the Germans to further their own ends. Can it be denied that a stubborn contest for the strictest observance of the treaty should have been their first line of defense? But since their main care was to anticipate all German wishes, they must have dreaded the tightening of the Nazi noose far less than the reactions of the French people and of the United States. They were concerned not so much to elude the grip of the conqueror as to dupe their own fellow countrymen.

Nevertheless, in that part of France designated as "free," the marshal was still looked upon as the very embodiment of patriotism by a substantial portion of the upper classes, of the high and middle bourgeoisie. In these circles he was no longer believed to be endowed with political wisdom, since British valor had falsified his expectations. But they still refused to question his good faith. Moreover, in the Vichy diplomatic corps, there were men who not only adopted the views of this minority but believed it to be the majority. Why did the evidence of events win credence so slowly in the early days of 1942?

The industrialists had regained the power taken from them in 1936. They ruled the roost in the governmental agencies of Vichy. That was no small matter. Moreover, all profits, all returns on their investments came to them from Germany. Were they not morally bound to keep their men on the pay roll? And no pay roll could exist apart from the Nazis. Only a few of them gave themselves up to the New Order, body and soul. But most of them were alarmed at the thought of an abrupt and total collapse of their business.

In the higher levels of French society outside the occupied zone (where day-to-day contact with the Nazis created a practically unanimous opposition) there was widespread hope that Pétain's authority would not crumble away. After all, the "French State" of his creation rested on sound social principles. In many respects was it not better than the old, ambitious, supposedly powerful Republic and its vicious credo? Besides, so long as the occupation continued, there was always the danger that the steam roller of some regime modeled on Hitler's might flatten the whole community if the old statue fell from its niche. A Laval or a Doriot would feel free to dare anything, a terrifying prospect!

As to those conservatives who believed in an Anglo-American-Russian victory, they also counted on the chief to prevent the return of the Popular Front or the second French revolution preached by de Gaulle. They wanted him to remain firmly planted on his pedestal. Thus they made excuses to all and sundry for even the most dubious and pernicious of the marshal's acts.

The village squires delighted in their revenge against the Radical-Socialist and Socialist mayors. For a full half century, except in Normandy and some other parts of western France, the populace had prevented them from exercising authority in local affairs. Once again they were enjoying the pleasure of giving orders which afforded them immense satisfaction.

Then there was this apprehension which spread wide and far. Were the Vichy structure to collapse, might not the Germans extend the occupation to the whole of metropolitan France? At the very thought a large number of southern Frenchmen, even though they scorned the marshal and swore to themselves they would throw him out the minute the Germans withdrew, condoned his dictatorship for the time being.

But all these elements added up to only a fraction of the French people. In gradually shifting away from the marshal, the masses were swayed by the following events. First, the immobility of the French African Army during Wavell's drive to Bengazi in February 1941—incidentally, it should be said that French astonishment at Weygand's failure to move was eloquent of the illusions entertained at that time; secondly, Russia's entry into the war and the effect of Communist propaganda which had, formerly, canceled itself out in condemnation of every sort of "imperialism"; thirdly, the establishment of the Japanese in Indo-China; and finally the cruel German levies of the second winter concomitant with American full participation in the war.

Only with great difficulty could the foreign diplomats inform themselves of popular feeling. Shut up tight in the Vichy Kremlin, where few could penetrate, they were really observers beset by all sorts of restrictions. Even supposing that the high officials with whom they generally associated had a clear understanding of things, they would scarcely choose the diplomats as recipients of their confidences. A story went the rounds of the Vichy embassies that, at least in the days of Laval's tenure in 1940, microphones had been scattered throughout the offices of the Ministry of Foreign Affairs and that private conversations were thus reported to the Cabinet. All the foreign envoys were not fooled by appearances. I could quote reports about Vichy's immediate future which were certainly pessimistic enough. But others persisted in seeing in the dictator with the seven stars on his sleeve the man who despite everything was best qualified to speak for the French nation.

Nothing is more difficult than to follow the process of being melted down and recast in a people whose historic features are indelibly imprinted upon one's memory. How can we guess what will be the new countenance to emerge after the ordeal? The admixture of its social components is all the more obscure in that men's feelings are not sincerely expressed; neither newspapers nor magazines nor books nor free discussion are at work day by day to shape public opinion, to disentangle it from the whims or the isolated communings of individuals and their tiny immediate groupings. The investigator is always wondering whether the particular fact he has grasped has a general significance or is merely accidental, whether a given man whose tales and prophecies astound him deserves to be taken seriously as a prognosticator of what is to come or merely as an impostor or as a fool. To fathom the secret of a cabinet discussion, however well guarded it may be, to unravel a policy which seeks to remain hidden—such things are mere child's play to the practiced observer. But guessing what will be the moral and social structure of forty million French people, hurled into the crucible, can spring only from intuition, historical knowledge, and reasoning by analogy. Out of common prudence, most of those who try hard to understand are reluctant to part with the "established values" they have known for so long. To them a member of the Institut de France is still a member of the Institut de France, an archbishop is still an archbishop, a general retains his general's authority, and a marshal can be nothing else but a marshal.

The case of the Americans who had to defend the cause of their own country as well as that of the United Nations at Vichy was somewhat peculiar. Above all, they realized after December 7, 1941 (Pearl Harbor) —as did their government—that thenceforward the French fleet was something which could tip the scales upon the seas and therefore was far more important than it might seem from its intrinsic fighting power. They were disturbed at the idea that a gust of ill temper or anger on the part of the marshal or Darlan could throw that fleet into the Axis clutches. Their natural instinct led them to try to win the good will of men who had it in their power to do incalculable damage. And but for a few individuals gifted with unusual toughness of character, diplomats are professionally inclined to flatter and praise the government to which they are accredited. To play up to Pétain, therefore, became the first order of the day. "Oh, if only the marshal knew all that is being done in his name! If only the truth could reach him! To keep the French fleet neutral, the best approach is to play upon the marshal's sense of honor." During the days when Anglo-American sea power was weak that sort of time serving could readily be understood. It did not necessarily involve, however, a favorable interpretation of the Pétain "enigma." Nor did it rule out, for the future, a policy of putting trust in the forces of popular sentiment. But this point deserves to be stressed. On all public buildings the motto of the Republic—Liberty, Equality, Fraternity—had been scraped off and replaced by the words: Fatherland, Family, Work—which stank of fascism. Americans who were convinced that their civilization would come out on top could see nothing in this new motto but ephemeral rhetoric. While sparing the feelings of present-day official France, they must have felt that a very different sort of France would emerge. Whenever they tried to perceive what the France of tomorrow would be like, the easiest way of approach for them was to hark back to the great figures of the defunct Republic regime, who seemed less unworthy than the rest. Thus they thought Herriot a potential tower of strength. After all, when Herriot served as Prime Minister, Pétain had long since been a marshal and the generals with whom they wined and dined were already on the General Staff. With such figures of the past they were on familiar ground, they knew where they stood. But as for the "Gaullist" movement, that was a rebellion. It was attacking the governing classes of today, but, however much it might refuse to recognize any laws save those of the Republic, it did not clearly link with the governing classes of yesterday. Some effort of the imagination was needed to understand the forces which might gather round the Gaullist rallying points. Unhappily that effort was never made.

The American attitude toward Vichy was perhaps never reduced to a clear-cut policy, but in its calculations it relied mainly on the men of recognized political and social standing. The courtesies showered upon the marshal, the humiliations inflicted upon General de Gaulle, the care exercised at certain junctures not to unreservedly identify the American cause with the British in French eyes—presumably for the sake of humoring Vichy and preserving the singular favor supposed to be enjoyed by the United States among the masses—such a demeanor did nothing to help the United Nations. Those Frenchmen who thought to thwart the government at the risk of their liberty and their lives were completely nonplused. By helping Pétain and his crowd to give their regime an outward veneer of respectability, America counteracted the pressure which had held them all in check from below and which up till then had restrained them whenever they tried to go too far on the road toward collaboration. That Vichy could think and say that Washington and London were not of a single mind and purpose in the struggle gave the "collaborationists" an immense lever. They were able to argue effectively that, after all, the United States was none too solidly united with England, that it was following its own policy in the war, and that, consequently, Germany would manage to elude defeat.[31]

The testimony which some American diplomats have thought fit to adduce on the deep-seated patriotism of the marshal—which, as they saw it, was merely awaiting some favorable circumstance in order to burst forth against Germany—is not supported by a single fact which cannot be accounted for by motives very different from nobility of heart.

The non-belligerence of the French fleet? It was not taken for granted earlier than in the summer of 1942. In order to prove Pétain's and Darlan's laudable intentions, reference is made to the scuttling orders given to our warships in June 1940. What better guarantee could have been found for the fulfillment of Hitler's solemn pledge, inserted in the armistice treaty, that our fleet would not be seized? It has already been explained why, in June 1940, Pétain and his people, feeling it necessary to soothe the British Cabinet and reassure the Washington government, arranged for this act of destruction in case of necessity. But with the passing of time the Nazis insisted more and more on obtaining French naval assistance. Thus it came about that the scuttling orders served another purpose than that of tranquilizing the British and dis-

---

[31] It dawned upon Laval that there might be a chink in the armor. He had the cheek to tell an American diplomat in April 1942: "I hope for a German victory in Europe and an American victory in Asia."

suading them from striking again as they had struck at Mers-el-Kebir. The preparations made for a huge naval suicide now began to play a part in the relations with Berlin.

The fleet was the last remnant of our military might. Whatever turn the war might take, a British victory, a German victory, a compromise peace, Vichy (deeply sunk in illusion as to the consequences of the two last possibilities) could not fail to reckon the fleet a precious asset. And yet Vichy foresaw that, in some conceivable set of circumstances, the fleet had better be completely destroyed than escape and survive. Vichy's motives are worth explaining.

The Vichy rulers never dared imagine that, against Germany, reprisals might have to be enforced to the length of ordering the French fleet to rejoin the British. Not even if Germany trampled upon all her promises under the Armistice, rushed her troops into the "free zone" and the French Empire, and canceled all the advantages which, in the judgment of Pétain and his friends, constituted the justification of the 1940 surrender. That would mean too much audacity on their part, placing too much confidence in the enemies of the Nazis—above all, putting the National Revolution in too much jeopardy. They were very alive to the danger that Germany would scrap the Armistice. But, in order to provide for a deterrent, the utmost they were prepared to do was to arrange for the automatic destruction of the most important prize which the conqueror could derive from the total occupation of France: the fleet and its arsenal. The most extraordinary point is that, as months went by, the above-said deterrent, as they saw it, became the regulator of the Franco-German intercourse.

Nothing had to be done in order to create this counterthreat to the Germans. To the knowledge of everybody, it had existed since June 1940, when it served to keep the British quiet, not only in the interest of the Pétain regime but also of the Nazi Empire.

It had grown more impressive, Vichy thought, as Franco-German cooperation developed. The Nazis would know that with the French fleet would vanish the whole system of defense organized to protect France's oversea possessions against any British or American attack. From the days of Mers-el-Kebir the French Navy had practically operated as a covering force for the Germans within the limits of the French Empire, and for that reason it had been fully armed in spite of the disarmament clauses of the Armistice. At the outset the scuttling orders were intended to be a surety for the fulfillment of Hitler's pledge not to seize the French fleet. Later on they were more than balanced by the instructions given to all French admirals to engage the British and Americans if they appeared in force in waters within French jurisdiction.

As far as the Germans were concerned, the scuttling order was meant to convey that only the future could tell whether our main instrument of military power could do more for them than it had hitherto been planned to do by preventive action. Implicitly Pétain and Darlan said to them, "You know our difficulties. We have often discussed them in our joint conferences. We are always ready to talk whenever you have any proposal to make to us. But please don't try to help yourselves, for then we should be unhappily obliged to prevent your getting what you wanted. You would lose the help we are now giving you which is not to be despised." What a vile and senseless policy!

By a fresh curtailment of French power Hitler was to be barred from enforcing the most predatory scheme. Only impotent men could have had recourse to such a course. They boasted of their word of honor given to England and made great play with it. But one may hazard the conjecture that the fleet would never have been scuttled as long as German fortunes were in the ascendant. In other words, unrestricted naval collaboration was the true logical outcome of Vichy's attitude. Save for Darlan's objections to French sailors being replaced in his ships by Germans and Italians, it is not so sure that at some date, in 1941 or 1942, the Germans would not have had their way. To enable the Nazi High Command to do what they liked with the ships, this measure could hardly be dispensed with, as the spirit of the French people was bound, sooner or later, to spread to the sailors. But Darlan could not be expected to condone such a substitution of German and Italian for French crews. He, the great feudal lord of the sea, could never tolerate to be deprived of his own kingdom and of the instrument of his political fortune. Never! Besides, once all limits were removed from French collaboration, Hitler, at the slightest provocation, could have done away with Vichy and the "free zone." The last drop of juice would have been squeezed out of the lemon, and it could be thrown away at any moment. In the autumn of 1942 that vile and senseless policy was about to be revised. Darlan, at any rate, was awakening to the premonitory signs of Germany's defeat. But to think in terms of a German ultimate triumph had, by then, become for most a second nature, and when the Allies landed in Africa the reversal had hardly begun.

There is really no Pétain enigma. His record is all too clear. And those who followed him day by day could only wonder that, far from responding to the pleadings of the Western Powers, France's traditional friends, he should have become petrified within the convention of June 1940, despite so many signs pointing to the ebb of the totalitarian tide.

7

Pétain and the Spirit of Revolt

I HAVE ATTEMPTED TO RELATE how Gamelin, Daladier, and Reynaud failed and fell. I have not compromised with truth. But the errors of Pétain, on the level of both political thought and action, were incomparably more criminal than theirs. Gamelin lost the battle of the frontier. Daladier proved unable to rescue the country from its internal discord, to temper and gird it for the hour of destiny. Reynaud edged over toward surrender when means for struggling on had not yet been exhausted. But in the first instance, at any rate, none of them can be accused of bad intentions. Gamelin, Daladier, Reynaud, all had faith in the greatness of their country. A wavering, a halfhearted faith, a faith which was inoperative or went astray, but still an undeniable faith. Not only must Pétain be held responsible for the dislocation of the French Army between 1919 and 1935, for the baneful doctrines which year after year pervaded the General Staff in the matter of tactics and strategy. He conceived and carried out the counterrevolution. He pairs with Laval.

Pétain dealt French moral unity a blow more serious than that it suffered from the Revolution of 1789. By wreaking upon the 1936 Popular Front an exorbitant revenge, a revenge that no final German victory, fortunately, will help to perpetuate, he has merely prepared the resurgence of the forces he was out to crush. And this time all patriots will be on their side. To form some idea of what that movement may be like, one needs only recall the swing of the pendulum, Right to Left, Left to Right, since World War I. Millerand's conservative regime was followed by the cartel of the Left in 1924. The moderate governments of 1926–36 brought on the sit-down strikes. Against the social experimenters of 1936–38, Pétain's dictatorship, with Nazi support, came in 1940 as a deadly counterstroke. On the day of liberation will the reprisals of patriotism, the vengeance of Pétain's victims operate on some comparable scale?

Let us hope that a vast majority of Frenchmen will repudiate Vichy and all it stands for. May Pétain, Laval, and their followers fade out of the picture without a fight and without gaining any measure of Allied support on the plea of maintaining public order. Then violence may be avoided, although the country's wounds will go on bleeding slowly for a long time. But should there remain upon our soil a stubborn and substantial minority devoted to the old man's cause, France is likely to be visited with one of the worst convulsions in her history. In any event, the issue is bound to be settled by national and popular forces. On the other hand, it must be confessed that apathy on the part of the French people on the day of liberation would be a sign of evil portent. The vitality of France itself might then seem open to doubt.

Starting in the summer of 1941, Pétain stripped himself of any appearance he might have retained of genial and kindly paternalism. He assumed the hateful countenance of a dictator—he will go down to history with it. I have pointed out that popular sentiment intervened between him and total collaboration with Germany, and that it got the better of him. But during the few months he thought German military successes enabled him to overcome what stood in his way he abandoned all restraint and gave free rein to the most ruthless among his followers. His repression of the French people was coupled with Nazi repression. Undoubtedly he did not deliberately seek this hateful connection, but once circumstances had produced it he did nothing to break it off. The stars on his sleeve are now red with blood.

On August 12 he spoke over the radio in a harsh and overbearing tone which had never before been his—at least to so marked a degree —outside the military sphere. He showed his annoyance that collaboration was moving so slowly, that the bulk of the French people were either openly or covertly hostile to his external or internal program. "Authority no longer springs from the people. There is but one authority —that which I delegate. In 1917 I put a stop to mutiny. In 1940 I put an end to rout. Today I want to save you from yourselves." Thereupon he proclaimed an intensification of fascist sternness. The next day, August 13, the Paris mob demonstrated noisily near the Gare St. Lazare and the Halles markets. The food shortage had much to do with it, but so also had the arrival of soldiers released in Syria. From then on acts of violence against the army of occupation multiplied. The Stuelpnagels and the Schaumburgs began their massacres.[1] Had not the op-

---

[1]That is, their public massacres. They had slaughtered people before, but had not advertised it. In evidence thereof, the 1940 Armistice Day, when a student was killed on

portunity then finally arisen for Pétain to bring into play that threat of the fleet and the empire which, at times, had been described in Vichy as impressive enough to keep the Germans in the occupied zone within the limits of decency? Pétain and Darlan never even thought of doing so. They made common cause with German terrorism on the ground that they might thus control it, restrain it, dilute it.

They greatly increased the number of tribunals of the star-chamber pattern. By a Law of July 21, 1941, military courts could constitute themselves as courts-martial to judge those who infringed the military code of justice and "ordinary penal laws." On August 14, 1941, special sections were attached to each military or naval court to smite down those who ran afoul of the penal code with "communist or anarchic intent." In the occupied zone, where such judicial bodies did not exist, the same function was assigned to a special section in each court of appeal. On September 10, 1941, in order to reach not only those actually guilty of criminal acts but also, "with even greater severity, those who directed or incited them," the state tribunals of Paris and Lyons set to work. Twelve of the fourteen judges were to be "freely chosen"—that is, were not necessarily members of the judiciary.

At the same time, of course, arbitrary warrants of arrest hailed thick and fast, as did the exactions of the newfangled police of the regime. It was trained in a special school on the same footing as the major state schools, and the marshal insisted that the first graduating class should be named after him. Pétain and Darlan were bespattered by the crimes of Pucheu, their Minister of the Interior after July 19, 1941. Up to that date, for five months, Darlan had been in charge of that department. He also had a direct hand in the bloody business. Someday the long train of his victims will be numbered.

"I shall crush my opponents," Pétain burst forth in a speech to the Council of State on August 21. How often were the marshal's officials requested by the Germans to select from among groups of hostages those who were going to face the firing squad? On October 22, in Châ-

---

the street and two others died of the treatment they received from the German police. In evidence thereof, Fernand Hollweg, the Sorbonne professor who had labored in our national-defense laboratories and who was brought home with his skull bashed in. These are but two instances. General von Stuelpnagel was appointed to Paris in April 1941. He was fairly representative of a military conception which, in the management of French affairs, was to gradually supersede the policy of Von Ribbentrop. In 1942 the generals had their own way in everything. Their watchword was that, to meet the requirements of the Russian campaign, all French resources had to be seized more ruthlessly than before. In its turn, by the summer of 1942, the Gestapo became the dominant power. In a detailed relation of the enforcement of the 1940 armistice those three periods ought to be given separate treatment.

teaubriant, was the list of twenty-seven names drawn up with their help? A diplomatic dispatch drafted at about that time recorded the boast of Pucheu: "Public order will be respected even if I have to put three Frenchmen out of every five in concentration camps." On July 27, Marx Dormoy, Léon Blum's Minister of the Interior, had been assassinated. A month later, to the very day, Laval and Déat were seriously wounded. Between Frenchmen, blood was paying for blood. Later on Giton, the turncoat communist, and Perengaux, Pucheu's chief of secretariat, were killed. A dose of civil war was injected into the struggle of the Germans against those Frenchmen who would not submit. The populace no longer made any distinction between the crimes of the Nazis and those of their toadies.

Pétain could not keep it up. He backed out from his threats of August 12. Pucheu, whose program was to hold off Nazi control by a great show of true National Socialist severity at home, did not long have the marshal's support. Pétain was not the hotheaded and passionate leader that such a policy required. He committed himself to its enforcement while success seemed quick and easy. He soon lost his nerve. "I want to save you from yourselves!" he had said. Now the words turned against him: the resistance of the mass cowed the master.

Darlan and his ministers were left to their own devices. On the one side, they doubled their police force, filled prisons and camps to overflowing. They made furious efforts to clean out the black market, but for every step forward they slipped back two. They sought new recruits for the Legion—Vichy's "one-party" system: whoever wished to obtain any trifling favor from the government had to enroll, and presently within its ranks was formed the already mentioned Service Corps— truly a pretorian guard. They wielded a formidable weapon against their internal foes: the ration card, renewable at regular intervals. On the other side, they set free one after the other such labor leaders as were willing to promise assistance or non-interference, and old-age pensions began to be paid to workers. After the whip, a paltry lump of sugar. But kindness had no more effect than violence.

Vichy's reforms were not taken seriously. That they would pass away as speedily as they had come in was a remark heard everywhere. The Labor Charter, promulgated on October 4, 1941, had been dismissed as a mere tool for securing the supremacy of the economic oligarchy: former socialists or union officials, now in the Vichy fold, were abandoned by the workers. Besides, Jouhaux, the head of the defunct General

Confederation of Labor, and his friends were unshakable: the German authorities strove in vain to beguile them.

Lucien Romier, commissioned to draft a new constitution, made no headway. The restoration of the monarchy fell through: the Count of Paris—who, to smooth his own path, blessed the marshal's policy, abjured the sound foreign policy long advocated in his review, the *Courier Royal,* and ate humble pie to please Charles Maurras—was fated to be soon put to shame. The Vichy State failed even to define its own character and constitution. It remained nothing but a shaky absolutism, a display of hollow rhetoric. The Church was afraid of falling back into the "clericalism" of an earlier day. In no guise did she wish a return to the old alliance between "throne and altar." Certain important prelates and some of the priests appointed to the municipal commissions which replaced elected bodies were not always discreet. However, the rank and file of the clergy in many parts of France—in Brittany particularly—was publicly rebuked by Darlan, and that tells a long story. The aphorism of the Cardinal of Lyons in 1940, "Pétain is France and France is Pétain," sank into oblivion. Archbishop Saliège of Toulouse, with Father Bruno de Solages, rector of the Institut Catholique at his side, became the true Primate of the Gauls, the fighting Gauls.

"Authority comes from above." Perhaps it did, but it did not filter down into the hearts of men. From the winter of 1941 underground movements began to crystallize, first around some ten centers and then, in the summer of 1942, around a council of resistance where the old political parties and trade-unions sent delegates. A true form of national union which did not exclude the Communists. Clandestine newssheets circulated from hand to hand.

Suddenly, over a silent France, exploded the Riom trial. Here was a mighty machine which, at the most unexpected moment, hurled deadly missiles against the government. True to type, Pétain had kept wobbling. He had realized at an early date that the magistrates of the Supreme Court (to the lasting honor of the French judiciary) were not governmental catspaws, and with the guidance of a "Court of Political Justice," named for the occasion, he therefore hastened, on October 17, 1941, to sentence Gamelin, Daladier, and Blum to life imprisonment. But Joseph Barthélemy could not wholly forget that, before being appointed Minister of Justice, he had taught law to generations of young men. Besides, he was well aware of the weakening of the regime. With his approval the legal proceedings begun in the summer of 1940 followed their course, even though it meant that the same men were to be tried twice for the same offenses. And the marshal must have nodded assent. The hearings, spread out between February 19 and April 17, need not be described here. Suffice it to say that the defendants keenly felt that an opportunity was at hand to strike at the dictatorship. They took a high hand with their accusers. They made it a point to incriminate Pétain again and again while the chief prosecutor failed to do much to shield him. Daladier had no difficulty in showing that the High Command, of which the Head of the State was a part, was primarily to blame for the defeat. Léon Blum's emphatic statement that the Popular Front had set rearmament in motion and that counterrevolutionary elements among the industrialists had contrived to slow it down could not be seriously refuted. "The Republic and Democracy are here on trial: we shall remain their defenders." In the subservient press of Vichy and the Paris newspapers, at the beck and call of the Nazis,[2] the defendants' speeches were only printed in a mutilated form and covered with abusive commentaries. What did it matter? The British broadcasted them to the world over the radio. From mouth to mouth they traveled into every village in France. Subtle forerunners of freedom, they stole in and out, laughed at locks and bars. The aged despot could guess what would become of him the day when all the gags were torn off.

No revolt broke out—none was physically possible. But already the spirit of revolt was alive. How distressing it had been to look at Rude's "Marseillaise" on the Arc de Triomphe during the days of the disaster, when the French people bestirred itself only to flee. The carvings had lost all life; they no longer moved men's souls. They seemed only a memory—a pathetic anachronism. But now the old lines were coming to life again. Once more they stirred the souls of Frenchmen because they were being sung by men going to their death. Pétain's National Revolution, even under Hitler's protectorate, had encountered something it was unable to withstand. On March 28 an English commando was hurled against the port of St. Nazaire. When the time came to re-embark, all the raiders could not be assembled again. The local population rushed out to join forces with these doomed fighters, and for three long days all battled side by side. The reprisals were pitiless. Not only in the town, but in the surrounding countryside, some fifty Frenchmen were shot daily throughout the month of April. With its blood the people sealed anew the British alliance which Pétain had betrayed.

In those last days of March, Hitler waxed more and more impatient

---

[2] Let it be mentioned that André François-Poncet, the former Ambassador to Berlin and Rome, was press co-ordinator in Vichy and Paris.

at the turn taken by the Riom trial. He had expected that it would provide his "new European order" with letters of legitimacy, that the French Government of 1939 would there be pronounced guilty of having started the war. But no judge had come forward to indict the prisoners on that count; the only spectacle presented for Hitler's edification was the confusion into which his French vassals had been thrown. He bethought himself that Pétain and Darlan had given the full measure of their ineptitude, that the experiment was conclusive. The attack on Russia was about to be renewed, and an Anglo-American invasion of the Continent seemed to be impending. The whole of France might be turned into a zone of operations for the German Army. The time had come to replace the crew which had promised to hand French souls over to him by the agency of Laval, who at least understood better how to hand over their bodies. At his father-in-law's behest, René de Chambrun came to Vichy to enlighten Pétain. Hitler's wrath would be terrible: his speech of March 15 was a final warning. To make it more emphatic he had called the Reichstag into session, a solemn procedure used only at the most serious junctures. The lord of Chateldon alone was of a stature to counter the threat. Perhaps our twelve or thirteen hundred thousand prisoners were in danger.

The marshal was not particularly disturbed. As was his wont, he went on damning the fallen politician whom he nevertheless received on March 26. "I shall never call him back," he told a foreign Ambassador two days later. However, Darlan was apparently not quite sure of the sequel. The crisis was drawing near and he was not blind to its implications. Still he bragged: "Ten chances out of a hundred that Laval will return—no more!"

On April 14, Pétain restored the Minister he had driven out as an unfaithful servant on December 13, 1940. At the bidding of a higher authority he bent the knee. He swallowed all the insults and accusations heaped upon the man. He not only restored Laval to the vice-presidency, but stripping himself of half his own title, the marshal set him up as the Head of the Government and, practically, as its immovable head, liable to dismissal only at the good pleasure or the ill fortune of the Führer. The dotard was determined to preserve his power at any price. Today he accepted Laval; tomorrow, in order to appease the Allies, it might be either Weygand, Reynaud, or anyone else, to the tune of "National Union."

What, then, was lacking in this infantry colonel whose promotion in the army and in public life since 1916 can today be considered as nothing less than a calamity? He lacked breadth of outlook and what may be termed imagination of the heart. On the level of intelligence and feeling, he was dull and commonplace. He could not expand beyond his narrow technical and human orbit which contracted further with old age.

The classic representation of patriotic steadfastness under adversity has been handed down to us by Livy. After the Battle of Cannae, which Schlieffen considered a model of the victory of extermination, Rome was stricken with terror. She was at Hannibal's mercy. Men of consequence talked of giving up the fight and fleeing. The surviving consul, Terentius Varro, had been forced upon the patricians in the Comitia. An incompetent leader in war, but a brave man, he tried to rebuild an army out of the wreckage of the legions. Coming back to the city, he expected to be called to account. Upon his arrival, however, factional strife subsided. The citizens closed their ranks and thanked their defeated chief for "not having despaired of the Republic." He had not despaired of the Republic: how the antique phrase, stammered out by generations of schoolboys, takes on new life when applied to the French counterrevolutionaries!

Reverse every detail of the picture and you have Pétain's story. Contrasted with Roman grandeur, it will signify, in the eyes of posterity, the humiliation, the breakup of a national community in the face of disaster.

EPILOGUE

The Gravediggers. North Africa. The New France in the Making. The Liberation

VICTORY for the United Nations is now dawning. But the French people, in its unspeakable plight, does not measure its hopes by facts duly verified. It leaps far beyond them in its yearning. It borrows against a happy outcome in order to steel itself against the intolerable privations of the present and the bitter memories of the past. A friend newly come from France remarked to me: "At home optimism is always ahead of what prudence enjoins upon England, the United States, Russia."

One of my liveliest recollections of childhood is the tale of an arch-bishop of Bordeaux who fell into a coma. Laid out upon his bed of state, he watched the preparations being made for his funeral, and he sur-vived for many years to describe the experience. I seem to remember reading somewhere that he made a speech on this subject before the Senate during the Empire. Like this prince of the Church, France, while yet alive, thought that she lay stricken among the dead. The grave-diggers are the men from whom she will demand a reckoning. Some of them bartered away her independence, her body, and her soul: they actually hollowed out her sepulcher. Some knew not how to save her. Some wrapped her in her shroud, believing or feigning to believe that she no longer breathed. Still others attempted only a halfhearted rescue. And the guiltiest of all rolled a great stone over her burying place, making out that they heard no sound or sign of life.

As I have already pointed out, the war of 1870-71 brought about in the mass of Frenchmen a rebirth of patriotism and of the military spirit. The nation redeemed itself from the slackness, the materialism which had set the prevailing tone under the Second Empire and even under the reign of Louis Philippe despite all its revolutionary ferment. For that reason the Third Republic possessed, in 1914, the best-managed diplomacy and an army without equal since the days of the great Napo-leon. The formative years of the Republic resounded with the beating of drums and the blare of bugles. With some ups and downs, the watch-fulness of the French people held out for more than forty years. Had not the disaster been vividly remembered, Poincaré would not have been elected to the presidency of the Republic in January 1913. For the sake of France's salvation, a sentiment keener, deeper, more powerful, more lasting than the bitterness of 1870 must grow out of the ordeal suffered after June 1940. The picture of the gravediggers must be stamped on every mind. Henceforth public affairs must be transacted in a fashion the very opposite of the example they have set us. In its freedoms re-gained (may we be spared any samplings of dictatorship!) the nation will be all the surer not to go astray.

The story I have tried to tell is complex and, in many of its ramifica-tions, hard to follow. For more than forty months that half silence, which tyranny always imposes, has weighed heavily upon France. All we could hear were the tales spun by the Germans and the endless apologia of the men of Vichy. Anything like the roughly accurate representation of the recent past which, in normal times, is almost automatically hammered out in periodicals and books, error being weeded out little by little as the new evidence comes daily to the surface, has not yet even begun. If the French people were called upon to vote in an election before it was adequately informed as to the causes of its misfortune, it would be nothing but a dangerous farce. The gravediggers will struggle desperately to save their skins. They will play upon men's ignorance to distort events. They will plead that their mistakes were the mistakes of the whole people. Every single one of them, except those most deeply involved, will shout out that they were the friends of England and the United States, held in check their eagerness only to help them and hid the true promptings of their hearts through political prudence, through a machiavellianism required by the national interest. They will set their secret intentions in contrast to their outward behavior. In 1942–43 they slipped into the baggage trains of the Allied Armies landing in North Africa. They will make capital out of Nazi severity toward them. Their friends have begun to do so. Weygand, Reynaud, and many others are today in German prisons. Can anyone question their patriotism or their loyalty?

The first of these arguments rests upon the open or tacit consent of the people, won by each successive government, at any rate, under the Republic, which, they implicitly claim, deprives the people of the right to judge the men responsible for the defeat, for the dishonor and for the temporary enslavement of the country. The leaders' acts had the approval of Parliament and of the electorate, or else they obviously corresponded to the wish of the majority. In fact, they maintain, the mistakes of those who governed, if indeed there were mistakes, cannot be separated from the mistakes of the governed. What a flimsy plea! Constituents never forego the right to judge ministers and politicians who succeeded in obtaining their mandates from them. The manner in which public men discharge their trust can never be laid down in advance and remains the sole responsibility of those in power. In any case, would anyone dare to assert that in June 1940 the problem of the separate armistice and the dictatorship was placed squarely before a terrorized people?

Any man having the responsibilities of government who failed to warn the multitude of its dire peril or to put it on guard against its own temperamental weakness must be accounted guilty even if he kept clear from criminal failures and criminal doings. To deny this is to imply that ministers, members of Parliament, and electors bear an equal measure of responsibility for the conduct of public affairs, which is tantamount to saying that no one is responsible for anything. Even universal suffrage cannot confer so handsome a gift on anyone. The community's instinctive urge, its will to survive, repudiate any such doctrine. In practice, the community claims the privilege of a constitutional king who can do no wrong; this is the prerequisite of its faith in its own destiny. The fact of the Nazis turning their wrath against the very people who in one way or another helped them, either because they did not get everything they expected or because they avenged themselves for injuries done them either before or after our catastrophe, can in no way affect the judgment which past acts have deserved. Kindliness and pity may attenuate the rigor of the punishment meted out, but the facts themselves are hard as granite, which these sentiments cannot soften. As to the other argument, the eleventh-hour shift to the Allied camp of men who had previously betrayed national independence and liberty, their case cannot be too summarily dismissed.

I have not tried to carry my narrative beyond that fourteenth of April 1942, when the old marshal scrapped what conscience, sense of honor, and personal power still remained to him and called back Laval. After that the view which we can obtain of events in France becomes dim and uncertain. Moreover, by that date, the gravediggers' features have become so sharply defined that their subsequent actions are easy to understand. Their likenesses are clearly portrayed by a description based on long observation. The plaster of Paris applied to their faces has yielded an image—which remains unchangeable in spite of their contortions and grimaces. Their countenances may vary, under the pressure of circumstances pushing them about right or left. In repose the masks remain the same. All that is needful is not to be deceived by appearances, not to assume that changes of attitude denote changes of character. A cursory glance at recent events will afford sufficient guidance.

In the spring of 1942 the Germans had good cause to require Laval's return. They felt that they had reached the end of their amazing run of military fortune. The ensuing summer, for the second time, they cast the dice in Russia, and, for the second time, they lost. The tidal wave of conquest began to ebb in the early autumn. El Alamein and Stalingrad were the turning points. Then followed a succession of surprises. On November 8 and 12, American and British expeditionary forces landed in French North Africa. On November 11, the anniversary of the 1918 Armistice, the Germans burst into the "free zone": in other words, they destroyed the Armistice Treaty of June 1940. The Vichy Government sank to the lowest level among the Quislings. On November 13 the formal agreement between Darlan and Eisenhower was signed. The Admiral of the Fleet, for five days virtually the prisoner of the Americans, finally decided to become the invaders' right-hand man. On November 27 the main portion of the French fleet, gathered at Toulon, was scuttled. By this time the Army of Vichy had been disbanded. Some thirty thousand "mobile guards," various bodies of police, and growing numbers of "volunteers" recruited under Laval's auspices, were left on sufferance to maintain public order. On December 24, Darlan was assassinated. Darlan—bolstered by an "Imperial Council" on which sat all the African proconsuls, Noguès, high commissioner at Rabat; Chatel, governor-general of Algeria; Boisson, governor-general of West Africa; General Juin, commander in chief; General Bergeret, former Air Minister,[1] and General Giraud, brought in from Gibraltar on November 9— was mobilizing all the great resources of our African Empire for the struggle.

What fine excuses for the gravediggers to seize upon! Listen to them! Of course they were waiting for the hour to strike, the hour of the British, of the Americans, of the Russians: they were playing a carefully planned two-faced game. They rushed to the succor of France's redeemers. They did not falter. They lined up under the banners of the United Nations.

---

[1]Bergeret was Air Minister starting September 6, 1940. At the time of the Syrian campaign he ordered Weygand to send the North African air force into action. General Odic, who was in command of these units (some 150 planes), protested, but Weygand insisted that he carried out Bergeret's orders. Yves Chatel, an insignificant official of the colonial service, the choice of Darlan, was replaced toward the end of January 1943 by Marcel Peyrouton, who had resigned from the Buenos Aires Embassy in April 1942, when Laval returned to power. Son-in-law of Louis Malvy, the 1914–17 Minister of the Interior who was convicted of forfeiture by the High Court in 1918, Peyrouton is a master of brutal and cynical police methods. As Minister of the Interior in December 1940, he executed Pétain's decision to scrap Laval. He shared the marshal's ideas on collaboration with the Germans and even on the re-establishment of the monarchy. As late as 1942, in Buenos Aires, he still gave himself out as a Royalist, but he hastened to add that, in the French drama, the last word would not rest with a king. With all that, had not the diplomats, his subordinates, remonstrated with him, he would have cabled a message of reconciliation to Laval when the latter was wounded in August 1942. While Minister of Colony, in 1924–25, Daladier, to please Malvy, took an interest in Peyrouton, then invested with a minor function in West Africa. As Prime Minister in 1933, Daladier made him resident general at Tunis, to subdue the Destour, the native intellectuals who clamored for some representative institutions. At Tunis, Peyrouton broke with the labor unions and with the Salammbo and Carthage lodges—that is, with Free Masonry. Léon Blum recalled him in 1936, and he was sent for the first time to Buenos Aires, in deference to Malvy's lingering influence with the Left. During the war Daladier restored to him his post in Tunisia. There he was an asset of counterrevolution. Boisson, a low-grade teacher, entered the colonial service after World War I on the strength of his brilliant military record. He owes his fame to the reverses inflicted on General de Gaulle and the British before Dakar in September 1940 and to his drastic repression of all local separatism (see page 458, note 6).

Their treachery was merely superficial; it concealed bold schemes. They allowed the conquerors time to exhaust themselves and the avengers time to get ready. To realize how much such talk deserves to be taken seriously, it is only necessary to probe the case of Darlan, the model reproduced in the present mass output of turncoats.

In the first place, a general remark may be made. Why did the grave-diggers—some of them as early as 1934–35—take up their picks and shovels in the service of Hitler and Mussolini? It was certainly not out of personal devotion to the persons of those tyrants. The gravediggers were out for the preservation of the established social order and of their own political careers. Little did it matter to them that the prophecy of Renan in his *Réforme Intellectuelle et Morale,* published after the war of 1870, should be fulfilled, the prophecy of a soft French com-munity, slack, accustomed to an easygoing way of life, abandoning to Prussia a monopoly of the military virtues and the task of policing Europe. Under a Nazi protectorate such fellows were prepared to per-form the tasks which, in the Italian twelfth century, fell upon the podestas borrowed by one city from another when it became weary of factional strife. But once Germany was shaken on the battlefield and clearly doomed to defeat, these modern podestas could be expected to ask for nothing better than to change sides and get out of the road lead-ing to the gallows. Why should the men of Vichy despise such a wind-fall? What is really surprising is not that they should have yielded to the new course of events, but that they should have struggled against it at all, causing bloodshed in Morocco, in Oran, in Tunis, and at least in one instance, at Toulon, turning a grand opportunity into disaster. The surprising thing is that the first victory of the Allies should not merely have had to take them by the hand but had to actually seize them and drive them along.

Now for the admiral.

Darlan spent the three weeks preceding the Anglo-American invasion putting the last touches to the defense of the French Empire, since, in the summer months, Berlin and Vichy had, except for the precise date, seen through the plans of the Western Powers. Vichy had kept only its fleet and its African army and obtained the release of Juin and other generals by promising to oppose with force any attacks on French terri-tory across the Mediterranean. This time, the admiral announced to the press, there will be no token fighting, as at Madagascar, but a real battle to the death. We are in a position to win, and it will not be long before the invader finds it out. The standing order to resist British and Americans came into play. Resistance developed. It greatly exceeded what would have satisfied "honor," both at Casablanca, at Port-Lyautey, at Fedallah, at Oran, etc.[2] On land in Morocco our troops used up all their ammunitions. At sea, before Casablanca, more than twenty units of the French fleet were sent out to destruction by Admiral Michelier, counted an old friend of Darlan's.

The American command was hard put to it. It must launch its advance toward Bizerte as quickly as possible in order to forestall the Germans there. And now it faced the necessity of scattering its rather slender forces in Algeria and Morocco, to safeguard lines of communication, to meet the desert guerrillas, to keep watch on Spain! Relying upon the assurances of Mr. Robert Murphy, the American command had believed that help would come from every side. In fact, out of all the negotiations long since carried on with military men in Africa and with General Giraud, through M. Lemaigre-Dubreuil,[3] there resulted only the fifth column, which, in vital spots, interfered for some precious hours with the setting in motion of the local defenses. A useful action but limited to the Algiers military area and incomplete, a mere preliminary.

The hardy men who volunteered to be the vanguard of the American Expeditionary Force—a mixed lot of Gaullists, royalists cut loose from the *Action Française,* and recent seceders from Vichy—performed wonders. But they were comparatively few in number. Since 1940 all nuclei of resistance had been destroyed under Weygand and Darlan. In the circumstances they could get only scanty help from the consuls and agents of the United States. They put under arrest generals reputedly loyal to the marshal, circulated false orders, took temporary control of the telegraph and telephone network. For half a day they delayed the reaction of the Vichy machine in the principal city of Algeria, and then American

[2]The fighting was hardest at Port-Lyautey; there the first regiment of Moroccan sharpshooters (Colonel Petit) hurled the American landing parties back into the sea. It had thirteen officers killed. At Oran, General Marshall's old regiment lost one third of its strength.

[3]Lemaigre-Dubreuil can be taken as the specimen of those industrialists who had all too often "collaborated" with the Nazis and, as early as 1941, paved their way toward the dollar. In the summer of 1942 they became aware of some gaps in Germany's source of supply, which emboldened them to take their chances. By marriage, Lemaigre-Dubreuil is related to the Lesieur family, owners of peanut-oil refineries spread from Dunkirk to Dakar. In his capacity as purveyor for Rommel's army he moved freely both in France and in the Empire. He boasts that his contacts with Robert Murphy began during the first half of 1941. American confirmation of the national revolution carried through thanks to Germany: that was the program in view. M. Lemaigre-Dubreuil was the former president of the Taxpayers Association, a body of agitators which came in for its fair share of responsibility on February 6, 1934.

troops marched in. They could do no more. For a while the outcome looked somewhat uncertain, and the enemy was left enough time to consolidate its foothold at Bizerte and Tunis. The resident general, Admiral Esteva, and the naval prefect, Admiral Derrien, were sticklers for military discipline. Their first impulse was to turn against the Germans, but they were called to order by Admiral Platon, a Secretary of State in Vichy, whose duties were not related to national defense. Platon had no business to interfere. Nonetheless, with the name of Pétain on his lips, he persuaded both admirals to help the Germans. Derrien delivered to them a dozen small warships. The military commander, General Barré, was of a more enlightened patriotism, but did little beyond taking his own troops out of the trap.[4]

Throughout the whole military administrative hierarchy only two men were found with the courage to revolt: General Mast at Algiers, the true leader of the local fifth column, and General Béthouart at Casablanca. The latter was promptly jailed since he had not found enough support around him to place Noguès under arrest. With many others the former[5] was saved from the clutches of the state police only by the somewhat belated arrival of American units. All the rest, and first of them Noguès, telephoned wildly to find out whether they had to deal with a large-scale American operation or with a brief commando raid. These wise men thought they faced nothing more than a commando. The amazing fact is that Anglo-American power bursting over Africa, with its wonderful promise of emancipation, should have been greeted by more bullets than handclasps. Weygand and his successors had placed the dissidents under lock and key. It was enough to sterilize the most prolonged political and economic preparations. How far remote all such scenes, from the spontaneous uprising of the people at St. Nazaire in March! Vichy-minded men in North Africa constituted a sort of jellylike protoplasm, not easily galvanized to action by the notion of national duty. They lived among fascist landowners and merchants who had made money out of the war, they were dominated by groups of fanatics, cynics, and irresistibly drawn to seek peace and quiet by passively obey-

[4]Vichy's land and sea forces had been concentrated in Morocco against the Anglo-American threat. But in Tunisia, which lay open to German and Italian initiative, there was only a small garrison. Which proves the hypocrisy of the shibboleth by which Weygand set so much store: Any aggressor, whoever he may be, will be held off! Esteva, a devout Roman Catholic, boasts that he never shaved and never married so as to give more time to his professional duties than any other sailor! He longed for the life of a hermit in the Sahara Desert. He wanted to emulate Father de Foucauld.

[5]He was locked up for several hours while the generals who themselves had been arrested the night before were set free.

ing Pétain's instructions. But, luckily, there was an unforeseen element. There was Darlan.

From Vichy he had returned to Algiers as a result of a telegram announcing the serious illness of his son. On November 8, at one in the morning, he was roused from his sleep by General Juin, who called him on the telephone with Mr. Murphy by his side. The American command might well feel disturbed about the unexpected resistance offered to the landing. Moreover, the day before, at Gibraltar, it had not been able to come to an agreement with General Giraud on operational methods.[6] Now Giraud's assumed popularity had been the yeast wherewith the American command had thought to leaven the French military dough. Giraud was not to arrive in Algiers until the ninth, two days later than had been arranged. His proclamations were issued before he set foot on African soil.

Darlan was given the choice between two courses: Either he would be taken into custody by the American command and become, for all practical purposes, a prisoner of war; or he would place his authority and influence over the armed forces at the disposal of the Allies and behave, so to speak, as the *deus ex machina* called in to resolve the crisis. Obviously, Giraud did not possess the magnetism with which he had been credited. Among military officers loyalty to Pétain threatened to prove stronger than any other collective feeling. The American com-

---

[6]General Giraud escaped from the Koenigstein fortress on April 17, 1942, to the great detriment of the negotiations then in progress between Laval and the Germans. On an earlier page the reader has already come across him (May 1940). As a member of the Superior War Council ever since 1938, Giraud shared the errors of the High Command, especially with regard to the use of tanks and planes. Earlier, when military governor of Metz, he was continuously at odds with his subordinate, Colonel de Gaulle, who headed a tank group. Politically, Giraud belongs to the extreme Right, and Gamelin had a difficult time saving him from the vengeance of Daladier, whom his impromptu speeches to officers on tours of inspection had deeply irritated. In Giraud's eyes Republican institutions were to blame for the disaster. Personally honest, but endowed with a rather narrow intellect, he was famed for his dashing spirit and the response to it he got from his men. Through Lemaigre-Dubreuil, Murphy singled him out for the battle of Africa, on the theory that the average Frenchman, equally disgusted with Pétain, with England, and with de Gaulle, would rally to the brilliant "escapist." And since they could not extract from General de Gaulle any commitment with regard to their frontiers, the Poles lent their support. One of their emissaries, General Kleber, spent several weeks with Giraud. In his report Kleber said: "He is perfectly willing to work *with the Americans* but not with the British." Indeed, exchanging letters with General Eisenhower, on November 2, Giraud specified that British troops were not to land in Africa except in case of need and with his own approval. Giraud's political innocence comes out in the letter he sent to Pétain on May 4, 1942, to pledge unbounded loyalty to the marshal. Therein he bestowed his blessings upon the policy of collaboration as carried out by Darlan and Laval under Pétain's guidance. Later Pucheu was to come to North Africa with Giraud's approval.

mand could find no better way of retrieving its fortune than by compelling Giraud to give way to Darlan, the very man whom Pétain had made supreme military commander on land, on sea, and in the air. Darlan did not relish being driven into such a hot corner. He was enraged. Then he cooled down, and for three days he thought it over. I am told that Darlan kept a political diary which was hastily extracted out of the safe in his office a few minutes after he died. Let us hope against hope that Darlan's intimate deliberations with himself were sincerely recorded in those pages and that the naval officer who purloined them will not tamper with the text for the sake of the admiral's posthumous justification. It ought to prove a wonderful human document.

The Admiral of the Fleet wondered, as did Noguès and so many others, whether he was confronted with a powerful American expeditionary force or merely with a transient foray. Some ten days earlier, at the time of his first trip through Algiers, he had told Mr. Murphy: "If ever your people come here, they had better come in strength!" Possibly he knew something of the impending German counterstroke and was impressed by the scope of Nazi preparations. Possibly he found the American Expeditionary Force grossly inadequate. But there were other considerations which must have preyed on his mind more deeply. Would it be possible for him, the promoter of the Vichy national revolution all through so many months, to bring his own subordinates round to the Allies' cause, at a few hours' notice, and to stop the fighting he had carefully prepared for so long? And even if he succeeded, would not a fearful Nemesis rise, sooner or later, from the victory of the Allies to visit him with retributive justice? Of course British and Americans would pledge themselves to protect him against the fury of a redeemed French nation. But such pledges could not always be fulfilled. Even now what had become of the agreement Giraud had concluded with Eisenhower? Nothing was left of it but a scrap of paper. Any arrangement Darlan might come to with the London and Washington governments, which were always disconcertingly amenable in the long run to the dictates of public opinion, was bound to be very precarious.

Looking at the future, how could he expect to clear himself of the charges which, on account of the policy carried out during his premiership, would be leveled at him in a France reborn to free institutions, once he had joined the Allies? So great a tergiversation in North Africa was enough to debar him from ever alleging that his unbounded devotion to the marshal and his absolute compliance with the rules of military discipline accounted for his whole conduct. Nobody, then, would stand by him. He would be abominated by everybody. He would be exposed as a leader utterly devoid of principle, as an out-and-out opportunist. He could not lay claim to any nobility of purpose whatever. Such was the train of ideas which revolved in Darlan's mind. No vigorous decision emerged from it. He sought refuge in duplicity. On the one hand, he gave the American command the assurances it insisted on getting from him, as he did not want to put up with the harsh treatment which would surely be meted out to a vassal of Pétain or to forsake altogether the chance of participation in an allied victory. On the other hand, he stood forth more than ever as the defender of the "national revolution" and paraded his conviction that all the steps he took were in accordance with the inner thoughts of the marshal. The worst of it was that he questioned his own ability to stop the mechanism of resistance to the Anglo-Saxon "invaders" he had personally devised. Thereupon his effort could not be wholehearted. There is some authority for the story that, from the very room where he was closeted with Murphy, Darlan managed to communicate with the admiral in command of coastal defenses and ordered him to train his guns on the "invaders." But I shall not build on this incident.

He had turned to the marshal as early as November 8, begging him to halt the fight. On November 10 he reiterated his appeal. On both occasions an injunction to hand over his military powers to Noguès was the only answer which he received. He had to make his choice between Vichy and the Western Powers. This time how could he avoid taking sides? A lesser opportunist would have been caught, but not he. Being as slippery as an eel, he escaped out of the dilemma. On November 11 he let it be known that a coded message from his right-hand man in Vichy, Admiral Auphan, had conveyed to him the secret approval of Pétain. November 11! On that very day the Germans had entered the free zone and Pétain became a closely guarded prisoner. It was open to Darlan to pretend that any public reproof issued by Vichy was only a concession to German pressure and should be treated as such.

Auphan's "coded message" bids fair to have been little more than a fiction invented by Darlan to further his own ends and to make it possible for him to pursue an ambiguous course.[7] Anyhow, it can be con-

---

[7] I am told from a responsible source that a message was actually received from a Commander Jouanin, a friend of Darlan and Auphan. It was rather cryptically drafted (*"Nous ferons Fort Chabrol"*) but could be construed as an indication that Vichy was going to resist the Nazis. Was Jouanin merely speaking for himself?

tended that the trick had beneficent results and was therefore to be considered a successful stratagem. Gathering courage, Noguès, Chatel, Bergeret, Boisson joined the Admiral of the Fleet and two days later, on November 13, agreed to serve under him in a newfangled government of North Africa. Darlan's friends can reasonably maintain that the game was worth the candle.

Reluctantly, on November 8, Darlan issued for the first time the order to cease fire. Reluctantly, on November 10, he renewed it—twenty-four hours after the fact had become known that, outside the perimeter of Algiers, fighting had continued as fiercely as ever. At last, French resistance having ceased in Morocco[8] and in the Oran area on the morning of November 11, did he then readily agree to concern himself with Tunisia, to interfere with Admiral Esteva, Admiral Derrien, and with General Barré? Not at all.

General Clark wrangled with Darlan on November 8, 9, 10. On November 11 he overcame the hesitation of the admiral regarding Tunisia only by going to the length of using threats. With Auphan's "coded message" supposedly in his pocket, Darlan pleaded complete helplessness on the ground that he was Pétain's obedient servant and, as such, not entitled to take any initiative of his own. And a few hours later, after he had given way, staff officers were there to intercept his orders and hold them in suspense on the pretext that Noguès would soon arrive in Algiers and that nothing could be done without him. As to the generals in command of the troops, they refused to have them entrained for Tunis and led them back to the barracks. At last, listening to the Vichy radio, they had understood that Pétain disowned Darlan. Tunisia would have to be reconquered.

In a similar but less tragic juncture Admiral Robert is reported to have said: "You don't realize how painful it is to have to choose between military honor and patriotic duty." High-sounding words, but uttered to conceal sordid sentiments and calculations, unsurpassed hypocrisy. For some months Darlan had foreseen that Americans and British would, someday, throw their net over North Africa, and with the opportunism ingrained in him he contemplated casting his lot with them. But he had not anticipated that such an early date as the first ten days

---

[8]Noguès informed Mr. William Stoneman (*Daily Telegraph,* February 15, 1943) that he brought resistance to an end after he had caused the German general who was head of the Disarmament Commission in Morocco to verify the fact that his means were exhausted. Therefore, on his own admission, he did not bow to Darlan's leadership as long as he could go on with the fight. On November 8 he retorted to Darlan, who first approached him on the telephone: "Is this not an American officer who is talking? How am I to know?"

of November had been selected nor a spot so far east as Algiers. He was allowed no respite to make his own arrangements. He was not ready to face the emergency. He did not boldly make up his mind. He finessed for three long days when quick and unflinching resolution was needed. In Morocco, in western Algeria, and in Tunisia, where on November 10 the Germans began to get a foothold, thousands of French sailors and soldiers have paid with their lives the price of Darlan's ignominy.

In the destruction of the main part of the French fleet, at Toulon, Darlan's responsibility is not less deeply involved. Darlan endeavored, on November 11, and perhaps even before, to bring that force to North African waters. But on the opposite shore of the Mediterranean, American power did not weigh with the admirals as it weighed with Noguès, Bergeret, Chatel, and Boisson. Instead the German menace hung over them. And in order to reject Darlan's entreaties they had only to quote Darlan's orders and instructions, both old and recent. The destruction of the fleet originated in the fact that the Darlan of November 11, 1942, was in conflict with an earlier Darlan.

In 1940, 1941, 1942, he had arranged for his ships to be scuttled to avoid their seizure by the Germans. It had never entered his mind that a day might come when even so hardened a collaborationist as he would wish the French squadrons to join the British and Americans. As late as February 1942 he was still ordering the *Dunkerque* back to Toulon. On November 11, taking suddenly a stand obviously not expected by anyone, his appeal fell in a vacuum. It has been said that there was not sufficient fuel available. But if the hypothesis of a resumption of the struggle against Germany had really been contemplated in a relatively near future, would not the small supplies needed have been built up, at least enough for a certain number of vessels to leave? It was not necessary for the ships to traverse thousands of miles in order to be safe. Darlan's appeal from Algiers evoked no response because it was in contradiction with all the instructions which he had issued during a period of thirty months. To be certain that those instructions would be carried out in all circumstances he had even secretly sent supplementary orders forbidding all concerned to obey if, in a crisis, he countermanded the steps planned so long before. You will have to consider, he wrote, that I am no longer free. No admiral was more intimately connected with Darlan than Auphan, Secretary of State for the Navy under Laval and chief of the General Staff. On November 11 he wrote to Grand Admiral Raeder begging him to "keep in mind what the French Navy had done since the Armistice" (some "fifty warships sunk or damaged and thousands of dead and wounded"), "to respect it and to respect also the independence of the marshal for which it had fought. . . ." On November 12, Raeder answered that "the German Commander did not intend to deny the French Navy the esteem it had deserved by its attitude. . ." Incidentally, reading these sentences, it is hard to believe that the same day Auphan conveyed to Darlan the encouragement of Pétain in the secret message already referred to. Auphan, who had parted with Darlan in Vichy less than a week before, was entitled to believe that, through disregarding Darlan's appeals, he remained true to him.[9]

The suicide of the French fleet proves how sincere Darlan had been at Berchtesgaden, in May 1941, when he offered Hitler his services. Naturally he feared then that the Germans might push him so far into collaboration as to be able afterward to dispense with his personal help, and he sought to forestall their extreme demands by confirming the scuttling orders of the preceding year. But he never paid any serious attention to the possibility of putting the fleet back into the war against the Nazis.

Our American friends are perhaps more inclined to rejoice that so many French ships rest on the bottom of the sea and that they never were incorporated in the German and Italian navies. A magnificent result, surely! The fate of the Nazis was so completely settled that Darlan himself crept out from under the deal made with Germany. The "free zone" evaporated—the free zone Vichy had purchased at the price of accepting the armistice and putting up with the most outrageous German demands. And still the main battle fleet, the last embodiment of French power, the impregnable citadel of French resistance, stayed at its moorings. So rigorous had been the measures devised by Darlan to keep it fixed there, so perverted in their patriotism were his subordinates,[10] that even he was not able, at a dire moment of the nation's need,

---

[9] Admiral de Laborde, the commander in chief of the High Seas Forces at Toulon, was a convinced fascist and no friend of Darlan. He ranked foremost among French admirals and yet, in the summer of 1940, he was cheated of the functions and honors heaped on Esteva, Decoux, Abrial, etc. In a communiqué to the staffs and crews under him, on November 15, he stigmatized as the work of foreign agents the current talk about German interference in Toulon and mentioned the admiration of the military authorities of the Axis for the heroism of the second light squadron (which had fought at Casablanca on November 8) and the other naval forces in North Africa!

[10] Vice-Admiral Michelier, in command at Casablanca, is a sample of the whole lot. He had served on the Wiesbaden Commission. It seems that he was in a temper with the Germans. Yet he obeyed Noguès rather than Darlan. Not only did he sacrifice his warships; he had a number of merchantmen scuttled, including the liner *Gouverneur Genéral Laferrière,* sunk close to Oran harbor against American ships.

to untangle the knot he had tied. Seemingly it would have taken an American commando raid on the spot to fill our vessels' bunkers and get them under steam.

That man had perhaps done more than any other in the creation of the magnificent 1939–40 Navy, finer than anything we had had afloat since the days of Colbert, certainly since 1850–60. He was the godson of Georges Leygues, repeatedly Minister of the Navy between 1917 and 1929. The Minister and his right-hand man, Darlan, were skillful enough in getting huge sums from Parliament. Let Darlan have due credit for it. But he made this navy into his personal tool. A general officer who knew him as an ensign on board the destroyer *Chamois,* in 1907, describes him as already pulling political strings to benefit his immediate superiors, his messmates, the officer his sister had married. This Gascon had politics in his blood. As far back as we look in his career he is invariably to be seen leading his gang.

A few more touches may be added to the portrait. In 1939, since he had not succeeded in having himself named chief of staff for national defense, he tried to make up for his disappointment by having an ancient title revived for him, "Amiral de France," the equivalent of "Marshal de France," as he chose to call it. He sought to drag Gamelin along with him in a joint plea to Daladier. Marshal of France Gamelin, Admiral of France Darlan! What imposing figures in the turmoil of the mobilization! And what magnificent statues to adorn the temple of Victory or its porticos in years to come! As a spur to the spirit of our soldiers and sailors on the eve of the war, there was surely nothing exaggerated in reviving an office which has not been awarded any man since the seventeenth century. Gamelin had the good sense to refuse any part in the scheme; Darlan could call himself by no higher title than Admiral of the Fleet. But when he became vice-premier in 1941 he hastened to have seven stars sewn upon his sleeves. He conferred upon himself the naval marshalship which he had first tried to ferret out among the ancient trappings of monarchy. And all this long-sustained intrigue only to send a squadron into action against the very life of his own country on November 8 and to stand by in tears, on the twenty-seventh, while Toulon turned into a graveyard of hulls! What admiral ever more shamefully lost the battles which he might have won? Darlan is the Bazaine of the sea.

He was assassinated on December 24. We know today what sort of vengeance nerved the arm which struck him down. Fernand Bonnier de Lachapelle was a member of the Youth Organization mobilized on

November 7 to do fifth-column work in the interest of the Allies. He had royalist affiliations and may have believed that Darlan's disappearance might help the Count of Paris to his throne. Anyhow, Darlan, as he saw him, was a traitor to national independence and a force still capable of jeopardizing France's salvation.[11]

The legendary good luck of the admiral was merely interrupted by the revolver which laid him down. In a sense this good luck continued after he was in the grave. The American emissaries had been working to clear the way on the idea that Noguès, Boisson, and others might be induced to desert Pétain. They had been frustrated by the cowardice of these people. Darlan unexpectedly provided them with a substitute. They eagerly fell back upon it and gladly merged the admiral in the setup which they had long been seeking to effect and which came to very little. They, therefore, endowed Darlan with the attributes of a leader whose fundamental patriotism could never be questioned and who, even though he had played with Hitler, was merely awaiting the happy moment, the lucky junction of the forces at his command with the swelling Anglo-American power, to save his country. What had in fact been only crafty bargaining with the Allies by a discomfited Darlan is now held up to us as a gallant assault upon the enemy.

How about the record of the rest of them in continental France when they were confronted with the turn of the Anglo-American tide? With the practical certainty or, at least, the likelihood of an allied victory, the men in responsible positions did not break the shackles of the marshal's discipline there any more than elsewhere, not even in Darlan's underhand and halting manner. Yet, since the summer, some of the industrialists, because of their closeness to events in Germany, had discovered her internal weakness, and Pétain had been kept informed.

One may ask how much could have been done. It would at least have been possible to save the fleet and to ship across the Mediterranean a few thousand officers, assets of valor and patriotic spirit, with which the Army of Vichy was more richly supplied than that of Africa. But as the

---

[11]Bonnier de Lachapelle was shot within forty-eight hours. All regular procedure was omitted. No investigation was made. Until the last minute he was induced to believe that nothing more than a mock execution was contemplated. The military authorities did not wish to know about the plot and its ramifications. A leader of the Youth Organization and a priest, a former Jesuit who had more or less broken with the discipline of the Church and as military intelligence officer shared in the work of the fifth column, wielded a powerful influence over the young man, the son of a local journalist and of an Italian mother. The Count of Paris hastened to Algiers in the naïve belief that the vacant presidency of the "Imperial Council" was about to devolve upon him.

Americans and the British did not appear on the scene to give the required push, the marshal's congenital apathy—all the greater under Laval's control—was not seriously disturbed. Only at the level of divisional commanders and below did the spirit of sacrifice and revolt give signs of life. Once again let us bow to General de Lattre de Tassigny and other leaders of unshakable faith.

The wooden image did not stir in its Vichy niche. All of a sudden the governmental setting so dear to Pétain's heart was blown away. It was a mendacious governmental setting, but he took it, or affected to take it, at its face value. The rhythm of his daily life in the little city on the Allier River went on undisturbed. His fleet was sunk, his army dissolved; nothing survived of the restricted autonomy his administrative machine had retained under the invader for twenty-nine months. France was turned into a fortress. Her coasts bristled with guns. The Germans spent, in these fortifications, the billions piled to their credit for which they had not been able to find any use. The daily tribute was raised from three hundred to five hundred millions. Did Pétain mind? Probably, but the outside world never knew. He was told that thousands and thousands of workers were trucked off to Germany,[12] that thousands and thousands of men, among them many officers, were sent into internment beyond the Rhine, that officials, advisers of his—Weygand, for instance—were taken away from French territory and assigned forced

---

[12]In his speech of June 22, 1942, Laval divulged the agreement for the "exchange" of war prisoners against workers he had to enforce by means of pressure which by degrees turned into sheer coercion. On June 11, at a ceremony staged by the Legion, Pétain had identified himself completely with Laval: "He has won my utter confidence, not only through his words but through his deeds. . . ." Emboldened by this tribute, Laval shortly afterward announced, "I want Germany to win." Here is a fairly complete survey of Laval's labor policy published in November 1943. The arrangement of June 1942 provided for the transportation to Germany of 350,000 French workers (including 150,000 skilled workers). The arrangements of December 1942 and April 1943 increased the above figures by 240,000 and 230,000 respectively. In the last batch 180,000 were marked out for service in the Todt organization and in German armament factories on French soil. Out of the total number of 820,000—750,000 had actually been taken away by August 1943. Moreover, 150,000 "volunteers" (including 50,000 foreigners living in France) had "enlisted" before June 1942 and 250,000 war prisoners had "agreed" to serve in German industry. Conscription of labor, which Laval enforced by law on February 16, 1943, fatally accounts for such brilliant results which mere administrative pressure would not have secured. The whole system was screwed up with the appointment of Joseph Darnand as "Secretary to the maintenance of order" (December 31, 1943). On the one hand, the Nazi and the reorganized French Gestapo tried hard to exterminate all defaulters, partisans, guerrillas. On the other hand, a form of national service was enacted. In March 1944, if records stolen from Vichy can be trusted, 3,300,000 Frenchmen were detained in Germany: 1,250,000 prisoners of war, 1,000,000 or more conscripted labor, 300,000 political deportees. Jews, Alsatians, and inhabitants of the northern departments made up the balance.

residences. He was told that more and more patriots fell before Hitler's firing squads—perhaps two or three or four tens of thousands up to this day. No protest ever came from him except in one case. He threatened to resign if the Nazis got hold of Jacques Rueff, dismissed in 1940 from his subgovernorship of the Bank of France because of his Jewish birth. Pétain is godfather to Rueff's little girl. Laval's government, his own government after all, has been turned into a factional government, a gangsters' government supported by the bands of Darnand, Doriot, etc. No word of disavowal on his part has been reported by any foreign ambassador. On December 31, 1943, Joseph Darnand became the French equivalent of Himmler, the head of a French Gestapo equipped with the same weapons as the German Gestapo. Repressive action under all its forms and the food rationing services were entrusted to him—a sinister combination of duties. Today some fifty thousand desperadoes are being embrigaded by Darnand, and they will be called upon, in the forthcoming crisis, to rescue what will remain of the National Revolution and its personnel. Did Pétain even notice it?

Had Pétain's silence been complete, he might be allowed the excuse of an implicit abdication, but that plea does not hold. On November 19, 1942, he delegated the signature of all decrees to Laval. The same day, on the radio, he urged the Army in Africa to repel the "Anglo-Saxon invasion." The marshal did not leave unanswered the messages which Hitler sent to him on November 11 and 26, before the invasion of the free zone and the entry into Toulon respectively. At least he affixed his name to the replies drafted by Laval. He declared himself ready to receive General von Rundstedt, the military administrator of France. Afterward, not more than before, did he live up to the theory, his theory, that the Head of the French State had disappeared on November 11, 1942, and that a prisoner of war—one among some twelve hundred and fifty thousand prisoners of war—survived on the ruins of the Vichy structure. By the middle of November 1943 he vainly attempted to address the French people on the radio. Was he to utter some proud words? No; he wished to tell them that at the earliest opportunity he intended to call back the National Assembly of 1940 and return to it the "mandate" forcibly wrested from a terrorized majority on July 10 of that year. That gesture (which did not materialize, owing to German interference) was not of Pétain's invention. Frightened politicians of the Moysset-Romier type planned it. They were in fear of the new governmental authority forming in Algiers. Pétain wanted all to know that the means had been found to prevent that authority from ever asserting itself. At last, in

April 1944, he was allowed to raise his voice, but for the special purpose of reminding the French nation that in the impending campaign of France it must loyally stand by the German Army.

In the Teutonic sense of the word, *marshal* originally meant a slave in charge of the horses. Pétain has dragged down the marshalship to its original significance.

The gravediggers may try to worm their way into the victory of the British, the Americans, and the Russians. The reconstituted Republic will deal with them as with men of death. Their lackeys would have us forget their criminal record. "The unity of France is at stake!" they cry. "If we try to set up a sort of last judgment there will be no end to it!" But unity is the very last word to use in connection with men like those of Bordeaux and those of Vichy, who themselves all but destroyed the very principle of unity, the soul of the nation.

The suggestion, then, is that these men should recover their positions and their influence in the commonwealth of tomorrow. But how can "extenuating circumstances" be granted to men who sold the freedom of the country cheap? Is it to be expected that, once more active in public life, they would beat their chests in self-reproach and turn into blameless patriots? Their aim seems rather to show their earlier behavior under a favorable light. They would make capital of everything to demonstrate that they were not so far wrong in the past. They would seek their revenge. They would try to befog that clear vision of a period packed with guilt and crime, without which there can be no salvation for our people. And their following would consolidate round them fast enough! The moment a Vichy number two seemed to be springing up in Africa under the patronage of the Allies, the human castoffs began to agitate and to speak once more, the same men who, at the sign of the forthcoming German defeat, had shrunk away to nothing. If "clemency" were to win the day, Vichy would not cease to exist. In some shape or form it would remain one of the poles of the Republic. The counterrevolutionaries of 1940 have deepened the schism of 1789. If the authors of defeat and dictatorship remain intact in any corner of the French world, this aggravated schism will become permanent.

Amnesty and national reconciliation are exclusive of each other. If, in the anxious moment which liberation necessarily brings with it, the French people do not feel that their government is animated by a new spirit, the old quarrels will automatically spring up all the more embittered by the recent dissensions. The only chance of reuniting the nation is to raise to power men speaking a language not yet heard in our political life.

Of course we cannot hope for unanimity. There will be too many victims, too many new poor, too much rancor among us. But the greatest possible measure of national reunion can be achieved only by a leadership which cannot be charged either with the faults of the Republic or the abominable actions of Vichy.

As for Vichy, the crime of those who belonged to it far exceeds the guilt of the émigrés in 1790–94. The latter remained loyal to an old France which was inconsistent with the France of the Revolution. They fought for a France which no longer existed, but they did not dream that France might disappear. What they did could have led to the ruin of the country, and they were rightly charged with treason, but in what they endeavored to do they were simply led astray by chimerical notions born of their yearning for a noble past. In contrast the ideology of the New Order was aimed at no such chimera. It failed of realization only by a hairsbreadth. All those who lamented what was called "traditional France" did not follow Maurras in his acceptance of the armistice. Many of them have proved it by their valor under the cross of Lorraine. Let us hope that even more of them, having suffered from the schism of our own times, will recognize how dangerous was the old schism dating back to the Revolution. But they would not have anything to do with a regime which sank back into the spinelessness of the Third Republic, into perpetual forgiveness of all sins.

II

At the close of this study it is impossible to evade the question so eagerly discussed all over the world. Is what happened in France a mere accident, or does it point to her decadence? Five times within less than six generations our country has been invaded, and four times our capital city has fallen into the hands of the enemy. Seen in such a perspective, the 1940 disaster resembles the final illness of a sick man whose reserves of strength have gradually been sapped and who recovers from each successive crisis only by a spasmodic effort. Military defeat, however complete, is only a passing evil, provided that it is not repeated. But are not four utter disasters in less than a century and a half symptoms of incurable weakness?

There is no need to dwell on the lessening of relative material power evidenced for more than a hundred years. The annual birth rate has indeed dropped by 40 per cent. In 1810 the French population amounted to 15 per cent of the population of Europe; in 1930, to only 8 per cent.

All too often French production has evinced that timidity, that fear of incurring risks, which go by the name of Malthusianism, and during the course of the transition from the agricultural to the industrial era, our country failed to hold its own. But, leaving all that on one side, is it not true that since 1918 men have come into power—we have seen them at work all through the sad pages of this essay—of whom the worst were traitors and the best were head and shoulders beneath their predecessors in public office? When did we see those entrusted with the responsibilities of government surrounded by a ruling class and a Parisian society so narrow in outlook, and so deep an apathy in the country as a whole in the face of mortal danger? Within less than one hundred and thirty years the constitution has been overthrown eight times, if not more. Every possible form of government has been tried out: an absolute and (for a few days) a liberalized form of imperial power, constitutional monarchy inclining to despotism, parliamentary monarchy, an almost socialist republic, a reactionary republic degenerating into dictatorship, an authoritarian empire, a liberal empire, a government of national defense imposed by the Parisian mob under the fast-growing shadow of German invasion, a National Assembly with the Commune at its heels, a conservative republic, a radical republic, a popular-front republic, and, under the fire of the enemy, a counterrevolution. Leaving the revolutionary period of 1789 aside, and counting only the nineteenth century, there are months, weeks, or days of civil strife to be found in 1815, in 1830-35, 1848, 1851, 1870, 1871. Behind all these phenomena is not to be detected an increasing debility of the spirit of sacrifice, of the collective resolve not to allow a great inheritance to perish, which are the true foundations of any commonwealth?

We are at a great turning point of human history. We can vaguely discern a new civilization in the making. Liberal institutions are on the wane. The trend is toward new forms of society which we cannot yet see clearly but which differ as much from the legacy of 1789 as it differed from monarchy by divine right. In the same way the monarchy of Louis XIV, consolidated and glorified, cut short the social, religious, and aristocratic disturbances of the fourteenth, fifteenth, and sixteenth centuries, while that turbulent era was in sharp contrast with the feudal world and, at an earlier remove, with Charlemagne's shriveled little universe. Four times within nine hundred years, starting with the day when Hugh Capet, the petty sovereign who carried "St. Martin's cope," went to and fro in his little realm, between Paris, Laon, Chartres, and Orléans, France has been ahead of others in trying now modes of government and ordered life.[13] And on the intellectual level, she has, more than any other country, assimilated and fructified the Greco-Latin heritage—the noblest and most lovely flower of human experience. Assuredly I have no desire to minimize Renaissance Italy, which recaptured the spirit of the ancient world. Still, perhaps more than those of any other country, our classic writers are the heirs of the Attic tradition. When it found its way once more to the surface, the fountain of Arethusa watered our soil by preference.

If she is to be true to herself, our country should today play the foremost part in shaping the coming age. And yet until 1940, before she fell, she had reacted badly to the new circumstances. Are we, then, at the end of France's history? With all its renown, will our people merely sink

[13]"If we observe the general state of European civilization after the Carolingian period, we see that nearly all its essential characteristics made their appearance in France earlier than elsewhere, and also that it was in France that they achieved their most perfect expression. This applies to religious as well as secular life. The Order of Cluny, the Order of the Cistercians, and the Order of the Premonstrants had their birth in France; the Order of the Chivalry was a French creation, and it was from France that the Crusades drew their most numerous and most enthusiastic recruits. It was in France, too, at the beginning of the twelfth century, that Gothic art suddenly rose as from the soil and imposed its supremacy on the world, and in France the first *chansons de geste* made their appearance. All these coincidences were not merely fortuitous. That so many eminent personalities should have existed in one country, that the basin of the Seine, from the tenth century onward, should have been the scene of so many achievements and so many innovations, means that there must have existed there, as in Greece, in the Attica of the fifth century, an environment which was peculiarly favorable to the manifestations of human energy. And it is a fact that the two great social forces which sprang from the ruins of the Carolingian Empire to constitute a new Europe—the monastic and the feudal system—were nowhere so active and so predominant as in northern France. . . . Thus the ascendancy of French civilization long antedated the ascendancy of the French monarchy." (H. Pirenne, *A History of Europe*.) And the Belgian historian goes on to cite the "courteous manners," the supreme part played by the University of Paris, foster mother of the University of Prague and thereby of the German universities, promoter of scholastic Latin, which spread from Paris, and of the *langue d'oïl*. Similar remarks could be made with reference to St. Louis and all he stands for, to Louis XIV and to the Revolution of 1789.

Doubtless France's contribution to civil and political liberties came later than England's. Once a centralized and absolute state had at one stroke been brought into being at Westminster by the Norman conquest, all the forces of emancipation conspired to limit the kingly power and to hedge it round with charters; whereas in Capetian France it devolved upon the same forces to uphold the monarch against the semi-independent principalities which tried to arrest the decay of the feudalism. The revolution of 1789, however, gave a universal and terribly dynamic expression to what had been, on the other side of the channel, a gradual process of regularizing and defining privileges. To say this implies no depreciation of England's contribution. One might even claim that public liberties won by aristocrats are more solidly established than those created by the legal mind. But I am here discussing merely the effect produced upon other peoples. Our revolution, with its unparalleled violence, exceeded all others in explosive power. In Ste.-Beuve's words it "popularized equalitarian principles."

into a state of vegetation? Will it lose caste like bankrupt noblemen who retire to an encumbered estate in the country and, little by little, with coats of arms carved in the wall, resume the manners of their peasant ancestors? Are those whom I have called the "gravediggers" merely the agents of ineluctable necessity? Such is the sum of what can be said to make us fear that our country will never recover.

For a Frenchman, even in the depth of today's humiliation, there is much to sustain his hopes that refuse to die. As regards the statisticians' demographic curves and their birth and mortality rates, we have only to apply them to Europe as a whole to feel less disturbed. It is not a problem peculiar to France. From decade to decade the population expanded all through eastern and southeastern Europe, while it stagnated in the west and in the north. France shares the fate of all the nations facing the Atlantic. Is it extravagant to think that after these years of agony the west will manage to solve this problem like many others? We are not here confronted with a specific sign of French decadence.

Nor are our upheavals of the nineteenth century in any way decisive. In comparison with the period between the accession of Charles IX and that of Louis XIV they seem mild enough. Almost four centuries ago people cried out in Paris, "Better the Spaniards than the Huguenots!" The tribulations through which a nation passes, the number and the fierceness of its gravediggers are not, in themselves, symptoms of weakness. If recovery is swift and violent, it offers the best proof of deep-rooted strength. It might indeed be argued that our "great century" was the outcome of the nine "wars of religion" and of the chaos of the two regencies, that the troubles of the period produced the strong public spirit of that age and fortified Henri IV, Richelieu, Mazarin, and Louis XIV in their achievements. If that be so, no true bill has yet been found against the France of our day.

Another fact deserves some attention. Only a quarter of a century ago our people proved on the battlefield that they were ready to make any sacrifice for the sake of their freedom. In 1918 no man could have said without incurring derision that the French were no longer worthy of their history, unable to defend their soil or to sustain their traditional part in world affairs. The vigor the French Army showed in the struggle so impressed the British and the Americans that they believed their allies were in a fair way to oppressing Europe and feared lest by their harshness and their inordinate demands they might provoke a desperate reaction on the part of the vanquished. As a result the British and the Americans took their stand with immense tenacity against so-called "French imperialism." No doubt they argued at times that, in respect of material resources, France was not cut on the same pattern as the really large empires and that the disproportion between means and aims might imperil the continent. But much more frequently heard was the assertion that French ambitions were altogether boundless and exaggerated. In short, the British and Americans considered us as unduly enterprising. Ten years ago they still denounced us for being the opposite of a power sunk in self-renunciation. Now these same people accuse our country of being "exhausted." Are we, then, to believe that in the course of one generation so fundamental a change has taken place, that a France whose expansion was a matter of British and American apprehension a generation ago, whose vitality was so recently taken for granted to such an extent that on her shoulders was placed almost the whole military responsibility for British and American security, has now been stricken by some mortal consumption? In its lasting values it is altogether probable that the French community of 1943 is very like the French community of 1918. The decay of a people which has lived through a thousand years does not materialize within a single generation. Ancient nations and empires which have perished did not fall so swiftly into the abyss. If the war of 1940 had not been preceded by the conflict of 1914–18 and today's collapse by the magnificent sacrifice of the Marne and of Verdun, our enemies might well proclaim that our great destiny has been forfeited. But the heroism of 1914–18 cannot be dismissed as just a spurt of flame flickering uncertainly among the embers of a dying fire.

The pessimistic thesis, upon which the gravediggers harp so readily, seems to derive some support from the strange character of the military disaster which we have suffered. On May 10, 1940, France was still, in the eyes of the world, a power capable of holding the brutal might of Germany in check. On May 14 the awful blow fell. Only for a very short while did the country make a show of rallying her forces. As we have seen, Gamelin broke down after three or four days of fighting. Physically and morally the country collapsed within a month. Napoleon's blitzkrieg occasionally produced far-reaching results in an equally short time, but war in 1940 aimed at a "total" destruction of the enemy which the men of 1805 and 1806 never conceived. The fall was almost instantaneous, the conquest unlimited both in extent and depth: in this our defeat was unique. Nobody, then, need wonder that so many exclaimed that France was nothing but a medieval suit of armor stuffed with cotton wool. At the first stroke of the mace the flimsy coating of iron was shattered into pieces. Long since there had been no knight in that coat of mail, and behind that shield France's power had survived in the world's esteem only by a kind of trickery. The same note is struck by the well-known theme of Charles Maurras: the French Monarchy never lost battles except insignificant engagements like Rossbach. To lose great battles like Sedan was the specialty of the regimes sprung from the Revolution, whether imperial or republican.

In reply to Maurras, all that need be said is that these two incapable generals whose 43,000 troops were routed by 24,000 Prussians in 1757 cannot lay claim to any credit because they did not bring about France's total ruin. The difference between what happened then and in our time does not lie in any greater strategical or political wisdom on the part of leaders, but rather in the simple fact that the concept of royal legitimacy and of a Christian commonwealth imposed limits on aggression. Moreover, the kingdoms of that era were not organized to play for unlimited stakes. Circumstances account for that state of affairs; kings, ministers, and warriors have nothing to do with it. It happens, however, that the rout at Rossbach recalls in many ways what we ourselves witnessed on the Meuse. Everything was settled within less than an hour and a half by thirty-eight squadrons of cavalry charging "with incredible speed." Apart from this, King Frederick made use of but seven infantry battalions, each man firing a mere five to fifteen rounds. His casualties totaled only 550 killed and wounded as against 7,700 on our side. Detractor Maurras might well have picked a more apposite battle. Moreover the Seven Years' War cost us India and Canada. The loss was therefore greater and more irreparable than that which followed the Sedan of 1870.

Let us dig deeper than any such superficial argument and ask whether from a military point of view France is no longer herself? In the first part of this book chapter and verse have been quoted to prove that our defeat was mainly the fault of the generals. Assuredly this contention of mine and of many others will provoke the retort that a people is collectively responsible for its leaders, that it gets the generals it deserves. If that be so, the most cursory glance at history obliges one to admit that the French people may have deserved the blows that they have had to withstand fairly frequently in the course of the centuries. At the head of the nation capable leaders in war were more numerous than the inept, but the latter have not been lacking. Bad generalship is not a distinctive feature of contemporary France.

Our military tradition is the oldest in Europe—probably because the feudal system developed earlier and more vigorously in northern France than elsewhere. One eminent historian even goes so far as to say that the knights, the professional soldiers of their age and constantly under arms, probably amounted to one tenth of the whole population. Consider the epic achievement of the Normans and Angevins in England, in Sicily, in continental Italy, on the eastern shores of the Adriatic, in Hungary, in Poland, not to mention the exploits of so many other warriors in Palestine, Syria, Constantinople, and Greece. The brilliance of our arms from the eleventh to the fourteenth century was equaled only by the campaigns of the Revolution and the Empire, and it was more lasting. All the same, French chivalry cut a pitiful figure in the Hundred Years' War, so much so that after Crécy and Poitiers its sorry failure played a part in the indignation and rebellion of the peasants, in the Jacquerie of 1358. Thus, even during the vigorous youth of our kingdom, victory sometimes deserted our banners, and, in the fourteenth and fifteenth centuries, with terrible consequences.

Much nearer our own time, similar ups and downs may be seen. Before the military renaissance which culminated in the victory of 1918, France had to put up with strategists alongside of whom Gamelin is a model of foresight, of methodical planning and of intellectual power. The reader need only consult the book written by General H. Bonnal, former commander at the Superior War College, on *The French High Command at the Outset of the Wars of 1859 and of 1870*.[14] He will be duly edified.

In the summer of 1857, when he was already thinking of making war on Austria, Napoleon III gathered the guard at the Châlons camp and, to get his hand in, ordered military maneuvers. "Making every allowance, spectacles comparable only to the military shows of the ancient hippodrome were witnessed day by day . . . In the evening marshals and generals met at Imperial headquarters and there—incredible but absolutely true—in the presence of the sovereign, Marshal Vaillant read to them accounts of the battles of the First Empire from the writings of M. Thiers . . ."[15] From the lessons of Napoleonic warfare, which the great chieftain had not committed to paper in systematic form and of

---

[14]Paris. *Editions de la Revue des Idées et Librairie Militaire*, R. Chapelot et Cie., 1905.

[15]Marshal Vaillant was War Minister. He was so potbellied he could not ride a horse which moved faster than a walk.

which the historian of "the Consulate and the Empire" could only supply a faint literary impression, the French General Staff had derived no living tradition. In their Algerian battles the generals had mastered the art of moving about a few thousand men and a few hundred horses. Their knowledge ended there. Therefore, after Sadowa, they were nonplused by the Prussian operation carried out in a mere eight days. They could not have done as much. Their successes at Magenta and Solferino did not blind them to their own inferiority. But, then, to cheer them up, the chassepot rifle and the first machine guns were introduced. The fire power of small arms, the tactical defensive, the cult of positional warfare in eighteenth-century style and of entrenchments would make good all their deficiencies and would lead them to victory in spite of everything. That is what they sought to believe.

Nobody is entitled to maintain that the French Command's incapacity in 1940 surpassed everything experienced in the past. Even Weygand's and Pétain's political preoccupations may be compared with those of Bazaine.[16]

Marshal von der Goltz's volume, *Rossbach and Iena,* published in 1883, depicts what was wrong with the French military system of 1940: "When in any army old ideas are still in force whereas the new are only beginning to break through in a form as yet undefined, the period of transformation which results is a crisis of the most dangerous sort." This sentence was written about the Prussia of Frederick-William III. The victory of Austerlitz, the author continues, produced among young Prussian officers a wave of reform which broke on the routine of the old generals and came to nothing.

The experience we had to endure on the battlefield, four years ago, is an old, old story. In appraising France's military "decadence," nothing more relevant can be said than this. Napoleon III and his lieutenants in June 1859 defeated the Austrian Army despite their incompetence because they were bold against any odds, because they could still unleash the *"furia francese"* of Fornoue and were ready to meet any challenge. Marshal von Moltke, in his book on the Italian campaign (1862), squarely

---

[16]I do not mean to say that the opportunities for victory which lay within Bazaine's grasp at Rézonville, on August 16, 1870, were likewise preferred to Weygand. But Bazaine, in command of an army, had dreams of an imperial regency. In this sense the leaders of 1940, obsessed with the idea of counterrevolution, are akin to him. Bazaine, shut up in Metz, lied outrageously. Reading his dispatches, one would think that all he sought was to cut his way out. General de MacMahon was ordered by Napoleon III to help him to extricate himself, and another French army was lost. Falsehoods intended to conceal specific weakness or shameful scheming have been known before 1940.

put his finger on the point:[17] "Even though the troops were dispersed and many of the men had lost sight of their colors, every soldier yearned to be in the thick of the fight. Victory was won by the tenacity of the individual French foot soldier, a hardy marcher, self-reliant, and ready to take the initiative." In 1861, Prince Frederick-Charles of Prussia did strike the same note: "No one in the French Army was capable of noticing the tactical errors committed by the High Command. The confidence of the troops in their leaders remained unshaken, whatever the latter did, and in the field the sheer daring of some, the headlong spirit of others, redeemed many a fault." But the General Staffs themselves went into the fight as though to a ball. "Silence, gentlemen; and then take away those flowers!" shouted General Regnaud de St. Jean d'Angely, the morning of Magenta, on the bridge of San Marino. He was addressing his officers "garlanded from head to foot by Italian women and chatting noisily." In a somewhat milder tone, half an hour earlier, General de MacMahon had scolded his own subalterns: "Come, come, gentlemen! Be serious! Don't you hear the artillery?"[18]

What a far cry between the French military world of 1859 and that of our own day! It is easy to see the change both in the leaders and in the rank and file. But need we be surprised? After all, the officers of 1859 had fought the Arabs for a quarter of a century without interruption, and the soldiers enlisted for seven years: in the Latin phrase, their weapons weighed no heavier upon them than their own arms and hands. They belonged to that military family which General de Gaulle wished to create anew in 1934 by means of his professional army.[19] Service by conscription bars all selection; it cannot yield homogeneous groups, the climate in which the "furia" can thrive. Nor should we forget the feeling of impotence instilled by the enemy's possessing equipment and tactics far surpassing our own. Against such inequalities huge sacrifices on the scale of Verdun, whose horrors had been told and retold by the older generation, must have seemed pure waste.

[17]We need not be surprised that the German military leaders should have followed the campaign of 1859 with avid attention. They were already looking ahead to their wars with Austria and France. And these two states provided them with a testing ground before they themselves went into action.

[18]German Bapst, *Le Maréchal Canrobert,* quoted by General Bonnal.

[19]In his book on "Suicide," published early during that century, Emile Durckheim, if I remember rightly, expressly points out that non-commissioned officers, discharged after long years spent in barracks, accounted for the largest single group of those who did away with themselves. Cut off from the old regiment, only painfully could they re-establish themselves in the community. Such was the strength of the regimental ties today destroyed.

Can it be said that seventy-five years of universal suffrage have got the best of the French nation and have left it an easy prey to the plottings of foreigners? Was democracy in France synonymous with national decline? That the French people will continue irresistibly inclined toward the pattern of government which, whatever happens, is likely to survive in what we call the "Occident" is certain. To assert that what happened to our country is attributable to the vices of French democracy would, therefore, amount to admitting that France will not recover but that like wonderful Athens she will perish.

Ernest Renan, in his *Intellectual and Moral Reform,* published in 1871 immediately after the Treaty of Frankfort, undertook to lay bare the deep roots of our misfortunes. The republican faction, he said, will never be strong enough to set up the regime close to its heart. And even if, in despite of wind and tide, it succeeded in doing so, that regime would never have an army or a diplomacy worth the name. Moreover, if it should have happened that the republican state, breaking with the principles of 1789, interfered with private enterprise and private contracts and began meddling with the regulation of industrial and commercial affairs, its ruin would be all the swifter, for "no socialist system has yet appeared with even a semblance of being a possible form of government." He went on to urge a return to the traditional hierarchies, to the former ruling classes, and professed to find salvation in a liberal monarchy which would know how to make the masses swallow the pill of political and social inequality required for the necessary division of labor.

Our experience with the Republic proves Renan mistaken. Universal suffrage and a Parliament were long compatible with a skilled diplomacy, and the army of 1914–18 was formed under popular legislation. Not only in France, but everywhere, the jurisdiction of the state has been steadily growing in scope. As for the break up of the military machine which followed the 1918 victory, and the inept preparations of 1939–40, readers of those pages cannot lay the principal blame on democracy. Our military leadership failed in its duty—a military leadership chosen under the dire test of battle, twenty-five years earlier, but which had become fossilized, at least at the top. The mistake of French ministers and members of Parliament was not to interfere with the High Command and make it feel the weight of its ill will or its dissatisfaction. By and large, all the appropriations requested from Parliament for national defense were voted, and at the Riom trial the state attorney had to register this fact in his bill of particulars. The true failure of French politicians lay rather in keeping aloof and in showing far too great a respect for the powers-that-were in the army, for its "fixed stars."

The same harsh judgment must be entered against other departments of French leadership, whether newly formed or of long standing. None of them lived up to its position of trust. Neither the financial leaders, nor the economic, nor the industrial, nor the legal (I am thinking of the Council of State and of the counterrevolutionary prefects Vichy so easily enlisted among its members), nor the elite entrenched in the Institute of France, nor that more amorphous elite which is dubbed Parisian society and which to a large extent determines the moral atmosphere which the government if not the whole country has to breathe. Alone among them all, the leaders of the Church, selected and encouraged by a great pope, and of the universities did not on the whole fail in their duty.

It will be claimed that the parliamentary leaders were no better. Yet they were thrown up by the ballot boxes, not by any examination or competitive system. They owned nothing to social influence or to the privilege of birth. Certainly I shall defend neither the Chambers elected between 1920 and 1940, of which so many monstrous examples figure in the pages of this book, nor the prevalent habits of French democracy: senators and deputies encroaching upon the business of the executive and making deals with officials around the ministers and in the administrative services far too freely, the repulsive vulgarity of the gang of "good fellows" who were said to run the Republic. The likeness to Plato's caricature of the free city is far too close: "Is not everyone free to do what he pleases in it?" But the parliamentary leaders of the nation were no worse than the rest.[20]

Contrary to Renan's prediction, the allegation cannot be sustained that Demos has always been in the wrong or that oligarchs of every breed and kind have always been in the right. During the period we have investigated the guilt of the many is less than the guilt of the fewer. Moreover, in extenuation of the masses' guilt, it must be said that they would have behaved better, both they and their immediate representatives, if

[20]The Oustric and Stavisky scandals created a widespread belief in the general rottenness of all legislators. In both Houses some thirty scoundrels could be enumerated, and everyone knew who they were. More than a half century ago the Panama Company is supposed to have "rewarded" 104 members for their votes. In the interval consciences for sale had not become more numerous; if there had been a change, it was rather the other way. But men of inferior ability had crowded into Parliament, and the level on which administrative services operated had become lower. Sluggishness and excessive tolerance with individual or group interests had filtered in everywhere. In his analysis of this spirit in a democracy, Plato (*The Republic*, VIII, 11) comes near describing the Stavisky scandal.

wiser counsel had been given them by the men whose social function was to clarify the great problems of the nation; if, in both Houses, those very men had not furthered the fortune of the meanest politicians. Why did our leadership thus go astray? Why did that liberal bourgeoisie which had supplied the Republic with so many good servants become suddenly sterile? Why did the standard of politicians decline after the death of Clemenceau and Poincaré? Only one answer suggests itself. The impact of socialism on the Republic unsettled, from one end of the community to the other, the propertied classes, both those long established and those of recent date. They did not make available to the country the latent statesmanship which might be in them. Men who would, normally, have taken their share of the responsibilities of government threw themselves into the extremist parties. They were lost to the nation's good. They shunned electoral contests. They fell back on the narrowest of ideas and interests and relied on means of influence outside Parliament. The very notion of public service thus was obscured or impaired in those circles where it should have found its citadel. We must conclude that France was betrayed by its supposedly conservative classes rather than by the democratic process. That is another good reason for not believing in the decadence of our country. Leadership failing in its task and calling for renewal is no new phenomenon in the life of peoples.

For France, once she is free, the problem will not be to devise a new constitutional framework (even though the 1875 structure cannot be left as it was) so much as to rear leaders who will break away from those who swarmed round the gravediggers. This undertaking is far more exacting than a mere revision of the constitution. It requires for its fulfillment something besides ink and paper. To some extent it will depend on luck and fate; it will need an operation of nature which nobody can dare predict, still less direct who does not indulge in schemes of party dictatorship. Eckermann records this remark by Goethe after Jena: "Universal pain and a feeling of shame have got hold of the nation like some demon." Will the French people be possessed by this demon? Nothing less will do if it is to be ridden of what was so greatly amiss in its republic. When peace comes the same problems will arise as in 1918, but in an infinitely aggravated form, and some of the solutions possible twenty-five years ago are ruled out today. This time, however, if we are not more successful, the country will be finally wrecked in civil strife.

The age-old fabric has tumbled into ruins. Had the German invasion been consolidated, slavery for as far as we can see into the future would have resulted. But as it ebbs back to its own boundaries the German invasion will nonetheless leave behind it a state of revolution. It has shaken men's ideas and their social conditions to the core. We do not delude ourselves on the losses already suffered and still to be suffered on that account. At least the demon of vengeance will work more at his ease in the rubble. If he were never unloosed, if the French people, on the plea of unity and of so-called national reconciliation, were to revert to its easygoing ways before the cataclysm, further disasters would be added in the peace to those already wrought by war. What we must hope for is a break with the past as clean as the break of 1789. For that reason, on the day we regain our freedom the fiction of a legal continuity with the foundered Republic need not be sought. To breathe new life into the assemblies, the central or departmental authorities which were debased long before July 10, 1940, even on the pretext of effecting a transition, would mean, for the people, going back to its own vomit.

Whose heart will not be straitened before the upheaval in his little corner of social life? But individual regrets count for little as against the redemption of the country. The bourgeoisie stands condemned insofar as it cannot get away from its moral complexion during the last fifty years. It is convicted by its carelessness, its lack of thoroughness, its lazy mandarinism manufactured out of examinations and competitions which in no case set a premium on character. It sank into an evil system of self-perpetuation, often excluding, crushing, almost always debasing men with any pride or strength. When they read these words many will squeak that Communism is on the way and re-echo the cry which the gravediggers have long sounded in our ears. But I do not believe that all spirit of enterprise stands a stronger chance of being locked into a concentration camp on our soil than it does in England, the United States, Holland, or Belgium. We pray for a change in the temperament of France, for the advent of a society less centered on the quest for lucre but dedicated above all to public service. The countries I have just mentioned will go through transformations similar to ours. May our vessel sail in company with theirs. Quite apart from theoretical bolshevism, it is self-evident that the Russian reconstruction of the last fifteen years offers an example not to be brushed aside.

To still our anxiety over the unknown political and social world which lies ahead, we need only consider the forty generations of Frenchmen from whom we are sprung. People have become accustomed to say there are two Frances. The France begotten by the Revolution and the France of the Monarchy. But indeed, in the centuries before 1789, three or four markedly distinct Frances, and not one, may be seen quite apart from the spiritual republic of writers and artists, above the turmoil of worldly affairs. From one France to another the change was sudden or gradual, violent or almost insensible, ever since civilization had to start afresh from the bare earth after the crumbling of the Roman heritage. The complete repose of which some of our contemporaries dream has never existed, unless it be at the raw beginnings in a state of complete destitution.

For three or four centuries, beginning with the sixth, any notion of profit approximating ours however faintly waned from men's memories. There were no manufactures, no markets, no cities. There was no currency. The only remaining recourse was to live off the soil. Thus the lands granted to the knights were in lieu of military pay. In these humble surroundings the feelings which helped to nurture the nascent community gradually asserted themselves: loyalty, piety, honor, with overtones to which man's soul in antiquity had not been attuned. Later on came the veneration of the king, the legacy of St. Louis, that is, attachment to the central power, and, even later, at the time of the Renaissance, the first allurements of trade, wealth, and luxury, the initial forms of capitalism, a broadening outlook on the world, bolder individual enterprise, the taste for an enlarged freedom exceeding the special liberties and restraints which had hitherto existed, and finally the emancipation of the spirit. Out of the continuous interplay of the human elements involved, out of the varying proportions in which they blended, came forth in each age the temperament of our people. Would it not be consistent with its history if, after the unspeakable ordeals, a new compound were precipitated, if a fifth or sixth France appeared, without anything being crushed in the fascist or communist fashion? How diverse, how rich is the substance of France, as seen in the ever-changing characteristics of each of her social classes! Has the divine mold been broken? Has it worn itself out in the course of a thousand years?

III

France will be saved through the victory of England, the United States, and Russia. "Our firm intention is to restore her in her independence and in her greatness," Mr. Winston Churchill wrote to General de Gaulle on August 7, 1940. Even more precise are the promises of the Washington Government, as much to the Fighting French as to those in authority at Vichy: maintenance of her territorial integrity, restoration of her sovereignty.[21] France, torn by the Allies from the grasp of the common foe, will hence be re-established both in her possessions and her status among the nations.

But the French would be grievously deceiving themselves if they were to rest shiftlessly content with these generous assurances. They will not come into their heritage, either material or moral, like some heir who fights opposing claims through the agency of a bailiff. The victors—and that is only consonant with justice—will have to convince themselves that France is of sufficient stature to mend her fortunes, to become once more a useful ally, that by her own efforts she will soon add unto the property titles restored to her that deed which, above all others, constitutes, in the long run, evidence of ownership: namely, the strength to defend her inheritance and even to win it back from the foreign hand which has roughly seized it. If France cannot fly on her own wings after a very short period of transition, if she loiters and dawdles under the shadow of the two great Western Powers, if she does not very quickly recapture her historic personality, she will be lost beyond recall.

It would not be wise to think of the years which will follow the armistice as necessarily free of jolts and jerks. I want to believe in the permanence of the forthcoming peace settlement. Schooled by misfortune, those who will be its architects and guardians would surely not revert to the faintness of heart of 1935–36 if the lovers of violence challenged them again. Today they know better. They have awakened to the fact that no international treaty can exist which, at some hours of crisis, ministerial infirmity of character cannot bring to ruin. And certainly they will grow used to the idea of preventive action. May they be truly great peacemakers! But there is no likelihood either that a European continent will speedily emerge with clean-cut lines after the earthquake or that the relations between the states which form that continent will be quickly integrated like some piece of clockwork. The ground will long remain "wet and softened after the flood." Only slowly will it harden within the mold set for it. Accidents may happen. The three great organizing powers—after all, strangers to this area of soft loam and clay and trying to put it in order from without—will, short of a twenty years' occupation, only be able to prevent them to the extent that concord between them endures. Much expediency will necessarily have to be mixed with the application of the "charters" formulated from above.

France's help will be needed, and her place among nations in after

<hr>

[21]Declaration of Mr. Sumner Welles, in the name of the United States Government, on March 2, 1942, a letter to M. Henry Haye of April 13 and assurances concerning Indo-China.

years is sure to be determined by what she is able or unable to do. From July 1940 onward the cross of Lorraine, the insignia of the Fighting French, has continuously been displayed in the battle waged by the British on land and on sea. In North Africa soldiers and sailors, forcibly torn from their allegiance to Vichy by the Anglo-American landing of November 8, 1942, have proved their mettle in the Tunisian campaign and seized Corsica. In Italy they have won glory (May 1944). Some ten French divisions provided with "lease-lend" equipment are now in position to respond to the call of the Allied commander in chief. Once more the destiny of our country is on the ascendant, but this time with a starting point located in North Africa, far away from its original cradle, the Ile de France. The time ought not to be very far distant when France will be the most efficient "associate," on the continent, of the three great powers.[22] Her European function cannot be left in abeyance.

But our keen disappointment cannot be concealed. Some eighteen months have gone by since the allied expeditionary forces seized Morocco and Algiers and set free a fraction of the French territory. Yet the French patriots who, all through the dark years, were the soul of French resistance, have been thwarted and kept by the Allies at arm's length rather than encouraged to go ahead with their task.

Invested with military and political power over the French African Empire by his own arrangements with the Washington Government, General Giraud, with Bergeret playing the part of a confidential adviser, set up the kind of regime branded in French annals with the name of "white terror"—terrorism as practiced by the so-called conservatives. Then, in addition to General Bergeret, such proconsuls as Noguès, Peyrouton and Boisson were confirmed in their functions, dignities, and influence, while the worship of Pétain went on unabated particularly among the officers of the Navy. Whence came this remarkable tolerance on the part of England and America? To account for it there are only two words: military necessity, the very expression already used in relation to Darlan. Most assuredly it was only too natural that military necessity should have its way with Germans and Italians still fighting bitterly in Tunisia. Such was not the time to make changes in the French higher command or upset discipline in the lower ranks. Nevertheless, next to immediate military necessity, the military interest of tomorrow and the political interest of the future deserved consideration. They required France's moral recovery as a condition of her lasting material recovery. The French problem to be faced in North Africa con-

[22] See Mr. Sumner Welles's speech on October 16, 1943.

sisted of two different sets of terms, one short range and the other long range. All long-range consideration of the problem made it imperative that some connection should be established with the forces of internal resistance. Those forces were overlooked in 1943 as they had been in Weygand's times, when the United States busied itself exclusively with building up that general into an anti-Vichy leader and sending supplies to the territories under his command.

I have always been under the impression that our American friends and some of our British friends, too, often missed the decisive point when discussing French affairs. Unless the men who never contemplated coming to terms with Pétain, Darlan, and Laval do wield public authority in France in the transitional period preceding a general election, and unless they use it most resolutely in order to do away once for all with the gangs responsible for the defeat, the armistice, and the policy of collaboration, unless they are given full scope to perform that cleansing operation as a preliminary to the polling day, too many Frenchmen, however well meaning, may again be led astray by vested interests. Had that point been better understood, General de Gaulle and his Fighting French Committee would not have had practically to force a passage to North Africa through numberless obstacles. After the French Committee of National Liberation had been set up as the outcome of a compromise (June 3, 1943), de Gaulle would not have found the business of getting rid of the Vichy retinue so exacting. The Committee itself would have expanded more quickly and easily into a true provisional government. When one thinks of General Georges landing from a British airplane at Algiers on the same day as General de Gaulle and boasting that he had been within an ace of bringing Pétain with him!

North African Vichy has been cleaned up. Peyrouton, Bergeret, Noguès and Boisson have been driven out and then locked up, except Noguès, who went abroad. General Giraud is out of the way. Pucheu has been shot. The laws of the Third Republic are in force. A consultative assembly met in Algiers on November 3 in the true spirit of the resistance movement. Perhaps no more than a few fragments of the broken mirror have been put together as yet, but others will be added, and gradually the whole image of the nation will be reflected. Will the same hard task have to be performed in metropolitan France? On June 6—henceforward a landmark in French history—the Allied troops assaulted the German defensive line in Normandy. The second battle of France is on. But the Washington and London governments do not yet see more clearly than in 1942–43 what is at stake. They mechanically repeat that the French people shall decide on their political institutions at a general election. This is a truism. It does not reach the heart of the issue. It falls short of an adequate program.

No program can be said to be adequate which does not fully provide for the immediate replacement of the rulers at Vichy, of their officials and appointees, for the transformation of the Algiers Committee with the popular support which surges up to the name of General de Gaulle[23] into a vigorous provisional government dedicated to the task of ridding French public life of the elements which are an offense to French patriotism. Are there any conceivable alternatives to that course of action? The selection of the new authorities by the Allied commander in chief? What an invidious responsibility for him to assume! Calling in the elder statesmen of the defunct Republic? They are all politically dead. Or the National Assembly of 1940? It stands as a dishonored body. Or delegates of the departmental councils in accordance with a garbled version of the Treveneuc Law? The most objectionable members of the National Assembly are entrenched in these departmental councils. I believe this conclusion to be inescapable. If the reform movement which originated in Fighting France and resistance groups doesn't, for one reason or another, sweep the land with enough authority and prestige to compel all Vichy men to cower, civil war is likely to break out. So far no other leader so well prepared as General de Gaulle to successfully appeal to the country and take drastic action has come forward. Of course there is no certainty that he is going to overcome all obstacles. For one thing, the lack of competent men around him gives Vichy-minded officials an opportunity to hamper him. With the elimination of General de Gaulle, what would become of the new France in the making remains, at least, very doubtful. Old divisions would reappear and Frenchmen fall back into opposite camps with a vengeance. Were the storm to be weathered and some compromise arranged for, a general relapse into the hateful past could be feared. Ultimately, Communists or Fascists might thrive on the disillusionment, the disgust, and the lassitude of the worthiest citizens.

To that line of argument the ever-recurring objection is that to allow an energetic center of government to be formed in France, months be-

[23]Let us place in record that public declaration of René Massigli, formerly French Ambassador at Ankara and one of the chief officials at the Ministry of Foreign Affairs, on his arrival in London, in February 1943: "For the French people all resistance has one name only: de Gaulle." Practically all public and resistance men coming out of France have confirmed that testimony.

fore a general election, can be called the equivalent of allowing a full-fledged dictatorship to creep inside the walls.

Plainly there is no denying that since the Republic was destroyed on July 10, 1940, and cannot be re-established until a popular vote has taken place, whoever is invested with public authority, during the process of liberation, will have to rule in a constitutional vacuum. In his day-to-day decisions he will make it a point to conform to the legislation of the Third Republic, to base his decrees upon the enabling acts once adopted by Parliament which made Daladier or Reynaud practically omnipotent. He will nevertheless not be legally entitled to rule; he will have no letters of legitimation to exhibit. In that sense a dictatorial power will be bound to exist. But any other possible arrangement will deserve the same appellation. So far as constitutional law is concerned, an interregnum cannot be avoided which must be arbitrarily filled. And the same state of affairs will be seen practically everywhere in Europe. In France the so-called dictatorship will be no more than the imperative action of French patriotism, with the restoration of republican institutions as its aim. At that juncture a timorous, wobbling, hastily improvised provisional government would be much more likely to lead to fascism than a group of men gathered around a definite plan, having set up months in advance a consultative assembly which in its methods of discussion conducts itself as a parliament of the usual pattern, the very opposite of a "single-party" system.

The Italian and the German totalitarian regimes have become such an obsession for us that we are apt to describe as outbursts of fascism any popular movement advancing behind a leader. By that token Danton himself would be dubbed a fascist. In the last resort the inner dispositions of a national community with a long record behind it are sure to prove the determining influence. I do not believe that General de Gaulle and his friends are aiming at securing permanent absolute power for themselves. But did they happen to evince anything like dictatorial propensities, I believe that they could never recruit among the French people the consistent "single party," which is the indispensable instrument of modern despotism. The most the Vichy rulers could achieve in the way of a "single party" was the "French legion of ex-service men," an indifferent force, and whatever success they had in that respect was due to the overpowering presence of the victorious Nazis and to French despair. In a redeemed France a powerful public opinion will be the only "Legion" available to governments. And public opinion will have ample opportunity to assert itself: within a twelvemonth, municipal, departmental councils, and two national assemblies will have to be elected.

France does not meet her liberators wearing a hair shirt, strewn with ashes, and reciting penitential psalms. Such apparel would ill befit her national pride, an asset worth saving and treasuring. When the Americans and the British grow impatient at its expression they should not forget that, without it, no moral or material reconstruction can ever be undertaken. "You had the Channel, you had the Atlantic to protect you; all we had was the Meuse." Our friends have already had to listen to such words, and they will have to listen to others like them. No man can accuse me of having withheld unpleasant truths. And, in years gone by, I never imagined that France would not be one with England and the United States. How should she not be one with them now that she owes them her very salvation? Once more it has been demonstrated, and more crushingly than ever before, that the natural interests of all the Western Powers are relentlessly convergent. I hope that around England a federation of western Europe will be evolved. On this record I feel authorized to display the *"Honni soit qui mal y pense"* motto and to remind these who might be prone to ignore it that France had no monopoly of gravediggers, even though in other lands they were more foolish than wicked. All responsibility does not rest with her. England and America must bear their share.

Were they not digging graves, those who persistently ignored for so long that French military power stood between their country, their civilization and the enemy, and who for fifteen years endeavored to whittle that power away? In the end they convinced the French that it was utter folly to try to be wise all by themselves. How often did Mr. Winston Churchill tell a shortsighted House of Commons, between 1932 and 1934: "You insist on France reducing her Army. God help us if ever that Army gives way!" How many men of peace wished to shatter with a sledge hammer the very shield which protected them! When this keystone was broken they were in a position to appraise the arch which fell with it. Soon the whole world was ablaze. Because the French soldier had not held his own, the Russian soldier and the American soldier had to step in. Is it not appalling that England should have waited until the end of 1936 grudgingly to concede a frontier guarantee, a truncated guarantee, grossly inadequate even on paper in response to the obviously impending menace of Hitler?

Were they not digging graves, those who in 1918 dragged France into a peace treaty at variance with the data of European experience, from which not a single French statesman or a single qualified diplomat expected any decent outcome?

What did France ask after having lost more of her substance on the battlefield than any other nation? The direct or hidden acquisition of the Rhineland was of questionable wisdom, I admit. But at bottom France was begging England for the tie which, twenty-three years later, in May 1942, was granted Soviet Russia by Mr. Winston Churchill and Mr. Anthony Eden, for the kind of solidarity which, in October 1943, was brought into being between the three great Allied nations. Our claim to the Rhineland was little more than a lever. France met with a check because her program ran counter to President Wilson's Covenant. When the British Cabinet recognized the justice of the Russian demands, when it geared the eventual system of collective security to the continued alliance of two or three leading states, having in the meanwhile tested its illusions of the period and found them wanting, it implicitly admitted that France had not been fairly treated, that she had not been given a square deal. This is being written without any idea of extracting justification from the past for the crime indicted on every page of this book —the jettisoning of the British alliance in June 1940 and the forfeiture of American friendship never broken in 160 years. It would, however, be failing in my duty to my country not to tell our English and American saviors without in any way detracting from our gratitude and affection: "Remember well that in 1919 you left your French ally in the lurch."

I do not want to end on what some might call a querulous note. The battle is raging in France. My thought goes to the American and British soldiers, to the French patriots in the back country who redeem the world from the Nazi bondage. Statesmen will follow in the steps of the warriors and rebuild the peace. The bad dreams of yesterday must not interfere with the hope of these who shoulder their task in the morning light.

Appendixes

Note on the Preface Written by Marshal Pétain for General Narcisse Chauvineau's Book: *Is Invasion Still Possible?*, See Page 12.

APPENDIX 1

Marshal Pétain quotes Chauvineau and agrees with him. "The attack must possess a superiority of three to one in infantry, six to one in artillery, twelve to one in munitions before it can hope to dominate the defense. Also incalculable superiority in the fighting quality of its effectives."

But Pétain does not stop there. In this anthology of error I note the following statements:

"A continuous front . . . inevitably results from the increased man power mobilized by the nation in arms, as it does from the technical properties of the new weapons. The reason for this lies in a humble truth—one might almost say in a sordid truth: no living creature can still run when, after being caught in the barbed wire of the defense system, he is hit in the head by a metal projectile fired by an invisible weapon. No patriotic enthusiasm, no moral fervor can stand up against this fact. No way to outflank this barricade of wire and automatic weapons exists where it has been extended to protect the whole field of operations. Means do exist to break the barrier: these means are tanks and heavy artillery. But they are costly and not available in great numbers. They are also relatively slow to bring into position. The scarcity of these instruments limits the fronts on which they can be used. The length of time necessary to develop their effective action can be employed by the defense in bringing up its reserves—the ease of this operation corresponding to the narrowness of the front.

"The effectiveness (of an air force) in a land battle is unreliable. It is indirectly, through its action behind the lines, that aviation is most efficient . . ." "The continuous front is a reality which it would be perilous not to recognize . . ."

"Never have the particular moral attitudes of military leaders, nor those of the peoples concerned, determined the main strategical and tactical characteristics of wars: today, as always, these characteristics are determined by precise and measurable factors—man power and armament."

And here is how Pétain deals with General de Gaulle's ideas: "The army composed of technicians, such as that which has been proposed, would be . . . completely armored and mechanized, and capable of going into action at nightfall at a point two hundred kilometers distant from where it camped in the morning. Moreover, it would be able to break through fortified lines and create panic behind them. It seems somewhat imprudent to accept these conclusions. Here perhaps is an effort in the field of tactics, to obtain decisive results through the offensive, but results which are apt to prove short lived if no precautions are taken to guard against its possible failure. Perhaps also too much is expected from tanks, too much reliance placed on the idea that they can be made subject to a commanding officer's close control. These matters have not been probed with sufficient thoroughness . . . Perhaps finally—to consider only the tactical use of these weapons—the hypothesis of the enemy's possessing a similar army for defense has not been taken into account . . . Up till now, and as far as operations on the ground are concerned, every new invention has been of greater benefit, generally speaking, to the defense than to the attack."

"Would not the tank itself—regarded today as the supreme instrument for attack and as the best weapon for breaking through a fortified front—find its effectiveness greatly increased were it used for defense, or in counterattack against enemy forces, even against armored forces, but forces which would be disorganized through the very fact of their advance?"

As for Chauvineau, carried away by his paradoxes, he goes so far as to argue that, thanks to the defensive front, small countries today enjoy unprecedented security, and so alliances are no longer needed.

Concerning this book of Chauvineau's, Gamelin was more cautious than Pétain. He went no further than to remark: "It's the exaggeration of a sound idea."

In contrast to this unfortunate preface of Pétain's, it is only fair to quote from a report made on January 26, 1940, by Colonel de Gaulle in a last attempt to enlighten the blind:

"Aviation and armored forces now possess such a tremendous potential of destruction and surprise in relation to exposed infantry, artillery and supply trains, that these cannot make a move in battle without risking immediate annihilation. . . . If the enemy is not already in possession of a mechanized force capable of breaking our defense lines, everything leads us to think that he is engaged in preparing such a force." And Pétain's courts condemned General de Gaulle to death!

APPENDIX 2

IT IS EASY TO GET LOST in the maze of military and ministerial councils of technical character in which the various problems of national defense and of politics, inextricably bound together, came under discussion. I list them here for the reader's convenience.

1. *Superior Council of National Defense.* The last meeting of this council took place several years ago. It was composed of the Premier, the Minister for Foreign Affairs, the Ministers heading the three branches of national defense, the officers commanding in chief the Army, Navy, and Air Corps, together with their chiefs-of-staff, etc. Marshal Pétain was a member. A large secretariat and several research

committees, administratively subordinated to the Premier's office, were at its disposal.

2. *Permanent Committee for National Defense.* Actually this committee replaced the Superior Council, found to be unwieldy because of its numerous membership. When it met at the request of the military authorities it included only the chiefs of the Army, Navy, and Air Corps, together with certain of their staff officers. When a meeting was called by the government, the Premier, the Minister for Foreign Affairs, and the ministers heading the three branches of National Defense were present in addition to the above. This committee met twice during Blum's tenure of office, at the Hotel Matignon, on which occasions the Socialist Premier and Marshal Pétain sat facing each other across the table. The committee used the secretarial services provided for the Superior Council.

3. *The War Committee.* This first met at the time of mobilization and superseded the Permanent Committee. It, too, used the Superior Council's secretariat. Under Article 40 of the Law of July 11, 1938 (general organization of the nation in time of war), the War Committee provides for "unity in the military conduct of the war and for coordination of effort on land, sea, and air."

Gamelin's authority in his capacity as chief of staff for National Defense not having prevailed, the War Committee, with the secretariat of the Superior Council for National Defense by its side was, in France, the nearest approach to the Wehrmacht's High Command. But obviously a deliberating body, even if it assigns to the generalissimo tasks extending beyond the scope of his normal authority, can scarcely be described as an instrument of command. Then, too, the "War Committee" held regular meetings only after Reynaud came to power.

The President of the Republic was in the chair, and its membership included the commanders in chief and staffs of the Army, Navy, and Air Force, as well as their respective ministers and the Minister for Foreign Affairs—who, however, was not accompanied by his technical adviser of ambassadorial rank, the secretary-general of the Quai d'Orsay. The Ministers of National Economy and Colonies also had the right to participate. Baudouin, Under Secretary of State for Foreign Affairs, succeeded in having the membership of the committee altered so that he belonged to it.

4. *The War Cabinet,* created by Reynaud. Roughly speaking, it was a separate meeting of the six ministers whose departments were concerned with national defense. War, Navy, Air, Foreign Affairs, Colonies, Blockade, together with the three officers commanding the three arms. But Gamelin, Darlan, and Vuillemin, basing their objection on existing legislation, refused to inform the War Cabinet as to their plans. Reynaud called only three meetings of this committee. An abortive attempt.

5. *The Economic Cabinet.* A committee of the Ministers of Finance, Economy, Commerce, Public Works, etc.

6. *The Superior War Council.* Presided over by the Minister for National Defense with the generalissimo as vice-president. It included the marshals of France and the generals who would be in command of armies in time of war. A peacetime organization only. All questions concerning the organization of the army, mobilization, operation plans, were submitted to it at the Minister's discretion. Between June 1936 and September 1939 this Council met only on three occasions and only once under Daladier's chairmanship (December 15, 1937). Daladier never forgot that on December 18, 1933, this Council had, at Weygand's urging, rejected the

plan he had set before it to solve the problems of the "hollow years" (see page 330). All the details given above are only approximately correct. I have not been able to collect all the decrees concerned.

APPENDIX 3

PERSONAL AND SECRET ORDERS No. 26,225, of March 24, 1918. (Transmitted, everything leads us to believe, for the hour is not indicated, at about 8 P.M., March 24.)

1. Information regarding the enemy.

(a) Having thrown back the British 3rd and 5th armies on the Fampoux, Bapaume, Péronne line (east of Arras) and the Somme, Crozat Canal line, during the days of March 22 and 23, and forced their way at Tergnier and Hamm on the evening or during the night of the twenty-second, the enemy crossed the river at Bethencourt during the morning of the twenty-fourth.

In the north the enemy has reached Cléry-sur-Somme, Combles, pushed beyond the Rancourt ridge, Sailly-Saillisel.

Moreover, our 3rd Army has involved its free units in a very hard fight along the Chauny, Commenchon, Neuville-en-Beine, Villeselve front, and to the west. South of the Oise our situation has not changed. Our artillery posted along this bank controls the valley and the slopes north of Chauny.

(b) The enemy seems to have as its objective:

Army Group of the Crown Prince of Bavaria: To cut the British 3rd Army from the 5th in the region north of Péronne and to drive back toward the north the principal body of the British armies.

Army Group of the Imperial Crown Prince: To shatter the right of the British 5th Army and thus clear the way to Amiens and Beauvais.

2. Intentions of the general commander in chief:

Above all to hold firm the structure of the French Armies as a whole, especially not to let the G.A.R. (Group of Armies in Reserve) be separated from the remainder of our forces. Then, if possible, keep in contact with the British forces.

The battle is to be conducted with this in mind.

3. Mission of the G.A.R.

The G.A.R. shall hold the enemy in check by supporting the 3rd Army's right at the Oise and, if necessary, by falling back on the general line: Noyon, Porquericourt, Lagny, Roye, which shall become the line where it will make its stand. The 1st Army, in accordance with circumstances and the way its units are disposed, (a) either shall extend to the left of the 3rd Army, to link it to the British right, should the latter continue to hold, (b) or reinforce and support the 3rd Army, either by occupying in advance positions on which to eventually fall back, or by counterattacking.

The cavalry, shifted to the left of our sector, shall reconnoiter and cover the left of the G.A.R. (primary mission) while trying to preserve contact with the British right (secondary mission).

4. Mission of the G.A.N. (Group of Armies of the North).

The G.A.N. shall at all costs hold the Ailette line to Manicamp, then to the south, west of the Oise, under all circumstances keeping in contact with the G.A.R.

PÉTAIN

Letter from General Foch to M. Georges Clemenceau, Minister for War and Premier.

Paris, March 24, 1918.

Given the present situation on the Franco-British front, the following can be said:

1. The enemy offensive looks as though it must have been stopped along the southern sector, from Tergnier to Péronne, which is crossed by the Crozat Canal.

2. Further north the terrain offers few natural obstacles up to Arras.

Consequently, in this region a renewed German offensive can develop with easy tactical successes and aim at strategical results of very great importance, such as cutting off the railroad and the highway from Amiens to Doullens and St. Pol, and, moreover, getting hold of our coal-fields area, Neux-les-Mines, Bruay, Béthune.

It is therefore in this region that for the time being will be settled the fate of the coalition.

We should and can ward off these dangers:

(a) Through an inch-by-inch defense of the terrain in the afore-mentioned region.

(b) It would seem to be possible at the outset to achieve this by means of the British forces still available, on condition that they are promptly realigned and set going to this purpose and that we are precisely informed as to their worth.

(c) Yet whatever may be the worth of these forces, their numerical inferiority as compared to the German mass requires the immediate assembling of a French mass, held in reserve in the region northeast of Amiens, in order to guard against all unforeseen events and, in case of need, to counterattack the German offensive.

From the preceding it follows that two regions seem entirely different from each other: that south of the Somme, toward Péronne, little threatened and easy to defend; that north of Peronne, full of danger, and where it now seems the die is cast. The defense of this region requires spending every British resource at hand and a large-scale supplementary spending of French forces.

Whence the necessity of providing for and organizing an enlightened and planned common action in the Péronne-Arras region.

It is therefore requested:

That the French general in chief be oriented, as indicated above, and without delay receive appropriate instructions;

That in like manner Marshal Haig be requested to manage his defense in the fashion indicated above and to hold firm until the time when French participation will come into play, meanwhile informing us without delay of his situation and resources;

That the organism directing the war, once it has given its directives, supervise their execution.

If this is not done, we run the risk, so far as the coalition is concerned, of having on our hands a battle of serious consequence, insufficiently prepared, insufficiently supplied, insufficiently managed.

APPENDIX 4

Facts and Arguments Produced by Daladier and Blum at Riom.

I

AT THE TIME I wrote this book the evidence given out at the Riom trial was known to me in part. About the equipment of the French Army I could avail myself only of the following sources of information: incomplete data derived from the Ministry of Armaments, those gathered in great quantity by the public prosecutor, the outcome of the searching investigations conducted by judges specially appointed for the purpose (*juges d'instruction*), and press clippings. Since then the testimonies heard in court and the statements made by the defendants have been divulged to some extent. In the case of Léon Blum a verbatim report is available. Those new elements do not invalidate the views I have expressed. Nevertheless, it would not be fair to leave them aside.

Fulfillment of the armament's program. Messrs. Daladier, Jacomet, and Blum stated repeatedly that the armament program was actually fulfilled ahead of schedule—by as much as six months on January 1, 1939, according to Daladier. Such an assertion runs counter to what I heard from all sides when Daladier was in office and people spoke the truth all the more readily because they believed in victory. Nor can it be reconciled with the speech Daladier himself delivered on December 22, 1939, to which reference is made on page 132. Are we to think that what Messrs. Daladier, Jacomet, and Blum had in mind was the initial program of 1936, considered without relation to the various plans of execution which subsequently enlarged its scope? I have it from a competent official that in 1938, when, to quote M. Jacomet, the output of the factories was at its peak, the shortage of machine tools was an established fact. Indeed, that official was sent on a mission to England in order to get some assistance.

In the winter of 1939-40, Daladier was so unfavorably impressed with what was going on in French industry that he planned to subsidize the expansion of American plants. Surely he would hardly have moved in that direction had he not been in doubt concerning the fulfillment of the program. Here is another fact: An inventory of French armament was undertaken in February 1940 and brought to completion two months later. The figures were kept secret by M. Dautry and his assistants. They do not even seem to have been officially brought to the knowledge of the High Command. On May 12, 1940, a Sunday, in the early afternoon, General Picquendar visited Dautry on behalf of the High Command and insisted on the swift delivery of twelve thousand tanks. He was then shown the data concerning armored forces and artillery. Were those data such as to enable Daladier, assuming that they ever reached him, to regard his speech of December 22, 1939, as unduly pessimistic? May one believe that Daladier, in the days following his dismissal from office, was more accurately informed than at the time the Ministry of National Defense was under his control?

Here are the arguments upon which Daladier has tried to build his case.

1. *In 1940 the French Army was provided with arms and ammunition on a much larger scale than commonly believed.*

I have compared the figures which M. Daladier submitted to the Court and found them more or less in keeping with those quoted in this book. M. Daladier mentions 13,000 grenade throwers and 360,000 light mines of the pattern used by the infantry, which, he said, were ready for use on January 1, 1940. The public prosecutor did not contradict him on that point. He declared that the requirements of the General Staff had been fully satisfied. Besides, Daladier never said that the grenade throwers were of recent make. As to the tanks, the count made by Daladier approximates ours: 3,615 tanks as against 3,446. It is in relation to anti-tank guns and air-defense artillery that all the data of which I have availed myself are at variance with those of the ex-Premier. In the first case he speaks of seventy-five hundred to eight thousand guns, including six thousand of 25 and twelve hundred of 47, and, in the second case, of thirty-seven hundred guns, among them twenty-five hundred of 25. Those figures border on the incredible. The point was not cleared up. As to air forces, the figures quoted at Riom from M. Guy la Chambre (1,710 planes maintained in first line on May 10, 1940) differ by four hundred from General Vuillemin's computation, but I happen to have listened to some explanations given orally by M. Guy la Chambre which tallied closely with the testimony of that military commander.

2. *The High Command squandered its armaments.*

This leitmotiv of M. Daladier runs through the first part of this book. As to the scattering of the armored matériel, M. Daladier has made great use of a report drafted by General Keller in July 1940. According to that authority, the forty battalions of tanks—that is the whole armored matériel which had not been incorporated in the four armored divisions and in the three light mechanized divisions —were dispersed from the North Sea to Switzerland at the rate of three or four in each army. "Even so they were not kept together but broken down into companies and into sections. Such small units were staked on hazardous and critical missions over bridges and highways, along the edge of forests, etc. That total bulk of some two thousand tanks could have been detailed into fairly heavy detachments of two hundred. Instead, in order to make up for the inadequate strength of the infantry, it was cut into insignificant fragments dispersed right and left, and thus doomed to face impossible odds and to be wantonly crushed."

3. *Quantities of war matériel were left unused.*

Attention has been called to the carelessness of the High Command in respect of the air forces (see page 28) and the Supply Service Corps (see page 29, note 10). M. Daladier maintained that four hundred tanks in good condition and four hundred and fifty anti-tank guns were forgotten in depots. Military officers testified that forty up-to-date tanks had been destroyed at Bazas, that shells for 75′ guns had been overlooked in army reserve stores and also millions of bombs and enough optical instruments to equip some twenty divisions, etc. General Keller belied Daladier. At Riom the various testimonies on those points were so conflicting that any definite conclusion had better be postponed.

4. *The armament program of the French Command was inadequate because the power of the German military machine had not been properly appraised. The program was fulfilled, but it did not meet the requirements of the French Army as they became known on the battlefield.*

The French High Command unquestionably erred in its estimate, both quantitative and qualitative, of the war matériel needed to stop the German onslaught.

Its responsibility is fully exposed in Marshal Pétain's foreword to the book of General Chauvineau, quoted in Appendix 1: "No offensive action has a chance to succeed that is not supported by three times the number of men, six times the artillery, and twelve times the munitions at the disposal of an enemy defense." At Riom, General Keller, duly drubbed and thrashed in combat, finally saw the light and stated the truth: "The enemy was left at liberty to choose the point of attack. Therefore it could not be resisted unless superiority in numbers was on the side of the army which kept on the defensive." This is to be taken as a supreme confession of failure. The French General Staff was not only wrong as to the nature of the weapons needed by its troops and the proper way to handle them. It did not realize how many of them had to be mustered to check the German onslaught.

But, when everything has been said, is Daladier entitled to censure the generals on the ground that they did not ask enough? He should first be cleared from the reproach that he did not supply even the modest requirements of the High Command.

5. *The matériel available to the Germans was not so plentiful as the French High Command would have us believe.*

At Riom it was the contention of General Julien Martin, whom General Keller had replaced as inspector of the armored forces, that in May 1940 a German armored division did consist of 304 tanks, not of some four hundred. Daladier went much further. He argued that tanks of eight, nine, and twelve tons, armored cars of six tons were included in that number. The most powerful German tanks, according to him, did not exceed twenty tons. And while General Keller credited the German Army, during the campaign of France, with six thousand or sixty-five hundred tanks, he cut down the figure to four thousand. Of course he was trying to demonstrate that a French Command alert enough to put to good use every weapon it had at hand would have managed to hold its own. It is worth noticing that this new argument put forward by Daladier detracts from the validity of argument No. 4.

In the same spirit M. Guy la Chambre attempted to explain that the Germans did not possess an air superiority of more than two to one over French and British —in truth, a deadly enough handicap.

Sooner or later the Germans will disclose their records and thus arbitrate between the disputants.

II

The speech delivered by Léon Blum at Riom on March 11 and 12, in vindication of his social reforms, is likely to remain as a monument of French political oratory. L. Blum's reasoning is crystal clear, and fire bursts forth in the impassioned tones. Nevertheless, the judgment passed in this book on the Prime Minister of 1936–37 must stand. It is not possible to approve of some of his arguments.

1. *The doctrine of the imperative mandate.*

To justify the drastic enforcement of the 1936 social legislation Léon Blum was not content to argue that no brake could have been applied to the strike movement which he found in full swing on his assumption of office, without endangering the whole structure of society. He insisted also that the promises given to the electorate had to be redeemed. The parliamentary regime, as he saw it, was impaired in France because electoral programs had been treated too often by previous governments as merely a means to ensnare the voters. The fascist plague was spreading all over Europe. It was in the general interest that free institutions should be rehabilitated through a faultless fulfillment of the commitments entered into during the electoral campaign.

To the plea of Léon Blum the answer is that the head of a government must remain in a position to adapt his policy to facts and circumstances as he sees them, once he has taken charge of the premiership, and become more thoroughly acquainted with them, that he ought not to have fettered himself in such a manner as to be compelled to act against his better judgment. It is bad enough that a candidate should make promises likely to impair the common weal. But it is worse to carry them out when their damaging effect has become evident. On the doctrine of the "imperative mandate," indiscriminately understood and practiced, free institutions are more likely to be wrecked than rehabilitated.

　　2. *Shorter working hours and greater industrial production.*

Improvements in industrial technique make it possible to shorten the number of working hours and yet maintain the level of production, but on the condition that the change is gradually and experimentally introduced, that the benefit expected from new tools or from new operative methods is first carefully estimated. Léon Blum declared at Riom that the true significance of the forty-hour law was to grant labor a "small dividend," taking the form of an increased salary for the same work or of more spare time for the same salary. Such "dividends" command approval in the light of what has occurred in the last hundred years. However, if too abruptly granted, they may impair the producing capacity of a nation in the same way that too large a distribution of reserve funds between shareholders may imperil the financial foundation of a great business.

　　3. *Duplicating or triplicating shifts to make up for shorter hours.*

Léon Blum admitted in so many words, in Riom, that skilled workmen, "specialists," could be formed only by long apprenticeship and training. Obviously, in 1936, they were not available in sufficient numbers to make it possible, at short notice, to run the factories on a two- or three-shift basis. A transitional period, therefore, was a necessity.

Léon Blum also laid down as a fundamental rule that, while reformers are free to treat human labor as a flexible element, machines should be constantly kept running. Léon Blum boasted that the forty-hour law complied with that rule. How, then, does he account for the "two Sundays a week," for the stoppage of all work on Friday night? "In effect, it worked out as though one 'specialist' out of every six at the disposal of French industry had disappeared." That pungent sentence came from M. Dautry and was quoted by the presiding judge.

　　4. *"Extra hours."*

Under the American New Deal, employers have been left free to make labor work extra hours on a 50-per-cent increased rate of pay. Why did not Léon Blum take that leaf out of Mr. Roosevelt's book and strike out, in the definition of the "dividend," the words "greater spare time for the same salary"?

In France, under the social legislation of 1936, the government kept for itself the right to grant or refuse extra hours. In Riom, Léon Blum said that "extra hours" were granted very niggardly and with some distrust, except in the case of national defense where, he continued, no limit was set and all that was required was that one of the three national-defense ministers (War, Air, and Navy) should have reached an understanding with the Minister of Labor. Thus Léon Blum admits that, except in war factories, the government did not really want extra hours to be granted, and we can well ask him whether the French nation could be adequately prepared for war with its economic activity revived only in some special compartments. But, as regards those "special compartments"—i.e., the war factories —Daladier, in circular instructions dated July 29, 1936, had plainly declared that "no extra hours were to be worked." In the following October, it is true, Daladier canceled those instructions, but it remains that a bad start had been made. And later, although we do not perceive who was at fault, it does appear that extra hours were not resorted to.

Moreover, after Léon Blum's premiership had come to an end, Daladier, who then insisted on labor working longer hours in war factories, had to cope with the persistent malevolence of the Metal Workers Federation. At the trial Léon Blum admitted as much and suggested that ulterior political motives might have actuated the Federation.

5. *Working hours at the time of the enforcement of the 1936 legislation.*

Here, perhaps, is the crux of the whole controversy. Léon Blum took the view that in 1936 the French industrial output had fallen so low that his reforms did not really bring about a reduction of hours effectively worked. And he added that the armament program of September 1936 did not call for "extra hours" in its first phase where only prototypes had to be produced. Extra hours, according to him, were not found necessary until later, when mass production of armaments had begun.

That argument was obviously introduced by Blum to explain why so little use was made of overtime. But if he did believe that for many months to come extra hours were to be nothing more than a theoretical possibility, we need no longer be impressed by his assertion that as early as October 1936 he made a generous allowance of them in the interest of national defense.

But when did French labor work the hardest? Before Blum's reform or afterward? In this book (see page 370) figures borrowed from the International Labor Office have been quoted. In Riom, Blum declared them inaccurate. I can only put on record that the Bulletin of General Statistics—an official publication—corroborates them except for some unimportant differences. What that bulletin says is that French labor, on an average, worked 44.5 hours in 1935; 45.8 hours in 1936; 40.4 hours in 1937; 39 hours in 1938; 41.14 hours in 1939, from January to July.

In addition, the census of men drawing unemployment compensation shows that the loss engendered by the relaxation of individual effort was not outweighed, to a satisfactory degree, by the rehiring of jobless men. June 1935: 402,900 unemployed; June 1936: 419,000; June 1937: 321,700; June 1938: 362,900; June 1939: 349,000.

Index